TRANSITIONAL JUSTICE

THE LIBRARY OF ESSAYS ON JUSTICE – SECOND SERIES

Series Editor: Tom D. Campbell

Titles in the series

Transitional Justice
Christine Bell

Restorative Justice
Theo Gavrielides

Victimology
Joanna Shapland and Matthew Hall

Environmental Justice
Steve Vanderheiden

TRANSITIONAL JUSTICE

The library of essays on justice – second series

Edited by
Christine Bell

Routledge
Taylor & Francis Group
LONDON AND NEW YORK

First published 2017
by Routledge

2 Park Square, Milton Park, Abingdon, Oxfordshire OX14 4RN
52 Vanderbilt Avenue, New York, NY 10017

Routledge is an imprint of the Taylor & Francis Group, an informa business

First issued in paperback 2020

British Library Cataloguing in Publication Data
A catalogue record for this book is available from the British Library

Library of Congress Cataloging in Publication Data
A catalog record for this book has been requested

ISBN: 978-1-4724-5041-8 (hbk)
ISBN: 978-0-367-59614-9 (pbk)

Typeset in Times New Roman
by Servis Filmsetting Ltd, Stockport, Cheshire

MIX
Paper from responsible sources
FSC™ C013985

Printed in the United Kingdom
by Henry Ling Limited

CONTENTS

ACKNOWLEDGEMENTS

The editor would like to thank DFID for their support. This publication is an output for the Political Settlements Research Programme, funded by UK Aid from the UK Department for International Development (DFID) for the benefit of developing countries. However, the views expressed and information contained in it are not necessarily those or endorsed by DFID, which can accept no responsibility for such views or information or for any reliance placed on them. Thanks also to Lars Waldorf, Catherine O'Rourke, Louise Mallinder and Gerhard Anders, who shared 'transitional justice' course outlines to give me a perspective of how different people were approaching the field, which assisted me in thinking through how I would approach the selection of essays. Mistakes which remain are my own.

The chapters in this volume are taken from the sources listed below. The editor and publishers wish to thank the authors, original publishers or other copyright holders for permission to use their material as follows.

Chapter 1: Paige Arthur, How "Transitions" Reshaped Human Rights: A Conceptual History of Transitional Justice, *Human Rights Quarterly*, 31, 2009, 321–67. Permission by the Johns Hopkins University Press.

Chapter 2: Ruti G. Teitel, Transitional Justice Genealogy, *Harvard Human Rights Journal*, 16, 2003, 69–94. Permission by *Harvard Human Rights Journal*.

Chapter 3: Christine Bell, Colm Campbell and Fionnuala Ní Aoláin, Justice Discourses in Transition, *Social & Legal Studies*, 13, 2004, 305–28.

Chapter 4: United Nations, The Rule of Law and Transitional Justice in Conflict and Post-conflict Societies: Report of the Secretary-General, UN Doc. S/2004/616, 2004, 3–24.

Chapter 5: Lia Kent, Introduction: The Global Celebration of Transitional Justice and the East Timor Reality, in *The Dynamics of Transitional Justice: International Models and Local Realities in East Timor*, 2012, 3–21. Permission by Taylor & Francis Ltd.

Chapter 6: Diane F. Orentlicher, 'Settling Accounts' Revisited: Reconciling Global Norms with Local Agency, *International Journal of Transitional Justice*, 1, 2007, 10–22. Permission by Oxford University Press.

Chapter 7: Concurring Opinion of Judge Diego Garcia-Sayán, Judgment of the Inter-American Court of Human Rights Case of *The Massacres of El Mozote and Nearby Places v. El Salvador* of October 25, 2012.

Chapter 8: Martti Koskenniemi, Between Impunity and Show Trials, *Max Planck Yearbook of United Nations Law*, 6, 2002, 1–35. Permission by Brill Academic Publishers.

Chapter 9: Leslie Vinjamuri, Review of Kathryn Sikkink's *The Justice Cascade: How Human Rights Prosecutions Are Changing World Politics*, *Journal of Human Rights*, 11, 2012, 283–88. Permission by Taylor & Francis Ltd.

Chapter 10: Priscilla Hayner, Confronting Past Crimes: Transitional Justice and the Phenomenon of Truth Commissions, *Unspeakable Truths: Transitional Justice and the Challenge of Truth Commissions*, 2011, 7–18. Permission by Taylor & Francis Ltd.

Chapter 11: Rosalind Shaw, Memory Frictions: Localizing the Truth and Reconciliation Commission in Sierra Leone, *International Journal of Transitional Justice* 1, 2007, 183–207. Permission by Oxford University Press.

Chapter 12: Pablo de Greiff, Vetting and Transitional Justice, in Alexander Mayer-Riechk and Pablo de Greiff (eds), *Justice as Prevention: Vetting Public Employees in Transitional Societies*, 2007, 523–44.

Chapter 13: Naomi Roht-Arriaza, Reparations in the aftermath of repression and mass violence, in Eric Stover and Harvey M. Weinstan (eds), *My Neighbor, My Enemy: Justice and Community in the Aftermath of Mass Atrocity*, 2004, 121–39.

Chapter 14: Ruth Rubio-Marín, Gender and Collective Reparations in the Aftermath of Conflict and Political Repression, in Ruth Rubio-Marín (ed.), *The Gender of Reparations*, 2009, 381–402.

Chapter 15: Mihaela Mihai and Mathias Thaler, Introduction, in Mihaela Mihai and Mathias Thaler (eds), *On the Uses and Abuses of Political Apologies*, 2014, 1–4.

Chapter 16: Nick Smith, Political Apologies and Categorical Apologies, in Mihaela Mihai and Mathias Thaler (eds), *On the Uses and Abuses of Political Apologies*, 2014, 32–51.

Chapter 17: Andrew Schaap, Reconciliation as Ideology and Politics, *Constellations*, 15, 2008, 249–64.

Chapter 18: Par Engstrom, Transitional justice and ongoing conflict, in Chandra Lekha Sriram, Jemima Garcia-Godos, Olga Martin-Ortega and Johanna Herman (eds), *Transitional Justice and Peacebuilding on the Ground: Victims and Ex-combatants*, 2012, 41–61. Permission by Taylor & Francis Ltd.

Chapter 19: Hugo van der Merwe, Transitions in the Middle East and North Africa: new trajectories and challenges for transitional justice?, in Kirsten J. Fisher and Robert

Stewart (eds), *Transitional Justice and the Arab Spring*, 2014, 226–38. Permission by Taylor & Francis Ltd.

Chapter 20: James E. Beitler, "Inescapable Networks of Mutuality": The Development of Transitional Justice in the United States, in *Remaking Transitional Justice in the United States: The Rhetorical*, 2012, 127–48. Permission by Springer.

Chapter 21: Catherine O'Rourke, Justice for What? Recognising a web of gender-based harms against women in transitional justice, in *Gender Politics in Transitional Justice*, 2013, 37–59. Permission by Taylor & Francis Ltd.

Chapter 22: Lars Waldorf, Anticipating the Past: Transitional Justice and Socio-Economic Wrongs, *Social & Legal Studies*, 21, 2012, 171–86. Permission by Sage Publications.

Chapter 23: Ruben Carranza, Plunder and Pain: Should Transitional Justice Engage with Corruption and Economic Crimes?, *International Journal of Transitional Justice*, 2, 2008, 310–30. Permission by Oxford University Press.

Chapter 24: Mark Kersten, Justice after the war: The International Criminal Court and Post-Gaddafi Libya, in Kirsten J. Fisher and Robert Stewart (eds), *Transitional Justice and the Arab Spring*, 2014, 188–207. Permission by Taylor & Francis Ltd.

Chapter 25: Rosemary Nagy, Transitional Justice as Global Project: critical reflections, *Third World Quarterly*, 29, 2009, 275–89. Permission by Taylor & Francis Ltd.

Chapter 26: Adam Branch, The Violence of Peace: Ethnojustice in Northern Uganda, *Development and Change*, 45, 2014, 608–30. Permission by John Wiley & Sons Ltd.

Chapter 27: Tshepo Madlingozi, On Transitional Justice Entrepreneurs and the Production of Victims, *Journal of Human Rights Practice*, 2, 2010, 208–28. Permission by Oxford University Press.

Chapter 28: Geoff Dancy, Impact Assessment, Not Evaluation: Defining a Limited Role for Positivism in the Study of Transitional Justice, *International Journal of Transitional Justice*, 4, 2010, 355–76. Permission by Oxford University Press.

Chapter 29: Colleen Duggan, "Show me your impact": Evaluating transitional justice in contested spaces, *Evaluation and Program Planning*, 35, 2012, 199–205. Permission by Elsevier.

Every effort has been made to trace all the copyright holders, but if any have been inadvertently overlooked the publishers will be pleased to make the necessary arrangement at the first opportunity.

Publisher's Note

The material in this volume has been reproduced using the facsimile method. This means we can retain the original pagination to facilitate easy and correct citation of the original essays. It also explains the variety of typefaces, page layouts and numbering.

SERIES PREFACE

Historically, justice is a core concept in law politics, and, after a period of neglect, has been at the fore of academic scholarship since the publication of John Rawls's path-breaking *A Theory of Justice* (Oxford University Press, 1971). Rawl's book triggered a flood of work on theories of justice, which is reflected in the volume Justice in the Dartmouth/Ashgate/Routledge series entitled 'The International Library of Essays in Law and Legal Theory' (1991) in which the editor, Thomas Morawetz, divides his selection of essays into four parts: 'Rawls's Legacy', 'Recent Jurisprudence', 'Distributive Justice' and 'Corrective Justice'.

Since that time, theories of justice have been supplemented by more specific topics, each with its own burgeoning literature. This prompted a further Ashgate/Routledge series entitled 'The Library of Essays on Justice' (2012), including the volumes *Procedural Justice, Intergenerational Justice, Distributive Justice, The Capabilities Approach* and *Global Justice*. This has now been extended into the second series of 'The Library of Essays in Justice' to take in four further areas of intense practical and theoretical interest with flourishing literatures, containing the volumes *Restorative Justice, Transitional Justice, Victimology* and *Environmental Justice*.

Restorative Justice, edited by Theo Gavrielides, develops the pioneering work of John Braithwaite, with an emphasis on equality and empirical testing. *Transitional Justice*, edited by Christine Bell, deals with post-war settlements after a range of conflicts, including sections on trials, truth commissions and reparations. *Victimology*, jointly edited by Joanna Shapland and Matthew Hall, contains a wide range of issues related to the recent move to focus more on victims and less on perpetrators of crimes, including the experience of victims in trials and compensation issues. The *Environmental Justice* volume, edited by Steve Vanderheiden, takes us to this relatively new and immensely important topic, with issues relating to the distribution of environmental risks, international and intergenerational issues and climate change.

Each volume represents a selection of published essays and chapters made by major scholars in their respective fields and contains a substantial introduction to the literature selected.

TOM CAMPBELL
Series Editor
Professorial Fellow, Centre for Applied Philosophy and Public Ethics (CAPPE)
Charles Stuart University Canberra

INTRODUCTION
THE FABRIC OF TRANSITIONAL JUSTICE

Binding local and global political settlements

> Looking for a new material that was tough, scientists developed one that also can stretch up to 20 times its original length without breaking. . . A typical hydrogel (a gel whose particles are dispersed in water) can stretch only a few times its length, if that. Even natural rubber can stretch only five to six times its length. But the new compound, made of alginate, polyacrylamide and water, proved to be far more stretchable and fracture-proof in tests. . . Incredibly enough, the stretchiness was just a side effect of the team's research, Suo said.
>
> (Live Science, http://www.livescience.com/22945-super-stretchy-material-also-super-strong.html)

Introduction

This *Transitional Justice* essay collection sits as part of a library of essays on different concepts of 'justice'. Yet transitional justice appears quite different from other types of justice. While a now established field of transitional justice clearly exists with specialist journals dedicated to it, fundamental ambiguities characterise the term and raise questions as to how it should sit alongside other concepts of justice. The adjective 'transitional' creates an ambiguous term that suggests three quite different ways in which it might be understood as a distinctive 'brand' of justice.

A first incarnation views the phrase transitional justice as a new philosophical concept of justice to operate in the peculiar situation of 'transition'. From this perspective transitional justice is a new concept of justice, aimed at a distinct set of legal and philosophical dilemmas involved in achieving political transitions. Like 'distributive justice' it is a normative concept whose contours are shaped by its function. A second possible meaning of the term views transitional justice as simply the justice issues raised by political transitions: a set of questions as to how bodies of law such as domestic criminal law, international human rights law, international humanitarian law, or even international criminal law apply in transitions. To borrow Posner and Vermule's phrase, transitional justice from this perspective is just 'ordinary justice' bowled in a slightly more tricky-than-usual fact-pattern, rather than a distinct and novel legal or philosophical concept (2004). A third conception of transitional justice posits it as a type of justice that is itself 'in transition': transitional justice as the movement of justice concepts and systems from one place or state to another. This is justice as the object of change rather than, or as well as, the subject of change (Bell, Campbell and Ní Aoláin 2004). From this perspective justice discourse itself is in transition: it is the concept of justice which is in transition.

The origin of the term, however, is one that derives as much or more from the field and practice (Editorial Note 2007) as from theory. From the practice-based field perspective, transitional justice is sometimes rejected as a normative concept at all, and talked of in terms of a 'tool-kit'. The United Nations in its 'The Rule of Law and Transitional Justice in Conflict and Post-conflict Societies' report defines transitional justice as merely a grab-bag full of tools. Transitional justice for the UN comprises 'the full range of processes and mechanisms associated with a society's attempt to come to terms with a legacy of large-scale past abuses, in order to ensure accountability, serve justice and achieve reconciliation' (2004: 4, para. 8). This tool-kit approach adds a fourth possible conception of transitional justice as a set of institutional choices relating to where and how to institutionalise a response to past atrocities. In attempting to avoid any suggestion of a distinct philosophical or legal conception, this approach tries to evade any need to locate a normative concept of justice as underlying institutional choice or design, or to elevate transitional justice to a concept of justice at all.

In this it is only partially successful: even the tool-kit approach cannot completely escape normative questions as to *when and where* these particular tools as opposed to others are to be used. When and under what circumstances is a truth commission a desirable or appropriate alternative to criminal trials? When should the International Criminal Court exercise prosecutorial discretion not to prosecute in the face of a peace process that may be undermined? These questions cannot be answered without some sort of decision as regards the normative imperatives underlying the choice. What normatively are these tools to be used for? Is the tool-kit to be understood as one which aims for 'accountability', or 'democracy', or 'peace' or even 'reconciliation'? Different decisions will lead to different results as regards what institutional alternatives to 'ordinary' criminal justice are permitted and even desirable. Or is the tool-kit to be understood as one which exists to enable trade-offs between these normatively driven outcomes or values, where they conflict? In a recent editorial attempting to capture the field, Makau Mutua argues that:

> Transitional justice is a subset, an offshoot, of the human rights movement. Its norms, devices – truth commissions, judicial processes, multisectoral reforms in the legal and law enforcement sectors, and open competitive political systems – carry a definite vision of the society they seek to create. The choice of transitional justice as the medium of change implies certain values and end results.
>
> (2015: 3)

However, its origins remain more contested than this (Bell 2009), and even if they were so settled, there is currently no real consensus as to what the values and end results of transitional justice should be.

The ambiguities and even confusion over what type of concept 'transitional justice' *is* has led to a field that is at once beguiling and frustrating. Transitional justice has become at once everything and nothing. Recent attempts to capture and evaluate the field of transitional justice talk in terms of the need to understand transitional justice as a justice concept ever caught between dichotomies: hope and disillusionment; promise and reality; principle and pragmatism; transformation and retrenchment; local and global politics (ibid.; Anders and Zenker 2014). These dichotomies appear and reappear throughout the current collection, I suggest because they are rooted in a concept that itself is generated by the fundamental dichotomy between the 'from' of the past and the 'to' of the future that transitional justice aims to navigate between (Bell and O'Rourke 2007). Indeed, reflexivity about the difficulty of finding agreement over the meaning or goals or politics of the concept is a characteristic of the field.

One consequence of transitional justice's ambiguous nature has been its resultant capacity to ever-expand in reach. In its ambiguities transitional justice takes on the capacity, like the hydrogel of the *Live Science* quotation at the start, of a miracle fabric whose warp and weave contain an almost infinite stretchiness because it can envelop all of its possible meanings so as to reach out to ever new political contexts. Transitional justice is capacious and seems to invite new concepts of justice, new concepts of 'transition' and new 'tools' within its folds. As a result, as a legal concept transitional justice is human rights, international criminal justice, humanitarian law, all merely finding instantiation in new institutional forms during transitions. As a normative concept, transitional justice is ordinary criminal justice, extraordinary criminal justice, distributive and procedural justice, global justice and intergenerational justice, all presenting as something extraordinary because of its distinctive setting in times of transition. As a set of tools it is trials, military tribunals, vetting, truth commissions, commissions of inquiry, amnesties, apologies or anything that deals with wrongs of conflicts past. At a politically normative level transitional justice is local justice, global justice, liberalising justice, transformative justice, restorative justice, depending on what we perceive and want it to be. Moreover, transitional justice in lacking a clear articulation of the 'transitions' to which it applies can be found in all sorts of transitions: transitions from authoritarianism, conflict, colonialism, slavery, child abuse, long-past state transformations, organised crime, and even perhaps from the ongoing transition that is any attempt to pursue democracy and justice as a practice in the most stable Western settings, as this collection illustrates. Like the hydrogel referenced at the start of this introduction, transitional justice as a concept has a resilience and strength that is closely connected to its stretchiness.

The essay collection and its impulses

What, then, to do with an essay collection on transitional justice that, unlike the field, has a very finite capacity? This collection attempts to capture and portray – inevitably in an emblematic rather than a systematic way – three different dimensions of the field. Part I addresses the origins of the field which continue to bedevil it. Indeed the origins themselves are increasingly debated in what is an emergent and contested historiography of the field that assists in understanding its contemporary quirks and concerns. Part II addresses and sets out – in a very partial way – some of the 'tool-kit' of transitional justice, which could be understood as the canonical research agenda of the field. Part III tries to convey a sense of the way in which the field is unfolding and extending to new transitions, new tools, new theories of justice, and all with a heavy dose of self-critique.

In approaching the collection in this way I have tried to remain true to a number of impulses. First was the impulse to convey something of where the phenomenon that is transitional justice has come from, including pieces that speak to its multiple origins in situations of authoritarianism, conflict and mass violence. This impulse is also one of conveying how the field has been generated by practice and academic legal argument working together to create and propel the concept. Part I tries to capture these dynamics and inter-relationships. The second impulse was to give as broad a sense as possible of what now stands within the transitional justice field, reflecting what might be the accepted 'canon' of transitional justice and also its unfolding new directions and the racy attempts to expand the field that characterise it. Parts II and III reflect this approach: Part I reflecting what might be considered the 'canon' of transitional justice and Part II the field's new directions. The third impulse was the impulse to give a sense of transitional justice's internal controversies, both at the level of specific debates, for example as regards the role of amnesty or trials in dealing with the past; and at the level of the discourse itself, where debates such as whether transitional justice is liberalising justice or transformative justice persist.

As a whole, the collection tries to walk a line between the two converse notions of the field: first, the idea that the field has a coherent remit and set of inquiries as a field; and second, that there is something more elusive and disturbing about the field and a justice concept whose normative and legal underpinnings and goals are so difficult to pin down. The collection aims to demonstrate both the common content of the field and its elusive quality.

I: The origins of the field: from whence did it come and why does it matter?

The term 'transitional justice' emerged as closely connected to transitions from authoritarianism to democracy of the early 1990s. Paige Arthur has suggested that the term was coined with reference to transitions to democracy in Latin America, where it 'helped to legitimate those justice claims that prioritized legal-institutional reforms and responses – such as punishing leaders, vetting abusive security forces, and replacing state secrecy with truth and transparency – over other claims to justice that were oriented toward social justice and redistribution' (2009: 321–2). One of the first publications to use the term 'transitional justice' was a three-volume set of books by Neil Kritz, entitled *Transitional Justice: How Emerging Democracies Deal with Former Regimes*, published by the United States Institute of Peace (1995). Volumes one and three dealt with different 'tools' of transitional justice, similar to Part II of this collection, while the middle volume provided case studies, many historical, focused entirely on transitions from authoritarianism to democracy. Ruti Teitel's early and foundational book *Transitional Justice* focused not just on South American debates, but also the authoritarian transitions of Eastern Europe, again pointing to the ways in which transitional justice aimed to mediate between a repressive past and a more liberal democratic future (2000; see also 2003).

All three works suggested – in different ways – that the concept of transitional justice that emerged was closely linked to the enterprise of moving from authoritarianism to liberal democracy.

Transitions from authoritarianism appeared to present a common set of dilemmas because, as Kritz's volume title suggests, there was a degree of consensus that these transitions were 'about' the move from authoritarianism to democracy. In some of the early violent conflicts in which transitional justice emerged this was also the case. Guatemala, El Salvador and South Africa clearly involved militarised intra-state conflict which any attempt to deal with the past had to reckon with; here too, however, the dominant and controlling international narrative of the conflicts understood armed conflict to be a symptom of lack of democracy and the authoritarianism of the state, rather than 'about' anything else. The language and mechanisms of transitional justice in these early conflicts, as with situations of authoritarianism per se, were understood to be in service to a liberal democratic transition, characterised by an attempted move to the political and legal institutions of liberal democracy. Transitional justice from this perspective was, as Mutua suggests, understood to be a product of human rights advocacy and closely related to the human rights project.

However, during this time the question of 'how to deal with the past' was also a central feature of attempted transitions from violent conflict in which the nature of the conflict, and the trajectory of the transition was much more contested. Peace processes in Northern Ireland, throughout Africa, and even in the Middle East, for example, all involved debate over how to account for past conflict atrocities, in contexts where the idea that everything would be dealt with by a straightforward domestic criminal justice application was understood to be impossible and problematic politically from the outset. As O'Leary and McGarry point out, any transition from conflict must reckon with 'the conflict about what the conflict is about' (the meta-conflict) (2004: 2). Accounts of the past are therefore inextricably linked with the future, because they prescribe a particular future 'cure' to the conflict.

In conflict settings a number of key differences with 'paradigmatic transitions' therefore pertained. First, the conflict settings in which transitional justice mechanisms were subsequently invoked were incredibly diverse, defying any 'one-size fits all' answer. The conflicts involved different levels of violence: from mass atrocity in full-blown civil war, such as Rwanda or Sierra Leone; to long standing low-level conflict such as Northern Ireland and Sri Lanka where the states denied that conflict existed, and responded using criminal law processes tweaked through emergency law provisions. A further conflict context for transitional justice involved conflicts which were international in nature, but which reinforced forms of internal conflict that then came to be the subject of transitional justice interventions. International intervention in Bosnia, Kosovo, Afghanistan, Iraq and Libya focused on regime change and created a need for substantial reconstruction in societies that were deeply divided internally. International actors attempted to promote forms of 'transitional justice' in some of these contexts, focused on accounting for abuses of the authoritarian regimes that had preceded the international intervention often using the name and 'tools' of transitional justice. Transitional justice here took place against the backdrop of inter-state conflict but saw international actors use transitional justice as a tool to address the ongoing internal conflict occasioned by the externally enforced regime change. These contexts were often also entangled with an international criminal legal process, or took place firmly within its shadow.

A second variation from the 'paradigmatic' authoritarian context for transitional justice was that these varied conflicts had distinct levels of international intervention, distinct regional dynamics and responses, triggered distinct international and domestic legal regimes, and distinct balances of power and moral dynamics that made any consensus about the nature and direction of the 'transition' difficult. Unlike authoritarian transitions, in these transitions it was much less clear that a transition to 'democracy' was in train and could justify moral and political arguments for a distinctive transitional justice rooted in the need for institutions that would enable democratic outcomes. However, it is also difficult to specify in advance of specific cases exactly which legal standards will apply to which parties for which phases of the conflict. While a notion of 'no blanket amnesty' took hold as a 'crystallising norm of international law', which drew its substance from a kind of 'composite' reading of different branches of international law, from a positive legal point of view it remained difficult to decide which legal standards apply in which context in any abstract way that might provide clear guidance to negotiators as to what is and is not legal in terms of international law. Moreover, as pieces in the collection acknowledge, human rights bodies have rarely had to adjudicate directly on how competing rights, for example to accountability or to non-repetition should be balanced in a context in which amnesty has been crucial to enabling a peace settlement.

Third, it was much less clear in transitions from conflict that human rights law was the key legal frame of reference and that human rights values were propelling institutional design. Novel institutional arrangements could be justified in paradigmatic transitions to democracy as in service to accountability, offering some accountability rather than none, and therefore a step towards rather than away from human rights, even if only a very small one. However, in transitions from conflict, institutional design relating to how to deal with the past focused much more explicitly around the 'justice versus peace' trade-off. The context involved deals that were often less about transition from one regime to another, and more about trying to get military-political elites at the heart of violent conflict, to share power in fragile compromises whose future normative trajectory was uncertain. In this context, transitional justice could not justify its departures from 'ordinary justice' in terms of a future democratic outcome. Rather it had to settle for the rather less noble justification of being 'the lesser of two evils', or the 'least bad choice', in situations where the choice appeared to be between a very imperfect peace and a very perfect war. As a result, the trade-offs between justice and peace appeared to have little normative basis but to be primarily linked to balance of power dynamics between the warring elites, and calculations as to what would best stabilise the emergent political settlement between politico-military elites. Whether transitional justice really was a part of the human rights project was much less clear, in part because how human rights law views these type of normative/pragmatist trade-offs is unclear.

Understanding the field's dual beginnings, I suggest, remains important to understanding the contemporary field, its preoccupations and its controversies. It points to the under-estimated connection of transitional justice to processes of political settlement.

There have been some attempts in the literature to disentangle the ways in which these different contexts have affected the take-up and impact of transitional justice mechanisms. Paige Arthur, at the end of her article, pointed to a need to consider further whether transition to 'peace' was different in kind to transition to democracy, requiring new normative aims and different institutional mechanisms for transitional justice (2009). Fionnuala Ní Aoláin and Colm Campbell (2005) considered in detail the relationship between authoritarian transitions as 'paradigmatic' transitions and transitions in 'conflicted democracies'. They suggested that there were indeed problems of 'translation' in terms of understanding the quite different challenges which transitional justice faced in 'conflicted democracies'. Fletcher, Weinstein and Rowen, in comparing transitional justice choices in practice, noted that distinctness in context significantly affects the choice of transitional justice mechanism and its operation in practice (2009). They examined how transitional justice mechanisms were taken up in seven quite different contexts, and produced an account of the 'dynamic system in which transitional justice interventions occur', suggesting eight factors or differences in context, which in their view influenced design. This work explicitly avoided distinguishing between paradigmatic or non-paradigmatic transitions, or trying to measure outcomes in terms of goals precisely because it recognised that any specification of goals would be putative and contested. Finally, I have suggested that the very existence and growth of a field of transitional justice is owed to its capacity to 'cloak' similar mechanisms all aimed in some way at 'dealing with the past', but operating in very different contexts as somehow dealing with similar problems in similar ways (2009). This is an idea that grounds this introduction and my approach to the collection, because it points to the ways in which different processes of political settlement start to give similar mechanisms very different meanings – an idea reflected in a number of essays.

However, the question of what motivates and 'creates' the field continues to haunt it. For example, a very recent report by the International Center for Transitional Justice and the Kofi Annan Foundation has attempted to address the failings of truth commissions as a mechanism (2014). It has questioned whether the mechanism had been too easily 'read across' from authoritarian contexts to conflict ones, with something crucial 'lost in translation'. The report viewed it important to understand what was 'lost' if different accountability outcomes for Truth Commissions that looked quite similar on paper, were to be understood and addressed.

Part I in its first two sections sets out foundational accounts of transitional justice that were themselves critical in shaping and 'creating' the field. Paige Arthur and Ruti Teitel provide explanations of the field's creation in terms of authoritarian-democracy transitions; while myself and my colleagues, and the pivotal UN Rule of Law and Transitional Justice Report of 2004 articulate the connections between transitional justice and conflict. Lia Kent's final piece in a sense pulls these threads together by making the connection to practice, illustrating how different conceptions and mechanisms of transitional justice played out in East Timor. She shows the 'daunting' set of goals that transitional justice is expected to achieve: 'providing "justice" to victims and their families, fostering healing, reconciliation and nation-building, acting as a deterrent to future human rights violations, and protecting the integrity of the UN itself' (2012: 11). She also demonstrates how globalised concepts and processes are given meaning in 'specific places and times', and how they may be reshaped in unexpected directions (ibid.: 17). Her observations again point to the resilience and strength of the discourse in meaning different things to different actors. Pointing to the connection between theory and practice Kent interrogates the appropriate and ethical research methods for investigating transitional justice, a matter that also recurs throughout the collection.

II: Transitional justice tool-kit: fencing in a coherent field

As the UN report in Part I demonstrates, one approach to understanding transitional justice as a coherent field of inquiry that offers either a way to embrace different accounts of its origins, or eschew them altogether, is to lay aside theoretical and 'field-origin' questions, and examine the mechanisms or 'tool-kit' of transitional justice. Part II, following Kritz's early work, is structured around the 'tool-kit' approach. This approach constructs the field as having a coherent research agenda and even a centre of gravity with a canon of work that cuts across contexts. There are many potential tools in the tool-kit and of necessity the collection focuses on a selection of tools choosing those that have been accepted as such since the field's inception: amnesty, trials, truth commissions, vetting and reparations. The inclusion of the newer tool of 'apology' reflects the growing repertoire of the field: apologies for 'the past' cut across not only authoritarian and conflict contexts, but began to bring apologies as diverse as the Irish state's apology for its involvement in institutional sexual abuse, or the Australian government's apology for the treatment of aboriginal people, within the transitional justice field. Part II, however, includes discussion of reconciliation, which I suggest below can be positioned as both a tool and a goal of transitional justice.

The pieces selected for each of these topics have been chosen from a vast repository of possibilities, as each 'tool' has its own sub-literature. I here tried to select pieces that both explain the tool and point to transitional justice's underlying controversies focused on how and when the tools should be used. Each of the tools in the tool-kit is often framed and discussed in terms of 'when and whether to choose it or not'. However, internal debates over whether, when and in what form to use criminal trials, amnesties or vetting quickly open up to more fundamental dilemmas over the normative consequences of these choices for transition that ensues.

Amnesties

Turning to amnesties – at the centre of the discourse, questions persist as to whether amnesties are always bad, or whether it depends on how they are framed. Questions include: when and how do they occur; when and under what circumstances are they legally permissible; do liberal democratic outcomes require tolerating them, or outlawing them? The amnesty debate continues to illustrate persistent questions over whether the validity of amnesty is different in conflict–peace transitions than in transitions from authoritarianism to liberal democracy. Hence, I have included Orentlicher's revisiting of one of her early foundational pieces (2007) regarding the legality of amnesties under human rights law this earlier piece having been key to arguments that post-transition accountability requirements remained post-transition (1991). I juxtapose the piece with the more contemporary revisiting of the relationship between transitional justice and peace in the concurring opinion of Diego Garcia-Sayán in the *El Mozote* case dealing with a massacre in El Salvador (2012). In this concurring opinion Garcia-Sayán suggests that the Inter-American court's existing amnesty jurisprudence is not automatically to be understood to apply to the context of a peace process with a justice versus peace dilemma, where a truth mechanism has been put in place along with a form of amnesty, as an attempt to move from conflict to peace. Garcia-Sayán argues that in post-conflict contexts, rather than considering amnesties as a violation of rights against impunity, they need to be considered in terms of a set of rights that include the right to non-repetition, not all of which will be able to be achieved simultaneously. Both Orentlicher and Garcia-Sayán grapple with the trade-offs between justice and peace, and between the different rights that are at play in transition. For Orentlicher the project is to counter the assumption that human rights obligations end with authoritarian regime change and ensure ongoing accountability. In democratisation contexts such accountability can be understood as part and parcel of the democratisation process with its commitment to rights and the rule of law. However, for Garcia-Sayán the project is to try to set out relevant factors that would help evaluate the legitimacy of an amnesty put in place to enable a transition from conflict to peace where commitments to justice appear to clash with commitments to peace (as in the ending of armed violence). In juxtaposition the two pieces not only illustrate the different considerations in the application of transitional justice in authoritarian and conflict contexts, but how human rights positions and political analysis of context and the application of transitional justice changes over time.

Trials

The desirability or undesirability of trials has similarly remained central to transitional justice discourse, whether domestic trials or international ones, and recurs in different ways throughout the essays. One of the originating questions of transitional justice was whether trials of former regime agents destabilised or stabilised a rule of law future. Surprisingly perhaps, a human rights movement that was deeply sceptical about criminal trials, punishment and deterrence with respect to 'ordinary decent criminals' in the domestic context often seemed to view criminal justice and punishment as the ultimate gold standard for former human rights abusers. Trials are here seen as synonymous with accountability and the rule of law. Sikkink, famously has talked of a 'justice cascade', in which human rights norms cascaded across contexts and from international to local level, in part through human rights activism focused on prosecuting former political leaders for past human rights abuses (2012). The justice cascade theory in a sense articulates and celebrates the successes of transitional justice as a global project of inaugurating democracy and the rule of law.

Challenges to this valorisation of the 'human rights trial' are varied. Vinjamuri's review of Sikkink illustrates a challenge to Sikkink's claim that such trials reduce repression, and to any idea of an uncontroversial normative link between trials, accountability and legitimacy (2012). Koskenneimi, in his account of the paradoxes of the 'show trial', points to a deep critique of the limits of the trial as linked to the limits of liberalism itself with respect to post-conflict political demands for accountability (2002). Many transitional justice debates have taken place against the backdrop not just of domestic trials, but of the Nuremberg trials, which are sometimes credited as an original jurisgenerative source of transitional justice. This retrospective discovery of transitional justice arises in part because the debate over whether and how to institute the Nuremberg court pre-rehearsed many of the post-conflict trial dilemmas of today. In his revisiting of Nuremberg, however, Koskenniemi points out how post-conflict 'show trials' in a sense embody the central paradox of liberalism itself: for the trial model to be vindicated it must contain the possibility of acquittal inherent in the rule of law notion of fair trial and due process. Yet, the political legitimacy of the legal institution and any rule of law and peace dividend, may require that what is 'known' politically – namely that the perpetrator is guilty – be validated by the court. In this way, the paradox of the trial can be understood as a microcosm of the paradox of liberal democracy itself. Liberalism premises its commitments and institutions on neutrality between political visions; however, at some point political threats to the liberal political order itself tempt it to abandon those commitments and institutions and in a paradoxical way move to dismantle itself to save itself. Ultimately, the flourishing of liberal democracy appears to either depend on an article of faith that 'good will out' or to require violating its own tenets where (paradoxically) political threats to liberal democracy appear to require it to.

Truth commissions

Truth commissions have often been offered as honourable alternatives to trials. In providing some accountability and forgoing the punishment end of criminal justice, they appear to offer a compromise between goals of accountability and negotiated ends to conflict: an institutional choice to square the circle, as Hayner's work illustrates. However, Shaw's work, like Kent's, demonstrates the complexity of the truth commission terrain when examined in its local context. Shaw argues that Truth Commissions have instituted 'redemptive verbal remembering' as a 'global paradigm that has acquired a strong momentum in practice' (2007: 186). Examining the truth commission in Sierra Leone, she interrogates the local–global dichotomy. She walks a line between viewing global paradigms as 'powerful forms of knowledge embedded in institutional and everyday practices' which 'reconfigure the field of action, subjugating alternatives and creating new forms of power and inequality', on the one hand, but acknowledging the capacity of local agency to subvert even powerful global paradigms, on the other (ibid.). However, Shaw also tells a story of the journey of the truth commission from tool of post-authoritarian transitions to liberal democracy, to 'truth *and reconciliation*' commissions as tools for transitioning from conflict to peace. She argues that they have inaugurated a new global approach of dealing with victims by focusing on inter-personal catharsis and 'coming-together' in public dramas of encounter, which were quite foreign to Sierra Leonean ways of processing trauma and memory. Through these dichotomies Shaw shows a truth commission that neither liberated Sierra Leoneans, nor subjugated them entirely, but in a sense muddled through without meeting the fundamental material needs that Sierra Leoneans persistently insisted and believed the truth commission should deliver, but which appeared unintelligible in terms of established transitional justice discourse.

Vetting

These types of dynamic permeate the other tools: de Greiff's discussion of vetting illustrates its norms and functions, but also how institutional arrangements must be crafted to meet competing demand of the future in particular converse demands for continuity and for change (2007).

Reparations

Reparations, like truth commissions, offer a mechanism that does not require a direct choice between accountability and stability. Rather, they would appear to be something which can sit alongside different modes of achieving accountability. Yet, like our other areas, institutionalisation of reparations embodies a variety of difficult choices as to how to achieve due process, how to ensure capacity to deliver and to pay, how to choose between individual and communal approaches to reparations, and how to ensure fairness in terms of how broader social needs are being met, as set out in Roht-Arriaza's essay. This essay also illustrates the technocracy of reparations and institutional choices as to 'how' to pay, illustrating how the reparations debate has also become intertwined with larger questions of how transitional justice deals with development and socio-economic rights issues addressed in Part III. Rubio-Marín's piece illustrates the relationship of reparations to gender, because patterns of combatants and victims are particularly constructed by gender and the relationship of gender to the conflict. In this her work represents a wider transitional justice turn to 'ask the woman question' picked up further in Part III. So here again, reparations both offer an example of the richness of each sub-debate and the dilemmas of institutional choice, but also illustrate how those dilemmas and choices open up much wider normative discussions as to the nature and direction of the transition and its inclusions and exclusions.

Apologies

Apologies are a more recent newcomer to the transitional justice field. In a recent collection Mihai and Thaler and Smith set out a political conceptualisation of apologies which again points to the relationship with political settlement, while trying to locate the normative content and function of different types of apology.

Reconciliation

Reconciliation perhaps sits uneasily in this section, as it looks much more like a putative outcome than a 'tool' in the tool-kit. However, reconciliation is often offered both as technique or tool as much as a justification for institutional choice. Shaw's piece on Sierra Leone again illustrates with its assertion that the act of verbalising is often equated with 'healing'. Similarly, the South African Truth Commission also was not only promoted as a means to reconciliation, but itself viewed as offering reconciliation in action through public testimony, catharsis and coming-together. However, Schaap re-frames debates over reconciliation by contrasting inter-personal reconciliation with 'political reconciliation' (2008). He draws a distinction between reconciliation as an ideological (usually conservative) concept, to reconciliation as an agonistic 'processing of a wrong, a demonstration of the fundamental wrong on which the polity is founded which is brought into view by the friction between reconciliation as ideology and politics'. His suggestion points to the possibility that political reconciliation may be at play in what look like individual reconciliation 'failures'.

Although Part II appears to set out a 'tool-kit'/canon approach to transitional justice, the essays selected very much point to the ways in which the choice between transitional justice tools is never just a technical institutional choice, but quickly exposes the tensions and dichotomies of the field that continue to define and mark it as a distinctive justice discourse, which in a sense elides between all three of the conceptualisations of transitional justice set out at the start of this essay.

III: The permeable boundaries of transitional justice: the politics of what is 'fenced out'

Having understood and set out some of the 'canon' of transitional justice by examining some of its core 'tools' or institutions, Part III turns to the alternative approach of understanding transitional justice in terms of competing normative inquiries. This section explores this approach by pointing to a number of seemingly possible boundaries for fencing in the field of transitional justice. However, in fencing in, we also fence out (cf. Conaghan 2009). Here, I have chosen a number of intersecting boundaries that also offer an opportunity to explore the current direction of travel of transitional justice as a field.

Which transitions?

The first permeable boundary is that of the type of transition to which transitional justice discourses apply. I chose to illustrate using three key 'new' contexts that have generated or are generating significant debate. The first is the question over whether and when transitional justice can be a tool in ongoing conflict. As Engstrom (2012) sets out, transitional justice is increasingly embedded in conflict resolution and peace-building efforts and increasingly there is a trend towards judicial intervention in ongoing conflicts. He suggests that this trend is owed to two developments, the intractability of armed conflict and the rise of the 'global accountability regime'. Engstrom's focus is primarily on international criminal law interventions. However, the scope of transitional justice in ongoing conflict is broader. Often cited as a key example is Colombia where after a series of failed peace processes, President Uribe negotiated a peace deal with right wing paramilitary groups who were alleged to have close connections to right wing governments, including Uribe's. He implemented a Law of Justice and Peace, under the guise of 'transitional justice', which set up a form of demobilisation linked to a form of truth-telling and de facto non-prosecution. Here the label of transitional justice was used, but also was contested, because there was no transition, and because the mechanism was understood not as a compromise between justice and peace but as a form of impunity with a self-interested dimension. However, Uribe's mechanism deliberately and cleverly deployed the 'tool-kit' and the discourse of transitional justice to achieve ends that seem antithetical to transitional justice as accountability or human rights. In some ways, this move exposed the difficulty of 'reducing' the discourse to a tool-kit, shorn of normative goals or justifications.

Since that time, transitional justice has been mooted as a tool in other quite different ongoing conflicts, from Sri Lanka, to Gaza, to Syria. But there have also been precursors, notably in the Bosnian war of the early 1990s. It is easy to forget that the International Criminal Tribunal for former-Yugoslavia, began life during the conflict as a mechanism for limiting the conflict but also for saving the face of an international community that was embarrassed by its impotency in ending the war. It was only when its operation was 'saved' into the Dayton Peace Agreement that it was secured as a post-conflict mechanism.

From a simple semantic point of view, it is unclear what makes innovative institutions for accountability in conflict a form of 'transitional' justice, beyond the fact that mechanisms traditionally associated with transitional justice – the tools in the 'tool-kit' – are reached for. What distinguishes transitional justice in conflict from any other pressure and mechanism to monitor and account for human rights atrocities during conflict or at any other time?

Closely related to this inquiry, is the new revolutionary/authoritarian/conflict context of the Middle East and North Africa (MENA). The 'MENA revolutions' of the Arab Spring constitute an attempt to apply transitional justice in contexts that in a sense cut across authoritarian and conflict transition-types. However, in their combination and complexity and their ongoing unresolved nature these uprisings and their aftermath also pose a new context completely. Here, key questions arise as to the relationship between the precise 'past' focused on by a transitional justice mechanism, and the extent to which there is ongoing 'conflict', or a pro-democracy transition in play which is serviced by labelling that particular 'past' as the unjust one to be transitioned from. I am writing in a week in which the 'post-conflict' Prime Minister Morsi, after being deposed in a second 'revolutionary coup', has been given a death sentence for escaping from jail during the pre-first-revolution regime of Mubarak, who himself was tried as a former political leader during the first phase of the revolution. It is difficult from a distance not to view Egypt as a battle ground and transitional justice as a discourse through which to gain strategic instrumentalist advantage in the battle. As van der Merwe points out, the Arab Spring does not just prove a challenge for the application of transitional justice but prompts questions about 'transitional justice's fundamental assumptions, methods and goals, as well as who does and who should define these' (2012). He identifies this as a pivotal moment for the field, which in his view needs a new consensus as to what transitional justice is trying to do.

In apparent stark contrast is the application of transitional justice in entirely settled contexts. Beitler's article on North America has been chosen as emblematic of this emerging practice, because it questions how different phases of state-building and constitutional development, and the justice inclusions and exclusions that characterised them, link to very local truth-seeking initiatives (2014). The wealth of initiatives Beitler presents in the US are interesting, as is his documentation of the link between these initiatives and transnational activism on truth-seeking, which he identifies as reaching transnationally to less settled contexts in an attempt to 'un-settle' historic narratives in the US.

Together these different contexts and their asserted 'peculiar' applications of transitional justice – itself already a 'peculiar' form of justice – illustrate the wide range of possible application of transitional justice inquiries. They also illustrate the tensions between an expansive approach to the field, and maintaining it as coherently a distinct 'field'. As I have pointed out the field is increasingly striking for the fact that no clear concept of 'transition' bounds it. Rather the 'transitions' of transitional justice are increasingly understood in a rather circular way, to be all those transitions in which the 'tool-kit' is used (Bell 2009).

However, such a fluid concept of transition carries risks. First, it points to the field as depending not on the integrity of the concept of transitional justice, but to the entrepreneurship of academics and activists. As such it is vulnerable to that entrepreneurship. Once everything is defined as transitional all justice becomes 'transitional' justice. Moreover, can a field be sustained that owes its existence and traction to the sociological dynamics of field creation, rather than consensus over some core normative propositions on which the field might be grounded? In fact, all politics involves ongoing political bargaining over the nature of the state, and the direction in which it is travelling in terms of essentially contested concepts such as 'democracy' or 'peace' or 'the rule of law' (Gallie 1956). These concepts are not simple 'things' to be achieved, but are dynamic and brought into being by the very arguments over what their essence involves. In some sense transitional justice mechanisms can be understood as contributing to a wider social negotiation as to what concepts such as democracy, peace or rule of law demand and should look like in the particular context.

Nonetheless, the capacity to frame almost any justice inquiry as a 'transitional justice' inquiry carries two risks. The first is that the field becomes a non-field – intellectually incoherent because it has little organising concept. That of course is an academic concern regarding academic activities. The second, however, is a practical concern relating to the apparent ease with which transitional justice can be strategically instrumentally used to pursue a variety of claims as to the future. The discourse of transitional justice in part has power because it can be used politically to 're-frame' assumptions as to what is 'settled' and suggest an alternative direction of travel. This can be a progressive re-framing, such as where transitional justice discourses in Spain are used to re-interrogate and push the compromises between democracy and authoritarianism that continue to shape, constrain and even trouble Spain's post-Franco political and constitutional settlement. However, it can also be a more negative re-framing, as with Uribe's use of transitional justice discourse and mechanisms in Colombia, which sought to reframe what might otherwise have been viewed as one-sided impunity for pro-state groups with close relationships to elements of government, as something more progressive and related to 'peace'. From this perspective, questions of which timeframe, which conflict, which transition, take on a deeper significance because they construct the rights and wrongs of the past and the associated consequences for the future direction of travel. The MENA transitional justice debates in particular have illustrated how contention over which timeframe, which conflict, which former regime themselves become a vehicle for competing strategic instrumental attempts to define the relevant 'conflict' from which the transition proceeds, in ways that stitch up the transition's nature and outcomes. Whoever defines the transition defines 'the peace'.

Which wrongs?

A second permeable line from which to interrogate the normative boundaries of transitional justice is from that of asking: 'which wrongs' does it apply to? This debate asks in a different way: to which conflict does the mechanism apply? This pushing out of the parameters of the discourse expands the reach of transitional justice by expanding the concept of 'conflict' or 'harm', rather than its geographic or historical reach. The three examples included in the collection represent two strong and persistent challenges and one more recent but growing one. O'Rourke's piece questions how we are to understand the gendered nature of the 'wrongs' recognised by transitional justice (2013). While transitional justice often has a 'from' and 'to' in mind, its articulation of the 'from' and 'to' is often deeply gendered. Rather than the harms of conflict and the non-harm of 'peace', O'Rourke – along with others – asks how women experience conflict and transition and points to the mismatch between an experience of women of continuities of violence whose form tends to mutate rather than disappear, and a discourse that assumes it 'knows' what the from and to comprise.

A second challenge to transitional justice's concept of harm questions its focus on civil and political rights to the exclusion of socio-economic rights. Transitional justice mechanisms have often been exclusively involved with the former – most of the 'tools' in the tool-kit implicitly engage with civil and political rights exclusively or disproportionately. This is a different form of presuming 'the wrong'. Increasingly, work challenges this focus to transitional justice. Waldorf considers arguments – made with increasing popularity – that transitional justice should focus more on socio-economic violations (2012). Even more recently, writing – of which Carranza forms an early example – is emerging considering whether transitional justice should engage with corruption and economic crimes – in a sense looking at the 'criminal' justice component of socio-economic rights (2008).

This second set of boundary dilemmas suggests that transitional justice discourse uses the wrong frame of vision when asking which wrongs to account for, so distorting the end goals that transition is focused on. In leaving out corruption, organised crime, socio-economic rights or the experience of women, the discourse is accused of understanding the conflict to be resolved in terms of merely one of its dimensions, and so reducing the potential for transformation. The critique operates not just as a critique of the remit of the field as currently constructed, but as a critique of the discourse more broadly.

However, the debates over 'which wrong' can also be understood as an attempt to have transitional justice engage with the mutating nature of conflict pre, during and even post ('the') conflict. Whether the focus is women, socio-economic development or corruption, each illustrates how conflict and forms of repression often mutate rather than being eliminated, and points to the connection between non-military 'wrongs' and the 'central' military conflict in complex ways. The 'what wrongs' question points to the uneven gains of peace processes and the variable geometries of violence. In this sense, this boundary discussion also grapples with 'what conflict' question, as it examines whether it is ever enough to deal with 'the' conflict which most overtly stands to be resolved, or whether we have to deal with the structural conflicts that come before it and come after it and are intimately bound up with it in complex ways. For some the broader approach is hopelessly utopian, while for others it is a necessity.

What political ends?

This brings us to our last boundary debate: the debate as to the actual and appropriate ends of transitional justice. In some senses this is the boundary debate implicit in all the others. While, as the debate over the origins of transitional justice illustrated, there was some consensus in authoritarian transitions as to what the nature and role of transitional justice was, this consensus is now under attack. Some attack transitional justice as something that has not achieved what it set out to achieve (whatever that 'it' is – one pays one's money and one takes one's choice). This attack suggests a failure in reaching the destination rather than the wrong choice of destination. However, the more fundamental charge here is that transitional justice institutions and mechanisms inevitably fail to deliver on their promise. This failure is often wrapped up in the wider failure of 'imposed' liberal democracy, often attributed to charges of lack of political will of international intervener, or lack of institutional capacity or competence, or all three, as Kersten's account of the International Criminal Court in Libya illustrates (2014).

However, others attack the project of transitional justice as having the wrong goals in the first place. Nagy's essay provides a succinct summary of the consequences of the boundary decisions over 'for what', 'for who' and 'when', pointing to transitional justice as 'depoliticised in its application', despite its considerable political power (2009). She calls for transitional justice to adopt a broader approach 'that encompasses structural violence, gender inequality and foreign involvement' within its purview (ibid.: 287).

Two last pieces mount slightly different attacks from specific case studies, focusing on the power of the discourse and forms of resistance to it. Branch examines traditional justice practices or 'ethno-national' justice in Northern Uganda, which he views as a reaction to the liberal critique of transitional justice (2014). Yet, he shows the limitations of how traditional practices are deployed as a transitional justice mechanism to exclude the pluralism of justice practices in a complex society, in favour of brands of traditional justice that offer forms of certainty and closure. In a sense Branch challenges the power of the transitional justice discourse to limit and constrain local development even when it overtly eschews global liberal projects. Madlingozi's piece on 'transitional justice entrepreneurs' and victims points to how a victim's group in South Africa tried to navigate the discourse's need to produce victims in a particular image (2010). He illustrates the complex 'dance' that local actors need to play, to respond to use global transitional justice norms and practices to meet local narratives and needs, again speaking to a discourse of constraint.

All three boundary debates can be understood in terms of the evolution of the praxis-based agenda by those who have found themselves excluded from the discourse, whether women, or victims of socio-economic rights violations. In fact, our first two boundary debates, in suggesting both new contexts and new 'wrongs' with which the discourse must reckon, use these boundary dilemmas as a form of challenge to what the discourse 'fences in' and 'fences out', and the political and justice consequences of this choice. These essays all explicitly challenge how the discourse constructs its power and the costs for individuals and for communities and societies. They suggest a complex interplay between global imposition and local resistance and agency that runs throughout the collection.

However, the critique can also be understood as part of a broader 'era of disillusionment' with transitions and their outcomes. If transitional justice emerged as a hopeful discourse linked to the possibility of progressive change, it now stands charged as yet another failed project. This charge is made by those who sought progressive transformation of oppressive and violent societies. However, it is also a charge made by some of the less progressive global forces that wish to replace what was a tentative move in the early 1990s towards negotiated ends to conflict with more force-based approaches. The move towards negotiated settlement was significant in replacing unthinking international endorsement of the state's monopoly on the use of force whatever the nature of the state, with an approach that understood shades of legitimacy and promoted negotiated peace as a better way to end conflict than either a wait-and-see approach of letting local parties fight it out, or a tilting-the-outcome approach of intervening militarily. Against this last backdrop there are also reasons to be critical of some critical approaches to transitional justice discourse, as themselves part of the sociology of field-creation and a 'coming of age' of the discourse as it shifts from praxis-based discourse rooted in human rights advocacy to 'legitimate area of academic study and critique' by those who have little connection to the praxis that was the originating dynamic of the field.

What effect?

This brings us to our last set of pieces. In response to emerging critique there has been a move towards attempting to 'measure' whether transitional justice mechanisms have delivered on the goals attributed to them. Do they achieve greater accountability? Do they correlate with more peaceful outcomes? Or more 'rule of law'? While in the early 1990s transitional justice's multiple goals could be lightly asserted to justify the adoption of new transitional justice mechanisms, 25 years on donors want to measure which mechanisms achieve which goals, and make future decisions on what transitional justice measures to support in the light of some sort of 'scientific' evidence. Transitional justice institutions and interventions are increasingly subjected to forms of evaluation or measurement. Yet, measuring outcomes presumes that we know what the goals of transitional justice are, and that those goals are measurable. The project of measuring and evaluating also implicitly assumes that we will learn how to 'do it better' from understanding gaps between goals and outcomes.

The question of measurement might not look like a 'permeable boundary' in transitional justice, but I suggest it is. The boundary is the one outlined at the start and that has run throughout the collection: between transitional justice as 'tool-kit' whose effectiveness can be measured, and transitional justice as a process and battlefield over what the normative content of justice is, which inevitably will remain unresolved and ongoing. Both Dancy and Duggan's pieces challenge any simple approach to 'measurement' that would deny the contested nature of the practice and its possible goals.

Conclusion

In conclusion I offer some thoughts of my own on what is now understood as a 'crossroads' for transitional justice (van der Merwe 2014). In this introduction and in my selection of essays, I suggest that transitional justice discourse has always stood at a crossroads: a crossroads between normative concept and tool-kit (to be used for good or evil), and a crossroads between local tool or globally imposed 'solution'. Having purveyed the field after being involved in it for many years, my own response to the 'crossroads' for transitional justice would be to in a sense relabel the project of 'transitional justice' as a project of 'contending with the past'. In my view, what best connects all the areas and debates outlined above is that they are all attempts to 'deal with the past' – or better still 'contend' with the past (Haass Report 2013). This re-labelling relieves transitional justice of its normative 'justice' burden, but also leaves us able to consider the types of normative, political, legal and moral function particular spaces and mechanisms for contending with the past play in their particular local and global context.

I suggest that we best make sense of the field by understanding transitional justice debates as attempts to examine the political and legal spaces in which societies can 'contend with the past' in ways that attempt to bridge to achieve the multiple goals necessary to stable inclusive and open political settlements. These goals include that elites pact successfully move from violence to political cooperation; that stable political and legal institutions are fashioned; that new aggrieved constituencies or 'spoilers' are not created; that a form of social transformation takes place capable of delivering peace as having some sort of meaning in terms of improved life capabilities.

From this perspective the key question for institutional design is not how to arrive at some sort of end-of-history communal moment. Rather, the key question is how to find spaces in which to contend with the past constructively and peacefully, in ways that lead away from that past rather than back to it. This approach will involve different institutional responses, with different relationships to law, at different stages of conflict and peace process, in different ways in different contexts. Reducing talk of 'transitional justice' and increasing the focus on 'how to contend with the past' would caution global actors to be prepared to adopt long-term views, and to live with mess and multiple institutional approaches, all the time aware of the ongoing connection of any attempt to contend with the past to the political economy of how actors are contending over the future. The past will need to be contended with on an ongoing basis, and it will need to be contended whatever the institutional choices of local or international elites. Often the very process of transitional justice design and implementation will involve contestation that is itself a process of contending with the past.

The key project question when deciding whether and how to establish a transitional justice mechanism is not how to define goals and tailor institutional design to achieving them. Rather, the key question is whether it is useful and important to have a constructed dedicated space in which to contend with the past, and how it can best be designed to improve the lot of those most damaged by the past, and lead to more justice rather than less in the future. In my view, this approach would lead to more modest and realistic approaches to what transitional justice can achieve. It would encourage people to view transitional justice spaces as ones where we create as much as apply justice, because justice must always be brought into existence by combining both universal global norms with particular local instantiations of justice. However, this more modest conceptualisation of transitional justice would also signal more clearly what is at stake in failing to address the past. Failure to provide constructive spaces for contending with the past will not lead to contention being postponed, or magically somehow disappearing. Rather, failure to provide space in which to constructively contend with the past will displace contention to other arenas. These are likely to be the spaces of the political and legal institutions of post-conflict state, who will face contention over their legitimacy whether peaceful or otherwise.

Bibliography

Anders, G. and Zenker, O. (eds) (2014) *Transition and Justice: Negotiating the Terms of New Beginnings in Africa* (Wiley).

Bell, C. (2009) 'Transitional Justice, Interdisciplinarity and the State of the "Field" or "Non-field"', *International Journal of Transitional Justice*, 3(1), 5–27.

Bell, C. and O'Rourke, C. (2007) 'Does Feminism Need a Theory of Transitional Justice? An Introductory Essay', *International Journal of Transitional Justice*, 1(2), 23–44.

Campbell, C. and Aoláin, F. N. (2005) 'The Paradox of Transition in Contested Democracies', *Human Rights Quarterly*, 27(1), 172–213.

Conaghan, J. (2009) 'The Making of a Field or the Building of a Wall? Feminist Legal Studies and Law, Gender and Sexuality', *Feminist Legal Studies*, 17(3), 303–07.

Editorial Note (2007) *International Journal of Transitional Justice*, 1(1), 1–5.

Fletcher, L., Weinstein, H. and Rowen, J. (2009) 'Context, Timing and the Dynamics of Transitional Justice: A Historical Perspective', *Human Rights Quarterly*, 31, 163–220.

Gallie, W. B. (1956) 'Essentially Contested Concepts', *Proceedings of the Aristotelian Society*, 56, 167–198.

Haass Report, 'Proposed Agreement, 31 December 2013, An Agreement among the Parties of the Northern Ireland Executive on Parades, Select Commemorations and Related Protests; Flags,

Emblems; and Contending with the Past' 2013, available at http://www.northernireland.gov.uk/haass.pdf

International Center for Transitional Justice & Kofi Annan Foundation (2014) *Challenging the Conventional: Can Truth Commissions Strengthen Peace Processes* (New York, available at http://www.kofiannanfoundation.org/sites/default/files/ictj-report-kaf-truthcommpeace-2014.pdf)

Kritz, N. (1995) *Transitional Justice: How Emerging Democracies Deal with Former Regimes* (Volumes 1–3) (United States Institute of Peace).

Mutua, M. (2015) 'What Is the Future of Transitional Justice?', *International Journal of Transitional Justice*, 9, 1–9.

O'Leary, B. and McGarry, J. (2004) *The Northern Ireland Conflict: Consociational Engagements* (Oxford University Press).

Orentlicher, D. F. (1991) 'The Duty to Prosecute Human Rights Violations of a Prior Regime', *The Yale Law Journal*, 100(8), 2537–2615.

Posner, E. A. and Vermule, A. (2004) 'Transitional Justice as Ordinary Justice', *Harvard Law Review*, 117(3), 761–825.

Sikkink, K. (2012) *The Justice Cascade: How Human Rights Prosecutions Are Changing World Politics* (W W Norton & Co).

Teitel, R. G. (2000) *Transitional Justice* (Oxford University Press).

Part I

ORIGINS AND CONCEPTIONS OF TRANSITIONAL JUSTICE

1

How "Transitions" Reshaped Human Rights: A Conceptual History of Transitional Justice

*Paige Arthur**

ABSTRACT

This article clarifies the origins of the field of transitional justice and its preliminary conceptual boundaries. I argue that the field began to emerge in the late 1980s, as a consequence of new practical conditions that human rights activists faced in countries such as Argentina, where authoritarian regimes had been replaced by more democratic ones. The turn away from "naming and shaming" and toward accountability for past abuse among human rights activists was taken up at the international level, where the focus on political change as "transition to democracy" helped to legitimate those claims to justice that prioritized legal-institutional reforms and

* I would like to thank the following people for graciously agreeing to be interviewed: Juan Méndez, José Zalaquett, Jaime Malamud-Goti, Margo Picken, Abraham Lowenthal, Tim Phillips, and Alice Henkin. Special thanks go to Tim Phillips for opening up the papers of the Project on Justice in Times of Transition to my research. Finally, thanks also owed to my ICTJ colleagues Pablo de Greiff, Mark Freeman, and Louis Bickford for comments on previous drafts of this article.

responses—such as punishing leaders, vetting abusive security forces, and replacing state secrecy with truth and transparency—over other claims to justice that were oriented toward social justice and redistribution. I end by discussing the many ways in which these initial conceptual boundaries have since been tested and expanded.

I. INTRODUCTION

Reflecting in 1989 on the question of how torture victims in Brazil, Uruguay, and repressive regimes around the world might find some measure of justice for their suffering, *New Yorker* writer Lawrence Weschler, with his usual eloquence, went straight to the heart of the matter. There was a "primordial moment which has desperately to be addressed—and as desperately by the torture society as by the torture victim." Questions needed to be answered: "Who was there? Who was screaming . . .? Who, even now, will dare to hear . . .? Who will be held accountable? And who will hold them to account?"[1] But, there was a problem. "Good people," he offered, "will disagree on how that holding to account ought to proceed in the context of real-life, often exceptionally precarious political situations."[2]

Weschler had been a part of a "remarkable group of activists and scholars," who, as he described it, convened in November 1988 to discuss how successor governments should deal with the crimes of their predecessors. The meeting, which was organized by the Aspen Institute and funded by the Ford Foundation, aimed to sort through the moral, political, and legal implications of recent trials, commissions of inquiry, purges, and other measures intended to hold previous regimes to account for systematic human rights abuses, as well as to foster a transition to democracy. "Over and over again," Weschler wrote, "countries as varied as Uganda, Argentina, South Korea, Chile, South Africa, Brazil, The Philippines, Uruguay, Guatemala, and Haiti (all of whom were represented at the Aspen Conference) and the Soviet Union, Poland, Czechoslovakia, and China (which were not) confront the same sorts of questions as they attempt to move from dictatorial to democratic systems of governance—in essence, the question of what to do with the former torturers persisting in their midst."[3]

The case of Argentina loomed large. With the collapse of the military dictatorship and the election of Raul Alfonsín in 1983, there had been a vigorous public debate about who should be punished for human rights

1. Lawrence Weschler, A Miracle, A Universe: Settling Accounts with Torturers 242 (1998).
2. *Id.*
3. Lawrence Weschler, *Afterword, in* State Crimes: Punishment or Pardon 89, 90, 92 (Justice and Society Program of The Aspen Institute ed., 1989).

violations and what should be done for victims of those violations. In the foreground of the debate, however, was always the threat to the stability of the new regime that such actions might pose. Alfonsín's government opted for limited prosecutions and, in a dramatic move, put the former junta leaders on trial. It also convened a commission of inquiry to find out what had happened to people who had been "disappeared" by the state security forces. Jaime Malamud-Goti, one of the chief architects, along with Carlos Nino, of Alfonsín's prosecutions policy, argued at the Aspen Institute conference that prosecutions were not only a response to victims' thirst for justice: "We agreed with the view that trying the perpetrators in the military of the worst crimes would contribute to the consolidation of democracy by restoring confidence in its mechanisms."[4] However, the administration was divided. The minister of defense, who had the most direct relations with the military, opposed the policy on the grounds that it risked a potentially disastrous political backlash—perhaps even a military coup.[5] Malamud-Goti and Nino worried that the judiciary, some of which was held over from the previous regime, would obstruct the prosecutions policy. Under severe pressure from the military, after a series of highly publicized trials and the publication of the commission of inquiry's report, *Never Again*, the government put an end to new prosecutions with the so-called Full Stop Law of 1986 and Due Obedience Law of 1987. A later government subsequently pardoned those still serving prison sentences.

The questions raised by the Argentine case were not only ones of justice: Whom to punish, by what authority, and on what grounds? What to do for victims and their loved ones? Rather, they were questions about justice *and* prudence: How to balance competing moral imperatives, reconcile legitimate claims for justice with equally legitimate claims for stability and social peace, and foster the relationship between justice for crimes of the past and a more just political order in the present.

A. A "Field" of Transitional Justice

At the Aspen Institute conference, José Zalaquett, a future commissioner of the Chilean National Commission on Truth and Reconciliation, reflected on the situation human rights activists faced in Latin American countries where repressive regimes had recently crumbled. "Experience has shown," he said, "that dealing with transitional political situations is a new area of

4. Jaime Malamud-Goti, *Trying Violators of Human Rights: The Dilemma of Transitional Democratic Governments*, *in* State Crimes, *supra* note 3, at 71–72.
5. Telephone Interview with Jaime Malamud-Goti, Director, Carlos Nino Institute, University of Palermo, Argentina (1 Oct. 2007).

human rights practice that poses some complex ethical, legal and practical questions"—questions that no one was yet in a good position to answer.[6] Six years later, at a conference on "Dealing with the Past" in post-Apartheid South Africa, he came to the conclusion that "[a] pool of world experiences is contributing to an understanding of the lessons to be learned about justice in the process of transition."[7] This essay examines the shift, implied in Zalaquett's observations, from the recognition of new practical dilemmas to the development of a knowledge-base to address those dilemmas through the emergence of a new field called "transitional justice."

In particular, this article looks at how a certain understanding of "transition" helped to shape the conceptual contents of a new field. The field of "transitional justice"—an international web of individuals and institutions whose internal coherence is held together by common concepts, practical aims, and distinctive claims for legitimacy—began to emerge as a response to these new practical dilemmas and as an attempt to systematize knowledge deemed useful to resolving them.[8] The field of transitional justice, so defined, came directly out of a set of interactions among human rights activists, lawyers and legal scholars, policymakers, journalists, donors, and comparative politics experts concerned with human rights and the dynamics of "transitions to democracy," beginning in the late 1980s.[9]

One window into understanding how transitions helped to structure this new field—which would later crystallize around such organizations as the US-based Project on Justice in Times of Transition (1993), the South Africa–based Justice in Transition (1994), and an international NGO called the International Center for Transitional Justice (2001), as well as pockets

6. José Zalaquett, *Confronting Human Rights Violations Committed by Former Governments: Principles Applicable and Political Constraints, in* State Crimes, *supra* note 3, at 26.

7. Aryeh Neier, José Zalaquett & Adam Michnik, *Why Deal with the Past, in* Dealing with the Past: Truth and Reconciliation in South Africa 1, 8 (Alex Boraine & Janet Levy eds., 2d ed. 1994).

8. For an application of the idea of "internal coherence" to transitional justice, see Pablo de Greiff, *Introduction: Repairing the Past: Compensation for Victims of Human Rights Violations, in* The Handbook of Reparations 1 (Pablo de Greiff ed., 2006).

9. This article does not represent an analysis of a field, in the sense advocated by field-theorist Pierre Bourdieu, but rather a conceptual history—which itself offers some clues for such an analysis. Thus, it does not advance a methodologically rigorous understanding of the word "field," in the sense of a structured set of relations among positions, occupied by actors with a particular set of dispositions, and which are hierarchically ordered and operate according to a distinctive, internal logic. However, the "looser" understanding of the word "field" used throughout this article does bear some resemblance to this concept, in that I identify as important features of the field of transitional justice the facts that it: 1) is clearly distinguishable from the field out of which it emerged, which is the field of human rights; 2) it implies a set of actors who have a set of common aims, and who are thus oriented toward one another in their practice; 3) it has developed institutions that advance those aims; and 4) it advances distinctive criteria of judgment and self-legitimation.

within other NGOs, universities, and international institutions—is a series of conferences that took place in the late 1980s and early 1990s. At the 1988 Aspen Institute conference, "State Crimes: Punishment or Pardon," the 1992 Charter 77 Foundation conference in Salzburg, Austria, "Justice in Times of Transition," and the 1994 Institute for Democracy in South Africa (IDASA) conference, "Dealing with the Past," political actors, human rights activists, and observers from around the world were convened in order to compare experiences and discuss options. Each of these conferences not only featured the same kinds of participants (in terms of professional competencies), but they also had many overlapping participants, including Zalaquett, Malamud-Goti, Aryeh Neier, Juan E. Méndez, Diane Orentlicher, Lawrence Weschler, Alice Henkin, Tim Phillips, and Adam Michnik.[10] Moreover, each was structured in a similar way: they dealt with a distinct set of measures—prosecutions, truth-telling, restitution or reparation, and reform of abusive state institutions—whose aims were to provide justice for victims *and* to facilitate the transition in question. The conferences optimized the possibility for comparative analysis of transitional "dilemmas."

In examining how transitions "mattered" to the emergence of a distinctive field, one goal is to offer some preliminary answers to the question of why a field of transitional justice emerged at the time that it did and in the form that it did.[11] However, this article focuses on only one aspect of this question: the particular and distinctive conceptual contents of transitional justice. Although some have dismissed the relevance of the word "transitional" as a kind of syntactical error, this article contends that the idea played an important role in shaping understandings of the dilemmas that actors faced, as well as in their justifications for their actions and judgments. "Transition"—and, more specifically, "transition to democracy"—was the dominant normative lens through which political change was viewed at this time, and thus attending to its distinctive contents should shed some light on the emergence of the

10. See the annex at the end of this article showing the overlap of participants, as well as a list of all participants at the three conferences.

11. It should be noted that my choice of the word "field" is made in contrast to Kathryn Sikkink and Carrie Booth Walling's word "network." Sikkink and Walling have done groundbreaking work on the question of how international human rights networks have been used to raise the salience of accountability claims made on the domestic level. This is not the question addressed in this article, however. This article describes how a distinct field of activity, known as "transitional justice"—and not just "human rights"—came into being. This question is related to the international human rights networks they address, but it is not reducible to it. That is, it is entirely possible that domestic human rights groups seeking to advance accountability claims could have leveraged their international networks to aid their causes—but without a distinct field of transitional justice ever coming into existence. *See* Kathryn Sikkink & Carrie Booth Walling, *Argentina's Contribution to Global Trends in Transitional Justice*, *in* Transitional Justice in the Twenty-First Century 301 (Naomi Roht-Arriaza & Javier Mariezcurrena eds., 2006).

field. Indeed, attending to what was understood by transition helps to clarify what was considered to be an appropriate justice measure. It explains why the measures of prosecutions, truth-telling, restitution, and reform of abusive state institutions—not some other measures of justice, such as those associated with claims for distributive justice—were recognized as *the* legitimate justice initiatives during a time of political change.

Though this is only one small part of the story, it is a significant one because these understandings were crucial to structuring the initial conceptual boundaries for the field. These are boundaries that have since been consistently pushed, sometimes in response to practical difficulties encountered in new political contexts, and sometimes through reflection on the part of those working within the field itself. Thus, this article does not look at the shifts in practice of human rights activists in the 1980s—that is for another essay. This article also explicitly avoids analysis of justice efforts in single countries (Argentina, for example), because the aim is to show that the field of transitional justice emerged at an international level.[12] Indeed, part of the distinctive character of the field is that its knowledge-base has always been comparative. It has attempted to devise typologies of experiences and systematic knowledge of (often disparate) country contexts. This fact can be seen in the early conferences: each of them was structured around the principle of comparing national experiences among a diverse group of international participants, rather than the principle of identifying (and exporting) an ideal-type.

To illustrate the argument, this article first makes a case for identifying the late-1980s to mid-1990s as the period when the field first began to emerge. A crucial piece of evidence here is the coining of the phrase "transitional justice." The term was invented as a device to signal a new sort of human rights activity and as a response to concrete political dilemmas human rights activists faced in what they understood to be "transitional" contexts. Having established this period as a plausible starting point, the article then turns to a consideration of what "transitions" meant at the time, in order to have a better understanding of how it might have shaped understandings of the kinds of justice claims that were considered legitimate or illegitimate in a period of transition. The article then weaves these strands together by looking at a particular case: the 1988 Aspen Institute conference, which was the first of a cluster of meetings that helped to clarify and solidify a conceptual framework for an emerging field. This conference brought together human

12. Thus, although Argentina's Center for Legal and Social Studies (CELS) was one of the key human rights actors pushing for justice measures during the Argentine transition, its international partner, Americas Watch, played a more central role in the emergence of an international-level *field* of transitional justice, particularly through the efforts of Juan Méndez and Aryeh Neier.

rights activists, philosophers, legal experts, and political scientists from Latin America, Uganda, Haiti, and South Korea in an effort to compare experiences of the pursuit of justice initiatives in varying transitional contexts. Some of the participants had been actors in transitional justice efforts (Malamud-Goti), some would become actors in such efforts (Zalaquett), whereas others were observers with varying degrees of interest in the outcome of any particular national situation.

This conference was not chosen because it represents a founding moment for the field of transitional justice, but because, in the words of its organizer Alice Henkin, it offered an "intellectual framework" that was previously absent for discussing issues that were raised in postwar Germany, Spain, Greece, Argentina, and other places.[13] The debates that took place and the participants involved thus give important insight into the conceptual underpinnings—if not the practical and institutional underpinnings—of an emerging field, one that came to be known several years later as "transitional justice." If human rights activists were developing a new set of practices, how did they—as well as the thinkers, policymakers, and donors with whom they interacted—conceive of those practices and shape them into the conceptual structure for a unique, new field?

B. Where to Start?

Where to start a history of the field of transitional justice is no easy question to answer. One thinks of the Allies' precedent-setting trials of Nazi war criminals at Nuremberg, or of the human rights policies of Argentinean President Alfonsín after the end of the military junta. But the measures we now associate with transitional justice certainly are nothing new. In *Stay the Hand of Vengeance*, Gary Bass recounts a history of war crimes tribunals that extends at least 200 years into the past.[14] In *Closing the Books: Transitional Justice in Historical Perspective*, Jon Elster has written about trials and purges more than 2,000 years ago, during political upheavals in ancient Athens.[15] So how do we decide where and when to start the story?

Perhaps simple is best; we should start by investigating the invention and acceptance of the term "transitional justice" itself. Interestingly, none of the existing accounts of the emergence of transitional justice explore the appearance of the term. Thus, for Ruti Teitel, the Nuremberg Tribunal is an

13. Interview with Alice Henkin, Director, Justice and Society Program, The Aspen Institute, New York, N.Y. (13 Aug. 2007).

14. Gary Jonathan Bass, Stay the Hand of Vengeance: The Politics of War Crimes Tribunals (2000).

15. Jon Elster, Closing the Books: Transitional Justice in Historical Perspective (2004).

important moment in the first "phase" of transitional justice, even though none of the actors involved would have described it as such.[16] Nor would those actors necessarily have ascribed the same meanings to what they were doing as Teitel and Elster do.

Here is where the question of methodology is important. An observer such as Elster, for example, treats transitional justice as a perennial problem, a timeless construct whose varieties can be understood and dissected across the ages—from ancient Athens to the present. Whatever meanings these various practices may have held for the historical actors involved (none of whom had ever heard the phrase "transitional justice") get swept into a universal, homogeneous conception of transitional justice, whose only meaning is identical to our conventional, twenty-first century understanding of it. This kind of approach, which in historical practice is called "anachronism," has been eloquently critiqued by Quentin Skinner, among many others.[17] In Elster's defense, he makes no claim to writing a history of transitional justice. The title of his book, which puts transitional justice "in historical perspective," as well as its contents, suggests otherwise. Those who take a genealogical approach, such as Teitel, fare better with respect to anachronism, but they still fall into the trap of imputing ideas about "transitional justice" to actors who, presumably, were unlikely to have held them, particularly in their discussions of the immediate post-World War II era.

It makes sense when one is writing a conceptual history to begin by examining the invention of a phrase itself, as representative of the emergence of a new position, as well as its subsequent acceptance as something distinct and meaningful. Such an approach has the advantage of avoiding anachronism, while providing a less arbitrary starting point.

Following from Skinner, the invention of new terms, or the shift in meaning of old terms, in a political vocabulary are responses to concrete problems faced in political life. Some of these political terms are, moreover, intersubjectively normative. As James Tully puts it, these are "words that not only describe, but, in describing, also evaluate"—according to the context in which they are invoked.[18] In a liberal-democratic context, for example, invoking terms such as "democracy," "dictatorship," "rational," "tolerant" implies an evaluation, a particular normative judgment. Calling another country "democratic" or another person "tolerant" is, in this context, a description that expresses approval—which, in turn, helps to legitimate the actions of those who invoke them. Thus, the appearance and apparent ac-

16. Ruti G. Teitel, *Transitional Justice Genealogy*, 16 HARV. HUM. RTS. J. 69, 70 (2003).

17. *See* Quentin Skinner, *Meaning and Understanding in the History of Ideas*, *in* MEANING AND CONTEXT: QUENTIN SKINNER AND HIS CRITICS 33–34 (James Tully ed., 1988).

18. James Tully, *The Pen is a Mighty Sword: Quentin Skinner's Analysis of Politics*, *in* MEANING AND CONTEXT, *supra* note 17, at 13.

ceptance of the phrase "transitional justice" is itself a response to a set of new problems and a means of legitimating the practices used to respond to those problems. Those practices were prosecutions, commissions of inquiry, purges, and restitution policies. This article seeks to sketch out the contents of "transitional justice" when the phrase was invented, and how those contents emerged.[19] This account will help answer some very basic questions about why transitional justice has resonated very strongly in some contexts, and has either been received with skepticism or completely ignored in others.

Not insignificantly, the first appearance of the term, in keyword searches of databases on international newspapers, law reviews, and social science journals, came in a *Boston Herald* article about the Charter 77 Foundation's 1992 conference in Salzburg, "Justice in Times of Transition." The reporter covering the conference noted in passing that this was to be "the first in a year-long series of meetings on transitional justice."[20] In the lead-up to the conference, its organizers, Tim Phillips and Wendy Luers, as well as other advisers such as Herman Schwartz and Ruti Teitel, used the phrase sporadically.[21] They ultimately opted, however, to describe their activities as "justice in times of transition." Indeed, they subsequently founded a new organization, the Project on Justice in Times of Transition (1993), a name that Alex Boraine, the future vice chair of the South African Truth and Reconciliation Commission as well as a co-founder of the International Center for Transitional Justice, then borrowed and adapted for his organization Justice in Transition in South Africa (1994).[22]

Whoever the original author of the phrase was, and there were probably several, most notable among them Teitel,[23] its transmission and acceptance

19. Skinner actually makes a much more sophisticated argument about the interrelationship between political vocabulary and political action. As Tully notes, "Using these terms in the conventional way serves to legitimate customary practices." Trying to use such a term in a *new* way, however, "will then serve to re-characterize, or re-evaluate, the political situation it represents; legitimizing a new range of activity or beliefs, delegitimizing or reinforcing the *status quo*, and so on." *Id.* This account does not rest on this broader set of claims, however, but rather only on the claims cited above.

20. Mary Jo Palumbo, *New Democracies Debate How to Punish Dictators of Past*, Boston Herald, 5 Apr. 1992, at 16.

21. *See, e.g.*, Letter from Wendy Luers in which she used the phrase "transitional justice," in Justice in Times of Transition Files, Folder, Background, to Justice Project (Early Proposals/Precursors) Cambridge, Mass (5 Dec. 1991) (copy on file with author).

22. Boraine had worked with the Project on Justice in Times of Transition, which enabled him to invite some of the international guests to the 1994 conference, "Dealing with the Past." When he left IDASA shortly after that conference, he formed his own organization, which was the occasion for adapting the Project on Justice in Times of Transition's name.

23. Ruti Teitel claims authorship of the phrase, and it is likely that she was among the very first to use it and was instrumental in its diffusion. *See* Ruti Teitel, *Editorial Note-Transitional Justice Globalized*, 2 Int'l J. of Transitional Just. 1 (2008). However, there are other usages around the same time, and some even earlier. In 1989, philosopher

was most significantly aided in the mid-1990s by the publication of Neil Kritz's four-volume compendium *Transitional Justice: How Emerging Democracies Reckon with Former Regimes* in 1995. Kritz had been in attendance at the 1992 Salzburg conference on Justice in Times of Transition. After his volumes' appearance, references to transitional justice steadily increased throughout the late 1990s. Among a range of scholarly journals in 1994, the first year in which there is any reference to transitional justice, there is only one reference to transitional justice—a citation of Kritz's volumes in Priscilla Hayner's article, "Fifteen Truth Commissions."[24] By 2000, a search of the same set of journals showed seventeen references. In major Anglophone newspapers uptake was slow, yet growing. Articles making reference to transitional justice appeared in the *Washington Post*, the *Los Angeles Times*, *Foreign Affairs* magazine, and *The Guardian* (UK).[25]

Kritz's volumes were reviewed by people with a range of institutional affiliations and competencies, and in a number of influential outlets. Both Timothy Garton Ash's review in *The New York Review of Books* and Richard Siegel's review in *Human Rights Quarterly* were substantial pieces of writing that set Kritz's work in the context of books on related subjects. Theodore Piccone, a US Department of Defense lawyer under the Clinton administration, wrote the review for the *American Journal of International Law*. Brief reviews also appeared in the *Washington Post* and the *United Nations Chronicle*. The

---

Milton Fisk used the phrase in a discussion of transitions to socialism, MILTON FISK, THE STATE AND JUSTICE: AN ESSAY IN POLITICAL THEORY 304 (1989). More significantly, in 1992 US-based Argentine sociologist Juan E. Corradi made reference to "transitional justice," in an essay he wrote for an edited volume on state terror in Latin America. For him, it was "a particular and intensive type of political justice: the trial by fiat of a previous regime." He continued:

> Transitional justice is both more and less than ordinary justice. It is more because it aims beyond the simple ordering of human relations: it seeks to achieve moral and political regeneration. It is less than ordinary justice because it is subject to serious irregularities, it is a political formula for the formal elimination of a scapegoat, it is imbued with problematic judgments by the power holders of the moment on the qualities and policies of their predecessors, and it is a constitutive act of a new regime.

Juan E. Corradi, *Toward Societies Without Fear, in* FEAR AT THE EDGE: STATE TERROR AND RESISTANCE IN LATIN AMERICA 267, 285–86 (Juan E. Corradi, et al. eds., 1992). Finally, there is a chapter entitled "Transitional Justice" in an obscure 1948 book on the US occupation of New Mexico: ARIE W. POLDERVAART, BLACK-ROBED JUSTICE (1948).

24. Priscilla B. Hayner, *Fifteen Truth Comissions—1974 to 1994: A Compartive Study*, 16 HUM. RTS. Q. 611, 622 (1994).

25. Lexis search for "transitional justice" from 1 Jan. 1950 to 1 Jan. 2001. Of course, the measures that, taken collectively, came to be known as transitional justice have a history of their own. For example, a similar search of the term "truth commission" yields negligible results (only eighteen mentions) before 1 Jan. 1990 (certainly owing to the fact that the Argentine commission did not call itself a "truth commission")—and then skyrocketed thereafter, mainly owing to reporting on the Chilean commission, the El Salvadoran commission, and the South African TRC. Between 1 Jan. 1990 and 1 Jan. 1994, there were 404 stories that mentioned "truth commission"; from 1 Feb. 1994 to 1 Jan. 1998, there were 1,759; and from 1 Feb. 1998 to 1 Jan. 2001, there were 1,377. The spike occurred at the time of the South African TRC.

only review to appear outside of the United States was Steven R. Ratner's essay in the *European Journal of International Law*.[26]

If Kritz's book represented a key driver in the early proliferation of the term transitional justice, then it would make sense to look at the volumes themselves to gain an approximate sense of the meaning given to the phrase, and whether the reviewers accepted that meaning. Importantly, the structure of the volumes suggests that transitional justice was a fully formed and rather well-understood set of practices in 1994—so much so, that one could compile a neat list of transitional justice measures and the controversies that might arise in undertaking them. These measures were commissions of inquiry, prosecutions, lustration or purges, and restitution or reparations programs.

What Kritz published was a canon of transitional justice literature—even before anyone was quite sure that a canon was needed. But what was that canon? The subtitle of the book provided a description of transitional justice: "how emerging democracies reckon with former regimes." Thus, transitional justice was something undertaken by "emerging democracies"— states that had undergone a change of regime. All of the reviewers, except one discussed below, accepted this definition uncritically. For Siegel, transitional justice "characterize[d] the choices made and quality of justice rendered when new leaders replace authoritarian predecessors presumed responsible for criminal acts in the wake of the 'third wave of democratization'"—making reference to Samuel Huntington's famous book on transitions to democracy in the late twentieth century.[27] For the *Washington Post*, the basic idea of Kritz's book "is to present the experiences of countries that have made a more or less successful transition to democracy—Belgium, Chile and Czechoslovakia, for example—for the benefit of those countries in the throes of the process."[28] For Piccone, *Transitional Justice* addressed "how new democracies have attempted to strike a balance between redressing the abuses of the former governments and integrating victims and perpetrators in a postconflict society."[29] Therefore, not only did the reviewers accept the utility of the term itself, but they also understood and accepted the contents of the term proposed in Kritz's work.

Ash was the only reviewer to call into question the utility of the linguistic invention of "transitional justice." For him, the book was "too narrowly titled," and in fact no word or phrase existed in English that captured the

26. Other outlets included *New Jersey Criminal Law Forum*, *Syracuse Journal of International Law and Commerce*, *Ethics & International Affairs*, and *Cambridge Quarterly*.
27. Richard Lewis Siegel, *Transitional Justice, A Decade of Debate and Experience*, 20 Hum. Rts. Q. 431, 433 (1998) (book review).
28. Nonfiction, Wash. Post Bookworld, 12 Nov. 1995, at X12.
29. Theodore J. Piccone, *Transitional Justice*, 90 Am. J. Int'l L. 540, 541 (1996) (book review).

full range of all of its attending processes. He suggested two German words that already had a history of usage in German: *Geschichtsaufarbeitung* and *Vergangenheitsbewältigung*. "These may be translated as 'treating' the past," he pointed out, "'working over' the past, 'confronting' it, 'coping, dealing or coming to terms with' it; even 'overcoming' the past. The variety of possible translations indicates the complexity of the matter at hand."[30] After surveying the various methods of dealing with the past—prosecutions, purges, and various truth-telling initiatives, from official commissions to the opening of archives—Ash asked who might best be equipped to do justice to the past. "The answer is, or at least should be, historians," he decided.[31] He continued, "Carelessly used, the records of a state that worked by organized lying, and especially the poisonous, intrusive files of a secret police, can ruin lives. To use them carefully tests the critical skills that historians routinely apply to a medieval charter or an eighteenth-century pamphlet."[32] Ash worried that "truth is a big word, so often abused," and he was keen to place limits on it.[33] "The evidence has to be weighted with very special care. The text must be put in its historical setting. Interpretation needs both intellectual distance and the essential imaginative sympathy with all the men and women involved, even the oppressors."[34]

I have discussed Ash's article at length because it offered actual resistance to the emergence of this new term. In particular, it challenged the idea that the contents of what Kritz had presented as "transitional justice" could capture real-world complexities. This dissension is significant in that it shows what was (perhaps surprisingly) lacking from the proposed canon at the moment of the term's invention: the famous German *Historikerstreit*, or historians' debate, of the 1980s. This debate was taking place in the media outlets of West Germany at the same time discussions in Latin American explored how to deal with former regimes. The historians' debate was a sophisticated, and highly public, conflict about how to interpret the Nazi era and the Holocaust. In particular it questioned how and when the memory of such events might be "overcome" or "mastered," and a more positive image of German history accepted. To a certain degree, the debate was also about who bore responsibility for the Nazi regime and its crimes—a small clique of elites who commandeered the state (making the Holocaust a historical aberration), or a broad swath of the population who actively or passively supported it (making it the end point in a "special historical path," or *Sonderweg*). Each position on this question was marked on the

30. Timothy Garton Ash, *The Truth About Dictatorship*, N.Y. Rev. Books, 19 Feb. 1998, at 35.
31. *Id.* at 40.
32. *Id.*
33. *Id.*
34. *Id.*

political spectrum. Those on the "right," such as Ernst Nolte, supported the argument that the Holocaust was an aberrational response to a particular set of historical conditions (in this case, the threat of communism). Those on the "left," such as Jürgen Habermas, argued that it was the result of deep-rooted cultural proclivities. Note that this debate took place after forty years of prosecutions, lustration processes, and reparation programs. Those historians most intimately involved with the production of truth about the past still disagreed about what the past meant, as did large segments of the German population.

This omission tells us something about Kritz's (and others') conception of transitional justice. Of the forty-two texts gathered in Kritz's thematic overview of transitional justice (Vol. 1), none were written by historians, and the German historians' debate merits only a single passing reference.[35] The reason for the omission is not hard to guess: historians simply were not involved in the production of Kritz's book, nor did they play an important role in discussions on the themes identified by Kritz—and implicitly accepted by most—as providing the conceptual content for transitional justice. Instead of "coming to terms" with historical complexities (as one might expect in an effort to deal with "the past"), transitional justice was presented as deeply enmeshed with *political* problems that were legal-institutional and, relatively, short-term in nature. So short-term, in fact, that they could be dealt with specifically during a "transitional" period.

This analysis is confirmed by Kritz's work. We can identify three areas of interest, sometimes distinct, and sometimes overlapping: human rights, law, and comparative political science. Among human rights activists who appeared in Volume I were José Zalaquett and Aryeh Neier; excerpts from publications by Human Rights Watch and Amnesty International were also included. Among the legal specialists were Diane Orentlicher, Carlos Nino, Thomas Buergenthal, and Theo van Boven. Finally, among the political scientists were Guillermo O'Donnell, Philippe Schmitter, Samuel Huntington, Juan Linz, and John Herz.

It is tempting to divide these groups into broad rubrics, under the headings of, say, morality, law, and politics—and then argue that transitional justice was an attempt to synthesize the three. Though not entirely inaccurate, this would oversimplify a complex and often contradictory process. Of particular interest here is the perhaps surprisingly central role accorded to comparative political analysis in what was considered to be a human rights agenda.

35. *See* From Dictatorship to Democracy: Coping with the Legacies of Authoritarianism and Totalitarianism, (John H. Herz ed., 1982), *cited in* Transitional Justice: How Emerging Democracies Reckon with Former Regimes, Vol. I, 132, 142 (Neil J. Kritz ed., 1995). It also appears, briefly, in Volume II. *See also* Lutz R. Reuter, *How Germany Has Coped: Four Decades Later, in* Transitional Justice, Vol. II, 63, 67 (Neil J. Kritz ed., 1995).

II. ON TRANSITIONS

As suggested, there was general acceptance of Kritz's definition of transitional justice as a set of measures undertaken specifically by "emerging democracies." Though Timothy Garton Ash criticized the narrowness of the term transitional justice," offering his own German-language alternatives laden with meanings from postwar German debates, he did not appear to dispute the idea that it is democracies that should or are more likely to undertake these measures.

This is an important point. As Elster's book shows, the measures we now associate with transitional justice have been around for a very long time. Yet it is only recently that they have been justified through appeals to universal norms such as human rights, or that they have been seen as legitimate only when undertaken by a democratic polity, or that they have been seen as having an underlying, determined connection related to the normative goal of promoting democracy. In order to understand why transitional justice emerged when it did and in the form that it did, we need to understand why it took on these particular contents.

Here is where "transition" surfaces as a crucial concept. After all, the term "transitional justice" could have been simply rejected. Other terms, such as "historical justice," "justice," or Ash's "overcoming the past" might have been proposed in its place. The term might have simply been ignored altogether—a conceptual failure without a legacy. Yet the term was accepted. Why was this so?[36]

On this point, it is important to shift from the questions of whether and how "transitional justice" resonated with its audience in the mid-1990s, to the question of how the capacity for that resonance was created—prior to the appearance of Kritz's volumes.

A. Human Rights and the "Ambiguities of Transitional Situations"

Up to the mid-1980s, the central aim of the international human rights movement had been to shame repressive governments into treating their citizens more justly. Since the regimes that organizations such as Human Rights Watch and Amnesty International investigated were, typically, repressive ones, the issue of accountability for violations had not been a central concern—since it was often impossible. The ending of repressive regimes in Latin America in the early to mid 1980s forced a shift in strategy and thinking. In a cer-

36. Of course, one could not only ascribe the "success" of the new field of transitional justice to its capacity to create resonances—an important part of the story is the creation of institutions and networks, which are not things treated in this article.

tain sense, the human rights movement might have lost—in these particular cases—what had been its central *raison d'être*.[37] Juan Méndez, an Argentine exile who was the Washington director of Americas Watch (now Human Rights Watch) in the early 1980s, and who is currently the president of the International Center for Transitional Justice, recalls that the common wisdom at the time was that there was "no role for us" after the fall of a dictatorship, since the country had "turned a new leaf."[38] However, in the aftermath of the dictatorship in Argentina, when claims for justice were being pursued by local human rights groups, "that wisdom did not last for very long."[39] According to Méndez, as the Alfonsín government mounted prosecutions of military leaders and formed a commission of inquiry into state-led abuse, human rights work "almost seamlessly turned . . . from an adversarial to a supportive position."[40] Indeed, the summary report that he authored in 1987, *Truth and Partial Justice in Argentina*, offered a clear picture of Americas Watch's positions on dealing with past state crimes—one that gave overwhelming attention to criminal prosecutions and an analysis and critique of the political reasons for which they had been limited and later stopped.[41]

José Zalaquett's seminal article, "Confronting Human Rights Violations Committed by Former Governments," written for the 1988 Aspen Institute conference, echoed Méndez's views on this shift in human rights actors' concerns. In it, Zalaquett spelled out the dilemma human rights advocates found themselves in by the early 1980s. He noted that although the human rights movement had been "a palpable presence internationally" during the fall of dictatorships in Greece, Portugal, and Spain in the 1970s,

37. It should be noted that the practices of "naming and shaming" that we associate with the international human rights movement have also been around a long time—one thinks of the anti-slavery campaign in Great Britain and other countries in the eighteenth and nineteenth centuries, as well as the anti-torture campaign in France during the French-Algerian War (1954–1962). However, these phenomena did not themselves constitute an "international human rights" movement, but were rather antecedents of it. *See* Samuel Moyn, *On the Genealogy of Morals*, The Nation, 16 Apr. 2007 (Review of Lynn Hunt, Inventing Human Rights: A History (2007)), *available at* http://www.thenation.com/doc/20070416/moyn.

38. Interview with Juan Méndez, President, International Center for Transitional Justice, New York, N.Y. (9 Aug. 2007). Margo Picken, the Ford Foundation program officer who helped to fund the Aspen Institute conference, recalls that many governments and donor agencies in the 1980s saw human rights organizations as troublemakers in these new regimes (which they supported). This perception resulted in a shift in funding away from human rights to conflict resolution organizations—a trend that was particularly striking in Latin America. Email interview with Margo Picken, Fellow, London School of Economics and Political Science (10 Dec. 2007).

39. *Id.*

40. *Id.*

41. Although Americas Watch strongly supported the aims of the National Commission on Disappeared Persons, its report devoted only three pages (out of sixty-four) to the commission. Juan Méndez, Americas Watch, Truth and Partial Justice in Argentina: An Update (1991). According to Méndez, the reason is that the CONADEP report was by that time very well known.

> the focus of human rights activism was on current abuses and only seldom on past abuses or on preventing the recurrence of human rights violations. . . . Starting in the 1980s, however, human rights organizations have had to focus much more centrally on the human rights issues related to political transitions.[42]

He claimed, moreover, that this turn in human rights activism posed new problems with no easy answers:

> The fragile character of the gains [in new democracies] made human rights organizations aware of the fact that measures which are straightforward from the standpoint of human rights norms could have undesired political implications, which in turn would affect human rights adversely. Human rights organizations were thus unavoidably drawn into the ambiguities of transitional situations.[43]

Political shifts, especially away from authoritarian rule, were the crucial new developments of the 1980s. The core of the debate at the Aspen Institute conference was formed around grappling with the opportunities and risks associated with these shifts. As such, political analysis and moral argumentation were the key discursive modes employed by the participants. Thus, a paper was commissioned from political scientist John Herz, a renowned scholar who had also been an actor in denazification efforts following World War II. It treated many of the same countries (Germany, Greece, Spain), that had been dealt with in his pioneering book *From Dictatorship to Democracy: Coping with the Legacies of Authoritarianism and Totalitarianism* (1982). The papers commissioned from Zalaquett and Jaime Malamud-Goti similarly considered the political implications of justice measures, and Zalaquett even proposed a typology of transitions that indicated the limits that each type would place upon justice efforts.

These political shifts were understood as taking, or were hoped to take, a particular form: transitions to democracy. This is not an inconsequential point. Changes in political regimes were in themselves nothing new. Where the changes would eventually lead was unpredictable and subsequent scrutiny has shown that many of the so-called transitions to democracy, heralded as part of the "third wave" of democratization, were no such thing. The fact that these changes were understood at the time, and almost universally, as "transitions to democracy" is a striking fact that demands an explanation.

---

42. Zalaquett, *Confronting Human Rights Violations*, *supra* note 6, at 24. It should be noted that although part of this article was republished in Kritz' *Transitional Justice*, Vol. 1, the opening sections, which are quoted here and which describe the reasons for a shift in human rights activism in the 1980s, were omitted from Kritz' excerpt.
43. *Id.* at 25.

B. Why a "Transitions" Paradigm

We have seen that the influential notion of a transition to democracy emerged as the principal paradigm by which to interpret the opening of authoritarian regimes. But what is a "transition," and why did it resonate so strongly? The varied instances of political change throughout the world since World War II resist categorization in a neat typology. Many terms might be used: perhaps some countries experienced "revolutions," others "transfers of power," others "regime change," or "restorations," or "independence," or "modernization," or "political development," or perhaps "transitions" of one sort or another. These terms encapsulate changes from capitalism to socialism, military dictatorship to civilian rule, authoritarianism to democracy, communism to liberal democracy, communism to a market economy, and more. The varieties of change are in fact quite staggering.

So how did one particular lens—that of a "transition to democracy"—become the dominant one through which political change was interpreted beginning in the 1980s? First, and most obvious, is the fact that democratic reform was a stated goal of important segments of the population in countries undergoing political change at the time. There may have been other goals, sometimes complementary, such as the establishment of civilian rule or the creation of a market economy, but claims for the democratization of political power were undeniable features of these events, regardless of the terms used to describe them.

Yet this point still leaves us with another question: why were these changes understood as "transitions" to democracy? Why were these phenomena not seen, for example, as merely the beginning of a long, open-ended process of establishing the social preconditions for democratic institutions—including a shift in socioeconomic structures, behavioral habits, and the structural conditions that would allow for a thriving public sphere?

This leads to a second reason for the "transitions" paradigm, much noted by observers, which is that earlier theories of democratization associated with modernization theory had lost their previous legitimacy and were due to be replaced. In the 1960s, for example, the heyday of modernization efforts, liberal Western policymakers and political scientists did not speak of "transitions to democracy," but rather of socioeconomic modernization as a precondition of an evolutionary process of political development. One well-known example of this theory was the work of W. W. Rostow, an economist, political theorist, and national security adviser to both the Kennedy and Johnson administrations, who suggested that societies passed through stages of social and economic growth, and that such growth was a precondition for the emergence of a society capable of sustaining democratic institutions.[44]

44. *See* W.W. Rostow, The Stages of Economic Growth: A Non-Communist Manifesto (3d. 1990). On the modernization theory and its impact on US foreign policy, see Nils Gilman, Man-

The notion that a democracy could be established in almost any country without much reference to socioeconomic conditions—that is, through a shortened "sequence" of elite bargaining and legal-institutional reforms rather than through long-term socioeconomic stages—was something new.[45]

Alongside critiques of modernization theory, there was a third reason: a corresponding rehabilitation of the term "transition," and a shift in its meaning. "Transitions" had long been discussed (and implemented) by Marxists as a series of concrete steps a society could take that would lead it, in a compressed (or "telescoped") period of time, to the establishment of a socialist or a communist society. In fact, Marxists had a virtual lock on the concept, using it as a device to understand and engineer various kinds of social transformations. Discussions of the transition from feudalism to capitalism, capitalism to socialism, and socialism to communism provoked much grand theorizing in the twentieth century, from the Bolshevik revolution to the Nicaraguan revolution.[46] These transitions, however, were typically understood as processes of social transformation—sometimes elite driven (by a "vanguard"), sometimes following a restructuring of the socioeconomic order—but always entailing changes at the structural level of society and economy. In recycling the concept of a "transition," analysts in the 1970s and 1980s recast it in terms of political reform, rather than social transformation. In this model, transitions were construed as taking place primarily at the legal-institutional level of politics.

Sociologist Nicolas Guilhot writes about this particular conceptual transformation, locating it mainly in a critique of functionalist explanations of political change. Beginning in the early 1970s, structural explanations for social and political development (such as modernization theory) were criticized in favor of models that stressed agency and choice—particularly among political elites. "The evolution of the comparative analysis of change in the 1980s," he writes, making reference to the studies of Juan Linz, as well as Guillermo O'Donnell and Philippe Schmitter, "indeed took the direction of inquiry into the role of 'institutional entrepreneurs' or elites." But it was not only modernization theory, prevalent in North American academic and policy institutions, that took a hit. Marxist-inspired models, such as dependency theory and world-systems theory, were equally under fire. Guilhot continues,

---

darins of the Future: Modernization Theory in Cold War America (2003); Michael E. Latham, Modernization as Ideology: American Social Science and "Nation Building" in the Kennedy Era (2000).

45. For a reference to the replacement of "stage" with "sequence" in theories of political development beginning in the late 1960s, see Gilman, *supra* note 44, at 90.

46. See Nicolas Guilhot, *The Transition to the Human World of Democracy: Notes for a History of the Concept of Transition, from Early Marxism to 1989*, 5 Eur. J. Soc. Theory 219 (2002).

> Grand theorizing had thus to be replaced by a more sectoral and policy-oriented approach whereby social change would no longer be an autonomous and all-encompassing phenomenon but could be seen as an *outcome* dependent upon the specific strategies and choices of a distinct political elite.[47]

Theories of socioeconomic evolution were replaced with technocratic approaches to engineering political change.

The final reason, which is related to this process of recycling the concept of "transitions" for the purposes of democratization, is the global decline of the radical Left during the 1970s and a concomitant ideological shift in favor of human rights. This deradicalization of social movements is as important in this story as the end of the Cold War, which it preceded by more than a decade. Across the Americas, as well as in Europe, left-wing ideological allegiances of the 1960s gave way to political setbacks and self-critiques. Having abandoned the Soviet Union, Cuba, and many African socialist states as desirable models in the 1970s, many on the Left turned against political ideology and toward the moral framework of human rights. Support for Eastern European dissidents became a focal point of advocacy, particularly in Europe—and such support was perhaps most vocal on the part of ex-communists or left-wing sympathizers who wished to correct their own past political errors.

Defending the rights of individuals was, in their view, the only appropriate response to the widespread abuses (and, indeed, carnage) wrought by both right-wing and left-wing forms of political repression.[48] In Latin America, among the oft-cited reasons for the decline of the radical Left's fortunes include the death of Che Guevara in Bolivia, disenchantment with the path of the Cuban revolution, the 1973 overthrow of Salvador Allende, and the defeat of urban guerilla movements. All of these events spurred re-evaluations of the radical Left's tactics (e.g., military action in some cases, nationalization and expropriation policies in others) in bringing about a transition to socialism, as well as an abandonment of commitments to revolution altogether.[49] Some have cited the specific impact of this shift among intellectuals—spurred either by exiles' admiration for social-democratic experiments they witnessed in Europe or by critical thinking within the domestic intellectual community itself. In Chile in the late-1980s and early-1990s, one influen-

47. *Id.* at 235.

48. *See* Nicolas Guilhot, The Democracy Makers: Human Rights and International Order (2005); Robert Packenham, The Dependency Movement: Scholarship and Politics in Development Studies (1992); Moyn, *supra* note 37.

49. These are complicated events to which I cannot do justice in just a few sentences. For an overview of the issues, see Norbert Lechner, *De la revolución a la democracia*, Ciudad Futura 2 (1986); Steve Ellner, *Latin American Studies Assoc.: The Latin American Left Since Allende: Perspectives and New Directions*, 24 Latin Am. Res. Rev. 143 (1989); Ronaldo Munck, *Farewell to Socialism? A Comment on Recent Debates*, Latin Am. Persp., Apr. 1990, at 113.

tial intellectual, Javier Martínez, noted that "the Socialist party completely changed its discourse because a group of intellectuals—sociologists, philosophers, historians—in part echoing the European discussion but basically taking seriously the problem of democracy, began to question the bases of Marxist-Leninist thought."[50] At any rate, as Guillermo O'Donnell remarked in reference to the 1980s transitions, "Never has the ideological 'prestige' of political democracy been higher in Latin American than now."[51]

Related to this shift was the increasing attraction and visibility of international human rights organizations. Militating against ideological bias that allowed some regimes' repression to go uncriticized, Amnesty International and the Watch Committees explicitly aimed to achieve "balance" in their coverage of abuses around the world.[52] Founders of the humanitarian group Médecins Sans Frontières argued that the organization should publicly take the side of victims, rather than that of any particular political agenda.[53]

In sum, the attractiveness of a transitions to democracy paradigm ought to be understood against the backdrop of four conditions: in most of the countries undergoing political change, democracy was a desirable goal for many people; the delegitimation of modernization theory; the transformation of the transitions concept from a tool of socioeconomic transformation to one of legal-institutional reform; and the global decline of the radical Left. This last phenomenon, I have suggested, had direct repercussions for the human rights movement, as many on the Left abandoned the language of class warfare to describe state violence in favor of the language of human rights. As Ronaldo Munck observes with respect to the disenchantment of the Latin American Left with socialism, "The struggle against military rule had centered largely around the issue of human rights, a defensive politics which took over from the vision of a socialist alternative."[54] Or, as James Petras has put it, "State violence was analyzed in terms of human rights violations, not

50. Jeffrey M. Puryear, Thinking Politics: Intellectuals and Democracy in Chile, 1973–1988, at 64 (1994).

51. Guillermo O'Donnell, *Introduction to the Latin American Cases, in* Transitions from Authoritarian Rule: Latin America 15 (Guillermo O'Donnell et al. eds., 1986).

52. Margaret E. Keck & Kathryn Sikkink, Activists Beyond Borders: Advocacy Networks in International Politics 88–90 (1998).

53. Bernard Kouchner, co-founder of MSF in 1971 and one of the leading lights of the Young Communists in France during the French-Algerian War, abandoned the "revolution vs. counterrevolution" framework through which he viewed struggles in the Third World upon a visit to Biafra in the late-1960s. For an exhaustive history of MSF's relationship to the radical Left, see Anne Vallaeys, Médecins Sans Frontières: La biographie (2004).

54. Munck, *supra* note 49, at 114. Munck continues, "The overwhelming presence of the state under the military encouraged a self-criticism of the left's own statism. . . . Above all, the logic of war as practiced by the military regimes led parts of the armed left to question its own past militarism." For Munck these self-critiques fed the turn toward human rights, democracy, and a concern with fostering civil society.

as expressions of class domination."[55] This was an important shift for those who had lived through (or taken part in) the political foment of the 1960s and early 1970s, and who had sympathized with socialist experiments.

C. Which Transition—And Why Does It Matter for Justice?

The ideological shift away from the politics of the radical Left is an important part of the story of transitional justice for yet another reason: the simple fact that transitions to socialism may entail very different kinds of justice claims than transitions to democracy. Mahmood Mamdani—a participant in the 1988 Aspen Institute conference—has written with some feeling of ambivalence about his own experience as a member of the first postcolonial generation in Africa. He describes the certainty he and his cohort felt with respect to their diagnosis of the most important legacy of colonialism: it was mainly economic, not political; it concerned social suffering, not individual human rights violations. "In the decade that followed African political independence," he writes, "militant nationalist intellectuals focused on the expropriation of the native as the great crime of colonialism."[56]

This claim, though sweeping, was true in many cases. As a corollary, the *rectification* of colonial exploitation was often claimed to be best accomplished through a set of economic and social policies that deliberately placed state power at the center of guarantees for social justice, and that were guided by socialist, rather than capitalist or liberal-democratic, models. Socialist transitions were advocated by leaders such as Kwame Nkrumah, Sékou Touré, and Julius Nyerere not necessarily because they felt an ideological affinity with the Soviet Union, although some of them did. Rather, leaders were concerned with—as Mamdani suggests—using the state to recapture economic power that had unjustly been taken and that still lay in the hands of foreign companies, governments, and persons.[57] Newly independent states

55. James Petras, *The Metamorphosis of Latin America's Intellectuals*, Latin Am. Persp., Apr. 1990, at 102, 104. Using an explicitly Marxist (Gramscian) frame of analysis, Petras argues that military regimes' persecution of intellectuals and scholars in the 1970s led to an increasing dependence of this "intellectual class" on foreign support, especially emanating from the United States and Europe. He charts the rise of externally funded research centers, such as CEDES (Argentina), FLACSO (Chile), and CEBRAP (Brazil), led by "local research entrepreneurs." These researchers constituted a "new class of 'internationally' oriented intellectuals . . . embedded in dependent relations with overseas networks." Although Petras only mentions one researcher by name—Guillermo O'Donnell—much of his analysis obviously refers to Fernando Henrique Cardoso, a leading thinker in the dependency movement, co-founder of CEBRAP, and later president of Brazil. *Id.* at 106, 112 n.3.

56. Mahmood Mamdani, *Beyond Settler and Native as Political Identities: Overcoming the Political Legacy of Colonialism*, 43 Comp. Stud. Soc'y & Hist. 651 (2001).

57. For a discussion of African socialism and a comparison of the ideas of Nkrumah and Nyerere, see Steven Metz, *In Lieu of Orthodoxy: The Socialist Theories of Nkrumah and Nyerere*, 20 J. Mod. Afr. Stud. 377 (1982).

sometimes used expropriation and nationalization as tools of rectification for past injustice and they spearheaded the effort to get social and economic rights recognized as equal counterparts to civil and political rights. Prosser Gifford and William Roger Lewis, editors of an influential two-volume work on "transfers of power" in Africa from 1940–1960, summarize what "breaking with the past" meant in these contexts. According to these countries, "a clean break must be made with the colonialist past." Gifford and Lewis suggest, "There must be a new beginning toward the restructuring of African societies on the basis of economic equality and social justice. It would be unwise for Western students of Africa to underestimate the lingering sense of outrage at the heritage of exploitation and inequality."[58] "Dealing with the past," in this context, meant something quite different from current, transitional justice evocations of it.

This alternative set of claims is mentioned not necessarily to argue for them, but mainly to offer an important rebuttal to histories of transitional justice that ignore them. It is generally a mistake to make broad claims about global post-World War II history only by reference to the Cold War. Ruti Teitel, in particular, argues that the incomplete internationalization of justice represented by the Nuremberg tribunal was foreclosed by the emergence of the Cold War. Thus, transitional justice went on hiatus for nearly forty years, until the establishment of the ad hoc international tribunals to judge crimes in Rwanda and the former Yugoslavia and Rwanda. Though the claim that international justice was cut short by the Cold War is not entirely incorrect, as Cold War tensions clearly played a role, this claim dangerously simplifies and effectively collapses decades of history. In the cases of Madagascar, Kenya, Indochina, and Algeria (to name a few) the lack of international accountability for systematic repression endured by civilian populations in the 1940s and 1950s was not a "consequence" of the Cold War. One might rather propose, as many did at the time, that the reason that a standing court to try international crimes had not been set up after World War II was precisely because great powers such as France feared their own soldiers would be tried for violations they committed in the colonies.[59] And one should not forget that the ex-colonial powers—especially France—continued to play strong economic and military roles in their former colonies, making the introduction of accountability measures very difficult.

58. Prosser Gifford & William Roger Lewis, *Introduction, in* Decolonization and African Independence: The Transfers of Power, 1960–1980, at xxv (Prosser Gifford & Wm. Roger Lewis eds., 1988).

59. A claim voiced, not least of all, by Jean-Paul Sartre during the course of the 1967 Russell Tribunal, when discussing why it was that a Nuremberg-style tribunal had not been set up to try members of the French government after the 1945 Sétif massacre in Algeria. *See* Jean-Paul Sartre, *On Genocide, in* Against the Crime of Silence: Proceedings of the International War Crimes Tribunal 615 (John Duffett ed., 1968).

These claims also demonstrate that there seems no reason to suppose that there are trans-historical contents to claims for justice after regime change. Postcolonial justice claims for the often massive and systematic violations of previous colonial regime existed—but they were often simply composed in a different key.[60] Yet they did not constitute what Kritz and others took to mean transitional justice.

D. Transitions from Authoritarianism to (Hopefully) Democracy

Understanding the key in which Kritz and many others composed transitional justice claims can be partly gained through an examination of the descriptions of political change that observers in the social sciences, sometimes called "transitologists," developed in the late 1970s and 1980s. Looking at these descriptions is useful for two reasons. First, they offer keen-eyed analyses of political events that help us to understand the practical difficulties that actors were facing in countries such as Argentina, Brazil, Uruguay, and elsewhere. Thus, their descriptions will help to clarify the political contexts out of which transitional justice claims emerged. Second, it is useful to understand them because they were influential in providing a conceptual vocabulary (e.g., "transitions," "breakdown," "consolidation," and "sequencing") that were appropriated by actors in the emerging field, culminating in Kritz's canonization of their works.

In 1978, Argentine political scientist Guillermo O'Donnell, American political scientist Philippe Schmitter, and Brazilian sociologist (and later president of Brazil) Fernando Henrique Cardoso honed in on "transitions" as a crucial area for exploration. The three were part of a newly formed advisory council for the Latin American Program at the Woodrow Wilson Center for Scholars, and with the help of the program's director, Abraham Lowenthal, they put together a ground-breaking new project. Thinking that research could help identify political opportunities to crack open authoritarian regimes and offer strategies for pushing change along, they developed a pro-

60. Not only ex-colonial states, but also ex-colonial powers demonstrated some interest in "transitioning" to socialism. During the Portuguese revolution in 1974–1976, nationalization and land expropriation policies were enacted, and the 1976 constitution proclaimed that the aim of the new republic was to ensure the "transition to socialism." French politics in the 1970s was also marked by a "Union of the Left" between the Socialist Party and the Communist Party, whose publicly stated goal was to nationalize more than 50 percent of the economy (the plan eventually put into effect by the Socialists in 1981 entailed vastly less than this). On Portugal, see Kenneth Maxwell, *Regime Overthrow and the Prospects for Democratic Transition in Portugal, in* TRANSITIONS FROM AUTHORITARIAN RULE: SOUTHERN EUROPE 109, 132–36 (Guillermo O'Donnell & Philippe Schmitter eds., 1986); on France, see BERNARD E. BROWN, SOCIALISM OF A DIFFERENT KIND: RESHAPING THE LEFT IN FRANCE (1982).

gram of papers, meetings, and conferences to take place under the auspices of the Wilson Center.[61] People involved in the project included the Chilean politicians and political scientists Sergio Bitar, Claudio Orrego Vicuña, and Manuel Antonio Garretón; Spanish political scientist and politician José María Maravall; as well as noted scholars Juan Linz, Terry Lynn Karl, and Adam Przeworski. Participants thus came from a range of backgrounds, and some, like Cardoso, were both scholars and political actors. Bitar (a former minister in Allende's government) and Genaro Arriagada (a political scientist who had been affiliated with the Wilson Center's Latin America Project) later mobilized a civil society coalition against the 1988 referendum to extend Pinochet's presidency by another eight years, and then became important political figures.[62] Orrego also continued a political career, whereas Garretón (whose brother is Roberto Garretón, a prominent human rights lawyer) has become a well-known expert on democratic transitions. Maravall, author of *La Transición a la Democracia en España* (1982), was also a minister in the Spanish government in the 1980s.

Members of this group of scholar-activists were often chosen precisely because of their dual credentials—something that was not extraordinary under Latin American dictatorships. O'Donnell himself was representative of this group, as he had been the leader of anti-Peronist students while pursuing a law degree in the 1950s and then went into politics upon graduation. Appointed the youngest deputy minister in Argentine history in 1963, his career was cut short by General Juan Carlos Onganía's coup in 1966, after which he left Argentina and ended up at Yale. There he undertook research that would lead to his now-classic work, *Modernization and Bureaucratic Authoritarianism* (1973).[63] O'Donnell's case was not unique. In Chile, for example, political repression had pushed opposition politicians into academia and research centers, as one of the few "liberal" spaces where they could meet and discuss—and where they could receive funding for their work from outside actors such as the Ford Foundation.[64] According to Bitar, there emerged "a kind of strange mixture of political intellectuals," meaning "intellectuals who take up politics and politicians who for the first time reflect from a more doctrinal perspective on great state issues."[65]

The privileged institutional location and the weighty intellectual and political capital associated with the Transitions project makes it of particular

61. Cardoso, though a principal architect of the project, was forced to scale back his participation when he became involved in electoral politics in Brazil in late 1978. Interview with Abraham Lowenthal, Professor, University of Southern California, via telephone (6 Aug. 2007).
62. *Id.*
63. *See* Guilhot, The Democracy Makers, *supra* note 48, at 123–24.
64. Puryear, *supra* note 50, at 57.
65. Sergio Bitar, *quoted in id.*

significance for grasping how transitions may have "mattered" to human rights. This is not to say that this project was the origin of a transitions concept or the only important actor in its proliferation—there was not just one such concept and there were other actors.[66] For example, a parallel effort was also underway at the time under the direction of John Herz, a participant in the Aspen Institute conference.[67] While this effort should also be acknowledged, this essay focuses on the Transitions project, mainly because it operated at a nexus of elite Latin American and US scholars with direct access to, and involvement in, policy and politics. A key actor in this nexus was Lowenthal, who was the director of studies at the Council on Foreign Relations before establishing the Latin American Program at the Woodrow Wilson Center, and who later developed, after consulting with Cardoso, the idea for the Inter-American Dialogue, a policy discussion group comprised of high-level politicians, business leaders, and academics from the Americas.[68]

The Transitions project resulted in the publication of the books *Transitions from Authoritarian Rule* (1986), which offer a rigorous and influential window onto the processes, risks, and challenges of democratic transitions—particularly in many of the cases, such as Spain, Argentina, Uruguay, and Brazil, that were important to the development of the field of transitional justice. Although O'Donnell and Schmitter remarked in their "tentative conclusions about uncertain democracies" that it was by no means assured that a transition away from authoritarianism would lead to democracy, they did

66. Nicolas Guilhot describes in much greater depth the vectors of transmission of the "transitions" idea in Guilhot, The Democracy Makers, *supra* note 48. He makes an important distinction between the left-leaning analysis of transitions evinced by actors such as the Woodrow Wilson group and the neoconservative analysis promoted by those associated with Reagan foreign policy.

67. Herz organized two meetings in 1979 and 1980 on a comparative analysis of "the breakdown of dictatorships and their transformation into successor democracies" at the City University of New York. The outcome was From Dictatorship to Democracy, *supra* note 35. This work, of course, excludes consideration of Latin American cases and focuses mainly on post–World War II transformations in Europe and Japan. It also considers Greece, Portugal, and Spain.

68. Interview with Lowenthal, *supra* note 61. Lowenthal recalls that the motivation for the Dialogue was to find a way to counterbalance the Reagan administration's policies in Latin America. During a trip to Chile and Peru in 1982, just after the Malvinas War, he was struck by how "flabbergasted" people were by the administration's obsession with Central America. Convinced that people were more agitated than he had ever seen them in his career since the 1960s, and that Washington was not paying attention, he wanted to find a way to inject their concerns into discussions in Washington. He made a last-minute lunch-time visit to Cardoso in Brazil, who then helped him to develop the idea. The first meeting of the Dialogue in November 1982 included an hour long exchange with Secretary of State George Shultz and ended with an hour and a half debriefing with Vice President George H. W. Bush. Today, the Dialogue includes among its members Cardoso, Alfonsín, Bitar, former Chilean President Ricardo Lagos, Joaquin Villalobos, Moisés Naím, plus a whole host of prominent US politicians and opinion-makers. *See* Inter-American Dialogue, *available at* http://www.thedialogue.org.

acknowledge that the normative impulse guiding their work was that a transition to democracy was a desirable outcome, and that they wanted to offer a "usable instrument" for those trying to effect a transition to democracy.[69]

One of the reasons why the project was so influential was because it decisively shifted focus away from an analysis of the structural conditions for democracy that had been the mainstay of earlier social science and policy concerns. These included issues such as the behavioral, institutional, social, or economic conditions of democracy—issues that tended toward structural rather than causal explanations of democracy. Indeed, Dankwart Rustow noted an important gap in structural accounts in a seminal 1970 article, "Transitions to Democracy: Toward a Dynamic Model," namely, that researchers had hitherto tended to

> ask the same sort of question and support their answers with the same sort of evidence. The question is not how a democratic system comes into existence. Rather, it is how a democracy, assumed to be already in existence, can best preserve or enhance its health and stability.[70]

Thus, the type of question almost universally asked is why it is that Anglo-Saxon and Scandinavian countries have smoothly running democracies whereas France and Germany are prone to crisis—instead of attempting to understand processes in countries "on the verge of democracy" such as "Ceylon, Lebanon, Turkey, Peru, or Venezuela."[71]

It was precisely this orthodoxy that the Transitions project challenged. Its key theme was that the origins of democracies are to be found in political choices rather than in structural conditions—and these choices are made by elites. Drawing on the case studies they had commissioned for the project, O'Donnell and Schmitter emphasized the inherent uncertainty of transitional outcomes, rejecting the contention that approaches applicable to stable periods were appropriate to transitional ones. They similarly placed enormous causal power in decisions taken, particularly by elites. They also emphasized the significance of bargaining on political outcomes, particularly in the form of pacts among elite groups. This latter point was one of the central elements of their argument. They divided the sequence of transitional "moments" into a series of pacts, each of which would offer various interest groups mutual guarantees of protection—starting with the army, and working toward business and political elites. Though inherently undemocratic in terms of procedures, pacts are the best method of maintaining the stability necessary to establish a democracy, they concluded.[72]

69. Guillermo O'Donnell & Philippe Schmitter, Transitions from Authoritarian Rule: Tentative Conclusions About Uncertain Democracies 5 (1986).
70. Dankwart A. Rustow, *Transitions to Democracy: Toward a Dynamic Model*, *in* Transitions to Democracy 14 (Lisa Anderson ed., 1999).
71. *Id.* at 340.
72. O'Donnell & Schmitter, *supra* note 69, at 37–39.

O'Donnell and Schmitter offered further refinements. They placed a strong accent on the resurrection of civil society and the necessity of "restructuring public space" during a transition. Of particular concern was that political identities were largely repressed under authoritarian rule, and thus modes of political participation had to be either created or created anew after the fall of the authoritarian regime.[73] As a corollary, they focused on "citizenship" as the key criterion for democracy—establishing or reestablishing equality before the law and possession of rights against a repressive state were crucial. Finally, O'Donnell and Schmitter's overwhelming focus in their "tentative conclusions" was on both averting a coup and on assuaging fears of a coup (even in those cases where it is unlikely).

O'Donnell and Schmitter also addressed the problem of "settling a past account," as they put it, "without upsetting a present transition." Focusing solely on prosecutions and purges of the state security forces, they asserted, "Transitional actors must satisfy not only vital interests but also vital ideals—standards of what is decent and just," and that "we believe that the worst of bad solutions would be to try to ignore the issue [of past violations]." Confronting past abuse, especially gross violations of human rights, were important in their view in order to transform the military's "messianic self-image" as *the* institution representing the interests of the nation, to combat impunity, and to reinforce the ethical values necessary to social health.[74]

Thus, given their synthesis of a range of country cases, the central usable instruments they recommended centered on the transformation of a repressive state security apparatus and the instauration of procedures and practices of democratic citizenship. The main actors involved in this transformation are, as mentioned above, elites who enter into a series of bargaining arrangements with one another as a means of managing risks to their interests. The main focus of these actors is legal-institutional reform, rather than transformation at the socioeconomic level. The outcome, if all goes well, would be a set of elections and the installation of party politics.[75]

This brief summary of the Transitions project at the Woodrow Wilson Center and O'Donnell and Schmitter's interpretation of transitions to democracy is not intended to displace the interpretations of those who were

73. In this respect, O'Donnell and Schmitter placed great weight on a few key elements: symbolic gestures of protest, often made by inspirational individuals; the activity of human rights organizations, which typically enjoy high prestige and moral authority in the wake of a political transformation; and the reactivation of working class and union identities hitherto suppressed by the regime. *Id.* at 48–49.

74. *Id.* at 28, 30, 31.

75. Given my argument above concerning the relevance of what is being "transitioned to," it is interesting to note that O'Donnell and Schmitter do not rule out the possibility (or desirability) of an eventual transition to socialism (or, as they call it "socialization"). For them, however, such a transition would best take place only after a transition to democracy has been consolidated. *See id.* at 11–12.

actually experiencing those events (although some of these people, such as Cardoso, Bitar, and Arriagada, were active participants, and others, such as O'Donnell, Garretón, and many others, were hardly disinterested observers). It is rather to provide a clearer picture of what a transition was understood to entail, even if it could never be guaranteed to happen. Thomas Carothers has argued that, in the US context at least, policymakers interested in democracy promotion came to much the same conclusions as O'Donnell and Schmitter, even if the direct influence of their work boiled down to nothing more than a lending of basic concepts and terms.[76] In any case, the question of direct influence is beside the point. The "transition" idea was indeed influential, and certainly did make its way into policy circles and domestic public spheres around the globe. Both Méndez and Zalaquett recall the concept of transition being borrowed from the social science research going on in the 1980s (both specifically cite the work of O'Donnell and Schmitter), even if a direct influence is difficult to trace.[77] Alex Boraine writes in his memoir that Aryeh Neier—who had been present at the Aspen Institute conference—"urged me not only to consider the examples in Eastern and Central Europe but also to look at the literature of recent transitions in Latin America and in particular in Argentina and Chile."[78] And, of course, the work of O'Donnell and Schmitter is cited in many seminal articles and books in the field and canonized in the Kritz volumes.

The intention in discussing O'Donnell and Schmitter is to better understand the contexts in which political actors operated as well as the specific political challenges they faced. Given the constraints and normative aims of these kinds of transitions in the 1980s, a normative agenda on issues relating to the transformation of an abusive state security apparatus and the reinstauration of democratic citizenship helped to shape the emerging field of transitional justice. It was this agenda that strongly colored perceptions of what justice entailed, or could become, during a time of transition.

76. See Thomas Carothers on relationship between policy and scholarly discussions on "transitions" in Thomas Carothers, Aiding Democracy Abroad: The Learning Curve 93 (1999). Given the much stronger links between academia and politics in Latin American countries than existed in the United States, perhaps there was more possibility for cross-fertilization.

77. Interview with Méndez, *supra* note 38; Telephone Interview with José Zalaquett, Professor, University of Chile, Santiago (9 Oct. 2007).

78. Alex Boraine, A Country Unmasked 16 (2000).

III. AN INTELLECTUAL FRAMEWORK FOR TRANSITIONAL JUSTICE

A. The 1988 Aspen Institute Conference

The 1988 Aspen Institute conference on state crimes was the brainchild of Alice Henkin, the director of the Justice and Society Program at the Aspen Institute. After hearing Julio Raffo of the important Argentine human rights organization Center for Legal and Social Studies (CELS) speak at an Americas Watch meeting about the "Full Stop" law, she telephoned Stephen Marks at the Ford Foundation. As it happens, Marks had just heard Raffo speaking on the same issue at the Ford Foundation offices, and his interest was piqued enough to recommend that his program should make an investment of $47,380 in order to investigate "the general problem of how countries in transition to democracy deal with past abuses."[79] Henkin promptly started canvassing people she knew such as Aryeh Neier and Juan Méndez at Human Rights Watch, an organization for which she was a board member.[80]

The reference to Raffo, CELS, and the Full Stop law in this negotiation was not simply fortuitous since, of course, the real origins of the conference were the dramatic events that had been taking place in Latin America and around the world in the 1980s, as well as the response to them on the part of those interested in promoting human rights. What the conference did—and this is the reason for which it is of historical interest—was to try to develop an intellectual framework that could grasp the common issues faced in Argentina, Uruguay, Brazil, the Philippines, and elsewhere. Specifically, the conference sought to clarify the political, moral, and legal challenges that those seeking justice for state crimes faced in the democratic transitions of the 1980s.

The people Henkin brought together had a range of experiences and competencies. Lawrence Weschler—who wrote about the conference in a 1989 *New Yorker* article about repression and impunity in Uruguay, as well as in the postscript of his 1990 book *A Miracle, A Universe*—was there. The philosophers Ronald Dworkin and Thomas Nagel were also present. Both of them had already been part of a group of five philosophers that Carlos Nino invited to Argentina in April 1986 (with funding from the Ford Foundation) to discuss human rights policy with himself and Jaime Malamud-Goti.[81] And

79. See Ford Foundation Archives, Grant No. 885-0149, § 4, Letter from Alice H. Henkin to Stephen Marks (26 Mar. 1987); Inter-Office Memorandum from Stephen P. Marks to Shepard Forman (17 Mar. 1987).

80. Interview with Henkin, *supra* note 13.

81. The group also included Owen Fiss, Tim Scanlon, and Bernard Williams. Interview with Malamud-Goti, *supra* note 5.

it was Nagel who, at the conference, came up with the now well-known distinction between knowledge and acknowledgment, the latter signifying the importance of official, public recognition of truths about past crimes.[82] Also there were political scientists such as Mahmood Mamdani (an Africanist), Margaret Crahan (a Latin America specialist), and Samuel Fitch (a specialist on civil-military relations). There were religious leaders such as Father Luis Perez Aguirre, whom Weschler famously wrote about in *A Miracle, A Universe*. There were other notables, as well, such as Diane Orentlicher, Paulo Sergio Pinheiro, Theodore Meron, and Hugo Fruhling.

The conference was anchored, however, around three papers written by Herz, Zalaquett, and Malamud-Goti. John Herz was a prominent political scientist who had edited *From Dictatorship to Democracy* in 1982, which was the first synthetic analysis of dealing with legacies of prior regimes (and which also, perhaps unintentionally, shared the title of Zalaquett's 1985 *New Republic* article). A German-Jewish émigré from Nazi Germany who arrived in the United States in 1938, Herz had been a major force in the emergence of the realist approach to international relations in the 1950s and 1960s, and also did work on comparative politics.[83] As he recounts in his article, however, he had the additional advantage of having been involved in US denazification policy following World War II. Herz was thus invited to give an overview of the issues from a "historical perspective" although he was not a historian.

According to Méndez, it was he and Neier who suggested to Henkin that she invite Zalaquett to write the centerpiece of the conference: an article laying out a theory of justice during transitional periods.[84] Zalaquett, a Chilean, had been a part of the Allende government overthrown in Chile in 1973, and he was arrested several times in conjunction with his work defending human rights as legal director of the interfaith Comite Pro Paz group, the forerunner of the important Vicaria de la Solidaridad. Exiled in 1976, he began to work for Amnesty International, holding a number of prominent positions within the organization until he was allowed to return to Chile in 1986. Through his work with Amnesty, Zalaquett had a privileged view on events: in 1984, he met with Alfonsín and the commission of inquiry that was looking into disappearances in Argentina. He also met with President Julio Sanguinetti just after the latter took power in Uruguay in 1985. Later, in 1987, the Ford Foundation asked him to visit Uganda, where Museveni was establishing a truth commission to examine abuses under Idi Amin. Zalaquett had also already begun to reflect on his experiences: in 1985,

82. Weschler, *supra* note 1, at 4.
83. M. Benjamin Mollov, Power and Transcendence: Hans J. Morgenthau and the Jewish Experience 4, 125 (2002).
84. Interview with Méndez, *supra* note 38; Interview with Zalaquett, *supra* note 77.

he published a cover story in *The New Republic* called "From Dictatorship to Democracy" (with the fitting subtitle of "Kicking out the generals is only the first chapter") in which he emphasized that the key element in political transformation of the military dictatorships in the Southern Cone was holding the armed forces accountable for abuses.[85]

Henkin also canvassed her husband, the influential Columbia University legal scholar Louis Henkin, who put her in touch with Malamud-Goti, who had been a visiting professor at Columbia lecturing on drug policy the previous year.[86] Malamud-Goti, as previously mentioned, was one of the architects of Alfonsín's prosecutions policy, along with Carlos Nino. In anticipation of the end of the dictatorship, he and Nino, who were both on academic fellowships in Germany, started to think about the issue of accountability. They began to "shop around" for a politician, and since Nino was already in Alfonsín's political party, they met with him, and Alfonsín subsequently invited them to be his advisers when he won the presidential election in 1983. Malamud-Goti recalls the prosecutions policy as a messy process marked by strong popular support as well as by sharp political setbacks and constraints—defined, in particular, by the capacity of military members and judges to close ranks and obstruct the process. Indeed, the article he wrote for the Aspen Institute conference was an adaptation of an argument he made in order to defend the Full Stop Law—the 1986 law, which he helped to author, that put an end to prosecutions of the armed forces.[87] Although he had spent years working on human rights issues in the Alfonsín government, this was his first expression of a reasoned justification for his views on prosecutions—in particular, for placing limits on them in the context of democratic transitions. This was thinking that responded directly to new dilemmas. Malamud-Goti's ideas were among those at the conference that expressed crucial stakes still under debate within the field today.

B. The Stakes of the Debate

The participants in the conference seemed to be aware that they were discussing something new. According to Henkin, those in attendance "were unanimous that the Conference was important, but only an important beginning." The goal of the conference was "to discuss the moral, political,

85. José Zalaquett, *From Dictatorship to Democracy*, New Republic, 16 Dec. 1985, at 17–21.
86. Interview with Henkin, *supra* note 13; Telephone Interview with Malamud-Goti, *supra* note 5. Malamud-Goti was actually recruited by Paul Martin, who worked with Louis Henkin at the Center for the Study of Human Rights at Columbia.
87. Malamud-Goti was responding to an article written by Julio Maier. Interview with Malamud-Goti, *supra* note 5.

and jurisprudential issues that arise when a government that has engaged in gross violations of human rights is succeeded by a regime more inclined to respect those rights."[88] In these discussions, the central issues were: whether there was an obligation under international law to punish violators of human rights; whether there was a minimal obligation of states to establish the truth about past violations; whether "discretion and prudence" should play a role in making decisions about justice measures; and how specifically to deal with human rights abuses by military authorities.

There were disagreements—often sharp ones—about the answers to these questions. The first question concerning the obligation under international law to punish violators of human rights was, however, fairly easy to dispatch. According to Henkin, "It was agreed that there was no general obligation under customary international law to punish such violators. Various international treaties, however, may require punishment expressly or by implication."[89] That is to say, the basis at the time was still rather thin. Following a panel discussion between Louis Henkin and Ted Meron on the relevance of international law, Méndez recalls Lawrence Weschler saying lightheartedly that the pair "reminded him of cavemen who rub sticks of wood together, and a little fire comes up only immediately to die out."[90] Although the Inter-American Court of Human Rights had just handed down its judgment in the important 1988 Velázquez-Rodríguez case, appeals to international law in debating these particular issues were difficult to make salient.[91] Moreover, a quick glance at the Americas Watch report (authored by Méndez), *Truth and Partial Justice in Argentina*, confirms that international law did not seem to enter into the calculations of actors pursuing justice initiatives in the Alfonsín government.[92] There is no mention of international law in the detailed descriptions of Argentina's human rights policies, indicating that the actors in Argentina themselves did not see a link, or at least did not rely on it. Where international law did come in, however, was in articulating Americas Watch's *own* positions with respect to justice in the Argentine case. For example, Americas Watch made specific appeals to Argentina's obligations as a signatory of the UN Convention Against Torture.[93]

88. Alice H. Henkin, *Conference Report, in* State Crimes, *supra* note 3, at 1, 9.
89. *Id.* at 4.
90. Interview with Méndez, *supra* note 38.
91. Angel Velásquez-Rodríguez was a student who had been detained by the Honduran police and then never seen again. The court ruled that the government had a responsibility under the American Convention on Human Rights to perform due diligence in preventing, investigating, and punishing disappearances. Since it did not do so in this case, it was obliged to pay compensation to the student's family. This ruling would be one of the bases for a later right to justice enshrined in the "Joinet Principles." *See* Mark Freeman, Truth Commissions and Procedural Fairness 9 (2006).
92. Méndez, *supra* note 41, at 59.
93. *Id.*

Real progress in this area would have to wait until the early- to mid-1990s, bolstered by Diane Orentlicher's groundbreaking 1991 article,[94] and then solidified by the elaboration of UN principles. Orentlicher recently recounted that the genesis for this article came directly from her participation in the Aspen Institute conference: "While some of my contemporaries had fairly well-developed views about what international law required, most believed that further study and analysis was needed. In the course of the Aspen seminar, many participants urged me to take up that challenge."[95] The 1997 publication of a UN-commissioned report on combating impunity known as the "Joinet Principles," which advocated for the rights to know, to justice, and to reparations, was also a signal event in this regard.[96]

As to whether states had a minimal obligation to establish the truth about past violations, there was a resounding consensus: there was indeed such an obligation. The stakes of the debate were not those of the oft-invoked "truth" versus "criminal justice" debate, in which truth-telling emerges as an alternative to prosecutions in cases where there has been an amnesty, thus making prosecutions impossible. Indeed, according to Henkin,

> There was common agreement that the successor government has an obligation to investigate and establish the facts so that the truth be known and be made part of the nation's history. Even in situations where pardon or clemency might be appropriate there should be no compromising of the obligation to discover and acknowledge the truth.[97]

Lawrence Weschler similarly affirmed,

> Over and over again, the same sorts of issues get played out, and over and over again, as the participants at the Aspen Institute Conference began to realize, the same two imperatives seem to rise to the fore—the intertwined demands for [criminal] justice and for truth.[98]

There were, however, some disagreements regarding the role of discretion and prudence in decisions to pursue justice measures. On the one hand, Herz, Zalaquett, and Malamud-Goti all affirmed the importance of political judgment in developing justice policies. As we already know, Zalaquett was

94. Diane F. Orentlicher, *Settling Accounts: The Duty to Prosecute Human Rights Violations of a Previous Regime*, 100 Yale L.J. 2537 (1991).

95. Diane F. Orentlicher, *Settling Accounts Revisited: Reconciling Global Norms with Local Agency*, 1 Int'l J. Transitional Just. 10, 12 (2007).

96. *See The Administration of Justice and the Human Rights of Detainees: Question of the Impunity of Perpetrators of Human Rights Violations (Civil and Political), Revised Final Report Prepared by Mr. Joinet*, U.N. ESCOR, Comm'n on Hum. Rts., Sub-Comm'n on Prev. of Discrim. & Protect. of Min., 49th Sess., Agenda Item 9, U.N. Doc. E/CN.4/Sub.2/1997/20/Rev.1 (1997). A brief overview of the development of international law and transitional justice can be found in Freeman, *supra* note 91, at 6–9.

97. Henkin, Conference Report, *supra* note 88, at 4–5.

98. Weschler, *Afterword*, *supra* note 3, at 92.

cautious about the "ambiguities of transitional situations" and the difficulties human rights advocates might have in navigating them. Malamud-Goti, who had navigated the treacherous political terrain in Argentina during the junta trials, also admitted that "the applicability of criminal provisions is largely a matter of political judgment" for transitional governments.[99] Indeed, in his view, decisions about whom to prosecute were political decisions, which explains the reference to "dilemmas of transitional democratic governments" in the title of his essay.[100]

Neier and Méndez, however, chafed at the idea that political concerns should limit justice. Many of the participants recall a vigorous debate between Neier and Zalaquett on the issue that was not represented in the conference report.[101] The disagreement essentially turned on whether there was a duty to punish human rights violators, and, if so, what the purpose of punishment should be. Neier defended the view that such a duty exists, and that allowing political struggles to impinge upon its fulfillment was wrong. This view had already been articulated strongly in Méndez's *Truth and Partial Justice* report. "We . . . recognize that statesmen have to make difficult judgments and that it lies beyond the capacity of an outside organization with a special agenda—the promotion of human rights—to evaluate all the factors that enter into that process," he wrote. He continued that, although this was the case, it was important to point out the "disturbing" way in which the prosecutions had been cut short: "We see a government and a Congress legislating under duress; under the ominous threat, by a powerfully armed elite, to eliminate the country's democratic process."[102] Of course, this chain of events was likely disturbing to many people; the question was how to remedy it. Neier thought that violators of human rights should be punished because they deserved to be punished, not for some other end. This was, as Méndez put it, Neier's "just deserts theory of punishment," and it fed expressly into a view that human rights principles agreed upon at the international level should stand as absolute values, incorruptible by politics.[103]

The answer to the final question—how specifically to deal with human rights abuses by military authorities—is a crucial one. In this conference, as well as in subsequent articles and conferences leading up to the publication of Kritz's compendium of "basic texts," there was a vague but discernible coherence at work. Dealing with human rights abuses by repressive states during a supposed transition to democracy entailed specific measures that have since been handed

99. Malamud-Goti, *Trying Violators of Human Rights*, *supra* note 4, at 76.
100. *Id.* at 72.
101. The only extant account of their debate is Weschler, A Miracle, *supra* note 1, at 243–45.
102. Méndez, *supra* note 41, at 60.
103. Interview with Méndez, *supra* note 38; Interview with Henkin, *supra* note 13; Telephone interview with Zalaquett, *supra* note 77; Telephone interview with Margo Picken, Fellow, London School of Economics and Political Science (11 Oct. 2007).

down as *the* legitimate transitional justice measures, in spite of their subsequent application to very different sorts of political and practical dilemmas.

C. An Implied Structure for Transitional Justice: Two Normative Aims

It was not by chance that the structure of conversations at this conference—and similar conversations at the 1992 Charter 77 Foundation conference and the 1994 IDASA-sponsored conference on dealing with the past in South Africa, as well as Kritz's work—consistently reflected an interest in a particular set of measures as objects of debate: prosecutions, truth-telling, transformation of an abusive state security apparatus, and rehabilitation or compensation for harms. Nor is it by chance that this structure implied that a comprehensive approach, including elements of all of these measures, should at least be considered by transitional regimes.

These measures fit closely with two normative aims that many of the participants expressed: first, the goal of providing some measure of justice to those who suffered under repressive state regimes and, second, the goal of facilitating an exit from authoritarianism and shoring up a fragile democracy. The argument here is *not* that these discussions were similar because the Aspen Institute conference influenced the shape of subsequent discussions, though because so many of the same people were involved it may have. Rather, these discussions were similar because the practical problems faced in various countries were understood in similar ways, and because the legitimate range of responses to those problems was defined similarly. This conceptual structure may have defined the emergence of the field, independent of whether individual participants were aware of it.

A brief look at each of these measures provides a picture of this structure and how it was justified, which will in turn help to draw out the connections between each of these two normative aims. Prosecutions, which may be considered the most contentious ethical question for a post-authoritarian regime given the potential political resistance to them, were intended to fulfill "a duty owed to the victims" that would "give significance to their suffering and serve as a partial remedy for their injuries," according to Henkin's summary.[104] They would also, in the words of Malamud-Goti, "provide a unique means by which to assert democratic values" through their five consequences: establishing tangible facts about past crimes, offering disapproval of official policies, promoting confidence in the new political arrangements, restoring to citizens full membership in society, and improving chances for a transformation of military/civilian relations.[105]

104. Henkin, Conference Report, *supra* note 88, at 3.
105. Malamud-Goti, *Trying Violators of Human Rights*, *supra* note 4, at 81–82. Although Herz also mentions that giving a "clear and unvarnished picture of the true character of the

Truth-telling efforts, which were acclaimed as a minimum requirement of justice by all the participants at the conference, "respon[d] to the demand of justice for the victims," according to Henkin's summary.[106] Without disclosure of the truth about what happened to their loved ones, "the actual suffering and indeed violation of the rights of the relatives of the victims" would be perpetuated, in Zalaquett's view.[107] Yet it would not be enough that only families of victims know the truth about what happened to their loved ones; all citizens must know, and the knowledge must be officially recognized. Zalaquett emphasized that official truth-telling is important in order to prevent "the military or other groups or institutions responsible for past abuses to escape the judgment of history and insist on exculpatory versions of what happened; new recruits will absorb an institutional tradition which has not expunged its most objectionable aspects. All this can only weaken efforts to prevent the recurrence of human rights abuses and to reinforce the rule of law."[108] Herz similarly argued for "the need for successor democracies to present to the people . . . a clear and unvarnished picture of the true character of the regime," precisely in order to act as a counterweight to the propagandistic character of official information given by the secretive authoritarian regime.[109] According to Henkin, truth-telling "facilitates national reconciliation."[110]

Transformation of the state security apparatus was argued by Zalaquett and others to be a necessary part of providing guarantees to victims that violations would not be repeated.[111] Beyond this aim however, such a transformation was argued to "create a democratic climate in a successor democracy," through activities such as prosecutions, purges, and human rights training. Also important was the reaffirmation of civilian authority over the military through the denial of the military ideologies of "national security" that were used to support practices such as disappearances, and the denial of security forces' claims that human rights abuses were mere "excesses," rather than systematic, sanctioned undertakings.[112]

Finally, rehabilitation and compensation for harms, though the least discussed and least developed theme of the conference, was nonetheless recognized as an essential element of coming to terms with an authoritarian

regime" was one of the aims of the postwar Allied trials, in fact, "they had little effect." John H. Herz, *An Historical Perspective*, in State Crimes, *supra* note 3, at 19–20.

106. Henkin, Conference Report, *supra* note 88, at 5.

107. Zalaquett, *Confronting Human Rights Violations*, *supra* note 6, at 31.

108. *Id.*

109. Herz, *An Historical Perspective*, *supra* note 105, at 19.

110. Henkin, Conference Report, *supra* note 88, at 5.

111. Zalaquett, *Confronting Human Rights Violations*, *supra* note 6, at 38.

112. Henkin, Conference Report, *supra* note 88, at 16, 6–7; Zalaquett, *Confronting Human Rights Violations*, *supra* note 6, at 60–61.

regime. For Zalaquett, even though repair for the damage caused to victims "cannot be fully achieved," it was desirable that "every possible effort . . . be made to compensate victims of human rights violations and their families."[113] Beyond the moral exigency to repair the harms of individual victims, however, such programs were claimed also to have broader public benefits. According to Herz, "Rehabilitation and indemnification of those who have suffered under the former regime is important for equity as well as for general symbolic and moral reasons."[114] He also pointed out the morally problematic way that reparations had been carried out in postwar Germany, where mainly Jews of German origin had been compensated, whereas others had not, and where wives of resisters who had been killed received no benefits while widows of high-ranking Nazis lived comfortably on government-supplied pensions.[115] Zalaquett further asserted that truth-telling and apologies operate as a form of reparation "for the victims, for the society and, not least, for the soldiers or policemen who did not participate in repressive activities or who were forced to implement illegal policies."[116]

In sum, it seems uncontroversial to say that the conceptions of justice that drew together these different responses to past human rights violations rested on two normative aims: achieving justice for victims, and achieving a more just, democratic, order. This latter aim placed an enormous burden on such measures. Sweeping claims about the capacity of justice measures to facilitate a political transition—and, in particular, to aid the instauration of practices of democratic citizenship and the reform of a repressive state security apparatus—suggested a general enthusiasm and optimism. It would remain to be seen whether such claims would be borne out empirically, or, after systematic investigation, possibly scaled back.

IV. THE PROBLEM OF TRANSITIONAL JUSTICE

This account of the conceptual foundations of the field of transitional justice began with an investigation into the origins of the term "transitional justice," and has ended by suggesting some of its conceptual contents at the time of its emergence. It has argued that "transitions" have mattered to human rights for two reasons: first, human rights practice had to adapt itself to new practical challenges; and second, that political change, understood as a "transition to democracy," had important effects for the kinds of justice claims that were considered legitimate. Indeed, the widespread acceptance of the

113. *Id.* at 36.
114. Herz, *An Historical Perspective, supra* note 105, at 20.
115. *Id.*
116. Zalaquett, *Confronting Human Rights Violations, supra* note 6, at 36–37.

reigning "transitions paradigm" and its focus on legal-institutional reforms and responses was a crucial factor in legitimizing the field of transitional justice. Transitions to democracy, for the many reasons discussed above, had become the dominant normative lens through which to view political change. Transitional justice fit into that lens.

A. The Distinctiveness of the Field

But is the field of transitional justice really new, or is it simply part of the human rights movement? This examination of the origins of transitional justice strongly suggests that it is a distinct field. Aryeh Neier's forceful disagreement with José Zalaquett at the Aspen Institute conference about the justification for punishment provides an important illustration of the distinction. For Neier, "punishment is the absolute duty of society to honor and redeem the suffering of the individual victim," and other aims, such as facilitating a transition, were either irrelevant or dubious. "I want to quarrel with the assumption that a principle reason for seeking justice, or criterion for evaluating its efficacy, should be the future stability of a reconstituted democracy," he asserted.[117] But this position, though important, was not the general one represented at the conference, nor the one that continued to animate the emergent field. In a way, Neier unwittingly identified the precise factor that makes the field of transitional justice distinctive: the second normative aim of facilitating a transition to democracy.

Unlike the broader human rights movement, transitional justice relies on two sorts of beliefs: principled beliefs, which are "normative ideas that specify criteria for distinguishing right from wrong and just from unjust"; and causal beliefs, which are "beliefs about cause-effect relationships which derive authority from the shared consensus of recognized elites, whether they be village elders or scientists at elite institutions."[118] The human rights movement has built its practical activity around advancing and defending norms, particularly at the international level. The field of transitional justice has also taken on this task of norm "entrepreneurship," but has added to it the burden of trying to systematize knowledge about the cause-and-effect relationships between justice measures and transitions. That is no easy task.

This article only tells part of the story. It has defined the emerging field of transitional justice as an international web of individuals and institutions

117. Weschler, A Miracle, *supra* note 1, at 244.

118. Judith Goldstein & Robert Keohane, *Ideas and Foreign Policy: An Analytical Framework*, *in* Ideas and Foreign Policy: Beliefs, Institutions, and Political Change 9–10 (Judith Goldstein & Robert O. Keohane eds., 1993). *See also* Keck and Sikkink's discussion of how "principled beliefs" are at the heart of human rights work. Keck & Sikkink, *supra* note 52, at 1.

whose internal coherence is held together by common concepts, practical aims, and distinctive claims for legitimacy. So far, there is no single theory of transitional justice, and the term does not have a fixed meaning. It remains to be explained how the elementary conceptual structure explored here interacted with the other elements of the emerging field. Moreover, the focus on these early discussions necessarily omits an important and ongoing development in the emergence of the field: the rapid expansion of international law on transitional justice issues throughout the 1990s.

B. Challenges to the Initial Conceptual Boundaries of Transitional Justice

In conclusion, this section addresses challenges to this initial structure that have since come to play an important role in understandings of—and debates about—the conceptual boundaries of transitional justice.

The first of these challenges arises with respect to the question of whether and how the chosen end point of a transition (e.g., democracy, socialism, enlightened despotism, etc.) may matter for the kinds of justice claims advanced. There was an explicit democratization frame for the initial conceptualization of transitional justice. What happens when a different frame is used? In the case of South Africa, for example, there has been a reactivation of distributive justice claims associated with transitions to socialism rather than transitions to democracy. Some critics of transitional justice have argued that justice for the crimes of apartheid requires more than the legal-institutional reforms required for an instauration of democratic citizenship and a transformation of an abusive state security apparatus; it requires a redistribution of wealth that was unjustly accumulated through an inhuman political and economic system. This challenge was, indeed, already recognized at the Aspen Institute conference. John Herz concluded his remarks by noting that in some contexts, democratic transitions (and the legal-institutional reforms that go along with them) may not mean very much: "Where, as in Brazil, Guatemala, El Salvador, and Haiti or the Philippines, land-owning is concentrated in large *latifundia*, with a dependent and impoverished peasantry, the overthrow of the Marcoses or the Duvaliers may mean little without a reform of the socio-economic system." He also concluded, however, that this problem represents "another story" from the one being told at the conference.[119] But on what grounds could one argue that such claims should not be considered transitional justice claims? If they can be considered transitional justice, then what specific form should they take, and which measures (nationalization, special taxation, expropriation, affirmative action, etc.) are most appropriate to their fulfillment?

119. Herz, *An Historical Perspective*, *supra* note 105, at 22.

Similarly, it must be asked whether a "transition to peace" really is different in kind than a transition to democracy, and if so whether a new normative aim must either replace or be added to the initial normative aims undergirding the transitional justice field. The practical dilemmas actors face in peacebuilding can be quite different from those involved in the instauration of democratic citizenship and the transformation of an abusive state security apparatus. Justice claims in such contexts are much more likely to revolve around reintegration of ex-combatants, ethnic cleansing, war crimes, internal displacement, property restitution, power sharing, wealth sharing, and claims for self-determination. The measures of prosecutions, truth-telling, reparations, and reform of an abusive state apparatus should not be assumed to map neatly onto these very different practical problems—if at all. Neier, for example, explicitly questioned the value of a truth commission in a post-conflict setting in a 1995 letter to the *New York Review of Books.*[120] For him, commissions were a logical response to the need to uncover tightly guarded state secrets. "What is it that a commission could tell us about the indiscriminate bombardment of Sarajevo or the radio-incited genocide in Rwanda that would assist in confronting such a past?" he queried.[121] Moreover, prosecutions and vetting are unlikely to be adequate measures in a post-conflict setting, where the problem of ex-combatant reintegration requires at least consideration of local-level, restorative justice approaches. Perhaps new norms and methods of realizing them need to be identified and refined. Should those working in transitional justice develop a new set of measures to address the specific justice concerns of transitions to peace? And if so, should they engage directly with social science literature on conflict resolution, state building, and peacebuilding to do so?

The second challenge is a response to the difficulties of transposing the regional diagnoses of Latin American observers to other parts of the world with different histories, cultures, and positions within the world economy. One of the most important critiques of the "transitions to democracy" literature was made in the mid-1990s by a group of Central and Eastern European regional specialists, who argued for the unique characteristics of the political transitions that took place in the post-communist countries.[122]

120. Aryeh Neier, *Do Trials Work?* N.Y. Rev. Books, 19 Oct. 1995 (in response to Timothy Garton Ash, *Central Europe: The Present Past,* N.Y. Rev. Books, 13 July 1995.

121. *Id.*

122. *See* Philippe C. Schmitter with Terry Lynn Karl, *The Conceptual Travels of Transitologists and Consolidologists: How Far to the East Should They Attempt to Go?,* 53 Slavic Rev. 173 (1994); Valerie Bunce, *Should the Transitologists Be Grounded?* 54 Slavic Rev. 111 (1995); Terry Lynn Karl & Philippe C. Schmitter, *From an Iron Curtain to a Paper Curtain: Grounding Transitologists or Students of Postcommunism?,* 54 Slavic Rev. 965 (1995); Valerie Bunce, *Paper Curtains and Paper Tigers,* 54 Slavic Rev. 979 (1995). Also of interest is Sarah Meiklejohn Terry, *Thinking About Post-communist Transitions: How Different Are They?,* 52 Slavic Rev. 333 (1993).

In these countries, "transition" had entailed sweeping social and economic reforms that could be characterized as revolutionary. Latin American countries in the Southern Cone had had strong capitalist classes independent of the state under their "bureaucratic" authoritarian regimes, whereas communist countries were single-party states where the party was uniquely responsible for economic decision making. Moreover, in their "pre-transition" phase, communist countries typically had more egalitarian class structures than their Latin American counterparts, meaning that class was unlikely to be mobilized as a political interest during the transition—instead, ethnic, national, or religious identities were more likely to become politically salient. Indeed, the critics point out that Latin American countries typically had established national identities, whereas post-communist countries did not. Finally, there is the fact that in the Southern Cone (Central American countries are considered an exception on this point), demands for social, economic, military, and administrative transformations were generally met sequentially—whereas in the post-communist states they occurred all at once, with little opportunity to prioritize among them.

Similarly, comparative research on African democratic experiments of the early- to mid- 1990s has also yielded alternative accounts of the most salient characteristics of sub-Saharan African political transitions. These accounts begin with a theory of the most prevalent type of autocracy in the region: neopatrimonialism, or "strongman" politics based on large, personal systems of patronage. In these cases, the very authority of the state rested on clientelist relationships that began to dissolve along with the austerity regimes imposed on so many debtor nations in the 1980s. These researchers stress that transitions from neopatrimonial-style states are likely to begin with mass protest, owing to the withdrawal of state subsidies to the vast clientele networks, rather than with elite pacts (with the exception of transitions away from settler oligarchies such as South Africa).[123] Such transitions sometimes lead to state fragility or failure, meaning that the very state institutions upon which transitional justice measures depend are weak or absent. Moreover, given the particularities of these kinds of states, corruption logically arises as one of the central justice issues of such transitions.

Given all of these differences, if it is agreed that the particular concerns and conceptual structure of transitional justice took shape in response to events in Latin America, to what degree can these concerns and conceptual structures be transposed to other regions?

Another challenge arises in the applicability of transitional justice in contexts where there is no discernible "transition." In many long-standing liberal democracies, for example, there remain important questions of "his-

123. *See* Michael Bratton & Nicolas van de Walle, Democratic Experiments in Africa: Regime Transitions in Comparative Perspective 118 (1997).

torical justice," which is discussed typically in cases where there has been long-term, systematic marginalization, often over centuries. The victims of the actual abuses may be dead, but the abuses live on by negatively structuring the life experiences and life chances of the victims' descendents. Examples include the legacy of slavery for African-Americans and of settler colonialism for indigenous peoples. It is far from clear, however, given that the initial impetus for the field of transitional justice was historically located in Latin American transitions from authoritarian rule, that claims for the rectification of historical injustices in mature democracies would best be satisfied through "standard" transitional justice measures. Indeed, many working in the field of historical justice have flatly rejected the relevance of anything so narrow as transitional justice. For these critics, transitional justice is intimately linked with measures specifically designed for the brief duration of a political transition. They emphasize the importance of long-term efforts at transformation that involve some element of social restructuring, such as affirmative action or land reform, which they see as fundamentally different from the limited aims of prosecutions, reparations, and the like.

Yet another challenge is the fact that, since the mid-1990s many observers have cast significant doubt on the transitions paradigm itself, mainly on empirical grounds—the observation that a number of countries that were supposed to be making a transition to democracy had ultimately failed to do so.[124] For these observers, the paradigm had raised false hopes, perhaps mostly among democracy promoters, of an easily identifiable, sequential path toward a new political regime. One critic of the post-communist aftermath in Russia, *Nation* columnist and Russian historian Stephen Cohen, excoriated the "near orthodoxy" status of the transitions paradigm among Western democracy promoters, whom he credited with a "Bolshevik-like experiment" that led not to democracy, but rather to an immense and unintentional redistributive scheme that skewed wealth fantastically at the top of the Russian social pyramid.[125] In another trenchant critique, Thomas Carothers advocated for the removal of a "transitions lens," as it did more to muddle political analysis than it did to clarify it. For him, those interested in democratization

> should start by assuming that what is often thought of as an uneasy, precarious middle ground between full-fledged democracy and outright dictatorship is actually the most common political condition today of the countries in the developing world and the post-communist world. It is not an exceptional category . . . it is a state of normality for many societies.[126]

124. *See* Fareed Zakaria, *The Rise of Illiberal Democracy*, 76 Foreign Aff. 22 (Nov.–Dec. 1997); Robert D. Kaplan, *Was Democracy Just a Moment?* Atlantic Monthly, Dec. 1997, at 55; Thomas Carothers, *The End of the Transition Paradigm*, 13 J. Democracy 5 (2002).
125. Stephen F. Cohen, Failed Crusade: America and the Tragedy of Post-Communist Russia 24, 94 (2001).
126. Carothers, *The End of the Transition Paradigm*, *supra* note 124, at 17–18.

Given the doubt cast on the very utility of the transitions paradigm, should justice measures continue to make empirical claims related to facilitating transitions? If so, then on what empirical basis can one claim that particular actions taken during a transition affect its outcome—and are such claims useful or even desirable?

A final challenge to this initial conceptualization of transitional justice would follow this critique of the transitions paradigm and simply reject the transitional framework altogether—perhaps on the grounds that it is too tainted by a specific political project (democratization) and by the support of specific institutional actors (US democracy-promoting organizations). One might be tempted to argue that the term "transitional justice" should be abandoned, and replaced with something along the lines of "mass atrocity" justice. The attempt to shift meaning in this way might make sense given the immense expansion of international principles and law on these issues since the late 1980s, and the emergence of an "anti-impunity" movement, which, though related to transitional justice, has a different history and conceptual background.[127] Should transitional justice be folded into an anti-impunity movement centered on the development of international norms and law, which would allow the contents of the word "transitional" simply to wither away?

This latter challenge echoes Aryeh Neier's comments at the Aspen Institute conference. His skepticism concerning the relationship between justice and a "reconstituted democracy," as well as his strong assertion that "punishment is the absolute duty of society to honor and redeem the suffering of the individual victims" may prove to have been quite prescient.[128] This final challenge has a distinct chance of succeeding, and in a sense it would represent an unsurprising historical outcome given the expansion of international law and principles—often called "international justice"—that has taken place since the Aspen Institute conference. It may be argued, however, that what made the field of transitional justice distinct from human rights was its addition of causal beliefs about facilitating a transition to the principled beliefs of human rights actors such as Neier about right and wrong. Resolving that tension by placing decisions about justice squarely in the sphere of international law might, on that definition, effectively announce the dissolution of transitional justice itself.

127. This movement has been analyzed in terms of a "justice cascade." *See* Ellen Lutz & Kathryn Sikkink, *The Justice Cascade: The Evolution and Impact of Foreign Human Rights Trials in Latin America*, 2 Chi. J. Int'l L. 1 (2001). *See also* Sikkink & Walling, *supra* note 11.

128. Weschler, A Miracle, *supra* note 1, at 244.

Annex: Attendees of Several Conferences, 1988–1994[129]

This chart is comprised of the participants at three conferences that treated the issues of justice in transitional periods. In the first part of the chart, I identify those people who attended more than one of these conferences. In the second, I listed all the other participants.

State Crimes: Punishment or Pardon? Aspen Institute Wye, Maryland November 4–6, 1988 Funder: Ford Foundation	*Justice in Times of Transition* Charter 77 Foundation Salzburg, Austria March 7–10, 1992 Funders: German Marshall Fund of the United States, the Charles Stewart Mott Foundation, the National Endowment for Democracy, Open Society, the Rockefeller Family & Associates, the Rockefeller Foundation, and the Charter 77 Foundation-New York	*Dealing with the Past* Institute for a Democratic Alternative for South Africa Somerset West, Western Cape February 1994 Funder: Open Society
Henkin, Alice H. The Aspen Institute, New York, USA	Henkin, Alice H.	
Malamud-Goti, Jaime Buenos Aires University, Argentina	Malamud-Goti, Jaime	
Méndez, Juan E. Americas Watch, Washington, D.C., USA		Méndez, Juan E.
	Michnik, Adam Editor-in-Chief of Wyborcza, Member of Parliament, Poland	Michnik, Adam
Neier, Aryeh HRW, New York, USA		Neier, Aryeh
Orentlicher, Diane Columbia University, New York, USA	Orentlicher, Diane	
	Sajo, Andras Legal Advisor to President Arpad Gönz, Hungary	Sajo, Andras
Weschler, Lawrence The New Yorker, New York, USA	Weschler, Lawrence	Weschler, Lawrence

129. State Crimes, *supra* note 3; Charter 77 Foundation, Project on Justice in Times of Transition, (Report of the Project's Inaugural Meeting), Salzburg, 7–10 Mar. 1992; Dealing with the Past, *supra* note 7, at 159. These lists are based on available sources, but may be incomplete.

State Crimes: Punishment or Pardon? Aspen Institute Wye, Maryland November 4–6, 1988 Funder: Ford Foundation	*Justice in Times of Transition* Charter 77 Foundation Salzburg, Austria March 7–10, 1992 Funders: German Marshall Fund of the United States, the Charles Stewart Mott Foundation, the National Endowment for Democracy, Open Society, the Rockefeller Family & Associates, the Rockefeller Foundation, and the Charter 77 Foundation-New York	*Dealing with the Past* Institute for a Democratic Alternative for South Africa Somerset West, Western Cape February 1994 Funder: Open Society
Zalaquett, José (Esq.) Santiago, Chile		Zalaquett, José
Bajeux, Jean-Claude Ecumenical Center of Human Rights, Port-au-Prince, Haiti	Alfonsín, Raoul President of Argentina, 1983–89	Adam, Heribert South Africa
Crahan, Margaret Occidental College, Los Angeles	Bence, Gyorgy Philosopher, Hungary	Asmal, Kader South Africa
Dworkin, Ronald New York University New York, USA	Biedenkopf, Kurt Minister President of Saxony, Germany	Boraine, Alex IDASA, South Africa
Fitch, Samuel University of Colorado, Boulder, USA	Bratinka, Pavel Member of Federal Assembly, Czechoslovakia	Burton, Mary South Africa
Fruhling, Hugo Academia de Humanismo Cristiano, Santiago, Chile	Degutis, Arunas MP, Lithuania	Calata, Nomonde South Africa
Henkin, Louis Columbia University, New York, USA	Errera, Roger Conseiller d'état, France	Canas, Roberto El Salvador
Herz, John H. City University of New York, USA	Garretón, Roberto Deputy Foreign Minister of Chile	Du Plessis, Lourens South Africa
Mamdani, Mahmood Makerere University, Kampala, Uganda	Goldman, Robert American University Law School Washington, D.C., USA	Du Toit, André South Africa
Meron, Theodor NYU, New York, USA	Grossman, Claudio American University Law School, USA	Gauck, Joachim Germany
Mulet, Edmond (Cong.) Guatemala City, Guatemala	Güttler, Vojen Justice, Constitutional Court of Czechoslovakia	Gcina, Paizoah South Africa

State Crimes: Punishment or Pardon? Aspen Institute Wye, Maryland November 4–6, 1988 Funder: Ford Foundation	*Justice in Times of Transition* Charter 77 Foundation Salzburg, Austria March 7–10, 1992 Funders: German Marshall Fund of the United States, the Charles Stewart Mott Foundation, the National Endowment for Democracy, Open Society, the Rockefeller Family & Associates, the Rockefeller Foundation, and the Charter 77 Foundation-New York	*Dealing with the Past* Institute for a Democratic Alternative for South Africa Somerset West, Western Cape February 1994 Funder: Open Society
Nagel, Thomas NYU, New York, USA	Holmes, Stephen Professor of Political Science, University of Chicago, USA	Goldstone, Richard South Africa
Nakchung, Paik University of Seoul, Korea	Huntington, Samuel Olin Institute Harvard University, USA	James, Wilmot South Africa
Pérez Aguirre, Luis (Father) Servicio Paz y Justicia, Montevideo, Uruguay	Laber, Jeri Executive Director, Helsinki Watch	Lapsley, Michael South Africa
Picken, Margo Ford Foundation, New York, USA	Luciani, Claudia Council of Europe	Motlana, Nthato South Africa
Pinheiro, Paulo Sergio Universidade de Sao Paulo, Brazil	Michelini, Rafael Deputy in Chamber of Representatives, Uruguay	Ntsebeza, Dumisa South Africa
Posner, Michael Lawyers Committee for Human Rights, New York, USA	Navasky, Victor Editor, *The Nation* USA	Osiatynski, Wiktor Poland/USA
Skweyiya, Lewis (Esq.) Durban, South Africa	Offe, Claus Professor of Political Science, University of Bremen, Germany	Petrova, Dimitrina Bulgaria
	Osiatynski, Wiktor Advisor to Polish government on drafting a new constitution, Poland	Rosenberg, Tina USA
	Petovar, Tanja HR Lawyer, Belgrade, Yugoslavia	Sachs, Albie South Africa
	Phillips, Tim Charter 77 Foundation, New York, USA	Schwarzenberg, Karel Czech Republic
	Rodrigo, Fernando Fundacion Ortega y Gasset, Madrid, Spain	Slabbert, Frederik Van Zyl IDASA, South Africa

State Crimes: Punishment or Pardon?	*Justice in Times of Transition*	*Dealing with the Past*
Aspen Institute Wye, Maryland November 4–6, 1988 Funder: Ford Foundation	Charter 77 Foundation Salzburg, Austria March 7–10, 1992 Funders: German Marshall Fund of the United States, the Charles Stewart Mott Foundation, the National Endowment for Democracy, Open Society, the Rockefeller Family & Associates, the Rockefeller Foundation, and the Charter 77 Foundation-New York	Institute for a Democratic Alternative for South Africa Somerset West, Western Cape February 1994 Funder: Open Society
	Roginsky, Arseny Board Member of Memorial, Russian Human Rights Organization Rupnik, Jacques Advisor to Mitterrand, France Schwartz, Herman American University Law School Co-chair, Project on Justice in Times of Transition, USA Steigenberger, Helmut Former Justice of the FRG Constitutional Court, Germany Szajer, Jozef MP, Hungary Teitel, Ruti New York Law School, USA Urban, Jan Journalist for Livdove noviny, Czechoslovakia	

2

Transitional Justice Genealogy

Ruti G. Teitel

Introduction

This Article proposes a genealogy of transitional justice.[1] Transitional justice can be defined as the conception of justice associated with periods of political change,[2] characterized by legal responses to confront the wrongdoings of repressive predecessor regimes.[3] The genealogy presented in this Article traces the historical pursuit of justice in periods of political flux, reviewing the political developments of the last half-century and analyzing the evolution of the conception of transitional justice.[4] This Article contends that a genealogy of transitional justice demonstrates, over time, a close relationship between the type of justice pursued and the relevant limiting political conditions. Currently, the discourse is directed at preserving a minimalist rule of law identified chiefly with maintaining peace.

The proposed genealogy is structured along critical cycles that divide along three phases.[5] This Article begins by briefly describing the phases, and then elaborates upon each phase as well as upon the critical dynamic interrelationships of the three phases within the genealogy.[6] The notion of genealogy presented in this Article is structured along the lines of and situated within an intellectual history.[7] Accordingly, the genealogy is organized

---

1. For a comprehensive analysis of transitional justice, see RUTI G. TEITEL, TRANSITIONAL JUSTICE (2000).

2. *See* GUILLERMO O'DONNELL & PHILIPPE C. SCHMITTER, TRANSITIONS FROM AUTHORITARIAN RULE: TENTATIVE CONCLUSIONS ABOUT UNCERTAIN DEMOCRACIES 6 (1998) (defining transition as the interval between one political regime and another).

3. For a helpful compilation, see TRANSITIONAL JUSTICE: HOW EMERGING DEMOCRACIES RECKON WITH FORMER REGIMES (Neil J. Kritz ed., 1997).

4. *See* TEITEL, *supra* note 1; Ruti Teitel, *Transitional Jurisprudence: The Role of Law in Political Transformation*, 106 YALE L.J. 2009 (1997).

5. The use of the term "phases" here should be considered primarily as a heuristic, to help understand the periodization of the various political and legal periods. This is not to say that there are acoustic separations dividing these phases. Indeed, there are overlaps among the three phases proposed here.

6. On the "critical" responses of transitional justice to predecessor political repressions, see TEITEL, *supra* note 1, at 216, 220–25.

7. Regarding genealogy, see Michel Foucault, *Nietzche, Genealogy, History* (Donald F. Bouchard &

along a schematic of the development of ideas associated with the three phases of transitional justice. These phases ultimately reflect the genealogy's link with the broader intellectual trend toward an increased pragmatism in and politicization of the law.[8]

The origins of modern transitional justice can be traced to World War I.[9] However, transitional justice becomes understood as both extraordinary and international in the postwar period after 1945. The Cold War ends the internationalism of this first, or postwar, phase of transitional justice. The second, or post–Cold War, phase is associated with the wave of democratic transitions and modernization that began in 1989. Toward the end of the twentieth century, global politics was characterized by an acceleration in conflict resolution and a persistent discourse of justice throughout law and society. The third, or steady-state, phase of transitional justice is associated with contemporary conditions of persistent conflict which lay the foundation for a normalized law of violence.

Phase I of the genealogy, the postwar phase, began in 1945. Through its most recognized symbol, the Allied-run Nuremberg Trials,[10] this phase reflects the triumph of transitional justice within the scheme of international law. However, this development was not enduring, due to its association with the exceptional political conditions of the postwar period: Germany's diminished sovereignty formed the basis for international nation-building. These political conditions were unique, and would neither persist nor recur in the same manner. Accordingly, this first phase of transitional justice, associated with interstate cooperation, war crimes trials, and sanctions, ended soon after the war. Beginning in the 1950s, the Cold War and a stable bipolar balance of power led to a general political equilibrium and an impasse on the question of transitional justice. Nevertheless, the legacy of the postwar trials that criminalized state wrongdoing as part of a universal rights scheme far exceeds the actual force of historical precedent, and this legacy forms the basis of modern human rights law.[11]

Sherry Simon trans.) *in* THE FOUCAULT READER 80 (Paul Rabinow ed., 1984). On genealogical politics, see WENDY BROWN, POLITICS OUT OF HISTORY, 91–120 (2001); MICHAEL CLIFFORD, POLITICAL GENEALOGY AFTER FOUCAULT: SAVAGE IDENTITIES 149–70 (2001).

8. On pragmatism, see Marion Smiley, *Democratic Justice in Transition*, 99 MICH. L. REV. 1332 (2001) (discussing pragmatic views of transitional justice and reviewing Ruti Teitel's *Transitional Justice*). *See also* Jack Snyder & Leslie Vinjamuri, *Principles and Pragmatism in Strategies of International Justice*, Presented at the Olin Institute National Security Seminar at Harvard University (December 2001) (on file with author).

9. For historical examples see TEITEL, *supra* note 1, at 31, 39–40; for earlier precedents see also MICHAEL WALZER, REGICIDE AND REVOLUTION: SPEECHES ON THE TRIAL OF LOUIS XVI (Michael Walzer ed., Marion Rothstein trans., 1992) (providing a historical account).

10. On the postwar period, see FROM DICTATORSHIP TO DEMOCRACY: COPING WITH THE LEGACIES OF AUTHORITARIANISM AND TOTALITARIANISM (John H. Herz ed., 1983). Of course, there are earlier examples in the century, but these are smaller-scale responses. *See* PHILLIPE C. SCHMITTER, TRANSITIONS FROM AUTHORITARIAN RULE: COMPARATIVE PERSPECTIVES (Guillermo O'Donnell et al. eds., 1986).

11. On the impact of the Nuremberg precedent, see Ruti G. Teitel, *Nuremberg and Its Legacy, Fifty Years Later*, *in* WAR CRIMES: THE LEGACY OF NUREMBERG 44 (Belinda Cooper ed., 1999). For an example of the impact of the postwar precedents in human rights law, see HENRY STEINER & PHILIP ALSTON,

Phase II is associated with a period of accelerated democratization and political fragmentation that has been characterized as a "third wave" of transition.[12] Over the last quarter of the twentieth century, the collapse and disintegration of the Soviet Union led to concurrent transitions throughout much of the world. Withdrawal of Soviet-supported guerrilla forces in the late 1970s fueled the end of military rule in South America.[13] These transitions were rapidly followed by post-1989 transitions in Eastern Europe, Africa, and Central America.[14] While these changes are often described as isolated developments or as a series of civil wars, many of these conflicts were fostered or supported by international power politics[15] and were therefore affected by the Soviet collapse, which ended the Cold War period of political equilibrium.[16]

While the post–Cold War wave of transition theoretically raises the possibility of a return to Phase I international transitional justice, the form of transitional justice that in fact emerges is associated with the rise of nation-building.[17] Moreover, rather than understanding rule of law in terms of accountability for a small number of leaders, the Phase II transitional model tends to rely upon more diverse rule-of-law understandings tied to a particular political community and local conditions.[18] However, this move toward more local or even privatized justice stands in tension with the potential of a broader conception of justice associated with transnational politics.

By the end of the twentieth century, the third steady-state phase of transitional justice emerges. This third phase is characterized by the fin de siècle acceleration of transitional justice phenomena associated with globalization and typified by conditions of heightened political instability and violence.[19] Transitional justice moves from the exception to the norm to become a paradigm of rule of law. In this contemporary phase, transitional jurisprudence

---

INTERNATIONAL HUMAN RIGHTS IN CONTEXT: LAW, POLITICS, MORALS (2000).

12. *See* SAMUEL P. HUNTINGTON, THE THIRD WAVE: DEMOCRATIZATION IN THE LATE TWENTIETH CENTURY (1991).

13. On the Latin American transitions, see PHILIPPE C. SCHMITTER ET AL., TRANSITIONS FROM AUTHORITARIAN RULE: LATIN AMERICA (1986); JAIME MALAMUD-GOTI, GAME WITHOUT END: STATE TERROR AND THE POLITICS OF JUSTICE (1996); LAWRENCE WESCHLER, A MIRACLE, A UNIVERSE: SETTLING ACCOUNTS WITH TORTURERS (1998); *see also* TRANSITION TO DEMOCRACY IN LATIN AMERICA: THE ROLE OF THE JUDICIARY (Irwin P. Stotsky ed., 1993).

14. See *supra* note 12.

15. On Latin America see LARS SCHOULTZ, NATIONAL SECURITY AND UNITED STATES POLICY TOWARDS LATIN AMERICA (1987) (discussing Latin America and the global balance of power); *see also* DAVID GREEN, THE CONTAINMENT OF LATIN AMERICA: A HISTORY OF THE MYTHS AND REALITIES OF THE GOOD NEIGHBOR POLICY (1971); WITH FRIENDS LIKE THESE: THE AMERICAS WATCH REPORT ON HUMAN RIGHTS AND U.S. POLICY IN LATIN AMERICA (Cynthia Brown ed., 1985).

16. This is, of course, not to offer unicausal theory, but rather to clarify shared factors in the multiple transitions that occurred in approximately the last quarter of the last century. For disciplinary reasons, scholarship in each area tends to be isolated.

17. There are exceptions in the turn to international justice regarding the conflicts in the Balkans and in Rwanda. *See infra* text accompanying note 133.

18. *See infra* text accompanying notes 53–73.

19. *See infra* text accompanying notes 128–145.

normalizes an expanded discourse of humanitarian justice constructing a body of law associated with pervasive conflict, which contributes to laying the foundation for the emerging law of terrorism.

I. Phase I: Postwar Transitional Justice

The first phase of a genealogy of transitional justice encompasses the post–World War II model of justice. However, the history begins earlier in the century, following World War I. During the inter-war period, the central aim of justice was to delineate the unjust war and the parameters of justifiable punishment by the international community. Questions confronted in this context included whether and to what extent to punish Germany for its aggression, and what form justice should take: international or national, collective or individual. Ultimately, the decision to convene international proceedings reflected the prevailing political circumstances, particularly the limits upon national sovereignty and the conceded international governance of that period.

A genealogical perspective situates postwar transitional justice in its own historical context, specifically the transitional justice of World War I,[20] and reveals the extent to which this preceding conception informs the critical response of post–World War II justice.[21] At least two critical responses emerge regarding World War II transitional justice. First, national justice was displaced by international justice. The administration of the post–World War I model of transitional punitive justice, characterized by failed national trials, was left to Germany.[22] Seen with the hindsight of history, it was clear that the post–World War I national trials did not serve to deter future carnage. In an evident critical response to the past, post–World War II transitional justice began by eschewing national prosecutions,[23] instead seeking international criminal accountability for the Reich's leadership.[24]

The second critical response concerned the post–World War I collective sanctions levied against Germany.[25] Seen through the lens of genealogy,

20. *See* Niall Ferguson, The Pity of War: Explaining World War I (2000).

21. Regarding the postwar Allied Trials program, see Telford Taylor, The Anatomy of the Nuremberg Trials: A Personal Memoir (1992); Sheldon Glueck, War Criminals: Their Prosecution and Punishment (Kraus Reprint Co., 1976) (1944).

22. For an account see Geo. Gordon Battle, *The Trials Before the Leipsic Supreme Court of Germans Accused of War Crimes*, 8 Va. L. Rev. 1 (1921).

23. On the history of the deliberations, see Robert I. Conot, Justice at Nuremberg (1983).

24. However, the subsequent Control Council Ten trials would be convened on a national basis. *See* Gov't Printing Office, Trials of the Major War Criminals Before the Nuremberg Military Tribunals under Control Council Law No. 10 (1953) (commonly known as the "green books").

25. The Versailles Treaty at Article 231 provides: "The Allied and Associated Governments affirm and Germany accepts the responsibility of Germany and her Allies for causing all the loss and damage to which the Allied and Associated Governments and their nationals have been subjected as a consequence of a war imposed upon them by the aggression of Germany and her Allies." According to the Treaty's "war-guilt" clause, all responsibility for the war was to be borne by Germany. *See* Treaty of Versailles, June 28, 1919, art. 231, pt. VIII, Consol. T.S. 225; *see generally* Nana Sagi, German Reparations: A History of the Negotiations (Dafna Alon trans., 1980).

these transitional responses clearly failed and came to be identified as a basis for the sense of economic frustration and resentment that fueled Germany's role in World War II.[26] Onerous sanctions and their crude undifferentiated impact raised profound normative questions.[27] This approach gave way to the critical response after World War II, and to the liberal focus on individual judgment and responsibility.

While the asserted aim of the transitional justice norm in this first phase was accountability, a striking innovation at the time was the turn to international criminal law and the extension of its applicability beyond the state to the individual. Moreover, through changes in the law of war and its principles of criminal responsibility, the international legal regime enabled holding accountable the Reich's higher echelons for the offenses of aggression and persecutory policy. While claims are made about the forward-looking nature of deterrence, it is clear that the Nuremberg prosecution was primarily intended to justify and legitimate Allied intervention in the war.[28] This use of transitional justice recurs in Phase III.[29]

The period immediately following World War II was the heyday of international justice. The critical turn away from prior nationalist transitional responses and toward an internationalist policy was thought to guarantee rule of law. However, whether deterrence would necessarily be better advanced by international accountability was debatable. Whereas international justice is commonly thought to incorporate the impartiality associated with the rule of law,[30] other rule-of-law values are seen as deriving from the local accountability associated with domestic justice.[31] Moreover, following World War II, the application of international justice involved legal irregularities which raised tensions for the rule of law, especially given its stated liberalizing aim.[32] Ultimately, the Phase I model would offer a very limited precedent. With the Cold War bifurcation, it became eminently clear that this model could not be readily exported. While a form of international justice does recur in Phase III,[33] this more contemporary internationalism has been transformed by the ongoing developments caused by globalization.[34]

The postwar turn to international law also reflected the sense that the relevant subject of transitional justice was an international legal response

26. *See* FERGUSON, *supra* note 20.

27. The uses of economic sanctions in the contemporary moment have raised similar concerns. On the U.S. sanctions debate, see Audie Klotz, *Norms Reconstituting Interests: Global Racial Equality and U.S. Sanctions Against South Africa*, 49 INT'L ORG. 451 (1995).

28. Transitional justice was used as a norm to distinguish between justified and unjustified military intervention. *See* TAYLOR, *supra* note 21, at 22–42 (discussing the Nuremberg ideas regarding whether launching an aggressive war should be considered a crime under international law).

29. *See infra* text accompanying notes 133–137.

30. *See* TEITEL, *supra* note 1, at 30–39; Stotsky, *supra* note 13.

31. These are discussed *infra* at Part II, notes 53–57, 58–73 and accompanying text. *See* TEITEL, *supra* note 1 at 36–40; *see generally* Stotsky, *supra* note 13.

32. *See* DAVID LUBAN, LEGAL MODERNISM 336 (1994).

33. *See* Teitel, *Transitional Jurisprudence*, *supra* note 4.

34. *See infra* text accompanying notes 132–137.

governed by the law of conflict. Over the years, this legacy has been mixed: the force of the precedent has hardly been reflected in other instances of international justice,[35] although this is arguably changing given the creation of the permanent International Criminal Court.[36] The postwar legacy's ongoing force has been evident in developments in international law, where dimensions of the precedent establishing international accountability for wartime abuses were entrenched in international conventions soon after World War II, such as the Genocide Convention.[37] Moreover, dimensions of the postwar precedent, such as its preeminent commitment to individual rights, have also informed domestic and comparative law, as evidenced in the heightened wave of related constitutionalism.[38] In the postwar phase, the exportation of forms of transitional justice occurred through legal transplants of treaties, conventions, and constitutionalism. The postwar period was also the heyday of the belief in law and development, and more generally in the belief in law as a tool for state modernization.[39]

The international justice associated with the postwar period returns in a new form in contemporary post-conflict circumstances, revealing transitional justice's critical dynamic. International justice recurs but is transformed by past precedents and a new political context. The subject and scope of transitional justice have expanded to transcend its operative action upon states and to operate upon private actors. Transitional justice has also extended beyond its historic role in regulating international conflict to regulate intrastate conflict as well as peacetime relations, comprising a threshold rule of law in globalizing politics.[40] The significance of these developments will be discussed further in Phase III.

---

35. *See* Teitel, *supra* note 11, at 44. The World War II–related prosecutions are still the largest precedents in criminal accountability. For a bibliography of war crimes trials, see WAR CRIMINALS AND WAR CRIMES TRIALS: AN ANNOTATED BIBLIOGRAPHY AND SOURCE BOOK (Norman E. Tutorow ed., 1986). *See* Symposium, *Holocaust and Human Rights Law: The Sixth International Conference*, 12 B.C. THIRD WORLD L.J. 191 (1992).

36. *See infra* notes 132–134 (regarding the Rome Statute).

37. *See* Affirmation of the Principles of International Law Recognized by the Charter of the Nuremberg Tribunal, G.A. Res. 95(1), U.N. GAOR, Doc. A/64/Add.1 (1946). For a discussion of the codification process and efforts of the International Law Commission, see M. Cherif Bassiouni, *The History of the Draft Code of Crimes Against the Peace and Security of Mankind*, *in* NOUVELLES ÉTUDES PENALES, COMMENTARIES ON THE INTERNATIONAL LAW COMMISSION'S 1991 DRAFT CODE OF CRIMES AGAINST THE PEACE AND SECURITY OF MANKIND 11 (M. Cherif Bassiouni ed., 1993); Convention on the Prevention and Punishment of the Crime of Genocide, Dec. 9, 1948, 78 U.N.T.S. 277 (entered into force Jan. 12, 1951); The Universal Declaration of Human Rights, G.A. Res. 217A (III), 71 U.N. Doc. A/810 (1948). For broader discussion of these post-war developments, see Ruti G. Teitel, *Human Rights Genealogy*, 66 FORDHAM L. REV. 301 (1997).

38. This is evidenced in the constitution-making of the postwar period. *See* LOUIS HENKIN, THE AGE OF RIGHTS (1990). On the emerging right to democracy, see Thomas M. Franck, *The Emerging Right to Democratic Governance*, 86 AM. J. INT'L. L. 46, 53 (1992).

39. John Henry Merryman, *Law and Development Memoirs II: SLADE*, 48 AM. J. COMP. L. 713 (2000). *See* John Henry Merryman, *Comparative Law and Social Change*, 25 AM. J. COMP. L. 457, 483 (1977); *see also* THOMAS CAROTHERS, AIDING DEMOCRACY ABROAD: THE LEARNING CURVE (1999).

40. *See infra* notes 128–140 and accompanying text.

II. Phase II: Post–Cold War Transitional Justice

The last two decades of the twentieth century have been characterized as a veritable wave of political transition. The collapse of the Soviet Union, the end of the bipolar balance of power, and the attendant proliferation of political democratization and modernization ushered in the post–Cold War phase of transitional justice.[41]

The decline and eventual collapse of the Soviet Empire sparked a wave of liberalization that began with the transitions in the Southern Cone of South America in the late 1970s and early 1980s, and continued throughout Eastern Europe and Central America.[42] While these regional developments are generally represented as independent of one another, a genealogical perspective illuminates the connection between these political transitions and illustrates how many local conflicts were supported by United States/Soviet bipolarism.[43] The end of this historical schematic does not imply that such conflict has also ended, as there remain numerous interconnected insurgency movements.[44]

When political transitions occurred in the 1980s, the question confronted by successor regimes was whether and to what extent to adhere to the Phase I model of transitional justice.[45] In the new democracies that emerged in South America following the collapse of repressive military juntas, it was unclear whether trials of leaders in the style of Nuremberg could be successfully followed in the Americas.[46] This question was first posed in Argentina after the Falklands/Malvinas War,[47] where the successor regime attempted to distinguish the context from that of international postwar justice and called for domestic trials.[48] Throughout Latin America, nascent demo-

---

41. Other works refer to this development as the "third wave" of democratization. *See, e.g.*, HUNTINGTON, *supra* note 12.

42. *See supra* notes 14–15; WALTER LEFEBER, INEVITABLE REVOLUTIONS: UNITED STATES AND CENTRAL AMERICA (1984).

43. For a review of this third wave of transition, see HUNTINGTON, *supra* note 12. *See also* SCHOULTZ, *supra* note 15, at 112–204 (discussing geopolitics and human rights regarding U.S. policy in Central America).

44. This was made very clear after the terrorist attacks on September 11, 2001. *See* AHMED RASHID, JIHAD: THE RISE OF MILITANT ISLAM IN CENTRAL ASIA (2002); *see also* Harold Hongju Koh, *A United States Human Rights Policy for the 21st Century*, 46 ST. LOUIS U. L.J. 293 (2002); *infra* notes 130–131 and accompanying text.

45. For a leading advocate of the "Nuremberg Model," see Aryeh Neier, *What Should Be Done About the Guilty?*, N.Y. REV. BOOKS, Feb 1, 1990; *see also* ARYEH NEIER, WAR CRIMES: BRUTALITY, GENOCIDE, TERROR, AND THE STRUGGLE FOR JUSTICE (1998).

46. *See* Ruti G. Teitel, *How are the New Democracies of the Southern Cone Dealing with the Legacy of Past Human Rights Abuses?*, in Kritz, *supra* note 3; Jaime Malamud-Goti, *Transitional Governments in the Breach: Why Punish State Criminals?*, 12 HUM. RTS. Q. 1 n.1 (1990). Other aspects of the precedent, such as reparations, were taken up later in the phase.

47. The war resulted in a crushing defeat of the country's military junta and allowed the transition to go forward. For discussion of the Argentine trials policy, see CARLOS SANTIAGO NINO, RADICAL EVIL ON TRIAL (1996); *see also* Carlos S. Nino, *The Duty to Punish Past Abuses of Human Rights Put into Context: The Case of Argentina*, 100 YALE L.J. 2619 (1991).

48. *See* Nino, *supra* note 47.

cratic governments struggled with national militaries over the chosen justice policy.[49] This provided a haunting reminder of the post–World War I period and again raised the question of whether the administration of criminal justice advanced the rule of law. In Phase II, modernization and the rule of law were equated with trials by the nation-state to legitimate the successor regime and advance nation-building.

Phase II manifests a similarly limited transferability to political contexts of radically different sovereignty as the Phase I model.[50] However, despite the general absence of international trials in Phase II, a review of the transitional jurisprudence demonstrates that international law can play a constructive role, providing an alternative source of rule of law to guide national trials in a transitional society.[51] In this regard, international legal norms serve to construct a perception of continuity and consistency in the rule of law.[52] The profound and permanent significance of the Nuremberg model is that by defining the rule of law in universalizing terms, it has become the standard by which all subsequent transitional justice debates are framed. Whereas the Phase I justice policy simply assumed the legitimacy of punishing human rights abuses, in Phase II the tension between punishment and amnesty was complicated by the recognition of dilemmas inherent in periods of political flux.

Transitional justice in its second phase reflected that the relevant values in the balance were hardly those of the ideal rule of law. Where the aim was to advance legitimacy, pragmatic principles guided the justice policy and the sense of adherence to the rule of law. Transitional jurisprudence was linked to a conception of justice that was imperfect and partial. What is fair and just in extraordinary political circumstances was to be determined from the transitional position itself.[53] Accordingly, multiple conceptions of justice emerged in Phase II.

The deliberations over justice in transition are best understood when situated in the actual political realities and in the transitional political context, which included the features of the predecessor regime as well as political, juridical, and social contingencies. The feasibility of pursuing justice and its ability to contribute to transitional rule of law depended upon the scale of prior wrongdoings, as well as the extent to which they were systemic or state-sponsored. The attempt to impose accountability through criminal law often raised rule-of-law dilemmas, including retroactivity in the law, tampering with existing laws, a high degree of prosecutorial selectivity, and a

---

49. *See* Alice H. Henkin, *Conference Report*, *in* STATE CRIMES: PUNISHMENT OR PARDON, PAPERS AND REPORT OF THE CONFERENCE, NOV. 4–6, 1988, WYE CENTER, MARYLAND 1 (1989).

50. *See* TEITEL, *supra* note 1, at 36–39.

51. *See id.*, at 20–23 (identifying and evaluating numerous instances where alternative rule of law values are drawn from international law and incorporated within the national law of transitional societies).

52. *See* Alvarez, *infra* note 56; Schabas, *infra* note 56.

53. *See* TEITEL, *supra* note 1, at 234.

compromised judiciary.[54] Therefore, to whatever extent imposing transitional criminal justice included such irregularities, it risked detracting from the contribution that justice can make to reestablishing the rule of law.[55] In fledgling democracies, where the administration of punishment can pose acute rule-of-law dilemmas, the contradictions to the uses of the law may become too great.[56] These profound dilemmas were recognized in the deliberations preceding the decisions in many countries to forego prosecutions in favor of alternative methods for truth-seeking and accountability.[57]

Given the tensions present in the administration of transitional justice in its second phase, the principles of justice associated with Phase I were increasingly questioned. In a critical response to the Phase I postwar justice project, Phase II moved beyond retributive justice as historically understood. The transitional dilemmas at stake in Phase II were framed in terms more comprehensive than simply confronting or holding accountable the predecessor regime, and included questions about how to heal an entire society and incorporate diverse rule-of-law values, such as peace and reconciliation, that had previously been treated as largely external to the transitional justice project. Accordingly, the move away from judgment associated with international justice reflected a shift in the understanding of transitional justice, which became associated with the more complex and diverse political conditions of nation-building.

---

54. Where prosecutorial strategy singles out individuals, it often fails to adequately express condemnation of the system that defines the modern repressive regime, potentially defeating a core purpose of transitional justice. *See* Jon Elster, *On Doing What One Can: An Argument Against Post-Communist Restitution and Retribution*, *in* Kritz, *supra* note 3, at 566–68. On selective trials, *compare* Teitel, *Transitional Jurisprudence*, *supra* note 4 (presenting selective trials as a limit in transitional punishment policy), *with* Payam Akhavan, *Justice in The Hague, Peace in the Former Yugoslavia? A Commentary on the United Nations War Crimes Tribunal*, 20 HUM. RTS. Q. 774, 774–81 (1998) (arguing for selective trials for their "truth-telling impact"), *and* Diane F. Orentlicher, *Settling Accounts: The Duty to Prosecute Human Rights Violations of a Prior Regime*, 100 YALE L.J. 2537 (1991) (offering an argument in favor of selective trials as on balance contributing to the rule of law).

55. *See* TEITEL, *supra* note 1, at 2016–30 (discussing rule of law dilemmas).

56. See TEITEL, *supra* note 1, at 36–39, 46–51. *See generally* Ruti G. Teitel, *Persecution and Inquisition: A Case Study*, *in* Stotsky, *supra* note 13, at 141. Failed trials in fledgling democracies such as Rwanda demonstrate the conflicts between the processes of national reconciliation and criminal justice. For an analysis of the Rwandan judicial system and the debate over UN Security Council Resolutions to create an international criminal tribunal in Rwanda, see NEIL J. KRITZ, U.S. INST. OF PEACE, SPECIAL REPORT, RWANDA: ACCOUNTABILITY FOR WAR CRIMES AND GENOCIDE (A REPORT ON A UNITED STATES INSTITUTE FOR PEACE CONFERENCE) (1995) *available at* http://www.usip.org/oc/sr/rwanda1.html (last visited Jan. 11, 2003). *See also* William Schabas, *Justice, Democracy and Impunity in Post-Genocide Rwanda: Searching for Solutions to Impossible Problems*, 7 CRIM. L.F. 523, 551–52 (1996) (citing S.C. Res 955, U.N. SCOR, 49th Sess., 3453rd mtg., U.N. Doc. S/RES/995 (1994)). Compare the international solution; *see* Jose Alvarez, *Crimes of State/Crimes of Hate: Lessons from Rwanda*, 24 YALE J. INT'L L. 365 (1999) (discussing the limits of international criminal tribunals).

57. South Africa is a prominent example. For a discussion of the state of the South African judiciary as a factor in South Africa's transitional amnesty agreement, see Paul Van Zyl, *Dilemmas of Transitional Justice: The Case of South Africa's Truth and Reconciliation Commission*, 52 J. INT'L AFF. 647 (1999). For a comprehensive analysis of the historical role of the judiciary under apartheid, see STEPHEN ELLMANN, IN A TIME OF TROUBLE: LAW AND LIBERTY IN SOUTH AFRICA'S STATE OF EMERGENCY (1995); David Dyzenhaus, *Transitional Justice*, 1 INT'L J. CONST. L. 163 (2003).

The post–Cold War phase stands in a critical position relative to Phase I transitional justice. In the Phase II context of a heightened wave of democratic transition and nation-building, transitional justice involved crucial rule-of-law compromises. Therefore, whereas Phase I transitional justice initially appeared to assume its potentially limitless and universal extension in the law, by its second phase transitional justice was more concededly contextual, limited, and provisional. Ultimately, the primary focus on local responsibility in post–Cold War transitions offered a partial, distorted perspective of the historically broader bipolar conflict. While the Phase II reliance on local or national justice constituted a critical response to Phase I, the post–Cold War model was ultimately not appropriate for later globalizing politics, in which national and international factors became interdependent contributors to political change.

A. *Juxtaposing Truth to Justice*

This Part elaborates upon the link between the chosen form of transitional justice response and political context. In Phase II, the central transitional dynamic responded to postwar transitional justice, while also differentiating itself from that period. Transitional justice responses in the second phase moved away from postwar international transitional justice toward alternative strategies. This was illustrated by the surge of hybridized law and the move to law and society responses.

The leading model in this phase is known as the restorative model. In this phase, the main purpose of transitional justice was to construct an alternative history of past abuses. A dichotomy between truth and justice therefore emerged. Thus, the Phase II paradigm largely eschewed trials to focus instead upon a new institutional mechanism: the truth commission. A truth commission is an official body, often created by a national government, to investigate, document, and report upon human rights abuses within a country over a specified period of time. While first used in Argentina,[58] the investigatory model is now associated with the response adopted in post-apartheid South Africa in the 1990s.[59] Truth and reconciliation commissions of various types have since been proposed or convened throughout the world and often garner significant international support.[60]

---

58. Argentina established the first official transitional commission of inquiry in the modern period. While it was a truth commission, it was not aimed at reconciliation. Indeed, the "Nunca Mas" commission inquiry was the first stage in Argentina's post-junta justice following the collapse of the military regime after the Falklands war defeat. For an account, see NINO, *supra* note 47. *See also* NUNCA MAS: THE REPORT OF THE ARGENTINE NATIONAL COMMISSION ON THE DISAPPEARED (Farrar et al. trans, 1986).

59. *See* TRUTH AND RECONCILIATION COMMISSION OF SOUTH AFRICA REPORT (Truth and Reconciliation Comm'n eds., 1999); Promotion of National Unity and Reconciliation Act, No. 34 (1995) (S. Afr.) (establishing the Truth and Reconciliation Commission). For an in-depth account of this history from a biographical perspective, see ALEX BORAINE, A COUNTRY UNMASKED (2000).

60. For a comprehensive discussion of truth commissions, see PRISCILLA B. HAYNER, UNSPEAKABLE TRUTHS: CONFRONTING STATE TERROR AND ATROCITY (2001). For a discussion of the South African Model, see BORAINE, *supra* note 59. For a critical interpretation of the truth commissions project, see

The appeal of the model is its ability to offer a broader historical perspective, rather than mere judgments in isolated cases.[61] Truth commissions are most popular where the predecessor regime disappeared persons or repressed information about its persecution policy, as was typical in Latin America.[62] In contrast, truth commissions have been of less interest in post-Communist Europe, where the use of history by various governments was itself a destructive dimension of Communist repression.[63] Accordingly, in Eastern Europe, the main critical response by the successor regime was not to create official histories but rather to guarantee access to the historical record.[64]

The second phase model did appear to advance some of the rule-of-law aims of criminal justice in transitional societies, in which legal institutions were functioning under stressed transitional conditions. Seen in a genealogical perspective, the primary aim of truth commissions was not justice but peace. This raised the question of the expected relationship between peace and furthering rule of law and democracy. While proponents of the South African model argued that peace was a necessary precondition to democracy,[65] building democratic institutions was not their primary goal.[66] It is not at all evident that short-term approaches to conflict management would further the rule of law.[67] Nevertheless, often a truth commission's purposes are deemed analogous to those of criminal justice, as both trials and truth commissions can be understood as primarily animated by deterrence.[68] In-

TEITEL, *supra* note 1, at 77–88.

61. *See* TEITEL, *supra* note 1, at 70 (discussing Foucaultian "truth regimes" and their inevitable association with a political regime).

62. *See* Teitel, *supra* note 46. *See also* THE REPORT OF THE CHILEAN NATIONAL COMMISSION ON TRUTH AND RECONCILIATION (Phillip E. Berryman trans., 1993) *available at* http://www.nd.edu/~ndlibs/eresources/etexts/truth/table_of_contents.htm (last visited Jan. 11, 2003).

63. On East Germany and its post-transition treatment of official file archives, see TINA ROSENBERG, THE HAUNTED LAND: FACING EUROPE'S GHOSTS AFTER COMMUNISM 261–394 (1996). *See also* TIMOTHY GARTON ASH, THE FILE: A PERSONAL HISTORY (1998).

64. Many countries in the region have enacted laws allowing victims and others access to the files. *See* TEITEL, supra note 1, at 95–103; *see also* Ruti Teitel, *Preface*, *in* TRUTH AND JUSTICE: THE DELICATE BALANCE: THE DOCUMENTATION OF PRIOR REGIMES AND INDIVIDUAL RIGHTS (1993).

65. *See* BORAINE, *supra* note 59; Margaret Popkin & Naomi Roht-Arriaza, *Truth as Justice: Investigatory Commissions in Latin America*, LAW AND SOC. INQUIRY, Vol. 20 (Winter 1995); KADER ASMAL ET AL., RECONCILIATION THROUGH TRUTH: A RECKONING OF APARTHEID'S CRIMINAL GOVERNANCE 12–17 (1997) (describing the Truth and Reconciliation Commission as "achieving justice through truth").

66. *See* GEORGE BIZOS, NO ONE TO BLAME: IN PURSUIT OF JUSTICE IN SOUTH AFRICA 229–39 (1998) (discussing the African National Congress' debate over the goals to be achieved by a South African truth commission).

67. For a related argument, see HUMAN RIGHTS IN POLITICAL TRANSITIONS: GETTYSBURG TO BOSNIA 13–31(Carla A. Hesse & Robert Post eds., 1999); *see also* Ruti Teitel, *Millennial Visions: Human Rights at Century's End*, *id.* 339–42.

68. *See* TEITEL, *supra* note 1, at 81. The establishment of the truth commissions does not necessarily imply that their investigative inquiries will be the government's complete and exclusive response to past injustices. For discussion of the Argentine process, see NUNCA MAS, *supra* note 58. In El Salvador and South Africa, Truth and Reconciliation Commission confessions were traded for amnesties. *See* The Truth Commission for El Salvador, *From Madness to Hope: The 12-Year War in El Salvador*, U.N. SCOR, Annex to letter dated 29 March 1993 from Boutros-Boutros Ghali to President of Security Council, U.N. Doc. S/25500 (1993), *available at* http://www.usip.org/library/tc/doc/reports/tc_elsalvador.html (last visited Jan. 11, 2003); Thomas Buergenthal, *The United Nation's Truth Commission for El Salvador*, 27 VAND. J.

deed, such commissions' mandates often include recommendations to prevent recurrence of rights abuses.[69]

The Phase II response transcended the single-minded focus on individual accountability in favor of a more communitarian conception. Nevertheless, this phase's aim was hardly a full-scale social justice project.[70] Instead, transitional justice's aims in this phase shifted from the earlier goal of establishing the rule of law through accountability to the goal of preserving peace.[71] This change in emphasis redefines the understanding of the purposes of transition.

Moreover, in this phase, the modality of transitional justice often became a private matter. Even when vested with government authority, transitional justice through truth commissions often became primarily a vehicle for victims to reconcile and recover from past harms, in consultation and with the assistance of various non-state actors. Transitional justice became a form of dialogue between victims and their perpetrators. There was a move away from the Phase I focus on universalizing judgment to a focus on rebuilding political identity[72] through rule of law, premised on local understandings of legitimacy.

The problem of judgment gave way to other responses, primarily national investigatory commissions which had the advantage of being able to inquire

---

TRANSNAT'L L. 497 (1994). A counter example would be Argentina, whose transition commenced with a truth commission, which then led to the formation of criminal justice policy, and finally to prosecutions. On the Latin American agreements see WESCHLER, *supra* note 13. Regarding the South African arrangement, see Promotion of National Unity and Reconciliation Act, *supra* note 59. On amnesty adjudication in South Africa, see TRUTH AND RECONCILIATION COMMISSION, AMNESTY DECISION TRANSCRIPTS, *available at* http://www.doj.gov.za/trc/amntrans/index.htm (last visited Jan. 11, 2003). For further remarks on the reconciliation process, see Abdullah Omar, *Truth and Reconciliation in South Africa: Accounting for the Past*, 4 BUFF. HUM. RTS. L. REV. 5 (1997).

69. *See* Popkin & Roht-Arriaza, *supra* note 65.

70. Of course, there are exceptions. When the South African transition first began, the African National League sought a broader redistributive program.

71. *See* Ruti Teitel, *Bringing the Messiah Through the Law*, in HESSE & POST, *supra* note 67, at 177–93 (discussing the conflict between the political business of peacemaking and the assertion of law in the International Criminal Tribunal for the former Yugoslavia).

72. There are a variety of related aims implied in this shift, including remembering, mourning, and recovering. There is a growing literature on the alternatives to punishment. *See, e.g.*, THE POLITICS OF MEMORY: TRANSITIONAL JUSTICE IN DEMOCRATIZING SOCIETIES (Alexandra Barahona de Brito et al. eds., 2001); GARY JONATHAN BASS, STAY THE HAND OF VENGEANCE: THE POLITICS OF WAR CRIME TRIBUNALS (2000); BORAINE, *supra* note 59; JOHN BORNEMAN, RULE OF LAW, JUSTICE AND ACCOUNTABILITY IN POST-SOCIALIST EUROPE (1997); HAYNER, *supra* note 60; Jennifer J. Llewellyn & Robert Howse, *Institutions for Restorative Justice: the South Africa Truth and Reconciliation Commission*, 49 U. TORONTO L.J. 355 (1999); MAHMOOD MAMDANI, WHEN VICTIMS BECOME KILLERS: COLONIALISM, NATIVISM, AND THE GENOCIDE IN RWANDA (2001); A. JAMES MCADAMS, JUDGING THE PAST IN UNIFIED GERMANY (2001); THE (UN)RULE OF LAW & THE UNDERPRIVILEGED IN LATIN AMERICA (Juan E. Mendez et al. eds., 1999); MARTHA MINOW, BETWEEN VENGEANCE AND FORGIVENESS: FACING HISTORY AFTER GENOCIDE AND MASS VIOLENCE (1998); MARK OSIEL, MASS ATROCITY, COLLECTIVE MEMORY, AND THE LAW (1997); Popkin & Roht-Arriaza, *supra* note 65; MARGARET POPKIN, PEACE WITHOUT JUSTICE: OBSTACLES TO BUILDING THE RULE OF LAW IN EL SALVADOR (2000); TRUTH V. JUSTICE: THE MORALITY OF TRUTH COMMISSIONS (Robert I. Rotberg & Dennis Thompson eds., 2000); DESMOND IMPILO TUTU, NO FUTURE WITHOUT FORGIVENESS (1999); RICHARD A. WILSON, THE POLITICS OF TRUTH AND RECONCILIATION IN SOUTH AFRICA: LEGITIMIZING THE POST-APARTHEID STATE (2001).

more systematically into a state's wrongdoings.[73] Despite the move away from the international criminal justice associated with the first phase, the Phase II response did incorporate the postwar model's human rights rhetoric, albeit in a broader, societal, restorative approach. The central dilemma associated with this phase was often framed in human rights terms, such as whether victims had rights to truth, and whether the state had a duty to investigate in order to reveal truth.[74] Within this framework, the core dynamic of "truth versus justice" suggested that there existed necessary conflicts among justice, history, and memory. This dynamic formulation is best understood as a critical response to the prior postwar model. However, the attempt to accommodate the international human rights rhetoric to a variety of broader social aims raises a number of contradictions and risks its likely misappropriation.[75]

However limited, transitional justice in its second phase enabled a form of preservative justice. The Phase II response allowed for the creation of a historical record while also leaving open the possibility of future judicial resolution. The emphasis on preservation conceded the existing constraints upon political sovereignty associated with modern democratization, globalizing political fragmentation, and other limiting political conditions at the core of contemporary transitional justice.

B. Trading Justice for Peace

A dynamic discourse that juxtaposed and even sacrificed the aim of justice for the more modest goal of peace emerged in Phase II.[76] This Part elaborates upon that discourse and reflects upon its place in the genealogy, largely in terms of its critical dynamic with the Phase I justice model. This Part ultimately contends that the Phase II model expanded the category of transitional justice, with implications for its future normalization.[77]

A jurisprudence of forgiveness[78] and reconciliation[79] is associated with the Phase II model. The truth and reconciliation project incorporated much of

---

73. For a comprehensive account of recent truth commissions and for an argument advocating investigation, see HAYNER, *supra* note 60; *see also* Kritz, *supra* note 3.

74. *See* Popkin & Roht-Arriaza, *supra* note 65, at 79; *see also* Rotberg & Thompson, *supra* note 72. Certainly there is no necessary conflict between investigation and justice, as is reflected in the first truth commission, convened during Argentina's 1983 political transition. *See* NUNCA MAS, *supra* note 58, preface.

75. For an argument that there is such an obligation, see Velasquez Rodriguez, Inter-Am. C.H.R. 35, at ¶ 166, OEA/ser. L/V/III.19, doc. 13 (1988) ("[T]he state must prevent, investigate and punish any violation of the rights recognized by the convention and . . . restore the right violated and provide compensation as warranted."). *See also* Torture Victim Protection Act, 28 U.S.C. § 1350 (1992).

76. *See* TEITEL, *supra* note 1, at 51.

77. *See* discussion *infra* at Part III.

78. *See* TUTU, *supra* note 72, at 260; MINOW, *supra* note 72; JACQUES DERRIDA, ON COSMOPOLITANISM AND FORGIVENESS 55–59 (Mark Dooley & Michael Hughes trans., 2001).

79. For a thoughtful philosophical justification of restorative justice, see Elizabeth Kiss, *Moral Ambitions Within and Beyond Political Constraints: Reflections on Restorative Justice*, *in* Rotberg & Thompson, *supra* note 72, at 68.

its normative discourse from outside the law, specifically from ethics, medicine, and theology.[80] Its purpose was not merely justice, but peace for both individuals and society as a whole.[81] The problem of transitional justice was reconceived across moral and psychological lines to redefine identity. The evident mix of legal, political, and religious language reflected both the conceit and the limits of the law. Phase II had its roots in Phase I and constituted a critical response to the broader postwar justice project. Whereas in its first phase the problem of transitional justice was framed in terms of justice versus amnesty, with amnesty considered exceptional to general adherence to the rule of law, the second phase adopted a broader amnesty policy with the aim of reconciliation.[82] The exception became generalized and reflected an explicit attempt to incorporate both mercy and grace into the law.

Both political activism and scholarship sought to move outside contemporary politics and history to represent conflict in timeless and universal terms.[83] Phase II did not resist the universalizing impetus associated with Phase I.[84] There was some continuation of the Phase I norm of deployment of universal rights as part of the justifying structure of Phase II. The form of law adopted offers a universalizing language about the aims of forgiveness and the possibility of political redemption.[85] While law as conventionally understood had almost disappeared, the alternative model was said to have universal applications and claimed general diffusion around the world.[86] Consider the extent to which the transitional justice being exported in the post–Cold War paradigm is a secularized religion without law.[87]

80. For a discussion of the turn to therapeutic language, see MINOW, *supra* note 72, at 21–22; Kenneth Roth & Alison Desforges, *Justice or Therapy?*, BOSTON REV., Summer 2002, *available at* http://bostonreview.mit.edu/BR27.3/rothdesforges.html. For an historical account of the turn to moral and religious language, see *infra* note 87; ASMAL ET AL., *supra* note 65, at 25.

81. On the uses of justice to advance peace, see Teitel, *supra* note 71, at 177–93. The Truth and Reconciliation Commission confronted "crucial questions of moral and political responsibility." ASMAL ET AL., *supra* note 65, at 25. *Compare* Popkin & Roht-Arriaza, *supra* note 65 (truth as route to peace), *with* Akhavan, *supra* note 54 (trials as route to peace). *See* HAYNER, *supra* note 60, at 134–35 (discussing complicated results of truth commissions for the aim of individual healing).

82. Most of the amnesties are pursuant to legislation, as in much of Latin America's Southern Cone. *See* Teitel, *supra* note 46. Others, as in South Africa, are handled on an individual basis but still pursuant to a broader transitional amnesty project. *See supra* note 59.

83. For example, there is an explosion of writing on the subject of evil. *See, e.g.*, ALAN BADIOU, ETHICS: AN ESSAY ON THE UNDERSTANDING OF EVIL (2001); SUSAN NEIMAN, EVIL IN MODERN THOUGHT: AN ALTERNATIVE HISTORY OF PHILOSOPHY (2002); JOHN KEKES, FACING EVIL (1990).

84. *See* STEINER & ALSTON, *supra* note 11 (discussing Nuremberg and the development of the universal human rights movement); *see also* HENKIN, *supra* note 38.

85. Indeed, this aim is made clear in the Truth Commission Reports. *See* TEITEL, *supra* note 1, at 69–72.

86. *See* BORAINE, *supra* note 59.

87. On the link between the corruption of political and legal authority and the move to moral and religious authority, see BORAINE, *supra* note 59, 340–78; *see also* LOOKING BACK, REACHING FORWARD: REFLECTIONS ON THE TRUTH AND RECONCILIATION COMMISSION OF SOUTH AFRICA (Charles Villa-Vicencio & Wilhelm Verwoerd eds., 2000) (discussing the religious character of South Africa's Truth and Reconciliation Commission).

In Phase II, there was an apparent conflation of the realm of ethics, generally considered to involve the private sphere rather than public choices,[88] and the realm of the political. This signaled the breakdown and interconnection of the private and the public spheres, a phenomenon associated with globalization.[89] Further, in the second phase, the relevant political actors changed from those with legal and political authority to those with moral authority in civil society. Whereas in its first phase justice was chiefly the purview of the successor regime and courts of law, in the second phase many of the relevant actors and institutions lay outside law and politics, and included churches, NGOs, and human rights groups that incorporated a variety of alternative forms of conflict resolution.[90]

Moreover, the Phase II model adhered only tenuously to conventional legal processes. This was illustrated by the move from the courtroom to the hearing room and the turn to discursive confessional testimonials. The choice of language had significant juridical and political implications. An ethical-religious discourse injected a moral basis into transitional justice. Yet the truth and reconciliation movement tended to eschew judgment and instead aimed to move beyond legal notions of guilt and responsibility. It contributed a political theology,[91] building a discourse that incorporated moral imperatives and had the potential to threaten the parameters of legitimate political discourse in liberalizing states, which conceives of the public sphere as a realm of free contestation.[92] Nevertheless, the truth commission was also associated with critical responses to globalization, where the perceived democratic deficit has led to the pursuit of a universalizing and legitimizing discourse.[93]

The evolution of the transitional justice discourse in the second phase highlighted a complex interaction between the dimensions of the universal, the global, and the local. While framing the problem in universalizing human rights terms suggested a form of justice that is abstracted from the interests and needs of societies, even the Phase II approach assumed conditions not formally present in many countries, with often dubious restorative re-

---

88. On the broader developments at this time toward an ethically driven public discourse, see THE TURN TO ETHICS (Marjorie B. Garber et al. eds., 2000); *see also* ZYGMUNT BAUMAN, POSTMODERN ETHICS (1993).

89. *See* DAVID HELD, GLOBAL TRANSFORMATIONS: POLITICS, ECONOMICS, AND CULTURE (1999); ULRICH BECK, WHAT IS GLOBALIZATION? (Patrick Camiller trans., 2000).

90. *See infra* notes 120, 123.

91. On political theology, see CARL SCHMITT, POLITICAL THEOLOGY: FOUR CHAPTERS ON THE CONCEPT OF SOVEREIGNTY (George Schwab trans., 1985). On the relationship of religion and violence, see HENT DE VRIES, RELIGION AND VIOLENCE: PHILOSOPHICAL PERSPECTIVES FROM KANT TO DERRIDA (2002); *see also* JACOB TAUBES, DIE POLITISCHE THEOLOGIE DES PAULUS (Aleida Assman et al. eds., 1993). For a related argument, see HANNAH ARENDT, THE HUMAN CONDITION 38–78 (U. Chi. Press 2d ed. 1998) (1958) (exploring the distinctions between the public and the private realms).

92. *See* JÜRGEN HABERMAS, THE THEORY OF COMMUNICATIVE ACTION: REASON AND THE RATIONALIZATION OF SOCIETY (1985).

93. The emergence of this form of transitional justice discourse at this time reflects its association with the politics of globalization, and the related challenges to the maintenance of a robust public sphere.

sults. Genealogical review illuminates the historical and political contingencies in the policy choices. It also shows the extent to which the Phase II juridical regime incorporated rule-of-law ideas that related closely to the legitimacy of local institutions, thus addressing the multiple aims associated with periods of political flux.

The politics associated with the post–Cold War transitional response are illustrative. The asserted aim of transitional policy was said to be the threshold goal of peace rather than democracy. The turn to alternative strategies, whether theological or therapeutic, was animated by the forward-looking aim of reconciliation. Forgiveness became a distinctive form of political apology,[94] understood as an act of contrition in a realm of unity politics.[95] A variety of conciliatory mechanisms emerged in many transitional societies, with the ostensible aim of stabilizing internal politics. These policies became the signs of an age of restoration of the rule of law in a global politics.

Nevertheless, there may well be long-term negative consequences to this type of reconciliation politics. For example, instigation of the settlement of claims can have conservative ramifications. The focus may subvert broader political reform[96] and generally cannot assist in laying the basis for development of democracy.[97] Moreover, as the responses discussed here have mostly implied national political resolutions, they often missed the broader structural causation associated with the bipolar balance of power. The Phase II discourse was being renegotiated at the same time as the debate on globalization reform. This appears to be more than historical coincidence. Even as the disparities between rich and poor associated with the free market economy have grown,[98] the impetus has been to resort increasingly to the transitional justice discourse and a project that is to some extent backward-looking and limited to restoration.[99] Presently, the extent to which transi-

94. For a discussion of some of the philosophical and sociological implications of forgiveness, see NICHOLAS TAVUCHIS, MEA CULPA: A SOCIOLOGY OF APOLOGY AND RECONCILIATION (1993); *see also* JEFFRIE G. MURPHY & JEAN HAMPTON, FORGIVENESS AND MERCY (1990); Michel Rolph-Trouillot, *Abortive Rituals: Historical Apologies in the Global Era*, *in* INTERVENTIONS: RIGHTING WRONGS, REWRITING HISTORY, vol. 2(2), at 171–86 (H. Bhabha & R. S. Rajan, eds., 2000).

95. On the role of forgiveness in the political sphere, see ARENDT, *supra* note 91, at 236–43. On South Africa, see BORAINE, *supra* note 59, 340–78, at 340–78 (discussing the need for "[f]acing up to collective responsibility"). On the expected role of the South African Truth and Reconciliation Commission, see ASMAL ET AL., *supra* note 65, at 143.

96. *Compare* Robert Meister, *The Politics and Political Uses of Human Rights Discourse: A Conference on Rethinking Human Rights*, paper presented at conference at Columbia (Nov. 8–9, 2001) (focusing on the model's effect upon the revolutionary project, rather than the democracy building project), *with* Jung & Shapiro, *infra* note 97.

97. In South Africa, the politics of reconciliation was associated with the politics of consociationalism. *See* S. AFR. CONST. ch. 15, § 251 (1993) (the "National Unity and Reconciliation" provision); Courtney Jung & Ian Shapiro, *South Africa's Negotiated Transition: Democracy, Opposition, and the New Constitutional Order*, 23 POL. & SOC. 269 (1995).

98. For a discussion of current tensions in the globalization of the market, see JOSEPH E. STIGLITZ, GLOBALIZATION AND ITS DISCONTENTS (2002).

99. For a discussion of some of the contradictions, see Meister, *supra* note 96.

tional justice has displaced other justice projects signals chastened political expectations responding to the failed experiments of a not so distant past.

C. *Fin-de-Siècle Transitional Justice and the Passage of Time*

This Part examines transitional justice over time. It explores the degree to which the discourse of transitional justice has become ever-present in politics. With apparently ongoing processes of transitional justice delayed, the very meaning of the category of transition has expanded over time to become a persistent trope.[100]

The developments described above have implications for human historical self-understanding. By the end of the twentieth century, it seemed that all justice had become transitional, *ex post*, and backward-looking. Among some theorists of the period, the post-Soviet dynamics and the related wave of transitions were expected to lead to political stabilization and, according to Francis Fukuyama, "the end of history."[101] Other theorists suggested that the Communist collapse left few political choices, and that therefore politics was past and all that remained was history. Thus, Jacques Derrida wrote about Marxism as a "ghost" to be mourned.[102] And while Derrida and Fukuyama shared little in the way of politics, they reflected a broad span of political writers whose work at century's end clearly memorialized a time when politics involved a pronounced revolutionary project.[103] However, these conclusions forecasting the end of history or the end of politics certainly seem inapposite.[104] Existing scholarship has not yet captured the prevailing dynamic of transitional justice or its nexus with ongoing political change.

The persistent discourse of the final years of the twentieth century was that of transitional justice. Developments seeking closure, associated with both the end of century and the end of millennium, reflected a pervasive sense of metatransition. At century's end, there was an evident increase of facing old injustices and of transitional justice delayed. There were persistent calls for apologies, reparations, memoirs, and all manner of account-settling related to past suffering and wrongdoing.[105] Examples of claim-

100. On the normalization of transitional justice, see *infra* Part III(A) and notes 130–147.

101. *See* FRANCIS FUKUYAMA, THE END OF HISTORY AND THE LAST MAN (1992).

102. *See* JACQUES DERRIDA, SPECTERS OF MARX: THE STATE OF THE DEBT, THE WORK OF MOURNING, AND THE NEW INTERNATIONAL (Peggy Kamuf trans., 1994) (discussing the remains of Marxism after the fall of communism).

103. *But see* ERIC HOBSBAWM, ON THE EDGE OF THE NEW CENTURY 95–107 (Allan Cameron trans., Antonio Polito ed., 2000) (discussing the changes in the meaning of the political discussion of left and right and in particular "progressive" politics).

104. Indeed, there is an evident post-Soviet fragmentation and disaggregation. For an argument that the contemporary world today appears more violent, see KEN JOWITT, NEW WORLD DISORDER (1992). For discussion of the role of law in circumstances of apparent perpetual conflict, see Ruti Teitel, *Humanity's Law: Rule of Law in the New Global Politics*, 35 CORNELL INT'L L.J. 352 (2002).

105. *See generally* John Torpey, *Making Whole What Has Been Smashed: Reflections on Reparations*, 73 J. MOD. HIST. 333, 334 (2001) (discussing the global spread of "reparations politics"); Sharon K. Hom & Eric K. Yamamoto, *Symposium, Race and the Law at the Turn of the Century: Collective Memory, History, and Social Justice*, 47 U.C.L.A. L. REV. 1747 (2000).

making and settlements abounded, including those related to assets and property lost during World War II,[106] reparations for slave labor,[107] and even more ancient injustices such as colonization, the Inquisition, and the Crusades.[108]

As a genealogical perspective illustrates, interest in the pursuit of justice does not necessarily wane with the passage of time.[109] This may be because transitional justice relates to exceptional political conditions, where the state itself is implicated in wrongdoing and the pursuit of justice necessarily awaits a change in regime. In recent years, this has been characterized by some as the "Scilingo Effect," for a confession given two decades after junta rule ended in Argentina that reopened the question of justice for crimes committed during the dirty war.[110] Transitional justice implies a non-linear approach to time. This phenomenon is reflected in legal responses taken, often in the form of delayed litigation, to extend the scope of transitional justice litigation on a case-by-case basis.[111] In the international sphere, this dilemma was resolved by the adoption of the UN Convention on the Non-Applicability of Statutory Limitations to War Crimes and Crimes Against Humanity, although this did not necessarily resolve the attendant political tensions.[112]

There is a complicated relationship between transitional justice, truth, and history. In the transitional justice discourse, revisiting the past is understood as the way to move forward.[113] There is an implied notion of progressive history. As a matter of intellectual historiography and human self-understanding, this notion is under siege.[114] However, transitions are rare

---

106. On the Holocaust as a standard and globalized model, see Torpey, *supra* note 105, at 338–42. *See also* Farmer-Paellmann v. FleetBoston Financial Corp., No. CV-02-1862 (E.D.N.Y. filed Mar. 26, 2002); Anthony Sebok, *Prosaic Justice*, LEGAL AFF., Sept.–Oct. 2002, at 51–53; Anthony Sebok, *The Brooklyn Slavery Class Action: More than Just a Political Gambit* (Apr. 9, 2002), *at* http://writ.news.findlaw.com/sebok/20020409.html (Findlaw's Legal Commentary); WHEN SORRY ISN'T ENOUGH: THE CONTROVERSY OVER APOLOGIES AND REPARATIONS FOR HUMAN INJUSTICE (Roy L. Brooks ed., 1999).

107. Declaration of the World Conference Against Racism, Racial Discrimination, Xenophobia and Related Intolerance, Durban, South Africa (31 August–8 September 2001), *at* http://193.194.138.190/pdf/Durban.pdf.

108. For historical discussion, see for example ELAZAR BARKAN, THE GUILT OF NATIONS: RESTITUTION AND NEGOTIATING HISTORICAL INJUSTICES (2002); JUSTICE DELAYED: THE RECORDS OF THE JAPANESE AMERICAN INTERNMENT CASES (Peter Irons ed., 1989); *see generally* ERIC YAMAMOTO ET AL., RACE, RIGHTS, AND REPARATION: LAW AND THE JAPANESE AMERICAN INTERNMENT (2001).

109. *Compare* Jeremy Waldron, *Superseding Historic Injustice*, 103 ETHICS 4, n.1 (1992) (arguing for "succession" of claims) *with* TEITEL, *supra* note 1, at 138–39 (discussing the paradox of the passage of time as concerns transitional justice, which generally involves state wrongdoing).

110. *See* MARGUERITE FEITLOWITZ, A LEXICON OF TERROR (1988) (discussing Argentina's "Scilingo Effect" of justice delayed).

111. *See infra* note 124 (regarding the Pinochet litigation).

112. Convention on the Non-Applicability of Statutory Limitations to War Crimes and Crimes Against Humanity G.A. Res. 2391, U.N. GAOR, 23rd Sess., Supp. No. 18, at 40, U.N. Doc. A/7218 (1968).

113. Indeed, this notion appears throughout the truth commission literature. In South Africa, the role of the Truth and Reconciliation Commission was envisioned as a "bridge" between the past and the future. *See* S. AFR. CONST. ch. 15, § 251 (1993) (the "National Unity and Reconciliation" provision).

114. For the most part such notions of history are associated with now largely passé perfectionist proj-

periods of rupture which offer a choice among contested narratives. The paradoxical goal in transition is to undo history. The aim is to reconceive the social meaning of past conflicts, particularly defeats, in an attempt to reconstruct their present and future effects.[115]

Transitions present a threshold choice. By definition they are times of contestation in historical narratives. Transitions thus present the potential for counter-histories. The question is posed anew after the passage of time, which underscores the threshold challenge of remaining in history as well as the limits to transformation. Indeed, the possibility of some minimal amelioration is often juxtaposed with the countervailing resistance to working within historical and political parameters for the possibility of change. The notion of a threshold choice following massive tragedy appears in works chiefly addressing responses to the Holocaust.[116] In this context, there is often resistance to the very idea of a transition, which would raise the possibility of political change. The problem concerns the propriety of further engagement after massive catastrophe, whether in the form of giving testimony, taking political action, or contributing scholarship.[117]

In the post–Cold War phase, historical production was fundamental to building a state's political identity,[118] and control over construction of an alternative history could lie with multiple actors, including historians, lawyers, journalists, and victims.[119] This raised the normative question of who should write the history of the transition. In this regard, Phase II transitional justice moved from a project dependent upon the leading role of the state to a process that often elided it. The devolution of state power reflected the broader political conditions associated with post–Cold War transitions and globalization. Given the fact that predecessor regimes were frequently implicated in past wrongdoing, the diminished role for political authority in Phase II managed to avoid many of the dilemmas associated with the more ambitious Phase I justice project.

---

ects such as Marxism. For a later critical presentation, see Walter Benjamin, *Theses on the Philosophy of History*, *in* ILLUMINATIONS: ESSAYS AND REFLECTIONS 253–64, at 257 (Hannah Arendt ed., 1968) (opposing progressive historical thought); *see also* FOUCAULT, *supra* note 7 (distinguishing genealogy from progressive histories).

115. On the notion of "working through history" or "vergangenheitsbewältigung," see Marc Silberman, *Writing What—for Whom? 'Vergangenheits Gewältigung' in GDR Literature*, 10 GERMAN STUD. REV. 527, n.3 (1987); Richard Evans, *The New Nationalism and the Old History: Perspectives on the West German Historikerstreit*, 59 J. OF MOD. HIST. 761, 785 n.4 (1987); *see also* Gordon Craig, *The War of the German Historians*, N.Y. REV. BOOKS, Jan. 15, 1987, at 16–19; CHARLES MAIER, THE UNMASTERABLE PAST (1988).

116. *See* JEAN AMERY, AT THE MIND'S LIMITS: CONTEMPLATIONS BY A SURVIVOR ON AUSCHWITZ AND ITS REALITIES (Stella P. Rosenfeld & Sidney Rosenfeld trans., 1980).

117. On the problem of post-Holocaust representation, in scholarly writing in particular, see for example PROBING THE LIMITS OF REPRESENTATION: NAZISM AND THE FINAL SOLUTION (Saul Friedlander ed., 1992).

118. *See* TEITEL, *supra* note 1, at 77–92.

119. On victims' testimony, see LAWRENCE L. LANGER, HOLOCAUST TESTIMONIALS: THE RUINS OF MEMORY (1993); MINOW, *supra* note 73.

This transforming context increased the possibility of various alternative and even competing transitional justice resolutions involving international, transnational, national, or private settlements. In Phase II, there were a host of new political actors[120] and a distinct privatization of the transitional response. The trend toward privatization took a number of forms, from its devolution to civil society to its relegation to private citizens via litigation.[121] These processes were partially related to globalization, and raised the question of the extent to which normative principles were available to guide transitional decision-making. The second phase policy reflected a struggle between local and global resolutions, even as globalization increased the interconnectedness of political decision-making. Genealogical, interdisciplinary, and comparative review reveals highly divergent approaches to the rule of law,[122] which in turn reflect different legal and cultural perspectives.[123] A profound normative question was raised in the interaction of transitional justice, globalization, and sovereignty: whether and to what extent the response to a harm should rightly remain under the control of the state where the harm occurred. In Phase II, actions related to transitional justice were increasingly taken independent of state actors. This unsettled earlier determinations, as illustrated in the landmark extradition case of General Augusto Pinochet.[124] Moreover, this case also demonstrated the expansion of transitional justice in time.[125] In a world that is increasingly economically, technologically, politically, and juridically interdependent, profound questions arise at the intersection of the principles of jurisdiction and sovereignty. Given the ongoing processes of globalization, this phenomenon will likely accelerate.[126] This seems to portend an expanded category of transitional justice.

---

120. On the growing role of transnational networks, see Martha Finnemore & Kathryn Sikkink, *International Norms Dynamic and Political Change*, 52 INT'L ORG. 887, 907 (1998); MARGARETH KECK & KATHRYN SIKKINK, ACTIVISTS BEYOND BORDERS: ADVOCACY NETWORKS IN INTERNATIONAL POLITICS (1998).

121. This is seen in the contemporary proliferation of lawsuits against multinationals. *See Developments in the Law—International Criminal Law: II. The Promises of International Prosecution*, 114 HARV. L. REV. 1957 (2001). On the problem of the relationship between state and individual responsibility, see STATE RESPONSIBILITY AND THE INDIVIDUAL: REPARATIONS IN INSTANCES OF GRAVE VIOLATIONS OF HUMAN RIGHTS (Albrecht Randlezhofer & Christian Tomuschat eds., 1999); Guillermo A. O'Donnell, *Democracy, Law, and Comparative Politics*, 36 STUD. COMP. INT'L DEV. 7 (2001).

122. Whereas the U.S. approach tends to delegate resolution of controversies to case-by-case litigation, the European approach generally focuses on rulemaking through legislation. For a comparative discussion of illustrations of the transitional rule of law, see TEITEL, *supra* note 1.

123. One illustration of these differences in transitional justice is postwar litigation, chiefly regarding the Holocaust, which has occasioned a reaction against the supposed export of the "American" approach to injury abroad.

124. *See* Regina v. Bow St. Metro. Stipendiary Mag., *ex parte* Pinochet Ugarte (No. 3) 1 A.C. 147 (2000).

125. For discussion of the relation of transitional justice to the passage of time, see *supra* text accompanying note 109.

126. For commentary on the potential of universal jurisdiction, see *infra* note 138; *see generally* HUMAN RIGHTS WATCH, 2001 WORLD REPORT, *at* http://www.hrw.org/wr2k1/index.html (last visited Jan. 13, 2003).

The association of post–Cold War transitional justice with a globalizing politics acutely reflected the constructivist dimension of the more limited Phase II approaches. Whereas the first phase conceived of the rule of law in universalizing terms associated with accountability for humanity, the Phase II model was instead concerned with advancing an opposing idea of the rule of law associated with the legitimacy of a country's national jurisdiction and sovereignty. This Phase II narrowing of the relevant scope of inquiry illuminated the political construction that correlated with this form of transitional justice, specifically responses that implicated local rather than international actors, and those lower rather than higher in the echelon of political responsibility and power. This signaled the Phase II response's constructive force and also showed the extent to which the Phase II model was amenable to politicization and ultimately depended upon promoting alternative values, besides universal rights and accountability, underlying the rule of law.

To the extent that the second phase moved away from traditional legal remedies, it challenged whether any threshold remained regarding what constitutes the predicate transitional rule of law.[127] These changes illustrate the normative implications of deploying a discourse of justice. The discourse can influence the legitimacy of the response by giving it the provenance and hence the democratic accountability of the successor regime, and by imputing the administration of the transitional response with the legality traditionally associated with judicial proceedings.[128] The question remains whether there are any transitional justice baselines or any threshold minimum beyond which historical, psychological, or religious inquiry ought to be characterized as justice-seeking. This genealogical review suggests that the relevant inquiry is not a metaphysical enterprise, but rather must be understood in its historical and political context. Still, there is an independent basis for critique which influences the nature of the emerging discourse and affects whether it is likely to simply assist in the immediate aim of conflict resolution or also contribute to the goals of democracy, nation-building, and the advancement of liberal political aims.[129]

III. Phase III: Steady-State Transitional Justice

A. *Transitional Justice All the Time*

The present phase can be characterized as steady-state transitional justice. The discourse has now moved from the periphery to the center. As discussed above, the new millennium appears to be associated with the expansion and normalization of transitional justice. What was historically viewed as a legal

127. *See* Teitel, *supra* note 1, at 213–28 (promoting an explicitly transitional rule of law that is not merely symbolic).

128. *See* H. L. A. Hart, The Concept of Law (2nd ed. 1997); *see also* Henkin, *supra* note 38, at 31–41.

129. On the evolution of transitional justice, see Teitel, *supra* note 1, at 223–28.

phenomenon associated with extraordinary post-conflict conditions now increasingly appears to be a reflection of ordinary times. War in a time of peace,[130] political fragmentation, weak states, small wars, and steady conflict all characterize contemporary political conditions.[131] These contemporary developments have spurred the attempted normalization of transitional justice, leading ultimately to ambivalent consequences. As a jurisprudence associated with political flux, transitional justice is related to a higher politicization of the law and to some degree of compromise in rule-of-law standards.

The most recognized symbol of the normalization of transitional jurisprudence is the entrenchment of the Phase I response in the form of the International Criminal Court ("ICC"), the new international institution established at the end of the twentieth century.[132] This court was preceded by the *ad hoc* international criminal tribunals convened to respond to genocidal conflicts in the Balkans and Rwanda.[133] Half a century after World War II, the ICC symbolizes the entrenchment of the Nuremberg Model: the creation of a permanent international tribunal appointed to prosecute war crimes, genocide, and crimes against humanity as a routine matter under international law.[134] The threshold global rule of law presently appears to be based on an expansion of the law of war.[135] Indeed, the move back to international humanitarian law incorporates the complex relationship between the individual and the state as a legal scheme which enables the international community to hold a regime's leadership accountable and condemn a systematic persecutory policy, even outside the relevant state.[136] Further, this particular form of international justice offers the potential for regime delegitimation that can support or even instigate transition.[137] Nevertheless, there are also

---

130. *See* DAVID HALBERSTAM, WAR IN A TIME OF PEACE: BUSH, CLINTON, AND THE GENERALS (2001).

131. For a more thorough discussion of law and politics in the post–September 11 political context, see Teitel, *supra* note 104.

132. Rome Statute of the International Criminal Court, U.N. Doc. A/CONF.183/9 (1998) *reprinted in* 37 I.L.M. 999 (1998) [hereinafter Rome Statute].

133. *See Statute of the International Tribunal for the Prosecution of Persons Responsible for Serious Violations of International Humanitarian Law Committed in the Territory of the Former Yugoslavia since 1991*, U.N. Doc. S/25704/Annexes (1993); *Statute of the International Criminal Tribunal for the Former Yugoslavia*, U.N. SCOR, 48th Sess., 3217th Mtg., U.N. Doc. S/RES/827 (1993), *amended by* U.N. SCOR, U.N. Doc. S/RES/1166 (1998); *Statute of the International Tribunal for Rwanda*, U.N. SCOR, 49th Sess., 3453rd Mtg., U.N. Doc. S/RES/955 (1994), *annexed to* U.N. Doc. S/IN-F/50 (1996). For discussion of the expectations of the *ad hoc* international criminal tribunals, see Teitel, *supra* note 71. For discussion of these tribunals' constraints, see Alvarez, *supra* note 56 (discussing the limits on international tribunals).

134. *See* Rome Statute, *supra* note 132, Preamble, at 1002 (affirming that "the most serious crimes of concern to the international community as a whole must not go unpunished").

135. *See United Nations Diplomatic Conference of the Plenipotentiaries on the Establishment of an International Criminal Court*, 17 July 1998, Annex II, U.N. Doc. A/CONF. 183/9, *reprinted in* 37 I.L.M. 999 (1998), *available at* http://www.un.org/icc.

136. *See supra* text accompanying notes 27–28.

137. *See* Teitel, *supra* note 71 (discussing the limited normative potential of such off-site tribunals); *see also* Christopher Rudolph, *Constructing an Atrocities Regime: The Politics of War Crimes Tribunals*, 55 INT'L ORG. 655, 684–85 (2001). Indeed, this is something of the theory for the Milošević trial, in light of the Kosovo Commission's conclusion that the NATO intervention in the conflict was "illegal but legiti-

many dilemmas and limits raised by the turn to the law of war in relative peacetime, as well as by the preference for international legal regimes. A dynamic tension emerges among adjudicatory fragmentation, the attendant potential for universal jurisdiction associated with transitional justice,[138] and the attempted centralization of accountability in the ICC.[139]

The normalization of transitional justice currently takes the form of the expansion of the law of war, as illustrated by the rise of humanitarian law.[140] Contemporary developments involve an appropriation of the discourse of the humanitarian law regime with twofold significance. The establishment of humanitarian law as the present rule of law constrains not only the conduct of war,[141] but also appears to expand the humanitarian regime to address broader aspects of the law of war, including the justification of its possible initiation. Further, the use of the international humanitarian regime to justify the NATO intervention in Kosovo appears to have established a precedent for expanding the legitimate bases for intervention, specifically a humanitarian basis for just war.[142] A juridical scheme in which the law of war forms the basis for international criminal justice resonates more deeply and offers a more thorough justificatory structure. Whether unilaterally or multilaterally, the expanded humanitarian law enables recognition of lapses in state action, but also appears to enforce state respect for human rights. This demonstrates the potential for sliding from a normalized transitional justice to the campaign against terrorism. The use of human rights law and the law of war has shifted after the move away from modern state theory to the period of globalization. The contemporary conflation of human rights law, criminal law, and the international law of war implies a pronounced loss for those seeking to challenge state action. Through the use of the transformed law of war and its rights enforcement scheme as a basis for intervention, the

---

mate." THE INDEPENDENT INTERNATIONAL COMMISSION ON KOSOVO, THE KOSOVO REPORT (2001), *available at* http://www.kosovocommission.org.

138. Certainly it is the legacy of Phase I postwar justice that is amplified in the globalizing context where greater international interconnectedness allows for the pursuit of offenders regardless of status or citizenship. *See* PRINCETON UNIVERSITY PROGRAM IN LAW AND PUBLIC AFFAIRS, THE PRINCETON PRINCIPLES ON UNIVERSAL JURISDICTION (2001); Kenneth C. Randall, *Universal Jurisdiction under International Law*, 66 TEX. L. REV. 785 (1988). On the effect of universal jurisdiction, *compare* Andrea Bianchi, *Immunity versus Human Rights: The Pinochet Case*, 10 EUR. J. INT'L L. 237 (1999), *with* Curtis A. Bradley & Jack L. Goldsmith, *Pinochet and International Human Rights Litigation*, 97 MICH. L. REV. 2129 (1999).

139. On the prospective role of the ICC and its likely interaction with domestic transitional justice, see Leila Nadya Sadat & S. Richard Carden, *The New International Criminal Court: An Uneasy Revolution*, 88 GEO. L.J. 381 (2000); Gwen K. Young, *Amnesty and Accountability*, 35 U.C. DAVIS L. REV. 427 (2002). On a related point regarding the Pinochet precedent, see Richard J. Wilson, *Prosecuting Pinochet: International Crimes in Spanish Domestic Law*, 21 HUM. RTS. Q. 927 (1999) (discussing implications of universality).

140. For elaboration of this current development, see Teitel, *supra* note 104.

141. On this distinction between *jus in bello* and *jus ad bello*, which has given rise to modern humanitarian law, see STUDIES AND ESSAYS ON INTERNATIONAL HUMANITARIAN LAW AND RED CROSS PRINCIPLES IN HONOUR OF JEAN PICTET (Christophe Swinarsky ed., 1984). On *jus ad bello*, see MICHAEL WALZER, JUST AND UNJUST WARS: A MORAL ARGUMENT WITH HISTORICAL ILLUSTRATIONS 21 (1977).

142. *See* THE INDEPENDENT INTERNATIONAL COMMISSION ON KOSOVO, *supra* note 137.

expanded humanitarian regime introduces new human rights dilemmas that bring to the surface the tension in the aims of justice and peace.

Under the label of "preemptive self-defense," a related discourse of apparently constant war is currently being appropriated to legitimate the next stage in the war on terrorism.[143] The rhetoric attempts to eviscerate the distinctions between war and peace, and between law and its exception. The notion of Phase III steady-state transitional justice is evident in the deployment of the humanitarian regime, which has expanded and merged with the law of human rights.[144] The appeal to a language of universal morality in humanitarian legal discourse resonates with recent developments in transitional justice. The apparent normalization of transitional justice is also evident in the toleration of greater political discretion,[145] politicization in the uses of justice, the rise of highly irregular procedures, and explicit departures from prevailing law,[146] all justified in humanitarian terms.[147]

The expansion of the transitional justice discourse to the issue of terrorism proves problematic due to the inadequacy of the analogies between terrorism and war or political crisis. Transitional justice tends to look backward in responding to the last conflict, and therefore it does not adapt easily to use as a template to guarantee prospective security. Any attempt to generalize from exceptional post-conflict situations in order to guide politics as a matter of course becomes extremely problematic.

Resisting the normalization of transitional justice is difficult. There is a significant loss in vocabulary from which to make any critique, since in the expanded discourse of transitional justice the law of war has merged with the law of human rights. Only time will tell whether and to what extent these developments pose a serious challenge to the rule of law or are associated with the present cycle of contemporary politics.

B. Transitional Justice: Discontinuity Versus Continuity

The remaining question that follows, given current trends in normalization, is what a genealogical perspective of transitional justice might convey about the conception of justice in ordinary times. To what extent is there continuity, and to what extent discontinuity, both descriptively and normatively? In recent years the question has been controversial, sparking a prolif-

143. *See* RICHARD TUCK, THE RIGHTS OF WAR AND PEACE 22–25 (1999) (discussing the historical justifications for preemptive attacks in the law of empire).

144. On this development, see Teitel, *supra* note 104.

145. This is seen in the lack of precise definition of the "enemy," other than in terms of executive discretion. *See* Detention, Treatment and Trial of Certain Non-Citizens in the War Against Terrorism, at § 1(e), 66 Fed. Reg. 57,833, 57,834 (2001) (military order of Nov. 13, 2001).

146. *See* DUNCAN KENNEDY, A CRITIQUE OF ADJUDICATION (1997). Compare with discussion of characteristics of rule of law in transition, *see* TEITEL, *supra* note 1, at 11–26.

147. On the general decline in adherence to the rule of law during this period, see Ruti G. Teitel, *Empire's Law: Foreign Relations by Presidential Fiat*, *in* SEPTEMBER 11TH: TRANSFORMATIVE MOMENT? CULTURE, RELIGION AND POLITICS IN AN AGE OF UNCERTAINTY (Mary Dudziak ed., 2003).

eration of scholarly writing. A number of scholars have challenged any conceptualization of transitions as exceptional in political life, claiming that the aspiration during transitional periods ought to be based on a general theory about the rule of law.[148]

This Article's genealogical review of the phenomena of transitional justice-seeking in periods of substantial political change suggests that this is a false dichotomy. Two political dimensions determine what signifies rule of law in periods of transition: the transitional context, specifically the circumstances relating to political and legal conditions associated with periods of political change, and other political factors, such as local context. Beyond the dimension of transition, local factors also affect the legitimacy of transitional responses. Thus, the mere exportation of ideal rule-of-law models does not provide sufficient guidance. While there is no clear boundary between ordinary and transitional periods, justice-seeking in periods of transition is differentiated by the rule of law associated with limited conditions of political flux. The central dilemma of transitional justice relates to the recurring issues that, even if not *sui generis*, are largely associated with the legal and political factors common to unstable periods of liberalizing political transformation.[149] To the extent that these political conditions are present in a successor regime, the circumstances will present rule-of-law challenges that are peculiar to or arise more frequently in the transitional context. Therefore, while in the abstract it might be desirable to insist that justice-seeking projects in transitional times emulate those of established liberal democracies, this exhortation will ultimately be of limited normative guidance. The rule of law capacity of transitional societies cannot be expected to function at the same level as states that have a consolidated liberal juridical apparatus.

Transitional periods, depending on the political and legal conditions in the relevant society, will fall somewhere along the continuum of the rule-of-law-established democracies. This observation should have implications for the impetus to entrench any particular form of transitional rule of law. To some extent, the dilemmas of transitional justice in its contemporary phases raise issues that resonate more generally with the efforts to establish rule of law in a globalizing world. These include how to shape law reform and justice projects in light of growing global interdependence, and to what extent to accommodate local structures to outside forces.[150]

---

148. *See* Martin Krygier, *Transitional Questions about the Rule of Law: Why, What and How?*, Presented before the Conference of the East Central Europe Institute for Advanced Study, Budapest (L'Europe du Centre Est. Eine wissenschaftliche Zeitschrift at Collegium Budapest) (Feb. 15–17, 2001); Dyzenhaus, *supra* note 57.

149. *See* TEITEL, *supra* note 1, at 11–18, 33–36.

150. *See* STIGLITZ, *supra* note 98. For discussion of globalization's effect on the third world, *see* Tina Rosenberg, *Globalization*, N.Y. TIMES MAG., Aug. 18, 2002, § 6, at 28.

Conclusion

This Article provides a genealogy of transitional justice over the arc of the past half-century. The genealogical perspective situates transitional justice in a political context, moving away from essentializing approaches and thereby illuminating the dynamic relationship between transitional justice and politics over time.

The genealogical inquiry highlights the relationship between juridical and political conditions during periods of political transformation. This inquiry indicates that transitional justice, while contingent upon local conditions and culture, also displays dimensions commonly associated with periods of political flux.

The genealogical approach contributes a needed perspective on the postwar model's enduring dominance in the field of transitional justice. It also illuminates the critical move in Phase II toward local, alternative approaches associated with nation-building and highlights the Phase II privatization and hybridization of the law, which also reflects trends in globalization. The post–Cold War focus on alternative methods for changing political identity was a strategy that responded critically to the post–World War II movement to internationalize and universalize the rule of law, but the strategy was also closely related to the particular national politics of the immediate post–Cold War moment. Change was therefore inevitable: roughly fifteen years after the end of the Cold War, we are now witnessing the normalization of transitional justice, as seen in the current expansion of humanitarian law to ordinary peacetime contexts.

Finally, transitional justice is an important part of broader political developments in recent international history. Thus, in Phase I, transitional justice adhered to juridical rights enforcement associated with liberal ideals of rule of law. However, as time passed, those normative assumptions were challenged, and similar trends emerged in both transitional justice and in the broader discussion of the concept of the rule of law. Just as postmodernist challenges generally offer better critiques than practical strategies,[151] in moving the discourse away from universalizing rule of law, the contemporary transitional justice model reflects a limited critical response. The genealogical method is no exception: it yields ongoing critical cycles rather than a progressive history of transitional justice.

151. On postmodernism as a source of critical theory, *compare* POSTMODERNISM & SOCIAL THEORY: THE DEBATE OVER GENERAL THEORY (Steven Seidman & David G. Wagner eds., 1992) (discussing the postmodern critique) *with* Jacques Derrida, *Force of Law: Mystical Foundation of Authority*, 11 CARDOZO L. REV. 919 (1990).

3

Justice Discourses in Transition

Christine Bell, Colm Campbell and Fionnuala Ní Aoláin

Abstract

This article asserts that 'transitional justice' analyses provide important tools in understanding how societies emerge from violent politics. It argues for a conception of transitional justice that goes beyond the question of dealing with the legacy of past human rights violations; rather, its focus is on a range of inter-related dilemmas relating to the role of law in transitional societies. Specifically, the article explores the pivotal and paradoxical role played by law and legal process in times of transition. It examines the tensions inherent in simultaneously reforming the law while utilizing legal form to bring about institutional transformation. These broad theoretical issues are addressed using Northern Ireland as a case study. The role of law is examined (and a reassessment of transition offered), through an exploration of five inter-linked areas: The relationship between law and conflict; the transformation of legal institutions; dealing with the past; political accommodation and minority rights; and the gap which occurs around gender and political transition. The article concludes by suggesting that only through a broader understanding of transitional justice, coupled with a nuanced reassertion of law's domestic and international legitimacy, can the role of law in transitional societies be adequately understood.

Introduction

'Transitional justice' analyses provide important tools in understanding how societies emerge from violent conflict. As generally understood, 'transitional justice' encompasses the legal, moral and political dilemmas that arise in holding human rights abusers accountable at the end of conflict. This article locates its exploration of the term in the considerable legal flux of the contemporary world. Viewed in these terms, we argue that 'transitional justice' can be used to examine a much broader range of dilemmas relating to the role of law in societies attempting to emerge from violent politics. We suggest that debates about how to deal with the past are only one part of a bigger question of how law and legal institutions assist (or not) in the move from violent conflict to 'peace' (conceived as non-violent political conflict) (Bell, 2000; Teitel, 2000). Indeed, we suggest that it is only within this broader context that debates about dealing with the past can be fully understood. In short, we argue that that transitional justice discourses are themselves in transition. In doing so, we further seek to define and explore the expansion of the transitional justice field, and to offer some views on its contours.

While the broader conception of transitional justice argued for in this article has implications for a range of conflicted and post-conflict societies, it uses the case study of Northern Ireland by way of specific illustration. Doing so not only emphasizes the point that transitional justice analyses may offer key insights into the region's peace process (Bell, 2000; Rolston, 2002; Campbell, Ní Aoláin and Harvey, 2003), it also illustrates how such processes may in turn be reshaping the boundaries of what is meant by 'transitional justice' (Teitel, 2003). The article, though, does not purport to resolve the dilemmas of the transitional justice landscape in Northern Ireland or beyond. Rather it seeks to reframe and take forward discussions about the potential and the limits of law in effecting transition, by mapping the shifting transitional justice terrain, both theoretically, and with relation to specific debates.

The analysis presented later of the complex relationship between law and contemporary transitions is tied to four important global realities (Campbell, 2000; Bell, 2003; Bell, 2004a). Firstly, there is the rise of negotiated settlements as the preferred way of dealing with internal conflict (Bell, 2000). In the last three decades of the twentieth century, internal conflict replaced inter-state conflict as the main type of conflict experienced globally. While the historical origins of transitional justice lie in the legacy of inter-state conflicts,[1] its reinvigoration can be located in the rise of the negotiated 'peace agreement' in internal conflict. Such settlements necessarily involve some compromise between violently conflicting parties, and this compromise is translated into the design of legal and political institutions. This gives rise to on-going dilemmas focused around law's possible role in achieving the transition from violence.

Secondly, there is the increased status of human rights law within and between states. This is demonstrated by more expansive understandings of what human rights entail, including civil and political rights (first generation), social economic and cultural rights (second generation), and people's or solidarity rights (third generation). The scope of human rights law, and its externality to the actors in a conflict, means that it offers increasing possibilities for mitigating the worst excesses of conflict. It also offers an increasing variety of tools, such as institutional blueprints, capable of assisting the negotiation of conflict endings. This points to a clear role for law in assisting a move away from violence to political accommodation.

Thirdly, there is an increased interface between human rights and humanitarian law as a way of dealing with the actions of both state and non-state actors in internal conflict. This has led to more emphasis on accountability and individual responsibility particularly in dealing with past human rights abusers (Campbell, 2000). Again, this raises the difficulty of how to reconcile normative legal standards with the pragmatics of making peace (Anonymous, 1996; Baker, 1996; 2001).

The final reality sits uneasily with the other three. In the wake of the atrocities of 11 September 2001 and of the invasions of Afghanistan and Iraq, and with the global 'war on terrorism' reaching into ever-increasing spheres, the world is a different place. Current US unilateralism, founded on unprecedented military and economic pre-eminence, has important implications for international law, most obviously for the capacity of such law to bind the US in any real sense (a point explored further later). The position is further complicated given the US appropriation of the language of 'transition' and 'democratization' in furtherance of an apparently global project, with few effective international legal constraints.

In the longer term, it is not clear how these dynamics will play out. It may be that US unilateralism will produce a seismic shift in international law, or it may be that countervailing pressures will emerge with time, producing a new international legal consensus. This article does not attempt to guess what the outcome will be; rather it explores the tensions around law and legal institutions generated in contemporary transitions by these sometimes dissonant realities.

The interplay between these realities suggests a distinctive relationship between law and politics in contemporary transition. Identifying such distinctiveness does not of itself assume a homogeneous view of law and legal process, either in a transitional or ordinary context. Rather we defend the view that in transitions particular legal institutions and norms are designed with a specific political task in mind: That of effecting and assisting transition. Typically, the starting point in transition is one in which the rule of law is either absent or degraded, while the end goal is one in which law plays its full role in a functioning liberal-democratic state. This begs the question explored in section A as to what is specific about the role of law in transition. What are the appropriate reference points for understanding it, and how different is law's role during the transition from that at its end-point? These theoretical debates are taken forward in section B of this article, where it is suggested that critical insights into the solution of the problem may lie in revisiting an under-explored relationship: That between law and pre-transition conflict.

The analysis then moves to explore how these debates play out in three areas typically addressed in peace agreements, but with a resonance across the broad spectrum of transitional situations: The challenge of institutional transformation (section C); measures aimed at dealing with the past (section D); and measures aimed at political compromise and accommodation (section E). Finally, section F makes the case for integrating gender studies squarely into the transitional justice landscape, as vital to understanding processes of conflict, processes of law, and transitional justice itself. The discussion in its entirety serves to illustrate the dilemmas for law in transitional situations, and the extent to which these are inter-related concerns, rather than discrete problems.

(A) MAPPING TRANSITIONAL JUSTICE THEORY: THE ROLE OF LAW

The interaction of law and politics in times of transition suggests a role for domestic law in situations of transition that is different from that occupied by law in more settled times. This is without prejudice to an understanding of law's role in a non-transitionary context as contested in many ways. Nonetheless we assert that rather than being related to well-established notions of order, stability and community, law in transitional societies has to engage with the imperatives of moving between radically different political contexts. The need to compensate for domestic rule of law 'gaps', coupled with internationally imposed imperatives, means that international law typically forms a heightened and important legal reference point during transition by virtue of its externality to the parties to the conflict (Hamber, 2003; Teitel, 2003). These reference points, together with the rhetoric in peace agreements and of the international community, suggest a paradigm of transition from a less liberal (more violent) context, to a more liberal (and less violent) one. The projected end-goal is thus some form of liberal-democratic state.

In practice, however, domestic parties almost invariably contest the processes and goals of transition. This contestation can take the form of a head-on attack either on democracy in its entirety, or on its 'liberal' dimension. Or it may be evident in more subtle disagreements over what democratic liberalization actually means or requires. One way in which this can manifest itself is in conflict as to the 'demos' in the democratic: What is the unit for the articulation of the democratic voice? At this point the argument shades into that on self-determination, as section D explores. Moreover, it is now more generally appreciated that positive movement towards democratic liberalization can be substantially offset by external geo-political factors, the limits of externally imposed 'off-the-peg' liberalism, or even the conflicting goals of the international community (Bell, 2004c).

The question mark over the international community's commitment to a democratic liberal direction for transitions looms ever-larger post-9/11. Even as democratic liberalism is promoted as the 'cure' for varied international problems (including despotic regimes, terrorism, ethnic conflict, and failed states), its central tenets are being concurrently challenged by the 'war against terrorism'.[2] This debate is writ large in the associated challenge to the primacy of international law, and in particular its human rights strand (Campbell and Ní Aoláin, 2003). Any 'externality' of international law turns on law having a degree of autonomy. Without this autonomy, international law would be unable to fulfil the kind of mediating role prescribed by Cassesse (1986), since mediation would be lost where a state was free to ascribe to international law whatever meaning suited it at a particular time. Time will tell how this mediating capacity of international law is affected by US unilateralism.

Any theory of 'transitional justice' therefore has difficult questions to grapple with, both domestically and internationally. The degrading of the rule of law in conflict situations means that in sociological and socio-legal terms there is likely to be a loss or absence of legal legitimacy (including the legitimacy of legal institutions) within communities at the sharp end of the conflict. The resulting crisis of legitimacy suggests that in transitional societies, law must be both the subject and object of change: It must simultaneously both produce change and be changed itself.

An initial question arises as to what the reference point for understanding the role of law in transition is. Can law and legal institutions created to facilitate a move from conflict be evaluated in terms of their capacity to buttress traditional concepts of order, community and stability? If not, what should the basis for their evaluation be? One possible answer is that they should be evaluated in terms of their capacity to assist in the kind of paradigmatic transition described above. Teitel (2000), for example, has justified the very *partiality* of transitional criminal justice mechanisms as serving the needs of transition viewed in such terms. She argues that debate over their compatibility with rule of law requirements can be assessed in terms of whether they enable or not liberal-democratic transition, in what amounts to a transition-specific conception of justice (p. 4). However, how to use this new notion of the rule of law so as to evaluate compromises made is not simple, either empirically or conceptually. Moreover, conceptualizing the contours of transition-specific justice is a formidable task, and as this article outlines, it may be a much more ambitious project than has previously been understood by academic and policy commentators.

There are, moreover, difficulties with evaluating legal mechanisms in terms of an accepted normative direction of transition towards a liberal-democratic future. Firstly, there is the problem adverted to earlier that in many post-conflict societies there is little consensus over what that liberal-democratic future should look like. A second practical difficulty in this context is the question of whether future evaluation requires a notion of when transition ends. Are legal institutions, such as bills of rights, to be designed with explicitly transitional goals in mind? If so, do they require to be replaced by more permanent documents at some point, and what would that point be? There would seem to be a danger that ongoing evaluation of legal reform in terms of instrumental transitional goals could, at some point, undermine the normative tenets of liberal democracy which these goals are aimed at.

This leads us to another question: How different, really, is law's role in times of transition, to its role in more liberal-democratic settings? Tully (1995), for example, in noting the modern challenges to liberal-democratic constitutionalism made by women, indigenous peoples, and minorities, argues for less static 'dialogic constitutionalism' which would enable social challenge to be better mediated in an on-going way. If transitional justice is merely a dramatic instance of social change, what are the implications of transitional justice responses for law more generally? It is possible that these discourses, in challenging traditional notions of the role of the rule of law, proffer creative possibilities for a much broader range of situations of social change.

Northern Ireland provides a valuable case study through which to probe the limits of contemporary transitional justice discourses both in its specificity from, and in its commonality with, other transitional situations. Part of its specificity lies in the liberal-democratic character of the UK (Campbell, Ní Aoláin and Harvey, 2003), with the implication that political and legal reform in Northern Ireland can be analysed from a 'democratic renewal' perspective. However, Northern Ireland's dysfunctional and conflicted democratic legacy (the region saw a half-century of one-party rule) also locates it at the transitional justice interface. In this it evidences greater similarity with other transitional situations, and borrows in its peace agreement from South Africa in particular (Harvey, 2001). The unique straddling of the categories of 'conflicted/transitional society' and 'western democracy' makes Northern Ireland a key case study in examining the extent to which the dilemmas and solutions of 'transitional justice' have a currency, both as regards other transitional situations, and processes of democratic renewal more generally.

(B) CONFLICT AND LAW

Paradigmatic transition is the transition from violent conflict to peace and democracy. Increasingly, both conflict and processes of resolution are being understood as fluid, with dynamics that change over time. Consequently, processes of conflict-prevention, peace-making and peace-building are now recognized as closely related (Boutros-Ghali, 1992; 1995; Brahimi et al., 2000). This relationship is built on two converse assertions. First, that greater understanding and acknowledgement of the relationship between law and the causes of conflict are necessary when designing legal mechanisms and institutions aimed at facilitating transition from conflict. And conversely, that 'transitional mechanisms' exhibited in societies emerging from violent conflict could have a constructive role elsewhere if promoted when conflict is at a nascent stage (Macedonian Framework Document, 2001). It is in the assumptions buried in these converse assertions, and indeed in challenges posed to them in conflict situations, that we would assert the claim for a distinctive notion of *'transitional'* justice lies.

Northern Ireland provides a prime example of a situation in which security responses, particularly in the early years of the conflict, frequently undercut the (often concurrent) legal responses seeking to eliminate the political causes of conflict. Yet, this phenomenon was denied by official discourses on emergency and anti-terrorist powers, which throughout the conflict were presented as 'the response of the liberal-democratic state to politically-motivated violence and terrorism' (*Report of the Commission to Consider Legal Procedures to Deal with Terrorist Activities in Northern Ireland*, 1972; *Report of a Committee to Consider, in the Context of Civil Liberties and*

Human Rights, Measures to Deal with Terrorism in Northern Ireland, 1975; McEvoy and Gormally, 1997). Thus incremental changes were at each stage justified in terms of a balancing calculation of the degree to which the ordinary liberties guaranteed by the liberal-democratic state should be limited in order to eliminate the violence, or at least to contain it within 'acceptable levels'. The problem and the response were separately compartmentalized and calibrated (with obvious post-9/11 resonance).

While challenges to the nature of specific balancing calculations are possible,[3] a more fundamental difficulty with the structure of argumentation was that it denied any link between state action and the causes of conflict. In situations such as Northern Ireland, emergency powers and the security policies operationalizing them could be argued not to be simply a response to the conflict, but in fact *partly constitutive of it.* While official discourses might project emergency legislation being introduced as a response to violent upheaval, in fact, 50-year old 'special' legislation pre-dated the most recent round of violence (National Council for Civil Liberties, 1936; Campbell, 1994). Repeal of this legislation was one of the core demands of the civil rights movement, generating street protests, the policing of which is generally seen as having contributed to the violent disintegration of the late 1960s (Boyle, Hadden and Hillyard, 1975). Particularly in the early 1970s it is empirically possible to demonstrate a correspondence between the escalation of violence and particularly harsh, military-based, security measures (Campbell and Connolly, 2003).

Official discourses obscured evaluation of the extent to which the state in Northern Ireland was not simply a bystander or referee in the conflict but a *participant* in it. This had obvious implications for perceptions of the law's neutrality and legitimacy, which any solution to the conflict would have to address, for the simple reason that in the liberal-democratic state, law matters. The mediating role of law, encapsulated in conceptions of the 'rule of law', is a key source of democratic legitimacy.

As already suggested, in such a situation there are possibilities for international law both to address the de-legitimation of law during conflict, and to provide a way around some of the legal dilemmas which arise at its end. However, the Northern Ireland conflict reveals difficulties for this role. If, as discussed earlier, international law is to play this mediating role,[4] it cannot be seen simply to endorse or accommodate whatever claims the state may choose to make as to its security needs during the conflict. The bite of international law can operate to buttress the autonomy of key legal norms such as the right to life, so as to affect how the state (and in turn opposition groups) conduct the conflict (Ní Aoláin, 2000b). However, in Northern Ireland, supranational legal supervision was not always robust. The relatively indulgent attitude adopted by the European Court of Human Rights to UK security claims in Northern Ireland during the actual course of the conflict suggests that international human rights norms, coupled with interpretative mechanisms which often gave deference to state fact-finding, were not always effective.[5] This poses the question of whether the liberal-democratic character of a state serves as a shield against international scrutiny.[6]

The question of the mediating role of international law arises even more starkly with relation to international humanitarian law (given that this is a conflict-specific body of law). Here the questions apply not just to the state, but also in relation to armed opposition groups or 'non-state entities'. Whether the violence in Northern Ireland amounted to an 'armed conflict' in the technical humanitarian law sense is a moot point. The UK went to great lengths to deny the possibility of the applicability of international humanitarian law to Northern Ireland, for instance, by delaying ratification of two 1977 Protocols to the Geneva Convention covering non-conventional armed conflict until the peace process was well in hand.[7] Non-governmental organizations were, over time, less reticent about drawing upon international humanitarian standards, though fudging the issue of whether the norms were strictly legally applicable.[8] Non-state entities, while making reference to the conflict as a 'war', did not claim adherence to either 1977 Protocol, nor indeed, did they conduct their own use of violence with appropriate or specific regard to humanitarian norms.

In short, difficulties with the applicability of international humanitarian law further evidence the complexities faced by the liberal-democratic state in coming to terms with the fact that it may have had an armed conflict of sorts taking place on its territory, and furthermore, that it may have been a participant in it. It also starkly highlights the activities of non-state actors and the gap between the invocation of 'war' rhetoric without regards to the observance of humanitarian norms. Despite these difficulties, humanitarian law would seem to have particular uses during transition, for example, with relation to provision for prisoner-release (1977 Protocol II provides for amnesty following high-intensity internal conflicts), and in providing norms capable of dealing with the experience of the past. Thus, humanitarian law provides one reference point to address both the behaviour of state and non-state entities at conflict's end.

This brings us back full circle to endorsing the view that an understanding of the relationship between conflict and law is vital to understanding the post-conflict transition. In many respects the success of the transition in a law-based state turns on a reversal of the kind of legal de-legitimation that occurred during the conflict: There is an attempt to rebuild the legitimacy of domestic law and of legal institutions. If rule of law deficits can be linked to conflict escalation, then rule of law cures play a vital part in any attempt to negotiate an end to conflict (Bell, 1999).

(C) INSTITUTIONAL TRANSFORMATION

Given the connection between conflict and law described earlier, transitional justice claims invariably implicate legal institutions. Any conflicted society is likely to exhibit sharp difference between communities in the confidence displayed in legal structures and processes. There may be conflicting views over the extent to which legal institutions have been complicit in the maintenance and management of conflict, and diverging views about the necessity and capability of reform. As a result, legal reform is debated not just in terms of the intrinsic value of reasserting the rule of law, but also as a form of broader political affirmation or denial of certain constitutional and political pasts and futures. The consequences of this bargaining dynamic around legal reform can be significant, indicating a need to maintain law's stability while simultaneously acknowledging its failings during the conflict, and redressing these in the form of institutional revisions.

Peace agreements frequently include legal and other institutional reforms that take account of this reality. As practice in multiple jurisdictions has demonstrated, the totality of reform cannot be contained in a peace agreement, and instead such reform tends to form part of the post-negotiation landscape. Thus, institutional reform can occur incrementally outside the initial, formal, negotiating process, and works to addresses the causes of conflict on a more piecemeal basis. This practical reality means that institutional reforms become intrinsically tied up with the ongoing experiment of political accommodation. This can operate to the detriment of a coherent reform process, as parties embrace or reject legal reform not on its own terms, but because of its capacity to reshape critical elements of the initial agreement towards their own vision of transition.

In Northern Ireland the contested dynamic that has emerged around institutional transformation is rooted in two aspects. First, there is a lack of shared narrative by all parties on the causes of conflict and its manifestations (an issue explored further in section E). This has led to markedly different views on the role and legitimacy of the actions of legal institutions and actors during the conflict. Second, there is a debate about the extent to which legal reform needs to be tied to a particular constitutional settlement.

These realities have substantial impact on the politics of institutional reform. If, on one view, the institutions of the state are viewed as having 'done a good job in difficult circumstances', then demands for reconfiguration are seen as charged political assault on the integrity and neutrality of legal form and structure. Change can only be countenanced as necessary when couched in managerialist language, with an emphasis on 'professionalism', 'efficiency' and 'modernization', and tied to developments in democratic jurisdictions elsewhere (and preeminently in the rest of the UK) (O'Rawe, 2003). On this view, change is not linked to the experience of conflict but rather to the kind of on-going economic or management imperatives that exist anywhere.

Others argue for substantial reform or innovation (frequently articulated in a language of 'transformation'), rooted in a view of enormous institutional failing, evidenced by multiple human rights abuses. Viewed in these terms, the challenge becomes that identified in section B: Building the legitimacy of the legal institutions of the new dispensation, producing an imperative for root and branch reconfiguration.

The institutional pattern of many peace agreements has been followed in the case of Northern Ireland. The Belfast/Good Friday Agreement (the 'Agreement') provided for a Criminal Justice Review, reform of policing, mechanisms for enforcing rights, (including a bill of rights), judicial reform, new equality legislation, and discrete measures relating to prisoners, victims, and language policy. Any one of these issues serves to illustrate the tensions described earlier, and attempts at reform have often tried to negotiate a middle way between competing understandings of the parameters of change. Thus, the Patten report on policing both addresses the problems of past legitimacy (but only implicitly), while reframing the debate around 'good policing' (rather than good 'police'), justifying many reforms as innovative good practice *per se* (Independent Commission on Policing for Northern Ireland, 1999). It has consequently been criticized as failing to deal adequately with the legacy of the past human rights abuses, but also for 'going too far', in a reconstructive agenda that cannot solely be justified as required by neutral managerial and efficiency requirements. The report could thus be viewed as an attempt to address the *legacy* of institutional delegitimation without an exploration of the *process* of delegitimation that an examination of the past might have produced. As such, assessment of its success as a transitional device is likely to depend in part on whether explicit acknowledgement of past failings is viewed as a necessary part of successful transition, or whether the kind of compromise in relation to the past represented by Patten is viewed as an acceptable cost of peace-building.

(D) DEALING WITH THE PAST

As the etymology of 'trans-ition' makes clear, the concept implies a journey, which in paradigmatic transition is from a conflict-laden past to an anticipated peaceful democratic future. Successful transitions in recent years have almost invariably been characterized by attempts to engage with this past, suggesting an important instrumental value for the exercise. Conversely, this experience warns that a failure to address the question adequately may hinder prospects for a successful transition.

Dealing with the past may be viewed as comprising two aspects, 'undoing the past', (typically by attempting to 'undo' the displacement of people and dispossession of land which occurred during the conflict), and 'accounting for the past' (for instance, through the use of truth commissions and domestic or international courts and tribunals) (Bell, 2000). In the Northern Ireland transition, the focus has been almost exclusively on the latter, though arguments are now being made that the significant population displacement which occurred at the start of the Troubles can be understood as a form of deliberate displacement akin to the recent experiences of other jurisdictions such as Bosnia, though on a much lesser scale.

Devising legal mechanisms for dealing with the past probes the limits of classical legal discourse. International law increasingly articulates a seemingly inflexible demand for trials of those responsible for major violations

(Orentlicher, 1991; Campbell, 2000), yet paradoxically, peace-making, reconciliation and truth-telling may be facilitated by a measure of immunity from prosecution (Cohen, 1995), and prisoner-releases have been a feature of most conflict-resolution processes (Gormally and McEvoy, 1995). Indeed, in the Northern Ireland process, prisoners are frequently presented as having played a major role in peace-making (McEvoy, 2001).

Truth commissions, with their novel approaches to accountability, may offer a way to square this circle, even if a degree of conflict with legal norms is involved (Roht-Arriaza, 1995). Yet such mechanisms cannot be said to represent an escape from law, since successful truth commissions almost invariably require a legal mandate (witnesses, for instance, need to be compellable) (Hayner, 2001). Others champion individual criminal trials as routes to truth and reconciliation (Akhavan, 1998). And yet others point (however critically) to alternative 'weeding out' (or lustration) mechanisms, whereby those involved in past violations (typically lower echelon functionaries) can be prevented by administrative or quasi-judicial means from public participation in the new institutions (such as in police forces) (Huyse, 1995).

The approach to the past in the Northern Ireland transition can be described as *ad hoc* and 'piecemeal' (Bell, 2003). There has been no unitary centralized mechanism for publicly re-examining the conflict, along the lines of the South African Truth and Reconciliation Commission. Nor is there widespread agreement on the institution of such a mechanism in the immediate future (Healing Through Remembering Project, 2002). Explicit acknowledgement of failure has been rare, though in some cases (as with the Patten report discussed earlier), the scale of change recommended contains an implicit narrative of institutional failure.

There are several instances, though, in which discrete conflict-related issues are being or have been addressed. Most prominent of these has been the continuing Saville Inquiry into the Army's 1972 Bloody Sunday killings (Hegarty, 2003). Another exploration has been through on-going criminal investigations in relation to criminal offences committed during the conflict, the most high profile of which produced the 'Stevens 3' report into collusion between elements in the security forces/services and loyalist paramilitaries (Stevens, 2003). Yet other initiatives have included a number of attempts to address the needs of victims (see, for example, Bloomfield, 1998; Department of Health and Social Services, 1998; Wilson, 1999; Healing Through Remembering, 2002): The provision of a de-facto amnesty through the early release of those convicted in special 'Diplock courts' (Northern Ireland (Sentences) Act 1998); the issuing of a number of apologies, (displaying greater or lesser degrees of apparent contrition) by paramilitary groups;[9] and the Cory inquiry, exploring whether further specific allegations of collusion require public inquiries.[10]

This piecemeal approach has had some instrumental benefits. Jurisdictions where a generalized exploration of the past has been agreed upon are generally those in which a high degree of societal consensus has emerged about the broad contours of that past (Bell, 2000; 2003). In Northern Ireland this consensus does not exist. Rather, as in many ethnic or quasi-ethnic conflicts, a conflict-about-the-conflict, or a 'meta-conflict' continues to exist (McGarry and O'Leary, 1995; Bell, 2000; Campbell, Ní Aoláin and Harvey, 2003). There remains no agreement as to what the conflict was about, or as to what caused it. Referring back to the earlier discussion of international legal regimes, there even remains a conflict as to whether any 'armed conflict' took place. And in a wide-ranging exploration, virtually all the parties have something to lose, particularly where questions of individual culpability for acts committed during the conflict may arise. In this environment, demands for an across-the-board exploration of the past might have proved an insurmountable obstacle to the peace process; the piecemeal approach circumvents this dilemma, allowing engagement with those issues for which there were specific political demands (Bell, 2003). And yet a generalized sense of unfinished business – a sense that closure on many conflict-related issues has not been achieved – persists in much of civil society (Healing Through Remembering, 2002). This poses the obvious question of whether achieving such a sense of closure is necessary, useful, or even possible. This in turn leads to the question of whether strategies of engagement with the past should be judged not simply in terms of their instrumental value in furthering transition, but perhaps in terms of a broader truth-telling imperative.

On the one hand, the lack of an overall narrative about the conflict impacts on on-going institutional reform in Northern Ireland. Every contestation in the reform process tends to become a surrogate continuation of the conflict, producing in turn an endless replay of the meta-conflict. On the other hand, it is arguable that to set out to establish the 'one great truth' about a conflict as complex as that in Northern Ireland may be to set the enterprise up for failure. It is possible to see a real problem here without retreating into the absolute relativism of the 'postmodernist black hole' (Cohen, 1995; Campbell, 2000: 33). It is also possible to see that a broader truth-eliciting process might be tasked with establishing particular truths that cumulatively, contribute to truth (rather than establishing *the* truth).

The problem of the past in the Northern Ireland transition reflects the classic dilemmas of established transitional justice discourses. These issues remain as relevant in the jurisdiction as elsewhere. There is at least one way though, in which the difficulties of instituting a unitary mechanism in Northern Ireland, and the consequent piece-meal approach, point to a disaggregation of broader dilemmas. If the stark choice sometimes presented between 'peace', 'justice' and 'truth' is unpacked, the Northern Ireland experience tends to suggest that the issue may be as much about timing as about substantive questions (Bell, 2003; 2004c). In these terms, the 'big problem' breaks down into questions of how interim mechanisms can be designed in such a way as not to preclude other possibilities in the future; questions of the timing of interim and overall initiatives; and technical questions springing from the need to keep past-focused initiatives operating in tandem with the political accommodation imperatives of the peace-building project.

(E) POLITICAL ACCOMMODATION AND MINORITY RIGHTS

As with 'dealing with the past', the question of law's relationship to political accommodation revolves around the issue of how to reconcile normative legal demands with the pragmatics of peace-making. Furthermore, the two are linked – hence the need to keep both operating in tandem.

At one level, political accommodation and the move towards compromise among competing groups over access to governmental power, may seem to have little to do with law or transitional justice. Yet, the inclusion of self-determination as a right within international human rights instruments, and an emerging body of minority rights law, have blurred the distinction between political and legal mechanisms.[11] Here again, the context of the conflict forms an important backdrop. As Berman (1998) has noted, international self-determination law does not stand above domestic law conflicts; rather 'the power of international law to shape the identity of the protagonists of such conflicts cannot be separated from even its principled activities to remedy them' (p. 28). International law's adjudication on self-determination positions during a conflict are integrally related both to the course of the conflict, and to eventual self-determination outcomes.

Self-determination law has been described as having two aspects: External and internal. External self-determination underwrites change in the status of states, for example, for colonial to independent, or from one state to two or more (Thornberry, 1993). Internal self-determination focuses on the 'relationship between a people and "its own" state or government', lifting the veil of the state to question its legitimacy and relationship to the will of the people' (p. 101). Only external self-determination has a clear legal basis, although, as Thornberry notes, the roots of a concept of internal self-determination can be found in most legal articulations (cf. Crawford, 1993).

Questions of self-determination centrally raise the question adverted to earlier, that of the demos in the democratic: Whose right is it, and what is the unit for its exercise? Increasingly, in internal conflict, difficult questions of external self-determination are being dealt with through ambiguous language that satisfies the international community's notion of what external self-determination law requires, while capable of quite different meanings to different parties to the conflict (Bell and Cavanaugh, 1999; Bell, 2000: 161–91). Simultaneously, the seemingly all-or-nothing requirements of external self-determination law are mediated by turning to a range of policy options aimed at accommodating competing demands for power, underwritten by a notion of 'internal self-determination'. These include autonomy regimes, consociational mechanisms (such as power-sharing government with vetoes), and 'corporate federalism' (whereby power is devolved to ethnic groups not on a territorial basis but over certain spheres of life, for example, education or culture). Thus, in Bosnia-Herzegovina the international community insisted on a unitary state within existing (post-Yugoslavian) boundaries, even as partitionist claims were controversially met by establishing ethnic entities to which nearly all power was devolved

(The General Framework Agreement for Peace in Bosnia and Herzegovina, 1995).

Although it is too early to talk of a legal 'right' to this broad concept of internal self-determination, the notion does find support in the proliferation of international instruments on minority rights, and is increasingly referred to by international bodies.[12] However, international law's attempt to provide blueprints for political institutions illustrates how some of the theoretical issues raised at the start of this article play out.

Firstly, there is the question of the normative requirements of self-determination law. Despite its notoriously ambiguous content, self-determination does have some clear normative content. Peace processes often implicitly pose the question of the extent to which that normative requirement can be ignored or manipulated. For example, in the Israeli/Palestinian conflict, the Oslo 'Declaration of Principles' was silent on the right of the Palestinian people to self-determination, thereby questioning whether an outcome consistent with Palestinian self-determination claims was even on the table.

Secondly, a fundamental question must be asked of situations in which the normative demands of self-determination law are less clear, as to whether it is useful for international law to aim to provide what are in effect self-determination blueprints. As Slaughter (1998) writes: 'The rise of group rights may be understood as the further colonisation of the political by the legal' (p. 134). However, she also notes that 'the relative success of informal efforts at mediating simmering ethnic conflicts suggests the value of expanding the repertoire of political solutions rather than searching for new rights and remedies.' (p. 129) And so the question must be posed as to whether international lawyers should strive to produce a normative response at all, or merely police the law/politics divide, acknowledging that where law ends, politics begins. At the minute the distinction between law and politics is to some extent being preserved by a distinction between hard law (external self-determination), and soft law (internal self-determination). However, soft law has a tendency to harden meaning so that this question is likely to become ever more pertinent in the future.

The use of a 'group rights' paradigm to address political institutions also raises difficult practical questions as to the relationship between group-oriented political structures and individual-oriented equality standards. Do power-sharing arrangements discriminate against the individual equality rights of 'others' who are not identified as members of the main political groupings (Wippman, 1998)? Do solutions fashioned around acknowledging one dimension of difference, namely ethnicity, marginalize equality for groups such as women? Or more positively, can addressing other types of difference, such as gender, contribute to addressing ethnic division by re-framing the problem? As discussed later (in section F), women have reason to be sceptical about the institutions of liberal democracy, and about the political and legal permutations which peace agreements produce, often in response to narrow definitions of 'the' conflict.

Finally, little work has been undertaken as to the *transitional* role which this form of constitutionalism takes (Teitel, 2000). In other words, are these mechanisms better viewed as permanent solutions to ethnic conflict, or temporary mechanisms, which, if successful, manage group conflict as non-violent, pending re-negotiation of the constitutional and territorial future?

Northern Ireland provides a good example of how these dilemmas play out in a classic example of constructive ambiguity (Bell and Cavanaugh, 1999). The Belfast/Good Friday Agreement's formulation in relation to external self-determination is that:

> it is for the people of the island of Ireland alone, by agreement between the two parts respectively and without external impediment, to exercise their right of self-determination on the basis of consent, freely and concurrently given, North and South, to bring about a united Ireland, if that is their wish, accepting that this right must be achieved and exercised with and subject to the agreement and consent of a majority of the people of Northern Ireland. (British and Irish Governments, 2003: Article 1(ii))

This formulation addresses the claims of both the main communal groups. For nationalists and republicans, self-determination is located by reference to the people of the entire island, while for unionists and loyalists, the fact that northern consent is required for re-unification means that a bar to this possibility exists, at least for the immediate future. Thus existing state boundaries remain intact for the immediate future, but British sovereignty over Northern Ireland is located not by reference to a UK claim as of right, but rather by reference to exercise of a right of self-determination involving the people of all the island.

In terms of the immediate exercise of political power – the sharp end of political accommodation – it is the internal dimension of the right to self-determination that takes centre-stage. This is true even if 'internal self-determination' is not the language explicitly used. In this regard, the Agreement stipulates a consociational form of government in which legislative and executive power is shared between the two communities, with a requirement that public power be exercised on the basis of 'parity of esteem'. Proof of the effect of these stipulations lies in the fact that the power-sharing Executive and Assembly have been suspended on four occasions. Moreover, as recent election results indicate (November 2003), a marked shift in the distribution of political representation is taking place within both nationalist and unionist communities, with benefits to Sinn Féin and the Democratic Unionist Party (unsurprisingly, suspension continues at the time of writing). Such internal political realignments are a feature of post-peace agreement landscapes in many jurisdictions. What should not be under-estimated is their capacity to undermine the broad accommodations reached in a prior comprehensive settlement, and their impact upon the course of the transitional process. Finally, straddling the external-internal self-determination divide is provision for North-South and East-West intergovernmental bodies, which some have considered 'confederal' in nature (O'Leary, 1999).

The consociational mechanisms of the Belfast/Good Friday Agreement are defended as a solution which by recognising competing nationalisms, enables their accommodation on the basis of equality (Eide, 1996; O'Leary, 1999). However, consociationalism is also under attack from a number of different perspectives. Some attack it as politically unnecessary, essentially denying that group accommodation is a problem in Northern Ireland. Thus, they argue for majoritarian devolution as in Scotland or Wales, often from a unionist perspective. Others argue, from a more legal viewpoint, that the mechanisms stand to ossify and entrench competing nationalisms, while excluding those who do not wish to be defined within these groups. These critiques leave it unclear whether there should be any attempt to accommodate competing group interests at all, or whether they view robust individual rights protections as sufficient to deal with minority rights. Interestingly, they draw on the Framework Convention's right 'not to be considered a member of a minority', exposing the tension inherent in minority rights documents between individual rights imperatives, and programmatic rights to group accommodation (cf. Wippman, 1998).

These debates, concretized by suspension and political deadlock in the post-election context in Northern Ireland, evidence yet another forum for the meta-conflict: On-going contestation as to what the problem is, and therefore what solutions will address it. However, while these debates play out politically, they also affect the design and reform of legal institutions, in ways similar to that of 'dealing with the past'. As regards the design of a proposed bill of rights, for example, debate has focused on the extent to which the bill should (a) underwrite consociational mechanisms entrenching them for the medium to long-term; (b) emphasize individual rights in a way which would put the consociational mechanism under legal attack, or (c) provide a programmatic standard relating to accommodation of groups on the basis of equality, which would underwrite the current mechanisms, and require the issue to continue to be addressed without requiring this particular mechanism in perpetuity (McCrudden, 1999; 2001; Northern Ireland Human Rights Commission, 2001). These debates can be considered the negotiation of a dilemma permanently present in any resort to a consociational formula in response to entrenched violent communal conflict: How to keep energy and innovation in the political system; how to create democratic stability without ossification and stagnation, and without working to the exclusion of groups (such as women) whose political voices have been silenced in the past.

(F) GENDER AND LAW IN SITUATIONS OF TRANSITION

Quandaries around consociationalism are but one example of a broader (and insufficiently researched) set of issues: The gendered dimensions of transition. Peace processes are typically deeply gendered, raising awkward questions about the neutrality of the transitional project. While women will often have been at the forefront of peace initiatives throughout a conflict, peace agreements are usually negotiated predominantly, if not exclusively, by men (Bell, 2004b). The conduct of violence and war is predominantly male, leading to a male bias in negotiations, and mediators are usually men (Askin, 1997; Yuval-Davis, 1997; Goldstein, 2001). This is despite the Platform for Action which emerged from the Fourth World Conference on Women in Beijing in 1995 which asserted that: 'In addressing armed or other conflicts, an active and visible policy of mainstreaming a gender perspective into all policies and programmes should be promoted so that before decisions are taken, an analysis is made of the effects on women and men, respectively' (World Conference on Women, 1995: para 141; UN SC Resolution, 2000).

Such exclusion has a double effect. Arguably, it operates to narrow the problems faced to a 'male' conception of conflict revolving around allocations of power and territory, and stopping certain forms of violence (Ní Aoláin, 1999; Bell, 2004b). These questions may impact only peripherally on many women's day-to-day lives. They may leave untouched socio-economic exclusions, and even violence, which women may not see as compartmentalized into 'conflict' and 'non-conflict' related, but rather experience as a continuum, only partially addressed by cease-fires (Cockburn, 1999). It also means that women rarely sit at the tables where the issues of post-conflict transition and reconstruction are addressed. This reinforces the 'conceptual exclusion'. As Chinkin and Paradine (2001) have pointed out, feminist discourse has shown women to have reason to be profoundly ambivalent about many of the basic tenets of liberal-democratic constitutionalism. Without women, these questions are less likely to be brought to the table.

Only relatively recently has the gendered dimension of war and of international law, in particular, been closely examined (Askin, 1997; Ní Aoláin, 2000a). This work has been supplemented by consideration of the gender dynamics of ethnic conflict, and internal conflict more generally (Yuval-Davis, 1997). We would argue that this body of research creates a baseline from which more nuanced analysis of the relationship between gender, conflict, transition, and peace can be undertaken. It also operates to reveal that there is a tangible link between the experience of women during conflict and the exclusions we have identified in the transitional context. A gendered understanding of peace processes is required to address how women can practically assert a presence at peace negotiations, while simultaneously reframing the questions these processes revolve around. Addressing gender is not just a matter of addressing women's needs. The experience of how women work can be vital to peace-making and peace-building. In particular women are often well positioned to further connections between civic society (where women often predominate) and political institutions (where men often predominate), and in so doing reshaping the notion of what is politics, and what is democratic participation.

The Northern Ireland transition offers a graphic illustration of many of the concerns outlined earlier. However, it also offers an example of an attempt to integrate a gender perspective into both the negotiation process and to the post-agreement political environment. This was achieved through three different types of intervention (Bell, 2004b). Firstly, through women creating networks across communal divisions during both the conflict and the peace process, enabled by their very political invisibility. Thus, women found ways to deal with communal difference without requiring its prior negation or elimination. Secondly, building on this experience, women worked together with other marginalized groups to create rainbow coalitions which were significant in placing a 'human rights and equality' agenda on the table, and ensuring that this agenda met real problems (McCrudden, 1999; Bell, 2004b). Finally, women worked both within their own political groupings and through the establishment of a women's political party – the Northern Ireland Women's Coalition – to input into the negotiations leading to the Belfast/Good Friday Agreement. The result of these combined strategies was an Agreement whose human rights and equality commitments went well beyond addressing the 'nationalist/unionist' communal divide to address other exclusions. Interestingly, each operated to mutual benefit: Reform which negotiators saw as aimed at addressing conflict divisions created stronger mechanisms for human rights and equality than would have emerged from the traditional British approach to each, while radical institutional reform became easier to present in 'good practice' terms rather than 'concessions to nationalists' the more it operated to benefit a broader range of communities, including women.

The case of Northern Ireland illustrates ways of opening up processes, both conceptually and practically, to ensure the participation of women. However, it also indicates some difficulties. Firstly, while Northern Ireland evidences some successes with relation to peace agreement provision for women, such provision is still relatively scant, evidencing the need for further models of good practice to be explored. Secondly, there is the difficulty of implementing any ensuing gender commitments, not least given the sheer volume of work which the Agreement has created for women's groups. Thirdly, is the difficulty that any emerging political consensus between opposing nationalisms, may, where women's issues are concerned, work to their detriment, as recent Assembly debates on reproductive rights evidence. Finally, the political realignments evidenced in Northern Ireland's Assembly elections have also operated to squeeze out the representational space that the Women's Coalition had gained in the post-Agreement elections. This is further evidence of the capacity of the transitional environment to operate in non-linear and illiberal directions, in antithesis to the interests of gender mainstreaming and the consolidation of women's political interests.

CONCLUSION

We finish where we began – with an assertion of the need for a much broader conception of transitional justice than one that focuses solely on 'dealing with the past' (particularly where this past is viewed in terms of male conceptions of harm). Hence the demand for a theory of law in transition that is not past-specific and that avoids the pitfalls of a gendered approach.

Part (though not all) of the solution may lie in seeing the transitional process in terms of the reversal of the delegitimation of domestic law and of legal institutions that occurred during the conflict. Thus the transition becomes a project of building the legitimacy of the law across the range of sites where rule of law deficits are evident in the conflict's wake. In doing so, we would assert that this does not limit the capacity of law and legal process to become a site of contestation in a post-conflict society, but it underscores the need for a degree of *a priori* legal legitimacy in order for that 'normal' contestation to take place. This approach is as applicable to the problems of institutional transformation and political accommodation as it is to dealing with the past. With it comes a particular focus on the experience of groups excluded during conflict, whether that exclusion was on the basis of politics, ethnicity or gender.

In building the legitimacy of domestic law and legal institutions, international law has a particularly important part to play by virtue of its externality to the parties to the conflict. This externality is directly related to the autonomous quality of international law – it is not an infinitely malleable set of standards, the meaning of which states are free to appropriate according to their whims at any particular time. We note, however, that in the post-9/11 world this autonomy is under particular threat. How this battle plays out will have important implications for the role of international law in situations of transition, particularly as the language of transition is increasingly invoked by the remaining superpower in a uni-polar world.

Northern Ireland provides intimations of some of these dilemmas. The UK's place as a leading western democracy meant that international law scrutiny of the state's behaviour during the conflict was not as robust as it might have been. This factor, together with a British strategy of avoidance of standards viewed as potentially troublesome (the 1977 Geneva Protocols are a case in point), meant that external checks, while important, were somewhat blunted. This attenuated external regime can be considered a contributory factor in the significant rule of law deficits that occurred during the conflict.

Addressing these deficits during the transition has not been an easy task, as the rocky record of the peace process illustrates. In some respects the very liberal-democratic character of the UK state has served, at least in the past, to hide the scale of the problem from itself. That said, the Northern Ireland transition does offer several positive lessons. Once its piecemeal approach to dealing with the past is seen as a work-in-progress rather than as the totality of the past-focused project, it may offer a way to satisfy the apparent clash between the needs of political accommodation and the imperative to deal with the past immediately. Questions of timing then become central. Initiatives around political accommodation during the transition display some success in addressing gendered deficits, and the formula in relation to self-determination suggests a creative exploration of the concept's internal and external dimensions. The consociational governmental model performed effectively in some respects, even if its future is unclear: In the short term because of suspension, and in the longer term because of possible political realignments. The ultimate success of initiatives around institutional reconfiguration will likewise take some time to measure, but at least some advances are clearly evident.

An overall assessment of the success or failure of the Northern Ireland transition is therefore some time off. Elaboration of the criteria for success will need to take account of shifting legal ground in the global legal and political environment. This will be no easy task. However, as this article has argued, central to this task is an understanding of the relationship between law and violent conflict, which cuts across pre- and post-transition landscapes, and acknowledges the complexity of the legal mechanisms required to manage, accommodate and overcome violence and its institutional legacies.

NOTES

1. The Nuremberg trials of the major German war criminals in the wake of the Second World War are probably the most important point of departure. For a roughly contemporaneous analysis, see H. Ehard (1949).
2. See UN Security Council Resolution 1373 (2001). Notable in this context is the amplification and expansion of draconian anti-terrorist legislation both by states experiencing conflict and by those which are relatively peaceful.
3. See *Murray v UK* (1996).
4. This issue is compounded by the realist assessment that without such relative autonomy, states would be free to use law in whatever way they wished, and there would be little point in examining the specific role played by law in transition. For a further exploration of this issue, see Campbell and Ní Aoláin (2003: 1210).
5. See *Ireland v United Kingdom* (1978) and *Brannigan and McBride v United Kingdom* (1993).
6. Contrast with *Aksoy v Turkey* (1996) and Greek case (1969). In *Brannigan and McBride v United Kingdom* (1993: paras, 14, 15 and 56), the Court made explicit reference to reviews of the PTA (Prevention of Terrorism Act) by Viscount Colville and others, which were conducted explicitly along the lines of the 'response of the liberal-democratic state' critiqued earlier in the article.
7. 1977 Protocol I covers both conventional wars and conflicts generally known as 'wars of national liberation'; 1977 Protocol II covers high-intensity civil wars. See Campbell, Ní Aoláin and Harvey (2003: 338).
8. Common Article 3 to the Four Geneva Conventions (1948). See Human Rights Watch (1991).
9. Combined Loyalist Military Command (CLMC) *Ceasefire Statement* (13 October 1994) and Irish Republican Army (IRA) *Statement of Apology* (16 July 2002).
10. See Northern Ireland Office/Department of Foreign Affairs (2001: paras 18–19).
11. See the UN Declaration on the Rights of Persons Belonging to National or Ethnic, Religious, and Linguistic Minorities, 1992, the Framework Convention for the Protection of National Minorities, 1995 and also the Lund Recommendations on the Effective Participation of National Minorities in Public Life, available at www.osce.org/hcnm/documents/lund.htm.
12. Ibid.

CASES CITED

Aksoy v Turkey (1996) Eur. Ct. H. R iv
Brannigan and McBride v United Kingdom (1993), 258 Eur. Ct. H. R. (ser. A) at 49
Greek Case (1969) Y. B. Eur. Conv. on H. R. 2 (Eur. Comm'n on H. R)
Ireland v United Kingdom (1978), 25 Eur. Ct. H. R. (ser. A) at 79
Murray v UK (1996), 22 Eur. Ct. H. R at. 29

STATUTES CITED

British and Irish Governments (2003) *British-Irish Agreement Amendment Act (1999)*, Statutory Instrument No. 378
Dayton Peace Agreement, 14 December 1995. UN Doc. S/1995/999 (1995), 35 I.L.M. 75 (1996)
Macedonian Framework Document, 13 August 2001
Northern Ireland (Sentences) Act 1998
The General Framework Agreement for Peace in Bosnia and Herzegovina, 14 December 1995

REFERENCES

Anonymous (1996) 'Human Rights in Peace Negotiations', *Human Rights Quarterly* 18: 249–58.

Akhavan, Payam (1998) 'Justice in The Hague, Peace in the Former Yugoslavia? A Commentary on the United Nations War Crime Tribunal', *Human Rights Quarterly* 20: 737–816.

Askin, Kelly-Dawn (1997) *War Crimes Against Women: Prosecution in International War Crimes Tribunals*. Dordrecht: Martinus Nijhoff.

Baker, Pauline H. (1996) 'Conflict Resolution versus Democratic Governance: Divergent Paths to Peace?', pp. 563–72 in Chester A. Crocker and Fen Osler Hampson with Pamela Aall (eds) *Managing Global Chaos: Sources of and Responses to International Conflict*. Washington, DC: United States Institute of Peace Press.

Baker, Pauline H. (2001) 'Conflict Resolution versus Democratic Governance: Divergent Paths to Peace?', pp. 753–64 in Chester A. Crocker, Fen Osler Hampson and Pamela Aall (eds) *Turbulent Peace: The Challenges of Managing International Conflict*. Washington, DC: United States Institute of Peace Press.

Bell, Christine (1999) 'Minority Rights and Conflict Resolution in Northern Ireland', pp. 305–23 in P. Cumper and S. Wheatley (eds) *Minority Rights in the 'New' Europe*. Dordrecht: Kluwer Law International.

Bell, Christine (2000) *Peace Agreements and Human Rights*. Oxford: Oxford University Press.

Bell, Christine (2003) 'Dealing with the Past in Northern Ireland', *Fordham International Law Journal* 26: 1095–147.

Bell, Christine (2004a) 'Peace Agreements and Human Rights: Implications for the United Nations', in N. White and D. Klaasen (eds) *The UN, Human Rights and Post-Conflict Situations*. Manchester: Manchester University Press.

Bell, Christine (2004b) 'Women and the Problems of Peace Agreements: Strategies for

Change', in R. Coomeraswamy (ed.) *Women, Peace-making and Constitutions*. New Delhi: Women Unlimited.

Bell, Christine (2004c) 'Negotiating Justice: Conflict Resolution and Human Rights', in J. Helsing and J. Mertus (eds) *Human Rights and Conflict*. Washington, DC: United States Institute of Peace.

Bell, Christine and Kathleen Cavanaugh (1999) 'Constructive Ambiguity or Internal Self-determination? Self-determination, Group Accommodation and the Belfast Agreement', *Fordham International Law Journal* 22: 1345–71.

Berman, Nathanial (1998) 'The International Law of Nationalism: Group Identity and Legal History', pp. 25–57 in D. Wippman (ed.) *International Law and Ethnic Conflict*. Ithaca, NY: Cornell University Press.

Bloomfield, Kenneth (1998) *'We Will Remember Them': Report of the Northern Ireland Victims Commissioner Sir Kenneth Bloomfield KCB*. Belfast: The Stationery Office Northern Ireland.

Boutros-Ghali, Boutros (1992) *An Agenda for Peace: Preventative Diplomacy, Peace-making and Peace-keeping, Report of the Secretary-General Pursuant to the Statement Adopted by the Summit Meeting of the Security Council on 31 January 1992*. New York: United Nations.

Boutros-Ghali, Boutros (1995) *Supplement to an Agenda for Peace, Position Paper of the Secretary-General on the Occasion of the Fiftieth Anniversary of the United Nations*. New York: United Nations.

Boyle, Kevin, Tom Hadden and Paddy Hillyard (1975) *Law and State: The Case of Northern Ireland*. London: Martin Robertson.

Brahimi, Lakhadar et al. (2000) *Report of the Panel on UN Peace Operations*. UN Doc. A/55.305 – S/2000/809.

Campbell, Colm (1994) *Emergency Law in Ireland 1918–1925*. Oxford: Oxford University Press.

Campbell, Colm (2000) 'Peace and the Law of War: The Role of International Humanitarian Law in the Post-Conflict Environment', *International Review of the Red Cross* 839: 627–52.

Campbell, Colm and Ita Connolly (2003) 'A Model for the "War Against Terrorism"?: Military Intervention and the 1970 Falls Curfew', *Journal of Law and Society* 30: 341–75.

Campbell, Colm and Fionnuala Ní Aoláin (2003) 'Local Meets Global: Transitional Justice in Northern Ireland', *Fordham International Law Journal* 24: 1201–23.

Campbell, Colm, Fionnuala Ní Aoláin and Colin Harvey (2003) 'The Frontiers of Legal Analysis: Reframing the Transition in Northern Ireland', *Modern Law Review* 66: 317–45.

Cassesse, Antonio (1986) *International Law in a Divided World*. Oxford: Oxford University Press.

Chinkin, Christine and Kate Paradine (2001) 'Vision and Reality: Democracy and Citizenship in the Dayton Peace Accords', *Yale Journal of International Law* 26: 103–78.

Cockburn, Cynthia (1999) *The Space Between Us: Negotiating Gender and National Identities in Conflict*. London: Zed Books.

Cohen, Stanley (1995) 'State Crimes of Previous Regimes: Knowledge, Accountability and the Policing of the Past', *Law and Social Enquiry* 20: 7–50.

Crawford, James (1993) 'Democracy and International Law', *British Yearbook of International Law* 64: 113–33.

Department of Health and Social Services (DHSS) (1998) *Living with the Trauma of the Troubles*. Belfast: The Stationery Office.

Ehard, Hans (1949) 'The Nuremberg Trials Against the Major War Criminals and International Law', *American Journal of International Law* 43: 223–45.

Eide, Asbjørn (1996) *A Review and Analysis of Constructive Approaches to Group Accommodation and Minority Protection in Divided or Multicultural Societies.* Dublin: Forum for Peace and Reconciliation.

Goldstein, Joshua S. (2001) *War and Gender*. Cambridge: Cambridge University Press.

Gormally, Brian and Kieran McEvoy (1995) *The Release of Politically Motivated Offenders in Northern Ireland: A Comparative Study of South Africa, Israel/Palestine, Italy, Spain, the Republic of Ireland and Northern Ireland.* Belfast: Northern Ireland Association for the Care and Resettlement of Offenders.

Hamber, Brandon (2003) ' Rights and Reasons: Challenges for Truth Recovery in South Africa and Northern Ireland', *Fordham International Law Journal* 26: 1074–94.

Harvey, Colin (2001) *Human Rights, Equality and Democratic Renewal in Northern Ireland*. Oxford: Hart Publishing.

Hayner, Priscilla (2001) *Unspeakable Truths*. London: Routledge.

Healing Through Remembering (2002) *The Report of the Healing Through Remembering Project*. Belfast: Healing Through Remembering Project.

Hegarty, Angela (2003) 'The Government of Memory: Public Inquiries and the Limits of Justice in Northern Ireland', *Fordham International Law Journal* 26: 1148–92.

Human Rights Watch (1991) *Human Rights in Northern Ireland*. New York: Human Rights Watch.

Huyse, Luc (1995) 'Justice after Transition: On the Choices Successor Elites Make in Dealing with the Past', *Law and Social Inquiry* 20: 51–78.

Independent Commission on Policing for Northern Ireland (1999) *A New Beginning for Policing in Northern Ireland*. Belfast: Independent Commission on Policing.

McCrudden, Christopher (1999) 'Mainstreaming Equality in the Governance of Northern Ireland', *Fordham International Law Journal* 22: 1696–775.

McCrudden, Christopher (2001) 'Not the Way Forward: Some Comments on the Northern Ireland Human Rights Commission's Consultation Document' *Northern Ireland Legal Quarterly* 52: 372–84.

McEvoy, Kieran (2001) *Paramilitary Imprisonment in Northern Ireland: Resistance, Management and Release*. Oxford: Oxford University Press.

McEvoy, Kieran and Brian Gormally (1997) 'Seeing is Believing: Positivist Terrorology, Peacemaking Criminology and the Northern Ireland Peace Process', *Critical Criminology* 8: 9–30.

McGarry, John and Brendan O'Leary (1995) *Explaining Northern Ireland: Broken Images*. Oxford: Blackwell.

National Council for Civil Liberties (1936) *The Special Powers Act of Northern Ireland: Report of a Commission of Enquiry Appointed to Examine the Purpose and Effect of Civil Authorities (Special Powers) Acts (Northern Ireland 1922 and 1933)*. London: NCCL.

Ní Aoláin, Fionnuala (1999) 'The Fractured Soul of the Dayton Peace Agreement: A Legal Analysis', *Michigan Journal of International Law* 19: 957–1004.

Ní Aoláin, Fionnuala (2000a) 'Sex-based Violence and the Holocaust – A Reevaluation of Harms and Rights in International Law', *Yale Journal of Law and Feminism* 12: 43–84.

Ní Aoláin, Fionnuala (2000b) *The Politics of Force: Conflict Management and State Violence in Northern Ireland*. Belfast: Blackstaff Press.

Northern Ireland Human Rights Commission (2001) *Making a Bill of Rights for Northern Ireland: A Consultation by the Northern Ireland Human Rights Commission*. Belfast: Northern Ireland Human Rights Commission.

Northern Ireland Office/Department of Foreign Affairs (2001) *Weston Park Document – Proposals for the Implementation of the Good Friday Agreement*.

O'Leary, Brendan (1999) 'The Nature of the Agreement', *Fordham International Law Journal* 22: 1628–67.

O'Rawe, Mary (2003) 'Transitional Policing Arrangements in Northern Ireland: The Can't and the Won't of the Change Dialectic', *Fordham International Law Journal* 26: 1015–73.

Orentlicher, Diane F. (1991) 'Settling Accounts: The Duty to Prosecute Human Rights Violations of a Prior Regime', *Yale Law Journal* 100: 2537–615.

Report of the Commission to Consider Legal Procedures to Deal with Terrorist Activities in Northern Ireland (Diplock Report) (1972). London: HMSO.

Report of a Committee to Consider, in the Context of Civil Liberties and Human Rights, Measures to Deal with Terrorism in Northern Ireland (Gardiner Report) (1975). London: HMSO.

Roht-Arriaza, Naomi (ed.) (1995) *Impunity and Human Rights in International Law and Practice*. New York: Oxford University Press.

Rolston, Bill (2002) 'Assembling the Jigsaw: Truth, Justice and Transition in the North of Ireland', *Race and Class* 44: 87–106.

Slaughter, Anne-Marie (1998) 'Pushing the Limits of Liberal Peace: Ethnic Conflict and the "Ideal Polity"', pp. 128–44 in D. Wippman (ed.) *International Law and Ethnic Conflict*. Ithaca, NY: Cornell University Press.

Stevens, John (2003) *Stevens 3 Enquiry: Overview and Recommendations*. Available at: http://news.bbc.co.uk/nol/shared/spl/hi/northern-ireland/03/stephens_inquiry/html/default.stm

Teitel, Ruti (2000) *Transitional Justice*. New York: Oxford University Press.

Teitel, Ruti (2003) 'Transitional Justice in a New Era', *Fordham International Law Journal* 26: 893–906.

Thornberry, Patrick (1993) 'The Democratic or Internal Aspect of Self-determination with Some Remarks on Federalism', pp. 101–38 in C. Tomuschat (ed.) *Modern Law of Self-determination*. Dordrecht: Martin Nijhoff.

Tully, James (1995) *Strange Multiplicity: Constitutionalism in an Age of Diversity*. Cambridge: Cambridge University Press.

UN SC Resolution (2000) 1325 of 31 October.

Wilson, John (1999) *A Place and a Name: Report of the Victims Commission*. Dublin: Stationery Office.

Wippman, David (1998) 'Practical and Legal Constraints on Internal Power Sharing', pp. 211–41 in D. Wippman (ed.) *International Law and Ethnic Conflict*. Ithaca, NY: Cornell University Press.

Yuval-Davis, Nina (1997) *Gender and Nation*. London: Sage.

World Conference on Women (1995) UN Doc. A/CONF. 177/20.

4

The rule of law and transitional justice in conflict and post-conflict societies

Report of the Secretary-General

Summary

Recent years have seen an increased focus by the United Nations on questions of transitional justice and the rule of law in conflict and post-conflict societies, yielding important lessons for our future activities. Success will depend on a number of critical factors, among them the need to ensure a common basis in international norms and standards and to mobilize the necessary resources for a sustainable investment in justice. We must learn as well to eschew one-size-fits-all formulas and the importation of foreign models, and, instead, base our support on national assessments, national participation and national needs and aspirations. Effective strategies will seek to support both technical capacity for reform and political will for reform. The United Nations must therefore support domestic reform constituencies, help build the capacity of national justice sector institutions, facilitate national consultations on justice reform and transitional justice and help fill the rule of law vacuum evident in so many post-conflict societies.

Justice, peace and democracy are not mutually exclusive objectives, but rather mutually reinforcing imperatives. Advancing all three in fragile post-conflict settings requires strategic planning, careful integration and sensible sequencing of activities. Approaches focusing only on one or another institution, or ignoring civil society or victims, will not be effective. Our approach to the justice sector must be comprehensive in its attention to all of its interdependent institutions, sensitive to the needs of key groups and mindful of the need for complementarity between transitional justice mechanisms. Our main role is not to build international substitutes for national structures, but to help build domestic justice capacities.

In some cases, international or mixed tribunals have been established to address past crimes in war-torn societies. These tribunals have helped bring justice and hope to victims, combat the impunity of perpetrators and enrich the jurisprudence of international criminal law. They have, however, been expensive and have contributed little to sustainable national capacities for justice administration. The International Criminal Court offers new hope for a permanent reduction in the phenomenon of impunity and the further ratification of its statute is thus to be encouraged.

But while tribunals are important, our experience with truth commissions also shows them to be a potentially valuable complementary tool in the quest for justice and reconciliation, taking as they do a victim-centred approach and helping to establish a historical record and recommend remedial action. Similarly, our support for vetting processes has shown them to be a vital element of transitional justice and, where they respect the rights of both victims and the accused, key to restoring public trust in national institutions of governance. Victims also benefit from well-conceived reparations programmes, which themselves help ensure that justice focuses not only on perpetrators, but also on those who have suffered at their hands. Strengthening United Nations support in all these areas will require efforts to enhance coordination among all actors, develop our expert rosters and technical tools and more systematically record, analyse and apply these lessons in Security Council mandates, peace processes and the operations of United Nations peace missions.

* Reissued for technical reasons.

I. Introduction

1. On 24 September 2003, the Security Council met at the ministerial level to discuss the United Nations role in establishing justice and the rule of law in post-conflict societies.[1] In an open meeting on 30 September 2003, Member States were invited to contribute to this process.[2] In a statement issued at the conclusion of the 24 September meeting,[3] the President, on behalf of the Security Council, noted the wealth of relevant expertise and experience within the United Nations system and highlighted the need to harness and direct this expertise and experience so that the lessons and experience of the past could be learned and built upon. The Council welcomed my offer to provide a report that could inform the Security Council's further consideration of these matters. At its 26 January 2004 meeting on "Post-conflict national reconciliation: the role of the United Nations", the Security Council invited me to give, in the present report, consideration to the views expressed in that debate.[4] The present report is submitted in compliance with those requests.

II. Strengthening the rule of law and transitional justice in the wake of conflict

2. The objective of the present report is to highlight key issues and lessons learned from the Organization's experiences in the promotion of justice and the rule of law in conflict and post-conflict societies.[5] Our experience in the past decade has demonstrated clearly that the consolidation of peace in the immediate post-conflict period, as well as the maintenance of peace in the long term, cannot be achieved unless the population is confident that redress for grievances can be obtained through legitimate structures for the peaceful settlement of disputes and the fair administration of justice. At the same time, the heightened vulnerability of minorities, women, children, prisoners and detainees, displaced persons, refugees and others, which is evident in all conflict and post-conflict situations, brings an element of urgency to the imperative of restoration of the rule of law.

3. And yet, helping war-torn societies re-establish the rule of law and come to terms with large-scale past abuses, all within a context marked by devastated institutions, exhausted resources, diminished security and a traumatized and divided population, is a daunting, often overwhelming, task. It requires attention to myriad deficits, among which are a lack of political will for reform, a lack of institutional independence within the justice sector, a lack of domestic technical capacity, a lack of material and financial resources, a lack of public confidence in Government, a lack of official respect for human rights and, more generally, a lack of peace and security. Over the years, the United Nations has accumulated significant expertise in addressing each of these key deficits. Departments, agencies, programmes and funds and specialists across the system have been deployed to numerous transitional, war-torn and post-conflict countries to assist in the complex but vital work of rule of law reform and development.

4. Of course, in matters of justice and the rule of law, an ounce of prevention is worth significantly more than a pound of cure. While United Nations efforts have been tailored so that they are palpable to the population to meet the immediacy of their security needs and to address the grave injustices of war, the root causes of conflict have often been left unaddressed. Yet, it is in addressing the causes of

conflict, through legitimate and just ways, that the international community can help prevent a return to conflict in the future. Peace and stability can only prevail if the population perceives that politically charged issues, such as ethnic discrimination, unequal distribution of wealth and social services, abuse of power, denial of the right to property or citizenship and territorial disputes between States, can be addressed in a legitimate and fair manner. Viewed this way, prevention is the first imperative of justice.

III. Articulating a common language of justice for the United Nations

5. Concepts such as "justice", "the rule of law" and "transitional justice" are essential to understanding the international community's efforts to enhance human rights, protect persons from fear and want, address property disputes, encourage economic development, promote accountable governance and peacefully resolve conflict. They serve both to define our goals and to determine our methods. Yet, there is a multiplicity of definitions and understandings of such concepts, even among our closest partners in the field. At an operational level, there is, for some, a fair amount of overlap with other related concepts, such as security sector reform, judicial sector reform and governance reform. To work together effectively in this field, a common understanding of key concepts is essential.

6. The "rule of law" is a concept at the very heart of the Organization's mission. It refers to a principle of governance in which all persons, institutions and entities, public and private, including the State itself, are accountable to laws that are publicly promulgated, equally enforced and independently adjudicated, and which are consistent with international human rights norms and standards. It requires, as well, measures to ensure adherence to the principles of supremacy of law, equality before the law, accountability to the law, fairness in the application of the law, separation of powers, participation in decision-making, legal certainty, avoidance of arbitrariness and procedural and legal transparency.

7. For the United Nations, "justice" is an ideal of accountability and fairness in the protection and vindication of rights and the prevention and punishment of wrongs. Justice implies regard for the rights of the accused, for the interests of victims and for the well-being of society at large. It is a concept rooted in all national cultures and traditions and, while its administration usually implies formal judicial mechanisms, traditional dispute resolution mechanisms are equally relevant. The international community has worked to articulate collectively the substantive and procedural requirements for the administration of justice for more than half a century.

8. The notion of "transitional justice" discussed in the present report comprises the full range of processes and mechanisms associated with a society's attempts to come to terms with a legacy of large-scale past abuses, in order to ensure accountability, serve justice and achieve reconciliation. These may include both judicial and non-judicial mechanisms, with differing levels of international involvement (or none at all) and individual prosecutions, reparations, truth-seeking, institutional reform, vetting and dismissals, or a combination thereof.

IV. Basing assistance on international norms and standards

9. The normative foundation for our work in advancing the rule of law is the Charter of the United Nations itself, together with the four pillars of the modern international legal system: international human rights law;[6] international humanitarian law; international criminal law; and international refugee law. This includes the wealth of United Nations human rights and criminal justice standards developed in the last half-century.[7] These represent universally applicable standards adopted under the auspices of the United Nations and must therefore serve as the normative basis for all United Nations activities in support of justice and the rule of law.

10. United Nations norms and standards have been developed and adopted by countries across the globe and have been accommodated by the full range of legal systems of Member States, whether based in common law, civil law, Islamic law, or other legal traditions. As such, these norms and standards bring a legitimacy that cannot be said to attach to exported national models which, all too often, reflect more the individual interests or experience of donors and assistance providers than they do the best interests or legal development needs of host countries. These standards also set the normative boundaries of United Nations engagement, such that, for example, United Nations tribunals can never allow for capital punishment, United Nations-endorsed peace agreements can never promise amnesties for genocide, war crimes, crimes against humanity or gross violations of human rights, and, where we are mandated to undertake executive or judicial functions, United Nations-operated facilities must scrupulously comply with international standards for human rights in the administration of justice.

V. Identifying the role of United Nations peace operations

11. Not all peace operations are mandated to address transitional justice and rule of law activities. Transitional administrations in Kosovo (United Nations Interim Administration Mission in Kosovo) and Timor-Leste (United Nations Transitional Administration in East Timor/United Nations Mission of Support in East Timor), however, have had direct responsibility for the administration of judiciaries, police and prison services. Others, including those in El Salvador (United Nations Observer Mission in El Salvador) and Guatemala (United Nations Verification Mission in Guatemala), as well as more recent operations in Côte d'Ivoire (United Nations Mission in Côte d'Ivoire/United Nations Operation in Côte d'Ivoire), Liberia (United Nations Mission in Liberia) and Haiti (United Nations Stabilization Mission in Haiti), have had important rule of law and justice components, illustrating the increased attention given by the United Nations to these questions.

12. At the Headquarters level, support for rule of law and transitional justice aspects of peace operations includes needs assessment, mission planning, selection and deployment of specialized staff and provision of guidance and support to rule of law components of missions. On the ground, our operations have worked, inter alia, to strengthen domestic law enforcement and justice institutions, facilitate national consultations on justice reform, coordinate international rule of law assistance, monitor and report on court proceedings, train national justice sector officials, support local judicial reform bodies and advise host country rule of law institutions. Our operations have helped national actors vet and select national police, judges and

prosecutors, draft new constitutions, revise legislation, inform and educate the public, develop ombudsman institutions and human rights commissions, strengthen associations of criminal defence lawyers, establish legal aid, set up legal-training institutes and build the capacity of civil society to monitor the justice sector. Peace missions have also helped host countries to address past human rights abuses by establishing tribunals, truth and reconciliation mechanisms and victim reparation programmes.

13. This range of activities would be demanding in any circumstances. The challenge is compounded by the fact that the United Nations is frequently called upon to plan the rule of law components of peace operations on extremely short notice, based on short assessment visits to the host country and with minimal human and financial resources. With limited staff devoted to rule of law and transitional justice issues, the United Nations has been stretched to address rule of law planning needs for new missions, while simultaneously providing support to rule of law activities in existing operations. Matching sufficient resources in the headquarters of relevant departments with the growing demands for rule of law support to peace operations is an issue that will require early and considered attention by the Secretariat. I intend to instruct the Executive Committee on Peace and Security to review these questions, with a mind to making proposals to Member States for the strengthening of these resources.

VI. Assessing national needs and capacities

14. In formulating recommendations for the Security Council, planning mission mandates and structures, and conceiving assistance programmes, it is imperative that both the Security Council and the United Nations system carefully consider the particular rule of law and justice needs in each host country. Accordingly, we must assess myriad factors, such as the nature of the underlying conflict, the will of the parties, any history of widespread abuse, the identification of vulnerable groups, such as minorities and displaced persons, the situation and role of women, the situation of children, rule of law implications of peace agreements and the condition and nature of the country's legal system, traditions and institutions.

15. Unfortunately, the international community has not always provided rule of law assistance that is appropriate to the country context. Too often, the emphasis has been on foreign experts, foreign models and foreign-conceived solutions to the detriment of durable improvements and sustainable capacity. Both national and international experts have a vital role to play, to be sure. But we have learned that effective and sustainable approaches begin with a thorough analysis of national needs and capacities, mobilizing to the extent possible expertise resident in the country. Increasingly, the United Nations is looking to nationally led strategies of assessment and consultation carried out with the active and meaningful participation of national stakeholders, including justice sector officials, civil society, professional associations, traditional leaders and key groups, such as women, minorities, displaced persons and refugees. In such cases, national bodies are taking the lead in carrying out diagnostics of the justice sector by mobilizing national legal professionals and are leading national consultations and assessments relating to transitional justice. In these processes, the United Nations can help facilitate meetings, provide legal and technical advice, promote the participation of women and traditionally excluded groups, support capacity-building and help mobilize

financial and material resources, while leaving process leadership and decision-making to the national stakeholders.

16. Similarly, the most successful transitional justice experiences owe a large part of their success to the quantity and quality of public and victim consultation carried out. Local consultation enables a better understanding of the dynamics of past conflict, patterns of discrimination and types of victims. Although the international community has, at times, imposed external transitional justice solutions, a more open and consultative trend is emerging, visible in places such as Sierra Leone and Afghanistan. Although the lessons of past transitional justice efforts help inform the design of future ones, the past can only serve as a guideline. Pre-packaged solutions are ill-advised. Instead, experiences from other places should simply be used as a starting point for local debates and decisions.

VII. Supporting domestic reform constituencies

17. Ultimately, no rule of law reform, justice reconstruction, or transitional justice initiative imposed from the outside can hope to be successful or sustainable. The role of the United Nations and the international community should be solidarity, not substitution. As discussed above, it is essential that these efforts be based upon meaningful public participation involving national legal professionals, Government, women, minorities, affected groups and civil society. Countless pre-designed or imported projects, however meticulously well-reasoned and elegantly packaged, have failed the test of justice sector reform. Without public awareness and education campaigns, and public consultation initiatives, public understanding of and support for national reform efforts will not be secured. Civil society organizations, national legal associations, human rights groups and advocates of victims and the vulnerable must all be given a voice in these processes. Most importantly, our programmes must identify, support and empower domestic reform constituencies. Thus, peace operations must better assist national stakeholders to develop their own reform vision, their own agenda, their own approaches to transitional justice and their own national plans and projects. The most important role we can play is to facilitate the processes through which various stakeholders debate and outline the elements of their country's plan to address the injustices of the past and to secure sustainable justice for the future, in accordance with international standards, domestic legal traditions and national aspirations. In doing so, we must learn better how to respect and support local ownership, local leadership and a local constituency for reform, while at the same time remaining faithful to United Nations norms and standards.

18. Support for reform must be cultivated among all groups in society, including elites, ex-combatants and (non-criminal) elements of former regimes, all of whom must be reassured that they will be protected from unlawful or unfair retribution and offered a real chance at reintegration into their society. Finally, in post-conflict situations and where transitional justice processes are under consideration, a particularly important constituency is the country's victims. The United Nations must assess and respect the interests of victims in the design and operation of transitional justice measures. Victims and the organizations that advocate on their behalf deserve the greatest attention from the international community.

VIII. Recognizing the political context

19. While effective rule of law strategies necessarily focus on legal and institutional requirements, due attention must be paid to political elements as well. Re-establishing justice systems, planning rule of law reforms and agreeing on transitional justice processes are activities of the highest public interest. They are therefore necessary subjects of serious public consultation and debate and, thus, as much political questions as technical ones. Institutions receiving international assistance cannot reasonably be evaluated in terms of their enhanced efficiency alone, without regard to their commitment to human rights or the responsibility of their public discourse. In some cases, State authorities have been more concerned with consolidation of power than with strengthening the rule of law, with the latter often perceived as a threat to the former. As such, my senior representatives in the field must give dedicated attention to supporting the political aspects of justice and rule of law reforms. Their good offices can be crucial to securing political space for reformers, insulating law enforcement from political abuse and mobilizing resources for the strengthening of the justice sector.

20. And yet, the international community has frequently underestimated the extent of political will necessary to support effective rule of law reform in post-conflict States and invested inadequately in public consultations on reform questions. As a result, justice strategies and assistance programmes have sometimes neglected to facilitate consensus among important stakeholders on the nature and pace of reforms and new institutions. Here too the United Nations has a role. Just as we have supported national consultations in the form of elections and referendums, so must we support and facilitate national consultations aimed at determining the national course for transitional justice or rule of law reform.

21. Equally important is the fact that rule of law reforms and transitional justice activities often occur simultaneously with post-conflict elections, as well as with the unfolding of fragile peace processes. Careful sequencing of such processes is vital to their success and legitimacy. Justice and peace are not contradictory forces. Rather, properly pursued, they promote and sustain one another. The question, then, can never be whether to pursue justice and accountability, but rather when and how. This means recognizing that United Nations peace operations, with some notable exceptions, are planned as short-term interventions, while accounting for the past, building the rule of law and fostering democracy are long-term processes. As such, strategic planning should, from the beginning, take account of the need for phasing and for post-mission international support in these areas, including long-term development assistance.

22. A related question is the timing of electoral processes. Recent experience has demonstrated that holding elections without adequate political and security preparation and disengaging too soon can undermine, rather than facilitate, the process of building the rule of law. Yet, the international community still sometimes encourages early elections in post-conflict States in an attempt to lend legitimacy to political leaders, processes and institutions. But premature elections can bring about only cosmetic electoral democracies, at best. In many cases, elections held in non-permissive security conditions exclude the meaningful participation of key groups, while exposing people to undue personal risk. In others, candidates and parties from the old political order, lacking a commitment to democratic principles and human

rights, use premature elections to consolidate their power. At worst, they can radicalize political discourse and even lead to renewed conflict.

IX. Embracing integrated and complementary approaches

23. Our experience confirms that a piecemeal approach to the rule of law and transitional justice will not bring satisfactory results in a war-torn or atrocity-scarred nation. Effective rule of law and justice strategies must be comprehensive, engaging all institutions of the justice sector, both official and non-governmental, in the development and implementation of a single nationally owned and led strategic plan for the sector. Such strategies must include attention to the standards of justice, the laws that codify them, the institutions that implement them, the mechanisms that monitor them and the people that must have access to them.

24. These are hard-learned lessons, drawn from decades of United Nations experience on the ground. For example, international efforts have sometimes focused on re-establishing police services, while paying scant attention to other justice sector components, such as legislative work, crime prevention, judicial development, legal education, prison reform, prosecutorial capacity, victim protection and support, civil society support, citizenship and identification regulation, and property dispute resolution. Yet all of these are essential to the rule of law and all are interdependent. Neglect of one inevitably leads to the weakening of the others.

25. In other cases, the international community has rushed to prescribe a particular formula for transitional justice, emphasizing either criminal prosecutions or truth-telling, without first affording victims and national constituencies the opportunity to consider and decide on the proper balance. The international community must see transitional justice in a way that extends well beyond courts and tribunals. The challenges of post-conflict environments necessitate an approach that balances a variety of goals, including the pursuit of accountability, truth and reparation, the preservation of peace and the building of democracy and the rule of law. A comprehensive strategy should also pay special attention to abuses committed against groups most affected by conflict, such as minorities, the elderly, children, women, prisoners, displaced persons and refugees, and establish particular measures for their protection and redress in judicial and reconciliation processes. For example, protection measures for children can include provisions for hearings in camera, pre-recorded testimonies, videoconferencing and the use of pseudonyms to protect the identity of child witnesses.

26. Where transitional justice is required, strategies must be holistic, incorporating integrated attention to individual prosecutions, reparations, truth-seeking, institutional reform, vetting and dismissals, or an appropriately conceived combination thereof. The United Nations must consider through advance planning and consultation how different transitional justice mechanisms will interact to ensure that they do not conflict with one another. It is now generally recognized, for example, that truth commissions can positively complement criminal tribunals, as the examples of Argentina, Peru, Timor-Leste and Sierra Leone suggest. And in Timor-Leste, the Serious Crimes Unit worked in close conjunction with the Reception, Truth and Reconciliation Commission, as provided for in Regulation

No. 2001/10 of the United Nations Transitional Administration in East Timor, which established the Commission's terms of reference.

X. Filling a rule of law vacuum

27. In post-conflict settings, legislative frameworks often show the accumulated signs of neglect and political distortion, contain discriminatory elements and rarely reflect the requirements of international human rights and criminal law standards. Emergency laws and executive decrees are often the order of the day. Where adequate laws are on the books, they may be unknown to the general public and official actors may have neither the capacity nor the tools to implement them. National judicial, police and corrections systems have typically been stripped of the human, financial and material resources necessary for their proper functioning. They also often lack legitimacy, having been transformed by conflict and abuse into instruments of repression. Such situations are invariably marked by an abundance of arms, rampant gender and sexually based violence, the exploitation of children, the persecution of minorities and vulnerable groups, organized crime, smuggling, trafficking in human beings and other criminal activities. In such situations, organized criminal groups are often better resourced than local government and better armed than local law enforcement. Restoring the capacity and legitimacy of national institutions is a long-term undertaking. However, urgent action to restore human security, human rights and the rule of law cannot be deferred. Thus, United Nations peace operations are often called upon to help fill this rule of law vacuum.

28. Indeed, in some cases, we have faced the difficulties of conducting peace operations where there are no functioning criminal justice mechanisms at all. In such situations, peacekeepers have encountered wrongdoers in the midst of committing serious criminal acts of a direct threat to civilians and to the operation itself. Military components typically lack the training, skills and resources to address such situations. At the same time, civilian components of peace operations, including police, are often too slowly deployed and are seldom mandated to undertake executive functions, such as arrest. Yet such lawlessness can seriously undermine the efforts of an entire peace operation. Given these realities, we must, together with Member Sates, rethink our current strategies for addressing the rule of law vacuum into which we are often deployed, including the role, capacities and obligations of military and civilian police components.

29. In some situations, where this problem has been most acute, civilian police in peace missions have been mandated to undertake executive functions, including powers of arrest and detention. While, in most cases, United Nations civilian police provide operational support and advice and are not empowered to carry out executive functions, their responsibilities have grown ever more complex. In every case, their role is central to the restoration of the rule of law and worthy of better support and more resources. The simple presence of law enforcement officials on the streets after a conflict can substantially reduce looting, harassment, rape, robbery and murder. After some 20 years of United Nations experience, this is an area that would benefit from a serious review, in order that we might consider ways to bolster our efforts.

30. But, as discussed above, while policing interventions in post-conflict environments are a crucial component of the rule of law continuum, they must be

linked to parallel support to the other institutions and functions of the justice system. Enhancing the capacity of police (or United Nations Civilian Police) to make arrests cannot be seen as a contribution to the rule of law if there are no modern laws to be applied, no humane and properly resourced and supervised detention facilities in which to hold those arrested, no functioning judiciary to try them lawfully and expeditiously, and no defence lawyers to represent them. Progress has been made in recent years to address such lacunae, including a number of dedicated projects to develop transitional codes, guidelines and rule of law policy tools, as recommended in the report of the Panel on United Nations Peace Operations.[8] In the coming months, many of these new tools will be finalized.

31. The establishment of independent national human rights commissions is one complementary strategy that has shown promise for helping to restore the rule of law, peaceful dispute resolution and protection of vulnerable groups where the justice system is not yet fully functioning. Many have been established in conflict and post-conflict societies with mandates including quasi-judicial functions, conflict-resolution and protection programmes. Recent examples include the national human rights institutions of Afghanistan, Rwanda, Colombia, Indonesia, Nepal, Sri Lanka and Uganda, each of which is now playing an important role in this regard. Exceptional fact-finding mechanisms have also been mobilized by the United Nations with increasing frequency, such as the ad hoc international commissions of inquiry established to look into war crimes committed in places such as the former Yugoslavia, Rwanda, Burundi and Timor-Leste.

32. Additionally, strategies for expediting a return to the rule of law must be integrated with plans to reintegrate both displaced civilians and former fighters. Disarmament, demobilization and reintegration processes are one of the keys to a transition out of conflict and back to normalcy. For populations traumatized by war, those processes are among the most visible signs of the gradual return of peace and security. Similarly, displaced persons must be the subject of dedicated programmes to facilitate return. Carefully crafted amnesties can help in the return and reintegration of both groups and should be encouraged, although, as noted above, these can never be permitted to excuse genocide, war crimes, crimes against humanity or gross violations of human rights.

33. Finally, better safeguards must be established to ensure that the very interventions designed to protect vulnerable and victimized groups, including women and children, do not result in their further victimization. In such situations, women often suffer from domestic violence in the home and targeted violence in the public sphere. Addressing the all too common sexual abuse, exploitation and traumatization of these groups in conflict and post-conflict settings requires special skills, resources and mechanisms to ensure that law enforcement personnel, peacekeepers and others who interact with them do not unintentionally contribute to or exacerbate their suffering. And it is critically important that those who seek to abuse or exploit them are held accountable. Indeed, if the rule of law means anything at all, it means that no one, including peacekeepers, is above the law. For this reason, I have issued a bulletin on special measures for protection from sexual exploitation and sexual abuse (ST/SGB/2003/13), setting out minimum standards of behaviour expected of all United Nations personnel, as well as measures necessary to prevent sexual exploitation and abuse.

XI. Developing national justice systems

34. While the international community is obliged to act directly for the protection of human rights and human security where conflict has eroded or frustrated the domestic rule of law, in the long term, no ad hoc, temporary or external measures can ever replace a functioning national justice system. Thus, for decades, a number of United Nations entities have been engaged in helping countries to strengthen national systems for the administration of justice in accordance with international standards.

35. Effective strategies for building domestic justice systems will give due attention to laws, processes (both formal and informal) and institutions (both official and non-official). Legislation that is in conformity with international human rights law and that responds to the country's current needs and realities is fundamental. At the institutional core of systems based on the rule of law is a strong judiciary, which is independent and adequately empowered, financed, equipped and trained to uphold human rights in the administration of justice. Equally important are the other institutions of the justice sector, including lawful police services, humane prison services, fair prosecutions and capable associations of criminal defence lawyers (oft-forgotten but vital institutions). Beyond the criminal law realm, such strategies must also ensure effective legal mechanisms for redressing civil claims and disputes, including property disputes, administrative law challenges, nationality and citizenship claims and other key legal issues arising in post-conflict settings. Juvenile justice systems must be put in place to ensure that children in conflict with the law are treated appropriately and in line with recognized international standards for juvenile justice. Justice sector institutions must be gender sensitive and women must be included and empowered by the reform of the sector. Legal education and training and support for the organization of the legal community, including through bar associations, are important catalysts for sustained legal development.

36. Our programmes must also support access to justice, to overcome common cultural, linguistic, economic, logistical or gender-specific impediments. Legal aid and public representation programmes are essential in this regard. Additionally, while focusing on the building of a formal justice system that functions effectively and in accordance with international standards, it is also crucial to assess means for ensuring the functioning of complementary and less formal mechanisms, particularly in the immediate term. Independent national human rights commissions can play a vital role in affording accountability, redress, dispute resolution and protection during transitional periods. Similarly, due regard must be given to indigenous and informal traditions for administering justice or settling disputes, to help them to continue their often vital role and to do so in conformity with both international standards and local tradition. Where these are ignored or overridden, the result can be the exclusion of large sectors of society from accessible justice. Particularly in post-conflict settings, vulnerable, excluded, victimized and marginalized groups must also be engaged in the development of the sector and benefit from its emerging institutions. Measures to ensure the gender sensitivity of justice sector institutions is vital in such circumstances. With respect to children, it is also important that support be given to nascent institutions of child protection and juvenile justice, including for the development of alternatives to detention, and for the enhancement of the child protection capacities of justice sector institutions.

37. Recent national experience suggests that achieving these complex objectives is best served by the definition of a national process, guided by a national justice plan and shepherded by specially appointed independent national institutions, such as judicial or law commissions. Our support for such processes and bodies can help ensure that development of this sector is adequately resourced, coordinated, consistent with international standards and nationally owned and directed. Where this is complemented with meaningful support for capacity-building within the justice sector, the interventions of our operations have the greatest hope for contributing to sustainable improvements for justice and the rule of law.

XII. Learning lessons from the ad hoc criminal tribunals

38. In the past decade, the United Nations has established or contributed to the establishment of a wide range of special criminal tribunals. In doing so, it has sought to advance a number of objectives, among which are bringing to justice those responsible for serious violations of human rights and humanitarian law, putting an end to such violations and preventing their recurrence, securing justice and dignity for victims, establishing a record of past events, promoting national reconciliation, re-establishing the rule of law and contributing to the restoration of peace. To these ends, a variety of institutional models has emerged. These have included ad hoc international criminal tribunals established by the Security Council as subsidiary organs of the United Nations for the former Yugoslavia (International Criminal Tribunal for the Former Yugoslavia) and Rwanda (International Criminal Tribunal for Rwanda); a mixed tribunal for Sierra Leone, established as a treaty-based court; a mixed tribunal for Cambodia, proposed under a national law specially promulgated in accordance with a treaty; a mixed tribunal (structured as a "court within a court") in the form of a Special Chamber in the State Court of Bosnia and Herzegovina; a Panel with Exclusive Jurisdiction over Serious Criminal Offences in Timor-Leste, established by the United Nations Transitional Administration in East Timor; the use of international judges and prosecutors in the courts of Kosovo, pursuant to regulations of the United Nations Interim Administration Mission in Kosovo; and a Commission for the Investigation of Illegal Groups and Clandestine Security Organizations in Guatemala, to be established by agreement between the United Nations and Guatemala, as an international investigative/prosecutional unit operating under the national law of Guatemala. The details of the agreement are currently under discussion.

39. Criminal trials can play an important role in transitional contexts. They express public denunciation of criminal behaviour. They can provide a direct form of accountability for perpetrators and ensure a measure of justice for victims by giving them the chance to see their former tormentors made to answer for their crimes. Insofar as relevant procedural rules enable them to present their views and concerns at trial, they can also help victims to reclaim their dignity. Criminal trials can also contribute to greater public confidence in the State's ability and willingness to enforce the law. They can also help societies to emerge from periods of conflict by establishing detailed and well-substantiated records of particular incidents and events. They can help to de-legitimize extremist elements, ensure their removal from the national political process and contribute to the restoration of civility and peace and to deterrence. Yet achieving and balancing the various objectives of criminal justice is less straightforward and there are a host of constraints in transitional

contexts that limit the reach of criminal justice, whether related to resources, caseload or the balance of political power.

40. Of course, domestic justice systems should be the first resort in pursuit of accountability. But where domestic authorities are unwilling or unable to prosecute violators at home, the role of the international community becomes crucial. The establishment and operation of the international and hybrid criminal tribunals of the last decade provide a forceful illustration of this point. These tribunals represent historic achievements in establishing accountability for serious violations of international human rights and humanitarian law by civilian and military leaders. They have proved that it is possible to deliver justice and conduct fair trials effectively at the international level, in the wake of the breakdown of national judicial systems. More significantly still, they reflect a growing shift in the international community, away from a tolerance for impunity and amnesty and towards the creation of an international rule of law. Despite their limitations and imperfections, international and hybrid criminal tribunals have changed the character of international justice and enhanced the global character of the rule of law.

41. The first modern international criminal tribunals, the International Criminal Tribunal for the Former Yugoslavia and the International Criminal Tribunal for Rwanda, have played a crucial role in advancing the cause of justice in the former Yugoslavia and in Rwanda. Indeed, in the absence of these tribunals, there would have been a massive justice deficit in the countries they served, as well as in the countries subject to the hybrid tribunals that must be recognized as progeny of the original tribunals. They have also made a global contribution by developing a rich jurisprudence in the area of international criminal law, thereby expanding and reinvigorating this key pillar of the international legal regime. As a result of their deliberations, legal efforts to hold violators to account will now benefit from greater clarity on questions of rape as a war crime and a crime against humanity, the elements of genocide, the definition of torture, the nature of individual criminal responsibility, the doctrine of command responsibility and appropriate sentencing. What is more, they have informed the development of hybrid tribunals elsewhere.

42. Of course, these gains have come with significant costs. The two ad hoc tribunals have grown into large institutions, with more than 2,000 posts between them and a combined annual budget exceeding a quarter of a billion dollars — equivalent to more than 15 per cent of the Organization's total regular budget. Although trying complex legal cases of this nature would be expensive for any legal system and the tribunals' impact and performance cannot be measured in financial numbers alone, the stark differential between cost and number of cases processed does raise important questions. Concerns regarding costs and efficiency have also emerged in cases being tried before the hybrid Tribunals. In addressing these cost-related issues, high priority should be given to consideration of the need to provide for an effective system for delivery of justice.

43. Partly in reaction to the high costs of the original tribunals, the financial mechanisms of the mixed tribunals for Sierra Leone and for Cambodia have been based entirely on voluntary contributions. While for the Extraordinary Chambers the viability of this mechanism is yet to be tested, in the case of the Special Court for Sierra Leone, my doubts about the sustainability and security of the court's operations being financed through voluntary contributions have been borne out. Less

than two years into its operation, and at the very moment when trials were about to begin, the Court has confronted a serious financial crisis.[9] As such, any future financial mechanism must provide the assured and continuous source of funding that is needed to appoint officials and staff, contract services, purchase equipment and support investigations, prosecutions and trials and do so expeditiously. Resort, therefore, to assessed contributions remains necessary in these cases. The operation of judicial bodies cannot be left entirely to the vagaries of voluntary financing.

44. The location of the Yugoslavia and Rwanda tribunals outside the countries where the crimes were committed has allowed them to benefit from more adequate operational facilities and has helped protect their security and independence. However, if security and independence are adequately maintained, there are a number of important benefits to locating tribunals inside the countries concerned, including easier interaction with the local population, closer proximity to the evidence and witnesses and being more accessible to victims. Such accessibility allows victims and their families to witness the processes in which their former tormentors are brought to account. National location also enhances the national capacity-building contribution of the ad hoc tribunals, allowing them to bequeath their physical infrastructure (including buildings, equipment and furniture) to national justice systems, and to build the skills of national justice personnel. In the nationally located tribunals, international personnel work side by side with their national counterparts and on-the-job training can be provided to national lawyers, officials and staff. Such benefits, where combined with specially tailored measures for keeping the public informed and effective techniques for capacity-building, can help ensure a lasting legacy in the countries concerned.

45. Lessons have been learned about the timeliness of trials, as well. Many suspects before the two ad hoc tribunals have had to spend lengthy periods in detention waiting for their trials to start. With regard to the ad hoc international tribunals, many of those trials have taken a very long time to complete, due in part to the complexities of prosecuting international crimes. The rules of procedure of the two ad hoc international tribunals have undergone revisions aimed at reducing delays. It was the recommendation of my Expert Group, when it reviewed the two ad hoc tribunals in 1999, that measures be taken to reduce the length of trials and expedite their completion, and that judges should take an active role and exercise a substantial degree of control over proceedings. It is highly desirable, then, that those nominated, elected or appointed to serve as judges in international and hybrid tribunals possess extensive criminal trial experience, preferably as a judge. To facilitate this, States should put in place career structures that make it easier to release serving members of their national judiciaries for service in international courts or tribunals and that give full credit for periods of service with such institutions. Moreover, adjudicating in international criminal proceedings is an arduous and stressful task, as the high number of casual vacancies that have arisen at the two ad hoc tribunals shows. It is accordingly essential that only those who are in good health be nominated, elected or appointed to serve as judges in international or hybrid tribunals. Consideration might also usefully be given in this connection to imposing an age limit on judicial service, as is done in many national jurisdictions.

46. In the end, in post-conflict countries, the vast majority of perpetrators of serious violations of human rights and international humanitarian law will never be tried, whether internationally or domestically. As such, prosecutorial policy must be strategic, based on clear criteria, and take account of the social context. Public

expectations must be informed through an effective communications strategy. Programmes must be in place to protect and support victims of gender and sexually based violence and to protect witnesses. And it is essential that, from the moment any future international or hybrid tribunal is established, consideration be given, as a priority, to the ultimate exit strategy and intended legacy in the country concerned.

47. Moreover, other transitional justice mechanisms, such as those discussed elsewhere in the present report, may need to be put in place in order to overcome the inherent limitations of criminal justice processes — to do the things that courts do not do or do not do well — in particular to help satisfy the natural need of victims' relatives to trace their loved ones and clarify their fate; to ensure that victims and their relatives are able to obtain redress for the harm they have suffered; to meet the need for a full, comprehensive historical record of what happened during the period of conflict and why; to promote national reconciliation and encourage the emergence of moderate forces; and to ensure the removal from the justice and security sectors of those who may have connived in the violation of human rights or aided and abetted repression.

48. Finally, efforts to hold violators to legal account for past abuses have not been limited to the courts of countries in which violations take place or international tribunals alone. Recent years have seen an unprecedented number of cases brought in the national courts of third-party States, under the universality principle, a previously little used element of international law that holds that some crimes are so grave that all countries have an interest in prosecuting them. Such universal jurisdiction has been invoked in cases relating to past abuses committed in all regions, with varying levels of success. To be sure, this exceptional form of jurisdiction is rightly reserved for the prosecution of only the most serious crimes and only in cases where the justice system of the country that was home to the violations is unable or unwilling to do so. What is more, its use raises complex legal, political and diplomatic questions. Nevertheless, it is a principle rooted in international law and codified in United Nations instruments and stands as a potentially important reserve tool in the international community's struggle against impunity. As such, the last decade's experiments with universal jurisdiction are worthy of careful review and consideration, in order that we might find ways to strengthen and preserve this important principle of justice and accountability.

XIII. Supporting the role of the International Criminal Court

49. Undoubtedly, the most significant recent development in the international community's long struggle to advance the cause of justice and rule of law was the establishment of the International Criminal Court. The Rome Statute entered into force only on 1 July 2002, yet the Court is already having an important impact by putting would-be violators on notice that impunity is not assured and serving as a catalyst for enacting national laws against the gravest international crimes. Already, some 94 countries have ratified the Rome Statute. It is now crucial that the international community ensures that this nascent institution has the resources, capacities, information and support it needs to investigate, prosecute and bring to trial those who bear the greatest responsibility for war crimes, crimes against humanity and genocide, in situations where national authorities are unable or unwilling to do so. The Security Council has a particular role to play in this regard, empowered as it is to refer situations to the International Criminal Court, even in

cases where the countries concerned are not States parties to the Statute of the Court. At the same time, I remain convinced that all States Members of the United Nations that have not yet done so should move towards the ratification of the Rome Statute at the earliest possible opportunity.

XIV. Facilitating truth telling

50. Another important mechanism for addressing past human rights abuses is the truth commission. Truth commissions are official, temporary, non-judicial fact-finding bodies that investigate a pattern of abuses of human rights or humanitarian law committed over a number of years. These bodies take a victim-centred approach and conclude their work with a final report of findings of fact and recommendations. More than 30 such truth commissions have already been established, including those of Argentina, Chile, South Africa, Peru, Ghana, Morocco, El Salvador, Guatemala, Timor-Leste and Sierra Leone. The Commissions of El Salvador, Guatemala, Timor-Leste and Sierra Leone have seen significant United Nations involvement and support and United Nations missions in Liberia and the Democratic Republic of the Congo are now engaged in supporting consultative processes for truth commissions in those countries. Truth commissions have the potential to be of great benefit in helping post-conflict societies establish the facts about past human rights violations, foster accountability, preserve evidence, identify perpetrators and recommend reparations and institutional reforms. They can also provide a public platform for victims to address the nation directly with their personal stories and can facilitate public debate about how to come to terms with the past.

51. Factors that can limit these potential benefits include a weak civil society, political instability, victim and witness fears about testifying, a weak or corrupt justice system, insufficient time to carry out investigations, lack of public support and inadequate funding. Truth commissions are invariably compromised if appointed through a rushed or politicized process. They are best formed through consultative processes that incorporate public views on their mandates and on commissioner selection. To be successful, they must enjoy meaningful independence and have credible commissioner selection criteria and processes. Strong public information and communication strategies are essential to manage public and victim expectations and to advance credibility and transparency. Their gender sensitivity and responsiveness to victims and to victims of discrimination must be assured. Finally, many such commissions will require strong international support to function, as well as respect by international partners for their operational independence.

XV. Vetting the public service

52. Vetting the public service to screen out individuals associated with past abuses is another important component of transitional justice for which the assistance of the United Nations has frequently been sought. Vetting processes help to facilitate a stable rule of law in post-conflict countries. In Bosnia and Herzegovina, Kosovo, Timor-Leste, Liberia and now in Haiti, our operations have been called upon to support vetting processes in various ways. We have helped, variously, to develop professional standards, set up oversight mechanisms and identify objective and

lawful criteria. Vetting usually entails a formal process for the identification and removal of individuals responsible for abuses, especially from police, prison services, the army and the judiciary. Parties under investigation are notified of the allegations against them and given an opportunity to respond before a body administering the vetting process. Those charged are usually entitled to reasonable notice of the case against them, the right to contest the case and the right to appeal an adverse decision to a court or other independent body. The inclusion of such due process elements distinguishes formal vetting processes from the wholesale purges practiced in some countries, involving wide-scale dismissal and disqualification based not on individual records, but rather on party affiliation, political opinion, or association with a prior State institution.

53. We have learned many lessons through our work in these areas. First, whether established as administrative or quasi-judicial bodies, legitimate vetting mechanisms should function in a manner respectful both of the sensitivities of victims and of the human rights of those suspected of abuses. Secondly, civil society should be consulted early and the public must be kept informed. Thirdly, vetting processes should include attention to the technical skills, objective qualifications and integrity of candidates. Fourthly, procedural protections should be afforded to all those subject to vetting processes, whether current employees or new applicants. Finally, where such mechanisms exist and are seen to function fairly, effectively and in accordance with international human rights standards, they can play an important role in enhancing the legitimacy of official structures, restoring the confidence of the public and building the rule of law. They are therefore worthy of international technical and financial support, where required.

XVI. Delivering reparations

54. The United Nations has also been seized of the question of reparations for victims. In the wake of the first Gulf War, the United Nations Compensation Commission processed more than 2.5 million claims, paying out more than $18 billion to victims of Iraq's unlawful invasion and occupation of Kuwait. In the Commission on Human Rights, a process is under way to develop "basic principles and guidelines on the right to a remedy and reparation for victims of international human rights and humanitarian law". And in peace operations across the globe, United Nations personnel are helping States to develop reparations programmes for common post-conflict challenges, such as the loss of property by displaced persons and refugees. Indeed, in the face of widespread human rights violations, States have the obligation to act not only against perpetrators, but also on behalf of victims — including through the provision of reparations. Programmes to provide reparations to victims for harm suffered can be effective and expeditious complements to the contributions of tribunals and truth commissions, by providing concrete remedies, promoting reconciliation and restoring victims' confidence in the State. Reparations sometimes include non-monetary elements, such as the restitution of victims' legal rights, programmes of rehabilitation for victims and symbolic measures, such as official apologies, monuments and commemorative ceremonies. The restoration of property rights, or just compensation where this cannot be done, is another common aspect of reparations in post-conflict countries. Material forms of reparation present perhaps the greatest challenges, especially when administered through mass government programmes. Difficult questions include who is included among the

victims to be compensated, how much compensation is to be rewarded, what kinds of harm are to be covered, how harm is to be quantified, how different kinds of harm are to be compared and compensated and how compensation is to be distributed.

55. No single form of reparation is likely to be satisfactory to victims. Instead, appropriately conceived combinations of reparation measures will usually be required, as a complement to the proceedings of criminal tribunals and truth commissions. Whatever mode of transitional justice is adopted and however reparations programmes are conceived to accompany them, both the demands of justice and the dictates of peace require that something be done to compensate victims. Indeed, the judges of the tribunals for Yugoslavia and Rwanda have themselves recognized this and have suggested that the United Nations consider creating a special mechanism for reparations that would function alongside the tribunals.[10]

XVII. Coordinating our efforts

56. Transitional justice and the rule of law represent broad substantive areas that have been the focus of attention by the United Nations for decades.[11] Outside the United Nations, an even greater number of actors are engaged in this work. In such circumstances, effective coordination is especially important.

57. Thus, in 2002, the United Nations Executive Committee on Peace and Security approved the final report of a system-wide, ad hoc Task Force to consider the Organization's approaches to justice and the rule of law in peace operations.[12] The Task Force identified a significant range and depth of rule of law resources and expertise available within the United Nations system,[13] as well as some gaps.[14] It provided recommendations on how we could best draw upon these resources and the resources of outside entities to better address rule of law issues through our peace operations. The report of the Task Force is a useful catalogue of resources available within the system and is already proving valuable for the coordination of our efforts. As a follow-up, a Rule of Law Focal Point Network has been established at Headquarters, comprised of specialists representing 11 departments and agencies, to facilitate coordination on rule of law issues and to strengthen our support to rule of law aspects of peace operations. Much more remains to be done. We need additional tools and mechanisms to promote gender justice. There is still no common database of the instruments, tools, experiences and best practices accumulated by the system and no web-based means to access them from the field. Developing such capacities will be a focus of our activities for the future. This year, we will issue a number of new rule of law policy tools and will convene technical meetings to collect and analyse relevant experiences, including a technical workshop on transitional justice experiences this fall. Preparation is under way for tools relating to justice sector mapping, transitional criminal codes, basic policy approaches to hybrid and domestic prosecution for serious violations, guidance on approaches to the creation of truth commissions, legal system monitoring methodologies, a review of reconciliation approaches and guidance on public sector vetting. Finally, planning has begun for the creation of a transitional justice web resource.

58. While our peace missions are sometimes called upon to play this role, coordination within the broader international community, including among bilateral and multilateral donors, aid agencies, non-governmental organizations, private

foundations and the United Nations is equally vital, yet remains a largely unresolved challenge. Inadequate coordination in this sector leads to duplication, waste, gaps in assistance and conflicting aid and programme objectives. Worse yet, the uncoordinated intervention of the international community can have the effect of distorting domestic justice agendas, wastefully diverting the valuable time of domestic justice sector actors and consuming precious development resources.

59. To remedy these problems, it is crucial that donors, peace missions and the United Nations system commit themselves to working jointly with each other in a collective effort led by key actors of the civil society and Government concerned. Mere information sharing is not enough. Rather, all partners should work through a common national assessment of needs, capacities and aspirations and a common national programme of transitional justice, justice reform and rule of law development.

XVIII. Building our roster of experts

60. Through the years, specialized United Nations staff have acquired significant expertise and experience in assisting post-conflict countries to establish transitional justice processes, restore shattered justice systems and rebuild the rule of law. Given the large (and growing) demand in this area, however, their numbers are not adequate for the task at hand. As such, we are increasingly drawing on external expertise to supplement the work of our expert staff. However, finding and deploying such personnel expeditiously presents a number of difficulties.

61. The first challenge is the lack of experts who combine the complementary skills required to do this work on behalf of the United Nations. Nor are there adequate cadres of civilian police, judges, prosecutors, lawyers, prison officials and so on. To be sure, there are plenty of persons who are expert in the workings of their own legal system, their own legislation and their own language. Such expertise is, however, of limited value to our activities. What is required is a mix of expertise that includes knowledge of United Nations norms and standards for the administration of justice, experience in post-conflict settings, an understanding of the host country's legal system (inter alia, common law, civil law, Islamic law), familiarity with the host-country culture, an approach that is inclusive of local counterparts, an ability to work in the language of the host country and familiarity with a variety of legal areas.

62. There is thus a clear need to develop a reliable international roster of individuals and institutions (including outside partners) reflecting the requirements and criteria above, in order to facilitate both efficient identification, screening, recruitment, pre-deployment training and deployment of high-quality personnel, as well as the agreement of effective institutional partnerships for our work in these fields. In doing so, we could draw from the various rosters developed and maintained by many of our partners, while maintaining our own screening and selection processes.

63. Once qualified personnel are identified, the next step is to ensure that they benefit from serious and systematic pre-deployment training, with core subjects ranging from the systems and traditions of the host country to the operations of the mission, to the norms and standards to be applied and to the standard of conduct expected of them. The United Nations has developed a number of training

programmes and materials for rule of law experts in various fields. Other international organizations and institutions in a number of Member States have done the same. More systematically coordinated efforts in this area would greatly assist our ability to identify, train and rapidly deploy qualified personnel to support justice and the rule of law in post-conflict countries.

XIX. Moving forward: conclusions and recommendations

A. Considerations for negotiations, peace agreements and Security Council mandates

64. Ensure that peace agreements and Security Council resolutions and mandates:

(a) Give priority attention to the restoration of and respect for the rule of law, explicitly mandating support for the rule of law and for transitional justice, particularly where United Nations support for judicial and prosecutorial processes is required;

(b) Respect, incorporate by reference and apply international standards for fairness, due process and human rights in the administration of justice;

(c) Reject any endorsement of amnesty for genocide, war crimes, or crimes against humanity, including those relating to ethnic, gender and sexually based international crimes, ensure that no such amnesty previously granted is a bar to prosecution before any United Nations-created or assisted court;

(d) Ensure that the United Nations does not establish or directly participate in any tribunal for which capital punishment is included among possible sanctions;

(e) Require that all judicial processes, courts and prosecutions be credible, fair, consistent with established international standards for the independence and impartiality of the judiciary, the effectiveness, impartiality and fairness of prosecutors and the integrity of the judicial process;

(f) Recognize and respect the rights of both victims and accused persons, in accordance with international standards, with particular attention to groups most affected by conflict and a breakdown of the rule of law, among them children, women, minorities, prisoners and displaced persons, and ensure that proceedings for the redress of grievances include specific measures for their participation and protection;

(g) Recognize the differential impact of conflict and rule of law deficits on women and children and the need to ensure gender sensitivity in restoration of rule of law and transitional justice, as well as the need to ensure the full participation of women;

(h) Avoid the imposition of externally imposed models and mandate and fund national needs assessment and national consultation processes, with the meaningful participation of Government, civil society and key national constituencies to determine the course of transitional justice and restoration of the rule of law;

(i) Where mixed tribunals are envisaged for divided societies and in the absence of clear guarantees regarding the real and perceived objectivity, impartiality and fairness of the national judiciary, consider mandating a majority of international judges, taking account of the views of various national groups, in order to enhance the credibility and perceived fairness of such tribunals among all groups in society;

(j) Insist upon full governmental cooperation with international and mixed tribunals, including in the surrender of accused persons upon request;

(k) Adopt an integrated and comprehensive approach to the rule of law and transitional justice, including proper sequencing and timing for implementation of peace processes, transitional justice processes, electoral processes and other transitional processes;

(l) Ensure the provision of adequate resources for the restoration of the rule of law and the establishment of transitional justice, including a viable and sustainable funding mechanism. Where United Nations-sponsored tribunals are to be established, this should include at least partial funding through assessed contributions;

(m) Consider the establishment of national human rights commissions as part of transitional arrangements.

B. Considerations for the United Nations system

65. I intend to instruct the Executive Committee on Peace and Security, building on the earlier work of its task forces, to propose concrete action on the matters discussed in the present report, for the purpose of strengthening United Nations support for transitional justice and the rule of law in conflict and post-conflict countries and to give consideration, inter alia, to:

(a) Making proposals for enhancing United Nations-system arrangements for supporting the rule of law and transitional justice in conflict and post-conflict societies;

(b) Ensuring that rule of law and transitional justice considerations are integrated into our strategic and operational planning of peace operations;

(c) Updating the current list of United Nations guidelines, manuals and tools on rule of law topics and supplementing those materials as needed;

(d) Proposing new or enhanced United Nations system mechanisms, including common databases and common web-based resources, for the collection and development of best practices, documentation, manuals, handbooks, guidelines and other tools for transitional justice and for justice sector development;

(e) Reviewing best practices and developing proposals for workable national-level rule of law coordination mechanisms involving justice sector institutions, civil society, donors and the United Nations system;

(f) Developing approaches for ensuring that all programmes and policies supporting constitutional, judicial and legislative reform promote gender equality;

(g) Convening technical-level workshops on the rule of law and on transitional justice experiences from around the world;

(h) Establishing arrangements for creating and maintaining an up-to-date roster/database of justice and transitional justice experts, based upon explicit criteria, reflecting geographic, linguistic, gender and technical diversity, and organized according to particular areas of expertise;

(i) Organizing interdepartmental staff-training programmes on the rule of law and on transitional justice;

(j) Ensuring systematic debriefing of personnel involved in rule of law and transitional justice operations.

Notes

[1] S/PV.4833.

[2] S/PV.4835.

[3] S/PRST/2003/15.

[4] S/PRST/2004/2.

[5] In response to a request from the Chairman of the Committee of 34, the Under-Secretary-General for Peacekeeping Operations sent a letter to all Member States on 25 November 2002, in which information was provided on both the available United Nations expertise and resources available as well as the gaps in this field.

[6] Already in 1948, the Universal Declaration of Human Rights affirmed that recognition of inherent dignity and of equal and inalienable rights is the foundation of freedom, justice and peace. Similarly, the International Covenant on Civil and Political Rights, ratified by 151 States, requires that, even during a state of emergency, the principles of legality and the rule of law must be upheld. In the administration of justice, the Covenant requires equality before the law, fair and public hearings, the presumption of innocence and certain minimum procedural guarantees. Countless United Nations treaties, declarations, guidelines and bodies of principles have been adopted by the Organization to define with particularity the international communities' obligations with regard to justice and the rule of law.

[7] The International Covenant on Civil and Political Rights, for example, obliges its States parties to "respect and to ensure ... the rights recognized" in the Covenant and to "take the necessary steps ... to give effect to the rights ...", including by ensuring an effective remedy for violations and by providing for determination of claims by competent judicial, administrative or legislative authorities, and to enforce such remedies when granted (art. 2). The rule of law loathes arbitrariness in the exercise of authority. The Covenant thus explicitly prohibits arbitrariness in the deprivation of life (art. 6), arrest and detention (art. 9), exclusion from one's own country (art. 12) and interference with privacy, family, home or correspondence (art. 17). The Covenant further guarantees fair and lawful process for arrest and detention (art. 9), imprisonment (art. 10), deportation (art. 13) and fair trial (art. 14). Importantly, article 26 recognizes all persons as equal before the law and entitles them to equal protection of the law without discrimination. Similarly, in ratifying the International Covenant on Economic, Social and Cultural Rights, States parties have undertaken to "take steps ... with a view to achieving progressively the full realization of the rights recognized ... by all appropriate means ..." (art. 2). To be sure, the rule of law is as vital to the protection of economic and social rights as it is to civil and political rights. For a legal system to ensure justice and the protection of the rule of law to all, it must incorporate these fundamental norms and standards.

[8] See A/55/305-S/2000/809.

[9] My request for a subvention to the Special Court was approved in the amount of $16.7 million, on the understanding that any regular budget funds appropriated for the Court would be refunded to the United Nations at the time of liquidation of the Court, should sufficient voluntary contributions be received.

[10] See S/2000/1063 and S/2000/1198.

[11] The matter has been on the agenda of the General Assembly since 1993 under the agenda item "Strengthening the rule of law". In the United Nations Millennium Declaration, heads of State and Government recognized a collective responsibility to spare no effort to strengthen the rule of law, as well as respect for all internationally recognized human rights and fundamental freedoms.

[12] See "Final Report of the Executive Committee on Peace and Security Task Force for Development of Comprehensive Rule of Law Strategies for Peace Operations" of 15 August 2002, approved by the Executive Committee on 30 September 2002. In response to a request from the Chairman of the Committee of 34, the Under-Secretary-General for Peacekeeping Operations provided a copy of the report to all Member States on 25 November 2002.

[13] Ibid., annex B.

[14] Ibid., annex C.

5

Introduction

The global celebration of transitional justice and the East Timor reality

The global celebration of transitional justice discourse and practice

It has become almost a truism to assert that societies emerging from protracted periods of conflict need to find ways of 'coming to terms' with past human rights abuses. In recent decades, a set of mechanisms and tools known as 'transitional justice' has been developed to assist states to confront the wrongdoings of repressive predecessor regimes and thereby make the shift from violent pasts to peaceful futures. Although transitional justice may encompass a broad range of measures such as reparations policies, institutional reform, lustration (the vetting of public officials), memorialisation, and reforms to police, prisons and judiciary, the most popular mechanisms are criminal trials and truth commissions. Transitional justice is more than just a collection of tools or mechanisms, however; it is also a 'discourse' that assumes a relationship between the promotion of the liberal values of individual rights and liberties, the rule of law and democracy, and the achievement of peace and stability in post-conflict societies. These assumptions are often taken for granted by transitional justice policymakers.

There is now a celebration of transitional justice practice – reflected in the proliferation of international courts and tribunals around the globe, including the recently created International Criminal Court (ICC), and the growing number of truth commissions. Indeed, as Stanley (2009: 56) observes, forty international courts and tribunals and over thirty-five truth commissions have been established over the last three decades. The emergence of non-governmental institutions, such as the International Center for Transitional Justice, in New York, and the birth of a new academic journal, the *International Journal for Transitional Justice*, are further testament to the growing popularity of transitional justice practice and discourse (see Moon 2008: 3).

The proliferation of transitional justice mechanisms has gone hand in hand with an expansion of the discourse regarding what these mechanisms can accomplish. Once viewed simply as a means of contributing to the redress of past violations and the development of an official historical record, transitional justice is now also claimed to facilitate broader processes of societal transformation and to contribute to ambitious goals such as reconciliation, nation-building and peace. Through the official investigation and public exposure of past human rights abuses, transitional justice is claimed to provide a rite of political passage towards the creation of a liberal political order that embeds values such as the rule of law and the rights of individuals.

Recent years have also seen a shift away from the dichotomous debate about the relative merits of truth commissions versus trials. Previously, proponents of truth commissions argued that the broad and flexible mandates of these mechanisms made them more 'victim-centred' than the adversarial and confrontational nature of judicial proceedings, and that they promote accountability, deterrence, reconciliation, truth and the rule of law more successfully than criminal tribunals (see Waldorf 2006: 16). By contrast, those who favour trials suggested that criminal accountability for human rights abuses provide more 'just' outcomes for victims than truth commissions, thereby creating a firmer basis for societal reconciliation. There is now a growing recognition that trials and truth commissions can positively complement each other and, recent transitional justice processes, including those established in East Timor, Argentina, Peru and Sierra Leone, have adopted a combination of mechanisms (see Lambourne 2009: 33; Leebaw 2008: 102; UNSG 2004: 9).

The current era is also marked by an apparent shift away from 'one-size-fits-all' approaches to transitional justice, towards a greater emphasis on 'local context'. Evidence of this can be seen in the 2004 report of the UN Secretary General, *The Rule of Law and Transitional Justice in Conflict and Post-Conflict Societies*, which calls for greater attention to indigenous and informal processes for administering justice or settling disputes on the basis that this will help to make transitional justice processes more meaningful to informal populations (UNSG 2004: para 36). The enthusiasm for incorporating local justice practices into formal transitional justice processes is apparent in the UN-sponsored truth commissions of both East Timor and Sierra Leone (Shaw and Waldorf 2010: 15; Waldorf 2006: 3).

In a different way, the renewed attention to local context is reflected in the UN's growing embrace of 'hybrid' or internationalised tribunals. Located within the country where the crimes were committed, and comprising both national and international staff and judges, hybrid tribunals are sometimes claimed to promise greater local legitimacy than international tribunals: they are said to be more economically sustainable, to contribute to the capacity-building of domestic legal systems and to make justice more meaningful to victims due to their proximity to the community (see, for example, UNSG 2004; OHCHR 2006). Hybrid tribunals, which have now been established in Kosovo, Sierra Leone, Cambodia and East Timor, can arguably also be understood as a response to what has been termed 'tribunal fatigue' within the UN and donor community, as a result of the expense and duration of international criminal trials (see, for example, UNGA 1999).

Somewhat paradoxically, alongside the UN's apparent eschewing of a 'one-size-fits-all approach' to transitional justice is the growing link between transitional justice and UN-sponsored state-building projects in states incapacitated due to conflict (see, for example, Fritz 2005). Transitional justice has become firmly entrenched as an essential component of the UN 'toolkit' for successful post-conflict recovery, underscored by the UN Department of Peacekeeping Operation's (UNDPKO) establishment of a Security Sector Reform and Transitional Justice Unit, the production of a number of UN documents and 'tools',[1] and the UN's sponsorship of recent transitional justice mechanisms, including those in East Timor and Sierra Leone.[2] This has meant that post-conflict states are now 'expected, encouraged or even coerced' to adopt transitional justice mechanisms (Subiotic 2009: 21). These developments can be seen as part of the surge in UN efforts to promote the 'rule of law' around the globe: a concept that the former UN Secretary General Kofi Annan has described as being at the very heart of the organisation's mission (UNSG 2004: 4).[3] Indeed, since the early 1990s, the UN and other international organisations have promoted transitional justice, human rights,

1 Recent UN documents include the 2004 report of the UN Secretary General, *The Rule of Law and Transitional Justice in Post-Conflict Societies* (UNSG 2004) and the 2006 publication of a series of *Rule of Law Tools for Post Conflict States* by the Office of the High Commissioner for Human Rights designed to help UN field missions and administrations emerging from conflict to establish transitional justice mechanisms (OHCHR 2006).

2 While East Timor's truth commission was established by the UN itself, in the case of Sierra Leone it received explicit endorsement from the UN. Various UN agencies have also provided transitional justice assistance and advice in countries such as Liberia, Afghanistan, Bosnia, Burundi and Herzegovina (Study by the Office of the United Nations High Commissioner for Human Rights on human rights and transitional justice activities undertaken by the human rights components of the United Nations system, UN Doc E/CN.4/2006/93, 7 February 2006 available at http://www.ictj.org/en/where/region3/507.html (accessed 2 February 2012)).

3 The UN Secretary General defines the rule of law as 'a principle of governance in which all persons, institutions and entities, public and private, including the State itself, are accountable to laws that are publicly promulgated, equally enforced and independently adjudicated, and which are consistent with international human rights norms and standards. It requires, as well, measures to ensure adherence to the principles of supremacy of law, equality before the law, accountability to the law, fairness in the application of the law, separation of powers, participation in decision-making, legal certainty, avoidance of arbitrariness and procedural and legal transparency' (UNSG 2004: 4).

the rule of law, good governance and democratisation as a key strategy of intervention, peacemaking and reconstruction in conflict and post-conflict societies (Humphrey 2005: 204; see also Carothers 2003; Sriram 2007). The assumption is that by granting an extensive role to the 'international community' in restructuring political, legal and economic systems, and introducing internationally recognised legal standards, post-conflict states will be assisted to become stable, liberal democracies that respect human rights and are integrated into the global economy (Paris 2004: 5; Rajagopal, 2008: 1346). These assumptions were certainly evident during the UN's post-conflict reconstruction of East Timor, which took place under the auspices of the UN following the 1999 referendum, and which, on the eve of the new nation's independence, was claimed as a 'success story'.

East Timor: from colonialism to 'transition'

The year 1999 was one of both extraordinary hope and terrible violence for the East Timorese people. While a UN-sponsored referendum on 30 August ushered in East Timor's transition to independence, and brought to an end the twenty-four-year oppressive Indonesian occupation of the territory, the year was also marred by killings, the burning and destruction of thousands of houses, and mass displacement. The primary perpetrators of this violence were East Timorese militia, mostly young men who had been armed and trained by the Indonesian military. Yet it is important to locate the events of 1999 within a much longer history of violence, disadvantage, poverty and exploitation that encompasses the Indonesian occupation and the period of Portuguese colonisation that preceded it. Considered in this light, the idea of 'transition' begins to lose its temporal certainties, and the concept of 'justice' comes to mean more than the prosecution of perpetrators of the 1999 violence (Figure I.1).

From the seventeenth century, East Timor was valued for its resources of sandalwood and coffee. Nonetheless, as one of the most remote of Portugal's colonies, it was relatively neglected, and received limited economic and political investment until the late nineteenth century (Taylor 1999: 1–3). At this point, Portuguese rule became more intrusive as the colonial power sought to consolidate its control over the territory in order to more systematically exploit its resources. One strand of its strategy involved the expropriation of large areas of agricultural land from local rulers to cultivate coffee and copra as cash crops for export, a system that was maintained by various methods of coercion, including a head tax and forced labour (Molnar 2010: 35). Another component pivoted around the introduction of policies to undermine the indigenous system of political alliances based on kinship and to replace it with a new administrative system (Taylor 1999: 10–11). The combined impact of these policies on East Timorese society was profound: the forced production of cash crops undermined the production of less profitable food crops that were vital to

Figure I.1 Aerial view of Dili after the post-referendum violence of 1999 (Ross Bird)

the food security of the East Timorese (Ramos-Horta 1987), while the creation of a system of government that deliberately pitted 'loyal' *liurai* (chiefs) against rebellious ones deepened pre-existing divisions amongst the population and fostered new ones (Taylor 1999: 11–12; Robinson 2010: 6).

The Second World War exacerbated the debilitating conditions in which much of the East Timorese population lived. Following Japan's attack on

Pearl Harbor in December 1941, Australian, British and Dutch troops took 'pre-emptive' action by landing in Portuguese Timor, concerned that Japan might use it as a base to launch attacks against Australia (CAVR 2005a: Part 3, 10). After Japan's invasion of Timor on 19 February 1942, many East Timorese fought alongside Australian soldiers, paying a heavy price for doing so. By the time the Japanese surrendered, some 60,000 East Timorese, or 13 per cent of the population, had died as a result of the war, most of East Timor's main towns and villages had been destroyed, livestock levels were greatly reduced and large numbers of people were starving (Taylor 1999: 14). As in other parts of Asia, there had also been widespread sexual slavery of East Timorese women by Japanese soldiers (ETAN 2008). As Gunn (1999: 235–7) highlights, despite the fact that many ordinary East Timorese suffered immensely during the war, there has never been an international investigation into war crimes committed by Allied or Japanese soldiers, nor have war reparations been paid to the East Timorese people.

After the war, Portuguese administrators re-established their control over the territory, even while many other southern nations were undergoing decolonisation (Molnar 2010: 37). East Timor remained a highly unequal society with a very limited infrastructure. For example, it was not until the 1960s that the capital city Dili was provided with electricity. By 1974, only a few main streets of Dili had been paved, while piped fresh water and medical facilities were not provided to towns beyond Dili until the early 1970s (Ramos-Horta 1987: 22). Education was also restricted: only one public high school existed in the territory in the early 1970s and 90 per cent of the population remained illiterate (Hughes 2009: 34; see also Gunn 1999: 247). Only a small number of privileged Portuguese-speaking *assimilados* (assimilated natives) were able to access seminary education. Educated in Portuguese history and literature, members of this elite group were also among the first nationalists in East Timor, and some went on to play key roles in the independence movement (Molnar 2010: 43–4).

The overthrow of the Caetano regime in Portugal in 1974 stimulated the growth of political parties in East Timor. Among the most prominent were the radical pro-independence FRETILIN (*Frente Revolucionária de Timor-Leste Independente* / Revolutionary Front for an Independent East Timor) and the more conservative UDT (*União Democrática Timorense* / Timorese Democratic Union), which favoured eventual independence, but only after a lengthy period of transition under Portuguese tutelage. In August 1975, in the context of covert Indonesian operations aimed at bringing about East Timor's integration with Indonesia, these parties were engaged in a brief, but brutal, conflict, which is often described as a civil war. After winning a military victory, FRETILIN declared East Timor's independence on 28 November 1975. The new nation was then invaded and occupied by Indonesian forces nine days later, and was subsequently incorporated into Indonesia as its 27th province. A tenacious armed and clandestine resistance struggle – which is discussed in Chapter 4 – was waged over the next twenty-four years.

Although the Indonesian invasion of East Timor in 1975 was widely condemned by the UN, the international community largely turned a blind eye to the repressive nature of the occupation. Many Western states acquiesced to the invasion, and played an ongoing role in sustaining the Indonesian occupation because it served their economic and strategic interests. Perhaps the most vigorous supporter of the Indonesian regime was Australia, which doubled its military assistance to Indonesia between 1975 and 1981, and granted *de jure* recognition to Indonesia's annexation of East Timor, necessary for its negotiations with the Indonesian government over the rights to the oil and gas deposits in the Timor Sea (Nevins 2002a: 629). Meanwhile, the United States continued to supply arms to Indonesia for use in maintaining 'internal security' (Nevins 2002a: 630).

According to credible estimates, the Indonesian occupation resulted in the deaths of an estimated 100,000–200,000 people out of a population of less than 800,000 (see Robinson 2003: 16; CAVR 2005a: Part 6; Kiernan 2003). While some deaths were the direct result of military assaults, more people perished of illness and starvation after being displaced, herded into camps or forcibly moved into Indonesian military-controlled resettlement villages, which, strategically, were located in zones far from areas of resistance (Taylor 1999: 84–92; Robinson 2010: 51). Poor conditions in resettlement villages, minimal supplies of food and medicine, and inadequate water sources were compounded by strictly curtailed freedom of movement and agricultural activities. These factors led directly to a devastating famine in the late 1970s, which claimed thousands of lives (Taylor 1999: 93; Robinson 2010: 51; CAVR 2005a: Part 7.3, 67). Throughout the occupation, the East Timorese population also endured arbitrary imprisonment, torture, assault and rape, repeated displacement, lack of access to basic needs including health care, and ongoing restrictions on freedom of movement (CAVR 2005: Part 7). Another pervasive feature of the occupation was the extensive militarisation of East Timorese society. A key aspect of the Indonesian regime's counter-insurgency approach involved the systematic recruitment of East Timorese into combat battalions, paramilitary groups and civil defence forces, and their employment as spies and informants, tactics that worked to undermine social bonds and to sow fear and distrust within local communities (see Robinson 2010; Larke 2009: 654; CAVR 2005a: Part 4).

The 1991 Santa Cruz massacre, in which up to 273 East Timorese lost their lives, many of them young people, marked a turning point in international awareness of Indonesian atrocities. Although similar atrocities had taken place before, what was different about Santa Cruz was that the actions of the Indonesian military were filmed by a British photojournalist who then managed to smuggle the film out of the country. The events were then shown worldwide (Taylor 1999: xiii). Nonetheless, real change was possible only following Indonesia's President Soeharto's fall from power in 1998 in the wake of the Asian Economic Crisis. The new President, B.J. Habibie, then unexpectedly announced his government's intention to conduct a referendum in which the people of East Timor would choose between autonomy within Indonesia and independence. Following negotiations between the UN and the Indonesian government, the United Nations Mission in East Timor (UNAMET) was established to organise a referendum. Despite evidence that the Indonesian military and police forces were collaborating with local militia groups to intimidate voters against voting for independence, the Indonesian police were put in charge of ensuring security for the referendum (Robinson 2010: 106). As the referendum date approached, the violence escalated and, on 6 April, members of the *Besih Merah Putih* militia group attacked a group of people who had taken refuge in the Catholic church compound in the town of Liquica. As many as sixty people were killed by militia as Indonesian military, police and Paramilitary Brigade (Brimob) troops stood by. Not long afterwards, on 17 April, militia members rampaged through East Timor's capital, Dili, killing more than a dozen people.

Despite the climate of intimidation, 99 per cent of registered East Timorese voted in the referendum. Within days of the announcement of the results, however, which demonstrated that an overwhelming majority of East Timorese people were in favour of independence, the territory was subjected to an intensified campaign of violence and abuse. Over 1,000 people were killed, houses and villages were burned and destroyed, around 400,000 people were displaced (including more than 200,000 into West Timor), and all significant government and commercial basic infrastructure was destroyed (OHCHR 2000; CAVR 2005a: Part 7.5, 48). A particularly brutal massacre took place in the town of Suai, Covalima, the day after the announcement of the referendum results, on 6 September 1999, when up to 200 unarmed civilians were killed at the *Nossa Senhora do Rosário* (Our Mother of Rosario) church, including refugees who had been sheltering in the church, together with three priests (Figure I.2). On 8 September, UNAMET was forced to withdraw most of its personnel from the territory due to grave concerns about their security, and it was not until 20 September that a multinational military force known as the International Force for East Timor (INTERFET) was deployed, under the operational command of Australia, to restore order (see UNSC 1999b). The UN then assumed the administration of East Timor, through the UN Transitional Administration for East Timor (UNTAET), until formal independence was declared on 20 May 2002.

The UNTAET mission represented one of the most ambitious state-building projects undertaken by the UN. Going beyond traditional peacekeeping and peace-building mandates, UN state-building is directed at 'constructing or reconstructing institutions of governance capable of providing citizens with physical or economic security' (Chesterman 2004: 5). In the case of transitional administration, these ends are accomplished by 'assuming some or all of the powers of the state on a temporary basis' (Chesterman 2004: 5). The

Figure I.2 Suai church, where up to 200 people were killed on 6 September 1999 (Lia Kent)

UNTAET mission was more expansive than previous UN transitional administrations because it represented the first time that the UN had exercised full sovereignty over territory independently of any parallel local authority (Chopra 2002: 28; Chesterman 2002: 46). As the UN Secretary General noted in early 2000, 'never before has the United Nations attempted to build and manage a state' (UNSG 2000a: para 64). Security Council Resolution 1272 establishing UNTAET gave the mission 'overall responsibility for the administration of East Timor' and the power 'to exercise all legislative and executive authority, including the administration of justice' (UNSC 1999a). With funding provided from the assessed contributions of UN member states and the voluntary contributions of foreign donor states and multilateral institutions, UNTAET was responsible for a daunting array of tasks. These included providing security and maintaining order, rehabilitating infrastructure, establishing an effective administration, assisting in the development of civil and social services, supporting capacity-building for self-government and reconstructing the justice sector (UNSC 1999a). The World Bank, in co-operation with the Asian Development Bank, had responsibility for facilitating economic reconstruction and development, and focused on the sectors of health, education, agriculture, transport, power and water supply, and private sector development (see Rohland and Cliffe 2002). East Timor's transition to independence was expected to take two to three years.

Dealing with the past

In response to widespread condemnation around the world of the post-referendum violence, UN statements, resolutions and reports were imbued with strong language about the need for criminal prosecutions of those responsible for the 1999 violence (see UNSC 1999a; UNSC 1999b; UNCHR 1999). This would be essential, it was argued, to provide 'justice' to the East Timorese and to facilitate a successful transition to democracy by acting as a deterrent against future abuses and helping to entrench a strong 'rule of law' culture. Thus the Security Council Resolution establishing INTERFET in September 1999 condemned all acts of violence and demanded that those responsible by brought to justice (UNSC 1999b).

Less explicitly, the prosecution of serious crimes perpetrators was also viewed as important to the international community as a whole, to restore basic 'universal values' that had been undermined by the Indonesian government's flagrant breach of the Security Council Resolution that had entrusted security for the referendum to the Indonesian police. Thus a report by the UN's High Commissioner for Human Rights, also in September 1999, concluded that:

> To end the century and the millennium tolerating impunity for those guilty of these shocking violations would be a betrayal of everything

> the United Nations stands for regarding the universal promotion and protection of human rights.
>
> (UNCHR 1999: para 48)

Despite these robust statements, there had been little pre-planning about how prosecutions would take place and who should take responsibility. To provide further guidance on these questions, a UN Commission of Inquiry (COI) visited the country in September 1999. It produced a report that, like that of the UN High Commissioner for Human Rights, was emphatic that the UN had a 'special responsibility' to ensure that the crimes committed in 1999 would not go unpunished, especially as Indonesia had breached a binding Security Council Resolution (OHCHR 2000: para 147). The COI report recommended the establishment of an international criminal tribunal along the lines of those created for the former Yugoslavia and Rwanda. In his letter of 31 January accompanying the COI report, UN Secretary General Kofi Annan endorsed the COI's findings, underscoring that 'the United Nations ha[d] an important role to play in this process [of bringing perpetrators to account] in order to protect the integrity of Security Council actions' (UNSG 2000b).

Yet, rather than following the COI's recommendation and establishing an international criminal tribunal, the Secretary General – responding to assurances from the Indonesian government – recommended that the Indonesian courts must first be given an opportunity to investigate and prosecute perpetrators in Indonesia. He justified this by explaining:

> The main thing is to put people on trial and make them accountable . . . If the Government has the capacity and the willingness to do it and is doing it, you don't want to create another tribunal.
>
> (UN Secretary General Kofi Annan, in Linton 2001: 213)

At the same time, the Secretary General declared that he intended to strengthen UNTAET's capacity to conduct investigations and to collaborate with the Indonesian processes, and, in April 2000, a Serious Crimes Investigations Unit (SCIU) was established in East Timor comprising international civilian and police investigators. The SCIU was mandated to investigate certain 'serious crimes', defined as genocide, crimes against humanity and war crimes, as well as certain domestic crimes including murder, torture and sexual offences. Two months later, in June 2000, a specialised 'hybrid' or internationalised tribunal was established, known as the Special Panels for Serious Crimes ('the Special Panels'), which was attached to the Dili District Court. Together, these investigative and prosecutorial functions are referred to as the Serious Crimes Process.[4] A Memorandum of Understanding (MoU)

4 See UNTAET Regulations 2000/11 and 2000/15.

between Indonesia and UNTAET was then signed with the purpose of ensuring co-operation in the exchange of evidence, requests for witnesses and making arrests, and ensuring the transfer of suspects when needed in the investigation and prosecution of serious crimes (RI/UNTAET 2000: Preamble). The MoU reaffirmed the commitment to 'hold accountable the perpetrators of serious violations of international humanitarian and human rights law in East Timor'. In response to international pressure, the Indonesian government eventually created another mechanism – the Ad Hoc Human Rights Court in Jakarta – to try within its own jurisdiction Indonesian perpetrators who had played a leading role in the violence.

UNTAET was also faced with the question of what to do with the thousands of other 'less serious' crimes, including looting, arson, theft and the destruction of property, committed immediately prior to and following the referendum of 1999. It was clear that the nascent domestic legal system, with its limited infrastructure and inexperienced legal actors, would not be capable of dealing with all of these issues. A related preoccupation at this time of both UNTAET and members of the East Timorese political elite – namely, leaders of the *Conselho Nacional de Resistência Timorense* (National Council for Timorese Resistance/CNRT)[5] – was how to ensure the safe return of the 120,000 Timorese who remained displaced in West Timor, who had the capacity to cause continuing instability. To respond to these concerns, in June 2000, UNTAET's Human Rights Unit, together with Uppsala University from Sweden, organised a workshop on transitional justice mechanisms to consider truth commission options, at which representatives of the International Center for Transitional Justice (ICTJ) provided expert advice (Larke 2009). The East Timorese leadership was also considering options for a truth commission and, in August 2000, a Congress of the CNRT recommended the need for a 'Commission for Resettlement and National Reconciliation', which should 'undertake fact finding to collect detailed data' (CNRT 2000a). The UNTAET Human Rights Unit then took the lead in convening a Steering Committee, which led to the establishment of the *Comissão de Acolhimento, Verdade e Reconciliação* (Commission for Reception, Truth and Reconciliation/CAVR), in July 2001, as an independent statutory body, by a legal act of the UN (UNTAET 2001). The body was then formally recognised within the East Timorese Constitution.

The CAVR had three main stated aims. The first was to establish the 'truth' about the twenty-four-year Indonesian occupation, by collecting statements

5 CNRT was formed in 1998 and was the major coalition of East Timorese political groups that resisted the Indonesian occupation of East Timor. The two most powerful among its constituent parties were FRETILIN and UDT. The president of CNRT was Xanana Gusmão. José Ramos-Horta – CNRT's international spokesman – was another powerful figure. CNRT was disbanded prior to the August 2001 elections.

from individuals throughout the nation and conducting public hearings. The second was to encourage the 'reception' and reintegration of former militia members who had committed so-called 'less-serious' crimes during 1999 back into their communities through an innovative community reconciliation process (CRP), which incorporated local dispute resolution practices. The third aim was to prepare a final report containing findings and recommendations to be presented to East Timor's President and Parliament following independence. Although it was developed quite separately from the Serious Crimes Process, the CAVR was nonetheless expected to play a complementary role and, in particular, the CRP was expected to relieve the pressure on an overburdened and underdeveloped East Timorese legal system.

While the Serious Crimes Process invoked 'universal' human rights values and the rule of law as means of addressing the past and deterring future human rights abuses, the CAVR promoted the values of community reconciliation and healing through truth-telling and restorative justice. It was also assumed that the CAVR's work would have other benefits: that enabling victims to tell their stories would help to restore their dignity, and that establishing the truth about East Timor's repressive past would contribute to national reconciliation, democracy and state-building, and act as a deterrent against future abuses. These multilayered expectations were articulated by the UNTAET Transitional Administrator, Sergio Viera De Mello, in January 2002:

> [The CAVR is a] vitally important initiative for the country. It will provide the East Timorese people with an official ear to listen to their grievances and acknowledge their past suffering. It will provide them with a historical record that is based on the experiences and stories of the people themselves. It will bring together those who have been in conflict in the past and give them a way forward, an opportunity for grievances and long-lasting reconciliation. It will further the cause of justice by offering a mechanism for dealing with many of the violations that were committed in this country during past conflicts, without burdening the court system that is already addressing the most serious cases.
>
> (Sergio Viera De Mello, in Huang and Gunn, 2004: 30)

In many ways, then, the transitional justice approach adopted in East Timor resonates with recent trends in transitional justice discourse and practice. Transitional justice was a central component of the UN's post-conflict reconstruction 'toolkit' applied to East Timor and, in addition, represented one of the first examples of an attempt to combine criminal prosecutions with a truth commission. Representing a shift away from international tribunals (in spite of lobbying by East Timorese leaders and human rights groups for this model), East Timor's 'hybrid' Special Panels for Serious Crimes were established as an adjunct to the domestic legal system; they comprised both East Timorese and international judges, and governed by a mixture of Indonesian and international law. This model was purported to combine the strengths of an international tribunal with the benefits of local prosecutions (Katzenstein 2003: 245–6). The CAVR, and in particular, the innovative CRP, represented a deeper attempt at engaging with East Timor's local context by building on pre-existing, village-based, dispute resolution practices. Endowed with an ambitious mandate, the transitional justice process as a whole was expected to accomplish a daunting range of goals, which included providing 'justice' to victims and their families, fostering healing, reconciliation and nation-building, acting as a deterrent to future human rights violations, and protecting the integrity of the UN itself.

Recent studies have shown that this approach had a number of fundamental flaws. A key issue was Indonesia's lack of co-operation with the UN's hybrid Serious Crimes Process; this meant that suspects based in Indonesia, among them senior members of the Indonesian military, could not be prosecuted. Relying on the Indonesian judicial system to prosecute war criminals also proved to be poor judgement on the part of the UN. Widely condemned as a failure by the international community, the Ad Hoc Human Rights Court indicted eighteen people, all of whom were eventually acquitted (Cohen 2003). By contrast, the CAVR has been judged to be more successful. Its nationwide community reconciliation process (CRP) adjudicated almost 1,400 cases of minor crimes, while, as part of its truth-seeking function, the CAVR held a series of hearings that were highly participatory and were broadcast widely on the radio and television. Yet many have questioned the extent to which the CAVR has responded to East Timorese expectations of justice, given that none of the principal Indonesian perpetrators of serious crimes have been arrested or prosecuted (Larke 2009; Kent 2004; Pigou 2004; Stanley 2009; Nevins 2005; Robinson 2010).

Following the conclusion of trials by East Timor's Special Panels in May 2005, and the completion of the CAVR's final report in late 2005, the slogan 'No reconciliation without justice' continues to be a rallying cry for national human rights NGOs and local victims' groups, who are waging persistent and vocal campaigns demanding prosecutions of the Indonesian military and reparations for victims. The enduring nature of these campaigns – which call attention to unfinished business and 'unreconciled' experiences – gives a preliminary sense of the widespread community disillusionment with the transitional justice process, and with the limited form of 'justice' it has provided. In the chapters that follow, I interrogate the dissonance between community expectations and institutional rhetoric in greater depth by unravelling the intersections, and at times collisions, between diverse narratives of justice circulating within the international, national and local spheres.

Producing a 'thick' study of transitional justice: methodology and conceptual approach

This book sets out to contribute what McEvoy refers to as a 'thick' exploration of transitional justice (McEvoy 2008: 17). In contrast to 'thin' or positivist studies, which emphasise the formal, instrumental or normative aspects of transitional justice, 'thick' explorations focus on its complex, multilayered and actor-oriented dimensions (ibid). They seek to engage with the messiness of transitional justice, including how globalised concepts and processes are given meaning in specific places and times, and how they may be reshaped in unexpected directions (see Shaw and Waldorf 2010: 3–4).

The book intentionally focuses on the *local* dynamics of transitional justice in East Timor. This emphasis means that the empirical material upon which the book relies is oriented primarily towards capturing the views of East Timorese survivors (as opposed to those of international state-builders, East Timorese leaders and transitional justice advocates). In other words, the book does not set out to provide a detailed examination of the political dynamics and conflicting narratives that played out *within* the UN and the transitional justice institutions themselves (although this would be a very interesting story in itself). Thus, while Chapters 1, 2, 3 and 4, which examine international and national justice narratives, draw on some interview material, they rely primarily on a critical analysis of key texts and documents including newspaper articles, speeches, press releases and UN reports. In reading these texts, I engage with a range of critical approaches to international law that seek to shed light on the deeper relations of power and particular worldviews that underpin the so-called 'universal', liberal assumptions of transitional justice *discourse*. I argue that these assumptions lead to particular retributive justice and restorative justice responses to conflict that may foreclose other, more nuanced ways of thinking about, and responding to, conflict. These power relations and exclusions may not always be visible to those who are formally involved in the practice of transitional justice, no matter how laudable their intentions.

The methodology for Chapters 5 and 6, which examine local justice narratives, draws on the results of extensive fieldwork. I seek to provide rich information about survivors' perceptions of the transitional justice process and to show how these perceptions are informed by the multiple, locally embedded meanings of justice. These chapters draw, in particular, on the findings of interviews conducted in the districts of Covalima, Lautem and Liquica over two fieldwork visits in 2007 and 2008. I conducted in-depth semi-structured interviews with approximately 100 individuals, primarily 'victims' or 'survivors' who had participated in the Serious Crimes Process or the CAVR, as well as community leaders, including *Chefes de Suco* (village chiefs) and *Chefes de Aldeia* (hamlet chiefs). These interviews were supplemented with informal conversations and observation. An analysis of fieldwork findings helps to further unsettle the liberal, universal assumptions of transitional justice discourse by showing how these processes are given meaning within specific political and social contexts (see also Dembour and Kelly 2007b). As Darian-Smith makes clear, empirical methodologies – and specifically ethnographic methodologies – are well placed to explore these intricacies because they illustrate that the 'law is not monolithic and universalistic in practice, that it does not correlate to any one culturally discreet unit, and that it is not devoid of sites of resistance, challenge and modification' (Darian-Smith 2004: 556).

Conducting cross-cultural research, particularly with individuals who have experienced violence and regarding painful subject matter, presents many ethical challenges and is fraught with issues of power and representation. The challenge, as post-colonial scholars have identified, is for researchers to seek to 'decolonise' their research practices (Tierney 2003: 306; Smith 2003: 7; Moreton-Robinson 2000). As Tierney acknowledges, while a commitment to 'naming' silenced lives or 'writing back' those who have been marginalised by dominant discourses is part of a decolonising approach, this, in itself, is insufficient (Tierney 2003: 306). What is needed is for researchers to engage in a process of 'reflexivity' in order to interrogate their own views and values and challenge Western research orthodoxies, which are often considered to be authoritative, neutral and universal (Rigney 2001: 3; see also Moreton-Robinson 2000; Tierney 2003).

A key aspect of a reflexive approach is an acknowledgement of the constructed nature of the research process, including the fact that researchers are not objective, impartial, recorders of facts, but have their own conceptual frames and worldviews, and interpret and mediate the data in a number of ways (Elliot 2005: 20; see also Tierney 2003). It also seeks to render visible, and challenge, the relations of privilege and power inherent in the research process (Tierney 2003; see also Stanley 2009: 16). Far from disavowing possibilities for change, this process can enable researchers to think more deeply about *what* they write and *why* they write (Tierney 2003: 318). The need for reflexivity is particularly important in the context of research on traumatic events, where trauma victims frequently become the objects of 'voyeuristic or triumphalist fascination' (Radstone 2007: 23), and where there can be a tendency to assume that providing an opportunity for interviewees to 'speak' may help be healing or therapeutic (Stanley, 2009: 13; see also Radstone 2007: 22). As Stanley observes, researchers can exacerbate experiences of marginalisation and inequality by turning stories into a 'commodity' for external consumption (Stanley 2009: 14–16; Tierney 2003: 318). Storytellers, she writes, 'can regularly lose ownership over their stories, a point intensified by unequal resources and access to global information flows' (Stanley 2009: 16).

Informed by these insights, where possible I attempt to consider the way in which my status as a white, female researcher from Australia – who speaks

Tetum – may have been perceived by interviewees, in order to unsettle assumptions about my 'neutral' and 'objective' status. This included being attentive, during fieldwork, to the reasons why some survivors may have expressed annoyance, or weariness, about the prospect of being interviewed, and why some of those I approached did not wish to speak to me. I also sought to understand why other individuals approached the interview task with a particular urgency, and recounted their stories in the style of a *testimonio* (testimony) in order to make a particular claim on my attention (see also Tierney 2003: 298–9). Like Stanley (2009: 15), who conducted research with East Timorese torture survivors, I found that, for many of my respondents, the interview process was not considered as an end in itself, but a form of political agency that was connected to a desire for concrete changes in their everyday lives. Reflecting on these issues led me to be particularly aware of the responsibilities inherent in the privileged role of 'researcher'. This entailed accepting that my role was not that of an 'objective' and 'neutral' recorder of facts, and that my position of privilege gave me a responsibility to be more than a 'spectator' to people's experiences (see Scheper-Hughes 1995). It meant that, where possible, I tried to assist individuals by clarifying basic facts about the transitional justice mechanisms and passing information back to these bodies regarding requests for information, public hearing books and feedback on certain cases.

Conceptually, the book works from a critical analysis of 'discourses' and 'narratives'. I understand discourse as a regulated way of thinking about and representing an issue through written and verbal forms, as well as socio-cultural practices (see, for example, Fairclough 1995). As Fairclough (1995: 82) has observed, discourses do not just represent the world, but are also ideologically invested because they contribute to the reproduction of relations of power. Some discourses can also be described as narratives. These are 'discourses with a clear sequential order that connect events in a meaningful way for a definite audience and thus offer insights about the world and/or people's experiences of it' (Hinchman and Hinchman, cited in Elliot 2005: 3). As Clare Moon (2008) has noted, transitional justice discourses can be understood as discursive narratives, in that they tell a story about 'transition' that has a clear beginning (conflict) and a clear end (peace or reconciliation). This story – which is a narrative of progress – evolves '*as if* in a linear and developmental trajectory' (Moon 2008: 7). Transitional justice narratives also render certain 'subjects' (namely, 'victims' and 'perpetrators') visible, and certain 'truths' (namely, a truth of individual human rights violations) central (Moon 2008: 6).

The public discourses of justice and nation-building promoted by members of the East Timorese political leadership can also be described as narratives. As will become clear in later chapters, these narratives tell their own story of progress, albeit of a very different kind. Theirs is a story of collective struggle and endurance against colonial occupiers and, ultimately, of liberation, in which certain subjects (namely, 'heroes' and 'traitors') are rendered visible. In a similar vein, the views and opinions of East Timorese survivors should be understood as 'narratives'. These tell very different kinds of stories from official narratives. They may be fragmented, non-linear and highly personalised stories, which, unlike official narratives, stress the continuing influence of the past in the present and emphasise a range of intertwined needs. Nonetheless, as will become evident in Chapters 5 and 6, local actors also embrace, transform and resist national and international narratives in a range of ways.

In analysing the views of East Timorese survivors in this way, I am informed by the work of feminist, Marxist, post-structuralist and post-colonial theorists interested in issues of subjectivity and identification. According to these theorists, our sense of self, or subjectivity, is not static, but fluid, and is 'constantly being reconstituted in discourses every time we think or speak' (Weedon 1987: 33). Rather than viewing individuals as autonomous agents who are capable of independently inventing themselves, these scholars understand individual lives as 'constant constructs embedded in societal and cultural forces that seek to constrain some and enable others' (Tierney 2003: 299). They do not assume that interview data provides objective, factual, information, but are interested in what this data reveals about the broader culture, framework and relations of power in which people make sense of their lives, and the everyday practices by which individuals construct and reconstruct their sense of identity (Elliot 2005: 28, 124). Informed by these insights, while I acknowledge interviewees' painful and very real personal experiences of past harm, I recognise that their lives 'cannot be considered independently of their social world and the discourses available to them to understand their experiences' (Powell 2007: 92). I am mindful, too, that local communities may replicate broader social inequities (McEvoy and McGregor 2008b: 9). In addition, I am interested not only in what interviewees say, but in *how* they frame, present and interpret their own stories, and the deeper meanings of these stories. Thus I consider such important questions as what is emphasised and what is left out of these stories? What is the purpose of telling stories? What do those who tell their stories expect from the listener? Who gets to tell their stories and who does not?

Finally, there are several terms I seek to problematise throughout the book. These include the terms 'international', 'national' and 'local'. Although I am interested in analysing the narratives of justice circulating within the international, national and local spheres, I am mindful that these spheres are not bounded and impermeable, but overlapping and interrelated. To suggest that East Timorese victims/survivors operate only in the 'local' sphere, while the staff of the CAVR and the Serious Crimes Process are 'international' and the East Timorese leadership is 'national', may overlook the extent to which international and national narratives circulate locally; international human rights discourses, for example, may be invoked by survivors in making justice claims, while East Timorese civil society organisations often have close links to international human rights organisations such as Amnesty International and Human Rights Watch. These terms may also obscure the extent to which 'local' problems often have global dimensions and causes (Merry 2006a: 212; see also Darian-Smith 2004: 552). East Timor's widespread and entrenched poverty, for example, is closely connected to a history of Portuguese colonialism and Western support for the oppressive Indonesian occupation. Thus, even as I use the terms international, national and local as broad terms of categorisation, I seek to unsettle them by exploring their internal tensions and their areas of intersection.

The terms 'victim' and 'perpetrator' may be similarly problematic. They may be analytically inadequate for attending to the multiple and changing identities that people assumed in the coercive context of the Indonesian occupation, when Indonesian military surveillance seeped into everyday life, permeating relationships, and fostered fear and suspicion amongst neighbours and families. As Shaw and Waldorf (2010: 8) note, the labels 'victim' and 'perpetrator' may also be profoundly depoliticising. The term 'victim', for example, often requires individuals to conform to a particular script of 'innocence' that defines them as 'passive objects of pity' and renders them 'dependent and subject to external interventions' (Gready 2011: 165). In the East Timor context, as I discuss further in Chapter 5, the extent to which an individual chooses to identify as a victim may also be shaped by a range of factors, including socio-economic status, gender and the extent to which they were involved in political resistance activities. Thus, during interviews, many activists and NGO workers did not wish to identify themselves as victims, associating this term with passivity and a lack of agency. To add another layer of complexity, even those who define themselves as victims in East Timor are far from a homogenous group: differences in gender, socio-economic status, political background, and experiences influence perceptions and views about justice. Conscious of these complexities, while I use the term 'victim' (or 'survivor') throughout this book to refer to individuals who had participated in the transitional justice process as a victim, I also seek to unsettle this category by considering who it includes and excludes, and reflecting on the forms of agency it enables and disallows. I also seek to engage with individuals not as passive victims, but as political actors: as 'living and breathing people attempting to make sense of their lives' (Hughes 2009: 21).

Part II

TRANSITIONAL JUSTICE 'TOOL-KIT' OR CONCEPTION OF JUSTICE?

(v) Transitional justice and reparations

(vi) Transitional justice and apology

(vii) Transitional justice and reconciliation

6

'Settling Accounts' Revisited: Reconciling Global Norms with Local Agency

Diane F. Orentlicher

Abstract

In the mid- to late-1980s, the discourse of transitional justice was shaped above all by the experience of countries in Latin America, where military forces continued to exercise autonomous power even after ceding formal authority to democratically elected governments. In this setting, while human rights professionals agreed that fledgling democracies should undertake prosecutions in accordance with their international legal obligations, they were divided over the question of whether further development of international obligations in respect of punishment was desirable. Nor was it clear what, precisely, international law already required.

Writing in the early 1990s, the author of this essay concluded that States parties to certain international treaties were in general required to prosecute specific crimes. More generally, she argued, wholesale impunity for atrocious crimes was generally incompatible with States' responsibility to ensure that individuals subject to their power enjoyed fundamental rights. But these duties, she wrote, should not be interpreted to require action incompatible with a nascent democracy's political or legal capacity.

In this essay, the author describes how her views have evolved in the past 15 years. Noting that international legal norms against impunity have grown increasingly strong and arguing that this trend has itself proved a powerful antidote to impunity, the author nonetheless affirms 'the central importance of promoting the broad participation of victims and other citizens in the process of designing as well as implementing programmes of transitional justice' and addresses the inherent tension between these values and norms.

Introduction

Among human rights professionals, few issues have proved as vexing as the set of challenges bound up in the notion of transitional justice. Should – must? – societies attempt to bring to justice those who bear key responsibility for past atrocities? Does justice inevitably entail prosecutions or does its meaning instead turn upon each society's historically and culturally specific experience? Besides trials, what roles can truth commissions, reparations programmes and other measures of transitional justice play in transforming a society that has been shattered by unspeakable crimes? Should – does? – international law constrain or shape

States' responses to crimes of the past? How do the answers to these questions turn upon the political constraints that define a nation's transition? These questions only begin a long, and ever-lengthening, catalogue of quandaries that vex societies confronting the challenges bound up in political transition and the professionals who seek to assist them.

Decades of practice toiling in the field of transitional justice have hardly eased its dilemmas. Instead, deepening global experience has brought home the unique complexity – and, often uniquely inspiring story – of each country's experience.

In this setting, the editors of the *International Journal of Transitional Justice* invited me to cast a backward glance at how my views on issues of transitional justice have evolved since the 'early days' of global human rights engagement with this subject. Although scarcely the only issue that has consumed my generation of participants in the global discourse of transitional justice, one question has long loomed large in our work and, certainly, much of my own: Is it helpful for international law to mandate particular responses to past atrocities and thereby narrow the scope of local variation in responding to similar atrocities? Or, instead, is the best response invariably particular to each society?

In large part because I am widely associated with a view that is supportive of a strong international duty to prosecute past abuses (though, as I will explain, many attributions of this position hardly correspond to my actual views), I will take this question as the organizing issue of this essay. I wish to make clear, however, that I do not consider this to be in principle the most urgent or important issue of transitional justice, although it may be just that in some societies.

The Early Days: Combating Impunity

For my generation of professionals addressing the challenges of transitional justice, the 'early days' unfolded in the 1980s, when transitions from military rule to nascent or restored democracy swept Latin America in particular while touching countries in other regions. This context is crucial in explaining not only the evolution in my thinking, but also that of many of my contemporaries. For while each country's story was unique, a common quandary defined most Latin American countries' democratic transitions and framed the central dilemma of transitional justice two decades ago: Although military juntas had formally ceded political power to democratically elected governments, armed forces continued to occupy an autonomous realm of power with the potential for imperiling their countries' fragile transition if the new government breached their citadel of impunity.

In many countries in Latin America, the price exacted for the end of military rule was society's acceptance of the outgoing junta's self-amnesty; in others, impunity for past crimes was the military's implicit but unambiguous price for remaining in the barracks as fragile democracies took root. Yet for the newly elected successor governments to honor nakedly self-serving claims of untouchability would betray the very principles they had pledged to restore and safeguard.

The dilemma thus presented was agonizing, and the professional human rights community was acutely conscious of the complexity of its challenges. Exploring these challenges at a landmark seminar in 1988 organized by the Aspen Institute, an international group of experts agreed on several core principles, notably including the central importance of establishing and acknowledging the truth about past violations. Thus while experience with official truth commissions – and international institutions' commitment to the 'right to know' the truth about past abuses – have grown exponentially in recent years, even in the 'early days' human rights and other professional experts saw disclosure of the truth about past abuses as a non-negotiable moral obligation of governments.

But if the Aspen assembly coalesced on this and other points, we staked out a range of views about the scope of states' moral and legal duties to punish violations of the past.[1] Even on this subject, however, there was broad agreement on two principles relating to prosecution of past abuses.

First, even those who favored broad scope for local determination in confronting abuses of a prior regime typically added an important qualification, reiterated so often that it soon took on a talismanic quality: Of course, they said, governments must comply with their international legal obligations.[2] But while some of my contemporaries had fairly well-developed views about what international law required, most believed that further study and analysis was needed. In the course of the Aspen seminar, many participants urged me to take up that challenge. I did, and my initial conclusions were published in a 1991 article in the *Yale Law Journal*, which I summarize below.

Another point of broad agreement emerged implicitly from discussion of a question that evoked a notably wide range of views among human rights professionals – whether the international community should press successor governments to mount at least some prosecutions of past atrocities. Implicit in the debate over this question was a broad, if ill-defined, consensus that successor governments *ideally* should undertake at least some prosecutions of a prior regime's atrocious crimes. This is, I believe, reflected in the way that José Zalaquett, one of the leading voices for broad local discretion in addressing past crimes, summarized his view of what the international community should demand of successor governments: 'The whole truth and as much justice as is possible.'[3]

As the second half of Zalaquett's formulation suggests, the fulcrum of debate 20 years ago did not concern the general desirability of prosecuting atrocious crimes (though we debated rather intensively the justifying aims of punishment in a context of transition). Rather – and here I am oversimplifying what was a far richer debate than I can reflect in this essay – the issue that vexed us most was whether it was prudent to press fragile democracies to mount prosecutions that they may not

1 See Alice Henkin ed., *State Crimes: Punishment or Pardon* (Queenstown: Aspen Institute, 1989).

2 See for example, José Zalaquett, 'Confronting Human Rights Violations Committed by Former Governments: Principles Applicable and Political Constraints,' in Henkin, ibid., at 23–69.

3 See Stanley Cohen, 'State Crimes of Previous Regimes: Knowledge, Accountability, and the Policing of the Past,' *Law & Social Inquiry* 20 (1995): 7–50, p. 43.

yet have sufficient power to survive. Indeed, even a brief dip into the literature of the time would reveal a preoccupation with issues of political power of successor democracies vis-à-vis the outgoing military regime.

This preoccupation did not displace other considerations: far from it. But in a fundamental way, it framed the transitional justice debate of the 1980s. For many of those who counseled caution in pressing transitional societies to mount prosecutions, the overriding paradigm was not so much one of transitional justice as transitional politics. If prosecutions threatened to imperil a transition to democracy, their potential value was outweighed by their attendant risks. For others, the dominant paradigm was one of impunity: If the principal reason for hesitating to prosecute those responsible for crimes against the basic code of humanity was the perpetrators' impunity, the task for international law and nongovernmental organizations (NGOs) was to mount effective strategies against impunity. Those who were strongly influenced by this paradigm – and I came to count myself among them – were hardly opposed to values, often associated with amnesties, bound up in processes of social reconstruction. But we came to regard with suspicion amnesties covering atrocious crimes that were justified as measures of national reconciliation. Grappling with these issues in the shadow of Latin American self-amnesties, there was ample reason to see 'reconciliation' as a watchword for impunity.

'Settling Accounts'

It was in this context that I wrote 'Settling Accounts: The Duty to Prosecute Human Rights Violations of a Prior Regime,'[4] whose principal aim was to identify the *scope* of states' obligations under international law when it comes to prosecuting human rights violations of a prior regime. The article also addressed the question of whether an international policy on prosecutions – reflected, ultimately, in law – was desirable. (Parenthetically, I have often regretted the article's subtitle, which may have contributed to a widespread – but quite inaccurate view – that my article found in international law a rigid and universally applicable duty to prosecute all human rights violations of a prior regime. A more accurate subtitle would have begun 'The *scope* of States' duties ...').

On the question of what international law required at the time of publication, in brief: 'Settling Accounts' found that States that had adhered to certain human rights treaties were generally required to ensure that criminal proceedings were instituted against those suspected of specified violations of human rights, such as genocide and torture. As for customary international law – the law that would apply to virtually all States, regardless of which specific treaties they had ratified – I concluded that States' general obligation to ensure the enjoyment of fundamental rights was incompatible with wholesale impunity for atrocious crimes but did not require prosecution of every offense.

[4] *Yale Law Journal* 100 (1991): 2537–2615.

Turning from general obligations[5] to the context of political transitions described earlier, I identified various ways in which international law should accommodate the constraints commonly confronted by democracies that succeed military regimes. Even with respect to States that had ratified treaties that seemed to require prosecution of every violation of its criminal prohibitions, I argued, States parties operating under the constraints commonly associated with political transition could satisfy their treaty obligations through exemplary prosecutions – focusing, for example, on those who appear to bear principal responsibility for systemic atrocities or on individuals believed to have committed notorious crimes that were emblematic of a regime's depredations. Asserting that governments should not be called upon to 'press prosecutions to the point of provoking their own collapse,'[6] I raised concerns about whether international law adequately takes account of the autonomous realm of power often occupied by military forces and the resulting constraints this imposed on a government's field of action.[7]

Even so, when it came to the perennially vexing question of how international law and policy should align itself in relation to the quandaries that then dominated the discourse of transitional justice, I placed striking confidence in international law itself. The crux of my argument in this regard was twofold: First, just as domestic law can take account of complexities, so too can international law. In effect, I argued, international law is capable of making appropriately nuanced judgments.

Second, and more fundamental to my claim, I argued that, through appropriately defined obligations, international law could assist rather than thwart the aims of fragile democracies tentatively seeking to reconstruct the norms and institutions of a full-fledged democracy. Although I did not put the case in these terms, I argued that international obligations in support of prosecutions could enlarge a fledgling democracy's political space for confronting past violators and that such prosecutions served important values as long as the effort did not provoke a reversal of hard won advances. In short, I saw international law as a potential counterweight, however limited, to the enduring power of impunity – not a panacea, but another weight added to the scales on the side of justice.

In pressing this claim, I took very much to heart the entreaties of colleagues from Argentina and other countries that had been reckoning with crimes of their recent past, some of whom had played leading roles in national efforts to mount prosecutions. These colleagues wanted me to understand, above all, that they would have been better equipped to confront the inevitable military backlash against prosecutions if international law stood firmly in their court – if, i.e., they

[5] Here I mean *general* in the sense of a rule that would ordinarily apply under its terms of application but which might be subject to exceptions rather than in the sense of a rule applicable to all States.

[6] Orentlicher, supra n 4 at 2548.

[7] Ibid., at 2606–12. In light of these claims, which were central to the position I developed in 'Settling Accounts,' I have been perplexed by some authors' attribution to me of a position that 'demands' prosecution no matter the consequences. See, for example, Helena Cobban, *Amnesty After Atrocity? Healing Nations after Genocide and War Crime* (Boulder: Paradigm, 2007), 198–99.

could credibly invoke a mandate for their work in international law. Some of the strongest claims in my article were, in fact, prompted by their views.[8]

At the same time, I had no illusions about the power of prosecutions by themselves to advance a fledgling democracy's transition – although, rereading my article, I can understand why some readers have discerned in my writing greater confidence in prosecutions as a centerpiece of a democratic transition than I ever possessed. I focused on prosecutions in 'Settling Accounts' because the scope of States' obligations in respect of punishment was the subject of my article, not because of a belief that prosecutions mattered more than any other measure of transitional justice[9] and certainly not because I believed that the potent alchemy of prosecutions could by itself transform a society that had descended into the abyss of State-organized depredations.

Still, my argument was profoundly shaped by a core belief that exemplary prosecutions, if prudently pursued, could help dispel the toxic effects of impunity. By condemning past crimes through the strongest sanction used by the institutions of government to condemn, exemplary trials could send a message to the future: This will not be tolerated again. Space does not permit a more elaborate account of the affirmative values I thought such trials could help secure, but one negative consideration played a key role in my thinking. Summarizing the 'case for prosecutions', I wrote: 'Above all, the case for prosecutions turns on the consequences of *failing* to punish atrocious crimes committed by a prior regime on a sweeping scale. If law is unavailable to punish widespread brutality of the recent past, what lesson can be offered for the future?'[10]

In the years since I wrote this, I have often been reminded of the profound importance of this point to victims of unspeakable crimes across the globe. As I write this essay, my mind echoes with the words of victims of 1990s-era 'ethnic cleansing' in Bosnia and Herzegovina, whom I have been interviewing in recent weeks[11] in an effort to understand what the work of the International Criminal Tribunal for the former Yugoslavia (ICTY) has meant to them. Virtually every person I interviewed spoke of his or her disappointments in the ICTY – yet all of them spoke passionately about what they considered the *necessity* of the Tribunal's work. Imagine, they implored, if the ghastly crimes they endured were to go unpunished! Whatever the Tribunal's shortcomings, the victims I interviewed believed its work essential (though hardly sufficient) to ensure their country's ability to restore fundamental norms of human decency and to secure the moral integrity of future generations.

[8] An example is the claim: 'Because trials secure preeminent rights and values, governments should be expected to assume reasonable risks associated with prosecutions, including a risk of military discontent.' Orentlicher, supra n 4 at 2548–49 (footnote omitted).

[9] To the extent it may suggest a view I never held, I regret the fleeting treatment of truth commissions in 'Settling Accounts,' which addressed this form of transitional justice principally by way of arguing that truth-telling processes should not be seen as a substitute for exemplary trials. See ibid., at 2546 n 32. As with many claims in 'Settling Accounts,' this one was responsive to a particular context – one in which truth commissions were sometimes presented as a 'second best' alternative to prosecution when the latter were seen to be too destabilizing.

[10] Ibid., at 2542 (emphasis in original).

[11] These interviews were conducted in Bosnia and Herzegovina in December 2006.

From an International to a Cross-Cultural Perspective

Inevitably, my views on transitional justice have evolved with the broadening and deepening of global experience. Some aspects of this evolution so nearly track broader trends in the field of transitional justice that I can briefly note them without substantial elaboration for the readers of this journal:

First, with others who have worked in fields bearing on transitional justice for an extended period, I inevitably have a deeper appreciation for the multifaceted nature of transitional justice and the special contribution that nonjudicial measures, when effective, can make to a broader process of political and social transition. If societies that have descended into the abyss of inhumanity bear a special burden of reckoning with their past, the work of highly respected truth commissions can facilitate a broader and more complex understanding of the machinery of mass atrocity than the circumscribed verdict of a criminal proceeding can do. At their best, moreover, truth commissions can advance a process of social inclusion and empowerment of previously marginalized – even brutalized – sectors of society, who may figure prominently in the work of a commission. Just as trials are not the stuff of magical transformation, no truth commission, however inspiring, can by itself set a country that has been deformed by widespread depredations right again. But an effective truth commission can engage society in an inclusive process of reckoning and repair. Truth commissions can, moreover, speak to the future through their recommendations for institutional reform.

If the passage of time has reinforced the need for a comprehensive approach in addressing systemic abuses of the past in which various measures – among them truth commissions; trials; institutional, social and economic reforms; and reparations programmes – play a distinct and unique part, it has also underscored the interdependence of these measures: to a considerable degree, the effectiveness of each of these measures turns upon the broader context in which it unfolds, including its relationship with other dimensions of transitional justice. Trials, for example, may seem an outsized expenditure of precious national resources if a society's basic social and economic needs remain unmet. And the expressive function of prosecutions will surely be undermined in the absence of public measures that institutionalize a government's commitment to fundamental rights. In larger perspective, as Laurel Fletcher and Harvey Weinstein have reminded us, 'an approach that does not integrate trials with . . . other capacity-building measures is insufficient to attend to social repair.'[12]

Recent experience has also brought home the need for concerted efforts to ensure that, when prosecutions or truth commissions are instituted, their work is known and understood by the societies on whose behalf they operate. If, with Bishop Berkeley, we might wonder whether a tree really fell in the forest if no one heard it fall, we may wonder whether prosecutions constituting a crucial pillar in

[12] Laurel E. Fletcher, and Harvey M. Weinstein, 'Violence and Social Repair: Rethinking the Contribution of Justice to Reconciliation,' *Human Rights Quarterly* 24 (2002): 573–639, p. 580.

a programme of transitional justice can play their intended role if they operate at a remote distance from the public and speak only in the largely inaccessible language of legal judgment. This point has, of course, assumed particular importance with the operation of international courts that operate outside the physical territory and political/legal culture of countries where atrocious crimes occurred, but is relevant as well to national and 'hybrid' courts. Indeed, if court officers and staff do not meaningfully engage with the communities most affected by their work, the field of interpretation may be occupied instead by local leaders bent upon distorting the work of prosecutions in the service of divisive political agendas.

Another important development since the 'early days' of global engagement in processes of transitional justice is the unprecedented, if still inadequate, attention to the special concerns of women, children and marginalized minority communities in programmes of transitional justice. Among the notable achievements in this regard, prosecutions before the International Criminal Tribunals for the former Yugoslavia and Rwanda (ICTY/R) have brought crimes of sexual violence – mostly ignored in postwar prosecutions – out of the proverbial shadows. In another arena of progress, their terms of reference have directed some truth commissions to give special attention to crimes of sexual violence; a number of recent commissions have held focused hearings on these types of abuse.[13]

These developments mark a sea change in public awareness; in the 'early days,' leading voices in the discourse of transitional justice were largely blind to these issues.(Unpardonably, I did not so much as allude to them in 'Settling Accounts'). Still, there remains a glaring need to invigorate efforts to incorporate the experiences of women, children and minorities into programmes of transitional justice. Even the pathbreaking precedents of the ICTY/R in addressing crimes of sexual violence have proved fragile: early achievements in this area hardly ensured that these crimes would receive similar attention in later cases.[14]

These points I believe to be relatively uncontroversial. Far more vexing issues are implicated in the question whether there are some core obligations of transitional justice that apply to all societies and, if so, under what conditions they should be subject to what international lawyers would call 'derogation' in the face of an overriding imperative, such as the desire to secure an end to armed conflict.

Before setting forth my own views, it may be helpful first to note the broad arc of relevant developments in international law and policy. Crucially in my view, in the past dozen years or so international law and policy have advanced on two tracks simultaneously, with inevitable tensions between the two paths they represent. As I will explain shortly, those tensions lie at the heart of my own thinking.

[13] See *Independent study on best practices, including recommendations, to assist States in strengthening their domestic capacity to combat all aspects of impunity, by Professor Diane Orentlicher*, UN Doc. E/CN.4/2004/88, ¶ 19(f) (27 February 2004).

[14] See Binaifer Nowrojee, '"Your Justice Is Too Slow": Will the ICTR Fail Rwanda's Rape Victims?' (United Nations Research Institute for Social Development, Occasional Paper 10, 2005).

On the one hand, international law and policy have provided increasingly strong support for the principle 'that the most serious crimes of concern to the international community as a whole must not go unpunished,' in the words of the preamble of the Rome Statute of the International Criminal Court (ICC). In 'Settling Accounts,' I reasoned that, to the extent that they foreclosed prosecution of certain human rights violations, amnesties would be incompatible with various human rights treaty obligations. In the years since I wrote this, relevant treaty bodies and other important sources have explicitly affirmed this position.[15] Moreover the establishment of several international and hybrid courts since 1993, including a permanent international court, is emblematic of international resolve to ensure that those most responsible for crimes against the basic code of humanity do not escape punishment.

Notably, the political bodies of the United Nations as well as human rights bodies have, in the words of the UN Security Council, affirmed the responsibility of States 'to end impunity and to prosecute those responsible for genocide, crimes against humanity and serious violations of humanitarian law.'[16] On the perennially challenging question whether there is an exception to this general rule in situations where an amnesty would bring an end to armed conflict, the UN Secretary-General summarized United Nations policy this way in a 2000 report: 'While recognizing that amnesty is an accepted legal concept and a gesture of peace and reconciliation at the end of a civil war or an internal armed conflict, the United Nations has consistently maintained the position that amnesty cannot be granted in respect of international crimes, such as genocide, crimes against humanity or other serious violations of international humanitarian law.'[17]

But while these trends signify powerful affirmation of a global norm in support of criminal accountability for atrocious crimes, professional practitioners of transitional justice are more aware than ever before that there cannot be a one-size-fits-all approach to transitional justice. So, too, are officials of the same United Nations that has affirmed with ever-strengthening conviction 'the position that amnesties cannot be granted in respect of international crimes.'[18] Given the extraordinary range of national experiences and cultures, how could anyone imagine there to be a universally relevant formula for transitional justice?

In recent years, when I have had the opportunity to contribute to the articulation of international standards in respect of transitional justice (principally through my appointment as a United Nations expert on combating impunity), I have been at pains to emphasize this point.[19] As I wrote in a 2004 UN report, 'The

[15] Some of these developments are summarized in *Independent study on best practices*, supra n 13.

[16] UN Doc. S/PRST/2002/41, p.1.

[17] UN Doc. S/2000/915, ¶ 22 (footnote omitted).

[18] Ibid., Notably, the Secretary-General affirmed both the inappropriateness of a one-size-fits-all approach to transitional justice and the United Nations' opposition to amnesties for international crimes in the same report. See *Report of the Secretary-General on the rule of law and transitional justice in conflict and post-conflict societies*, UN Doc. S/2004/616, p. 1; 10, 32 (2004).

[19] See, for example, *Report of the independent expert to update the Set of Principles to combat impunity, Diane Orentlicher*, UN Doc. E/CN.4/2005/102 ¶ 9 (18 February 2005); *Independent study on best practices*, supra n 13.

unique historical experience of each society that has endured [serious violations of human rights] will inevitably shape its citizens' understanding of justice.'[20]

Closely related to this point, I believe passionately in the central importance of promoting the broad participation of victims and other citizens in the process of designing as well as implementing programmes of transitional justice. I summarized some of the reasons why in a 2005 UN report:

> Their participation helps ensure that policies for combating impunity effectively respond to victims' actual needs and, in itself, 'can help reconstitute the full civic membership of those who were denied the protection of the law in the past'. Broad consultations also help ensure that policies for combating impunity are themselves rooted in processes that ensure public accountability. Finally, programmes that emerge from national consultations are, in the words of a recent report by the [UN] Secretary-General . . ., more likely than those imposed from outside 'to secure sustainable justice for the future, in accordance with international standards, domestic legal traditions and national aspirations.'[21]

This emphasis reflects something of an evolution in my thinking. In 'Settling Accounts,' I challenged the view that an amnesty would be legitimate if, among other conditions, it were democratically approved. My principal reason turned on the operation of a relevant rule of international law[22] but I also argued that a political majority should not be able to surrender the rights of a minority and that vulnerable minorities typically figure prominently among victims of past atrocities.[23] While this approach asserted the primacy of a victims' perspective, it did not reflect the emphasis I would now place on victims' agency in defining their own interests and preferences and in participating in national processes aimed at designing policies of transitional justice.

This perspective naturally raises the question, where does this leave the previously mentioned norms of international law that generally seem to require prosecution of at least those who bear primary responsibility for atrocious crimes? If victims' agency is a crucial value, does it not follow that victims should be able opt out of these international norms if, say, in their culture and immediate circumstances they would prefer to reintegrate rebels who have committed atrocities into their community through a traditional ceremony of reconciliation than to prosecute them?

As I write, this issue looms large in the context of the ICC Prosecutor's indictment of five members of the notoriously savage Ugandan rebel group, the Lord's Resistance Army (LRA), including its leader, Joseph Kony. The ICC Prosecutor undertook his investigation of the LRA after the Ugandan government referred the situation to the Court in January 2004. His indictment apparently provided the incentive for LRA leaders to agree to a truce (long-standing negotiations

[20] Ibid.

[21] Ibid., (footnotes omitted).

[22] See Orentlicher, supra 4 at 2595–96.

[23] Ibid., at 2595 n 260.

between the Ugandan government and the LRA had thus far been unable to achieve this much). But the indicted commanders reportedly refuse to follow through on a peace settlement unless the ICC indictments are dropped.[24] Meanwhile, even before the imperatives of peace and justice reached this level of apparent tension, leaders of the Acholi people, who have been principal victims of LRA atrocities, asked the ICC Prosecutor to withdraw his arrest warrants and defer instead to traditional Acholi ceremonies of reconciliation and forgiveness.[25]

Earlier in this essay, summarizing the position I advanced in 'Settling Accounts,' I wrote: 'By condemning past crimes through the strongest sanction used by the institutions of government to condemn, exemplary trials could send a message to the future: This will not be tolerated again.' The position I advanced in 'Settling Accounts' thus assumed that prosecutions are the 'strongest sanction used by the institutions of government to condemn' – a premise that I still believe accurately captures a norm common to most countries, assuredly including those whose experiences shaped my 1991 article. Suppose, though, a fundamentally different normative approach prevails among the Acholi? If, in their culture, a traditional ceremony of reconciliation and forgiveness is more likely than prosecutions to secure the end of savage armed conflict, how can international actors insist that prosecutions are indispensable?

As thus framed, the situation in northern Uganda seems to present a particularly compelling case for staying the hand of prosecution in deference to local preferences *and* peace imperatives. But the dilemma raised by this situation is more complex than I have suggested so far. To begin, it is not obvious that the views of Acholi leaders can be taken to represent those of 'the Acholi people.' An extensive survey of attitudes toward justice and peace undertaken in northern Uganda in 2005 found that most of those surveyed, including Acholi respondents, believed that those who had committed abuses should be tried judicially.[26] Among those who favored trials, 66 percent believed that LRA leaders should be tried.[27]

The broader question of cultural relativism is, moreover, just as complex in respect of the perennial 'amnesty vs. prosecution' dilemma as in other contexts. In

[24] 'Will Kony come out of the bush? It will be hard to reconcile peace with justice in northern Uganda,' *The Economist*, October 21, 2006, 56–57.

[25] Ibid.

[26] International Center for Transitional Justice and Human Rights Center, University of Berkeley, California, *Forgotten Voices: A Population-Based Survey on Attitudes about Peace and Justice in Northern Uganda*, 2005, 30. Among the four communities surveyed, the percentage responding affirmatively to the question whether those who had committed abuses should be tried judicially ranged from 67 and 76 percent respectively in two Acholi districts to 86 and 90 percent respectively in two non-Acholi districts, ibid. The same survey found that a majority of those surveyed supported amnesty, ibid., at 28. While this might suggest that most respondents prefer judicial punishment but would choose amnesty if necessary to achieve peace, the survey found that overall support for amnesty increased only slightly when respondents were asked, 'If the only road to peace was amnesty, would you accept that?,' ibid., at 29. A possible clue to the puzzle may lie in the fact that respondents were not asked how they understood the meaning of amnesty, ibid., at 28 n 47. In any event, the large percentage of respondents who support judicial punishment belies reports that Acholi as a cultural group eschew prosecutions in favor of traditional forms of reconciliation.

[27] Ibid., at 30.

principle, I believe that an approach toward the LRA that is rooted in local culture is inherently more likely to be meaningful to victims – and in other important respects to 'work' – than prosecutions that seem alien to Acholi culture. But to the extent this would entail wholesale amnesty for those who bear primary responsibility for horrific crimes, my views have also been shaped by my African colleagues' efforts to overcome what they consider an enduring weakness in many of their countries – a culture of impunity conducive to violence.[28] In much the same way that many of my colleagues and I came to regard with suspicion attempts to justify Latin American amnesties as measures of 'reconciliation,' many of my African colleagues are disposed to regard with suspicion claims of African exceptionalism when it comes to international norms concerning justice. As I turn the prism from one vantage point to another, then, a fundamentally different frame comes into view.

In a similar vein, if asked whether I would insist on prosecutions if doing so would block a peace agreement that would end human carnage, I would respond (as I always have), 'Of course not!' Still, I would resist changing the normative default rule of international law in a way that may *encourage* the granting of amnesties to the extent they encompass atrocious crimes, at least with respect to those who bear leading responsibility for unleashing systemic violence. Norms matter: they are the indispensable foundation of the whole enterprise of combating atrocious behavior.

Conclusion

This is the place where, by reasonable expectation, I should set forth what I consider to be the best way to reconcile these competing normative pulls. Yet the complex considerations on which I have briefly touched do not admit of any facile reconciliation. Indeed, I can hardly imagine reaching a nirvana moment when the dilemmas of transitional justice appear to dissolve.

And yet, decisions must be made in the face of real-world dilemmas of transitional justice. Turning from practice to further normative development, I have from time to time been tasked with clarifying international legal norms (so far principally in the form of United Nations-endorsed principles) – a charge that requires some measure of resolution, however tentative, of the dilemmas to which I have alluded.

Thus far, I have resolved them by maintaining support for the broad trend in international law supporting criminal accountability for those who bear principal responsibility for atrocious crimes, while, as I have noted, insisting on the importance of local agency in fashioning and implementing policies of justice. Although the first part of this approach is informed by many considerations, three have

[28] These efforts loom large in the Africa programme of the Open Society Justice Initiative, on whose board I am a member. See generally Craig Timberg, 'Impunity on Trial in Africa,' *Washington Post*, May 2, 2006.

loomed especially large: First, across diverse cultures, I have seen human rights victims thirst for justice in the form of prosecutions. This is not to say that all victims want the same thing but it is to say that many who have endured unspeakable crimes have a powerful need for justice and, I have found, increasingly turn to the international community to stand with them in their pursuit of justice against seemingly insurmountable challenges.

Second, I have been repeatedly astonished to see how effectively human rights advocates have utilized the norms enunciated by the United Nations and other international bodies to breach seemingly impregnable barriers to accountability for atrocious crimes committed in their countries. Similarly, the work of global courts as well as States' increased resort to universal jurisdiction have had a remarkable impact in countries where the crimes concerned actually occurred. Augusto Pinochet's 1998 arrest in London ultimately did not lead to his prosecution abroad but it catalyzed efforts to hold him to account in Chile, where he had long remained legally untouchable for crimes committed during his rule. Although Pinochet died without facing trial, he spent his final years fending off a raft of investigations into human rights violations committed decades earlier. Likewise, efforts to prosecute former Chadian leader Hissène Habré in Belgium inspired African countries to act to ensure his prosecution in Senegal.

Finally – and related to the second point – experiences in Chile, Argentina and other countries have shown that societies that are unable to mount prosecutions (or, as the case of Argentina suggests, to sustain them) during the early years of their democratic transition may have greater political space to do so with the passage of time. Crucially, international legal norms concerning prosecution of atrocious crimes have played an important role in enabling such countries to overcome otherwise insurmountable barriers to prosecution.

Examples could be multiplied at some length, but the point is simple enough: International legal norms affirming that atrocious crimes ought to be punished have provided a powerful antidote to impunity. While there are of course times when those same norms cannot be enforced, it has seemed preferable to say 'not yet' than to reframe global norms in terms that suggest prosecuting atrocious crimes is nothing more than an option. For if we were to move entirely away from the language of legal obligation, we would take from those operating on the frontlines of their countries' struggle for decency one of the most potent weapons in their arsenal.

7

CONCURRING OPINION OF JUDGE DIEGO GARCIA-SAYÁN JUDGMENT OF THE INTER-AMERICAN COURT OF HUMAN RIGHTS CASE OF *THE MASSACRES OF EL MOZOTE AND NEARBY PLACES v. EL SALVADOR* OF OCTOBER 25, 2012

1. On several occasions, the Inter-American Court of Human Rights has referred in its judgments to the issue of amnesties in relation to the protection of human rights and the obligation of the State to investigate and, as appropriate, punish serious human rights violations.

2. For a long time, the question of amnesties has been a significant issue in international law, in international relations, and in the examination of non-international armed conflicts. In Latin America, throughout the twentieth century, amnesties were routinely used as a tool to end civil wars, outbreaks of violence, failed coups d'état, and different armed conflicts. At least until the early 1990s, these amnesties were used without any preliminary discussion or analysis.

3. In more recent times, they are a matter of growing relevance in international human rights law, as indicated in various judgments of the Inter-American Court that refer to the issue. The problem concerns horrendous events and contexts that usually give rise to these controversial responses by the law. Authoritarian or dictatorial regimes, political transition processes, internal tensions or armed conflicts, among other matters, within frameworks that are usually very complex, from a political and social perspective, usually provide the objective conditions based on which amnesties are proposed.

4. Regardless of the decision in previous cases, the question of amnesties and their relationship to the obligation to investigate and punish serious human rights violations requires an analysis that provides appropriate criteria for a considered opinion in contexts in which tensions could arise between the demands of justice and the requirements of a negotiated peace in the framework of a non-international armed conflict. This concurring opinion addresses precisely these issues, based on the Court's judgment in this case.

5. It is well-known that the "exemplary" case establishing what, for some, is the Court's interpretation of this issue is the *case of Barrios Altos v. Peru* decided on March 14, 2001. In the most known and most quoted paragraph of this judgment, the Court established that:

> *"41. [...] amnesty provisions, provisions on prescription and the establishment of measures designed to eliminate responsibility are inadmissible, because they are intended to prevent the investigation and punishment of those responsible for serious human rights violations such as torture, extrajudicial, summary or arbitrary execution and forced disappearance, all of them prohibited because they violate non-derogable rights recognized by international human rights law."*

6. In that specific case, this approach was in response to two laws enacted in Peru in 1995, which the Court described in its judgment as "self-amnesties." The condition of "self-amnesty" of the laws examined was so relevant, that it appeared that the Court had limited its interpretation to that type of amnesty.[1]

---

[1] This interpretation could arise from the considerations in paragraph 43 of this judgment: "43. That is why the States Parties to the Convention that adopt laws that have this effect, <u>such as self-amnesty laws</u>, incur in a violation of Articles 8 and 25 in relation to Articles 1(1) and 2 of the Convention" (underlining added).

7. On that occasion, the concurring opinions of Judges García Ramírez and Cançado Trindade, whose reasoning I share, emphasized the contradiction between the "self-amnesty laws" and *"the general obligations of the State under the American Convention on Human Rights."*[2] It was affirmed that *"[t]he so-called self-amnesties are, in sum, an inadmissible offence against the right to truth and the right to justice (starting with the very access to justice)"*;[3] that *"[...] the perverse modality of the so-called laws of self-amnesty, even if they are considered laws under a given domestic legal order, are not so in the sphere of international human rights law of"*;[4] that *"[...] 'laws' of this kind are devoid of a general nature, as they are measures of exception"*[5], and that *"[...] the so-called "laws" of self-amnesty are not truly laws: they are nothing but an aberration, an inadmissible affront to the juridical conscience of humanity."*[6]

8. Since then, the Inter-American Court has had the opportunity to examine and rule on different cases on amnesty laws and their application. In these cases, the Court focused on the substantive incompatibility between the amnesty provisions and the State's obligations in relation to human rights violations. This was based on the underlying purpose of the law, its *ratio legis:* to leave these grave violations unpunished, rather than on the process of the adoption of the law or the authority that enacted it. These are the cases of *Almonacid Arellano et al. v. Chile* (2006), *La Cantuta v. Peru* (2006), *Gomes Lund et al. v. Brazil* (2010) and *Gelman v. Uruguay* (2011). In these cases, the Court followed its case law in the *Barrios Altos* case and further developed some aspects. In general, it reiterated what it had already indicated regarding the *"the incompatibility of amnesty laws relating to serious human rights violations with international law and the international obligations of States"*[7] and that the provisions of amnesty laws that prevent the investigation and punishment of serious human rights violations have no legal effects and, therefore, cannot obstruct the investigation of the facts and the identification and punishment of those responsible for human rights violations.[8]

9. Each of the cases on amnesty laws examined by the Court up until the massacres of El Mozote and nearby places had its own characteristics, nuances and emphasis, either with regard to the context in which the law originated or its scope. However, they all had in common that none of these amnesty laws was created in the context of a process aimed at ending, through negotiations, a non-international armed conflict.

10. This amnesty case arises from a different context to all the previous ones. This has implications for the analysis and legal characterization of the facts, and for the Court's concepts and considerations on this amnesty law enacted following an armed conflict and a peace negotiation process. That is why, according to the Court's reasoning, it has been necessary to take into account not only the norms and principles of international human rights law, but also the relevant provisions of international humanitarian law in view of the context in which the events occurred.

11. As described throughout this judgment, the facts of the massacres of El Mozote and nearby places occurred in the context of a non-international armed conflict. As it developed throughout the 1980s it had reached a point at which the global and regional

2 Concurring opinion of Judge Sergio García Ramírez, para. 1.

3 Concurring opinion of Judge Antonio A. Cançado Trindade, para. 5.

4 Ibid., para. 6.

5 Ibid., para. 7.

6 Ibid., para. 26.

7 *Case of Gomes Lund et al. (Guerrilha do Araguaia) v. Brazil.* Judgment of November 24, 2010, para. 147.

8 *Case of Gelman v. Uruguay.* Judgment of February 24, 2011, para. 232.

conditions arose coalesced to seek and achieve peace through negotiation. Under the Esquipulas II Agreement, signed in August 1987, the Presidents of five Central American countries agreed to seek a solution to the internal armed conflicts underway in El Salvador and other Central American countries. Among other matters, dialogue and reconciliation were proposed as solutions to the conflicts, and the cessation of hostilities and the democratization of Central American societies were counseled.[9]

12. The Salvadoran peace negotiations began, as the judgment recalls,[10] after the Central American Presidents requested the intervention of the Secretary-General of the United Nations. In September 1989, an agreement was signed between the Government of El Salvador and the Farabundo Martí National Liberation Front (FMLN) to initiate a dialogue process and to end, by political means, the armed conflict in El Salvador. Following the signature of the partial agreements (the first was the Human Rights Accord signed on July 26, 1990), the peace agreement was finally completed on December 31, 1991, and was formally signed on January 16, 1992, at Chapultepec Castle in Mexico City.

13. As this was a negotiated end to a long and intense armed conflict, it was no surprise that the question of what to do about the past was raised. First in the process that led to the signature of the peace and its implementation and, then, within the framework of the on-site verification by ONUSAL, the United Nations Mission in El Salvador. Thus, the Mexico Accords of April 27, 1991, referred specifically to the effects of the violence during the armed conflict and, to this end, established the creation of the Truth Commission, whose recommendations the parties undertook to comply with. In the final peace accord of January 16, 1992, there was agreement on "*the need to clarify and to overcome any indication of impunity regarding the officers of the Armed Forces, especially in cases where there was a commitment to respect human rights*" and the Truth Commission was cited to this end, emphasizing that events of this kind must "[...] *be used as exemplary action by the courts of justice.*"

14. A few days after the signature of the Peace Accord,[11] the "National Reconciliation Law" of January 23, 1992, was adopted. It granted amnesty to those who had "*participated as masterminds, perpetrators or accomplices in committing ordinary political offenses and ordinary offenses committed by no less than twenty persons, prior to January 1, 1992, with the exception, in all cases, of the common offense of kidnapping, defined in article 220 of the Criminal Code.*"[12] The same law excluded from this pardon those who "*[...] according to the report of the Truth Commission, had participated in serious acts of violence since January 1, 1980, whose impact on society demands public awareness of the truth with greater urgency, irrespective of the sector to which they belong.*"

15. Subsequently, the Truth Commission explained[13] the need to meet the requirements of justice in two ways: "*[o]ne is the punishment of those responsible; another is the*

[9] Among other aspects, the Esquipulas II Agreement contained an explicit reference to amnesty: "In every Central American country, with the exception of those in which the International Support and Verification Committee determines that it is not necessary, amnesty decrees shall be issued that shall establish all the provisions that guarantee the inviolability of life, liberty in all its forms, property and the safety of the people to whom these decrees apply. Simultaneously with the issue of the amnesty decrees, the irregular forces of the respective country shall release all those who are in its power. "

[10] Para. 266 of the Judgment.

[11] Para. 274 of the Judgment.

[12] National Reconciliation Law. Legislative Decree Nº 147, published on January 23, 1992.

[13] Para. 290 of the Judgment.

reparation due to the victims and their families." Thus, according to the agreement reached by the parties, the route proposed by the Truth Commission, whose recommendations the parties had undertaken to comply with, was that of justice and reparation with regard to the cases it handled. This was consistent with the spirit and letter of what the parties had negotiated and specified in the Peace Accord. Nevertheless, within days of the publication of the Truth Commission's report, the General Amnesty Law was enacted with a very different purpose.

16. A context such as the one outlined here – and that is described in more detail in the judgment – is different from the one that preceded the other amnesty laws to which the Court's case law has referred. Thus, as previously indicated, the Court's analysis and reasoning has characteristics that led it to incorporate elements of international humanitarian law elements to produce an interpretation that harmonized with the obligations established in the American Convention, in order to make a juridical assessment of amnesty in a context such as this one.

17. There is no norm in positive international law that has explicitly prescribed any kind of amnesty. The only explicit mention of amnesty in a multilateral treaty is contained in article 6(5) of Protocol II Additional to the Geneva Conventions of August 12, 1949.[14] In the commentaries to that article, the International Committee of the Red Cross (ICRC) indicated that its purpose "[...] *is to encourage a gesture of reconciliation that will help restore the normal course of life in a people that has been divided."*[15] According to the Proceedings of the Diplomatic Conference in which Additional Protocol II was adopted in 1977,[16] the meaning of that norm was to grant immunity to those detained or punished for involvement in the armed conflict.

18. Pursuant to the foregoing, in this judgment, the Court has indicated that, even though amnesties may be permitted as a component of the ending of a non-international armed conflict, they have a limit which is in relation to war crimes and crimes against humanity, so that these crimes cannot remain unpunished or be forgotten (see paragraphs 285 and 286 of the judgment). These limits are also found in what some call *"sources implicitly related to amnesty."*[17]

19. Moreover, within the United Nations it has been stated *"that peace agreements approved by the United Nations can never promise amnesties for genocide, war crimes, crimes against humanity or gross violations of human rights."*[18] For its part, the Rome Statute of the International Criminal Court, although applicable only to crimes falling within its competence and jurisdiction, entails the obligation of the States parties to hold

[14] Article 6(5) of Protocol II, establishes that *"at the end of hostilities, the authorities in power shall endeavour to grant the broadest possible amnesty to persons who have participated in the armed conflict, or those deprived of their liberty for reasons related to the armed conflict, whether they are interned or detained."*

[15] ICRC. Comments to the Protocol of June 8, 1997, additional to the Geneva Convention of August 12, 1949, relating to the protection of victims of non-international armed conflict. Colombia. 1998. Page 168.

[16] Proceedings of the Diplomatic Conference on the Reaffirmation and Development of International Humanitarian Law Applicable in Armed Conflicts, Geneva (1974-1977). Volume 9. Geneva, Switzerland.

[17] Freeman, Mark. Necessary Evils. Amnesties and the Search for Justice. Cambridge University Press. 2009. Page 36. It underscores Article I of the Convention on the Prevention and Punishment of the Crime of Genocide of 1948, certain regulations contained in the Geneva Conventions and Protocol I on international conflicts, Article 7 of the Convention against Torture and other Cruel, Inhuman or Degrading Treatment (1984); Article 6 of the Convention to Prevent and Punish Torture 1985; Article IV of the Inter-American Convention on Forced Disappearance of Persons,1994, and the International Convention for the Protection of All Persons from Enforced Disappearances, 2006.

[18] Report of the Secretary-General on the rule of law and transitional justice in societies experiencing or emerging from conflict. U.N. Doc S/2004/616. 3 August 2004. para. 10.

credible trials for the crimes defined therein (genocide, crimes against humanity and war crimes).

20. The fact is that, in the specific context of processes of widespread violence and non-international armed conflicts, amnesties may lead, at least in theory and according to the specific case or circumstance, in different directions. Consequently, this creates a whole range of possible outcomes that can delimit the exercise of assessing the interests at stake in order to combine the aim of investigating, punishing, and repairing gross human rights violations, on the one hand, with that of national reconciliation and a negotiated solution to a non-international armed conflict, on the other. There is no universally applicable solution to the dilemmas posed by these opposing forces, because it depends on the specific context, although there are guidelines that must be taken into account.

21. Based on international human rights law and, particularly the American Convention, some fundamental criteria can be outlined in order to deal with these opposing forces, which are basically justice and reconciliation.

22. A first and obvious starting point is that the anomalous and exceptional situation of a non-international armed conflict signifies that there are many thousands of violent offenders and, above all, victims. This exceptional situation usually requires exceptional mechanisms of response. The crucial element is to develop a method of assessment that deals, to the greatest extent possible, with this tension between justice and the ending of the conflict. To this end, several components must be taken into consideration, both judicial and non-judicial, that are focused, simultaneously, on seeking the truth, justice and reparation. This is because the demands that arise from massive violations, the responses to the aftermath of the conflict, and the search for long-lasting peace, require both the States and society as a whole to apply concurrent measures that permit the greatest simultaneous attention to these three rights.

23. In this context, the rights of the victims to truth, justice and reparation must be understood as interdependent. Only the integrated application of measures in favor of victims in all these areas can achieve results that are effective and consistent with the inter-American human rights system. Thus, the simple application of criminal sanctions, without these implying a serious effort to find and report the whole truth, could become a bureaucratic process that does not satisfy the valid objective of the victims to obtain the greatest possible truth. Furthermore, the award of reparations without knowledge of the truth about the violations that occurred, and without establishing conditions for a lasting peace, would only produce an apparent relief for the victims, but not a change in the conditions that would permit a recurrence of the violations.

24. These fundamental components can serve, in whole or in part, in the design of procedures that are suitable for the specificity of a process of negotiated solution to a non-international armed conflict. This, within a perspective in which the greater or lesser severity of the facts can make a specific processing of the facts viable – or not. Thus, for example, facts that can be categorized as war crimes or crimes against humanity in the definitions of the Statute of the International Criminal Court should merit being processed specifically and with priority, and this is not necessarily the same for the other crimes or human rights violations.

25. As for the truth component, in addition to the essential issue of the "judicial truth," which I discuss below in relation to the element of justice, on many occasions, this has led to the implementation of mechanisms such as truth commissions. However, the concept of "truth" is not unique and opens the door to different interpretations. Alex

Boraine,[19] former vice-chairperson of the Truth and Reconciliation Commission of South Africa conceptualized the "truth" in this type of situation at three levels: factual truth, personal truth, and social truth. The "factual" truth gives the family specific information on the whereabouts of the mortal remains of the victim or on what happened. The "personal" truth seeks a cathartic effect on the person who expresses or manifests that truth. The "social" truth is that which is adopted by society through dialogue and debate. In pursuit of this "social truth", an important role is played by measures such as access to the documentation held by the State, the revision of scholarly texts, and the construction of museums or memorials relating to what happened.

26. With regard to the element of justice, the State's legal obligation to investigate and punish the most serious human rights violations is - as the Court has repeatedly stated – an obligation of means and forms part of the obligation of guarantee established in the Convention. Thus, States must make adequate remedies available for victims to exercise their rights. However, armed conflict and negotiated solutions give rise to various issues and introduce enormous legal and ethical requirements in the search to harmonize criminal justice and negotiated peace

27. This harmonization must be carried out by weighing these rights in the context of transitional justice itself. Thus, particularities and specificities may admittedly arise when processing these obligations in the context of a negotiated peace. Therefore, in these circumstances, States must weigh the effect of criminal justice both on the rights of the victims and on the need to end the conflict. But to be valid in international law, they must abide by certain basic standards relating to what can be processed and implemented in several ways, including the role of truth and reparation.

28. It can be understood that this State obligation is broken down into three elements. First, the actions aimed at investigating and establishing the facts. Second, the identification of individual responsibilities. Third, the application of punishments proportionate to the gravity of the violations. Even though the aim of criminal justice should be to accomplish all three tasks satisfactorily, if applying criminal sanctions is complicated, the other components should not be affected or delayed.

29. The right of the victims and of society to access the truth of what happened acquires a special weight that must be considered by an adequate assessment in order to delineate the specifics of justice in such a way that it is not antagonistic to the transitional justice required in peace and reconciliation processes. In that context, specific guidelines can be designed for processing those responsible for the most serious violations, opening the way, for example, to giving priority to the most serious cases as a way to handle a problem which, in theory, could apply to many thousands of those held for trial, dealing with less serious cases by other mechanisms.

30. In this context, it is necessary to devise ways to process those accused of committing serious crimes such as the ones mentioned, in the understanding that a negotiated peace process attempts to ensure that the combatants choose peace and submit to justice. Thus, for example, in the difficult exercise of weighing and the complex search for this equilibrium, routes towards alternative or suspended sentences could be designed and implemented; but, without losing sight of the fact that this may vary substantially according to both the degree of responsibility for serious crimes and the extent to which responsibility is acknowledged and information is provided about what happened. This may give rise to important differences between the "perpetrators" and those who performed functions of high command and gave the orders.

---

[19] Boraine, Alex. *A Country Unmasked: Inside South Africa's Truth and Reconciliation Commission*, Oxford University Press. Oxford and New York, 2000.

31. It is relevant to consider the shared responsibilities of those involved in an armed conflict with regard to serious crimes. The acknowledgment of responsibility by the most senior leaders can help promote a process of clarifying both the facts and the structures that made such violations possible. Reduction of sentences, alternative punishments, direct reparation from the perpetrator to the victim, and public acknowledgment of responsibility are other ways that can be considered.

32. Full reparation is the third essential element of transitional justice in such a context. It aims to restore relationships of trust within society and seeks to lay the foundations for processes that prevent the repetition of the tragedy that violated this trust, because of the non-international armed conflict. Evidently, this is based on the principle that all violations of international law entail an obligation that they must be repaired and, in this respect, the case law of the Inter-American Court of Human Rights has made a significant contribution.[20] Regarding reparations, there is an extensive array of options that range from pecuniary compensation to measures of rehabilitation and satisfaction, among others.

33. As has been noted in some studies, the component of reparation has its own difficulties – and even impossibilities – in the case of massive and widespread violations of the human rights.[21] In these situations, it would seem that the objectives of these massive programs of reparations is not so much to reinstate the victims to the *status quo ante,* but rather to provide clear signals that the rights and dignity of people will be fully respected.[22] In any case, the legitimacy and effectiveness of reparation programs in these circumstances requires, as an essential ingredient, the design and implementation of effective mechanisms for the participation of those people at whom the programs are directed.[23]

34. Finally, an essential ingredient of reparation, not only for the victims but also for society as a whole, consists in the apologies and accounts of the perpetrators and the acknowledgments of responsibility. The full confession of the facts for which they may have been responsible is an inevitable ingredient - but not the only one - for reparation. It is also a message to society in order to close the door on violence as a way to deal with political or social differences. These "didactic monuments,"[24] as they are an account of atrocities, remind society about what can happen when an armed conflict breaks out and reinforce the capabilities of society in the face of future threats that something like that could happen again.

35. The acknowledgment of responsibility by senior State officials has been introduced consistently in the case law of the Inter-American Court. This is an essential ingredient of transitional justice that seeks to reconstruct the conditions for democratic institutional viability in a society. Although there are many precedents for this kind of act, they multiplied in certain parts of the world at the end of the Cold War.[25] Tony Blair in Great

---

[20] International law has established this principle explicitly, not only in Articles 10, 63 and 68 of the American Convention, but in many other international instruments such as the Universal Declaration of Human Rights (Article 8), the European Convention on Human Rights (art. 50), the International Covenant on Civil and Political Rights (Article 9), and the Convention against Torture and other Cruel, Inhuman or Degrading Treatment (art. 14).

[21] De Greiff, Pablo. *Repairing the Past: Confronting the Legacies of Slavery, Genocide, & Caste*. Yale University, Connecticut. October, 2005. Page 8.

[22] Ibid. Page. 10.

[23] Ibid. Pages 10-11.

[24] Osiel, Mark. *Mass Atrocity, Collective Memory and the Law.* Transaction Publishers, New Brnswick, 1999. Page. 4.

[25] Hazan, Pierre. *Measuring the impact of punishment and forgiveness: a Framework for evaluating transitional justice.* International Review of the Red Cross. Volume 88, Number 861. March 2006. Page 24.

Britain apologized for British responsibility in the nineteenth century Irish famine, Jacques Chirac for the deportation of French Jews to Nazi concentration camps during World War II, and Bill Clinton for the inaction of the United States government during the Rwanda genocide or for the support to dictatorships in Latin America.[26] In the context of processes of transition from internal armed conflict to peace, these acknowledgments acquire special relevance and significance as an ingredient that strengthens and sustains the others.

36. Thus, according to the context derived from the conclusion of the armed conflict, societies can demand that mechanisms exist that are complementary to the obligation of criminal justice and that satisfy the aspirations of the victims to a greater or lesser extent. Truth commissions, instruments for integral reparation, mechanisms to provide care and attention, the protection of vulnerable populations, purges in the public sector, and institutional reforms are some of the options that legislators and leaders have when deciding State policies, in combination with the application of criminal justice developed within a framework of weighing the elements.

37. A negotiated solution to the internal armed conflict raises several issues regarding the weighing of these rights, within the legitimate discussion on the need to conclude the conflict and put an end to future serious human rights violations. States have a legal obligation to address the rights of the victims and, with the same intensity, the obligation to prevent further acts of violence and to achieve peace in an armed conflict by the means at its disposal. Peace as a product of a negotiation is offered as a morally and politically superior alternative to peace as a result of the annihilation of the opponent. Therefore, international human rights law should consider that peace is a right and that the State must achieve it.

38. Thus, in certain transitional situations between armed conflicts and peace, it can happen that a State is not in a position to implement fully and simultaneously, the various international rights and obligations it has assumed. In these circumstances, taking into consideration that none of those rights and obligations is of an absolute nature, it is legitimate that they be weighed in such a way that the satisfaction of some does not affect the exercise of the others disproportionately. Thus, the degree of justice that can be achieved is not an isolated component from which legitimate frustrations and dissatisfactions can arise, but part of an ambitious process of transition towards mutual tolerance and peace.

Diego García-Sayán
Judge

[26] Ibid.

8

Between Impunity and Show Trials

Martti Koskenniemi

When former President Milosevic began his defence at The Hague on Tuesday, 12 February 2002, there was no reason to be surprised by his chosen tactics. By turning the accusing finger towards the West, in particular the members of the North Atlantic Treaty Organization (NATO), for their alleged complicity in first destroying what Milosevic called "mini-Yugoslavia" (Bosnia-Herzegovina) and in 1999 conducting an aggression against his own country, he aimed to avoid conducting his defence under conditions laid down by his adversaries. At the same time, his manoeuvre highlights, once again, the difficulty of grappling with large political crises by means of individual criminal responsibility and gives reason to question the ability of criminal trial to express or conserve the "truth" of a complex series of events involving the often erratic action by major international players, Great Powers, the European Union, the United Nations, and so on. The Milosevic trial – like international criminal law generally – oscillates ambivalently between the wish to punish those individually responsible for large humanitarian disasters and the danger of becoming a show trial.

I. Why Punish?

Bringing Milosevic to The Hague has been celebrated as the most significant event in the international efforts to end the culture of impunity, under way since the establishment of the Yugoslavian and Rwandan war crimes tribunals in 1993 and 1994, the adoption of the Statute of the International Criminal Court in 1998 and the commencement of criminal procedures in several countries against former domestic or foreign political leaders. The record of these events is mixed. But there is no doubt that they manifest a renewed urge today to think about international politics in terms of domestic categories. The universalisation of the Rule of Law calls for the realisation of criminal responsibility in the international as in the domestic sphere. In the liberal view, there should be no outside-of-law: everyone, regardless of place of activity or formal position, should be accountable for their deeds.[1]

Yet, as Hannah Arendt pointed out during the Nuremberg trials, "[h]anging Göring is certainly necessary but totally inadequate. For this culpability ... transcends and destroys all legal order."[2] What she meant, of course, was that sometimes a tragedy may be so great, a series of events of such political or even metaphysical significance, that punishing an individual does not come close to measuring up to it. In nearly all the criminal prosecutions concerned with crimes against humanity committed during or after World War II, some observers have doubted the ability of the criminal law to deal with the events precisely in view of their enormous moral, historical, or political significance.

The philosopher Karl Jaspers, for instance, wrote to Arendt in 1960, a few months before the opening of the Eichmann trial, pointing to the extent to which the events for which he was accused "stand outside the pale of what is comprehensible in human and moral terms" and that "[s]omething other than law [was] at stake here — and to address it in legal terms [was] a mistake."[3] The same argument was heard occasion-

---

1 The description of the campaign for ending the culture of impunity as an aspect of the legalist-domestic analogy is usefully discussed in G. Bass, *Stay the Hand of Vengeance. The Politics of War Crimes Tribunals*, 2000, 8-36.

2 Quoted in N. Frei, "Le retour du droit en Allemagne. La justice et l'histoire contemporaine après l'Holocauste – un bilan provisoire", in: F. Brayard (ed.), *Le génocide des Juifs entre procès et histoire 1943-2000*, 2000, 57.

3 L. Kohler/ H. Kohler (eds), *Hannah Arendt – Karl Jaspers. Correspondence 1926-1969*, 1996, 410. Quoted also in L. Douglas, *The Memory of Judg-*

ally in connection with the more recent trials in France of Klaus Barbie, "the butcher of Lyon" in 1987, and of the two Frenchmen Paul Touvier and Maurice Papon, in 1994 and 1998 respectively. And today, it seems clear that whether or not Milosevic goes to prison is in no way an "adequate" response to the fact that over 200.000 people lost their lives – while millions more were affected – by the succession of wars in the former Yugoslavia. If the trial has significance, then that significance must lie elsewhere than in the punishment handed out to him.

Because this is so plainly evident, it is often argued that trials involving genocide or crimes against humanity are less about judging a person than about establishing the truth of the events. While the prosecution of Eichmann in Jerusalem in 1961, for example, was almost universally held to be necessary, few thought that the necessity lay in the need of punishing Eichmann, the person. He was, after all, only a cog in the Nazi killing machine. Instead, the trial was held to be necessary in order to bring to publicity the full extent of the horrors of the "Nazi war against the Jews",[4] especially as that aspect of the German criminality had, in the view of many, received only insufficient attention in the Nuremberg process. For the State of Israel, the trial was to bring to light a central aspect of the nation's history, and to take a step towards explaining how it all could have happened.[5] What was to be Eichmann's fate after the trial would be of secondary consequence. Indeed, Elie Wiesel suggested that Eichmann should be simply set free, while Arendt advocated handing him over to the United Nations.[6] His death would in no way redress the enormity of the crime in which he had been implicated. It might even diminish the extent to which the special nature of that crime lay in its collective nature as part of the official policy of the German nation.

---

ment. Making Law and History in the Trials of the Holocaust, 2001, 174-175. Here Jaspers was undoubtedly drawing upon his *Die Schuldfrage*, 1946.

4 In her *The Nazi War Against the Jews: 1933-1945*, 1975, Lucy Davidowicz stresses the extent to which the Holocaust was not an accidental offshoot but a deliberate choice of the Hitler regime.

5 This was certainly the perspective taken by the Prosecutor, Gideon Hausner, whom Arendt saw as simply "obeying his master", David Ben-Gurion, the Prime Minister; H. Arendt, *Eichmann in Jerusalem. A Report on the Banality of Evil*, rev. and enlarged edition, 1963, 5. For an excellent recent discussion of this aspect of the trial, cf. Douglas, see note 3, 97 et seq., 150-182.

6 Arendt, see above, 270-271.

The view of criminal justice – also the Milosevic trial – as an instrument of truth and memory has been stated precisely in response to criticisms about criminal law's apparently obsessive concentration on the accused. This aspect of it was highlighted during the early years of the Yugoslavia Tribunal as it proved impossible to bring those accused of war crimes to trial in The Hague. The Tribunal resorted to the procedure that allows the reading of the indictment in open court and the issuing of an international arrest warrant in the absence of the accused.[7] The reasoning behind a "tribunal de verbe" as the procedure was opened on 27 June 1996 against Karadzic and Mladic has been summarised as follows:

> "Incapable jusqu'ici de rendre la justice, contraint de laisser sans châtiment des crimes contre l'humanité et un génocide, le travail du TPI prenait subitement une réelle consistance: la vérité pouvait au moins être dite devant les juges et les victimes reconnues comme telles, face au monde."[8]

Recording "the truth" and declaring it to the world through the criminal process has been held important for reasons that have little to do with the punishment of the individual. Instead, it has been thought necessary so as to enable the commencement of the healing process in the victim: only when the injustice to which a person has been subjected has been publicly recognised, the conditions for recovering from trauma are present and the dignity of the victim may be restored. Facing the truth of its past is a necessary condition to enable a wounded community – a community of perpetrators and victims – to recreate the conditions of viable social life.[9] Nuremberg, Eichmann and the three French trials (as well as more recent processes focusing on torture in Algeria) have each been defended as necessary for didactic purposes,

---

7 Rule 61 of the Rules of the Tribunal: "Procedure in case of failure to execute a warrant."

8 P. Hazan, *La justice face à la guerre. De Nuremberg à la Haye*, 2000, 134.

9 Cf e.g. J. Verhoeven, "Vers un ordre répressif universel?" *AFDI* 45 (1999), writing about criminal justice in terms of "une fonction qui l'on dirait 'consolatrice', d'ordre thérapeutique et pédagogique...la quiétude et la sérénité ," 55 et seq., (60). In regard to the Rwandan genocide of 1994, D.D. Ntanda Nserko, "Genocidal Conflict in Rwanda and the ICTR", *NILR* 48 (2001), 62 et seq.

for establishing an impartial account of the past and for teaching younger generations of the dangers involved in particular policies.[10]

It is hard to assess the psychological credibility of such justifications. In Germany, the didactic effects of Nuremberg have been obscure. At the time of the process itself 78 per cent of the German population regarded the trial as "just" while a similar poll four years later showed only 38 per cent to have this opinion. Many reasons must have contributed to such change of perception: allied policy in occupied Germany, attitudes towards de-Nazification and the sense of Nuremberg as victor's justice.[11] German legal literature of the immediate post-war period usually treated the International Military Tribunal as an occupation court (*Besatzungsgericht*) rather than as an international tribunal.[12] The trials held in the American occupation zone during 1946-1949, too, were intended "to reform and re-educate the German people."[13] However, they were compromised from the outset. Influential members of the US judiciary – including judges from the tribunals themselves – had serious doubts about the constitutionality and procedural fairness of the trials and congressional support for them was thin. Under such conditions, little sympathy could be expected for the trials from the German population.[14] In 1952, only 10 per cent of Ger-

---

10 For a summary of such justifications, cf. A. Cassese, "On the Current Trend towards Criminal Prosecution and Punishment for Breaches of International Humanitarian Law," *EJIL* 9 (1998), 2 et seq., (9-10).

11 Frei, see note 2, 62-67.

12 S. Jung, *Die Rechtsprobleme der Nürnberger Prozesse*, 1992, 89-92, 109-111.

13 F. M. Buscher, *The U.S. War Crimes Trials Programme in Germany, 1946-1955*, 1989, 69.

14 During 1946-49, twelve US military tribunals sitting in Nuremberg heard cases of 185-199 defendants (numbers vary according to source) while a US Army European Command set up its own process, conducted at Dachau that tried 1672 individuals. The trials were vehemently criticised by various United States and German organisations. Though the processes ended in a large number of convictions, most of the sentences were later reduced and a large number of the convicted amnestied in 1951. The summary of the history of those trials is negative: "... the war crimes programme did little to change German attitudes. Cries of foul play and 'victor's justice' accompanied the proceedings ... The constant attacks against the Allies, especially the United States as the main instigator of those proceedings in the late 1940's by Germany's church leaders, politicians, veterans' and refugee organizations demonstrated that the war crimes programme had not re-educated and democratized the Germans," Buscher, see note 13, 22. For the

mans approved of them.[15] "To be tried by a Nuremberg Military Tribunal signified at least in the Federal Republic of Germany no dishonour."[16]

Over the years, the German government, communities and individuals have taken far-reaching steps to keep alive and come to terms with the memory of the crimes of the Hitler regime.[17] But criminal justice has not been at the forefront of *Vergangenheitsbewältigung*. The Auschwitz process that terminated in Frankfurt in 1965 had only slight popular response, despite widespread press and TV coverage. In that same year, the Ministries of Justice of the Länder commenced a systematic effort to prosecute Nazi criminals: though the annual number of new dossiers arose in peak years to over 2000, the highest number of annual convictions was 39, and declined by 1976 to fewer than ten a year.[18] Empirical confirmation about the positive effects of truth-telling is not much more available from other sources, either. The most significant effort in this regard, the South African Truth and Reconciliation Commission (TRC), was hugely controversial when it was set up, and much of that controversy persists. In a recent poll in South Africa, only 17 per cent of the interviewed persons felt that process had had a positive effect while altogether two-thirds expressed the opinion that race relations after the TRC had deteriorated.[19]

Undoubtedly, many kinds of truth may be sought through criminal trials. The "denial of the Holocaust", for instance, has been criminalized in a number of countries in part to honour the memory of the victims, in part to uphold the conventions of truthfulness and good faith that found the discursive basis of the state. The 1985 law in the Federal Republic of Germany that prohibits "lying about Auschwitz" not only seeks to preserve the memory of the Holocaust but also and perhaps

domestic US critiques, cf. ibid., 29-47. For the uses of administrative reviews and amnesties, cf. ibid., 49-89.

15 Buscher, see note 13, 91.

16 Jung, see note 12, 5.

17 For a detailed review, cf. e.g. A. Grosser, *Le crime et la mémoire*, 1989, 87-132.

18 Cf. A. Rückerl, *NS-Verbrechen vor Gericht. Versuch einer Vergangenheitsbewältigung* 1984, 330; Grosser, see note 17, 112-113, 121.

19 E. Kiss, "Moral Ambition Within and Beyond Political Constraints. Reflections on Restorative Justice", in: R.J. Rotberg/ D. Thompson, *Truth v. Justice. The Morality of Truth Commissions*, 2000, 88 and Rotberg, "Truth Commissions and the Provision of Truth, Justice, and Reconciliation", ibid., 19.

above all the legitimacy of the new Germany by keeping open the gap between it and its Nazi predecessor.[20] The more distant the events, the more fragile their truth becomes and thus, it may seem, the more necessary to protect it by the law. And yet, as Lawrence Douglas points out, the agnostic formalism of the law that accepts all historical accounts as *prima facie* of equal value may, in an adversarial process, end up inadvertently legitimating "negationism" as a position on which reasonable men may disagree.[21]

In a similar way, the strategy chosen by Milosevic in The Hague reveals the danger of thinking about international criminal trials in historical or didactic terms. This was the gist of Arendt's controversial critique of the Eichmann trial. For her, the trial's problems arose from the introduction of historical, political, and educational objectives into it.

> "The purpose of the trial is to render justice, and nothing else; even the noblest ulterior purposes – 'the making of a record of the Hitler regime...' can only detract from the law's main business: to weigh the charges brought against the accused, to render judgment and to mete out due punishment."[22]

By contrast, Arendt wrote, the Eichmann trial had become a "show trial",[23] staged by the Prime Minister, David Ben-Gurion to support political motives which had nothing to do with criminal trials as Arendt understood them, as being about the guilt or innocence of individuals.

But should Arendt have the final word? Many of the problems of applying criminal law in response to massive injustice have become evident in the reactions to her critiques. Surely, as many of those involved in the process that led to the signature of the Statute for the International Criminal Court in 1998 seem to have assumed, the value of the new court lies in its deterrent message, the way in which it serves to prevent future atrocities.[24] The force of this argument is, however,

---

20 L. Douglas, "Régenter le passé: Le négationnisme et la loi", in: Brayard, see note 2, 218-223.

21 Douglas, see note 20, 227-238.

22 Arendt, see note 5, 251.

23 Arendt, see note 5, 4-5.

24 Thus one advocate: "...punishment of war criminals should be motivated primarily by its deterrent effect, by the impetus it gives to improved standards of international conduct," C.M. Bassiouni, *Crimes against Humanity in International Law*, 1992, 14. A particularly thoughtful argument is in P. Akhavan, "Beyond Impunity. Can International Criminal Justice Prevent Future Atrocities?", *AJIL* 95 (2001), 7 et seq.

doubtful. In the first place, if crimes against humanity really emerge from what Kant labelled "radical evil", an evil that exceeds the bounds of instrumental rationality, that seeks no objective beyond itself, then by definition, calculations about the likelihood of future punishment do not enter the picture. Indeed, there is no calculation in the first place. But even if one remained suspicious about the metaphysics of "radical evil" (as Arendt herself later became) the deterrence argument would still fail to convince inasmuch as the atrocities of the 20th century have not emerged from criminal intent but as offshoots from a desire to do good.[25] This is most evident in regard to the crimes of communism, the Gulag, the Ukraine famine, liquidation of the "Kulaks". But even the worst Nazi nightmares were connected to a project to create a better world. Commenting upon the speeches of Heinrich Himmler to the SS in 1942, Alain Besançon concluded that even the death camps were operated "au nom d'un bien, sous le couvert d'une morale."[26] But if the acts do not evidence criminal intent, and instead come about as aspects of ideological programmes that strive for the good life, however far in future, or to save the world from a present danger, then the deterrence argument seems beside the point.[27] In such case, criminal law itself will come to seem a part of the world which must be set aside, an aspect of the "evil" that the ideology seeks to eradicate.

As criminal lawyers know well, fitting crimes against humanity or other massive human rights violations into the deterrence frame requires some rather implausible psychological generalisations. Either the crimes are aspects of political normality – Arendt's "banality of evil" – in which case there is no *mens rea,* or they take place in exceptional situations of massive destruction and personal danger when there is little liberty of action.[28] This is not to say that in such cases, people act as automatons, losing capacity for independent judgement. Many studies have elucidated the way individuals react to pressure created by either normality or exceptionality, and are sometimes able to resist. But it is implausible to believe that criminal law is able to teach people to become heroes, not least because what "heroism" might mean in particu-

---

25 Cf. especially T. Todorov, *Tentation du bien, mémoire du mal*, 2000.

26 A. Besançon, *Le malheur du siècle. Sur le communisme, le nazisme et l'unicité de la Shoah*, 1998, 45.

27 Cf. J. Klabbers, "Just Revenge? The deterrence Argument in International Criminal Law", forthcoming in *Finnish YBIL* 11 (2000).

28 For a recent analysis, cf. I. Tallgren, "The Sensibility and Sense of International Criminal law", forthcoming in *EJIL* 13 (2002).

lar situations is often at the heart of the confrontation between the political values underlying the criminal justice system (perhaps seen as victor's justice) and the system that is on trial.

And then there is of course the very politics behind the establishment and functioning of a tribunal in the aftermath of a great crisis that may not always support the grandiloquent rhetoric that accompanies, on the victors' side, the work of justice, so conveniently underwriting their views and post-conflict preferences. By the end of the 1940's, Allied preferences had shifted dramatically. There was no political support for the trials of German industrialists and proceedings against high-ranking professional soldiers were followed with some embarrassment. Fear of communism, Germanophilia, sometimes antisemitism , as well as administrative problems connected with further punishments, made the principal Allied powers wary of further purges in Germany and keen to establish normal relations with it.[29] At least some of this supported the widespread German opposition to the Allied war crimes trial programme of 1946-1949: "Germans saw themselves as victims and not as perpetrators."[30]

In the Yugoslavian situation, too, it may not be exclusively the result of manipulation by the local leaders that the populations often seem to have little faith in the truth propounded by the Tribunal. The fluctuation of Western support, the visible impunity enjoyed by a large number of important Balkan war criminals, and the failure to prosecute the NATO bombings of Serbia of 1999 have provided space for cynicism and denial. Four years after the horrors of Srebrenica, Serbs residing in the area persist in claiming that "[n]othing happened here ... It is all propaganda."[31]

For such reasons, studies on the transformations of authoritarian regimes into more or less liberal democracies in central and eastern Europe, South America and South Africa have suggested a much more complex understanding of the role of criminal trials as not merely about punishment or retribution, nor indeed about deterrence, but as an aspect of a larger "transitional justice" that, in the words of one commentator, sometimes "perform [...] a successful 'final judgement' in the religious sense, a performance that would ultimately enable the state it-

---

29 Cf. D. Bloxham, *Genocide on Trial, War Crimes Trials and the Formation of Holocaust History and Memory*, 2001, 38-56.

30 Buscher, see note note 13, 110.

31 Hazan, see note 8, 245-247.

self to function as a moral agent."[32] Under this view, it is the symbolism of the criminal trial – and the eventual judgement – that enables the community ritually to affirm its guiding principles and thus to become a workable "moral community."

But no uniform jurisprudence has emerged on the use of criminal trials of former political leaders in transition situations. Perhaps the main generalisation that can be made is that such trials have been few, they have been targeted very selectively, the convictions have been moderate and amnesties have been widely used.[33] The legal principles have been vigorously contested, the main controversy focusing on to what extent such trials are only political instruments to target former adversaries on the basis of laws that were not in force at the time they were acting.

But whether the trials use superpositive law (such as the "Radbruch formula" in Germany) or retrospective interpretation of pre-transition law,[34] it seems clear that in order to attain the symbolic, community-creating effect it is supposed to have, criminal law need not be applied to everyone. It is sufficient that a few well-published trials are held at which the "truth" of the past is demonstrated, the victims' voices are heard and the moral principles of the (new) community are affirmed.[35]

This may sometimes become a logistic necessity, too. In 1946, for instance, over 100.000 suspected war criminals resided in the British and American occupation zones in Germany. And in 2001 the Rwandan prisons housed approximately 120.000 detainees. A full trial of each individual was in both cases an impossibility. In the Rwandan situation, an attempt is being made to use "Gacaca courts", popular tribunals akin to truth commissions to expedite the work of justice and the prospect of reconciliation.[36] Clearly, at least sometimes victims do not so much

---

32 J. Borneman, *Settling Accounts. Violence, Justice and Accountability in Postsocialist Europe*, 1997, 23.

33 Cf. R. G. Teitel, *Transitional Justice*, 2000, especially 51-59.

34 For this controversy after German unification, especially in relation to the GDR border guard trials and the trials of Honecker and the former Politbüro members, cf. J. McAdams, *Judging the Past in Unified Germany*, 2001, 23-54.

35 Teitel, see note 33, 46-49, 66.

36 Cf. K.C. Moghadli, "No Peace without Justice. The Role of International Criminal and Humanitarian Law in Conflict Settlement and Reconciliation," paper given at a conference "From Impunity to a Culture of Accountability," Utrecht 26-28 November 2001.

expect punishment (though of course that is not insignificant) but rather a recognition of the fact that what they were made to suffer was "wrong", and that their moral grandeur is symbolically affirmed.[37] For such purposes, "show trials" are quite sufficient, especially if they are supplemented with other measures such as compensations, disqualifications, administrative measures, truth commissions, opening of archives etc. However, such supplementary measures are not available at the international level. And here is the problem with the analogy between international courts and transitional justice. The reasons that make "show trials" – that is to say, trials of only few political leaders – acceptable, even beneficial, at the national level, while others are granted amnesty, are not present when criminal justice is conducted at the international plane. When trials are conducted by a foreign prosecutor, and before foreign judges, no moral community is being affirmed beyond the elusive and self-congratulatory "international community." Every failure to prosecute is a scandal, every judgement too little to restore the dignity of the victims, and no symbolism persuasive enough to justify the drawing of the thick line between the past and the future.[38]

In other words, if the argument of deterrence is unpersuasive as a justification of international criminal justice, and if the symbolic, community-creative rationales can be invoked only with the greatest difficulty, the temptation is great to see the point of the Milosevic trial in its truth-telling function, against the critiques by Arendt and others. Perhaps, the argument might go, the trial is important neither because it may end up punishing Milosevic, because it makes potential dictators or their henchmen think twice, nor because it enables the recreation of Balkan societies as moral communities. Perhaps, we might think, the significance of this "trial of the century" lies in the way it will bring to general knowledge the truth of what really happened – however and by whom that "truth" is then used by anyone at the national or the international level.

II. Of Truth and Context

As criminal lawyers have always known, legal and historical truth are far from identical. The wider the context in which individual guilt has

37 Cf. e.g. P. Bouretz, "Prescription: table ronde du 22 janvier 1999", *Droits* 31 (2000), 53.

38 For this criticism in regard to the ICTY, cf. Hazan, see note 8, 239-263.

to be understood, and the more such understanding defers to the contingencies of historical interpretation, the more evident the limits of criminal procedure for reaching the "truth."[39] One of the few uncontroversial merits of truth commissions *vis-à-vis* criminal justice has been stated to lie in the way the former are able to canvass much more widely and deeply the criminality under scrutiny and thus to offer more "opportunities for closure, healing and reconciliation."[40] This is not to say that there would be no intrinsic relationship between the two types of truth, historical and criminal. In the domestic society, and in the context of a domestic criminal trial, that relationship rarely becomes questioned. Even if a crime is exceptionally shocking – "serial killing" for example – there is normally little doubt about how to understand the relevant acts in their historical context. The only problem is "did the accused do it"? No further question about how to understand what he did, how to place his behaviour in relation to the overall behaviour of those around him, emerges. The truth of the broader context is one, or at least relatively uncontested. In transitional periods, however, the debate about past normality takes on a contested, political aspect. How to deal with the routine spying by citizens of one another, shooting at those wishing to escape, or systematic liquidation of political opponents? How to judge the actions of individuals living and working in a "criminal" normality"(*Unrechtsstaat*): how much "heroism" is needed? What about (mere) passivity? And last but not least – can those judge who have not lived under such conditions?[41]

Much of this applies in the international sphere, too, where problems of interpretation are even more difficult. For any major event of international politics – and situations where the criminal responsibility of political leaders is invoked are inevitably such – there are many truths and many stakeholders for them. In the Milosevic trial, for instance, the narrative of "Greater Serbia" collides head-on with the self-determination stories of the seceding populations, while political assessments of "socialism" and "nationalism" compete with long-term historical and even religious frames of explanation. Much of the West-

---

39 Cf. M. Wildt, "Des vérités qui diffèrent. Historiens et procureurs face aux crimes de Nazis", in: Brayard, see note 2, 251-257. Cf. also D. Lochak, "Prescription, remarques dans une table ronde du 22 janvier 1999", *Droits* 31 (2000), 49-54.

40 Kiss, see note 19, 69.

41 For discussion of this difficulty in the German situation, cf. Bornemann, see note 32, 80-96, 99-100; McAdams, see note 34, 47-54.

ern view depends on a (liberal) understanding of the sombre effects of the allegedly atavistic irrationalism underlying the different Balkan identifications – a view that dramatically plays down the political aspects of the conflict and the role of interest-groups (including the liberal one) in fomenting ethnic hostility. How to understand the actions of the leaders of the Yugoslav communities – whether they were "criminal" or not – depends on which framework of interpretation one accepts.[42]

Political Realists such as Hans Morgenthau always highlighted the weaknesses of the legal process in coming to grips with large events of international politics. Already in 1929, Morgenthau concluded that the role of formal dispute settlement had to remain limited in the international context because it inevitably focused only on some in itself minor aspect of an overall situation. A legal "dispute" for him was always just a part – and sometimes a very marginal part – of what he called a political "tension."[43] The narrower the focus, the less the process would convey any in-depth understanding of the situation and the less reason to think that it will bring about a credible political result. Because the legal process inevitably distorted the political context, it was not only useless but counterproductive for the purpose of providing a basis for peace and reconciliation.

The effort to end the "culture of impunity" emerges from an interpretation of the past – the Cold War in particular – as an unacceptably political approach to international crises. Focusing on the individual abstracts the political context, that is to say, describes it in terms of the actions and intentions of particular, well-situated individuals. Indeed, this is precisely what the Prosecutor in the Milosevic trial, Carla del Ponte, said she was doing in The Hague in February 2002. The (Serb) nation was not on trial, only an individual was. But the truth is not necessarily served by an individual focus.[44] On the contrary, the meaning of historical events often exceeds the intentions or actions of particular individuals and can be grasped only by attention to structural causes,

---

42 For the role of such interpretations in the Milosevic trial, cf. K. Čavoški, "Juger l'histoire" in: P. Marie Gallois/ J. Vergès, *L'apartheid judiciaire au TPI, arme de guerre*, 2002, 77-89.

43 H. Morgenthau, *Die internationale Rechtspflege, ihr Wesen und ihre Grenzen*, 1929, 62-72 and *passim*. For the general context and a discussion, cf. M. Koskenniemi, *The Gentle Civilizer of Nations. The Rise and Fall of International Law 1870-1960*, 2002, 440-445.

44 Wildt, see note 39, 251.

such as economic or functional necessities, or a broad institutional logic through which the actions by individuals create social effects. Typically, among historians, the "intentionist" explanations of the destruction of European Jewry are opposed by "functional" explanations that point to the material and structural causes that finally at the Wannsee conference of 1942 – but not until then – turned Nazi policy towards full-scale extermination. When Arendt and others were criticising the Eichmann trial, they pointed to the inability of an individual focus to provide an understanding of the way the Shoah did not come about as a series of actions by deviant individuals with a criminal mind but through *Schreibtisch* acts by obedient servants of a criminal state.

This is why individualisation is not neutral in its effects. Use of terms such as "Hitlerism" or "Stalinism" leaves intact the political, moral and organisational structures that are the necessary condition of the crime.[45] To focus on individual leaders may even serve as an alibi for the population at large to relieve itself from responsibility. Something of this took place in the trials of Nazi criminals in Germany after World War II. The failure of the Allied powers to agree on a "trial of industrialists" may have reflected emerging concern in the West about the appearance of a new enemy – the Soviet Union – and the need to enlist a democratic Germany on their side. But it dramatically downplayed the degree of participation by German economy and society in the Nazi crimes.[46] As the prosecutions moved to German courts, Allied legislation, particularly Control Council Law No. 10, was set aside as contrary to the principle of non-retroactivity. Recourse was made to the German Penal Law whose relevant provisions had to do with murder and manslaughter. These described the relevant criminality in purely individual terms. Murder, under the interpretation of the *Bundesgerichtshof*, had to take place with a "murderous intent" (*Mordlust*) or "in a malicious and brutal manner" in a way that completely failed to grasp the kind of writing desk action of which most Nazi criminality consisted and in which individuals could (rightly) believe themselves as fully replaceable if they did not carry out their tasks in accordance with the rules that themselves were criminal.[47] By the time of the Auschwitz trials in Frankfurt in 1963-65, the crime of manslaughter had already

---

45 As pointed out in Grosser, see note 17, 76-77.

46 Cf. Bloxham, see note 29, 28-32.

47 For an account of the procedural difficulties in prosecuting former Nazis in Germany under the common criminal law, cf. Rückerl, see note 18, 261-288.

been subject to the statute of limitations so that the defendants could only be tried for murder, and because of a definition of murder that referred to individual intent failed to apply to any but the most brutal operators of the extermination system, most of the Nazis not only escaped judgement but were integrated as loyal citizens of the Bonn republic.[48]

The point here is not to try to settle the epistemological controversy about whether the individual or the contextual (functional, structural) focus provides the better truth but, rather, that neither can *a priori* override the other and that in some situations it is proper to focus individuals while in other cases – such as Nazi criminality, and perhaps in taking stock of *Stasi* collaboration in the GDR – the context provides the better frame of interpretation. But if that is so, then there is no guarantee that a criminal process *a priori* oriented towards individual guilt such as the Milosevic trial necessarily enacts a lesson of historical truth. On the contrary, it may rather obstruct this process by exonerating from responsibility those larger (political, economic, even legal) structures within which the conditions for individual criminality have been created – within which the social normality of a criminal society emerges.

As the German historian Martin Broszat has pointed out, the "one-sided personalisation" and rigid conceptualisation of criminal categories may lead not only to a different kind of truth but also a different way of distributing accountability from that produced by a contextually oriented historical study in a situation such as Germany under the Hitler regime.[49] If one is participating in a collective venture with a sense of historical mission and a moral purpose ("happiness of mankind") such as "communism", for instance, then little is gained by a retrospective interpretation of the effects of that effort – between 85 to 100 million innocent killed – in terms of the evil acts of some number of individuals. The logic of "tentation du bien, mémoire de mal" at work in communism can only be reached through trying to grasp the collective process that combines utopianism and scientism with a revolutionary spirit.[50]

---

48 Cf. D. O. Pendas, "'Auschwitz, je ne savais pas ce que c'était'. Le procès d'Auschwitz à Francfort et l'opinion public allemande", in: Brayard, see note 2, 85-93. Cf also Douglas, see note 3, 188-190.

49 H. Graml/ K.D. Henke, *Nach Hitler. Der schwierige Umgang mit unserer Geschichte. Beiträge von Martin Broszat*, 1987, 47-49.

50 Todorov, see note 25, 36-41; Besançon, see note 26, 59-64.

But in the end, individualisation is also impossible. After all, the defences available to the accused refer precisely to the context in which his acts were undertaken. Was there an acceptable motive or an alternative course of action? Did the victim contribute to the action?[51] What about the acts of the Croatian Militia in Krajina or Eastern Slavonia at the beginning of the war, or the UCK in Kosovo? What was the chain of command that led to the Omarska camp or the Srebrenica massacre? As a journalist commenting on the Racak inquiry during the Milosevic trials observed: "Even among experts who loathe Mr. Milosevic, there are worries over whether the proceedings may look like victors' justice and whether the prosecutor, Carla Del Ponte, can deliver the evidence that draws a direct line between Mr. Milosevic and bodies like those uncovered here."[52] To create that chain will, in the absence of written orders, have to involve broad interpretations and assumptions about the political and administrative culture in the territory, including personal links and expectations between the various protagonists. In this way, even focus on individuals presumes a larger context in which particular individuals rise to key positions and in which their choices and preferences are formulated and come to seem either as "normal" or "deviant". The acts of former Nazis or the Communist Party *Politbüro* – or perhaps more mundanely, *Stasi* agents or members of *apartheid* hit-squads – were not anti-social in the way of regular criminality but part of the political "normality" of criminal societies. This is precisely why Milosevic is able to reveal the hypocrisy in the Prosecutor's position: the trial is a trial of the Serbian nation inasmuch as his acts were part of (and not a deviation from) the social normality of Serbia's recent past.

It is at this point that the strategy chosen by Milosevic receives its full significance, and tends to demonstrate the limits of the criminal trial as an instrument of material truth and political reconciliation. When a trial concerns large political events, it will necessarily involve an interpretation of the context which is precisely what is disputed in the individual actions that are the object of the trial.[53] To accept the terms in

---

51 Even the individualisation of guilt is a policy – namely a policy of collective impunity. "We have to individualize the guilt," said Ivan Djordjevic, a former dissident lawyer and an official in Serbia's Ministry of Internal Affairs. "Otherwise we have this feeling of collective guilt, that this whole nation had the goal of eliminating other people and killing. Not all of us supported this," New York Times 11 February 2002.

52 New York Times, 11 February 2002.

53 As Charles Leben has observed, in large political crimes, the ordinary relationship between fact and context breaks down. Judges may no longer

which the trial is conducted – what deeds are singled out, who is being accused – is to already accept one interpretation of the context among those between which the political struggle has been waged. This is what Jean-François Lyotard has famously called a *Différend* – a situation in which to accept a method or criterion of settlement is already to have accepted the position of one's adversary:

> "A case of differend between two parties takes place when the 'regulation' of the conflict that opposes them is done in the idiom of one of the parties while the wrong suffered by the other is not signified in that idiom."[54]

In case of differend, everything is at stake and the context is always a part of the dispute itself. To understand the German bombing of Coventry and Birmingham in November 1940, with their over 1200 victims as a war crime, but not to see one in the carpet bombing of Germany that resulted in perhaps 600.000 civilian deaths is possible only if one already accepts the truth of the Allied view. Not to condemn Germany, and only Germany, would have put to question the justice of the Allied cause itself. The Nuremberg idiom presumed that the war had been launched as Axis aggression and that every atrocity came about as a consequence of it.

If individual criminality always presumes some context, and it is the context which is at dispute, then it is necessary for an accused such as Milosevic to attack the context that his adversaries offer to him. This is where a trial becomes inevitably a history lesson, and the dispute at the heart of it a political debate about the plausibility of the historical "interpretations." Blaming the destruction of Yugoslavia, and the atrocities committed in what had been its territory, on Western policy, as done by Milosevic, plays upon complex structural causalities and long-term interpretations which are hard to consider within a formal trial. But it is imperative to notice that as long as the chain of causality to individual atrocities has not been established (and so far this has not been the case) to put the blame on Milosevic plays upon equally complex assumptions and interpretations. The fact that Milosevic is on trial, and not Western leaders, presumes the correctness of the Western view of the political and historical context. And because the context is part of the political

confine themselves within the former, historians within the latter: in judging the facts, judges also judge the context, "Remarques dans un débat de table ronde le 22 janvier 2000", *Droits* 31 (2000), 64.

54 J.F. Lyotard, *The Differend. Phrases in Dispute*, translated by G. Van Den Abbeele, 1988, 9.

dispute, the trial of Milosevic can only, from the latter's perspective, be a show trial participation which will mean the admission of Western victory.

There is no doubt that the The Hague trials are an effect of Western policy. The Tribunal would not have come to existence without pressure from the Clinton administration and quarters in the French government.[55] But the West should not be allowed to remain confident that its version of the recent history of the Yugoslavian populations will be automatically vindicated. A trial that "automatically" vindicates the position of the Prosecutor is a show trial in the precise Stalinist sense of that expression. This, after all, was the source of the embarrassment of the Western judges at Nuremberg when their Soviet colleague at the beginning of the trial toasted to the prospect that "they will all hang."[56] To avoid looking like Vyshinsky, the judges not only must allow Milosevic to speak, but take what he says seriously. They will have to accept being directed by Milosevic into the context within which he will construct his defence in terms of patriotic anti-imperialism. As the political and historical "truth" of the Balkans becomes one aspect of the trial, then the West must accept that some – perhaps quite a bit – of responsibility will be assigned to its weak and contradictory policy. The bombing of Serbia in the spring of 1999 that caused around 500 civilian casualties will become one of the relevant factors.[57] The Tribunal cannot ignore the question of whether that was a reasonable price to pay for flying at high altitudes so as to avert danger to NATO pilots.[58] But who can tell how far in the past the chain of political causality leads, and what will turn up as Milosevic will reveal his interpretation of why the West rejected him as an acceptable interlocutor?

In the course of the trial Milosevic has conducted his defence less in order to save himself than in order to get his version of truth across to

---

55 For the diplomatic history, cf. Hazan, see note 8, 55-77.

56 Vyshinsky, as reported in T. Taylor, *The Anatomy of the Nuremberg Trials. A Personal Memoir*, 1992, 211.

57 For the view of the Prosecutor that although "some mistakes" were made, no violations of humanitarian law were involved, cf. the Annual Report of the ICTY, Doc. A/55/273, 30-31, para. 192. The legality of the bombing has, however, been severely contested within humanitarian organisations, among them the ICRC. For the contents of a confidential memorandum by the ICRC, cf. Hazan, see note 8, 219-223.

58 Cf. Comparution de M. Slobodan Milosevic, Les incohérences du Tribunal pénal international, Le Monde Diplomatique (20 juillet 2001) par Catherine Samary, http://www.monde-diplomatique.fr/cahier/kosovo/samary0701.

the public in Serbia, as well as to "history" by and large. He portrays himself not unlike the Armenian Tehlirian who in Berlin in 1921 shot to death Talaat Bey, one of those responsible for the Armenian genocide of 1915, and gave himself up to the police so as to be tried and in the trial to have the occasion to give publicity to the cause of the Armenian people. We may agree that the punishment of one man is incommensurable with the atrocities committed in the Former Yugoslavia. But we are not entitled to forget that this man, too, may share the sense of his own insignificance, and choose to play not for acquittal, but for truth and history.

Having finally moved away from the Scylla of impunity – however incoherently and in response to external pressure – the West is now heading either towards a lesson in history and politics in which its own guilt will have to be assessed, or to the Charybdis of show trials.[59] Whether or not Milosevic was finally indicted only because the West had decided that it no longer needed him, and to provide support for its bombing campaign, once the trial had commenced, it had lost full control of where it might lead. The West may have erred in believing that the international "truth" is one in the same way as domestic truth. Now that the trial will be about the context, the West can no longer remain confident that its version will be automatically vindicated – unless, of course, it would prefer to have a show trial.

III. A Brief History of History Lessons

The idea of the trial as a didactic process, a process of learning the truth about the events on trial has frequently been voiced. The French Prosecutor François de Menthon, for example, addressed the Nuremberg Tribunal with the following words:

> "The work of justice is equally indispensable for the future of the German people. These people have been for many years intoxicated by Nazism ... Their re-education is indispensable ... The initial condemnation of Nazi Germany by your High Tribunal will be a first lesson to these people and will constitute the best starting point

59 For aspects of that guilt, cf. M. Koskenniemi, "'The Lady Doth Protest too Much" Kosovo, and the Turn to Ethics in International Law," *The Modern Law Review* 65 (2002), 159 et seq.

> for the work of revision of values and of re-education which must be its great concern during the coming years...."[60]

But the truth to which the Germans were to be educated at Nuremberg followed from controversial choices about how to focus the Allied case. In his four-hour indictment, de Menthon himself referred to the destruction of the Jews in only one sentence and not once to the Vichy régime, thus helping to build the Gaullist myth of the French nation united by *résistance*.[61] Above all, however, the energetic pursuit of United States' priorities by Justice Jackson in preparing the trial led to the principal charge becoming that of the Nazis having prepared and carried out an aggressive war. As a consequence, the atrocities against the civilians – "crimes against humanity" – were divested of an independent role and became relevant only to the extent they had been carried out after 1939 and "in execution of any crime within the jurisdiction of the tribunal." As Jackson himself put it in June 1945:

> "Our case against the major defendants is concerned with the Nazi master plan, not with individual barbarities or perversions which occurred independently of any central plan."[62]

Such an emphasis – until the end disputed by the French Judge Donnedieu de Vabres – downplayed the significance of the attacks on civilian populations and especially the racially motivated persecutions, carried out alongside and to a large extent independently of the war effort. Since the controversial charge of "common plan or conspiracy" under which members of Nazi organizations were to be tried was finally and perhaps somewhat absent-mindedly linked only to the aggressive war charge (thus undermining the original idea of covering also the pre-1939 persecutions),[63] the result was an interpretation of the Nazi regime as predominantly one of aggressive militarists that put its racist and genocidal character in a secondary and at times almost invisible role.[64] For instance, Belzec, Sobibor and Treblinka at which 1.7 mil-

---

60 Quoted in M. Marrus, *The Nuremberg War Crimes Trial 1945-46. A Documentary History*, 1997, 90.

61 Marrus, see above, 88; Bloxham, see note 29, 101-102. But de Menthon's alternate Edgar Faure went to great detail in researching and describing the persecution of the Jews and other crimes against humanity in the West. Cf. A. Wieviorka, "La France et le procès de Nuremberg," in: A. Wieviorka (ed.), *Les procès de Nuremberg et de Tokio*, 1996, 62-77.

62 Jackson, '6 June 1945' as cited in Marrus, see note 60, 42.

63 Cf. Taylor, see note 56, 75-76.

64 For a critique, cf. Douglas, see note 3, 48-56.

lion Jews were destroyed shared between them only one fleeting reference during the trial.[65] The industrial mechanism of mass killings was completely overshadowed by the Prosecution's concentration on the "common plan" and "aggression" charges. As the historian Michael Marrus has observed: "Distortion and exaggeration were indeed the results – creating an unreal picture for subsequent historians."[66]

The historical truth of Nuremberg came about through a complex play of national priorities, available evidence and interpretation. Among the trial's more embarrassing moments was a partial accommodation of the Russians' wish to avoid references to the Ribbentrop Pact that had divided the spheres of interest between Germany and the Soviet Union in August 1939 and whose existence was only indirectly affirmed through the examinations of Ribbentrop himself and Ambassador Ernst von Weizsäcker.[67] The British, too, had their skeleton in a closet, and it was only due to the defence counsels' persistence that it transpired in Admiral Erich Raeder's examination, that the reason for Germany's attack on Norway in 1940 was to forestall a planned attack by Britain. "On these matters", Telford Taylor later observed, "the tribunal was engaging in half-truths, if indeed there are such things."[68]

Nuremberg demonstrates the limits of criminal trial as an instrument of "truth" above all in its treatment of the destruction of European Jewry. As Lawrence Douglas has recently shown, when the documentary *Nazi Concentration Camps* which was made directly after the liberation of the camps and which includes the famous images of mountains of naked bodies bulldozed into mass graves, was screened in Nuremberg for the first time, the voice behind the images spoke of excesses in war and political brutality, thus highlighting war crimes instead of crimes against humanity.[69] It is not necessary to interpret this

65 Bloxham, see note 29, 108-110.

66 Marrus, see note 60, 127. For a sustained description and criticism of the emphasis in the IMT and the successor trials, cf. Bloxham, see note 29, especially, 57-128.

67 Marrus, see note 60, 134-139.

68 Taylor, see note 56, 555. Cf. also M. Messerschmidt, "La quête de la responsabilité...", in: Wieviorka, see note 61, 91-92. Other famous "oversights" include the Allied terror bombing of German cities and of course Hiroshima and (especially) Nagasaki. For the embarrassing treatment of the Katyn massacre, cf. A. Viatteau, "Comment a été traité la question de Katyn à Nuremberg", in: ibid., 145-155 and A. Tusa/ J. Tusa, *The Nuremberg Trial*, 1983, 410-412.

69 Douglas, see note 3, 57-63.

as manipulation of the evidence. It took years until the full extent of the Jewish catastrophe was revealed to the victors. But it does highlight the problem that as a trial writes history in the immediate aftermath of the events, its interpretation will necessary be based on fragmentary evidence and influenced by interpretations by contemporaries with a concrete stake in the result.[70]

The *Eichmann* trial attempted to correct what was felt in Israel as insufficient weight given at Nuremberg to the Nazi policy against the Jews. This time, *Nazi Concentration Camps* was screened as evidence of the atrocities against Jews. But this was not its only purpose and many observers have criticised the way the trial was used to bolster the self-confidence of the newly created Israeli state by focusing away from the image of Jews as helpless victims driven like lambs to slaughter and to bring to light stories of Jewish resistance and heroism.

In this regard, the story of the French use of the concept of "crimes against humanity" in the controversial trial of Paul Touvier is perhaps even more illustrative. In 1964, when the prospect of former Nazi criminals escaping trial due to passing of the 20-years' prescription period appeared on the horizon, the French National Assembly enacted a law on the non-prescription of crimes against humanity.[71] What were to be held as such was later defined by the *Cour de Cassation* in 1985 as:

> "all inhuman acts and persecutions which, in the name of a state practising a policy of ideological hegemony, have been committed systematically, not only against persons because of their membership in a racial or religious group, but also against the opponents of this policy, whatever the form of their opposition."[72]

---

70 The increasing criticism and decreasing use by historians of Nuremberg documentation is pointed out e.g. in B.F. Smith, *Reaching Judgment at Nuremberg*, 1977, xv-xvi. One aspect of the cold war interpretation lay in the legend about the *Wehrmacht's* innocence in the crimes of the SS, necessary so as to prepare military cooperation with the West. Cf. Bloxham, see note 29, 129-133.

71 Law No. 64-1326 of 26 December 1964. For a discussion of the debates surrounding the adoption of this law, cf. A. Laquièze, "Le débat de 1964 sur l'imprescriptibilité des crimes contre l'humanité", *Droits* 31 (2000), 19-40.

72 Cour de Cassation, Judgment of 20 December 1985. For an extensive analysis of the drafting of this language, cf. L. Sadat Wexler, "The Interpretation of the Nuremberg principles by the French Court of Cassation: From Touvier to Barbie and Back Again", *Col. J. Transnat'l L.* 32 (1994),

Now Touvier was a Frenchman who had been at the service of the Vichy *Milice* and in this capacity participated in the shooting of seven hostages at Rillieux-la-Pape, close to Lyon, on 29 June 1944. His trial brought for the first time to justice the nature of Vichy complicity in the atrocities during the German occupation. As Leila Wexler points out in her detailed study of the case, there was a sense in which it was to be "the trial of the whole French society and not just one man."[73] Was French society ready to stand trial?

Touvier had been condemned to death in absentia in 1946 and 1947. After these sentences had prescribed in 1969, however, he surfaced in France and was, two years later, granted pardon from the remaining convictions by President Pompidou. He was brought to trial anew in 1973 on the basis of the 1964 law and, after several turns, his case came to the Paris Court of Appeals, which in a decision of 13 April 1992, applied the above quoted definition by the *Cour de Cassation* so as to conclude that there was no cause to prosecute him as the Vichy regime had not conducted an "policy of ideological hegemony." The decision caused a tremendous uproar, not least among French historians who were "scandalised over the way the judges permitted themselves to write history and to characterise the ideological nature of the French State".[74] The judgement was partially reversed by the Criminal Chamber of the *Cour de Cassation* on 27 November 1992. However, in applying the definition the Court did not attribute Touvier's acts to Vichy France but to Germany, by pointing out that although Touvier was a member of the French Militia he was acting at the instigation of Gestapo, and "in the interests of the European Axis countries" as defined in article 6 of the Nuremberg Charter. Thus, finally, the Court managed to uphold an interpretation of the nature and role of the Pétain regime during the occupation period that did not conflict with the Fifth Republic consensus about an unbridgeable gap between France and the Hitler regime.[75]

---

287 et seq., (338). Cf also G. Binder, "Representing Nazism: Advocacy and Identity in the Trial of Klaus Barbie", *Yale L. J.* 14 (1989), 1321 et seq., (1337-1338).

73 Wexler, see above 72, 346.

74 Wieviorka, see note 61, 83.

75 Touvier was finally condemned to life imprisonment by the Versailles appeals court on 19 April 1994. For the relevant part of the act of accusation, cf. S. Chalandon/ P. Nivelle (eds), *Crimes contre l'humanité. Barbie, Touvier, Bousquet, Papon*, 1998, 160-163. For a description and critique of the

This consensus was, however, fragile. Work by historians of Vichy contemporaneous to the trial brought out increasing evidence of the enthusiasm with which French administrators collaborated with the Nazis, initiating legislative action that disqualified Jews from public service and required their registration in a way that greatly facilitated rounding them up for transport to the death camps. The deportation of 75.000 Jews from France was largely organised by the French themselves, sometimes without pressure from Germany. Particularly notorious in this regard was the Vel d'Hiv roundup in July 1942 when 7000 internees were held in a sports stadium in the 15th arrondissement in atrocious conditions for four days before being sent to the Drancy internment centre and then to the death camps.[76]

The policy of Vichy France itself was brought to trial in 1997-98 when Maurice Papon, the Secretary-General of the Gironde prefecture in Bordeaux in 1942 was indicted for his role in the deportation of almost 1600 Jews from the Bordeaux region. Papon, a Frenchman and, unlike Touvier, a white-collar administrator at the service of "*L'État français*" had organised the roundups, kept lists of Jews and provided transport and police protection to the convoys.[77] He had also enjoyed a successful career in post-war France, having been Prefect of Paris in 1958, member of the National Assembly in 1968 and even Minister of Finance in the French Government in 1978. There had been higher Vichy officials who had participated in the persecutions, such as René Bousquet and Jean Leguay, but both had died in the course of the proceedings against them in the 1980's. It was thus clear to most Frenchmen that to bring Papon to trial was to aim at Vichy France itself.[78] The

1992 judgments, cf. Wexler, see note 72, 344-353 and 361-367. Cf. also Annex II of the article which contains the reasoning of the Paris Court ending up in the conclusion that Vichy France was not exercising "a policy of ideological hegemony," ibid. 376-379.

76 Cf. especially M. Marrus/ R.O. Paxton, *Vichy France and the Jews*, 1983, 250-252.

77 L. Sadat, "The Legal Legacy of Maurice Papon," in: R.J. Golsan (ed.), *The Papon Affair. Memory and Justice on Trial*, 2000, 141-142.

78 This theme is treated in most of the essays in Golsan, see above. But cf. especially R.O. Paxton, "Vichy on Trial", 169-170; A. Lévy-Willard/ B. Vallaeys, "Those who Organised the Trains Knew There Would be Deaths," Interview with R.O. Paxton in: Libération 3 October 1997, ibid. 181 and N. Weill/ R. Solé, "Today, Everything Converges on the Haunting Memory of Vichy," Interview with P. Nora in: Le Monde 1 October 1997, ibid. 176-177. That to judge Papon was to judge Vichy France was even an as-

fact that he was sentenced, on 2 April 1998, to only ten years' imprisonment, and that French authorities did anything but hurry with the execution of the sentence, throws only a slight shadow on the clarity of that message.

Eichmann, *Touvier* and *Papon* were each about avoiding impunity. But they were also about historical truth and memory. As such, they entered the terrain where national identities are constructed out of interpretations of the nation's past – in these cases those of Israel and Fifth Republic France. But there is no agreement on such identities. What "Israel" or "modern France" stand for are issues of fundamental political controversy among nationals and non-nationals. The engagement of a court with "truth" and "memory" is thus always an engagement with political antagonism, and nowhere more so than in dealing with events of wide-ranging international and moral significance. Historians disagree on the interpretation of such events. So it is no surprise that judges may find it difficult to deal with them. But no matter how much judges may seek to proceed in good faith towards their judgements, the context of the trial cannot – unlike the history seminar – be presumed to manifest good faith on everybody's part. This is not a disinterested enquiry by a group of external observers but part of the history it seeks to interpret. Much is at stake for the protagonists – that is the nature of the trial – and no truth can remain sacred within it.

IV. The Politics of Truth

In order to attain "truth", and to avoid a show trial, the accused must be allowed to speak. But this creates the risk of the trial turning into a propaganda show. This was the great concern at Nuremberg and remains a predominant worry as the United States will bring to trial the prisoners from its terrorism war in Afghanistan, presently detained in Guantanamo. One of the reasons for setting up a Military Court instead of an ordinary civil procedure is precisely to avoid such embarrassment.[79] In this regard, Nuremberg was only partly successful. As

---

pect of Papon's defence. Cf. his final statement to the Bordeaux Appeals Court on 1 April 1998, cf. P. Nivelle, "Le procès papon", in: Chalandon/ Nivelle, see note 75, 510-513, 515.

79 Cf. Jackson's Report to the President, 6 June 1945 quoted by Marrus, see note 60, 41.

Jackson's cross-examination of Göring got out of hands, the latter later gloated with satisfaction: "I had the best legal brains of England, America, Russia and France arrayed against me in their whole legal machinery – and there I was, alone".[80]

There is no reason to think that historical truth in a trial such as that of former President Slobodan Milosevic would come about through obedient co-operation of the accused. A criminal trial is defined by adversity and the construction of the historical context is part of the antagonism between the prosecutor and the defence. In the Milosevic trial, the battle on the historical-didactic terrain clearly outweighs in importance the issue of whether or not the accused is found guilty. So far, his behaviour has well reflected this. Here is a reporter's summary:

> "Il fait le spectacle, tantôt boudeur, tantôt blagueur, toujours agressif et défiant face à des juges impassibles et des procureurs appliqués. Il bouscule chaque témoin produit par l'accusation. Il use et abuse des contre-interrogatoires au grand dam de l'accusation ... Parallèlement, l'accusé ne rate pas une occasion de s'emparer de cette tribune pour diffuser sa parole politique à son opinion publique."[81]

When the list of names that formed the group of Milosevic' legal advisers was published, it was clear that much of the trial would be conducted on this terrain. That list included the name of the controversial French advocate Jacques Vergès, known not only as the counsel for Klaus Barbie, "the Butcher of Lyon", the high-profile terrorist "Carlos" and a supporter of Palestinian activists, but also as the theorist of the "trial of rupture" in which the defence is conducted entirely as an attack on the system represented by the prosecution case.[82] In contrast to the trial of "connivance" in which the accused seeks merely to put the facts in question, a strategy of rupture starts from the existence of what I earlier referred to as a *différend* – two incompatible frameworks of interpretation, and directly attacks the opponent's framework:

> "La rupture bouleverse toute la structure du procès. Les faits passent au deuxième plan ainsi que les circonstances de l'action; au premier plan apparaît soudain la contestation brutale de l'ordre public."[83]

---

80 Quoted in Marrus, see note 60, 118.

81 C. Châtelot, "Le procès Milosevic s'enfonce dans la routine," Le Monde 25 Mai 2002, 15.

82 Cf. J. Vergès, *De la stratégie judiciaire*, 1968.

83 Ibid., 86-87.

The trials of Socrates, of Louis XVI, and of the Communist, Dimitrov, accused by the Nazis of the *Reichstag* fire of 1934, each involve aspects of this strategy – as indeed does the posture of Prometheus, declining to defend himself under Divine law, or Zola's attack on the prosecutors of Dreyfus: *J'accuse*. Dimitrov's strategy was published in the *Pravda* on 4 March 1934 in terms of taking initiative, making the prosecutor, as well as the high representatives of the state called to the witness stand, seem ridiculous. The sole objective in the trial, as described by Vergès, was to advance the cause of the proletariat. Everything else, including Dimitrov's own fate – he refused to rely on an alibi of being away from Berlin on the night of the fire – was secondary.[84]

The trial of Klaus Barbie in Lyon in 1987 is an exemplary case of the use of such a strategy. For most observers, the prime significance of that trial, too, had to do with truth and memory, educating a new generation of Frenchmen in the facts of Nazi policy under the occupation. "The trial was necessary" wrote André Frossard, member of *l'Académie française*, former member of the resistance and prisoner of war to the Germans, saved only by the fact of his ascendancy having been qualified as no more than "three quarters" Jewish, in the immediate aftermath of the trial:

> "la jeune génération d'aujourd'hui ne savait presque rien du passé où l'histoire devenue folle était sortie du monde connu pour séjourner quelque temps en enfer. Le procès Barbie l'a instruite."[85]

For giving this lesson, Barbie was an excellent candidate. He had been the head of the Information Section of the Gestapo in Lyon in 1942-1944, managed to escape trial after the war by participating in US counter-intelligence in Germany and fled then to Bolivia "where he spent the next three decades managing business and unapologetically touting Nazi and other militaristic causes".[86] He was finally abducted by the French Secret Police from Bolivia in 1982 and the trial against him commenced a couple of years thereafter. Among the charges two were particularly important. In April 1944 Barbie had organised the delivery to Auschwitz of 44 Jewish schoolchildren who had been staying at a religious *Foyer des enfants* in the village of Izieu, 75 km from Lyon,

---

84 Ibid., 104-112.

85 A. Frossard, *Le crime contre l'humanité*, 1997, 40. On the reception of the Barbie trial in France, cf. also the very useful account in H. Rousso, *The Vichy Syndrome. History and memory in France since 1944*, translated by A. Goldhammer, 1991, 191-216. Interesting is also Binder, see note 72.

86 Douglas, see note 3, 187-188.

together with their five teachers. None of the children and only one teacher returned. And he was known as the Gestapo officer having captured and tortured – sometimes to death – members of the resistance, among them the resistance hero Jean Moulin.

Two aspects of the Barbie trial bring strikingly to surface the politics of a trial conducted for historical or didactic purposes. There was, on the one hand, the question of whether the French statute of limitations was applicable to Barbie's activities against the members of *la résistance.* That statute limited the prosecution for the most serious crimes of the common law (such as murder) to 20 years. An exception was, however, created by the 1964 law, referred to above, which integrated "crimes against humanity" into French penal law and made them imprescriptible. In 1985, the Lyon court (*Chambre d'accusation*) interpreted the notion so as to allow only prosecution for the deportation of "innocent Jews" – the children of Izieu together with four other counts for action against Jewish civilians – but not for the torture and killing of Jean Moulin, the latter being a "war crime", and thus not covered by "crimes against humanity."[87]

Under pressure from organisations of former resistance members, especially those close to Jean Moulin, the indictment was appealed to the Criminal Chamber of the *Cour de Cassation* that chose a less restrictive interpretation of "crimes against humanity." As we have seen, the High Court defined the concept so as to include in the notion also crimes against the "opponents" of a "state practising a policy of ideological hegemony whatever the form of their opposition."[88] This definition enabled the Court to focus not only on the Jewish victims but also the action taken by the Gestapo against the resistance members, a determined preference for many politicians in the Fifth Republic. France was to be remembered not only as a land of victims and collaborators but also as a country of heroes and fighters, as argued by many of the civil parties in the Lyon hearings.[89] Through this means, however, as

---

87 Decision of 4 October 1985. For extracts from the act of accusation of the Lyon Court, cf. Chalandon/ Nivelle, see note 75, 17-28.

88 Judgment of 20 December 1985. Cf. also the quote at page 22 and references in note 72.

89 Cf e.g. the account of the statement of the counsel for the *Ligue des droits de l'homme*, Henri Noguères, experiencing "shock of witnessing a discrimination between the Jews and the non-Jews that had been thrown into the last train from Lyon to Auschwitz on 11 August 1944,"in: S. Chalandon, "Le procès de Klaus Barbie," in: Chalandon/ Nivelle, see note 75, 125.

Frossard points out, the notion of "crimes against humanity" was diluted so that almost any Frenchman could have invoked it against any German under the occupation.[90] Unlike the judgement of the Lyon Court, the broader view of the *Cour de Cassation* was open to criticism on account of its equating the two historical facts that formed the background of the trial – the destruction of the Jews and the work of the resistance. By so doing, it seemed to erase the special horror of the Jewish genocide, captured in an understanding of "crimes against humanity" as taking place only if, to quote Frossard once more, someone is killed "under the pretext of having been born."[91]

In effect, this confusion goes some way to supporting revisionist interpretations on Nazi policy that sometimes seek to explain the action against the Jews as directed against some kind of opposition or a "danger" to Hitler's regime. When a German historian of international law, for instance, fails to say a word about the Shoah in an account of the conduct of the belligerent powers in the World War II, instead pointing to actions against civilians by "both sides", highlighting the "sad role" that mass executions played in the activities against "partisans", he is engaged in a particularly distasteful act of historical revisionism that could be by-passed as yet another negationist apology, did it not come from the discipline of international law from which the notion of "crimes against humanity" once emerged.[92]

The second aspect of the politics of history in the Barbie trial is even more immediately relevant for the Milosevic case. The declared tactics of Barbie's counsel, Jacques Vergès, was to use the trial for the purpose of attacking the hypocrisy of the French State in accusing Barbie of acts that had been routine parts of its own colonial warfare and particularly

---

90 Frossard, see note 85, 17.

91 Frossard, see note 85, 70. In her thorough commentary of the case, L. Sadat takes the position that Frossard's definition, which coincided with the Lyon Court's restricted view, was both "illogical" and possibly "insensitive", see note 77, 137. Cassese, too, supports the wider definition – but oddly defends this on the basis that the targeted persons were chosen "only because they belong to the enemy" (instead of being belligerents), A. Cassese, *Law and Violence in the Modern Age*, 1986, 112. But surely the Jews were not targeted because they were the enemy. And surely that is precisely where the speciality of the Nazi genocide resides, as Frossard argues, and what is lost from the wider definition.

92 Cf. W. Grewe, *The Epochs of International Law*, translated by M. Byers, 2000, 626 and my book review in *ICLQ* 51 (2002), 746 et seq., as well as *Kritische Justiz* 35 (2002), 277 et seq.

of French policy in the Algerian war (1954-62). Himself of Vietnamese origin, Vergès was an *ancien combattant* in the decolonialist cause who had married an Algerian woman once savagely tortured and condemned to death by the French military. In his pre-trial statements, Vergès had stated that the real battle lay not in attaining the release of his client but in achieving control of the historical and didactic aspects of the trial – far more important questions than the fate of an old Nazi.[93] In fact, he declared, the original indictment had been formulated so as to cover only acts against Jewish civilians so as to avoid the obvious parallel between Nazi action against resistance members and the French suppression of Algerian opposition as well as to keep hidden the names of the resistance members – assumed to occupy high positions in contemporary France – that had delivered Moulin to the Gestapo on 21 June 1943.[94]

To conduct his "trial of rupture", Vergès invited two African lawyers to accompany him on the defence bench, the Algerian Nabil Bouaïta and the Congolese Jean-Martin Mbemba, as if to suggest that whatever happened to the Jews in Europe was about intra-European guilt, "a drop of European blood in the ocean of human suffering which, therefore, only concerned the white man."[95] The Barbie team did not attempt to exculpate Barbie for what he had done, look for mitigating circumstances or point to his marginal role in the Gestapo. Its main concern was to develop the *tu quoque* to maximal public effect, to demonstrate that in essence, there was hardly any difference between what Barbie had done in Lyon and French racism during the years of its colonial wars. Why weep over the dead in the white colonialist's internecine struggles, arrogantly labelled a "World War"? Did not the Barbie trial demonstrate that white man's pity extended only to another white man, his compassion turned into narcissism, exhausting his emotional energy and perpetuating his racism towards everything not-European?[96] "Racism", Vergès argued in his closing statement to the Lyon Court, "we know what it is. We bow our heads also in front of

93 For Vergès career and pre-trial statements, cf. Binder, see note 72, 1356-1359 and Cassese, see note 91, 113-115.

94 Rousso, see note 85, 208-209.

95 A. Finkelkraut, *La mémoire vaine. Du crime contre l'humanité*, 1998, 51-52.

96 Finkelkraut, see above, 61-63.

the martyrdom of the children of Izieu because we remember the suffering of the children of Algeria."[97]

In the end, Barbie's counsel did not go into systematic detail in producing evidence of the tortures committed as part of the official policy of France in the Algerian war or reveal much that was unknown regarding Moulin's arrest. Yet, he restated his main argument over and over again. Acts of colonial brutality in Africa and Indo-China were brought in as aspects of the historical context within which Barbie's actions were to be interpreted: on the day of allied victory, on 8 May 1945, French troops massacred 15.000 Algerian demonstrators in the town of Sétif who joined the celebration of victory with a call for national self-determination.[98] There was no reason – apart from racist reasons – to single out Nazi policy from the historical patterns of continuing violence exercised by Europe on everyone. There was no reason to deny the Holocaust, only to put it in the correct historical frame – in which its significance became automatically relative.

The defence tactic in the Barbie trial was to accept it as being about historical truth. By then choosing an appropriate interpretative context – European colonialism – the actions of the accused would necessarily appear as a relatively "normal" episode in the flow of racist persecutions and massive suffering of which European history has consisted. This has been the choice of Milosevic in the Hague as well. By turning his accusing finger against the Tribunal and the forces that lay behind its creation and his own downfall, Milosevic, too, seeks to write the history of the most recent Balkan wars as a continuation of the Great Power policy that had over and over again torn the peninsula into pieces, throwing its peoples against each other as part of a ruthless game of European domination.

When the debate is moved at that level, then of course it becomes much harder to receive closure by the trial. The opposing evaluations and assessments about how to think about Balkan history will not cease to exist when the judgement is read. The judgement will not provide the only prism through which the events succeeding the dissolution of the former Yugoslavia will be read. On the contrary – and this gives the accused his idiom – the judgement will become part of the complexities of Balkan history. If Milosevic succeeds in becoming a representative of one, perhaps disputed but still respectable view of that history, then he will have attained two victories.

---

97 Vergès 1 July 1987, as reported in Chalandon/ Nivelle, see note 75, 138.

98 Ibid. 139-140.

First, he will have escaped the full force of the legal judgement. The judgement will seem to manifest only one among several interpretations of the past and to receive its validity above all from the power of the forces that were behind it. It would be no more than "victors' justice." The condemnation of the accused would then not seem to carry universal moral significance. It would seem that he was found guilty, as Göring put it in Nuremberg, "because he was on the side that lost the war."

In the second place, by articulating and giving concrete appearance to the particular historical vision that he claimed was on trial, he will have strengthened that vision, providing it with the aura of an iconoclasm that seemed critical enough to have been subjected to the extraordinary measure of a formal trial. The martyrdom that will be the condemned man's private image will reflect on the historical truth that he represents as its secret critical force, its revolutionary power.

V. "Show Trial"?

It is precisely because Realist theorists such as Morgenthau or E.H. Carr had been right about the need always to look for the broad context that pure "individualisation" cannot be carried out. A legal system that did not hold the killing of the innocent a crime would be unacceptable. But equally, and more importantly, not every killing of the innocent is a crime. As the ICJ observed in its *Legality of the Threat or Use of Nuclear Weapons* opinion in 1996, article 6 of the Covenant on Civil and Political Rights prohibits only the "arbitrary" taking of lives and it cannot be determined whether the death of innocent civilians in some situation is an atrocious crime or an inevitable by-product of action that was necessary to protect some more fundamental interest.[99]

But as soon as the law tries to make an assessment about that larger interest, and evaluate the relevant contextual data, it will move onto an area of indeterminacy and political conflict. Are the Balkan wars to be interpreted by reference to ethnic animosities or the interests and alliances of the Great Powers in the region? It has been observed that a

99 Legality of the Threat or Use of Nuclear Weapons, ICJ Reports 1996, 226 et seq., (239-240, paras 24-25). Cf further M. Koskenniemi, "The Silence of Law/ The Voice of Justice", in: L. Boisson de Chazournes/ P. Sands, *International Law, the International Court of Justice and Nuclear Weapons*, 1999, 488 et seq., (490-498).

number of the total of 271 historical facts of which the Tribunal took judicial notice in the 1998 Galic case involved contentious assumptions that were disputed among historians.[100] A Court cannot avoid taking judicial notice of a certain number of background facts. But the moment it does this, it will seem to be conducting a political trial to the extent that what those facts are, and how they should be understood, is part of the conflict that is being adjudged.

Yet, success is not necessarily guaranteed by the opposite technique of refusing to take any of the disputed facts as granted, either. Trials against "Holocaust deniers" have brought to surface the dangerous weakness in the adversarial process: did the witness *really* see who gave orders to the massacre while he or she was hiding behind the barn? And if nobody saw it, did the massacre take place at all? Nobody may have *actually seen* Jews gassed at Auschwitz and lived to tell about it: so did gas chambers really exist? Even Raoul Hilberg's extensive minutiae on the extermination process and Christopher Browning's detailed accounts of the participation of "ordinary men" in the *Einsatzgruppen* are only "hearsay" and thus perhaps inadmissible as evidence in a criminal trial.[101] The more you try to prove such facts in court, the more fragile they become. Witnesses contradict themselves and each other, memories change, or remain inscribed in the words that have been used to give shape to them, lose their immediacy and turn into myth. A vigorous cross-examination leads even the most reliable witness to a state of confusion. In the end, memory may not have been served but undermined – not to say anything of the dignity of the victims who, like the young woman who survived the Racak massacre in January 1999, testified about it in the Hague in May 2002, and whose evidence was reduced to a series of panicky "I don't know" statements by a bullying Milosevic.[102] The tribunal – any tribunal – is here between the difficult choice of accepting some facts as commonly known (and integrat-

100 Čavoški, see note 42, 77-89.

101 Cf. the account of the trial of Ernst Zundel, over his pamphlet "Did Six Million really Die?", in Toronto, Canada, in 1988, in: Douglas, see note 3, 226-254. Through the aggressive cross-examination by Zundel's advocate, D. Christie, "memory was ridiculed, the survivor transformed into an amnesiac at best, and outright liar at worst," 240. For the enormous risks involved in trying to prove "sacred facts" through the banality of the legal process, cf. also D.D. Guttenplan, *The Holocaust on Trial. History, Justice and David Irving Libel Case*, 2001, 307-308.

102 Cross-examination of Ms Drita Emini on 28 and 30 May 2002, Transcript of the Milosevic trial, 5747-5764.

ing the controversies concerning the adequacy of what is "commonly known") and constructing facts out of what the procedural techniques – including cross-examination – happen to bring forward. Here the line between justice, history, and manipulation tends to become all but invisible.

The objective of "educating" people of "historical truths" through law emerges from our contemporary wish to accommodate the Realist insight about the need to take account of the context but also from our rejection of the Realists' conclusion – namely that law cannot be of use here. To speak of a duty of memory is fine, but "memory" may not be something that can be authoritatively fixed by a legal process. To document and to testify is necessary. But documents and testimony are not memory as such. The organisation of archives and the interpretation of testimonies so as to construct coherent narratives involves selection and emphasis that are aspects of the historical craft. "L'historien écrit et cette écriture n'est ni neutre ni transparente," writes the historian Pierre Vidal-Naquet in his polemic against Holocaust revisionism,[103] thus making also explicit the difficulty of conceiving courts as instruments of history and memory. A court rules – and must rule – over individual guilt and innocence and in so doing must strive for neutrality and transparency. Whether it succeeds can only be assessed from the outside, perhaps like in Nuremberg, only after decades of assessment and criticism. One type of memory involves precisely that assessment and criticism, an active interaction with the past from the perspective of one's personal recollection and experience, a memory that looks into the past but opens into the future, poised for transgression, possibly reconciliation. This contrasts with another kind of memory, labelled by the philosopher Alain Finkelkraut "vain memory", in which we outsiders admire our own moral sensibilities and capacity for quick compassion, a memory serving our personal and social projects, far removed from the events on trial[104] – perhaps the construction of an "international community" out of the tragedies of others.[105]

---

103 P. Vidal-Naquet, *Les assassins de la mémoire*, 1987, 148.

104 Cf. Finkelkraut, see note 95.

105 It often seems that the memory for which the trial in the Hague is staged is not the memory of Balkan populations but that of an "international community" recounting its past as a progress narrative from "Nuremberg to the Hague," impunity to the Rule of Law. This "community" would construct itself in the image of a "public time" (in analogy with "public space") in which it would contemplate its past and give a moral meaning to disas-

So far, the dry and bureaucratic procedures at the ICTY have made little impression on the communities in the territory of the former Yugoslavia. There is not much evidence of a developed sense of culpability among the populations. The spectacle of the Milosevic trial has been followed with varying interest in the press and on the terrain. After five months, other concerns seem to have set in. This is in the nature of the criminal trial, the famous tedium of Nuremberg so frustrating for a journalist but indispensable in a complex legal proceeding. Yet, one cannot fail to wonder to what extent a process conducted in front of foreign judges in the Hague is able to attain the didactic purposes hoped for; to what degree Balkan memory may be constructed or directed by an international process. Already antagonised by the absence of the death penalty, and the celebration as a hero of a condemned war criminal on his return to Zagreb after serving his two and half years' sentence,[106] the victims will have to accept being taught by a hypocritical West that has made sure its own guilt would not be formally adjudicated in the process. On the perpetrator side, the articulation of the Milosevic story gives it a measure of respectability that it might otherwise never have received. All this follows as a matter of course in criminal trial that looks for punishment. Anything more – "truth", "lesson", "catharsis", "reconciliation" – depends on how the tribunal will be able to deal with a constitutive paradox at the heart of its job.

This is the paradox: to convey an unambiguous historical "truth" to its audience, the trial will have to silence the accused. But in such case, it ends up as a *show trial*. In order for the trial to be legitimate, the accused must be entitled to speak. But in that case, he will be able to challenge the version of truth represented by the prosecutor and relativise the guilt that is thrust upon him by the powers on whose strength the Tribunal stands. His will be the truth of the revolution and he himself a martyr for the revolutionary cause.

---

ters such as Rwanda or Srebrenica as implying a promise of radiant future. On the idea of "public time", cf. S. Villavicencio, "Sans même un procès. L'impunité et les identités collectives," in: J. Poulain, *Qu'est-ce que la justice? Devant l'autel de l'histoire*, 1996, 216-217.

106 Cf. Hazan, see note 8, 243-247.

9

Review Symposium

Review of Kathryn Sikkink's *The Justice Cascade: How Human Rights Prosecutions Are Changing World Politics*

LESLIE VINJAMURI

The Justice Cascade is an ambitious book that traces the global diffusion of human rights trials over three decades. Its first claim, that justice is widely embraced and increasingly legitimate, is bold and masks intense contestation that the justice process has generated in Cambodia, Sudan, Kenya, Uganda, Kosovo, Serbia, and beyond. Its second claim, that "prosecutions *may* deter human rights violations," is more modest but based on an even more ambitious project. Together with coauthor Hun Joon Kim, Sikkink evaluates the impact of human rights trials on improvements in human rights. Many who read *The Justice Cascade* will share its enthusiasm for human rights trials. The evidence presented in *The Justice Cascade*, though, is unlikely to service the trope that international tribunals deter atrocities. Some leading human rights advocates have become wary of relying on the still prominent claim that trials and tribunals deter atrocities to justify war crime trials. Juan Mendez (2008), who figures prominently in Sikkink's story, argues for a renewed focus on trials for their role in establishing guilt and innocence.[1] Scholars, students, and practitioners who read *The Justice Cascade* will not find clear evidence of deterrence, but they will find plenty to debate.

Those familiar with Sikkink's writings will recognize *The Justice Cascade*. In its careful tracing of the work of individuals, nongovernmental organizations (NGOs), and networks to embed ideas in political life, it resembles the strength of Sikkink's earlier work. Empirically, though, this book goes much further. Qualitative comparisons of Argentina, Greece, and Portugal are followed by a statistical study of human rights trials. Theoretically, *The Justice Cascade* is less ambitious than Sikkink's earlier work, which sought variously to theorize about advocacy networks, the relative resonance of alternative norms, and the barriers that alternative institutional structures created for efforts to spread new ideas (Sikkink 1991; Keck and Sikkink 1998). Instead, *The Justice Cascade* describes in rich detail the role of dedicated individuals who worked tirelessly to advance justice and accountability first in Argentina and later abroad. Sikkink then counts the growth of human rights trials across

Leslie Vinjamuri is Lecturer in International Relations and Co-Director of the Centre for the International Politics of Conflict, Rights and Justice in the Department of Politics and International Studies at the School of Oriental and African Studies.

Address correspondence to Leslie Vinjamuri, Centre for the International Politics of Conflict, Rights and Justice, Centre for International Studies and Diplomacy, SOAS, Thornhaugh Street Russell Square, London WC1H 0XG, United Kingdom. E-mail: lv@soas.ac.uk the globe, details the treaties and institutions that have developed around this norm and develops a complex picture of the international and domestic linkages that have contributed to the diffusion of human rights trials.

On the face of it, Sikkink's claim that human rights trials have spread across the globe seems uncontroversial. She argues neither that human rights trials are more or less popular than, say, amnesties for human rights crimes, reparations, or truth commissions, nor that they are more or less successful than these other tools. Few are likely to argue with this basic aggregate finding, though some various lines of inquiry are imaginable; for instance, some may ask whether more trials are simply the product of more human rights abuses in that same country, in which case the cascade may be less significant as a proportion of the phenomenon it is designed to deal with. Sikkink's data also reveal a significant global imbalance: Latin America has had far more domestic human rights trials than any other region (Sikkink 2011: 22). Although the impression one is left with after reading *The Justice Cascade* is that justice has cascaded globally, Sikkink's own data raise real questions about the significance of human rights trials in Asia and Africa.

Latin America is central for Sikkink in more than one way. Like others who have written about transitional justice in Latin America, Sikkink explores the trials held by Argentina during its transition (Nino 1996). In a footnote at the start of Chapter Two, Sikkink "brackets" the successor trials that followed the Second World War, turning instead to emphasize the role of Argentina, and indeed of several notable Argentines, as the first diffuser of human rights trials (Sikkink 2011: 283). Unlike Portugal and Greece, which also held trials as part of their transitions, Sikkink argues that Argentina wanted to spread this practice abroad. Sikkink traces the role of Argentine advisers who travelled to South Africa to give advice about justice and accountability. South Africa rejected a legal strategy for establishing accountability and opted instead for a truth-telling process that served as a condition for amnesty applications. This truth-for-amnesty strategy enabled the political bargain between the African National Congress (ANC) and the de Klerk government that lay at the heart of the South African transition (Sikkink 2011: 94). Sikkink embraces this as an example of an Argentine-led transnational diffusion of individual criminal accountability.

If *The Justice Cascade* does an exemplary job of tracing the role of individual advocates in pressing for accountability, it says little about the importance of particular types or categories of atrocities in generating global advocacy campaigns and pushing the diffusion process forward. After all, Argentina may have held some of the earliest human rights trials and Argentines certainly did considerable work sharing their expertise, but transnational anti-apartheid activism had deep historical foundations and predated the work of Argentine activists. South Africa was important to the justice cascade not only for its particular response to apartheid but also because of the global outrage that apartheid produced. The power of the South African truth commission as a symbolic response to a situation that had already galvanized considerable global outrage led to normative diffusion that probably outweighed what emerged from the Argentine experience. Indeed, the recent history of transitional justice suggests an alternative hypothesis to Sikkink's, namely, that the global diffusion of a norm that perpetrators of mass atrocities should face justice has been pushed forward less by particular individuals with great passion (though one cannot and would not deny the fruits of their labor) and more by injustices that have sparked the deepest moral outrage. Three situations stand out: the Holocaust crimes of the Second World War, apartheid in South Africa, and ethnic cleansing in Bosnia, each marked by an official radical intolerance defined along racial or ethnic lines.

Still, Sikkink's account of the cascading of justice is a compelling one so long as one reads this less as *the* story and rather as *one* story of the justice cascade. Undoubtedly, Juan

Mendez and others whose role Sikkink highlights have played a powerful role in shaping international justice initiatives. But Sikkink's account says less about the legitimacy of individual criminal accountability than about the practice. Although Sikkink defines the justice cascade as a shift in the legitimacy of the norm of individual criminal accountability and an increase in human rights trials on behalf of that norm, her focus is almost exclusively on the latter (Sikkink 2011: 5). Sikkink states from the outset that legitimacy is difficult to measure and so she turns her efforts instead to a very ambitious global counting of human rights trials. Although this reads as a minor methodological choice, this is perhaps Sikkink's greatest capitulation and was no doubt driven by the desire to develop a comprehensive dataset in a timely fashion, no small achievement. But by abandoning the effort to establish the legitimacy of human rights trials, Sikkink cedes her ability to critically evaluate the real significance of the justice cascade and also, perhaps, to investigate the durability and limits of this cascade especially in those parts of the globe where human rights trials are less practiced, more contested, and less institutionalized. This is where the future of the justice cascade hangs in the balance.

Despite scattered remarks that justice is sometimes slow, delayed, or political, Sikkink's treatment of the justice cascade reads as a fairly uncomplicated, if time-consuming, "diffusion" of justice. As many advocates of justice will no doubt attest, justice has not cascaded easily and often it has been manipulated or obstructed (Eckel 2011). Sikkink's controls for this are not entirely obvious. At one point, she notes that she counts human rights trials in those countries where they "should" be able to take place fairly (Sikkink 2011). Even more problematic for the project of a dataset is the question of how to weigh those trials that are effectively obstructed against those that go forward. By my reading of Sikkink's coding system, if Prime Minister Hun Sen succeeds in his efforts to obstruct justice in Case 003, Cambodia would still be counted as part of the justice cascade in 2012 because Case 002 (the trial of Nuon Chea, Ieng Sary, and Khieu Samphan) was ongoing in that year (Eckel 2011).

Even among those who embrace human rights, peace, justice, reconciliation, and democracy as core values, the prospect of human rights trials has often been contested. Many of the biggest disputes have focused on who has the right to try perpetrators, international or local authorities. Sikkink's general claim that justice has cascaded glosses over the contestation that has taken place over questions of whose authority is legitimate. Many prominent international trials have been rejected by nationals as illegitimate (Belgrade Centre for Human Rights 2004). The ongoing struggle by governments in Uganda, Kenya, and now Libya to rest control over the prosecution of indicted war criminals from the International Criminal Court (ICC) underscores the importance that states, and often citizens, continue to attribute to national sovereignty. These struggles suggest that the legitimacy of human rights trials is contingent on the question of authority (who prosecutes) and is not linked in a linear fashion to an increase in the aggregate number of trials. The shift from state to individual accountability that is highlighted by human rights trials is not synonymous with the claim that sovereignty matters less; in debates about justice, it appears to be more relevant than ever.[2] And, over time, greater restrictions have been placed on the power of foreign and international authorities to convene trials. The Rome Statute of the International Criminal Court, at least in theory, grants greater control to states through its complementarity principle than either the Yugoslav or Rwandan tribunal. As Sikkink notes, universal jurisdiction trials (foreign trials by Sikkink's terminology) have been subject to greater restrictions over the past decade. Indeed, sovereignty remains central to the pursuit of individual accountability through the medium of "citizenship" and "nationals" that shape questions of jurisdiction at the International Criminal Court.

The question of legitimacy also extends beyond that of who has authority to convene human rights trials. The legitimacy of the concept of justice embedded in human rights trials has also been contested. Many affected by atrocities have advocated for justice strategies that are underpinned by alternative conceptions of justice stressing reconciliation or forgiveness. In some cases, these proposals have been pursued in response to international trial initiatives and represent a fundamental rejection of criminal justice in favor of strategies that stress forgiveness, reconciliation, or restorative justice (Philpott 2007).

Normative contestation over justice has also centered on questions of sequencing. In ongoing conflicts, debate has centered on whether trials are likely to reinforce or undermine efforts to secure peace, to reconcile society, and to rebuild states. Sikkink says relatively little about the conditions that shape when justice has taken place quickly and when it has been deferred. It also isn't clear whether justice always contributes to more robust human rights practices, or whether this is the case only when institutions are strong, spoilers are contained, and governments generally favor democracy and the rule of law anyway. Sikkink does argue that "widespread diffusion of the norm of individual criminal accountability, when it is embedded in law and institutions ... can help prevent or deter human rights violations in the future" (Sikkink 2011: 231). But it is still unclear whether this is a general or a specific claim; do human rights trials deter human rights abuses only in countries where the norm is embedded in law and institutions *or* do they deter human rights abuses even in states with weak institutions; do trials that are held locally deter human rights abuses that take place abroad? The answers to these and many other questions are crucial not only for academic debates that Sikkink engages with but also most importantly for practice. If the trial *in absentia* of former Tunisian president Ben Ali, or the trial of former Egyptian president Mubarak are anything to go by, one imagines that justice that comes quickly on the heels of a transition may also look very different. Even among those who agree about the inherent value of accountability, debates about sequencing have been central.[3] Crisis Group, a human-rights-oriented NGO whose current president, Louise Arbour, was formerly Chief Prosecutor of the International Criminal Tribunal for the former Yugoslavia, carefully distanced itself from the Security Council's referral of the ICC to Libya and the ICC's swift move to accept this case during the NATO air campaign and ongoing conflict.[4] The fact that Sikkink finds far more domestic human rights trials in Latin America where democratic transitions occurred far earlier than in Africa or Asia is not surprising; one suspects that a high percentage of the Latin America trials, and especially the domestic trials, were significantly delayed or took place in states where spoilers had considerably less power.

Sikkink's account though is not limited to this description of a justice cascade. In a time when many distinguished human rights advocates have begun to distance themselves from grand claims about the deterrent impact of trials and tribunals, it is also remarkable that a leading constructivist scholar has written a book arguing that the results of her multidecade, multicountry dataset demonstrate that human rights trials *can* prevent or deter repression. Sikkink has in effect responded to a growing chorus of human rights funders and pragmatists who call on human rights advocates to demonstrate the value of human rights by evaluating their impact on political life. The prospect that human rights may deter repression is attractive, but arguing for justice on this basis may turn out to be problematic if it turns out not to be true. This is especially true for those who believe in the essential value and inherent legitimacy of human rights trials. Sikkink shifts the terms of debate away from one that centers on the question of legitimacy without providing a rigorous justification for why a consequentialist justification should triumph or what is at stake in adopting this position (Vinjamuri 2010). The danger of course in justifying human rights on these terms is obvious. It conditions support for trials on the ability to empirically confirm their positive impact. If the data are challenged and turn out not to provide the kind of proof that the author hopes to have discovered, the alternatives may not be appealing for human rights advocates: first, to abandon the practice of individual criminal accountability; second, to shift the terms of the debate back to deontology, not a problem in and of itself but one that would require a kind of capitulation; or third, to get mired in another round of data analysis that may or may not yield evidence that is valid or valuable.

At the end of the day, though, the claim made by this book—that human rights trials deter repression—is almost too general to be helpful. Sikkink makes little effort to evaluate empirically the mechanism through which trials contribute to respect for human rights and suggests, without any attempt to confirm, that it is likely due to socialization and deterrence. But this ducks an essential debate. Several mechanisms have been debated among advocates and skeptics alike. Yet here we are left uncertain, for example, whether fear of punishment, the shame of being named and indicted, or the creation of robust legal institutions matter. Are convictions necessary for deterrence? On all of these questions, Sikkink has little to say for the time being. She also avoids a more systematic comparison of the impact of justice in different contexts, something that NGOs committed to transitional justice have begun to research.[5] We are told generally that human rights deter but given little concrete sense of the conditions under which this is likely to be the case. In many places around the globe, human rights trials have had their most demonstrable effects only after democratic transitions have taken place; it would lend greater weight, and also greater credibility, to Sikkink's findings if she were to say more about the relative impact of human rights trials that have taken place in fragile states when compared to those that have more effective and especially democratic institutions, for example. Much of the controversy surrounding human rights trials has to do with the timing of these trials. On this, Sikkink says little about whether trials pursued during conflict or immediately after a transition are more or less likely to deter than others. She does, though, argue that there is no reason to oppose delayed justice; a claim that is potentially sympathetic with those "trial skeptics" she critiques who find little problem with pursuing trials in stable democratic states.

Sikkink's view of human rights trials as an instrument rather than simply a morally important practice is also evident in her bold claim that human rights trials can be a cost-effective substitute for the use of force. This claim is especially notable given the strength of cynicism surrounding the Security Council's 1993 decision to authorize a tribunal and not the use of military force for war-torn Yugoslavia. Indeed, it is difficult to think of a situation where force and trials have been so clearly interchangeable. Instead, trials have often depended on the prior use of military force to secure peace. In the former Yugoslavia, no trials were pursued until several years after military force had been strategically deployed to help secure a successful peace agreement. In Libya, military force (both by rebels and by NATO) has been a crucial precursor for any trials that might take place. Similarly, in Rwanda it is virtually inconceivable that trials could have been pursued in the absence of a military victory by the Rwandan Patriotic Front, which depended crucially on its use of force. Peace in Sierra Leone was aided by Britain's military intervention and the Special Court took up its work only after this. Except in those circumstances where belligerents have simply run out of steam or willingly put down their arms, it is difficult to think of a case where either international or local uses of force have not preceded human rights trials.

In the end, Sikkink's claims are both bold and modest. This may prove to be the value of *The Justice Cascade*. They are bold because they claim the widespread legitimacy of human rights trials, a claim that may be less obvious the closer one looks. They are modest because they recognize that deterrence remains an unconfirmed aspiration of trial advocates. The expectation that trials should deter repression sets a high bar for a practice that may have inherent value for other reasons. This bar is an important one, in situations where the cost of pursuing trials may be prolonged conflict, loss of life, or other human rights abuses. In fact, as advocates of peace with justice (Sikkink's so-called trial skeptics) have suggested, human rights trials may be best when they are promoted by reformers who have the benefit of a secure institutional base that can ensure the stability that allows trials to succeed (Snyder and Vinjamuri 2003).

Notes

1. Also see Neier (2011) and Orentlicher (2008).
2. Others such as Teitel (2011) have noted the shift to individual accountability.
3. In fact, sequencing has become such a source of contention that Human Rights Watch recently devoted an entire report to this topic. See Human Rights Watch (2011).
4. At a time when others were calling for the ICC to get involved in Libya, Crisis Group deliberately stopped short of calling for Libya to be referred to the ICC. See International Crisis Group (2011).
5. The Research Unit at the International Center for Transitional Justice is among those NGOs most engaged in researching this question.

References

BELGRADE CENTRE FOR HUMAN RIGHTS. (2004) *Public Opinion in Serbia: Attitudes towards ICTY* (Belgrade, Serbia: Belgrade Centre for Human Rights).

ECKEL, Mike. (2011, July 20) Cambodia's Kangaroo Court: Why isn't the U.N. tribunal to prosecute genocidal Khmer Rouge war criminals going after more bad guys? *Foreign Policy Magazine*. [Online]. Available: http://www.foreignpolicy.com/articles/2011/07/20/cambodias_kangaroo_court

HUMAN RIGHTS WATCH. (2011) *Seductions of sequencing: The Risks of Putting Justice Aside for Peace* (New York: Human Rights Watch).

INTERNATIONAL CRISIS GROUP. (2011) *Immediate International Steps Needed to Stop Atrocities in Libya* (Brussels, Belgium: International Crisis Group). [Online]. Available: http://www.crisisgroup.org/en/publication-type/media-releases/2011/immediate-international-steps-needed-to-stop-atrocities-in-libya.aspx

KECK, Margaret E., and SIKKINK, Kathryn. (1998) *Activists Beyond Borders: Advocacy Networks in International Politics* (Ithaca: Cornell University Press).

MENDEZ, Juan E. (2008) Truth and justice. In *Doughty Street Chambers* (London).

NEIER, Aryeh. (2011) New research on transitional justice. In *Harriman Institute* (Columbia University). [Online]. Available: http://www.harrimaninstitute.org/events/event_videos.html

NINO, Carlos S. (1996) *Radical Evil on Trial* (New Haven, CT: Yale University Press).

ORENTLICHER, Diane F. (2008) *Shrinking the Space for Denial: The Impact of the ICTY on Serbia* (New York: Open Society Institution).

PHILPOTT, Daniel. (2007) Religion, reconciliation, and transitional justice: The state of the field. In *Social Science Research Council Working Papers* (New York, NY: Social Science Research Council). [Online]. Available: http://www.global.ucsb.edu/orfaleacenter/luce/luce08/documents/Philpott_SSRC-working-paper.pdf

SIKKINK, Kathryn. (1991) *Ideas and Institutions: Developmentalism in Brazil and Argentina* (Ithaca, NY: Cornell University Press).

SIKKINK, Kathryn. (2011) *The Justice Cascade: How Human Rights Prosecutions Are Changing World Politics* (New York, NY: W. W. Norton).

SNYDER, Jack, and VINJAMURI, Leslie. (2003) Trials and errors: Principle and pragmatism in strategies of international justice. *International Security*, 28(3).

TEITEL, Ruti G. (2011) *Humanity's Law* (Oxford: Oxford University Press).

VINJAMURI, Leslie. (2010) Deterrence, democracy and the pursuit of international justice. *Ethics and International Affairs*, 24(2): 191–211.

10

Confronting Past Crimes

Transitional Justice and the Phenomenon of Truth Commissions

The 1986 publication of *Transitions from Authoritarian Rule*, a major four-volume work focused on Latin America and Eastern Europe, helped to define the terms of a still-new field, that of studying how (and under what constraints) democratic transitions take shape after a period of repressive rule.[1] While the question of "settling past accounts," as the authors call it, is not the central focus of the study, they note a difficult tension between the desire to bury the past, in order to avoid provoking the ire of powerful wrongdoers, and the ethical and political demand to confront the crimes of the prior regime. The authors highlight this dilemma as one of "immense difficulty" for which they have no satisfactory resolution, and posit in a footnote that an essential difference between this and other transitional problems is that this dilemma is one that "simply cannot be avoided and one that the leaders must attempt to resolve."[2]

The writers then suggest that the "worst of bad solutions would be to try to ignore the issue," and that the least worst strategy, based on ethical and political considerations, is to hold trials for the wrongdoers. Leaving aside questions of international law, which the writers are silent on but which today often frame these issues, what is most interesting in this discussion is the narrow scope of options presented to respond to such crimes. When the book was completed, the National Commission on the Disappeared in Argentina was just getting under way. There was still virtually no international recognition of non-judicial truth-seeking as a transitional justice tool, nor was there much recognition of other non-judicial strategies now commonly considered during post-authoritarian transition. Within ten years, by the mid-1990s, this had already changed dramatically. Now, almost twenty-five years since the publication of this first collection, the new field of "transitional justice" is widely referred to, there is extensive literature on almost every aspect of the subject, and questions of justice for past crimes help to frame most major political transition the world round.

Countries are confronting questions of justice and accountability in a wide range of political contexts, following the end of a military regime or repressive government, or after a civil war. It is now perfectly clear that there are many needs arising out of these circumstances that cannot be satisfied by action in the

8 *Confronting Past Crimes*

courts—even if the courts function well and there are no limits placed on prosecuting the wrongdoers, which is rare. Thus, complementary approaches to criminal justice have slowly taken shape. Many needs of victims and communities that were damaged by the violence will not be addressed through such prosecutions, except perhaps in providing some solace if the perpetrators are successfully convicted. The institutional or societal conditions that allowed the massive abuses to take place—the structures of the armed forces and the judiciary, or the laws that should constrain the actions of officials, for example—may remain unchanged even as a more democratic and less abusive government comes into power. Many questions may remain open about exactly what took place during the years of repression, and tensions between communities may fester, or deepen, if these are left unaddressed.

It is with these many and multifaceted issues and problems in mind that the field of "transitional justice" has taken shape over recent years. The basic question, that of how to reckon with massive past crimes and abuses (either by the state or by the armed opposition), raises a wide range of difficult issues. The field has developed in response to the demands and differing circumstances of many transitional states around the world, and the increased expectation that accountability is due after atrocity. It is now widely believed that the legacy of these massive crimes cannot simply be buried, and must somehow be addressed.

A state may have a number of objectives in responding to past abuses: to punish perpetrators, establish the truth, repair or address damages, pay respect to victims, and reform institutions to prevent further abuses. There may be other, larger aims as well, such as promoting national reconciliation and reducing conflict over the past, or highlighting a government's concern for human rights and thus gaining the favor of international partners. Likewise, there are a variety of mechanisms or policies to reach these objectives: holding trials; purging perpetrators from public or security posts; creating commissions of inquiry; providing individualized access to security files; providing reparations to victims; building memorials; or implementing military, police, judicial, or other reforms.

Justice in the courts is usually the first and most prominent of demands, but also the most difficult. Many attempts to prosecute and punish those responsible for severe abuses under a prior regime have seen little success. Sometimes the political transition has involved political compromise, and these compromises have included some form of immunity from prosecution for the repressors of old, perhaps even preserving some of their power or incorporating them into the new government. These immunities, however, have not always held over many years, as the international reach of the law—and the global understanding of acceptable national law—has turned against immunity for the most serious crimes. However, even where there is no legal bar to prosecutions, and despite what are sometimes the best intentions of the new authorities, post-transition justice in the national courts is not easy and is not common. Where there are trials, they are usually few in number and sometimes fail to convict even those who everyone "knows" are guilty. The judiciary may be in shambles: judges politically compromised, corrupt, or timid; expertise lacking; and resources few. The numbers of accused perpetrators can be overwhelming and investigations time-consuming, leaving many perpetrators untouched.

Trials in international courts have also been limited. Again, a relatively small number of persons have been prosecuted in the various international or "hybrid" tribunals that have been created since the early 1990s. These tribunals hope that prosecuting the "most responsible" might have a significant deterrent effect. But the challenges have been great and the impact of these courts at the national level has been mixed.

Some Eastern European states employed a strategy of "lustration," which removed persons from public employment because of their affiliation with the prior regime. Yet this practice has been criticized for lacking due-process guarantees and for relying on the sometimes faulty intelligence files of the prior regime. Many lustration policies were implemented without much consideration of how to best protect those wrongly accused, or those whose affiliation with the prior regime was very limited or brief.[3] Such lustration policies—removing people from their positions solely on the basis of past political affiliation—has been rare outside of Eastern Europe. In most circumstances, this would not be possible, because it is unusual for a regime to keep such detailed records of collaborators, and the records that do exist are destroyed during the course of a transition, and because negotiated transitions sometimes include an agreement that civilian employees of the former regime will not be punished or purged.

Some other states have, however, tried to purge those with a record of human rights abuses from security forces and other public positions, generally referred to as a program of "vetting." El Salvador set up a special commission on this matter, the Ad Hoc Commission, as part of the peace accord that brought its twelve-year civil war to an end. This commission recommended that over one hundred senior members of the armed forces be removed; after considerable pressure from the international community (and with the support of the truth commission report that followed), they were all eventually retired from their posts. [4] When Haiti abolished its army and created a new civilian police force, it made an effort to screen applicants and exclude those from the previous force who were known to have been abusive. Liberia was assisted by the United Nations in individually screening all members of the police force, and a similar vetting program was implemented in creating the new national army.

Only in Eastern Europe has individual access been granted to former state security files (the best-known such program is in Germany, in relation to the East German Stasi files). Because the repression in Eastern Europe was dependent on vast networks of informers, accessing these files revealed many unexpected collaborators with the former regime. Individual victims were able to find and personally confront those who informed on them, all too often their own friends or family members.[5] But again, either because such files are not available or because the nature of the repression and the transition has been different in other regions, such a system of providing individualized access to intelligence and security files has rarely been considered in transitional states outside of Eastern Europe.

Reparations programs for victims, or for communities disproportionately affected by violence, have increased in number and in sophistication in recent years. In some countries, these programs have resulted from the work of truth commissions, as explored in Chapter 12. Transitional justice may also focus on robust programs to reform institutions that were involved in abusive practices, or the laws that allowed such practices to take place. Finally, in many contexts symbolic measures such as official apologies or the construction of memorials offer an important sense of acknowledgment of wrongs.

The field of transitional justice has also begun to address a broader array of issues, such as more careful attention to specific groups of victims, as well as the impact more generally on society beyond direct victims. For example, children may be perpetrators as well as direct victims in a war, raising complex questions of responsibility, accountability, and recovery. There has been greater attention to this issue by scholars and practitioners alike, as seen in the criminal charges brought against commanders for the use of child soldiers, by those working to reintegrate former combatants, and in truth commissions that have designed special procedures for children's participation.[6] Truth commissions and those designing reparations programs have also begun to address the economic impact of conflict and even the much broader question of economic rights.

The Emergence of Truth Commissions

Defining Parameters

The first widely known truth commission was set up in Argentina in 1983, but this body was not referred to as a "truth commission" at that time. Rather, it was and still is referred to as CONADEP, the National Commission on the Disappeared. "Truth commissions" as a term of art did not emerge until almost ten years later, after the National Commission on Truth and Reconciliation in Chile and the Commission on the Truth in El Salvador, which concluded in 1990 and 1992, respectively.[7] Classifying all these specialized truth investigations as similar kinds of exercises allowed a comparison between them, a means to assess their success, and the possibility of setting standards for such inquiries in the future.

But given the variation between these many inquiries, it is not always clear which bodies should be considered within the group for comparison. There is still no single, broadly accepted definition of what constitutes a truth commission. Thus, published lists and databases of truth commissions differ, with some researchers liberally including a broad range of inquiries, and others insisting on a more rigorous and narrow definition and thus a smaller number of commissions.[8]

The definition that I first suggested in 1994 is still often cited, though it has some limitations.[9] Slightly modified here for clarity, this defined a truth commission as (1) focused on the past; (2) set up to investigate a pattern of abuses over a period of time, rather than a specific event; (3) a temporary body, with the intention to conclude with a public report; and (4) officially authorized or empowered by the state.

But this is somehow insufficient. Perhaps the greatest difficulty is that this definition may simply be too broad, potentially including so many commissions of inquiry—set up in a wide range of countries but not perceived at the time as "truth commissions"—that the very meaning begins to be lost. Some analysts have also criticized the simplicity of this definition as missing key elements. Legal analyst Mark Freeman suggests a much more detailed set of qualifiers: that the definition should also explicitly state that (1) a truth commission focuses on severe acts of violence or repression; (2) the acts occurred during recent periods of abusive rule or armed conflict; (3) these commissions describe the causes and consequences of the violations; (4) they investigate violations that occurred in the sponsoring state and (5) the commissions themselves are based in that state; (6) these bodies are "victim centered"; and, finally, (7) they operate relatively independently from the state.[10] Freeman offers a definition that includes these elements.[11] While most of these elements are accurate most of the time, these may be descriptive rather than definitional points, and in some cases would exclude commissions unnecessarily; further, the length and complexity of such a definition makes it unwieldy for common usage.

Freeman also suggests another point of analysis for determining whether a commission is a truth commission: that of the perception by the local (and sometimes global) population. This is useful, though subjective, and may also be too limiting. Other analysts have emphasized adding just one element to the original 1994 definition: that a truth commission always engages broadly with victims and survivors. Finally, some have suggested that all truth commissions have the explicit intention to advance reconciliation or even democracy-building.

Thus, there remains a need for more careful delineation, to provide some parameters to the phenomenon under study. I suggest the following: what is special about truth commissions is their intention of affecting the social understanding and acceptance of the country's past, not just to resolve specific facts. While there is increasingly a focus by truth commissions on promoting "reconciliation," this was not always the case for early truth commissions and should not be a definitional element. It does seem, however, that the intention of truth commissions is part of what defines them: to address the past in order to change policies, practices, and even relationships in the future, and to do so in a manner that respects and honors those who were affected by the abuses. This can be captured in the following slightly revised definition:

> A truth commission (1) is focused on past, rather than ongoing, events; (2) investigates a pattern of events that took place over a period of time;

> (3) engages directly and broadly with the affected population, gathering information on their experiences; (4) is a temporary body, with the aim of concluding with a final report; and (5) is officially authorized or empowered by the state under review.

Thus, a truth commission can easily be distinguished from a governmental standing human rights body, or from a judicial commission of inquiry that aims to clarify the facts of one narrow event. On the other hand, there are truth commissions that are established, may work for some time, but fail to accomplish their objectives—ending before completing their report, or failing even to begin to collect information from victims and others. This may be due to financial or political constraints, or a lack of know-how or commitment on the part of the commissioners, given the extraordinary challenge and the evident risks and resistance they may meet. Such weak examples (or outright failures) must be included in our tally of experiences, as they may suggest important lessons.

For purposes of comparison and learning, it is also important to avoid defining the concept too rigidly. The interest of this book is to explore and understand the increasing use of this form of inquiry, the differences and similarities between such bodies working in very different contexts, the challenges they confront, and, ultimately, the impact that they have. I am aware therefore that I include in my comparative inquiry (and in my list of truth commissions) some commissions that fall outside certain aspects of the above definition. This is important to do for two reasons: First, some of these are extremely interesting new models, examples of the way that "truth commissions" are being relied on in new ways and new contexts, and it is likely that similar kinds of inquiries may be created elsewhere. Second, some of these bodies that strictly fall outside of this definition were nonetheless set up very self-consciously as "truth commissions," using this name and looking to other prominent truth commissions around the world for lessons and guidance. The Truth and Reconciliation Commission in Greensboro, North Carolina, in the United States, is such an example. It was largely (but not entirely) an unofficial process, and focused largely (but not entirely) on a specific event in 1979. But as I shall explain, it is important to include it here.

Truth commissions have been established under many names. For example, there have been "commissions on the disappeared" in Argentina, Uganda, and Sri Lanka; "truth and justice commissions" in Ecuador, Haiti, Mauritius, Paraguay, and Togo; a "truth, justice, and reconciliation commission" in Kenya; a "historical clarification commission" in Guatemala; and, of course, "truth and reconciliation commissions" in South Africa, Chile, Peru, and other countries. Others have been created in Germany, El Salvador, Chad, Timor-Leste, South Korea, Morocco, and elsewhere. While there is much in common between these various bodies, their specific investigatory mandates and powers have differed considerably, reflecting the needs, possibilities, and political realities of each country.

On the other hand, the term "truth commission" is now being applied to many kinds of inquiries that do not seem to fit the general model we are looking at here. In 2009, Scotland's faith community created a Poverty Truth Commission,[12] and in the same year Colombia concluded a quite serious Truth Commission on the Palace of Justice.[13] While the Colombian inquiry comes close to fitting into our scheme, its single-event focus makes it seem closer to a classic commission of inquiry, especially given that Colombia's broader history of violence was excluded. Three bodies that I list as truth commissions in the previous edition of this book are not included here. The two inquiries by the African National Congress are fascinating and well deserving of study, but ultimately the fact that these were undertaken by a non-state armed opposition group sets them apart. Further, the International Commission of Inquiry in Burundi that was established by the UN Security Council was not a national endeavor sponsored by the state under review, even if a request for its establishment formally came from the government. It was an important effort at the time, but is not a good fit with the parameters of truth commissions that we are studying here.[14]

Truth, Justice and Peace

Because truth commissions cover many events that could also be subject to trials, their relationship to the criminal justice system is sometimes misunderstood. But they should be seen as quite separate and independent. On one level, truth commissions clearly hold fewer powers than do courts. They cannot put anyone in jail, they cannot independently enforce their recommendations, and most have not had the power even to compel anyone to appear for questioning. To date, the South African commission has been the only one to offer individualized amnesty, whereby some perpetrators provided detailed accounts of their abuses. Most truth commissions do not interfere with or duplicate any tasks of the judiciary. Yet despite their more limited legal powers, their broader mandate to focus on the patterns, causes, and consequences of political violence allows truth commissions to go much further in their investigations and conclusions than is generally possible (or even appropriate) in a trial. Indeed, the breadth and flexibility of a truth commission are its strength. For example, truth commissions are usually able to outline the full responsibility of the state and its various institutions that carried out or condoned repressive policies—including not only the military and the police, but also the judiciary itself. Truth commissions' focus on victims, usually collecting thousands of testimonies, and honoring these truths in a public and officially sanctioned report, represents for many the first acknowledgment by any state body that their claims are credible and that the atrocities were wrong.

As will be explored in Chapter 8, the relationship between truth commissions and criminal prosecutions has varied, but most commissions have had every intention of strengthening prosecutions. In some cases, these truth inquiries have worked in the context of an amnesty that is already in place, or where a biased and corrupt judiciary makes trials unlikely, and the commission itself has been considered at least a minimal step toward accountability.

Meanwhile, at the broadest international policy level the increasing emphasis on justice during difficult political transitions has met with some concern. Insisting on accountability for past crimes may upset a fragile peace, or make a peace agreement impossible, some say. These concerns are not entirely unreasonable, given the strong reaction and reverberation that have resulted from a number of truth commission reports, or, more precisely, from the prospect that speaking the truth may lead to criminal accountability. Whether emerging from army generals or recently disarmed rebel warlords, tough truth has sometimes (though rarely) brought open threats of breaking the peace, as well as, ominously, death threats against commissioners. This classic "peace versus justice" tension has been present in the context of many post-war truth commissions, as well as in many post-dictatorship contexts if the powers of old still hold sway. These tensions must be recognized.

On the other hand, the proposal for a truth commission has generally not upset peace negotiations, and it has been common for both rebel and government negotiators to agree with relative ease to such a proposal.[15] True, they may be looking for a weak inquiry, or one that they hope to control; there are certainly examples of this. But once agreed, such a commission may become one of the most prominent initiatives of a transition, unexpectedly prying open public space to address long-hushed topics, and intent on pushing for serious reforms.

Other Kinds of Official Inquiries: Underappreciated?

There are a range of other kinds of official inquiries into past human rights abuses that have not been understood as truth commissions, but they have served a very important role and indeed may be a better approach than a truth commission, in some moments and in some contexts.

In Australia, for example, the government asked its permanent human rights monitoring body, the Human Rights and Equal Opportunity Commission, to look into the record of state abuse against the country's population. Its year-long investigation documented decades-long state policies of forcibly removing Aboriginal children from their families and placing them with white families in order to assimilate them into mainstream Australian society. These practices continued until the early 1970s. With the release of the commission's report, *Bringing Them Home*, in 1997, the story became a national scandal and ultimately a central issue in national elections, as the Australian public was outraged by this previously little-known practice, while the government refused to offer a formal apology in the name of prior governments.[16] Sixty thousand copies of the report were purchased in the first year after its release. An annual "Sorry Day" was created, as recommended by the commission, and "sorry books" were made available for signature by the public. Within a year, over 100,000 Australians had signed these books, filling hundreds of volumes.

Canada was also moved to review its policies and relationships with indigenous communities, also long based on forced assimilation through mainstreaming children in "residential schools." After an initial five-year commission of inquiry, resulting in significant reparations to survivors, Canada ultimately decided to establish a full-fledged truth commission to further address this legacy (described in Chapter 5).

The United States has also established various inquiries that aim to acknowledge a history of government abuse. In 1994, the energy secretary appointed an Advisory Committee on Human Radiation Experiments to look into the experiments conducted on unknowing medical patients, prisoners, and communities in the United States from the mid-1940s to the mid-1970s. The report of this committee provided an "unprecedented insight into a murky area of American history," according to one observer.[17]

In another case, with the intention to finally provide reparations, the U.S. Congress created a Commission on War-Time Relocation and Internment of Citizens in 1982 to study the policies and effect of placing Japanese Americans in internment camps during World War II. Many of the recommendations of this commission's report were implemented, including a formal apology from the government and the passage of legislation providing $1.2 billion in compensation to survivors.[18]

There have been other U.S. government practices for which reparations or apologies were offered many years after the fact, though without a formal government inquiry. For example, decades after the press reported on a secret syphilis study done on unknowing black men in Tuskegee, Alabama, which began in 1932 and continued into the 1970s, President Bill Clinton offered a formal apology in 1997. The experiments had been well documented by independent writers and the media, and the government had already paid the men and their families over $9 million in an out-of-court settlement, and thus no government inquiry was seen as necessary.[19]

There are other examples of official or semi-official inquiries into past human rights violations that serve some truth-commission-like functions. Some of these are undertaken during political transitions and served important roles in their respective political contexts, but were limited in authority or scope, or were undertaken only as a precursor to a possible full-fledged truth commission to follow. For example, after receiving pressure from the families of victims and from the press, Leo Valladares, the national commissioner for the protection of human rights in Honduras, a government-appointed ombudsman, independently undertook an investigation into 179 disappearances caused by the armed forces in the 1980s and early 1990s. Yet Valladares worked under his own initiative, received no assistance from the authorities, and based his investigations primarily on press accounts and other public information. He continued to call for a full truth commission even as he published his report in 1994 documenting the disappearances.[20]

Several years before the 1994 genocide in Rwanda, ethnic-targeted violence led to an agreement for a commission to investigate past atrocities, part of a negotiated peace accord between the government and the armed opposition. When the government took no action to set up the commission, Rwandan human rights groups invited four international human rights organizations, from the United States, Canada, France, and Burkina Faso, to undertake such an inquiry. Despite the president's public statement welcoming this non-governmental commission and the assistance provided by some government ministries, it was clear that the president and armed forces resented these investigations, and some witnesses were attacked, possibly in retaliation for their cooperation with the inquiry. The commission's report, released in 1993, had the greatest impact on European governments, especially France and Belgium, which were actively supporting the Rwandan government.[21] Yet the report and its recommendations failed to prevent the genocide that came just one year later.

There are other interesting models of international inquiries that have an official or semi-official flavor and overlap with the work that is typical of truth commissions. For example, an International Panel of Eminent Personalities to Investigate the 1994 Genocide in Rwanda and the Surrounding Events was created by the Organization of African Unity in late 1998, completing its report in 2000. Its research was focused on the history and circumstances of the conflict in Rwanda that led up to the genocide of 1994 and the resulting impact of the violence, basing its conclusions in part on research papers commissioned from experts. The Rwandan government cooperated with the inquiry.

Finally, there have been a number of war crimes investigations, often referred to as international commissions of inquiry, war crimes commissions, or commissions of experts, which can also be distinguished from truth commissions. These bodies, such as those established to look into events in the former Yugoslavia, Rwanda, and Timor-Leste, have been set up by the United Nations for the purpose of evaluating the evidence available for possible international prosecutions.[22] These commissions collect evidence, sometimes including testimony from victims, and submit a report, but they have not been authorized by the state under investigation, nor are they aimed at studying the overall patterns, causes, and consequences of the violence. Rather, they evaluate evidence of criminal wrongdoing and violations of international law. In a number of cases, these commissions have led to the creation of an ad hoc international tribunal, such as in the former Yugoslavia and Rwanda.

Unofficial Inquiries That Result in Broad Truth-Telling

The authorization by the state, which partly defines a truth commission, may provide better access to official sources of information, increased security, and a greater likelihood that a commission report and recommendations will receive serious attention. However, there are many examples of significant non-governmental projects that have documented the patterns of abuse of a prior regime. In some cases, these projects have taken on considerable proportions, gathered significant information, and concluded in sweeping and nearly authoritative reports, despite limitations such as restricted access to government records.

In Brazil, for example, a team of investigators was able to secretly photocopy all of the official court papers documenting political prisoners' complaints of torture—some one million pages in total. Working quietly, and with the support of the archbishop of São Paulo and the World Council of Churches, the team relied on this material to produce *Brasil: Nunca Mais*, a report analyzing the military regime's torture practices over a fifteen-year period.[23] In Uruguay, the non-governmental Servicio Paz y Justicia (SERPAJ) published *Uruguay: Nunca Más*, a far stronger report than that resulting from an earlier parliamentary inquiry, which had worked under a very limited mandate and with little political support.[24] The Human Rights Office of the Archbishop of Guatemala undertook an extensive project to document decades of abuses and massacres in advance of the official truth commission.[25] In Russia, the non-governmental organization Memorial was set up in 1987 to promote accountability and fact-finding around past events. Its staff gathered extensive archives on state abuses going back to 1917, and published several books with lists of victims' names and an analysis of state policies of repression.[26]

National Context

Many different factors may shape a country's transitional possibilities and constraints, and thus its post-transition reality. These include the strength of those groups or individuals who were responsible for the abuses and their ability to control transition policy choices; how vocal and organized is a country's civil society, including victims' and rights groups; and the interest, role, and involvement of the international community. In addition, the transitional choices will be affected by the type and intensity of the past violence or repression and the nature of the political transition. And finally, the national political and social culture—an indefinable set of preferences, inclinations, beliefs, and expectations—will help shape the parameters of whether and in what manner the past is confronted.

But the actual number of victims does not seem to determine how heavily the past will weigh on the future, or the intensity of interest in accountability. In some countries, the existence of a very small number of victims of government abuse has resulted in serious political repercussions and a strong emotional response from the public. Even with such relatively small numbers, the pressure for full truth and justice can be as great as in those countries where hundreds of thousands were killed.

The term "truth commission" is uncomfortable for some. But it has now become a term with a generally understood meaning: an official investigation into a past pattern of abuses. It is certain that more countries will be turning to official truth-seeking in the coming years, and that these inquiries will be shaped in many different ways, with powers, mandates, and expectations determined by local circumstances and priorities. In virtually every state that has recently emerged from authoritarian rule or civil war, and in many still suffering repression or violence but where there is hope for a transition soon, there has been interest in creating a truth commission—proposed either by officials of the state or by human rights activists or others in civil society.

The task of these truth bodies will never be easy. Truth commissions are difficult and controversial entities; they are given a mammoth, almost impossible task with usually insufficient time and resources to complete it; they must struggle with rampant lies and denials to uncover still-dangerous truths that many in power may resist. At the end of a commission's work, a country may well find the past still unsettled and some key questions still unresolved. Yet despite the inherent limitations, both the process and the product of a truth commission can make a critical contribution in the midst of a difficult transition, fundamentally changing how a country understands some of the most contentious aspects of its recent history.

11

Memory Frictions: Localizing the Truth and Reconciliation Commission in Sierra Leone

Rosalind Shaw

This paper concerns the frictions of engagement when transitional justice mechanisms are implemented in local contexts. My focus is the practice of truth-telling as part of a global paradigm of redemptive memory. I first trace the genealogy of this paradigm, examining how it came to appear 'natural' and 'universal.' Second, I explore struggles over memory that ensued when Sierra Leone's Truth and Reconciliation Commission (TRC) assertively promoted this paradigm in a region in which alternative memory techniques reflected popular priorities in an unstable context of 'no peace, no war.' These struggles were rooted not only in the contested content of memories, but also in a perceived incommensurability between contrasting memory projects believed to have divergent implications for processes of reconstruction. Finally, I examine the significance of reparations both for local practices of post-war memory and for the local effectiveness of the TRC.

Introduction: Local Engagements

Come blow your main, come clear your chest. Truth and Reconciliation – The Commission we come for help, make peace sidon na Salone [Truth and Reconciliation Commission (TRC) radio and television jingle, Sierra Leone].

After more than a decade of civil war in Sierra Leone, a TRC began its first public hearings in April 2003. Funded through and coordinated by the UN's Office of

[1] My field research visits to Sierra Leone from 2001 to 2004 were funded by Tufts University's Faculty Research Awards Committee (2001, 2002 and 2003), the Mellon-MIT Inter-University Program on NGOs and Forced Migration (2001 and 2003), the Marion and Jasper Whiting Foundation (2002), a Research and Writing Award from the John D. and Catherine T. MacArthur Foundation (2004) and the United States Institute of Peace (2004). Earlier drafts of this article were written when I held a Jennings Randolph Senior Fellowship at the United States Institute of Peace in Washington, DC (2003–04), a MacArthur Research and Writing Award (2004–05) and a nonstipendiary Fellowship at Harvard University's Carr Center for Human Rights Policy (2004–05). I would like to express my sincere gratitude to all Sierra Leoneans who have shared their experiences of the war and of the TRC with me; to the staff and Commissioners of Sierra Leone's Truth and Reconciliation Commission, who were unfailingly generous with their help; to Rafael Abiem, Andreas Brandstatter and Bjorn Pettersson of the United Nations Assistance Mission in Sierra Leone (UNAMSIL); to Monsignor George Biguzzi, Bishop of Makeni; and to Virginia Bouvier of the United States Institute of Peace. Earlier versions of this paper were presented at the MIT International Studies Center Migration Seminar, the University of Chicago's Anthropology Seminar, the University of Michigan's Africa Workshop, the United States Institute of Peace, Harvard's Carr Center for Human Rights Policy and Uppsala University's Anthropology Department Seminar.

the High Commissioner for Human Rights (OHCHR) in Geneva, and assisted by consultants from the International Center for Transitional Justice (ICTJ) in New York, TRC staff in Freetown sought to create a Commission appropriate to Sierra Leone.[2] Posters, leaflets, radio and television skits and jingles like the one above translated the truth-telling goals of the TRC into Sierra Leone's lingua franca, Krio, urging survivors and perpetrators to '*Come blow your main* [mind],' to vent their thoughts and feelings. '*Blow main*,' according to the TRC, not only gives voice to survivors and addresses the impunity of perpetrators, but also transforms subjectivities by generating '*kol at*' ('a cool/settled heart'), making peace '*sidon na Salone*' ('stay in Sierra Leone') and rebuilding the nation. 'We and the international community want to give a new face to Sierra Leone...' said the Chair of the Commission, Bishop Joseph Humper; 'I believe Sierra Leone will become a new Sierra Leone.'[3]

In the TRC's nationwide exercise in truth-telling from late 2002 to August 2003, memories of violence were gathered as written statements, narrated during public hearings and broadcast on the country's electronic media. The Commission collected more than 8,000 statements. But Sierra Leoneans were divided as to the desirability and timing of such public remembering. While some enthusiastically embraced the TRC's message that *blow main* would bring about *kol at* at both a personal and national level, most of those to whom I spoke during my ethnographic research visits from 2001 to 2004 remained skeptical. Repeating the English expression, 'forgive and forget,' they argued that healing and reconciliation depend on forgetting rather than truth-telling. In some communities, survivors and witnesses of the violence agreed together that they would not give statements telling of what they had suffered during the war. In most of the public hearings, audiences were lower than expected (although they rose dramatically when ex-combatants spoke), relatively few ex-combatants testified and it became clear that a substantial portion of the victims and survivors who testified had done so in the hope that this would give them access to economic assistance. The International Crisis Group (ICG) writes that 'the surprising indifference shown by much of the population to the TRC' raises 'doubts [as to] whether [the hearings] served one of their main purposes: to develop understanding of what happened and so lead to healing.'[4]

2 Sierra Leone's Truth and Reconciliation Commission was mandated by Article XXVI of the 1999 Lomé Peace Agreement, and was established when Sierra Leone's Parliament passed the Truth and Reconciliation Act in 2000. Since the Lomé Accord gave all combatants in Sierra Leone's war a blanket amnesty, the TRC was intended to provide an alternative form of accountability. Although this was a national commission, OHCHR was closely involved in its establishment, helped to draft its legislation, recommended the three international Commissioners, approved the secretariat and was responsible for fundraising and cash flow. See, Richard Bennett, 'The Evolution of the Sierra Leone Truth and Reconciliation Commission,' in *Truth and Reconciliation in Sierra Leone*, ed. UNAMSIL (Freetown, 2001), 37–60. For further information on Sierra Leone's TRC and the TRC Act of 2000 see, UNAMSIL, ed., *Truth and Reconciliation in Sierra Leone* (Freetown, 2001).

3 TRC Tonkolili District Hearings, Magburaka, 7 July 2003.

4 International Crisis Group (ICG), 'Sierra Leone: The State of Security and Governance,' (Freetown/Brussels, 2003), 1 and 12.

In this paper, I am concerned with truth-telling as practiced in truth commissions – a practice that has become part of a globalized discourse of memory as redemptive on both personal and national levels. I will first trace the genealogy of this model of redemptive memory, examining how it came to appear 'natural' and 'universal,' and grew into a global paradigm. Second, I will explore what happened when Sierra Leone's TRC – which assertively promoted this paradigm – was implemented in a region in which alternative memory techniques had been developed as a means of dealing with a violent past. Third, I examine the significance of reparations for both the local effectiveness of the TRC and local practices of post-war memory.

Those who planned and implemented Sierra Leone's TRC sought to create an exemplary performance of truth-telling in the public hearings as part of a process that would (it was hoped) establish individual accountability, foster reconciliation, prevent a recurrence of violence and help rebuild Sierra Leone. Here, the practice of testifying before the Commission formed part of a struggle over memory. But this struggle was fought not only, as is usual in truth commissions and tribunals, over the contested content of the memories of those who committed violations and those who survived them. It was also rooted in a perceived incommensurability between alternative *projects* of memory that many believed to have divergent implications for processes of personal and national reconstruction.

A great deal was – and is – at stake in these contested memory projects. During the country's 11 years of civil conflict from 1991 to 2002, tens of thousands of people were killed or mutilated. The vast majority of Sierra Leone's population of four and a half million were displaced at least once, either as refugees in neighboring countries, as internally displaced persons (IDPs) in towns and formal camps or as groups living in hidden bush camps.[5] Sierra Leoneans experienced displacement, looting, burning, rape, torture, amputation and the killing and abduction of family members; while many ex-combatants (large numbers of whom were youth and children) were themselves abducted, displaced, tortured, raped, drugged and made to loot, burn, rape, kill, abduct and amputate.[6] Each of the four main Sierra Leonean combatant groups – the Revolutionary United Front (RUF) rebels, the Sierra Leone Armed Forces, the Armed Forces Ruling Council (AFRC) junta and the pro-government Civil Defense Forces (CDF) militia – committed (to varying degrees) acts of physical mutilation; abduction and conscription of children and youth; and sexual violence against women and young girls. In addition, the

[5] Displacement figures for Sierra Leone typically do not include the vast and undetermined numbers of people forced to protect themselves by living in the bush. Almost everyone from the Provinces to whom I spoke had had to live in the bush at some point, either hiding there until they could return to their homes or traveling through it to reach a town in which to settle.

[6] For analyses of Sierra Leone's civil war see, Ibrahim Abdullah, ed., *Between Democracy and Terror: The Sierra Leone Civil War* (Dakar: Council for the Development of Social Science Research in Africa [CODESRIA], 2004); David Keen, *Conflict and Collusion in Sierra Leone* (Oxford: James Currey, 2005); Paul Richards, *Fighting for the Rain Forest: War, Youth and Resources in Sierra Leone* (Oxford: James Currey, 1996).

mostly Nigerian troops in the Economic Community of West African States Monitoring Group (ECOMOG), the ceasefire monitoring group of the Economic Organization of West African States (ECOWAS), summarily executed large numbers of civilians accused (often arbitrarily) of belonging to the RUF or AFRC. For several decades, moreover, Sierra Leone has not been a functioning state in any real sense.[7] Its state infrastructure is propped up by donor funds, and it is regularly ranked last in the UN's Human Development Index. How do people live together and reconstruct their lives under these conditions?

The expanding field of transitional justice has sought to answer these questions and to design and implement practical mechanisms – truth commissions, tribunals, reparations and alternative forums such as Rwanda's Gacaca courts – as a basis for post-conflict or post-authoritarian reconstruction. According to the model on which these mechanisms are based, a full acknowledgement of the past through verbal testimony not only forms an essential basis for justice but also facilitates healing and helps rebuild the nation. While most of those involved in policy and planning recognize that transitional justice needs to be adapted to particular settings,[8] the model of redemptive verbal remembering on which transitional justice mechanisms are based has become a global paradigm that has acquired a strong momentum in practice.

Before embarking upon this examination of how a global 'universal' developed and how it was locally engaged through a transitional justice mechanism in Sierra Leone, let me locate my approach to the study of rights- and justice-based interventions and the 'universals' they carry with them. I suggest that we need to hold in tension two opposed standpoints. Some scholars have examined how such interventions form one manifestation of what Foucault called 'governmentality,'[9] in which powerful forms of knowledge embedded in institutional and everyday practices reconfigure the field of action, subjugating alternatives and creating new forms of power and inequality.[10] Transitional justice, moreover, is realized within a context in which geopolitical asymmetries shape the allocation of culpability: the violence of some states is more readily categorized as a crime against humanity, for example, than that of others.[11] Other scholars have noted that external interventions are not juggernauts that prevail over all before them; they are appropriated and transmuted in new ways by local agency.[12] Just as 'universals' never fully

[7] See, William Reno, *Corruption and State Politics in Sierra Leone* (Cambridge: Cambridge University Press, 1995).

[8] See for example, Kofi Annan, 'Report of the Secretary-General to the Security Council: The Rule of Law and Transitional Justice in Conflict and Post-Conflict Societies,' UN Doc. No. S/2004/616, 23 August 2004, 14–16, 25, 64(h); Judy Barsalou, 'Trauma and Transitional Justice in Divided Societies,' United States Institute of Peace Special Report No 135 (Washington, DC: USIP Press, 2005), 8.

[9] See, Graham Burchell, Colin Gordon and Peter Miller, ed., *The Foucault Effect: Studies in Governmentality* (Chicago: University of Chicago Press, 1991).

[10] See for example, Harri Englund, 'The Dead Hand of Human Rights: Contrasting Christianities in Post-Transition Malawi,' *The Journal of Modern African Studies* 38 (2000).

[11] Nandini Sundar, 'Toward an Anthropology of Culpability,' *American Ethnologist* 31 (2004).

[12] Steven Archibald and Paul Richards, 'Converts to human rights? Popular debate about war and justice in rural central Sierra Leone,' *Africa* 72 (2002).

succeed in being universal, interventions are never fully realized as they were intended: when engaged in particular places with particular histories, they are invariably driven in unexpected directions. This second position, we should note, neither balances nor resolves the first one: geopolitical and regional inequalities are changed but not neutralized through the local appropriation of globalizing and universalizing interventions.

Neither of these last two standpoints alone, I suggest, is adequate for an understanding of the instabilities, contradictions and unintended consequences of intervention. In order to grasp the abrasive, unequal and unpredictable ways in which universals – human rights, justice, democracy, capitalism, environmentalism – actually travel through particular locations and histories, Tsing uses the metaphor of 'friction.' 'A wheel turns because of its encounter with the surface of the road,' she argues; 'spinning in the air it goes nowhere.'[13] Thus:

> Attention to friction opens the possibility of an *ethnographic* account of global interconnection. Abstract claims about the globe can be studied as they operate in the world. We might thus ask about universals not as truths or lies but as sticky engagements ... Universals are effective within particular historical conjunctures that give them content and force. We might specify this conjunctural feature of universals by speaking of engagement. Engaged universals travel across difference and are charged and changed by their travels. Through friction, universals become practically effective. Yet they can never fulfil their promise of universality. Even in transcending localities, they do not take over the world.[14]

It is only through the 'sticky' grip of material engagement, then, that transitional justice and its universalizing concepts – impunity, accountability, truth, justice – assume concrete form as institutions and mechanisms that move from one part of the world to another. The 'stickiness' of their practical implementation, however, can dissolve, unmake and remake what 'transitional justice' actually *is* and how it works. Attending to the 'frictional' travels of transitional justice mechanisms requires us to attend to both of the standpoints I outline above – in which interventions may be both repressively top-down *and* locally integrated in creative ways – as we explore, on the ground, how transitional justice is practically engaged in a specific place and time.

Before I discuss the frictional engagement of the TRC in Sierra Leone, however, I will outline the ethnographic methodology through which I conducted my research.

Ethnographic Travels

In order to examine how the TRC moved through local terrains, I carried out ethnographic research in four TRC District Hearings in Makeni (Bombali District),

[13] Anna Lowenhaupt Tsing, *Friction: An Ethnography of Global Connection* (Princeton: Princeton University Press, 2005), 5.

[14] Ibid, 6-8.

Kambia (Kambia District), Magburaka (Tonkolili District) and Moyamba (Moyamba District) from May to July 2003.[15] In ethnographic research, which typically consists of a combination of participant observation and informal ethnographic interviews, anthropologists and others seek to understand particular processes, events, ideas and practices in an informant's own terms rather than ours. This entails building up relationships rather than making a single visit, and spending time in ordinary conversation and interaction, preferably before introducing the more directed form of an interview. When we listen to people on their own terms by developing relationships and by observing and participating in events, the answers we receive are often more revealing than those that people give in an interview. This is both because we exert less control over the conditions of their production, and, in interviews that build upon participant observation, we tend to ask better questions. What we learn through ethnography thus has more potential to challenge our assumptions, often forcing us to unlearn as much as we learn. It is this that makes ethnography such a powerful tool for challenging received wisdom and for understanding events and processes on the ground.

Ethnographic research is, moreover, especially appropriate in sensitive situations. In some post-violence situations, for example, people may have good reason to be suspicious of anything resembling official information gathering, such as a survey. In others – such as an impoverished, war torn country – people may wish to connect themselves to the national or international organization funding a survey, perceiving this as a potential source of assistance and answering the questions accordingly.[16]

During my field research on the TRC, I observed the hearings, conversed and conducted informal interviews both with members of the audience and with people outside the hearings. It was important to pay attention to people beyond the physical space of the hearings, some of whom hung around outside the hall without going in, others of whom went about their normal business in town. It was also important to conduct research in towns and villages outside the District capitals in which the TRC hearings were taking place. Thus during the hearings I also examined the TRC's impact on civilians and ex-combatants in the town of Lunsar, the village of Mamamah (both in Port Loko District), the village of Magbonkane (Bombali District) and Freetown, the national capital. At that time I did not seek to meet or interview those who testified before the TRC: I did not know what impact giving testimony and being questioned during the hearings would have upon them, and did not wish to intrude with additional questions. But the following year, in July and August 2004, I conducted follow-up ethnographic

[15] In addition, I studied an audiotape recording of the Port Loko Distict Hearings held in April 2003.

[16] Thus even a thoughtfully designed survey in Sierra Leone on ex-combatant views of the TRC and the Special Court yielded misleading results, finding a high degree of ex-combatant support for these mechanisms. These results were belied a year later, when all but a few ex-combatants kept away from the TRC hearings that I attended, afraid that these were covert conduits for the Special Court. See, PRIDE and International Center for Transitional Justice, *Ex-Combatant Views of the Truth and Reconciliation Commission and the Special Court in Sierra Leone* (Freetown, 2002).

research in Makeni and other parts of Bombali District with seven witnesses who had testified before the Bombali District Hearings.

Traditionally, ethnographic research has been conducted in a single site. Recently, however, multi-sited ethnographies and 'traveling ethnographies' such as the one I conducted as I followed the TRC hearings through different districts have become common in order to track translocal processes and examine connections and contrasts across different places and times. While I attended one of the TRC District Hearings in the south (Moyamba) for purposes of comparison, most of my research has been conducted in locations (both urban and rural) in northern Sierra Leone.[17] My findings in this article thus apply with particular force to the north, but are also consistent with my more limited research in Moyamba and Freetown.[18]

Remembering and Healing: A Genealogy

In Sierra Leone, the TRC's model of redemptive remembering through truth-telling was central to the friction of its local engagement. In order to understand how this model became foundational to transitional justice, we need to trace the genealogy of truth commissions, which have proliferated throughout the world over the past 20 years in the wake of political and intrastate violence. The *locus classicus* of truth commissions was that of transition from violent state repression during and shortly after the Cold War.[19] In particular, Latin American regimes that were US allies during the Reagan era developed forms of violence and repression, most notably disappearances, torture and death squad killings that were covert and therefore deniable.[20] At a time when Cold War alliances often precluded the criminal prosecution of predecessor regimes, truth commissions enabled victims to challenge the state's official version of the past through personal testimonies of suffering that became one of the most significant weapons against human rights abuses. If '[i]gnorance of those who have disappeared undermines the reality of the world,'[21] then the denials and other official lies about the disappeared created – through words – a set of alternate realities,[22] a distorted hall of

[17] The Northern Province has historically been (and remains currently) disadvantaged relative to the rest of the country in terms of development and education. Its capital, Makeni, was in addition the headquarters of the RUF/AFRC occupation toward the end of the war, and still retains a large concentration of ex-combatants.

[18] This research, in addition, builds upon fieldwork carried out during two visits prior to the TRC hearings, in 2002 and 2001. In 2002, I examined the work of memory in local practices for the reintegration of child ex-combatants in northern Sierra Leone, and in 2001 I examined processes of Pentecostal healing among war-affected youth in Freetown. This post-war fieldwork forms part of a long-term commitment to Sierra Leone through research visits conducted over 27 years from my initial 15 month doctoral fieldwork in 1977–1978.

[19] See, Ruti G. Teitel, 'Transitional Justice Genealogy,' *Harvard Human Rights Journal* 16 (2003).

[20] Aryeh Neier, 'Rethinking truth, justice, and guilt after Bosnia and Rwanda,' in *Human Rights in Political Transitions: Gettysburg to Bosnia*, ed. Carla Hesse and Robert Post (New York: Zone Books, 1999), 40–42.

[21] Zbigniew Herbert 1985, quoted in Eric Stover, *The Witnesses: War Crimes and the Promise of Justice in The Hague* (Philadelphia: University of Pennsylvania Press, 2005), 33.

[22] See, Marguerite Feitlowitz, *A Lexicon of Terror: Argentina and the Legacy of Torture* (Oxford: Oxford University Press, 1998).

mirrors that had to be smashed through words. In the politics of memory that operate in truth commissions following such crimes, the narration of personal memories becomes a site of redemption, of moral accountability.[23] Truth commissions sought to make leaders morally and politically accountable, to expose abuses that had been obscured by a miasma of lies and to acknowledge the stories of individuals whose own realities had been denied. In such contexts of clandestine, state-sponsored violence, forgetting what had happened would feed the miasma and compound the abuse.[24]

During the 1990s, truth commissions were recast as truth and reconciliation commissions (TRCs), of which South Africa's was the most influential in shaping an internationally compelling template for healing, redemption and closure. Although this Commission was not particularly effective in serving the needs of those most affected by the violations of the apartheid era,[25] it has 'become the paradigmatic international model of how to "work through" a violent past and in so doing, to "heal the nation."'[26] Here the dominant image of the truth and reconciliation process was Archbishop Desmond Tutu's metaphor of the cleansing of infected wounds. In the TRC's Final Report, he wrote:

> There were others who urged that the past should be forgotten – glibly declaring that we should 'let bygones be bygones.' This option was rightly rejected because such amnesia would have resulted in further victimization of victims by denying their awful experiences ... The other reason amnesia simply will not do is that the past refuses to lie down quietly. It has an uncanny habit of returning to haunt one. 'Those who forget the past are doomed to repeat it' are the words emblazoned at the entrance to the museum in the former concentration camp of Dachau. They are words we would do well to keep ever in mind. However painful the experience, the wounds of the past must not be allowed to fester. They must be opened. They must be cleansed. And balm must be poured on them so they can heal. This is not to be obsessed with the past. It is to take care that the past is properly dealt with for the sake of the future.[27]

This image of a sentient, feeling body suffering from infected wounds that must be reopened and cleansed through truth-telling represents the TRC as both a surgical procedure and a form of spiritual healing through the application of biblically resonant substances such as balm and oil. The identity of the body in question – whether that of the individual giving testimony before the TRC or of the suffering South African nation – is blurred, suggesting that the healing efficacy of truth-telling operates simultaneously on personal and national levels that

[23] Jennifer Cole, 'The work of memory in Madagascar,' *American Ethnologist* 25 (1998): 626.

[24] See for example, Martha Minow, *Between Vengeance and Forgiveness: Facing History after Genocide and Mass Violence* (Boston: Beacon, 1998), 5.

[25] Fiona C. Ross, *Bearing Witness: Women and the Truth and Reconciliation Commission in South Africa* (London: Pluto Press, 2003); Richard Wilson, *The Politics of Truth and Reconciliation in South Africa* (Cambridge: Cambridge University Press, 2001).

[26] Brandon Hamber and Richard Wilson, 'Symbolic Closure through Memory, Reparation and Revenge in Post-conflict Societies,' *Journal of Human Rights* 1 (2002): 35-53.

[27] Archbishop Desmond Tutu, foreword to the *Truth and Reconciliation Commission of South Africa Report*, Vol. 1(London: Macmillan, 1999), 7.

are homologous. This ambiguity was productive for national purposes, observes Wilson, turning South Africa's TRC into a nation-building process in which 'individual suffering was valorized and linked to a national process of liberation.'[28]

South Africa's TRC redefined truth commissions by shifting the emphasis from justice to health.[29] Subsequently, it has provided a global template for TRCs as part of an international 'first aid kit' in the expanding post-Cold War field of transitional justice.[30] In the ensuing introduction of TRCs to address Peru's Shining Path insurgency; Sierra Leone, Liberia and Burundi's civil wars; and Indonesia's suppression of East Timor, this model of truth, healing and reconciliation came to be applied in the aftermath of quite disparate contexts of human rights violations outside truth commissions' original *locus classicus* of violent institutional silencing.

The truth that re-wounds but also cleanses, and upon which it is assumed that healing and reconciliation depend, is understood in terms of a painful verbalization of memories of violence. How did this understanding of truth-telling develop? The English word 'amnesty' derives from the Greek *amnestia*, meaning 'oblivion': both 'amnesty' and 'amnesia' share the same Indo-European root, '*men*,' 'to think,' and the prefix that negates it.[31] The etymology of 'amnesty' suggests that reconciliation depends on a condition of 'not thinking,' of containing and controlling that form of memory that would foster retribution – a concept that continues to circulate through the English expression 'forgive and forget.' There has long been a broad range of 'Western' responses to memories of violence and suffering, but much of this range has been obscured by an increasingly dominant discourse of remembering.

Any understanding of the historical process through which pain and the verbalization of truth became a compelling model for healing must begin with Christian practices of confession. As we know from Talal Asad's genealogy of discipline and power in the Church, Christian confessional, juridical and other disciplinary practices have often been expressed in terms of a medical metaphor in which spiritual sickness requires treatment through pain and purging.[32] Archbishop Tutu was far from being the first to use the image of cleansing infected wounds. A 6th century treatise on penitence titled *Liber de Penitentia*, for example, casts verbal confession as healing for the wounded soul:

> How art thou to be cured, if thou do not lay bare what things are hidden within thee? [T]hy penitent confession is thy medicine, which cures thee and gives thee life; and

[28] Wilson, supra n 25 at 119.

[29] Minow, supra n 24 at 22 and 63.

[30] See for example, Catherine Jenkins, 'A Truth Commission for East Timor: Lessons from South Africa?' *Journal of Conflict and Security Law* 7 (2002): 233–252. Some aspects of South Africa's TRC have provided an effective model for other commissions however. According to Salomon Lerner, Chairman of Peru's TRC, the complexity of the South African TRC's mandate made it appropriate to Peru's situation during the planning for Peru's Commission. 'Briefing on Peru's Truth and Reconciliation Commission,' United States Institute of Peace, Washington, DC, 9 April 2004.

[31] I am grateful to Jennifer Cole for bringing this connection to my attention.

[32] Talal Asad, *Genealogies of Religion: Discipline and Reasons of Power in Christianity and Islam* (Baltimore: The Johns Hopkins University Press, 1993), 83–167.

which suffers not thy wound to retain its corruption, but when thou hast groaned awhile, replaces this by a knotty scar.[33]

In the medieval Church, Asad points out, new forms of authority and experience were created by making the practice of verbal confession a universal discipline for every Church member. Just as inquisitorial confession produced truth through the application of torture (or the threat of torture) to the body, mandatory annual private confession produced truth through the fear of future pain in the afterlife. In both cases 'confession was ... a unique process that linked the idea of bodily pain (here, or in the hereafter) with the exchange of question and answer in the pursuit of truth.'[34] To verbalize, through pain, what lay hidden within the conscience was to produce the truth that restored the confessing sinner to spiritual health.[35]

Later, the disciplinary power of verbalization (minus the application of pain) was attached to Enlightenment concepts of language and violence as antithetical discourses opposing the powers of modern reason to those of primordial hatred.[36] If violence is understood in primitivist Hobbesian terms of *brute* force and *mindless* acts of destruction, it must be transformed by the civilizing power of language. This longstanding idea of language as a bulwark against violence is implicit in much contemporary legal discourse, as Minow suggests when she writes that, '[g]roping for legal responses marks an effort to embrace or renew the commitment to replace violence with words.'[37]

A further strand of this discourse of verbalized truth stems from the 19th and early 20th century growth of psychoanalysis and psychiatry. Here a different kind of connection developed between pain – now internal and emotional rather than physical – and the production of truth. Thus psychoanalytic ideas of repressed memories, of initial pain and cathartic release when these memories are consciously confronted, and of the threat of the 'return of the repressed' when they are not, have all seeped into American and European consciousness through the development of 'therapy culture' and recent controversies about recovered memories. Converging with these is the psychiatric construction of 'post-traumatic stress disorder' and its treatment by verbal processing, which entails the painful narrative recapitulation of traumatic events from the past.[38] Together, these constructs have established discursive (and typically painful) verbal remembering as a prerequisite for personal healing in many parts of the world in which

[33] Quoted in Oscar D. Watkins, *A History of Penance*, Vol. 2 (Longman: London, 1920), 565.

[34] Asad, supra n 32 at 96.

[35] Ironically, then, the painful imperative to verbalize truth in truth commissions shares a genealogy with religious torture.

[36] See, Uli Linke, 'Archives of Violence: The Holocaust and the Politics of German Memory,' in *The Anthropology of Genocide*, ed. Alexander Laban Hinton (Berkeley: University of California Press, 2002), 260.

[37] Minow, supra n 24 at 2.

[38] Allan Young, *The Harmony of Illusions: Inventing Post-traumatic Stress Disorder* (Princeton: Princeton University Press, 1995).

psychoanalysis and psychiatry have become powerful forms of knowledge. Through these therapeutic models, for example, journalist Antjie Krog construed the often painful practice of giving testimony in the human rights violations hearings of the South African TRC as part of the therapeutic process, writing, 'this particular memory at last captured in words can no longer haunt you, push you around, bewilder you, because you have taken control of it – you can move it wherever you want to.'[39]

This dominant memory discourse has been further developed in response to the Holocaust, which has become the paradigmatic modern atrocity in American memory.[40] In the face of denials and revisionist history, remembering the Holocaust has become imperative 'so that it will not happen again.' This imperative to remember is repeatedly invoked in relation to atrocities elsewhere.[41] By returning again and again to the time of atrocity, memory becomes an apotropaic process that instils a rational and progressive historical self-consciousness that is assumed to be inimical to violence.

In South Africa's TRC, all of these strands of a hegemonic, historically constituted Western memory discourse were brought together in friction with South Africa's apartheid history, its social and cultural terrain and its political predicament in the early 1990s. The recounting of memories of atrocity was recast as a civilizing, transformative and 'African' process that reclaimed peace and healing from past violence. But for many – if not most – of those who testified before South Africa's human rights violations hearings, the verbalization of unspoken memories was not a healing process. According to the Trauma Centre for Victims of Violence and Torture in Cape Town, between 50 and 60 percent of those who testified experienced difficulties afterwards, and many regretted testifying.[42] For women in particular, as Fiona Ross explains, 'the equation of speaking self with healed subject ... [does] not do justice to the range of women's experiences of harm and the diversity of efforts to cope.'[43] Yet so internationally compelling was the model that linked the painful verbalization of memory with personal empowerment and national redemption, and so successful was the publicizing of individual cases that appeared to confirm this model, that the frictions of the TRC's actual engagement in South Africa were all but erased. A new paradigm for transitional justice had been created, and awaited its own frictional travels to other parts of the world.

[39] Antjie Krog, *Country of My Skull* (London: Vintage, 1999), 64.

[40] Lawrence Langer, *Holocaust Testimonies: The Ruins of Memory* (New Haven: Yale University Press, 1991); Peter Novick, *The Holocaust in American life* (Boston: Houghton Mifflin, 1999); James E. Young, *The Texture of Memory: Holocaust Memorials and Meaning* (New Haven: Yale University Press, 1993).

[41] John Borneman, 'Reconciliation after Ethnic Cleansing: Listening, Retribution, Affiliation,' *Public Culture* 14 (2002): 290.

[42] Suzanne Daley 1997, cited in Priscilla Hayner, *Unspeakable Truths: Facing the challenge of truth commissions* (New York/London: Routledge, 2002), 144; see also, Brandon Hamber 1996, cited in Wilson, supra n 25 at 121.

[43] Ross, supra n 25 at 165.

Arts of Forgetting in Sierra Leone

> A person's resilience can really be measured by the power to forget ... Whether a Lethe flows somewhere I do not know, but what I do know is that this art can be developed. Yet it does not at all consist in the total disappearance of particular impressions; for the art of forgetting is not the same as forgetfulness ... Forgetting is the shears with which one clips away what one cannot use – though, mind you, under the overall supervision of memory. Forgetting and memory are thus identical, and the skillfully achieved identity is the Archimedean point with which one lifts the whole world.[44]

In Sierra Leone, during the rainy season of 2002, almost everyone seemed nervous about the upcoming TRC. That year marked the official end of the civil war, and a lot of people felt uneasy about a process that would activate memories of the violence that still seemed so close. The teenaged ex-combatants among whom I conducted fieldwork that year regarded this process with trepidation: some feared it would disrupt their integration into civilian society, and all dreaded the return of their own memories. 'I don't want a lot of that kind of talk – I want to forget what happened,' said Joseph, a 15-year-old former member of the Civil Defense Forces, sitting with his mother in the house his family was trying to rebuild after their town, Kondembaia, had been burned four times. In Freetown, an old friend, John, was adamant that although he approved of people confessing their crimes, he would not want to hear details of how rebels had killed his son during the AFRC junta's occupation of Freetown in 1998. Some people worried about the potential for vengeance when civilians heard ex-combatant testimonies about former acts of violence to themselves, their family members or their property. Others were anxious about the potential for retaliation when ex-combatants heard civilian testimonies that implicated them in atrocities. Michael, a friend from an NGO upcountry, summed up many of these concerns as we sat in a bar in Freetown:

> I am skeptical, seeing these people coming to confess. Someone coming to tell a story that he is trying to forget. It makes them start to think again ... I have committed a crime against you, and I come and say, 'Rosalind, I have killed your father.' It is another trauma. But Sierra Leoneans, they are flexible. There are some people who like to come and talk anyway. They say the TRC is a healing process. But it can add to the wound, after I have tried to forget.

What did Michael, Joseph and others mean by 'forgetting'? They did not mean the erasure of personal memories, but their containment in a form that would enable them to recover their lives. One of the people who brought this meaning of 'forgetting' home to me was an 18-year-old secondary school student I will call 'Jonas' in the north-central town of Magburaka. A few years before, a man who had once made unwelcome sexual advances toward Jonas' mother subsequently joined the RUF rebels and brutally attacked her with a cutlass during a raid. Jonas' brother and

[44] Søren Kierkegaard, *Either/or: A Fragment of Life* (ed. Victor Eremita, abridged, translated, and with an introduction and notes by Alastair Hannay, London: Penguin Books, 1992), 235. I am most grateful to Artemis Christodoulou for drawing my attention to Kierkegaard's distinction between forgetting and forgetfulness.

sister found her on the ground, fatally wounded, the next morning. Before she died, she told them her killer's identity. On the same day, the civilian militia, the Kamajos, took over their village. When Jonas' brother and sister told them what had happened, they summarily killed the man Jonas' mother had named. When my research assistant, Moses, asked Jonas if he had thought about giving a statement or testifying before the TRC, he responded, 'I don't remember it any more ... There's no need for me to talk about it. I have forgotten what they did to me.' He paused and added, '[j]ust let God help me when I learn my book [study at school].'

Jonas' horrifying memories were clearly still there. Kierkegaard's distinction between forgetting as an art that can be developed and forgetfulness as an involuntary disappearance of memories is especially useful in helping us understand what Jonas meant when he claimed to have forgotten his mother's murder.[45] What Jonas articulated was an 'art of forgetting' that forms part of the work of memory in northern Sierra Leone. Here, as Cole describes for communities in east Madagascar, the work of memory is not primarily to store and retrieve information but to create a relationship between oneself and a remembered event or person: the verbal recollection of violent events (especially in public) is undesirable because it makes that violence present and connects it to the person remembering.[46]

When Sierra Leone's civil war was over, what Cole terms 'directed forgetting' was widely practiced.[47] The English expression 'forgive and forget' spread even in rural communities, and parents told their children not to talk of the war outside the confines of the house. In many communities, people sought to displace explicit verbal memories of this violence through a range of social and ritual practices – sacrifices, prayer, exorcism, funerals, ritual healing, church services – the purpose of which was to create 'cool hearts' that form the basis for life in a community.[48] The verbal recounting of recent violence – especially in public – was widely discouraged except in ritually framed confessions that formed part of a broader process of containing and 'unmaking' the violent past.[49] Directed forgetting, then, is part of the post-war work of memory, continually practiced and therefore continually remembered in order to reach 'the Archimedean point' with which one can transform one's world.[50]

[45] Ibid.

[46] Jennifer Cole, *Forget Colonialism? Sacrifice and the Art of Memory in Madagascar* (Berkeley: University of California Press, 2001).

[47] Ibid.

[48] See for example, Rosalind Shaw, 'Displacing violence: Making Pentecostal memory in Postwar Sierra Leone,' *Cultural Anthropology* 22 (1) (2007).

[49] In Temne-speaking communities in north-central Sierra Leone, earlier periods of violence have also been subject to directed forgetting. Several historical layers of violence – the Atlantic slave trade, the 19th century trade wars and the imposition of a colonial protectorate in 1896 – are remembered nondiscursively in the landscape, ritual practice and visionary experience, but rarely in discursive verbal form. When asked, some chiefs and ritual specialists are able to narrate memories of these dangerous times in words, but before doing so they invoke the protective presence of the ancestors. See, Rosalind Shaw, *Memories of the Slave Trade: Ritual and the Historical Imagination in Sierra Leone* (Chicago: University of Chicago Press, 2002), 62–67. For the concept of 'unmaking' war see, Carolyn Nordstrom, *A Different Kind of War Story* (Philadelphia: University of Pennsylvania Press, 1997).

[50] Kierkegaard, supra n 44 at 235.

Many people, however, were unable to reach this Archimedean point of forgetting through the direction of memory. 'I cannot forget,' I was told again and again, 'when I cannot rebuild my house/cannot get married again/cannot get a job/cannot feed my children/cannot pay my school fees.' Jonas, remember, concluded his claim to have 'forgotten' what was done to his mother with the words, '[l]et God help me when I learn my book.' For Jonas, as for most Sierra Leoneans, the art of forgetting depended on the ability to build a future.

Memory Frictions

> The object for which the Commission is established is to create an impartial historical record of violations and abuses of human rights and international humanitarian law related to the armed conflict in Sierra Leone, from the beginning of the Conflict in 1991 to the signing of the Lomé Peace Agreement; to address impunity, to respond to the needs of the victims, to promote healing and reconciliation and to prevent a repetition of violations and abuses suffered.[51]

Sierra Leone's TRC Act of 2000 states that the TRC would 'help restore the human dignity of victims and promote reconciliation by providing an opportunity for victims to give an account of the violations and abuses suffered.'[52] Giving testimony was assumed to be a need in and of itself, to which the Commission would respond by providing an opportunity for victims to give their accounts. As Fiona Ross comments about South Africa's TRC, the implication was 'that "stories" of violation were intact, awaiting only the opportunity to be told.'[53]

As the truth commission model was locally engaged, frictions arose. One official involved in the TRC told me later:

> In Sierra Leone, initially, people were not interested in what happened and didn't happen. They just wanted peace. But there was a very strong vocal minority that thought that people needed to talk about what happened.[54]

The statement-taking stage of the TRC's operations, which began in late 2002, guided people in the TRC's new work of memory. In each District the statement

[51] Sierra Leone's Truth and Reconciliation Commission Act (2000), Part III.6.1, available at https://www.usip.org/library/tc/doc/charters/tc_sierra_leone_02102000.html.

[52] Ibid, Part III.6.2a. As Sierra Leone's TRC Act suggests, this Commission was modeled on South Africa's, although without powers to grant amnesty, and without separate human rights violation hearings and amnesty hearings. One of South Africa's former TRC Commissioners, Yasmin Sooka, was selected as one of Sierra Leone's three international commissioners, and a consultant from South Africa's TRC, Ilan Lax, was hired during the preparation stage in 2002. Yet the presence of experts from South Africa's Commission did not necessarily mean the univocal imposition of an external template. Thus Ilan Lax writes in an essay explaining methods of truth seeking in Sierra Leone's TRC, 'we are not in the business of selling models or stock solutions. Each conflict has its own conditions, dynamics and cultural issues.' Ilan Lax, 'Strategies and Methodologies for Finding the Truth,' in UNAMSIL, supra n 2 at 63.

[53] Ross, supra n 25 at 6.

[54] The strong, vocal minority to which he referred consisted of local human rights activists, initially in the Sierra Leone Human Rights Committee and subsequently in the National Forum for Human Rights and the National Commission for Democracy and Human Rights. See, Bennett, supra n 2 at 39.

takers traveled from town to town in Land Cruisers with the TRC logo, wearing printed TRC t-shirts and caps, bearing supplies of posters and leaflets and inviting people to come and tell them what had happened to them during the war. Aminata, a young woman who had been a statement taker in one of the northern Districts, told me of how she spoke to those who agreed to talk to her:

> I sensitize them. I explain what the TRC is. 'Have you heard about the TRC on the radio? Let you come and clear your chest. The bad things that they did to you during the war, you should come and say them out.' I tell them the objectives of the TRC: 'All the statements we collect will make one big book, to make history ... What they have done to you, it did not happen in vain.' Then normally they ask, 'what will the government give me now?' They expect something. I tell them, 'If you know what happened during the war [say it]. We don't want that kind of thing again ... When someone does you wrong, he comes and says he is sorry. You forgive him. So peace will come.'

According to Aminata, most of those who gave statements viewed this practice of textualizing their memories of violence as part of an exchange that would bring them material benefit. The purpose of directed forgetting, following a violent past, is to be able to reconstruct one's life, and is undermined by the absence of material resources to do so. People hoped to be able to put the TRC's memory practice of textualized truth-telling to the same purpose. The TRC was, in fact, struggling for funds. But in the context of Sierra Leone's severe economic deprivation, combined with its rapid UN-ization and international NGO-ization, the TRC – with its international funding, its foreign Commissioners and consultants, its national media presence and its white, logo-bearing Land Cruisers – was widely perceived as a site of resources, opportunity, modernity and reconnection back to the international community from which war-torn Sierra Leoneans had long felt severed. The memory practices that it introduced were connected to powerful transnational forms of knowledge, the force of which derived from the global political economy of post-war reconstruction. Armed with these potent forms of knowledge and practice, and despite widespread concerns about the upcoming hearings, the TRC's statement-taking exercise was broadly successful in countering the practice of directed forgetting. The statement takers collected more than 8,000 statements. But as it moved through the statement-taking phase and into the hearings phase, the friction of the Commission's engagement both with local arts of forgetting and with expectations of material resources proved strong and sustained.

From May to July 2003, during the TRC Hearings, I interspersed my traveling ethnography of the District Hearings with fieldwork visits outside the district capitals, in places where the TRC was present mainly in radio broadcasts and (at most) the visits of statement takers. Most people I asked in these locations were not convinced by the TRC's sensitization campaign. In the northeastern town of Lunsar, for example, a former iron mining town that had since fallen into abject decline and decay, two men ran up to my vehicle and led my research assistant and I to a palm wine bar off the side of the road, where 15 young and middle-aged men sat on wooden benches under the shade of trees behind the palm wine seller's house. They told me they wanted me to hear their views, and launched into a discussion that they, borrowing the language of NGO workshops, termed a 'program.' Reversing the usual top-down flow of sensitization from white expatriates, *they* wanted to sensitize *me*. What follows are excerpts from their program:

The TRC is too public.

I have forgotten and have forgiven, so no need for the TRC.

I support the TRC, even though it comes too early. We will know exactly what caused this war. Plenty of things happened. ... The TRC comes out with secrets, so that history will not repeat again.

These things repeat if you talk about them too much.

We don't want the TRC because the TRC is only word of mouth. But if you will give me what I've lost, then the TRC will hold water. How will I go and talk on the radio about what they've done to me, when I get no [material] benefit from that? I'll feel shame. I don't want to let the public know what they've done to me.

We all decided not to talk to them. The president talked to us – 'forgive and forget.' Then they [the TRC] said they come to take statements, but no [material] benefit! We discussed this before they came. We decided to avoid them.

When you talk about what happened, you feel worse, not better.

One of my palm wine bar instructors – a teacher – disagreed with his friends, affirming the TRC's message that telling your story would help to heal you and to rebuild the country. With this one exception, what struck me about this discussion was not the content of the arguments (which I heard again and again throughout my research), but their strongly critical tone. I had heard plenty of hostility about the TRC from ex-combatants and plenty of concern and cynicism from civilians, but was surprised to hear, in addition, such strong civilian antagonism – especially as civilians had suffered a great deal under the RUF occupation of Lunsar during the last years of the war. What had made these men especially resentful was the amount of expenditure allocated to a Commission that was introduced to help survivors of the war, the vast majority of whom had had little or no opportunity to rebuild their lives. Yet the TRC would offer them nothing tangible in compensation for the pain of narrating their memories in public: 'They came with their Land Cruiser, bluff [boastful, arrogant] TRC. Big men for themselves, not for us ... If they want to heal the wounds, let them send jobs.' These men were angry because they felt insulted.

The TRC, in the meantime, moved from district to district on its travels through the country. And the friction of these travels would, as Tsing puts it, 'change everyone's trajectory.'[55]

Recasting Memory in the District Hearings

In the TRC's District Hearings, a standard physical layout connected dilapidated provincial town halls, school assembly halls and court buildings to national and transnational spheres of justice, rights, peacemaking and nation building. At the front of a hall stood three tables: one for the Commissioners, one for the Leader of Evidence, and, between them, a table for the witness, who was supported by an interpreter and a counselor giving comfort and guidance as needed. Behind stood two blue, white and green Sierra Leonean flags, while in the center of the wall a large banner in the national colors announced: 'THE TRUTH AND RECONCILIATION COMMISSION PUBLIC HEARINGS 2003.' Posters around the walls framed the space with the premises of the Commission, underscoring the positive outcomes of truth-telling and warning of the future violence that would be unleashed by failing to speak: 'Truth hurts, but war hurts more'; 'Truth today! Peaceful Sierra Leone tomorrow'; and '*Tru at fo tok, but naim nomo go bring pis*' ('It's hard to speak the truth, but only this will bring peace'). Together, the posters, the flags and TRC banner located the hearings' truth-telling process within the project of rebuilding the nation. On one side of the hall sat stenographers entering witness's testimony into computers, on the other the technical crew monitored sound and recording equipment for simultaneous radio broadcast, while a videographer recorded the proceedings for later broadcast in news segments on national television. The impression that the eyes of the nation and the world were upon this space of truth-telling was reinforced when Commissioners told witnesses that as a result of their testimony, 'everyone will know your story.' The hall was filled with chairs and wooden benches for an audience that, except during the testimonies of notorious ex-combatants, consisted overwhelmingly of adult men. Apart from members of formal women's organizations, women giving testimony and female TRC staff, most women I asked outside the hearings regarded the Commission as a political space of the state and the international world that was removed from them.[56] Similarly, apart from members of formal youth and children's organizations, young people tended to hang around outside or sit at the back of the hall, feeling peripheral (and sometimes hostile) to the proceedings.

Before the hearings proper began, the opening ceremonies provided an opportunity to educate the residents of the Districts in the memory project that both personal healing and national reconstruction required. In many of the opening speeches, TRC Commissioners and staff and some local officials and religious leaders presented truth-telling as a process that would bring about healing, liberation and peace. During his speech in the opening ceremony of the Kambia District Hearings on 9 June 2003, for example, Franklyn Karifala Tarawalie, District Officer for Kambia, drew upon both the Bible and the first line of the TRC radio jingle to promote truth-telling as personal liberation and civic duty:

[56] Cf. Chris Coulter, 'Being a Bush Wife: Women's Lives Through War and Peace in Northern Sierra Leone' (Ph.D. diss., Uppsala University, Sweden, 2006), 269–80.

> As the Bible says, the truth will set you free. The memories of these rebel attacks in Kambia District, which destroyed so many lives, the shattering of so many families, the deaths of so many people, it is fresh in our memories. When you tell your truth, you will have cleared your chest, as the saying goes. It is a conversation you have at home. Then with a neighbor, then with a friend. You will tell what your husband has done. You will be free. You will be representing the people of Kambia, because you have cleared your chest.

Bishop Joseph Humper, Chairman of the TRC, borrowed from the TRC's South African genealogy, paraphrasing Archbishop Tutu's metaphor of truth-telling as the cleansing of infected wounds:

> Why do we come and open the wounds again? Why do we come and recall the past? We have to reopen the wounds because they have not healed. Superficial healing will allow the wounds to explode again. We have to revisit the events so that we can heal properly.

The testimonies themselves were another opportunity for a reeducation in the proper work of memory. As Kelsall observes of most 'victim' testimonies in the Tonkolili District Hearings, these typically bore little resemblance to cathartic outpourings:

> Most of the testimony was delivered in a rather detached and clinical way ... There seemed to be a process of dissociation at work, in which facts were willfully cordoned off from feelings; the impression being given that emotions were dammed up or held in check ... Victims stared implacably into the middle distance, or into their laps, as they testified.[57]

Similarly, when I arrived in Makeni for the Bombali District Hearings in May 2003, the flat, factual tone of testimonies reminded me of the tone of local politicians' speeches. This was not the venting of thoughts and feelings that usually constitutes *blow main*. Although witnesses were engaged in the discursive public remembering of horrific acts of violence, most were doing so in a way that reduced, as far as possible, the reentry of that violence as a tangible experience in the present.

Through their comments and questions, some of the Commissioners coached those giving testimony by affirming a connection between truth-telling and healing or reconciliation. 'Whatever you did during the course of the war,' Bishop Humper told an ex-combatant in the Bombali District Hearings, 'you have to share with us so that we can set the record straight, in order to achieve reconciliation.'[58] When a witness in the Kambia District Hearings called the RUF rebels the derogatory term 'bush people,' Bishop Humper responded: 'Thank you for venting your feelings. That is part of healing.'[59] When a woman in the Moyamba District Hearings described the burning alive of her mother, grandfather and uncle by troops from the Sierra Leone Army, Commissioner Laura Marcus-Jones

[57] Tim Kelsall, 'Truth, Lies, Ritual: Preliminary Reflections on the Truth and Reconciliation Commission in Sierra Leone,' *Human Rights Quarterly* 27 (2005): 367–69.

[58] Bombali District Hearings, Makeni, 30 May 2003.

[59] Kambia District Hearings, Kambia, 9 June 2003.

told her:

> Talk to [the counselor] when you leave, and she will be able to help you. Now that you've come to talk here, and people all over will be able to hear your experience, you will feel a little better.[60]

Requests for aid, however, were less easy to respond to. The Commissioners sometimes urged witnesses to come forward and testify by assuring them that this would enable the TRC to make recommendations to the government and the UN to address their needs. To many of those who testified, such statements often sounded like a promise to address their personal needs, even though they were told that the Commission could not pay them.[61] Almost without exception, witnesses who spoke in the District Hearings I attended ended their testimony with pleas for material assistance, often expressing these pleas in a strongly felt manner more characteristic of *blow main* than their testimony itself had been: 'I have nothing! What will be given to me?' And almost without exception the Commissioners responded, in tones ranging from empathy to impatience, that such assistance was not part of the TRC's mandate, but that they would bear such requests in mind when they made their Final Report to the Government of Sierra Leone. It became clear that most of the people who testified had done so because of their expectations that the TRC, the government or the international community would help them rebuild their lives.[62] In the Tonkolili District Hearings at Magburaka, the widow of a section chief who was killed and thrown into the river by members of the Kamajo Civil Defense Forces, ended her testimony as follows:

> I have noone to assist me. Now, I'm very, very sick. Sometimes I do not have the chance to eat – only if people give me. Last year, when people came to build houses, I was not there, so I did not get one. I am alone with God! So when I heard of the Commission, I decided to come and testify.[63]

Speaking in a bland, unresponsive tone, one of the Sierra Leonean Commissioners sidestepped her plea by attempting to reconfigure her words in line with the TRC's goal of nation building through painful truth-telling:

[60] Moyamba District Hearings, Moyamba, 12 June 2003.

[61] Kelsall, supra n 57.

[62] In his TRC Report on the Kono and Pujehun District Hearings, Bjorn Pettersson of UNAMSIL wrote: 'The hearings in Koidu, as in many other districts, signaled that many Sierra Leoneans come to the TRC motivated by the prospect of some kind of concrete reparation. Over time, the Commissioners have gotten used to the 'shopping lists' presented to them at the end of each witness session and do not always try to minimize expectations but rather routinely promise to include witnesses' material priorities in the recommendations of the Final Report ... There is however an inherent risk in simply piling up the requests without actively pursuing the establishment of a reparations programme ... One witness in Koidu had two children killed and her leg amputated. As so many others, she asked the TRC for help to make a living. Clearly, she was not impressed to hear that the Commissioners do not have a mandate or the resources to provide support but that they would make recommendations that will reach the Security Council. And she is far from the only witness frustrated with the lack of a reparations programme for victims. There is therefore a risk that if the TRC process does not result in at least limited concrete benefits to the cooperating communities, reconciliation and healing might not be long lasting.' Bjorn Pettersson, *Human Rights Section Weekly TRC Report*, 23–27 June 2003, 2–3.

[63] 10 July 2003.

> We know that it's not very pleasant to remember such events in one's life. But we know you have decided it would be in the interests of the country for you to testify before the Commission.

By not only failing to respond to her plea but also claiming to 'know' her feelings and intentions and renaming these as a contribution to an abstract national recovery, he was effectively shutting down her experience and concerns. Thus for this widow, testifying did not consist of replacing silence with voice, but of being silenced by the TRC's model of redemptive memory.

Although, as we shall see in the next section, many of those who testified had integrated the TRC's message that *blow main* would facilitate *kol at*, *blow main* alone was not enough. For them, the memory practice of public testimony had a second purpose, and one that was crucial for the achievement of *kol at*: that of opening access to resources for rebuilding their lives. To their great disappointment, this second purpose of public remembering was replaced by the abstract notion of rebuilding the nation and the vague promise of government action in some unspecified future.

'I Can't Be Struggling and Say that I Am Living in Peace'

When I returned to Sierra Leone in 2004, a year after the TRC hearings, people still regularly told me that they had 'forgiven and forgotten.' But increasingly over the preceding two years this expression had been countered by another response that was closer to the message of remembering and reconciliation promoted by the TRC: 'I can forgive, but I cannot forget.'

I searched for the 17 witnesses who had testified before the TRC's Bombali District Hearings in Makeni the year before, finding and interviewing seven of them: four (two middle-aged women and two 18-year-olds) from amputee and war-wounded settlements, two formerly prosperous traders (one man and one woman) and one ex-combatant. For the ex-combatant, a former RUF Military Police Investigator, testifying before the Commission had been a positive experience in spite of widespread fears of a hidden connection between the TRC and the Special Court for Sierra Leone. 'I was so happy,' he told me. 'I expressed apology on behalf of the Movement [the RUF]. People blessed us and accepted us.' He had been able to convert both his disarmament, demobilization and reintegration (DDR) skills training and his testimony before the TRC into employment as the assistant of a local political leader. Most ex-combatants have not been so fortunate: in Makeni, the reconstruction of which lags behind that in equivalent southern towns, few ex-combatants have been able to convert their skills into sustainable livelihoods.

The civilians who had testified were more ambivalent. Verbalizing the violence and abuses they had suffered before the TRC had been a difficult experience for them, but they had been coached to interpret this pain as part of the ultimately productive process of 'clearing their chest.' None claimed, when I asked, to have 'felt bad' after talking to the TRC, and all but one (the male trader) said that they had felt better afterwards. But – with the exception of the female trader, who had been able to rebuild her business – they were disappointed by the TRC. Their hopes that the TRC might help exchange their painful memories of the past for a sustainable future were not realized: 'Up to this time, nothing. They said that they would tell the international community, pass on my request to them.' Their expectations were very similar to those of survivors of Peru's conflict who testified before that country's TRC. For witnesses from the devastated Ayacucho region, according to Laplante and Theidon,

> ... there is an implicit contract established in the giving and receiving of testimonies about a painful history of sustained political violence. When victim-survivors speak about their suffering and losses, they place a responsibility on their interlocutors to respond: testimony is a demand for acknowledgement and redress.[64]

Before the TRC hearings, many amputees and war-wounded had been provided, through international humanitarian programs, with houses in special settlements. Three of these were on the outskirts of Makeni. Their residents were pleased with the houses themselves – small cement structures, arranged in neat parallel rows, with standpipes that provided running water – but found it difficult to pursue a viable livelihood so far out of town, and so far from networks of social support in their home communities. In 2003, the TRC had appeared to offer a solution.

One of those who testified before the Bombali District Hearings in Makeni was Isatu. In 1998, she was shot in an RUF raid in a village a few miles to the north; when she was taken to hospital she was told she would die. But she survived, and when the war ended she was given a house in a settlement for the war-wounded. Her husband left her, however, and she is raising her four children alone. In a skills training program she was taught to weave high quality local 'country cloth,' and she showed me, laughing, how she worked her loom in the small parlor of her house. The price Isatu obtains by selling her cloth, though, is too low to provide a viable livelihood for her and her children, even when supplemented by the garden of peppers she grows to sell in the market. She had thought that testifying before the TRC would bring her much-needed assistance:

RS: *Ya Isatu, why did you want to talk to the TRC?*

I: One, I went to clear my chest. If I just go and sit down and don't talk, it would burn my heart more and more. But if I go and talk it in public, I will feel better in my heart. That's what they told me, and it was true.

RS: *How did you feel?*

I: I didn't feel bad at all.

RS: *What was the second thing you expected?*

[64] Lisa J. Laplante and Kimberly Theidon, 'Truth with Consequences: Justice and Reparations in Post-Truth Commission Peru,' *Human Rights Quarterly* 29 (1)(2007): 231.

I: I felt glad the TRC asked me to go and talk [because] I felt they would give me money.

RS: *Did they tell you that you wouldn't get money if you went to talk?*

I: Yes, but I didn't believe it. I felt in my heart that they would give me some.

RS: *How did you feel afterwards?*

I: The TRC told me, no money. So I felt bad. I wasted time from seven in the morning until five o'clock. My heart was spoiled [disappointed]. But I'm glad that I cleared my chest.

RS: *If you had known you wouldn't get money, would you still have gone to talk?*

I: If I had known, I would have said, 'Let me not waste my time to go.' But at the time I talked, I was glad.

Isatu adapted very easily to the memory practice of public testimony. She had internalized the TRC's messages about the harms of directed forgetting ('it would burn my heart') and the healing powers of publicly remembering the raid and its aftermath ('if I go and talk it in public, I will feel better in my heart'), and had translated these into experience. But at the same time she integrated the TRC's ideas of the benefits of 'talking it in public' with understandings of healing as forgetting: 'I'm not able to do hard work,' she told me, 'so if I have someone to help me, I can forget. I am straining.' For Isatu, however, 'forgetting,' healing and reconciliation (*kol at*) were built upon a foundation of material reconstruction. In spite of the TRC's disclaimers about payment, it had been inconceivable to her that a body with the TRC's national reach and international funding would not remunerate her for giving up a day's work to do as they asked her.

A few miles away from Isatu lives Adama, a lively middle-aged woman in an amputee settlement just off a highway. Originally from Kabala to the north, Adama and her husband had been living in the diamond district of Kono to the east when they, together with 24 others who were hiding in the bush, were captured by 'juntas' (members of the ex-AFRC junta). The juntas amputated both of her husband's hands and both of his ears; he later died from his wounds in hospital. They amputated Adama's left hand, but she lived. She is raising four children, supporting them through petty trading, soap making, processing palm oil and cultivating cassava and corn for the market. Whenever I visited the settlement I found Adama working – spinning thread, making soap or pounding food in a mortar.

During one of my visits I asked Adama about her experience of testifying before the Commission:

RS: *Ya Adama, when you talked to the TRC, how did you feel?*

A: When I was talking, I felt bad. But when I finished talking, I didn't feel bad any more. Because everyone knew what had happened to me.

RS: *What did you think would happen after you talked?*

A: I thought that when I talked, people would know my problems, and that I could sit in my house and see people coming to help me.

RS: *Has this happened?*

A: No. The TRC told the government to help us, but up to now, there's no help.

R: *Why did you feel bad when you talked?*

A: What happened to me, I didn't want to explain it too much.

R: *Are you glad or sorry that you talked?*

A: I am glad.

RS: *Has the TRC helped you get a cool heart?*

A: I got a cool heart – a little. Because what they put on paper to pass on to the government, I haven't seen any result ... If I get help, I'll forget about the war. But if you don't have help, you'll remember the war all the time. Now I remember because noone helps me ... What happened to the paper carried to the government? Right now, we're taking care of ourselves.

As a memory practice, Adama's experience of truth-telling had been shaped by the TRC counselor who guided her before and after her testimony. Publicly verbalizing her horrific memories of her husband's and her own amputation, and her husband's subsequent death, had indeed been difficult, but the pain had not persisted afterwards. What had helped her recover from the pain of testifying, however, was the expectation of assistance. When Adama said that she 'didn't feel bad any more' because 'everyone knew what happened to me' when she testified, by 'everyone' she meant staff from NGOs and the government. For her, telling her story before an audience (and, via the radio, before the nation and the world) was neither an act of remembering for its own sake, nor a preexisting 'need,' but part of what she hoped would become a reciprocal relationship. By participating in this national and international forum, she had hoped to become part of a circuit connecting her to the national and international resources that would help her rebuild her life and raise her children. *This*, rather than the reliving of her memories of mutilation and death, would bring about healing. And, as for Isatu and the other witnesses to whom I spoke, such healing consisted of forgetting: 'If I get help, I'll forget about the war.' Adama and the other witnesses had effortlessly transformed the TRC's memory work into a new art of forgetting. What they lacked, however, were the material resources that would allow them to sustain this art.

In Adama's questions to the Commission after her 2003 testimony before the Bombali District Hearings, she connected her struggle to raise her children with the struggle for a sustainable peace in Sierra Leone. Her words were selected for quotation in the TRC's Final Report:

> We the amputees, how are we in the world now? I am not speaking for myself here. The government should not leave our case behind. It is not for us, it is for our children. If

> my child grows up and asks me who chopped off my hand, I shall say these people did it to me. That will bring the war again. If you say peace should come, we the amputees should bring the peace. I cannot be struggling and say that I am living in peace. That is why our case should be pushed forward. If our problem is left behind, the war will not end. We the amputees, we all have children.[65]

Adama's comments clearly resonated among the authors of the Final Report, who used them to illustrate the urgency of a reparations program.[66] These recommendations, however, have so far been met with standard stonewalling by the Government of Sierra Leone. In a 2005 white paper, the government stated, in the typically vague language of a stalling maneuver, that it would 'use its best endeavours' to implement the reparations, 'taking into consideration the resources available.'[67]

Conclusion

As Sierra Leone's TRC took tangible form in jingles, posters, statement forms and hearings that traveled through the country's districts, it carried with it a genealogy from South Africa, Latin America and beyond. This genealogy, crystallized as exemplary global knowledge and driven by the political economy of post-war transition, naturalized the project of truth-telling as a tool that would cut through conspiracies of silence, create accountability, restore voice and dignity, 'talk out' trauma and rebuild the nation. This naturalization of the concept of redemptive remembering and the 'universal' status it is accorded made it seem imperative for the TRC to intensify the friction by opposing rather than building upon local techniques of forgetting in Sierra Leone.

But people built upon them anyway. Michael, my friend from an NGO upcountry, had been right: while many Sierra Leoneans stayed away from the TRC, others were flexible and engaged with it. If '[f]orgetting is the shears with which one clips away what one cannot use,'[68] then the TRC taught those who testified that they could use verbal memories of violence that were previously considered deleterious. Although the TRC set about the process of 'sensitizing' Sierra Leone's war-torn population to its model of redemptive verbal memory in a top-down manner, this is not just a story of the subjugation of alternative forms of knowledge and

[65] *Sierra Leone Truth and Reconciliation Commission Report* 2004, Vol. 2, Ch. 4, 239, available at http://www.trcsierraleone.org/drwebsite/publish/index.shtml.

[66] Ibid. The Final Report was presented to the Government of Sierra Leone in October 2004, but because of internal disagreements about its contents it was returned to the publisher and revised. It was released to the public in August 2005.

[67] 'SIERRA LEONE: Civil society criticises "vague" government plan for post-war reform,' *IRIN*, July 13, 2005, http://www.irinnews.org/report.aspx?reportid=55429. The implications of this unresponsiveness for the process of social repair and restorative justice are serious. Again, there are close parallels with Peru, where, 'more than two years after the publication of the TRC's Final Report in August 2003, there is a high level of disappointment due to the government's failure to implement the recommendations made by the TRC. Among the most disappointed – those who outrightly reject the work of the TRC – are victim-survivors who mistakenly believed their testimony would result in immediate compensation for their suffering.' Laplante and Theidon, supra n 64 at 241.

[68] Kierkegaard, supra n 44 at 235.

practice. For the friction between local arts of forgetting and the TRC's transnational techniques of truth-telling was in some ways productive, creating new forms of remembering and forgetting. Those who testified before the Commission verbalized their memories of horrific violence before a local, national and international audience. But they testified in their own way, holding back from a full *blow main* expression of their experience, and integrating their testimony into prevailing understandings of healing as forgetting. Thus from the very beginning their truth-telling diverged from that of a simple duplication of TRC ideals: transformed by its context, truth-telling became a new technique of forgetting.[69]

But if this is not just a story of subjugation, neither is it just a story of triumphant local creativity. The friction of a globalized universal traveling through a particular place and time may enable wheels to turn, but sometimes those wheels may get stuck. For those who testified before Sierra Leone's Commission, it was not enough to have turned 'clearing your chest' into an art of forgetting when the conditions of their post-conflict lives remained as a constant mnemonic for violence and loss. So far, the best creative efforts of the survivors who testified, and of the authors of the Commission's Final Report who listened to them, have been unable to turn the TRC into a mechanism that would, in fact, 'respond to their needs.'

[69] Some proponents of truth-telling argue that forgetting is, in fact, a product of truth-telling. I did not hear such arguments as part of the Sierra Leonean TRC's promotion of truth-telling however.

12

Vetting and Transitional Justice

Pablo de Greiff

Various measures that can be loosely grouped under the label of "vetting" have long been a part of common practice in post-conflict and post-authoritarian transitional situations. Although we will tighten the meaning of the term below, one only has to recall the massive purges of collaborators that took place in many countries in the aftermath of World War II; or that a good number of the countries in the "third wave" of democratization, to use Huntington's term, including Greece, one of the countries with which the wave started, implemented vetting measures.[1] And the practice continues apace despite the fact that it remains largely understudied, and that frequently the measures implemented are acknowledged to be less than successful even in generous interpretations of "success."[2] The lack of clarity and the obfuscation that pervade the general issue cover not only questions about the potential and limitations of vetting measures, or basic questions about implementation—which the thematic chapters in this volume address—but also questions about the justification and the ends of vetting.

This chapter concentrates on the latter set of issues, on questions of aims and justification. Among other things, it will try to clarify the purposes that can legitimately be sought through vetting measures.[3] Two caveats are in order. First, of course, a complex practice can always be set in place in order to achieve more than one aim. Second, the defining aims of a practice always underdetermine the shape the practice should take. This chapter does not assume a reductionistic position concerning the ends of vetting—accepting that it can pursue plural ends at the same time—nor a normatively naive position according to which, having defined the aims of a practice, its "blueprint" follows as if through simple deduction—accepting, of course, that there are different means of satisfying a given aim. Having said this, however, questions about ends and justification do set some constraints on practice and implementation. And precisely because vetting is a practice that, both in the distant and in the recent past, has known so many examples of *unrestraint*, this is an important exercise. This chapter will defend an understanding of vetting that emphasizes its preventive aims (and deemphasizes both the punitive and the deterrent justifications) and will seek to clarify the relationship between vetting and other transitional justice measures by examining the potential of vetting as an enabling condition of the other transitional justice measures, and, at a more conceptual level, by examining its potential to foster the trust of citizens in the institutions of the state.

VETTING AND IMPUNITY

The idea of ridding institutions of abusers and collaborators in the aftermath of conflict or authoritarianism, as is well known, has a long (but not necessarily distinguished) history.[4] At the most general level this is an expression of the desire for a new beginning, or at least a renewal, which is perfectly understandable under such circumstances. However, there is no such thing as a "new beginning" and the idea of renewal is nothing more than shorthand for something that requires articulation. Consequently, not just any means for satisfying these inchoate desires will be the object of consideration here. I will follow recent efforts to distinguish vetting measures from massive, summary dismissals or purges, and will use the term "vetting" to refer to processes for assessing the integrity of individuals to determine their suitability for continued or prospective public employment.[5] The reason why purges and massive, summary dismissals should not be considered forms of vetting, properly speaking, has nothing to do with numerical considerations, but rather with the criteria used for dismissals and the procedures and guarantees that are applied in either case; vetting here designates processes in which the criteria of assessment relate to *individual* behavior, which therefore calls for individual review, and for offering individuals some procedural guarantees. Mere membership in groups, including political parties, should not be the primary criterion of exclusion. Clearly, just as many—or few—people can be excluded through vetting as through purges; the numbers ultimately depend, to begin with, on how widespread the perpetration of violations may have been. What is critical, from the standpoint of justice, is, precisely, to select criteria designed to track individual abusive behavior.[6]

VETTING AS A PUNITIVE, DETERRENT, AND PREVENTIVE MEASURE

Regardless of where the exact boundaries of vetting may be set, various aims have been ascribed to the practice, and these aims have been used to ground justificatory arguments. Given the manifest "impunity gap" faced by societies emerging from conflict or authoritarianism, it is not surprising that vetting as well as other transitional justice measures have been thought to address this gap. My aim in this chapter is not to counter the positions I will review, but to subject them to scrutiny. However, I do not take these positions to be equally plausible or convincing. I have ordered them in increasing order of plausibility.

That vetting has a punitive dimension can be easily seen. In fact, this is part of what justifies our concern with offering procedural guarantees to those who are subject to it.[7] Vetting subjects people to loss of jobs and income, never an indifferent loss, but particularly not under circumstances, all too common in post-conflict and transitional societies, in which economies are in crisis and job creation is stagnant if not receding. The effects of such loss are particularly severe for members of the security sector, most of whom may not be particularly highly skilled or have skills that can be easily transferred to other economic activities. But beyond that, vetting typically subjects people to shaming;[8] being vetted out of a job is not the same as suffering the impact of, say, downsizing. The more public the exclusion, the greater the potential for becoming the recipient of the public's opprobrium.[9]

However, punishment as the main rationale for vetting should be seen as problematic, at least if it is meant as an exhaustive account. In the end, a mainly punitive interpretation of vetting highlights the impotence of the criminal justice system. Imagine a transition in which even the worst offenders, against whom there is sufficient evidence to initiate prosecutions, get off with nothing worse than being relieved of their jobs and whatever shaming that leads to. This would require some explanation, and what such explanation would try to do is to provide an account, precisely, of why these people do not receive more severe punishment.

Another way of expressing the point is the following: even if there were a society that espoused a completely nonpunitive approach to its transition, it might find good reasons to vet some of its institutions. Naturally, it would do so for reasons other than punishment.

None of this is an argument against the punitive use of vetting. The point, rather, is that the punitive rationale does not seem to capture the whole reason (or better, all the reasons) that we engage in vetting. Some of these reasons are spelled out in what follows.

Vetting, as other justice measures, could also be thought to be a deterrent. This seems to me to be either a purely aspirational claim, or an empirical one, and as such it stands or falls on empirical evidence. The problem is that gathering such evidence is peculiarly difficult, for it would have to be of the counterfactual sort; in other words, it would require comparing outcomes (the behavior of some people with and without vetting in place) and this is the sort of experiment that we do not know how to carry out directly. Support for the proposition can be gained by proxy (for example, through comparative analysis), but this will always be a debatable ground. Leaving this epistemic problem aside, there are reasons to think that attributing strong deterrence powers to vetting is not particularly plausible: if, for example, more severe forms of punishment (including the death penalty) in "well-established," efficient, and expeditious legal systems have dubious deterrent value, it is not far fetched to think that deterrence is not the strongest defense of vetting in the midst of all the uncertainties of a transitional situation.[10]

Vetting is also often said to have a preventive function[11]—and prevention is not the same thing as deterrence. Rather than focusing on the possible reactions of individuals to particular measures, as the deterrent argument does, this claim operates at a different, more structural level. The argument takes vetting to be something akin to an anti-Mafia measure. Thus, its purpose is not primarily to send signals to *individuals* (i.e., that they will lose their jobs and social standing if they engage in certain behavior), but to disable *structures* within which individuals (who, by the way, may have refrained from criminal activity were it not for those structures) in fact carried out criminal acts. This is a more defensible position than the preceding one, fundamentally because it need not commit itself to controversial assumptions about the behavior of individuals given certain incentives. The most controversial assumption the preventive argument can simply eschew has to do with a claim about recidivist tendencies, namely that those who have committed certain offenses are more likely than others to commit them in the future. This is a questionable assumption on its own terms (for, among other reasons, it abstracts from peculiar social conditions that enable criminal activity, conditions in the absence of which many individuals may have refrained from participating in crime, and which are also, precisely, the typical conditions in conflict situations), but it also conflicts with a commitment to "meliorism"—the idea that autonomous individuals have the power to improve themselves—which is a part of the liberal doctrine that constitutional democracies try to institutionalize.[12] Vetting, then, is defended on the grounds that it may prevent the recurrence of violations, not necessarily because the sanctions it metes out (loss of job, public prestige, etc.) are sufficient to deter individuals, but because it dismantles networks of criminal activity, even if it does not reach each and every participant in activities that violate the rights of others.

VETTING AS AN ENABLING CONDITION

Up to this point the analysis of the possible aims and justification of vetting has proceeded largely in abstraction from other transitional justice measures, such as criminal prosecutions, truth telling, reparations for victims, and other forms of institutional reform. In trying to situate vetting in a transitional context, it is important to start with some caveats.

First, there have been plenty of transitions in which no formal vetting procedures, not even of rule of law institutions, have been established (e.g., Chile, Argentina, Guatemala, South Africa). There have also been transitions with very modest and sector-specific vetting (El Salvador, Greece, etc.). Thus, we should not overstate the importance of vetting in transitions.

Second, the relationship between vetting and other transitional justice measures depends on many factors, which include whether the different measures are deliberately designed to relate to one another, and also on how they are sequenced. This is in turn a complicated issue that hinges on many factors that are irreducibly contingent and contextual. In what follows, and for the sake of clarity in the presentation of the *potential* that vetting has to contribute to other justice measures, I assume that vetting can be implemented early on in a transitional process.[13] Needless to say, this will not always be possible.

Third, even if, as I will argue, vetting can be considered an enabling condition of other transitional justice measures, obviously when it is botched—and there are plenty of ways of getting it wrong, including doing it through processes that offer few guarantees, that are overly expansive in their attribution of responsibility, and so on—vetting may also make the implementation of these measures more difficult. Thus, to illustrate, among transitional justice measures, arguably vetting is the one that has lent itself more frequently to political manipulation. I cannot offer a full account here of why I think this is the case, but the following factors are part of that account: post-conflict or transitional prosecutions are infrequent to begin with, and they generally involve sufficient due process guarantees so as to raise a shield against easy political manipulation; and truth-telling exercises, particularly by way of truth commissions, are also extraordinary events and the publicity that surrounds them is one among many factors that have kept such commissions from falling into the trap of partisan politics. Vetting, on the other hand, usually involves thousands of people, and the processes more often than not take place with little public scrutiny, offer weak procedural guarantees, and, contrary to even the best outcome of prosecutions or truth telling, what hangs in the balance is (some degree of) control of public institutions—a strong incentive to engage in it for partisan political purposes.[14]

Vetting may also create difficulties beyond making the implementation of transitional justice measures more complicated if the process is plainly defective. That possibility needs to be acknowledged. It is often claimed that vetting may create governance vacuums.[15] Perhaps the claim is overstated, given that, unlike indiscriminate purges, most vetting procedures do not lead to the dismissal of massive numbers of people.[16] But that is not to say this cannot or that it has not happened. In two post-conflict cases (and also cases that may be closer to purges than to vetting as defined in this chapter), namely post-World-War-II Germany and "de-Baathified" Iraq, governance gaps appeared, leading to the rehiring of people formerly expelled from their jobs. Another difficulty that is frequently attributed to vetting is an increase in criminality. This claim may also be overstated, in particular because in very complex and fluid transitional and post-conflict situations it is not easy to isolate the effects of a single initiative. Be that as it may, it is undeniable that in some countries (e.g., Haiti) the participation in criminal activities of former members of the security forces who have been vetted has increased, and that in itself is a worrisome trend.

Fourth, and once again in the spirit of tempering naive hopes, we do well to remember that under most circumstances vetting, like the other transitional justice measures, will only weed out the worst elements in an institution, leaving plenty of "undesirables" in place.

Having said all of this, however, it is still possible that vetting may indeed facilitate the application of measures such as criminal prosecutions, truth telling, reparations for victims, and other forms of institutional reform. That is, vetting may be thought of as an "enabling condition" of other transitional justice measures.[17] Local human rights NGOs in Morocco, for example, have claimed that the lack of cooperation with the recent truth commission, the *Instance Equité et Réconciliation* (IER),[18] on the part of some sectors of the security forces can be explained by the continued presence of officials who should have been vetted. Thus, the absence of vetting made truth telling more difficult, and, the claim is, by contrast, that the IER would have been more effective in its truth-telling function if, as is likely had these officials been vetted, it could have accessed these institutions' archives and have had more unhindered access to other members who would then have been willing to give testimony.[19]

Similarly, there are instances in which vetting may facilitate criminal prosecutions. Argentina may be a case in point. As is well known, the prosecutorial efforts started by President Raúl Alfonsín—which led to the trials of the junta leaders[20]—came to a halt in that country after a series of coup attempts.[21] Had some of the military officers been vetted, perhaps it would have been more difficult for them to organize the uprisings. The fact that the rebellious officers were mostly junior increases the plausibility of the thesis. Of course, it is possible that they may have revolted by virtue of the mere chance of being vetted, but in the calculus of probabilities the fact that vetting, for all its punitive effects, is *not* the same as a criminal sentence must be factored in, even if by itself this may have been insufficient to tip the scales against the officers organizing the revolts. The question is open in this instance, but the general point remains: it is not unreasonable to think that security forces that have been vetted may collaborate more with, or at least impede less, prosecutorial efforts.

The relationship between vetting and reparations is slightly more complicated, but here again similar conclusions may be reached, even if through a more indirect path. One can imagine situations in which an argument analogous to that made to show how vetting can facilitate the implementation of truth telling and prosecutions could plausibly be defended regarding reparations. To begin with, to the extent that reparations are a form of recognition of state responsibility,[22] those who are responsible for the abuses are likely to oppose the establishment of reparations programs. Thus, vetting those responsible for the abuses may weaken one of the sources of resistance to reparations.

However, unlike criminal prosecutions and even truth telling, which cannot be successfully implemented without thereby affecting fundamental interests of those responsible for the violations (hence their opposition to these measures), it is sometimes thought that reparations *can* be successfully implemented without the perpetrators having to pay this price. Indeed, reparations have sometimes become the object of a proposed bargain (rarely so grossly articulated, but real nevertheless): reparations benefits of a certain magnitude are offered to victims in exchange for leniency in the domains of prosecutions and truth telling. Thus, for example, in the aftermath of Pinochet's return from detention in England, when it was clear that criminal prosecutions against members of the military were in the cards for Chile, the political party aligned with him, the *Unión Demócrata Independiente* (UDI), traditionally lukewarm on the topic of reparations, suggested a major restructuring of the reparations programs that had been in existence for more than ten years, so as to expand their coverage, and, importantly, to significantly increase the magnitude of their benefits, but with one catch: beneficiaries had to waive all claims against perpetrators.[23] Fortunately, this proposal did not prosper. This is by far not the only example of this sort of bargain. Arguably, a bargain of this sort underlies the law passed in Colombia in 2006 to demobilize paramilitary forces known to be responsible for gross human rights violations.[24] Although neither of these two cases involved vetting directly, they show how reparations can become the subject of peculiar political dynamics that sometimes lead perpetrators or their backers to *support* the implementation of reparations measures (but only as part of a quid pro quo). Clearly, this is "support" that reparations can do without, so even in cases such as these, vetting may facilitate the implementation of legitimate and effective reparations programs.

Finally, it is reasonable to think that vetting may also facilitate the broader sorts of institutional reform measures that are often called for in the aftermath of conflict and in transitions to democracy.[25] The argument again is that vetting may weaken sources of opposition and resistance to reform especially regarding, for example, the restructuring, downsizing, and rationalization of security forces; predictably, this will be easier to accomplish once entrenched interests in maintaining the status quo have been dislodged from positions of power.[26]

It is important to reiterate that the preceding arguments are not meant to yield *predictions*. Whether vetting in fact enables or impedes the implementation of other transitional justice measures is an empirical matter that cannot be decided a priori. All sorts of intervening causes and incentives play a significant role in leading to specific outcomes. The arguments presented here also assume what must be acknowledged to be a simplistic relationship between vetting and other transitional justice measures: that these measures are sequenced in a particular way, with vetting coming early in the process or at least sufficiently earlier than other measures so as to allow them to benefit from its results, something which cannot be taken for granted either. Nevertheless, my hope is that to the extent that the arguments are reasonable, they help to clarify the reasons why it makes sense for post-conflict and transitional societies to try to vet their security forces, as well as one particular way in which vetting can relate to other transitional justice measures.

VETTING AND A HOLISTIC CONCEPTION OF TRANSITIONAL JUSTICE

In order to fully understand the place of vetting in a transitional justice policy, one has to go beyond contingent pragmatic relationships, as important as these may be. In the final part of this chapter I will argue that there is a compelling conceptual argument to think of vetting as part of a holistic transitional justice policy. Despite the fact that each of the measures that form a part of such a policy—criminal prosecutions, truth telling, reparations, and institutional reform (of which vetting is one modality[27])—has its own specific goals, they share two mediate goals, namely, to provide recognition to victims, and to foster civic trust.[28] Now, these goals are closely related to justice, being both conditions and consequences of the achievement of justice. Achieving justice through the legal system presupposes that those whose rights have been violated are recognized as having standing, and this means that they are recognized as individuals, as victims, and more fundamentally as rights bearers. At the same time, the achievement of justice contributes to entrenching these forms of recognition. Similarly, civic trust is both a condition and a consequence of justice. Legal systems presuppose a certain level of trust, and at the same time, at least in part by stabilizing expectations, help lower the risks associated with trust.[29] So, beyond the commonality of ends, what ties together the different elements of a transitional justice policy is the peculiarity of these ends, namely that they are justice related in just this way. This is what makes the different measures part of a *holistic* conception of transitional justice.

Having this as a background, since the main goal of this chapter is not to present a particular conception of transitional justice but to clarify the practical and conceptual relations between vetting and other transitional justice measures, I will concentrate here on its trust-inducing potential.[30]

VETTING AS A TRUST-INDUCING MEASURE

In societies emerging from conflict or authoritarianism, vetting may have trust-inducing consequences. This is important for several reasons, which I will elaborate after a brief description of a norm-based account of trust. These reasons include that trust facilitates social interactions and there is a strong connection between trust and justice.

A NORM-BASED ACCOUNT OF TRUST[31]

Before attempting to explain how vetting may be thought to induce trust, it will be necessary to specify a conception of the type of trust in question. Trust in general, as a disposition that mediates social interactions, "is an alternative to vigilance and reliance on the threat of sanctions, [and] trustworthiness...an alternative to constant watching to see what one can and cannot get away with, to recurrent recalculations of costs and benefits."[32] Trust, then, at a general level, contrasts with the sort of constant monitoring and appeals to sanctions that speak of suspicion.

Still, it can be said that while trusting someone involves relying on that person to do or refrain from doing certain things, trust is not the same thing as mere predictability or empirical regularity. If that were so, the paradigm of trust would obtain in our relationship with particularly reliable machines. That reliability is not the same as trustworthiness can be seen in our reluctance to say that we *trust* someone about whose behavior we feel a great deal of certainty but only because we both monitor and control it (e.g., through enforcing the terms of a contract), or because we take defensive or preemptive action.[33] Trust, far from resembling a sort of "mechanical reliability," involves an expectation of a shared *normative* commitment. I trust someone when I have reasons to expect a certain pattern of behavior from her, and those reasons include not just her consistent past behavior, but also, crucially, the expectation that among her reasons for action is the commitment to the norms and values we share. In this sense, although trust does not involve normative symmetry—trust is possible within largely asymmetrical relationships including those within deeply hierarchical institutions—it does involve normative reciprocity: trust develops out of a mutual sense of commitment to shared norms and values. This explains both the advantages of trust and the risks it always involves: dispensing with the need to monitor and control facilitates cooperation immensely, and not only by lowering transaction costs; but as a wager (no matter how "safe"), that at least in part for *normative reasons* those we trust will not take advantage of our vulnerabilities, we risk having our expectations defeated.

Now, the term "civic" in "civic trust" I understand basically as a limiting qualifier. Trust can be thought of as a scalar relationship, as one that allows for degrees. The sense of trust at issue here is not the thick form of trust characteristic of relations between intimates, but rather "civic" trust, which I take to be the sort of disposition that can develop among citizens who are strangers to one another, and who are members of the same community only in the sense in which they are fellow members of the same political community. True, the dimension of a wager is more salient in this case than in that of trust towards intimates, since we have much less information about others' reasons for actions. However, the principles that we assume we share with others and the domain of application of these principles are much more general. To illustrate, the loyalty that binds me to intimates is significantly thicker than the loyalty to, for example, a common political project that binds me to fellow citizens.

TRUST AND SOCIAL INTERACTION

Despite its thinness, some form of civic trust is crucial for large-scale social interactions. This is most obvious in the domain of economics, where the effects of distrust have long been studied: weak networks of trust severely limit the range of options of action available to economic agents. An environment characterized by mistrust is one that requires agents to make large investments in information, monitoring, and sanctioning.[34] The opportunity costs of such investments may be large enough by themselves to put more than a dent in economic productivity. Hence, it is not surprising to find that "interpersonal trust is strongly linked with economic development."[35] Of course, the effects of distrust can go far beyond increasing transaction costs; it is an understatement to say that in such contexts certain actions are considered as live options—as opposed to merely theoretically possible courses of action—only to be discarded because they have become "too expensive." What likely happens under these circumstances is that the range of options to be considered is significantly constrained, and even preferences themselves are adapted downwards.[36]

There is no reason to believe that these effects of the lack of trust are confined to the economic sphere. Indeed, in the domain of democratic politics, in which gathering information about what others are doing, monitoring their activities, and relying on sanctions become not simply "expensive" but may undermine both the legitimate means and ends of democracy, the absence of trust is particularly pernicious. Given democratic constraints, it is especially true that interpersonal trust is essential to the cooperation with strangers that is a prerequisite for the large-scale political organization on which modern democracies are based.

TRUST AND JUSTICE

The literature on social capital is full of illustrations of the many ways in which trust facilitates all sorts of important social interactions.[37] This alone justifies taking an interest in measures that can promote trust. However, since the discussion thus far has taken place at a high level of generality and has pertained mostly to "horizontal trust," that is, trust among citizens, rather than "vertical trust," that is, trust between individuals and the institutions by which they regulate their common lives, some additional steps are called for.

Let us then return to the argument that civic trust is at one and the same time a condition and a consequence of achieving justice through a legal system. There are myriad ways in which a legal system relies on the trust of citizens.[38] At the broadest level, a legal system works only on the basis of citizens' generalized norm-compliance. In other words, the legal system can cope with norm-breaking behavior only when it is exceptional. This means that most social interactions are not directly mediated by law, but rather, at some level, by trust between citizens. Closer to home, however, all legal systems rely not just on the trust that citizens have towards one another but on the trust that they have in the systems themselves. In the absence of total(itarian) surveillance, criminal legal systems must rely upon citizens' willingness to report both crimes that they witness and crimes that they suffer.[39] And this willingness to report, of course, rests upon their trust that the systems will reliably produce the expected outcomes. This is actually a complex sort of trust: in police investigations, in the efficiency of the court systems, in the honesty of judges, in the independence of the judiciary (and therefore in the executive's willingness to protect and promote that independence), in the at least minimal wisdom of the legislature, and in the strictness (but perhaps also the simultaneous humaneness) of the prison system, and so on. Needless to say, each of these objects of trust can be further analyzed.

On the other hand, it is not just that legal systems rely upon the trust of citizens both among one another and in the system itself. Legal systems, when they operate well, also catalyze trust, once again both among citizens themselves and in the system itself. Indeed, John Rawls takes the rule of law's ability to generate social trust—which he understands in terms of the reliability of expectations—as a definitional aspect of the rule of law:

> A legal system is a coercive order of public rules addressed to rational persons for the purpose of regulating their conduct and providing the framework for social cooperation. When these rules are just they establish a basis for legitimate expectations. They constitute grounds upon which persons can *rely on one another* and rightly object when their expectations are not fulfilled.[40]

To the extent that law helps to stabilize expectations, and that it helps to diminish the risks involved in trusting others, especially strangers, it contributes to the generation of trust among citizens.

As for the catalytic role of law in generating trust in legal institutions, the underlying argument should be clear: legal institutions, insofar as they are reliable, provide further reasons for citizens to rely upon them for the resolution of their conflicts. This simply follows from the fact that trust is something that is earned, rather than arbitrarily bestowed, and this is true just as much for institutions as it is for individuals. The easier way of seeing this is by noticing attitudes towards law in societies where the legal system is perceived as inaccessible or otherwise unreliable.

But, if we are going to be precise and consistent with an account of trust that centers on norm-based behavior, our task is not done, for it is not clear what, on this account, trust in institutions might mean. Strictly speaking, if trust is a relationship that cannot be reduced to mere empirical regularity, but one that involves an awareness of mutual normative reciprocity, this is possible only among individuals, and then there is no such thing as trust in institutions. Nevertheless, we trust institutions, and the people who inhabit them. How so? Claus Offe offers the following explanation:

> "Trusting institutions" means something entirely different from "trusting my neighbor": it means *knowing* and recognizing as valid the values and the form of life incorporated in an institution and deriving from this recognition the assumption that this idea makes sufficient sense to a sufficient number of people to motivate their ongoing active support for the institution and the compliance with its rules. Successful institutions generate a negative feedback loop: they make sense to actors so that actors will support them and comply with what the institutionally defined order prescribes.[41]

By way of contrast, people mistrust institutions because they suspect (correctly) that the values embodied by those institutions do not "make sufficient sense to a sufficient number of people to motivate their ongoing active support for [these institutions] and the compliance with [their] rules." Trusting an institution amounts to knowing that its constitutive rules, values, and norms are shared by its members or participants and that they regard them as binding.[42]

The argument that I am interested in exploring is that well-designed vetting measures can be trust inducing, that they can promote trust in institutions.[43] The initial plausibility of this claim is easy to see if we start with the oft-reported effects on victims and others of encounters with former perpetrators still in positions of authority.[44] Particularly chilling examples are often reported by women who encounter police officers who abused them, sometimes as they searched for missing relatives. Predictably, it will be impossible for an institution inhabited and operated by such personnel to garner the trust and confidence of those it is intended to serve, when the latter had become their victims.

This commonsensical explanation of the untrustworthiness of institutions that have not vetted their personnel after periods of widespread abuse is fine—as far as it goes. But it risks underdescribing the sources of distrust in these institutions; distrust under such circumstances usually does not target the particular individuals known (or suspected) to be responsible for violations, but the institutions as a whole. Why is this the case? The norm-based account of trust sketched above suggests an answer: the continued presence of known violators in the ranks of the police and other security forces, for example, betrays that the basic rules of the legitimate exercise of power, and specifically of the use of force, do not "make sufficient sense to a sufficient number of people to motivate their ongoing active support for the institution and the compliance with its rules." Again, the critical point is that the lack of commitment to rules is not just that of the perpetrators, but rather a broader, systemic problem; the institution is distrusted for having employee retention "policies" that keep these people in their jobs; for having a culture of cronyism that protects perpetrators from being sanctioned; for having weak oversight structures; for having a lack of commitment to the prevention of the recurrence of abuses, and so on. If trust is plausibly accounted for in terms of commitment to norms, given the generality of the relevant norms, it is easy to see how breaching them impacts on the trustworthiness not only of the rule breaker, but of the institution of which she or he is a member.

Conversely, vetting those responsible for human rights abuses signals seriousness and commitment that goes beyond issues of personnel selection alone. The general point is that although, as Alexander Mayer-Rieckh has argued in this volume, vetting should properly be seen as part and in need of a broader array of institutional reform tools, and as an instrument that concerns mainly personnel, choices about the latter can be, with good reason, taken to reflect institutional commitments to norms. "Repeopling" abusive institutions with new faces (and, of course, under reliable and transparent procedures), then, is not a bad indication of whether basic norms have acquired the requisite sense to make institutions *trustworthy*. This is important in its own terms, and also as a contribution to, and a consequence of, the application of soundly designed, holistically conceived transitional justice measures.

Modesty about the reach of vetting with, but particularly without, other transitional justice measures is called for: re-peopling unreconstructed institutions with new faces will obviously not, by itself, correct all institutional defects: thus, in a country in which there are many different institutions in the area of security with overlapping mandates and attendant weakening of oversight and accountability, leaving these institutions unmodified is unlikely to significantly transform their trustworthiness in the short or the long run, no matter how many new faces are brought in. Similarly, no matter how much personnel is renovated and how thoroughly institutions are reformed, unless these reforms are accompanied by other transitional justice measures such as prosecutions, truth-telling, and reparations for victims, there will always be a significant sense in which important claims to justice would remain unredeemed. This is one of the implications of arguing that although institutional reform (including vetting) can make a contribution to transitional justice, on its own, of course, it cannot bear the full weight of the multiple and various claims to justice that arise in post-conflict and post-authoritarian transitional situations.

NOTES

I have benefited from comments offered by Roger Duthie and Alexander Mayer-Rieckh, and from discussions during the meeting of authors held at the Rockefeller Foundation's Bellagio Study Center. The views expressed in this paper do not necessarily represent the ICTJ's position.

1 See Samuel Huntington, *The Third Wave* (Norman: University of Oklahoma Press, 1993). For a salutary, "revisionist" account of vetting in Greece, see the chapter by Sotiropoulos in this volume.

2 With the appearance of two ambitious studies of reparations for victims of human rights violations, which add to the copious literature on criminal prosecutions and the growing one on truth commissions, it is now even truer than ever that vetting is the least studied transitional justice measure. To be sure, after the great transformation of the Eastern and Central European countries post-1989, academic interest in "lustration" followed, but since then the topic has garnered remarkably little attention. Some of the earlier studies on vetting are reproduced in Neil Kritz, ed., *Transitional Justice* (Washington, DC: United States Institute for Peace, 1995), vol. 1. The two recent studies on reparations are Pablo de Greiff, ed., *The Handbook of Reparations* (Oxford: Oxford University Press, 2006) and K. de Feyter, S. Parmentier, M. Bossuyt, and P. Lemmens, eds., *Out of the Ashes. Reparation for Victims of Gross and Systematic Human Rights Violations* (Antwerpen: Intersentia, 2006). On criminal prosecutions see Aryeh Neier, *War Crimes: Brutality, Genocide, Terror, and the Struggle for Justice* (New York: Times Books, 1998), and now, the articles in a dedicated journal, the *Journal of International Criminal Law*. On truth commissions, see Priscilla Hayner, *Unspeakable Truths: Facing the Challenge of Truth Commissions* (New York: Routledge, 2001).

3 This chapter examines questions of the aims and justification of vetting primarily from a human rights perspective. In the literature on state building, for example, vetting is defended on grounds of security, of the orderly management of governance institutions, and of the "signaling effect" of vetting, that is, its use to indicate a regime change. I will not examine these arguments here.

4 See, for instance, Herbert Lottman, *The Purge: The Purification of the French Collaborators After World War II* (New York: William and Morrow, 1986), and the papers in part 2 of Jon Elster, ed., *Retribution and Reparation in the Transition to Democracy* (Cambridge: Cambridge University Press, 2006).

5 International Center for Transitional Justice, "Vetting Public Employees in Post-Conflict Settings: Operational Guidelines," Sections I and IV.E, in this volume.

6 "Abusive behavior" is used instead of "criminal behavior," mainly because there may be circumstances in which gross violations of human rights, serious crimes under international law, or other forms of serious misbehavior have not been locally criminalized, and yet may become vetting criteria.

7 On this topic, see chapter by Andreu-Guzmán in this volume.

8 The shaming potential of vetting measures can be enhanced or diminished through different design features; people with "positive" vetting records (i.e., those whose records provide grounds for exclusion) can be given the opportunity to resign and their records kept confidential (as in Hungary), or they can be fired and their records made public. In Argentina, which does not have a formal vetting procedure, military promotions can be impugned in a process that involves public hearings in the Senate. See the chapters by Barrett, Hack, and Munkási in this volume.

9 Whether the potential is realized is a factual, empirical, and highly contextual matter. In Poland, for example, the vetting procedure, to which candidates for public office among others had to submit, did not punish collaboration with the communist secret services, but only making a false vetting declaration. This meant that the collaboration of many candidates became a subject of public knowledge. The expectation of the framers of the law was that this would dissuade the electorate from voting for candidates with a record of collaboration. But for many reasons, which may include the long time lag between the relevant activities and the coming into effect of the law, that the relevant "crimes" were not violent crimes but the giving of information to the former secret services, and that this was something that tens of thousands of people did, a good number of candidates in these situations were actually elected, despite their previous collaboration. See chapter by Czarnota in this volume.

10 The forms of uncertainty that are relevant for this argument are at least twofold. The first is about the course of the transition. The fact that, especially at the pre-transitional stage and even in the early stages of the transition, it is rarely a foregone conclusion that a new regime intent on vetting will be able to consolidate its hold on power may weaken the deterrent potential of any proposed measure (and may actually generate incentives to block the transition). The second has to do with uncertainties (doubts) about the probabilities of being subject to *any* justice measure. It has been observed in the criminological literature that beyond a certain threshold, more than the length of sentence, what ends up having deterrent potential is the degree of certainty of being apprehended, tried, and convicted, and hence having to serve *a* sentence. In countries where the security and justice sectors have been left in disarray, this is highly unlikely. It is doubtful that vetting has a significant deterrent power.

As for the general deterrence power of the death penalty, obviously the greatest penalty, see the materials of the Death Penalty Information Center, on whose website one reads:

> Even as the use of the death penalty continued to decline in the United States, the number of murders and the national murder rate dropped in 2004. According to the recently released FBI Uniform Crime Report for 2004, the

> nation's murder rate fell by 3.3%, declining to 5.5 murders per 100,000 people in 2004. By region, the Northeast, which accounts for less than 1% of all U.S. executions, continued to have the nation's lowest murder rate, 4.2. The Midwest had a murder rate of 4.7, and the murder rate in the West was 5.7. The South, which has carried out more than 80% of all U.S. executions, again had the nation's highest murder rate, 6.6.

See http://www.deathpenaltyinfo.org/article.php?did=2065 (accessed November 1, 2006).

11 See Mayer-Rieckh's chapter on vetting and other institutional reforms in this volume.

12 For a succinct account of meliorism as a liberal commitment, see John Gray, *Liberalism* (Minneapolis: University of Minnesota Press, 1995).

13 For the view that vetting is better done early in a transition or not at all, because postponing it increases the risk of partisan political manipulation of the process (a view largely based on Central and Eastern European experiences), see Charles Bertschi, "Lustration and the Transition to Democracy: The Cases of Poland and Bulgaria," *East European Quarterly* 28, no. 4, (1995): 435–51, and Carmen González-Enríquez, "Decommunization and Political Justice in Central and Eastern Europe," in *The Politics of Memory: Transitional Justice in Democratizing Societies*, ed. Alexandra Barahona de Brito, Carmen González-Enríquez, and Paloma Aguilar (Oxford: Oxford University Press, 2001), 218–47.

14 The targeting of thousands of people, the uneven publicity, and the weak procedural guarantees are features that vetting shares with many reparations programs. However, the partisan political stakes of vetting are significantly higher, which might explain why despite the similarities the claim that vetting has lent itself to more political manipulation than reparations remains plausible. For a review of the politicization of lustration processes in Central and Eastern Europe, see Cynthia Horne and Margaret Levi, "Does Lustration Promote Trustworthy Governance? An Exploration of the Experience of Central and Eastern Europe," in *Building a Trustworthy State in Post-Socialist Transition*, ed. Janos Kornai and Susan Rose-Ackerman (New York: Palgrave, 2004), 52–74.

15 See, e.g., Bruce Ackerman, *The Future of the Liberal Revolution* (New Haven, CT: Yale University Press, 1993).

16 Even in the Czech Republic, whose vetting system applied quite extensively, the numbers of people actually removed from their jobs was comparatively small. See chapter by Priban in this volume.

17 Again, notice the modality. This is not a predictive claim. Whether vetting facilitates the application of other transitional justice measures is an empirical matter.

18 Morocco's *Instance Equité et Réconciliation* (IER) was established in 2004 by King Mohammed VI to investigate human rights violations (forced disappearances, arbitrary deten-

tion, torture, sexual abuse, deprivation of the right to live as a result of unrestrained and inadequate use of state force, and coerced exile) during the period 1956 to 1999—a period which overlaps almost completely with the reign of the King's father, Hassan II, who ruled from 1959 to 1999. This was not a truth commission operating in a situation of "regime change." In addition to a great deal of institutional continuity in the country, there was also lingering personnel continuity. Most of the worst abusers had retired by the time the IER started its investigations, but not all. No vetting has taken place in Morocco to this date, and this is one of the demands of human rights NGOs. Interviews conducted in Rabat, with various human rights organizations during 2005–2006.

19 The IER itself complained of "inadequate cooperation" on the part of some authorities. In its summary of findings, it says: "The Commission faced obstacles in its truth-seeking mission, including the limitations of certain oral testimonies and their fragility. However, these were overcome by referring to written sources. Other difficulties relate to the deplorable state of national archives and the inadequate cooperation of certain authorities, whereby certain officials gave incomplete answers about cases they were questioned about, while certain former, retired officials refused altogether to contribute to the efforts to reveal the truth." IER, "Summary of the Findings of the Final Report" (Rabat, n.d.), 6.

20 In December 1985 the trial of the nine heads of the military juntas in Argentina ended with the following results: General Jorge Videla and Admiral Emilio Massera were sentenced for life; General Roberto Viola to seventeen years in prison; Admiral Armando Lambruschini to seven years; Brigadier Raúl Agosti to four-and-a-half years; General Leopoldo Galtieri, Brigadiers Rubén Graffigna and Basilio Lami Dozo, and Admiral Jorge Anaya were absolved. Although all of them benefited from the pardons extended by President Carlos Menem in 1989, as it turns out this was not the end of their confrontation with the criminal justice system. The literature on Argentina is extensive. See, e.g., Alexandra Barahona de Brito, "Truth, Justice, Memory, and Democratization in the Southern Cone," in *The Politics of Memory: Transitional Justice in Democratizing Societies*, ed. Alexandra Barahona de Brito, Carmen González-Enríquez, and Paloma Aguilar (Oxford: Oxford University Press, 2001), 119–160.

21 On the military uprisings in Argentina, see Deborah Norden, *Military Rebellion in Argentina: Between Coups and Consolidation* (Lincoln: University of Nebraska Press, 1996).

22 As I have argued they *ought to be* if the benefits are to count, legitimately, as reparations; see Pablo de Greiff, "Justice and Reparations," in *The Handbook of Reparations* (Oxford: Oxford University Press, 2006), 451–477.

23 See, for example, "La Paz Ahora" (UDI's proposal), published in *La Nación*, June 20, 2003; http://www.lanacion.cl.

24 Law 975, 2006.

25 Mayer-Rieckh, in his chapter on vetting and other transitional reforms in this volume, insists again on the importance of seeing vetting as only one narrow measure in the domain of institutional reform, and one that frequently needs to be accompanied by others if its effects are to be significant and long lasting.

26 Vetting's potential to help implement these different transitional justice measures in the first place is enabling in a different way: as Mayer-Rieckh has argued, vetting may improve the efficiency of rule of law institutions so that they investigate crimes, render justice, provide reparations, and so on. The point is that the contribution that vetting can make to a transition goes beyond removing obstacles that may lie in the way of putting transitional justice measures in place. Vetting can contribute positively to the operation of institutions that are rarely created de novo or totally and thoroughly transformed.

27 I am following Mayer-Rieckh in thinking about vetting as a form of institutional reform, without rehearsing his argument. See his chapter on vetting and other transitional reforms in this volume.

28 In this chapter, both for reasons of space and of clarity, I will elaborate the argument about the trust-inducing potential of transitional justice measures in reference to vetting. I will be very brief about how the different elements of a holistic transitional justice policy provide recognition, for as far as possible, I want vetting, and not a general conception of transitional justice, to remain the focus of this paper. Thus, the following will suffice: the various transitional measures can be interpreted as efforts to institutionalize the recognition of individuals as rights bearers. Criminal justice can be interpreted as an attempt to reestablish the equality of rights between the criminal and his or her victim, after the criminal severed that relationship with an act that suggested his or her superiority over the victim. Truth telling provides recognition in ways that are perfectly familiar, and which are still probably best articulated by the old difference proposed by Thomas Nagel between knowledge and acknowledgment, when he argued that although truth commissions rarely disclose facts that were previously unknown, they still make an indispensable contribution in acknowledging these facts. The acknowledgment is important precisely because it constitutes a form of recognizing the significance and value of persons—again, as individuals, as citizens, and as victims. Reparations are the material form of the recognition *owed* to fellow citizens whose fundamental rights have been violated, manifesting that the state has taken to heart the interests of those whose rights went previously unrecognized. Finally, institutional reform (to which vetting aims to contribute) is guided by the ideal of guaranteeing the conditions under which citizens can relate to one another and to the authorities as equals. For a full elaboration of this argument, see my "Justice and Reparations."

In addition to serving justice in general and the two mediate goals of recognition and civic trust, transitional justice measures also share two final goals: first, social reconstruction or reconciliation, and, second, making a contribution to processes of democratization, but I will not discuss this here. On reconciliation, see my "The Role of Apologies in National Reconciliation Processes," in *The Age of Apologies*, ed. Mark Gibney and Rhoda Howard-Hassmann (Philadelphia: University of Pennsylvania Press, forthcoming).

29 For an elaboration of this argument, see my "Truth telling and the Rule of Law," in *Telling the Truths: Truth Telling and Peace Building in Post-Conflict Societies*, ed. Tristan Anne Borer (Notre Dame, IN: University of Notre Dame Press, 2006).

30 Obviously, the fact that vetting has this potential is significant on its own terms, independent of the particular conception of transitional justice sketched in this chapter.

31 The material in this section borrows from my "Justice and Reparations," "Truth telling and the Rule of Law," and "The Role of Apologies in National Reconciliation Processes."

32 Annete Baier, "Trust and Its Vulnerabilities," in *Moral Prejudices* (Cambridge, MA: Harvard University Press, 1994), 133.

33 Laurence Mordekhai Thomas illustrates the point with a telling example: "Trust does not amount to prediction: if I put everything under lock and key and invite you into my home, I can quite confidently predict that you will not steal anything, yet nothing is clearer than that I do not trust you." "Power, Trust, and Evil," in *Overcoming Racism and Sexism*, ed. Linda Bell and David Blumenfeld (Lanham, MD: Rowman and Littlefield, 1995), 160.

34 Claus Offe, "How Can We Trust Our Fellow Citizens?" in *Democracy and Trust*, ed. Mark E. Warren (Cambridge: Cambridge University Press, 1999), 42–87. The economic limitations that follow from distrust go beyond those that stem from the high costs of information gathering, monitoring, and sanctioning. In the early days of the post-Soviet period, firms in the former Soviet republics, for example, conducted business only on the basis of prepayment schemes, a notoriously inefficient strategy (albeit contextually reasonable). Furthermore, these firms solved disputes via private protection rackets, which manifested, sustained, and encouraged illegal activities. See Vadim Radaev, "How Trust is Established in Economic Relationships when Institutions and Individuals Are not Trustworthy: The Case of Russia," in *Creating Social Trust in Post-Socialist Transition*, ed. János Kornai, Bo Rothstein, and Susan Rose-Ackerman (New York: Palgrave, 2004).

35 It goes without saying that this correlation is a complex one. Ronald Inglehart not only recognizes that "trust shapes economic development rates, as well as the reverse," but he is also emphatically interested in examining other factors that might affect levels of trust, such as religion and the history of political institutions. See his "Trust, Well-being and Democracy" in *Democracy and Trust*, ed. Mark E. Warren (Cambridge: Cambridge University Press, 1999), 88–120, 91ff.

36 Both Robert Goodin and Cass Sunstein have argued that at every level of income, but notoriously among the poor, preferences are accommodated to perceptions of possi-

bility in order to avoid the acute dissonances that would follow the awareness that there is in fact no direct relationship between effort and success. See Goodin, "Laundering Preferences," in *Foundations of Social Choice Theory*, ed. Jon Elster and Aanund Hylland (Cambridge: Cambridge University Press, 1986), 75–101, and Sunstein, "Democracy and Shifting Preferences," in *The Good Polity: Normative Analysis of the State*, ed. Allan Hamlin and Phillip Pettit (Oxford: Polity Press, 1989), 196–230.

37 See, for example, Robert Putnam, "The Prosperous Community: Social Capital and Public Life," *American Prospect* 13 (1993): 35–42. In the literature on conflict, see Nat J. Colletta, Teck Ghee Lim, and Anita Kelles-Viitanen, *Social Cohesion and Conflict Prevention in Asia: Managing Diversity through Development* (Washington, DC: The World Bank, 2001).

38 For a closer analysis of this issue and of how truth-telling efforts, in particular, can contribute to the rule of law in transitional situations precisely by fostering civic trust, see my "Truth telling and the Rule of Law."

39 From the perspective of well-ordered societies it is hard to conceive of circumstances in which people would not bother reporting even serious crimes like murder. But this indeed happens. In Colombia, for example, during the late 1980s more than 35% of murders were never even reported. See Mauricio Rubio, *Crimen e Impunidad* (Bogotá: TM Editores, 1999).

40 John Rawls, A *Theory of Justice* (Cambridge, MA: Harvard University Press, 1972), 235. My emphasis.

41 Offe, "How Can We Trust Our Fellow Citizens?" 70–71.

42 Tom Tyler and Yuen J. Huo provide the results of empirical research that confirm that "judgments about the motives of the particular police officers and judges with whom people have personal experiences have more influence on whether people accept the decisions of these legal authorities than do evaluations of the favorability of their outcomes.... [W]hen people's actions develop out of a trust in the motives of the authorities with whom they are dealing, they consent and cooperate with those authorities' directives." *Trust in the Law* (New York: Russell Sage Foundation, 2002), 75.

43 Notice again the modality of the claim. This is not a prediction. The argument is about what it is reasonable to think vetting *can* achieve. Whether vetting achieves this, in fact, is of course an empirical question that depends on many factors.

44 See chapter by Sotiropoulos in this volume.

13

Reparations in the aftermath of repression and mass violence

Naomi Roht-Arriaza

It is a basic maxim of law that harms should be remedied. Every legal system insists on it, in some form. Under international law, states are obliged to provide remedies for violations of human rights, both as a matter of treaty law and as part of the general rules of state responsibility. Recent United Nations (UN) formulations view restitution, rehabilitation, and compensation as interlinked but distinct state obligations.[1] Not only states must remedy past harms: the statute of the newly created International Criminal Court allows for individual offenders to pay reparations to victims, as well as for the creation of a trust fund to be used where individual awards are impracticable.

Despite these remedies, few reparations have actually been paid to victims of war crimes and human rights abuses in the wake of mass violence. So far, Germany has paid the largest reparations (for Nazi-era crimes). The United States paid reparations to surviving Japanese-American internees, but other claims from the Second World War, like those against Japan for "comfort women" and slave laborers, have fared less well. Outside the context of the Second World War, examples of large-scale reparations programs become scarcer. Chile and Argentina provided compensation, rehabilitation, and services to some (but not all) of the victims of their respective military dictatorships. The UN set up a compensation mechanism for victims of Iraq's invasion of Kuwait, some of whom suffered what could be characterized as violations of human rights. The International Criminal Tribunal for the former Yugoslavia (ICTY) allows victims to pursue compensation claims in their national courts. Truth commissions in South Africa, Guatemala, El Salvador, and Panama have recommended reparations programs, but to date the governments of those countries have been slow to act on their proposals. The Rwandan government has an elaborate plan for reparations for victims of the 1994 genocide, but it is too soon to tell if the process will work effectively.

Why the discrepancy between word and deed? If reparations are so universally accepted as part of a state's human rights obligations, why have so few states emerging from periods of armed conflict or mass violence put viable programs into place? In this chapter I consider some of the difficulties in thinking about reparations in the wake of genocide and other forms of mass violence, both in general and in the context of poor countries where there may be many victims and multiple claims on scarce resources. I also examine past practices for ideas and insights that might be applicable in the context of mass violence. In a final section, I propose three distinct yet interrelated ways of thinking about reparations, all of which eschew the classic view of individual, court-ordered reparations in favor of more community-oriented, flexible approaches.

Defining reparations

There is a basic paradox at the heart of the idea of reparations: they are intended to return victims to the state they would have been in had the violations not occurred – something that it is impossible to do. They are also supposed to be the physical embodiment of a society's recognition of, and remorse and atonement for, harms inflicted. This view of reparations emerges both from the law of civil wrongs and from the law and jurisprudence around state responsibility for wrongs done, at least initially, to other states. But what could replace lost health and serenity, the loss of a loved one or of a whole extended family, a generation of friends, the destruction of culture or an entire community?

Reparations serve multiple functions. They are both backward- and forward-looking. They aim to recompense for loss and to restore the good name of those defamed, but also to reintegrate the marginalized and isolated into society so that they can contribute to the future rebuilding of the country. Reparations can be both moral and material. Material reparations for an individual victim can include restitution of lost or stolen property, a job, a pension, or a person's good name. If needed, they can provide rehabilitative services to victims, including medical, psychiatric or occupational therapies. They can encompass monetary compensation in the form of a one-time payment, a pension, or a package of services for victims and survivors. For collectivities such as a village or religious community, restitution can include restitution of cultural or religious property, communal lands, and education and health facilities, and compensation in the form of money or services to the community.

History has shown that moral reparations are essential for victims and, in some cases, more important than material ones. They can encompass the disclosure of the facts of a victim's mistreatment or a loved one's death, and the public naming of those responsible for these crimes. They can include official apologies and acknowledgment of wrongdoing and, most importantly for many victims, judicial proceedings or administrative procedures, including the removal of perpetrators from positions of power.

Moral reparations can be as fundamental as the exhumation and identification of the remains of victims, and assistance in reburials and mourning ceremonies. They can have a collective aspect, including public memorials, days of remembrance, parks or other public monuments, renaming of streets or schools, preservation of repressive sites as museums, or other ways of creating public memory. Reform of education, re-writing of history texts, and education in human rights and tolerance embrace the notion of reparations. However, there is a danger that such moral reparations can be used politically to stigmatize and marginalize those groups whose members perpetrated the abuse. Reparations must be offered in ways that acknowledge the suffering of victims but do not victimize others who did not actively engage in the violence.

Modalities of reparations

Reparations to victims can come about through complaints filed in the courts, or through specially designed administrative schemes. Most reparations programs have elements of both approaches. In a number of cases, settlements of court cases have included or have triggered administrative compensation schemes. In addition to national courts, which hear claims based on acts committed in the victim's home country and, occasionally, abroad, regional courts in Europe and the Americas have assessed damages against states, and friendly settlements of cases before regional bodies have sometimes provided for individual reparations.

Court-based mechanisms function best when the plaintiffs are single individuals or, at most, small numbers of victims. In situations where large numbers of people were affected but only a few sue, a few victims can receive large amounts of compensation while others, similarly situated, receive nothing because they never filed claims. Better-educated, middle-class victims often have greater access to courts than those in the lower echelons of society. Court procedure often can be protracted or obscure, or seem to favor defendants. Judgments may be hard to collect. Moreover, individual reparations may fail to capture the collective element of the harm in situations of mass conflict or repression. In counter-insurgencies and civil conflicts, those who plan and carry out atrocities often target specific communities in an effort to end the community's support for rebels, to disperse any organized opposition, or to force the population to flee. Military forces may seek to make local civilians complicit in atrocities, forcing them to watch or even to participate in the violations of their families' or neighbors' basic human rights. These harms to community life and trust cannot easily be redressed through individual awards. For all these reasons, access to courts, national or regional, will be insufficient in most cases of mass violence.

Few governments have instituted administrative schemes to pay reparations to victims and survivors of massive violations of human rights. In general, existing reparations programs have involved relatively well-off countries, or those where there is a limited and easily identifiable set of victims. They also have involved abuses committed by state security forces against a largely unarmed opposition, such as those in the Southern Cone of South America or Eastern Europe.

German reparations to the victims of the Holocaust have served as the model for subsequent reparations programs. Claimants who could prove they had survived a concentration camp received a lump sum for deprivation of liberty, while another lump sum went to a coordinating body of Jewish organizations for the settlement of Jewish victims living outside Israel.[2] Compensatable categories of harm included loss of life, damage to health, and loss of liberty. Despite the billion-dollar sums involved, many victims remained unsatisfied with the German effort. The administrative procedure was intimidating and degrading, officials tried to weed out claims rather than support victims, and professionals were treated far better than ordinary workers. Retraumatization and a sense of injustice followed, and the lesson that design and attitude matter carried forward to more recent reparations efforts.

In the wake of military dictatorships during the 1970s and 1980s in Chile, Argentina, and Brazil, the newly elected civilian governments of those countries agreed to institute reparations programs for victims of the human rights abuses of the dictatorship. The scale of the programs, like the scale of the repression, differed greatly from one country to the next. For example, following the 1973 military coup in Chile, security forces killed some 3,000 people, and over 1,000 disappeared. The Chilean Congress agreed to provide a lump-sum payment equal to a year's pension, and a monthly pension, based on the average wage, for the spouses, parents, and children of those killed or disappeared. Scholarships for the children of those killed or disappeared, and free medical and psychological care were also available. Argentina compensated political prisoners and the families of the over 10,000 disappeared, and created a legal figure of "absent due to forced disappearance" which allowed the families of the disappeared to remarry or claim inheritance rights without having to concede that the disappeared person was dead.[3] In addition, both Chile and Argentina have provided some degree of moral reparations, including official acknowledgment and public memorials.

In the 1980s, several Eastern European countries established compensation for those killed or imprisoned under Communist regimes. Meanwhile, South Africa's Truth and Reconciliation Commission (TRC), formed to investigate gross human rights violations during the years of *apartheid* rule, recommended payment of some R50 million (approximately US $8 million at the current exchange rate) to 18,000 people as immediate interim reparations, and individual reparation grants of about US $3,500 a year for six years to victims, an amount the commission considered "sufficient to make a meaningful and substantial impact on the quality of [victims'] lives."[4] It also recommended provision of medical and psychological care, fulfillment of significant personal and community needs (like health care, mental health facilities, education and housing, and headstones for graves), and symbolic reparations.

Truth commissions in El Salvador and Guatemala recommended a range of reparatory measures, few of which have been carried out. The Salvadoran Truth Commission, made up entirely of non-Salvadorans, called for the creation of a Special Fund, financed by government and international aid funds, to pay compensation to victims. It also recommended moral reparations and a follow-up body to monitor compliance with the recommendations. In Guatemala, the UN-backed Commission on Historical Clarification (CHC) called for official acknowledgment, construction of parks and monuments, naming public buildings after victims, a day of remembrance, and restoration of Mayan sacred sites. It also recommended a National Reparation Program, to include restitution of material possessions, especially land; compensation for the "most serious injuries and losses"; psychosocial rehabilitation; and moral and symbolic reparations. However, neither of the parties to the conflict has expressed much interest in carrying out these recommendations.[5]

Administrative reparations also can include restitution of land and property. In Bosnia and Herzegovina, the Dayton Peace Agreement included provisions delegalizing transfers of property made under threat or duress or otherwise connected to ethnic cleansing, and created a special Commission on Real Property Claims to provide restitution or compensate citizens who lost land and property during the 1992–1995 war. In South Africa, the government established Land Claims Courts. Under the South African Restitution Act, plaintiffs must show that they are communities or individuals who themselves or through their forebears had land rights of which they were dispossessed after June 19, 1913 by racially discriminatory laws or practices. The difficulties of proving land rights that go back generations and where land was often held communally and without written title are formidable, and the Land Claims Courts have used testimony from historians and anthropologists, as well as local elders, to substantiate claims. Remedies can include full ownership, partial rights to the land, rights to equivalent land, or compensation. The present landowners are compensated by the state at market value.[6]

Another compensatory mechanism is the creation of trust funds at a national or international level. In the wake of Iraq's invasion of Kuwait in 1990, the UN established a Compensation Commission to provide reparations to foreign governments, corporations, and individuals injured by Iraq's actions. The compensation comes from sales of a fixed percentage of Iraqi oil, held in a fund. The UN has a number of trust funds, including one for victims of torture. Sierra Leone set up a Special Fund for Victims, which it hopes to finance through international donations.

These compensation schemes share a number of vexing problems. First, and perhaps most difficult, is defining who is a "victim." At least in three countries, the results have not been very satisfying. In Chile, the government decided to focus solely on those killed and disappeared by the security forces, leaving aside the vastly larger number of those who were tortured while in detention and survived, and those who were forced into exile. While justified as a way to spend limited funds on the "worst" violations, the effect was to infuriate survivors, who read this as a lack of recognition of the severity of their own suffering and an attempt to paper over the extent of the crimes.[7] In South Africa, the TRC defined "victims" as those who suffered from the gross violations – killing, torture, abduction – prohibited under South African and international law. Critics pointed out that this limited mandate excluded the legal pillars of *apartheid*: forced removals, pass laws, residential segregation, and other forms of racial discrimination and detention without trial.[8] By doing so, it shifted the focus from complicity in and the benefits of *apartheid* as regards whites as a group to the misdeeds of a smaller group of security force operatives, easily characterized as "bad apples." In this case, individual guilt promoted a myth of collective innocence for the beneficiaries of the *apartheid* system. Finally, in Guatemala, members of the paramilitary Civil Self-Defense Patrols ((PACs), who were used as human shields and to do the military's dirty work, claimed compensation for their unpaid government service. The government agreed to pay each PAC member some Q5,000 (US $675), while reparations for civilian victims of war crimes languished. In all three cases, the identification of "victimhood" has been highly contested.

The range of reparatory measures may also be open to debate. The largest study to actually interview victims was carried out by the Chilean human rights organization CODEPU under the auspices of the Association for the Prevention of Torture. The study interviewed about 100 individuals and groups of family members of disappeared and summarily executed victims in Chile, Argentina, El Salvador, and Guatemala (it relied on secondary research for a section on South Africa). The study emphasized that, for the victims, moral and legal measures of reparation are fundamental, while monetary compensation is controversial and problematic. One striking finding of the CODEPU study is the emphasis that survivors placed on education for the children of those killed.[9]

Why collective reparations?

In recent years, episodes of genocide and mass violence involving the deaths of tens or even hundreds of thousands of people usually have taken place in poor countries with scarce resources. Often they follow or coincide with a civil conflict that has devastated the country's infrastructure and displaced large segments of the population. In these situations, individualized monetary reparations are difficult to imagine without a substantial financial commitment from the international community.

Because the number of victims is so large, episodes of mass violence can exacerbate the limitations of individual reparations schemes. Reparations through courts or administrative compensation schemes require a generally functioning system, not one suffering massive breakdowns in every facet of life and governance. Moreover, in mass conflicts, the collective nature of the harm becomes more salient. Where there is attempted genocide, the harm is defined in terms of an attempt to destroy a group, and so reparation should be similarly defined. Genocidal (or large-scale political conflicts) often have been characterized by the displacement and destruction of whole communities, the setting of neighbor against neighbor, the breeding of forced complicity, and of atomization and distrust. In such situations the lines between victim, bystander, accomplice, and perpetrator are often blurred.

By and large, courts have been reluctant to award collective reparations in the wake of mass violence, and in any case have found themselves ill-equipped to do so. For example, the International Criminal Tribunal for Rwanda (ICTR), through the Office of the Registrar, attempted at one point to provide minimal support for witnesses coming before the tribunal. In September 2000, the Registrar's office launched an initiative to provide legal advice, psychological counseling, physical therapy, and monetary assistance to the Taba Township. In this locality, where the mayor had been convicted of genocide, there were hundreds of survivors, most of them destitute women. However, the tribunal soon found that the needs far exceeded its capacity, that it was ill-equipped to design and administer reparations schemes, and that to do so adequately would require amendment of the tribunal's statute and rules. The effort was scaled back, although the judges and prosecutor agreed that the UN Security Council should amend the tribunal's statute to allow it a greater role in compensation.[10] This dilemma raises the important question of whether an international court should differ in its responsibilities to victims and their communities from domestic courts, where collective harm is usually minimal (see also Stover, Chapter 5, and Fletcher and Weinstein, Chapter 1, in this volume).

Court-based mechanisms tend to function most effectively for individual litigants or small groups. Nevertheless, the Inter-American Court of Human Rights (IACHR or the Court) has taken some steps in a number of cases to use the court system to award collective reparations. In one case involving summary executions in Suriname, the IACHR awarded collective reparations by ordering the construction of a school and medical dispensary as part of a formal judgment, while denying monetary compensation to the affected community as a collective.[11] In a massacre case in Guatemala, the parties agreed on collective as well as individual reparations, to be decided by a community consultation process.[12] In each of these cases the limitations of court-based procedures for granting collective awards is apparent: only a relatively small number of actual victims were involved in either case, and significant amounts of time passed between the violation and the reparations settlement or judgment.

The most comprehensive collective reparations program has been the German payments to Jewish organizations and to the State of Israel following the Holocaust. Jewish organizations asked for collective reparations to compensate for the damage caused to the "very fabric of the Jewish people's existence," including the loss of life, destruction of property, and suffering of those with no living heirs or dependants.[13] Germany eventually paid a total of approximately US $824 million to Israel for acts against the Jewish people, in addition to substantial amounts of compensation to other European states, and to individual victims and survivors.

Other group claims relating to the Second World War have fared less well. For example, after decades of silence, Asian "comfort women" began in the late 1980s to organize to seek redress for their sexual enslavement by the Japanese army during the war. The women unsuccessfully sought official acknowledgment and apologies, a memorial, compensation for survivors and their families, and changes in the teaching of history in Japanese schools. In 1991, one woman, Kim Hak Sun, filed suit against the Japanese government. While the government refused to provide individual compensation, it did attempt a form of collective reparations. Eventually, an Asian Women's Fund (AWF) was established through private donations to improve the livelihoods of the women. Some survivors have criticized this approach as being based on socio-economic need rather than on moral restitution. They have held out for individual reparations fully funded by the government and accompanied by a formal apology from the Diet (Japanese Parliament).[14] The Japanese government's resistance to collective reparations may reflect on-going denial of responsibility for the actions of Japan during the Second World War, covert racism, or a reflection of the role of women in Japanese society. Whatever the explanation, this kind of governmental resistance sends a message that the wrong has not been acknowledged; the victims are not likely to feel relief and are revictimized.

Modalities of collective reparations

Collective reparations in the wake of mass violence can fit into three broadly defined and overlapping models: reparations as community development, reparations as community-level acknowledgment and atonement, and reparations as preferential access. I will explore the advantages and complications of each in turn.

Community development

Communities affected by mass violence are usually poor. In some cases, the key underlying causes of the violence have been poverty and inequality. In these situations, widespread destruction of property, crops, infrastructure, and services only exacerbates poverty. Women and children are particularly vulnerable and often are the majority of victims. In some countries, property and inheritance laws that disfavor women may leave widows landless. Economic development at the community level is thus a sorely needed commodity.

Community development as a form of reparation can have several benefits. Projects, such as the construction of schools and community centers, can provide recognition of the wrong done to a community as a whole and give members of divided communities a focus around which to begin rebuilding the fragile ties among neighbors stretched or broken during the conflict. It is essential, however, that the beneficiaries themselves participate in defining the priorities and design of such projects.[15]

The most attractive feature of linking collective reparations with local development is that it avoids the dilemma of choosing between reparations and other, equally pressing, spending priorities like water or housing. The South African government, for example, justified the small size of its proposed individual reparations grants for victims of *apartheid*-era abuses by arguing that the overall goal of fundamental social transformation is paramount, and that the TRC's reparations proposals could only be accommodated within that larger goal.[16]

Reparation as a form of development has a number of drawbacks. First, it conflates two separate obligations of government: to make reparation for wrongs and to provide essential services to the population. Why should governments, which are obligated to improve the well-being of their citizenry, be allowed to slap a "reparations" label on a development project and get off cheaply? Human rights groups have objected to this conflation of obligations as an abdication of a state's legal obligation to respond to past injustices.

Second, it is often impossible to appropriately target development projects as reparations to the victims and survivors. Where the country is ethnically or politically divided along geographic lines, it may be possible to funnel development aid and projects to the hardest-hit areas, where most victims and survivors reside. Doing so may foster new resentments over perceived favoritism, however. The development of new infrastructure and services may even tend to disproportionately favor those with the economic and social power to take most advantage. In countries like Rwanda, where Hutu and Tutsi live intertwined, services and infrastructure cannot feasibly be reserved to the "victim" group, and so development projects framed as reparations are of equal benefit to victims, bystanders, and even, at times, perpetrators. The Guatemalan Truth Commission recognized this conundrum and advised in its report that:

> Collective reparatory measures for survivors of collective human rights violations and acts of violence, and their relatives, should be carried out within a framework of territorially based projects to promote reconciliation, so that in addition to addressing reparation, their other actions and benefits also favor the entire population, without distinction between victims and perpetrators.[17]

Depending upon the country's unique characteristics, the nature of the conflict, and the structure of the post-conflict government and of other development efforts, collective reparations must carefully consider the balance between acknowledging the special claims of some and avoiding the creation of new inequalities and resentments.

Finally, the "reparations as community development" paradigm can potentially negate or underrate the moral or symbolic elements of reparations, which studies have shown are the most important for victims.[18] Governments could add a commemorative element to their provision of basic services, such as naming a new school or health center after victims, combining the road opening with a monument. But this has to be done conscientiously, and the project has to be framed not just as development but also as redress. This is particularly important in rural areas where such projects, although no substitute for individualized reparations, may be the best that can be expected.

One of the obstacles to pursuing a "reparations as community development" framework is the differing mandates, cultures, and conceptualization of goals that exist among the various institutions usually involved in post-conflict reconstruction and development. On one side are human rights and survivors' organizations that often view reparations and accountability for past crimes as a priority. Even here, our studies (see Biro et al. Chapter 9 and Longman et al. Chapter 10 in this volume), suggest that the relationship between trauma and justice is not straightforward. On the other side are governments, which may wish to avoid dredging up old animosities, and international development agencies, which wish not to become bogged down in political issues.

These two visions have moved closer together in recent years, as the UN Development Programme (UNDP) and the World Bank, as well as major European, Canadian, and US development agencies, have realized the need for a more comprehensive approach to their post-conflict interventions. The UNDP, the World Bank, and national development agencies such as the United States Agency for International Development (USAID) now have specific units or bureaus devoted to post-conflict recovery and reconstruction. The UNDP's list of recovery priorities includes "reduction of conflict and promotion of reconciliation," while the World Bank's human rights manifesto lists "victims of war and violence" as among the vulnerable groups most needing protection.[19] The integration of post-conflict reconstruction and collective reparations seems, therefore, promising. However, difficulties persist based on differences in vocabulary, professional biases, restrictive mandates, and ease of goals. Neither the UNDP nor the World Bank frames issues in terms of justice or dealing with legacies of the past, but rather in terms of repair and economic growth. In part, this may be due to the predominance of lawyers in framing reparations issues, and the predominance of economists and engineers in the development assistance world. Post-conflict work also involves merging the different perspectives of conflict management, humanitarian assistance, human rights monitoring, and traditional development cultures, each with its own "turf," time frame and policy prescriptions. Development aid involves different, often shorter-term, and more measurable goals. As a World Bank report stated in 1998: "It is easier to rebuild roads and bridges than it is to reconstruct institutions and strengthen the social fabric of a society."[20] It is also easier to quantify payback periods and break-even points in the former enterprise than the latter.

A reparations perspective, especially if politically sensitive, might also be considered interference in the political affairs of a state, which is prohibited by the World Bank's Articles of Agreement.[21] To the extent that identified victims and all local residents benefit from projects, this problem would be mitigated. The World Bank has come a long way toward recognizing human rights, considering "rights-based" approaches to its work, and incorporating demobilization of former combatants and reintegration of displaced groups into its mandate.[22] However, the kind of market-opening, social-service-restricting, large project development often espoused by agencies like the World Bank and the International Monetary Fund (IMF) may actually run counter to the local-level, service-providing, participatory focus of a reparations policy. Development strategies such as micro lending and small grants seem better suited to integrating development into a reparations perspective – and reparations into a development plan.

Community-level acknowledgment and service

Collective reparations in the aftermath of genocide and other forms of mass violence form only a small part of a larger agenda for social reconstruction. That agenda, explored in the rest of this volume, includes such mechanisms as prosecutions; disclosure of the nature, pattern, extent, and consequences of abuses through various approaches; removal of those responsible for past crimes from positions of public trust; psychosocial interventions; education reform; refugee returns; community-building; and commemoration.

In a number of post-conflict countries – Rwanda, East Timor, Sierra Leone – the new governments have turned to quasi-traditional mechanisms to provide some measure of justice while fostering the reintegration of low-level offenders into local communities. Although discussed mainly in terms of punishment, such quasi-traditional mechanisms have a clear reparatory element, one which should be further emphasized and developed. For example, in Rwanda (as described by Karekezi et al. in Chapter 3 in this volume), the post-genocide government opted to revive the gacaca system of traditional justice. The courts consist of some tens of thousands of elected lay judges who hear testimony from assembled villagers on the participation of suspects in genocide, and may sentence them to jail time or, in the case of property crimes, to compensatory payments. The primary emphasis is on restoring some of the damage done to the community, but the public hearings also allow for truth-telling; confrontation of victims and accused; and opportunities for acts of contrition and apology on the part of perpetrators and bystanders; and, when possible, acceptance by victims. During the public village hearing, civil claimants can make their case for compensation, and the accused, or others, can present arguments against the civil claim.[23] The gacaca judges compile a list of victims who suffered material losses or bodily harm, and create an inventory (including an amount) of losses according to a schedule set out by law. This list is to be forwarded to a compensation fund, which will be in charge of implementation. The compensation fund is to be financed by a combination of state funds, voluntary foreign contributions, reparations taken from individual offenders tried in the domestic courts, and profit from community service works. Because the amounts awarded by thousands of gacaca courts may well exceed the amount collected for the fund, the fund's board can draw up a scale of payments, and payments may be made in decreasing installments.[24]

If the suspect (except for leaders and organizers) confesses, half the sentence may be converted to a community service order; for lesser (Category 3) offenders the whole sentence may be replaced by community service. A draft decree on community service would create "Committees for Community Service" which will place prisoners in host institutions. Community service may involve rebuilding destroyed schools, houses, or clinics, maintenance work on buildings, roads, or gardens, crop cultivation to feed the prison population, educational and motivational activities, first aid, or personal care. Thus, a form of collective reparation would replace punishment. Ideally, this will be of benefit both to victims and perpetrators, and thus encourage the social reconstruction of community life.

However, there are a few potential drawbacks: while the labor may be free, many building and maintenance materials still have to come from somewhere, and it is unclear whether adequate state resources will be available. In addition, community service by mostly Hutu offenders may reawaken memories of old injustices, when Belgian colonialists imposed forced labor "uburetwa" on the mostly Hutu peasantry.[25] It is unclear whether enough judges with clean hands or witnesses can be found or, as Karekezi and colleagues describe, that the population will be willing to participate in a process that can be time-consuming and take years to complete. Finally, the gacaca courts do not have a mandate to examine crimes committed by the Rwandan Patriotic Front (RPF); this leaves victims of RPF abuses unrecognized and unacknowledged (see Des Forges and Longman, Chapter 2 in this volume).

A traditional approach to reparations has also been undertaken in East Timor, where widespread looting and burning, along with murder and rape, accompanied the 1999 rampage of pro-Indonesia militias, a culmination of years of repressive acts and human rights violations by the

Indonesian military following its 1974 annexation of the island nation. After the violence ended, a national Commission for Reception, Truth, and Reconciliation was formed to assist in reconciliation. The Commission has the normal truth-seeking, statement-taking, and report-writing functions, but it contains a significant innovation. Those who committed less serious crimes (theft, minor assault, house-burning, stealing or destroying crops or animals) may approach the Commission and ask it to convene a meeting with victims and local community members. These parties are to discuss the crimes and propose an agreement whereby the perpetrator agrees to undertake some form of community service, including community work, a repayment or public apology, or to undertake some other "act of reconciliation." Once this process is completed, the District Court is to enter an order that those acts cannot be prosecuted or be subject to civil liability in the future, and the community is to agree that the perpetrator may return home without fear. Failure to fulfill the agreement is itself a criminal offense punishable by up to one year's imprisonment and/or a fine, while failure to apply to the Commission process leaves the offender at risk of future prosecution. Serious crimes, including rape, murder, organizing or planning crimes, and crimes against humanity are dealt with separately by a Serious Criminal Offenses Panel.[26]

The hearings have been ceremonial affairs making extensive use of traditional symbols and rituals, including traditional law-givers. Before a panel of community elders and the assembled village, including the victims, those seeking reintegration tell their story and respond to questions. Victims then are able to respond, the public can contribute additional information about the deponents, and negotiations ensue over appropriate reparatory acts. In the hearings to date, these have ranged from a formal apology, to payment in livestock, traditional fabric, coins, and liquor. In a few cases, the accused have agreed to work repairing a school (together with the victim after he volunteered to help) or building a church. According to one observer, "[d]eeply embedded in the strong local culture and custom, community members affirmed that this process had real meaning for their lives – that it was important for them to publicly acknowledge what had happened in the community and to deal with the rift that had divided them."[27]

These types of local-level community reconciliation program might prove an effective form of reparation where there are many low-level perpetrators, where victims and perpetrators (and everyone in between) must coexist, and where neither the state nor the perpetrators have the resources to pay monetary compensation. These approaches emphasize moral reparations to the community as a whole, a recognition that wrong was done both to individual victims and to the fabric of community life.

Other attractive features include the perpetrators' public recognition and atonement for their wrongs, and the involvement of the whole community in the process of hearing and challenging the defendant/deponents' story, and in the ultimate resolution and reintegration of all concerned. These efforts allow victims to confront those who harmed them, and encourage apologies and atonement. They also are able to reflect and affirm local cultural traditions and values, and can be tailored to the specific dynamics of each culture.

And yet, to date, the primary focus has been not on reparations but on punishment (Rwanda) and reconciliation (East Timor). There is the danger that issues of reparation could be short-changed, and that victims could feel pressured not to demand too much from perpetrators in order not to interfere with community reconciliation. Community reparations programs like these will also work well only where there is a sense that the higher-ups who perpetrated the violence are being adequately dealt with elsewhere. Finally, there may be certain cultural preconditions for such programs. In rural societies like East Timor, for example, community unity and harmony may be more salient values than, say, in cities in Bosnia or in Latin America. Cultural determinants may condition these kinds of community service/reconciliation program.

Preferential access

A third way of thinking about reparations after genocide or mass violence is the provision of preferential access to services and public goods to victims: a "go-to-the-head-of-the-line" approach. From a position of ostracism and marginalization, the victims' status as worthy members of society is restored and acknowledged, through priority access to government services such as state-subsidized or state-built housing, education, public transportation passes, and the like.

Most countries provide their war veterans with preferential access to certain state benefits. It takes only a small leap of the imagination to analogize the risks and burdens borne by veterans with those borne by victims of state repression or targeted by *génocidaires*. Like veterans, victims of mass atrocity have made extraordinary sacrifices; they arguably deserve a privileged place in rebuilding society. Indeed, in the Gorbachev-era Soviet Union, many cities awarded survivors of the Gulag the privileges enjoyed by veterans, including the right to shop in special stores, free passage on local transport, and priority access to better housing and medical care.[28]

The approach in practice may not differ much from a "reparations as development" paradigm, but the underlying rationale is focused on repairing individual harms and on foregrounding recognition that society owes a debt to victims. It also allows an emphasis on the educational and health benefits that victims and survivors seem to value most highly, with less focus on more controversial monetary compensation. It does not confuse the state's obligation to all inhabitants to provide infrastructure and public services with its separate obligation to remedy past harms to some.

A preferential access approach does, however, entail certain risks and drawbacks. To begin with, if a large enough percentage of the population qualifies as "victims," there may be little point to being moved to the front of a very long line for services. It is also unclear how long such programs should last before the debt is paid, and what kind of administrative apparatus is needed to register the individual's special status. More fundamentally, a preference-based approach can create new resentments and a sense of victimization among those who are not the beneficiaries of preferences. Moreover, in some circumstances, victims may not want to have to publicly identify themselves as such in order to gain access to services. It is hard to imagine, for example, Tutsi victims of the Rwandan genocide wanting to carry any identification giving them preferential access to government services, after identification cards marked with ethnic identity served as death warrants during the 1994 genocide.

Conclusion

States may combine elements of these three approaches to reparations in cases of mass violence. Rwanda's compensation fund, for example, contemplates payment in services as well as cash. One could imagine preferential access to microcredit as a combination approach. Much will depend on the specific culture and the relationships among organized state power, perpetrators, and victims. The use of one or more of these three approaches should keep the focus on inclusion, moral reparation, community-level solutions, and access to necessary resources. A constant under all these approaches is the need to involve the victims and their organizations in discussions about what reparations, like other post-conflict strategies, should look like.

Reparations are also part of a larger, multi-faceted approach to post-conflict justice and social reconstruction, and should be seen within that context. Reparations may be the most tangible and visible expression of both acknowledgment and change, and in that sense an important contributor to reconciliation and social reconstruction. Reparations also serve as a bridge between the notions of reparatory and distributive justice, between the spheres of political/moral life and economic well-being. Much empirical research on the effects of different kinds of reparations policy on victims, perpetrators, and the larger society remains to be done before we can pinpoint the contribution of reparations to the larger goals of peace, justice, and equity. It will take a good deal of experimentation and flexibility, as well as adherence to the principle that reparations must eventually be provided to victims of mass violence, to find the right approach for each society.

NOTES

1. Sub-Commission on the Protection and Promotion of Human Rights, *Basic Principles and Guidelines on the Right to a Remedy and Reparation for Victims of Violations of International Human Rights and Humanitarian Law*, UN Doc. E/CN.4/2000/62 (18 Jan. 2000) (annex).
2. Kurt Schwerin, "German Compensation for Victims of Nazi Persecution," *Northwestern University Law Review* 67 (1972): 479–527; Dinah Shelton, *Remedies in International Human Rights Law* (Oxford: Oxford University Press, 2000), 334–336.
3. Marcelo Sancinetti and Marcelo Ferrante, *El Derecho Penal en la Protección de los Derechos Humanos* (Buenos Aires, Ediciones Hammurabi, 1999), 360–377.
4. South African Truth and Reconciliation Commission, "A Summary of Reparation and Rehabilitation Policy, Including Proposals to be Considered by the President," available at http://www.doj.gov.za/trc/reparations/summary.htm.
5. Victor Espinoza Cuevas, Maria Luisa Ortiz Rojas, Paz Rojas Baeza, "Comisiones de Verdad: Un Camino Incierto? Estudio Comparativo de Comisiones de la Verdad en Argentina, Chile, El Salvador, Guatemala y Sudáfrica desde las víctimas y las organizaciones de derechos humanos" (Santiago, Chile: CODEPU/APT, 2002), 139. Available at http://www.apt.ch/pub/library/Estudio2.pdf.
6. South Africa Restitution Act, as amended by Land Restitution and Reform Laws Amendment Act 63 of 1997, available on World Wide Web at http://www.polity.org.za/html/govdocs/legislation/1997/act63.pdf.
7. Cuevas, Rojas, and Baeza, "Comisiones de Verdad."
8. Richard A. Wilson, "Justice and Legitimacy in the South African Transition." In Alexandra Barahona de Brito et al., eds. *The Politics of Memory* (Oxford: Oxford University Press, 2001), 207; Mahmood Mamdani, "Reconciliation Without Justice," *Southern African Review of Books* (1996), 45.
9. Cuevas, Rojas, and Baeza, "Comisiones de Verdad."
10. United Nations Security Council, "Letter Dated 14 December 2000 from the Secretary General Addressed to the President of the Security Council," S/2000/1198, December 15, 2000. The ICTY came to similar conclusions – see United Nations Security Council, "Letter Dated 2 November 2000 from the Secretary General Addressed to the President of the Security Council," S/2000/1063, November 2, 2000.
11. Aloeboetoe et al., Judgment of 10 Sept. 1993, 15 Inter-Amer. Ct. H. R. (ser. C) (1994).

12. Report 19/97, Case 11.212, *Juan Chamay Pablo v. Guatemala* (Colotenango case), 13 March 1997.
13. Elazar Barkan, *The Guilt of Nations: Restitution and Negotiating Historical Injustices* (Baltimore: Johns Hopkins University Press, 2000), 6.
14. K. Parker and J. F. Chew, "The *Jugun Ianfu* ('Comfort Women') System." In R. L. Brooks, ed. *When Sorry Isn't Enough: The Controversy over Apologies and Reparations for Human Injustice* (New York and London: NYU Press, 1999), 89.
15. The Guatemalan and South African Truth Commissions recognized the need for community involvement and empowerment. Commission for Historical Clarification, "Memory of Silence: Report of the Commission for Historical Clarification, Conclusions and Recommendations" (Guatemala: Commission for Historical Clarification, 1999), recommendations, para. 11. Available on World Wide Web at http://shr.aaas.org/guatemala/ceh/report/english/recs3.html; Hlengiwe Mkize, "Introductory Notes to the Presentation of the Truth and Reconciliation Commission's Proposed Reparation and Rehabilitation Policies, 23 Oct. 1997." In Brooks, ed. *When Sorry Isn't Enough*, 501.
16. See, eg, Matome Sebelebele, "Mbeki Says No to 'Wealth Tax'," *BuaNews*, April 15, 2003. Available on World Wide Web at http://www.safrica.info/ess_info/sa_glance/constitution/wealthtax.htm.
17. Commission for Historical Clarification, "Memory of Silence."
18. Cuevas, Rojas, and Baeza, "Comisiones de Verdad."
19. The UNDP has a Bureau for Crisis Prevention and Recovery, while the World Bank has a Conflict Prevention and Reconstruction Unit. The US Agency for International Development's Office for Transition Initiatives plays a similar role. See the website on World Wide Web at http://www.undp.org/erd/recovery/recoverypriorities.htm; World Bank, Conflict Prevention and Reconstruction Unit, "Post-Conflict Reconstruction: The Role of the World Bank," available on World Wide Web at http://lnweb18.worldbank.org/ESSD/sdvext.nsf/67ByDocName/FrameworkforWorldBankInvevolvement-inPost-ConflictReconstruction/$FILE/pcr-role-of-bank.pdf; World Bank, *Development and Human Rights: The Role of the World Bank* (Washington, D.C.: World Bank, 1998).
20. World Bank, *Development and Human Rights*, 8.
21. See Maurizio Ragazzi, "Role of the World Bank in Conflict-Afflicted Areas," *The American Society of International Law Proceedings* 95 (2001): 240–244.
22. World Bank, *Development Cooperation and Conflict Operational Policy 2.30* (Washington, D.C.: World Bank, 2001), para. 2.
23. Stef Vandeginste, "Victims of Genocide, Crimes Against Humanity, and War Crimes in Rwanda: The Legal and Institutional Framework of Their Right to Reparation." In John Torpey, ed. *Politics and the Past: On Repairing Historical Injustices* (Lanham, Md.: Rowman and Littlefield, 2003), 249–276.
24. Ibid.
25. Ibid.
26. Information about the Commission and its work can be found on World Wide Web at http://www.easttimor-reconciliation.org.

27. Kieran Dwyer (observer at a November 2002 hearing), "Report on a Community Reconciliation Process in Suco Lela-Ufe, Nitibe, Oecussi on 22 November 2002," reported in Commission for Reception, Truth, and Reconciliation in East Timor, "Update: October–November 2002," available on the World Wide Web at http://www.easttimor-reconciliation.org/Update-OctNov.htm#English.
28. Kathleen Smith, "Destalinization in the Former Soviet Union." In Naomi Roht-Arriaza, ed. *Impunity and Human Rights in International Law and Practice* (Oxford: Oxford University Press, 1995), 117.

14

Gender and Collective Reparations in the Aftermath of Conflict and Political Repression*

Ruth Rubio-Marín

When the rebels attacked Kingtom, we ran into hiding but unfortunately, someone told the rebels that we were in the mosque.... They located us, killed six people, chopped off my sister's head, raped me, tied me up and amputated my foot... for four days I was there alone and maggots started coming from my foot.... Later I was rescued by some ECOMOG soldiers who took me to the hospital where I learnt I had become pregnant and had to do an abortion.[1]

Ideas of "reconciliation" and "transitional justice" have rapidly diffused around the world in the past two decades, intended to help post-authoritarian or post-conflict societies deal with the legacy of gross human rights violations. Much of the debate to date has focused on the status and treatment of the offenders, and in particular whether they should be prosecuted for their actions or accorded some form of amnesty or forgiveness in the name of national healing and reconciliation. However, there are equally important developments regarding the status and treatment of the victims, and in particular whether they should receive some form of reparations.

Indeed, reparations for victims of gross human rights violations are becoming an increasingly common feature of transitional processes. We can see this trend in the recommendations of various truth commissions and in the

* This article was first published in *The Politics of Reconciliation in Multicultural Societies*, ed. Will Kymlicka and Bashir Bashir (Oxford: Oxford University Press, 2008), 192–214. I want to express my thanks to the editors of that volume for insightful and useful input that helped shape the article.

[1] A 15-year-old girl testifying to the Truth and Reconciliation Commission of Sierra Leone during closed hearings in Freetown, *The Final Report of the Truth and Reconciliation Commission of Sierra Leone*, Volume B: Chapter 4: Children and the Armed Conflict in Sierra Leone, para. 120. Cited in Dyan Mazurana and Khristopher Carlson, "Reparations as a Means for Recognizing and Addressing Crimes and Grave Rights Violations against Girls and Boys during Situations of Armed Conflict and under Authoritarian and Dictatorial Regimes," Chapter 4 of this volume.

emerging jurisprudence of national and international human rights adjudication bodies,[2] and it has recently been endorsed by the UN in its *UN Basic Principles and Guidelines on the Right to a Remedy and Reparation for Victims of Gross Violations of International Human Rights Law and Serious Violations of International Humanitarian Law* (2005).[3] Transitional justice mechanisms have been supplemented with reparations initiatives and programs for victims in South Africa, Germany, Chile, Brazil, and Argentina.[4]

These reparations programs serve a dual function. Looking backward, they are intended to repair a past wrong. Reparations programs are typically structured around the definition of "victims" or the selection of a list of violations or crimes that took place in a certain predetermined period of the past, and they seek, as a general inspirational aim, to "repair" the wrong that has been done. But they also have a forward-looking goal of helping rebuild society. In allocating benefits, both material and symbolic, reparations programs rest on future-oriented notions of rehabilitation, satisfaction, and reintegration, tracing an end-station through which victims will be dignified. More importantly, at least in those scenarios self-reflectively identified as "transitional," discussions about reparations tend to coincide with broader structural, political, legal, and institutional reforms seen as foundational to a "new democratic order." The needs of redress, recognition, and compensation to victims are therefore pondered jointly with the larger political aims of societal healing and national reconciliation.

This dual function of reparations has implications for the kinds of reparations that are adopted. A purely backward-looking focus would presumably aim to provide remedies to individuals in strict proportion to the harm they have suffered. Case-by-case remedies in strict proportion to harm might be best decided by courts. But the enormous range of violations, the number of victims, and the fact that societies that emerge from conflict or long periods of authoritarian rule are often faced with a wide set of competing reconstruction and development needs, make the idea of compensation in strict proportion to harm illusory.[5] Moreover, such an exclusively backward-looking focus

[2] This includes the European and the Inter-American Courts of Human Rights.

[3] Resolution 2005/35, E/CN.4/2005/L.48. The UN principles refer to restitution, compensation, rehabilitation, satisfaction, and guarantees of nonrepetition as categories of reparations measures.

[4] See Pablo de Greiff, ed., *The Handbook of Reparations* (Oxford: Oxford University Press, 2006) [*The Handbook*, hereafter].

[5] See Pablo de Greiff, "Justice and Reparations," in *The Handbook*, 451–477; Naomi Roht-Arriaza, "Reparations in the Aftermath of Repression and Mass Violence," in *My Neighbor, My Enemy: Justice and Community in the Aftermath of Mass Atrocity*, ed. Eric Stover and Harvey M. Weinstein (Cambridge: Cambridge University Press, 2004), 121–137; Richard Falk, "Reparations, International Law and Global Justice: A New Frontier," in *The Handbook*, 478–503.

ignores the contribution reparations can make to building a new democratic order.

In both the theory and practice of reparations, therefore, the idea that reparations should not only or primarily be seen as means to provide individual remedy to the victims (so as to restore them to the situation prior to the violations) has been gaining support.[6] When confronted with a legacy of mass and grave violations, acts of reparation should be thought of not only as means to provide remedy but also as an expression of commitment to a system of rights and, thus, as acts of affirmation and (re-)creation of the democratic state. Granting adequate recognition to victims as equal right holders by turning them into reparations beneficiaries serves this wider purpose of contributing to the creation of the new democratic order.[7]

Conceived in this way, the goal of reparations is not to address every consequence of the breach of a person's rights and try to restore her to the *status quo ante* (the situation prior to the violation). Rather, reparations become a measure that promotes both interpersonal trust and trust in the institutions of the "new state" as well as in its overall legitimacy and efficacy. Reparations become an expression of the recognition of victims as human beings and as equal citizens in the new political order, an admission of past or future responsibility for certain types of conduct, and, at the same time, a symbolic expression of the deontological code of the new political system. In this lies their potential, however modest, for contributing to democratic state building.

The shift from judicial reparations directed at individual victims to broader reparations programs is therefore not just a concession to practical considerations. It also reflects a broadening of the underlying normative goals and ideals of reparations, supplementing the traditional goals of restitution and compensation with broader ideals of affirming equal citizenship and strengthening a more democratic and inclusive political order.

One dimension or implication of this shift has been the increased use of *collective* reparations. Again, this is partly a matter of administrative convenience, given the scarcity of resources and the urgent need for development and reconstruction measures, and the difficulty of making individual-level judgments about harm. However, the increasing interest in collective reparations may also reflect a modest but growing recognition of the group-based nature of past rights violations, and it may in fact be useful in contesting the inherited stigmas and hierarchies that often underpin those rights violations in order to build a new democratic order. Sensitivity to the group-based nature of violence and the group-differentiated impact of violations is also reflected in

[6] de Greiff, "Justice and Reparations."

[7] Ibid.

the increasing trend to recognize that reparations must be gender sensitive and that they must address the specific needs and concerns of women, indigenous peoples, and other marginalized populations.[8]

I believe that these shifts toward broader reparations programs, including the use of collective reparations, are potentially important contributions to the (re-)building of democratic societies. However, these shifts also raise a number of dilemmas, since the different functions or justifications of reparations may pull in different directions. In particular, there is a potential conflict between what I will call the *corrective* dimension of reparations (namely, giving adequate redress to victims) and the *transformative* dimension of reparations (advancing the consolidation of a more inclusive democratic system).

These tensions remain largely unaddressed, in part because the notion of collective reparations has not yet been systematically explored in the transitional justice literature. In this chapter, I will explore the corrective and transformative dimensions of reparations and the tensions that are likely to appear between them. To do so, I will focus in particular on women and gender-based reparations. The multifaceted group-based harms done to women during conflict and under authoritarianism can give rise to claims for collective reparations. It is important, therefore, to consider the possibilities for a project of reparations that seeks both (corrective) redress for victims and (transformative) progress in dismantling patriarchy. As we will see, however, combining the corrective and transformative dimensions of collective reparations in the context of gender is not easy. Policies of compensation, restitution, or rehabilitation of victims can be used to help transform inherited gender-based stigmas and hierarchies that predated the conflict, but they can also affirm and reproduce those stigmas and hierarchies.

I begin by exploring the notion of collective reparations as reparations to encapsulate group-based harm (Section I). I then consider violence against

[8] Examples of this trend include the Reparations Program recommended in the Final Report of the Truth, Reception and Reconciliation Commission in East Timor, handed down to Parliament in November of 2005, which includes gender equity as one of five guiding principles that inspires its overall conception (see Galuh Wandita, Karen Campbell-Nelson, and Manuela Leong Pereira, "Learning to Engender Reparations in Timor-Leste: Reaching Out to Female Victims," in *What Happened to the Women? Gender and Reparations for Human Rights Violations*, ed. Ruth Rubio-Marín (New York: Social Science Research Council, 2006) [*What Happened?* hereafter], 308). Similarly, Morocco's Equity and Truth Commission (IER), set up in 2004 and with a mandate that lasted until December 2005, made gender mainstreaming one of the priorities in its reparations policy (see the final report of the *Instance Equité et Réconciliation* [IER], available in Arabic, French, and Spanish at http://www.ier.ma). Finally, Colombia's current Commission on Reparations and Reconciliation (CNRR) has established a specific unit with the task of ensuring that all of the policies and recommendations of the Commission take into account the specific needs of women and other marginalized groups.

women as an important example of the sort of group-based harm that collective reparations might remedy (Section II), and I identify some of the dilemmas between the corrective and transformative dimensions of gender-based reparations (Section III). I conclude with some reflections that draw links between this discussion and the wider debate on the relationship between democracy and reparations politics (Section IV).

I. COLLECTIVE REPARATIONS AND GROUP-BASED HARM

What, then, are collective reparations? In the reparations literature in the transitional justice domain it has become a commonplace to distinguish between symbolic and material reparations, on the one hand, and between individual and collective reparations, on the other. In spite of this, there is little conceptual clarity as to what exactly collective reparations are about.

Sometimes it seems that the narrative of collective reparations is deployed to deny the need for reparations altogether. For example, it is sometimes said that in the aftermath of conflict or widespread repression, it makes better sense to preserve scarce resources for development and general reconstruction to the benefit of the entire society. At other times, it seems that collective reparations are endorsed not as a substitute for reparations but as a *modality of distribution*, collective here meaning that instead of being given to each victim individually, the benefit is given to a "group" or to certain "groups" of victims. A third use of the expression is that which reflects the nature of the benefit when what is given as a form of reparation is a *public* or *nonexcludable* good, in the sense that, once put in place, it benefits not only victims but a wider population. On some other occasions, the idea of collective reparations is used to describe the option of concentrating reparative efforts on certain *geographical regions*, generally those most severely affected by a conflict and hence with a larger number of victims. Finally, there is a growing but still diffuse sense that when the violence inflicted on individuals is tied to their *group membership* (such as the violence inflicted on indigenous people or ethnic groups), this results in harms that are collective in nature and therefore need collective forms of redress.[9] This last notion of collective reparations is the one that I will explore here.

Collective reparations can indeed be a response to group-based violence. Group-based violence is the violence victims experience when it is linked to

[9] An example of this is Guatemala's National Reparations Program, which includes cultural reparations measures seeking to promote the revitalization of the cultures affected by the internal armed conflict, mainly the Mayan culture (see Claudia Paz y Paz Bailey, "Guatemala: Gender and Reparations for Human Rights Violations," in *What Happened?* 113).

their belonging to certain groups or collectivities (along the lines of gender, sexual orientation, race, ethnicity, religious beliefs, language, etc.). In particular, group membership might be connected to either the rationale for or the form of expression of the violence. Think of genocidal violence where people are persecuted *because* of their ethnicity and the way such violence can contribute to shaping ethnic identities and social perceptions thereof. Think also of gender-specific forms of violence that happen to women *because* they are women in times of conflict and repression; these are the kind that we will explore in the sections that follow. Collective reparations in this sense would refer to the need to redress the harm to the identity and social status of the targeted individuals as well as the diffuse harms ensuing to the entire group. Reparations benefits could include public goods for the entire group. Measures of redress would be inspired by the need to reshape social meanings and allow present and future members of those groups to preserve their identity, status, culture, and sense of self-worth, thereby reducing the chances of exposure to ongoing widespread societal discrimination and violence.

One paradigmatic example of collective reparations in this sense would be reparations for the violation of collective or group-based rights, meaning those rights specifically recognized to certain groups as such. A useful illustration drawn from the jurisprudence of the Inter-American Court of Human Rights is the granting of reparations for the destruction of and displacement from villages occupied by indigenous populations.[10] However, this category of collective reparation is not exhausted by the notion of remedy for the infringement of

[10] The Inter-American Court of Human Rights has embraced an evolutionary interpretation of the right to property under article 21 of the American Convention as including communal property. This has allowed it to decide the need for collective reparations for collective harm experienced by native communities who are forced out of their village and suffer cultural harm, including the disarticulation of their local structures of power, the impossibility to perform death rituals for their deceased loved ones, and the transmission of culture across generations. See, for instance, *Moiwana Village v. Suriname* (June 2005) and *Yakye Axa Indigenous Community v. Paraguay* (June 2005). The Court has also interpreted the right to cultural and religious freedom as having a collective dimension. Thus, in *Plan de Sanchez Massacre v. Guatemala* (April 2004, Reparations decision November 2004), the Court found that the massacre of 268 members of various Mayan Achí communities by Guatemalan armed forces during the internal armed conflict in the country violated both the individual right to life of those killed and the collective right of the Maya Achí community to cultural and religious freedom. This latter finding was based on the facts that survivors were forced to abandon the area for years and were unable to bury the dead or practice other religious or cultural rites and that the death of women and the elderly foreclose the possibility of passing on the Maya Achí culture to the next generations. The Court ordered the payment of pecuniary damages for individual survivors as well as collective measures such as community development in affected areas, the funding of the study and dissemination of the Maya Achí culture in the affected communities, and the publication of the decision in the relevant indigenous language.

collective or groups-based rights. This is so for three reasons. First, as a matter of law, many groups or collectivities are not accorded any form of group rights and yet are specifically targeted in some conflicts. Second, group-based harm may result from the violation of individual rights and not only from those more traditionally conceptualized as group rights or collective rights.[11] Finally, the notion of group-based harm includes harms done to people who are not commonly recognized as the sorts of collectivities that might be entitled to group-rights, such as women or sexual minorities, even though it often is the case that belonging to such groups is in fact related to either the rationale for or form of violence they experience.

Here I want to argue that a conception of reparations that places the focus on giving victims recognition as *equal* citizens, thereby contributing to the creation or affirmation of a more inclusive and democratic political ethos, must capture the group-based dimension of violence and hence include collective reparations. This is so because in those cases victims can be recognized as equal citizens only if they feel that they are not being penalized for belonging to certain groups or collectivities, which requires that these be treated with equal respect instead of oppressed, systematically marginalized, or structurally subordinated. Without the latter, the former is not conceivable. People killed, maimed, tortured, or raped because of their religion, race, or ethnicity are being denied the status of equal citizens not only because their inalienable rights to life and physical and moral integrity are infringed, but also because they are being persecuted on the grounds of their race, ethnicity, or religion. The violence they experience sends a message to them, and to other members of the group and to the wider society, about the lack of worthiness of their identity or condition.

II. THE GENDERED MEANINGS OF VIOLENCE AGAINST WOMEN AND THE VIOLENCE CONTINUUM

In the light of this meaning of collective reparations, we can now ask whether it makes sense to consider women as their potential beneficiaries. Are women appropriately identified as a distinct category of victims to whom collective reparations are owed? And, if so, what form of reparations would serve both

[11] This was recognized in *Yatama v. Nicaragua* (June 2005), a case in which the Inter-American Court, having found that Nicaragua did not adopt the necessary measures to ensure the individual rights of the Yatama people to run for candidates in local elections without discrimination and that this generated collective harm, ordered collective reparations both monetary and nonmonetary.

to correct (to right the wrong) and to transform (to build a more inclusive democratic order)?

From a structural perspective, leaving the group dimension of large-scale violence and political repression unaddressed, and presenting the violent period as a sum of separate violations of individual rights, is an insufficient response. It misses a historic opportunity to spell out true guarantees of nonrepetition for victims, to engage in a conversation about what forms of institutional reform might be called for to accommodate minority or oppressed groups in the "new" democratic order, and to discuss which of the possible democratic models best ensures its inclusiveness. The promise of a common set of individual rights that will not be violated in the future is important for the recognition of victims as equal citizens, but it is also likely to leave unaddressed ingrained prejudices, misperceptions, and structural imbalances that were among the root causes of the group-specific violence. When the structural causes of the violence remain unaddressed, the real chances that in the new democracy those citizens will in fact enjoy equal rights and freedoms without sacrificing their identity and unique forms of cultural and communal life are reduced. Collective reparations, then, from this perspective, are measures specifically targeted to capture and redress the group-based harm both to individual victims as well as the entire group they belong to.

To explore this question, we need to consider in more depth the nature of the group-based harms that women suffer in war or under authoritarian regimes. There is an increasingly rich literature on women under authoritarian regimes and women in war describing the manifold forms of victimization of women.[12] Women, of course, suffer from operations that randomly target the civilian population. Like men, they are detained, imprisoned, extrajudicially executed, and subject to torture or inhuman and degrading treatment for fighting in resistance movements. Women are also frequently punished for their family or communal links. They are harassed, sexually assaulted, and

[12] See, for instance, Meredeth Turshen and Clotilde Twagiramariya, eds., *What Women Do in Wartime: Gender and Conflict in Africa* (London: Zed Books, 1998); Sheila Meintjes, Anu Pillay, and Meredeth Turshen, eds., *The Aftermath: Women in Post-Conflict Transformation* (London: Zed Books, 2001); Susie Jacobs, Ruth Jacobson, and Jennifer Marchbank, eds., *State of Conflict: Gender, Violence and Resistance* (London: Zed Books, 2000). See also Margaret Randolph Higonnet, Jane Jenson, Sonya Michel, and Margaret Collins Weitz, eds., *Behind the Lines: Gender and the Two World Wars* (New Haven: Yale University Press, 1987). On women under Apartheid, see Diana E. H. Russel, *Lives of Courage: Women for a New South Africa* (New York: Basic Books, 1989). On women under the Pinochet dictatorship in Chile, see Marjorie Agosin, *Scraps of Life: Chilean Women and the Pinochet Dictatorship*, Cola Franzen (trans.) (Trenton, NJ: The Red Sea Press, 1987). On women under fascism, see Victoria de Grazia, *How Fascism Ruled Women: Italy 1922–1945* (Berkeley: University of California Press, 1992).

held in prison for being family members of men involved in the conflict or simply for belonging or being perceived as belonging to and sustaining communities suspected of collaboration. Women are also persecuted, raped, forcefully impregnated, sterilized, or killed because of their ethnicity, race, nationality, or religion. By oppressing women in times of political turmoil, the state, subversive groups, and civilian self-defense groups rely on forms of violence that are common to men and women as well as on other forms much more specifically tailored for women, such as sexual and reproductive violence or domestic and sexual exploitation. Boys and girls are included among the pool of victims, and some of the violence they experience is also gendered in that either the reason for or the modality of the violence is conditioned by their gender.

A systematic analysis of the most common rationales and modalities of violence against women shows that, beyond killing, maiming, traumatizing, and exploiting human beings, such violence harms women *as women* because it rests on and exacerbates social meanings that feed the construction of gender relations as a system of dominance. In reinforcing sexual hierarchies, this type of gender-specific violence undermines women's chances to live a life with self-respect and free of prejudice and subordination.

There are at least four different but interrelated meanings underlying either the "why" or the "how" of violence against women *as such*.[13] They are neither mutually exclusive nor exhaustive: there are undoubtedly other factors explaining why women are targets of violence in scenarios of mass atrocity or systematic political repression. However, these four meanings do capture the group dimension of the harm done to women in these situations and therefore allow us to lay the ground for the quest for collective forms of redress.

First, much of the violence women encounter in these contexts is essentially an *assertion of female subordination*. Men are the speakers, women the audience. Women are subject to sex-specific and sexual forms of violence that target both the physical and moral attributes of the female condition more than other less sex-specific forms of violence, the act of violence being at the same time an opportunity for the affirmation of sexual hierarchies. Common examples include sexual forms of torture and violence; the amputation of female attributes; and the infliction of pain by making women feel that they fail in their primordial roles as mothers (as when their children are removed from them while in prison, or when women are threatened with the infliction

[13] Walker develops a slightly different typology from the one sustained here, which has, nevertheless, largely benefited from the former. Margaret Urban Walker, "Gender and Violence in Focus: A Background for Gender Justice in Reparations," Chapter 1 of this volume.

of pain on their children or forced to witness such pain). The speech that this type of violence expresses is directed by the perpetrator not only at the individual victim, but at the female condition. Indeed, this explains its systematic use, such as when women are systematically raped before being massacred. That the meaning conveyed transcends the individual women sacrificed is rendered vivid by the fact that some of the most abhorrent sex-specific practices are performed on women after they have been killed, such as the opening of assassinated women's wombs to extract and destroy their fetuses.

Related to such violence, but with a different audience in mind, is the violence that women and girls endure as a means for men to assert or show their masculinity and, often and related to it, to *assert their absolute or relative male power*. Compared with the previous form, one could say that women here are "downgraded" in an act of ruthless reification: from despised and subordinated interlocutors to mere instruments of assertion of male power in front of themselves and in relation to other men. Whereas on some occasions violence against women simply constitutes an opportunity for male bonding ("this is what we men do"), more frequently violence against women is a form of expression of relative social power: "this is what we do to (your) women to show our power over you." Killing and raping the women of the enemy men, often in their presence, is a way of emasculation that consists of humiliating these men by showing them that they have failed in their manly role to protect women as honor, property, or reputation.

Much of the violence that women and girls are subject to can be understood as sheer acts of *appropriation and exploitation that rest on women's prior reification*. Indeed, women and girls are often treated as objects for male sexual satisfaction or as labor at men's disposal. When taken from others, then, their labor and bodies become stolen "property" and the act of theft possibly also a form of male affirmation. When taken as a price for conquest, they become war booty. The abduction of girls and women, their forced recruitment, their sexual or domestic enslavement and exploitation, as well as the practice of forced prostitution, are all-too-common examples of gender violence as a form of appropriation.

Finally, because women are often perceived and defined primordially as engines of social, cultural, and biological reproduction, certain forms of violence against women are commonly intended as forms of *biological and cultural engineering*. Forced displacement, massacres, mass rape, forced pregnancies, abortion, and sterilization are all tools to destroy morale as well as the actual chances of a community to reproduce itself. "Ethnic contamination," cultural humiliation, or extinction of the community may be behind the efforts to control women's reproductive capacity or to spoil them as repositories of tradition, culture, and collective honor. Both this and the previous meaning of gender violence share the construct of women as subordinate and functional. In the first case, women are primordially there to serve and be used by men. In the second, they serve their communities. They can be sacrificed to either.

So now we know better why and how women and girls become targets of violence in times of political repression and widespread conflict. But what distinguishes this from the forms or meanings of violence that women are *ordinarily* subject to? This question has given rise to what is known as the *violence continuum thesis*. It is widely accepted in the gender and conflict literature that the distinction between "ordinary" and "extraordinary" violence, as applied to women, constitutes a misrepresentation of what women and girls endure before, during, and after times of conflict or political repression. According to the violence continuum thesis, violence against women is better understood as a continuum stretching from "the gender violence of everyday life, through the structural violence of economic systems that sustain inequalities and the repressive policing of dictatorial regimes, to the armed conflict of open warfare."[14] This assertion rests on the fact that, as Margaret Walker puts it, violence against women is still *normative*, by which she means that men's aspiration to control women's lives – including their productive, sexual, and reproductive activities and capacities, as well as their speech and self-expression – remain, to a greater or lesser extent, a rather undisputed fact in human societies.[15]

Having said this, Walker herself warns that the violence continuum thesis might not be the right paradigm to capture "the sense of enormity and outrage, or the terror, despair, and social ruin" that many victims experience in actual instances of violence in conflict.[16] According to her, the key is remembering that "normative social behaviors and positions, by their nature, constitute an *order*, and that order is in many and profound ways suspended, deformed, or destroyed in conflict situations."[17] The idea that violence against women is normative, then, does not imply that all forms of subordination, exploitation, and oppression of women are more or less familiar or expected for women. Some forms of violence clearly imply the breakdown of an order, and hence the suspension of the limits and whatever protection the old order used to offer. This is why, seen from the victims' perspective, their experiences may well be

[14] Cynthia Cockburn, "The Continuum of Violence: A Gender Perspective on War and Peace," in *Sites of Violence: Gender and Conflict Zones*, ed. Wenona Giles and Jennifer Hyndman (Berkeley: University of California Press, 2004), 19.

[15] Walker, "Gender and Violence in Focus."

[16] Ibid.

[17] Ibid.

one of extreme and traumatic "discontinuities" and why, from that perspective, it may still be relevant to distinguish the ordinary from the extraordinary.[18]

Identifying continuities of violence for purposes of analysis and theoretical reflection may not be adequate to capture victims' experiences of rupture. Instead, the theoretical construct of a continuum is a reminder that violence against women "is primarily about control, where controlling women – either one's own or those of other men – is emblematic of masculine power. This factor predicts features of pre-conflict, conflict, and post-conflict situations for women as targets of violence."[19] This includes the retrenchment of masculine and feminine roles with men as leaders before the conflict, the escalation beyond normative bounds during conflict of the forms of coercion that are common in everyday life, and the increase in violence against women after the conflict, when men may find themselves with the "need to reassert control over women . . . [or] to reestablish their place in masculine groups and hierarchies."[20]

Although the idea of a violence continuum has a role to play in explaining the sequence and forms of violence women are subject to, it accounts for victims' experiences only imperfectly. This becomes even clearer when we focus on the collective dimension of the experience. Moving beyond the individual victims, and thinking in terms of harm to the group linked to the extraordinary forms of domination and violence that women are subject to during conflict and authoritarianism, we can identify two main forms of such harms. On the one hand, in many ways the extraordinary is simply an exacerbation of the ordinary, and so the gendered meanings underpinning ordinary violence inflicted on women are reasserted in times of conflict and political repression. On the other hand, the new experiences of violence also represent a disruption of a gendered order – an order that sanctions female subordination but also contains its forms and modalities of expression defining what is "normal" for women to expect but also what is *not*. This new experience of unbound violence and domination disrupts the ordinary by further dehumanizing women, broadening the imagination as to what women are for, who women belong to, what can be done to women, what causes women can be sacrificed for and what is a woman's proper place in society. Moreover, all of this works to the detriment of women's overall social status *as women*, and often, as women belonging to certain religious, ethnic, or racial groups also. If this is so, then increased violence against women in the

[18] Ibid.
[19] Ibid.
[20] Ibid.

aftermath of a conflict in which women have experienced extraordinary forms of violence may be not only collateral damage in the process of reconstructing a system of a gendered social order, but also the expression of new forms and degrees of violence that have been normalized and hence become less "unthinkable" in a post-conflict society.

This double dimension of "extraordinary" violence against women (as both affirmation and subversion of preexisting meanings and orders) makes the project of reparations for survivors one that is inevitably ridden with tensions. On the one hand, the disruption of a preexisting order may be the source of corrective claims of victims to have it reestablished and affirmed (going back to "normal"). On the other, victims and women in general may also have legitimate expectations to push a transformative agenda when asking for reparations so as to question sexual hierarchies that were embedded in the "ordinary" accounting for many of the forms of violence they experienced in their normal lives. This possibility of advancing a transformative agenda is likely to present itself only when the wider societal conditions allow for a fruitful dialogue between the process of historical clarification and rectification, on the one hand, and, on the other, the ongoing challenge of strengthening and deepening democracy by making the contestation of inherited gender stigmas and hierarchies a paradigmatic expression of democratic progress.

III. GENDER-BASED VIOLENCE AND COLLECTIVE REPARATIONS: FROM VICTIMS TO AGENTS OF CHANGE

We now have a better sense of the tensions that may surface in a project of reparations that tries to address both the individual and collective effects of gender violence. Because reparations for women have not figured prominently in the reparations agenda of most countries, these underlying tensions have received little attention to date.

It is widely acknowledged that women play an essential role during periods of violence and its aftermath, working to sustain and reconstitute families and communities, demanding justice for their loved ones, and trying to revert life back to normalcy. Nonetheless, reparations programs in transitional societies have, for the most part, not been explicitly designed with a gender dimension in mind. The inroads of feminism in international law, especially since the 1990s, coupled with the trend of more participatory processes of reparations, has raised awareness that something "has to be done about the women." However, all too often this has meant more meetings in which women meet other women, but not many of the decision makers, who continue largely to be male. Until very recently feminist organizations and women's rights organizations tended to be largely absent from the discussions of reparations, even in those cases where they had been actively involved in discussing the conflict and fighting for peace. This is partly due to the fact that women's groups are often of a different social, cultural, or ethnic background than victims. Also, the energies of women's groups in times of transition often go toward seizing the window of opportunity for structural and institutional future-looking and long-term reforms, which are often more inspired by global feminist movements than by women's extraordinary suffering in the past, even fairly recent suffering.

Thus, it is not surprising that although there is an increasing interest in exploring collective forms of reparation, there is virtually no discussion of how this interest and that of "engendering" reparations may intersect in ways that are conducive to pushing forward the agenda of "engendering" democracy. Can collective reparations (such as those for group-based harm to women) serve to promote a more democratic order (including a more gender-inclusive democracy)? As discussed earlier, the notion of collective reparations is used to refer to a variety of things, and it is unlikely that there will be one single answer to this question. Here I would like to focus on the one meaning of collective reparations that I have explored and defended above – namely, collective reparations as those measures that address and attempt to *redress the harm to identity and status resulting from group-based violence*, in this case from gender-based violence.

We saw above that the violence women experience during times of "extraordinary" conflict and authoritarian repression asserts gender meanings in ways that both confirm and expand those underlying "ordinary" violence against women. It was argued that, as a result, structural oppression and subordination of women is reaffirmed to the detriment not only of individual victims but of women in general and of those belonging to certain ethnic, religious, or racial groups in particular. I would now like to argue that addressing the broad implications of gender-based violence allows us to connect the "backward-looking" reparations agenda to the "forward-looking" institutional and legal reform agenda. This potential connection is greatest precisely in those moments that tend to be identified as moments of "democratic state building," and I believe that the notion of collective reparations can be especially apposite for drawing this connection. At the same time, though, I will show that the case of gender-based collective reparations reveals the complexities involved in trying to combine the corrective and transformative dimensions of a reparations project.

So what could be some forms of collective reparations for women? How could women's past experience of violence (and the analysis of its underlying and enabling structural conditions) contribute to reforms aimed at ensuring women equal citizenship in more inclusive democracies? Answers to such questions must be context specific and will probably be determined both by the specific history and forms of female subordination and by the prevailing conception of democracy in each society. Short- and long-term measures of collective reparations could include things as diverse as sensitization campaigns regarding women's human rights or violence against women; training of the army and police forces on these matters; vetting of the public-order forces that engaged in the worst forms of gender violence; gender-sensitive school programs; symbolic reparations (such as a collective apology to the women); and reforms of the constitutional and legal systems to remove traces of formal discrimination against women as well as to facilitate women's equal opportunities. Gender quotas or political parity measures to ensure women's effective political representation would also count. Other legal reforms and structural measures to address women's economic subordination (such as reform of patriarchal land tenure, ownership, or inheritance rules) or their reduced chances of a life free of violence and sexual abuse are also relevant examples. These would all have to be supplemented with measures designed to address the harm in status and identity resulting from those violent actions that targeted women both as women and as members of certain national, ethnic, or religious minorities.

If defined with the participation of victims, and if meaningfully implemented, these measures of cultural, social, institutional, and legal reform could connect collective and individual reparations processes. Thus they could bring up the status of women in general, and of those belonging to minority groups in particular, enhancing their chances to live a life with self-respect and free of prejudice and subordination. They would also reduce the odds of repetition for victims by helping stop cycles of violence and vulnerability.[21] Finally, the adoption of such reforms could also give victims, especially those involved in the process of defining reparations, a sense of satisfaction in that it would recognize them as agents of social change, something that could facilitate their rehabilitation process. Indeed, contributing to the creation of a better, more just society in which their children and the generations to come will be spared the injustice they had to experience can be a source of meaning, especially in the case of lives otherwise dramatically truncated by the disruption of violence.

[21] In fact the Inter-American Court of Human Rights (the international human rights adjudicatory body that has thus far gone the furthest in articulating the right to monetary and nonmonetary reparations for victims of human rights violations) has on several occasions ordered states to engage in certain legislative or institutional reforms or to adopt certain policies for the sake of nonrepetition. For concrete examples, see Arturo J. Carrillo, "Justice in Context: The Relevance of Inter-American Human Rights Law and Practice to Repairing the Past," in *The Handbook*, 527.

At the same time, though, it is important to keep actual victims' legitimate claims, including those of restitution and compensation, in the picture. Using victims' experiences of unspeakable pain and anguish only or primarily as material for pedagogical future-looking nation building or political re-foundation, without doing anything concrete to help victims out of their devastation, would be perceived at best as a purely instrumental use of victims and at worst as an exercise of empty rhetoric. It is only when the two processes go hand in hand that victims may gain a sense of satisfaction from the fact that their pain was not in vain and their lives were not entirely wasted. But the two goals may not always be easy to reconcile, as some of the expectations of victims to have their broken lives restored may entail the affirmation (rather than transformation) of preexisting gender hierarchies.

Several examples can illustrate the complexity. Within reparations parlance, *restitution* measures seek to restore the victim to the original situation before the violation and may include restoration of employment and return of property. One common problem is that often employment opportunities and property rights were not equally recognized to men and women to start with (precisely because women were seen as subordinate to men or as male extensions rather than as citizens and full subjects of rights). What to do, then, with the all-too-common post-conflict scenario where female-headed households are suddenly multiplied? Here "meaningful" restitution can only be transformative. Men can't be brought back to life. To the extent that restitution is embraced, it must mean "transformative restitution," bringing the victim not to where she was but to where she ought to have been. Restoring a discriminatory system of property and employment would be of little avail to females who suddenly find themselves alone in heading households (often with more dependants than before), or to women more generally. This is an example of how, under certain circumstances, the transformative solution may be to the advantage of both victims and the wider group of women.

Think of *compensation* measures now. Compensation is often provided as a form of reparation. It can simply involve a token recognition of the fact of a rights violation, or it can aim at redress in proportion to harm or, if not in strict proportion to harm, at least aim to be sensitive to the seriousness of the violation and attuned to the affected good, the ensuing harms, and the lost opportunities. The idea of compensating women for the violation of rights or in proportion to harm presents interesting challenges not only, as the previous example shows, because women are often simply denied some rights, but also because what something is "worth" is often the result of external sources of evaluation. Take the example of women who are subject to sexual and reproductive violence and, as a result, lose their virginity or their capacity to bear children. On the one hand, assessing the harm done to victims of sexual and reproductive violence in terms of loss of virginity or loss of reproductive capacity, far from being transformative, reinforces the notion that women are primarily to be valued for their sexual purity or as reproductive vessels. On the other, women and girls who have lost virginity or the capacity to conceive children, or who have been forced to marry the enemy or bear their children, do find their chances of marrying significantly reduced. They also commonly experience family and communal ostracism. And all of this means that their opportunities to achieve equal status, protection, and income are severely undermined. Measuring this harm in terms of lost opportunities seems to convey and perpetuate the "wrong gender meanings," and refusing to measure compensation in this way may seem like an act full of promise for future generations of women. Yet such a transformative stance would do little to help actual victims avoid dire material destitution. Where restitution through reconstructive surgeries may not be a sufficient solution, pensions might be a good way to address the "disability" that women are left with in societies whose patriarchal cultures can't be changed all at once.

Let us take an example drawn from another modality of reparation: *rehabilitation*. To some extent rehabilitation may actually require a degree of social and cultural transformation. The best example may again be that of victims of sexual violence, because in most scenarios the violence these victims endure at the hands of their perpetrators is only the prelude to additional forms of violence through stigma, abandonment, isolation, and ostracism coming from their partners, families, villages, and communities. Healing, then, can come only from a transformed society that stops the process of holding victims themselves (partly) responsible for their own victimization. The fact that such transformation can take place only at a certain pace represents one of the most daunting challenges for the full psychosocial rehabilitation of women who have been sexually abused and exploited.

On the other hand, rehabilitation may also require a certain measure of corrective reparation, whatever its shortcomings for advancing a transformative agenda. Indeed, to the extent that its goal is reinserting women back into their societies and allowing them to recover a functional life, rehabilitation must be attuned to victims' felt experiences of trauma, and these often involve the sense of a prior order being disrupted. The area of symbolic reparations illustrates this. Brandon Hamber and Ingrid Palmary explore the role of apologies and memorials as forms of symbolic reparation and recognition in helping rehabilitate victims and give them a sense of satisfaction.[22] These scholars have pointed out the fact that women's manifold forms of agency

[22] See Brandon Hamber and Ingrid Palmary, "Gender, Memorialization, and Symbolic Reparations," Chapter 7 of this volume.

during times of conflict are rarely recognized in memorials, and that, when portrayed as victims, the focus is on women's suffering as mothers and wives. This can be criticized for reproducing sexual stereotypes that "depoliticize" women's lives and life within the family. Indeed, memorials and statues that emphasize women's experiences *only* as mothers and wives during times of political turmoil send out wider messages about proper male and female roles that are likely to reinforce patriarchy. However, it is also true that people's experiences of loss, pain, and trauma are partly shaped through social meanings that must be acknowledged if we want victims to *feel* duly recognized. We can and maybe should insist that in the aftermath women reclaim more space to analyze the ways in which they both participated and suffered beyond their roles as mothers and wives. But this cannot mean silencing women's articulated pain and sense of loss as mothers or wives by judging it primarily as an expression of false consciousness or indoctrination.[23]

In short, restitution, compensation, rehabilitation, and satisfaction measures must help victims connect past and future and enable them to move on with their lives. Keeping in mind victims' experiences and the societies and cultures that act as vehicles for the meanings through which those experiences are interpreted is crucial. A policy of reparations that takes place at a given point in time cannot entirely and immediately reconstruct victims' experiences or their societies from scratch in the light of transformative conceptions of gender relations. A balance must be drawn. Focusing only on "restoring" victims to a place as close to the one where they were before "the events" is clearly insufficient, for several reasons. It fails to address the cumulative effects of the (often-intertwined) ordinary and extraordinary forms of subordination women experience; it does not pay due attention to the fact that gender violence results in harms to all women and not just victims of certain atrocities; and it misses the importance of conceptualizing gender subordination as fundamentally incompatible with the promise of inclusive democracy. Reparations must, therefore, include transformative as well as restorative dimensions. On the other hand, optimizing only the transformative dimension of reparations (by privileging those concrete reparations benefits that would best suit the new conception of a more emancipated woman in a more egalitarian society) is equally inadequate. It betrays victims to the extent that the system of meanings

[23] See also Fionnuala Ni Aolain, "Sex-based Violence during the Holocaust – A Reevaluation of Harms and Rights in International Law," *Yale Journal of Law and Feminism* 12 (2000): 19–20, arguing that refusing to address the harm of maternal separation under the Holocaust as a genuine harm to women for fear of essentializing the female as mother shows the dangers of creating "totalizing theories of harm that fail to account the specific and lived experiences of the victims . . . shunning the concrete in pursuit of universal truth."

underlying gender-normative violence is unlikely to change fast enough and in ways that are concrete enough to allow victims to make sense of their past and future lives. In some respects, then, the most that can be asked from victims is that they take an active role, if they so wish, to act as facilitators of change for the benefit of future generations. Procedurally, this can be done only when reparations are shaped through a deliberative process that includes victims' voices and visions of a better society.

IV. CONCLUDING REFLECTIONS: ON REPARATIONS AND DEMOCRACY

All of the above suggests that reparations should not be seen as an attempt at closure aimed at settling once and for all the debts of the past, tracing a rigid line that historically divides the "evil past" from the "redeemed present and future." Rather, the struggle for reparations can be seen as an ongoing struggle for recognition aimed at achieving ever-more inclusive democratic orders. After all, the political life of reparations is often fluid. In many countries, including Chile and Argentina, reparations policies have evolved in a piecemeal way rather than as part of an encompassing plan decided once and for all. And although we have focused in this article on scenarios self-reflectively defined as "transitional" because of their recent departure from authoritarianism or armed conflict, many of the countries that pride themselves on being consolidated democratic regimes are also addressing reparations claims as part of larger efforts to tackle long-standing forms of exclusion (e.g., in Australia, the United States, Canada).

The ongoing struggle to redefine the "demos" in a way that allows for the contesting of hegemonic discourses and patterns of exclusion requires meaningful recognition and redress of a past characterized by the systematic denial of equal citizenship linked to group membership. After all, many of the countries in which transitional justice practitioners work are not only societies coming to terms with past massive human rights violations – they are also societies coming to terms with ethnic, religious, or linguistic divisions and patriarchal orders that may have been at the root of the violations themselves. As Pablo de Greiff argues compellingly, we have a duty to remember collectively what we cannot reasonably expect our peer citizens to forget.[24] And this includes the fact that certain groups among us have been systematically oppressed and marginalized and the concrete ways in which such oppression has deeply affected their lives and those of their descendants. Such a recognition might be essential to reconstructing a shared political memory that enables a renewed political

[24] See Pablo de Greiff, "The Duty to Remember," unpublished manuscript, forthcoming.

"we" as well as to triggering social change and transformation to ensure the overcoming of domination and hierarchy.

This reconstructed "we" would not necessarily rest on the possibility of the "healing of a preexisting people," on the prospects for reconciliation as an inner spiritual process, or, for that matter, on the chances to achieve a new *common* identity through the act of reconciliation. Rather, reparations are (more modest) acts of recognition of people as equal citizens and right-holders that, paraphrasing Andrew Schaap, will facilitate the recognition of the other as "sharing a space for politics within which citizens divided by memories of past wrongs could debate and contest the terms of their political association."[25] Women, sexual minorities, religious minorities, racial or ethnic minorities, and indigenous peoples can use the banner of reparations to contest the terms of their political association if they do not limit themselves to pressing claims to have a certain order of things restored but instead push to have that order transformed in ways that are identified by multicultural and deliberative theories of democracy. In this sense, reparations politics and multicultural and deliberative theories of democracy can be seen as potentially supplementing each other in their joint, never-ending search for ever-more inclusive and egalitarian political systems. More specifically, reparations struggles remind us of the need to explore continuities between past and present patterns of exclusion, a need which is too often ignored under the uplifting but delusional effects of the promise of a clean slate epitomized by gender-, race-, sex-, language-, and religion-neutral rights and institutions of the liberal state.[26] At the same there is growing awareness that the potential healing effects of reparations measures cannot be achieved unless society is taking measures to address the structural problems that gave rise to the conflict.

Reparations can also contribute to a more inclusive deliberative process. Reparations debates are discursive instruments that can give voice to the

[25] Andrew Schaap, "Political Reconciliation as Struggles for Recognition?" *Social and Legal Studies* 13, no. 4 (2004): 538.

[26] See also Bashir Bashir, "Accommodating Historically Oppressed Social Groups: Deliberative Democracy and the Politics of Reconciliation," in *The Politics of Reconciliation in Multicultural Societies*, ed. Will Kymlicka and Bashir Bashir (Oxford: Oxford University Press, 2008), 48–70; Paul Muldoon, "Reconciliation and Political Legitimacy: The Old Australia and the New South Africa," *Australian Journal of Politics and History* 49, no. 2 (2003): 195–196, for whom reconciliation should also be viewed as a conversation forum for public deliberation about the past and its links to the present; and Lawrie Balfour, "Reparations *After* Identity Politics," *Political Theory* 33, no. 6 (2005): 802, arguing, in the context of the struggle for slavery and Jim Crow in the United States, that reparations politics provides "a critical discourse that serves as a counterweigh to race-blind language and incorporates acknowledgment of the past into present practices."

historically oppressed, who often find mainstream institutions particularly inaccessible. Such debates give groups a say on what it is that they need in order to feel that their past has been adequately recognized, thereby allowing them to move forward and be reconciled as members of a shared political space.[27] The increasing awareness within transitional justice initiatives about the need to guarantee victims' participation in the process that leads to reparations coincides with the claims of participatory models of democracy, which argue that, in general, it is not enough that citizens in liberal democracies are bearers of rights entitlements. There is a need to adopt measures that will enable citizens also to be participants in the democratic dialogue.[28] Clearly, victims of historical injustices (or reparations commissions claiming to articulate their views, or courts claiming to defend their rights) do not have the unilateral right to define or implement on their own broader structural, institutional, or legal reforms that will shape not just the future of victims but also that of the entire society. But giving victims a voice in the process of defining measures of redress and nonrecurrence can enhance the inclusiveness of the democratic process, whose long-term legacies of systemic discrimination against historically oppressed and silenced groups cannot be erased in a single moment. Indeed, most victims experience the possibility of expressing and voicing their grievances "officially" as having in itself a reparative dimension, from which they draw a renewed sense of dignity.[29]

In summary, debates about reparations should not be seen as expressing an inherent flaw or insufficiency of democracy in a "post-political" era but can rather be interpreted as opportunities to discuss our democratic hopes. In post-conflict or post-authoritarian situations, they provide a forum to discuss what it is that democracy requires in a period self-identified as "transitional"; in consolidated democracies, they provide a forum to discuss whether the democratic aspirations once embraced have in fact delivered the promise of equal citizenship. In particular, reparations discussions offer the possibility to address historical injustices against groups that have been adequately recognized thus

[27] This is of course not to deny the obvious fact that admission of responsibility for historical injustices requires a relative political strength on the part of victims to start with. Rather, it is to suggest that such power should also take the form of agency. See Elazar Barkan, "Restitution and Amending Historical Injustices in International Morality," in *Politics and the Past: On Repairing Historical Injustice*, ed. John Torpey (Lanham, MD: Rowman and Littlefield, 2003), 93.

[28] Jürgen Habermas, *Between Facts and Norms: Contributions to a Discourse Theory of Law and Democracy*, William Rehg (trans.) (Cambridge: Polity Press, 1996), ch. 9, esp.

[29] Martha Minow, *Between Vengeance and Forgiveness: Facing History after Genocide and Mass Violence* (Boston: Beacon Press, 1998), 93, 99.

far, and to draw lessons about the measures needed to prevent discrimination and ensure intergroup equality (including group rights).[30] The conclusions and deficits identified in each national conversation stirred up by reparations claims will vary, in part because there are competing and changing conceptions of what equal citizenship means. These variations show how, although inspired by a universalist ethos, democracy remains a historically grounded and shaped venture, always open for revisitation with an eye both to the past and the future.

This becomes even more obvious when we underscore the fluid boundaries between the "ordinary" and "extraordinary" forms of violence, marginalization, and exclusion signaling the "before" and the "after" of a certain historical episode collectively understood as "the dark ages." Rather than taking place at one single point in time with final closure as a necessary end station, the struggle for reparations can recur whenever sufficient progress in either democratic conviction or practice has been made to "signal" a foundational break with the past, enabling a collective reinterpretation of the meaning and relevance of both past and present forms of exclusion. For women, who have thus far rarely been the protagonists of discussions about historical injustices and reparations,[31] this opens up the possibility that, in time, all of the gender-based forms of systemic discrimination, violence, and subordination will come to be judged as "extraordinary" and, hence, as essentially antithetical to the democratic promise, triggering, among other things, a call for reparations.

[30] In fact claims of reparations and restitution have been crucial to push indigenous people's agenda for broader recognition of group rights including self-government rights. See Barkan, 94–97.

[31] According to John Torpey, it is primarily the "Holocaust analogy" that has allowed race and ethnicity to have a greater intuitive appeal as criteria for determining membership in a victim group and therefore accounts for the predominance of ethnicity and race-based reparations movements over those which have or could have focused on different criteria of victimization, including gender or class (John Torpey, "'Making Whole What has Been Smashed': Reflections on Reparations," *The Journal of Modern History* 73, no. 2 [2001]: 351–352). It seems to me that an insufficient analysis of the gendered dimensions of episodes predominantly portrayed as "religion, race or ethnicity-based," including the Holocaust, suggests that the root causes for the historical neglect of gender based violence may be only partially explained by the lack of a Holocaust-type analogy. On gender and the Holocaust, see Leonore J. Weitzman and Dalia Ofer, eds., *Women in the Holocaust* (New Haven, CT: Yale University Press, 1998).

15

Introduction

Mihaela Mihai and Mathias Thaler

In the last few decades, numerous liberal democratic states have offered public apologies for past violations of human rights[1]. A gesture formerly associated with weakness is nowadays perceived as a marker of moral strength.[2] Crimes such as enslavement, displacement, violation of treaties, war crimes, ethnic discrimination, cultural disruption and many other types of human rights abuses have led to public expressions of regret.[3] Whereas politicians have traditionally been unwilling, or at least hesitant, to offer apologies for historical injustices at the hands of the state, we are currently witnessing a veritable wave of apologies around the world. Academic research has rapidly picked up on these changes, so much so that the nature of state apologies has become a subject of inquiry for a number of key disciplines in the social sciences and humanities, including philosophy, political science, theology, history and sociology.[4]

Structurally, state apologies can be classified as 'many to many' or 'many to one'. Whenever state officials offer an apology to another collective, we speak of a 'many to many' situation. This is the case even if the apology is uttered by an identifiable person – for instance, the Prime Minister – because this individual acts as a spokesperson for a greater community.[5] A 'many to one' situation obtains when a state issues an apology to an individual. As an example, consider the apology by the Canadian Prime Minister Stephen Harper in 2007 to Maher Arar, a Canadian citizen who had been abducted and tortured with assistance from Canadian intelligence services.[6]

Another way of classifying political apologies is according to the contexts in which they take place: domestic, international and postcolonial. In the domestic realm, political apologies address injustices committed against citizens under the aegis of the state. Canada's apology and compensation to Canadians of Chinese origin for the infamous 'Chinese Head Tax' law and the US's apology and compensation to American citizens of Japanese descent for the witch hunt they were subjected to during the Second World War are relevant examples. In the international realm, political apologies are important diplomatic tools and usually address injustices committed during wartime. Consider here Japan's 'sorry' for the abuse of Korean and Chinese 'comfort women' and Belgium's expression of regret for not having intervened to prevent the genocide in Rwanda. Finally, one can identify postcolonial relations as a context, somewhere between the domestic and the international realm. Just think of Australia's and Canada's apologies to their Aboriginal communities for forced assimilation policies, Queen Elizabeth's declaration of 'sorrow' for Britain's treatment of the Maori community, and Guatemala's apology to victimised Mayans.

But the normalisation of apologies as a standard mechanism for addressing state-sponsored violence is not uncontroversial. Fierce public debates have accompanied their emergence and proliferation. The controversy in Britain surrounding the apology for its participation in the Atlantic slave trade illustrates the divisive nature of such practices. The facts are known: between the 16th and 19th centuries, Europeans traded approximately 8 million slaves out of Africa, 2.5 million of whom were transported on British ships.[7] The slave trade was extremely profitable for the colonial powers as it strengthened the economic interdependence of the territories bordering the Atlantic. The first country to officially make slave trading illegal was Denmark in 1792, but today Britain appears to be the most vocal in claiming credit for leading the way. In 1807, following efforts by a minority of intellectuals and members of the Quaker community, the British Parliament passed an act that abolished British participation in the trade of enslaved Africans.[8]

The conjunction of the bicentenary of the 1807 Abolition of the Slave Trade Act, apologies by the Anglican Church, by the Mayor of London, Ken Livingstone, and by the City of Liverpool made it impossible for Prime Minister Tony Blair to keep silent. In an article published in *New Nation* in November 2006,[9] and during subsequent commemorative events at the Elmina castle in Ghana,[10] Blair expressed 'deep sorrow' over Britain's participation in the slave trade, a practice he equated with a crime against humanity.

The Prime Minister's statements divided the British public. On the one hand, advocates of a more comprehensive apology found Blair's efforts wanting in terms of taking responsibility and making a commitment to redress the derivative economic, political and cultural disadvantages. Blair's story left out many of the systematic atrocities committed by the British against Africans, focused on the pioneering role that Britain played in abolishing the slave trade, and asymmetrically celebrated white abolitionists while effacing the memory of Black resistance. Many felt indignant and disappointed.[11]

On the other hand, a series of vehement objections were raised against the idea of apologising for the past. Concerned with Britain's self-image, critics pointed out that an apology would focus attention on negative aspects of the country's history, to the detriment of its merits in eliminating oppression. Some groups, encouraged by the evasiveness and ambiguity of the Prime Minister's statement, highlighted the country's pioneering role in fighting slavery worldwide. They thought the apology tarnished the country's image and unnecessarily denigrated its achievements. In their eyes, it constituted an incomprehensible and dangerous effort to rewrite history and to portray the British Empire as an active force of injustice. Conservative commentators and public figures concerned about the state's remarkable tradition and history objected to the irrational degradation of its accomplishments. Sustained efforts were made to underline Britain's decisive role in the abolition movement and to promote a positive image of its history.

This case is illustrative of the normative and prudential dilemmas that political apologies pose for liberal democratic societies. Broadly speaking, the most heated controversies revolve around the collective character of such practices, their contestation of a glorious national history and the issue of sincerity. Let us briefly unpack each of these areas of dispute.

First, concerns have been raised about the very idea of a state (collective) apology. As one of our authors has aptly remarked, apologies offered by collectives add 'a few more coats of grey'[12] to a subject matter that, even on the individual level, cannot be sketched in strokes of black and white. What does it mean for a state to apologise? Can a state feel regret or remorse? Can the state as an institution be sincerely sorry for something that happened in the past? All these questions point to the thorny issue of collective and intergenerational responsibility.

Second, there is often a fear that discussing the past might distort and damage the community's self-image. Besides the case discussed above, two other notorious examples are Turkey's refusal to acknowledge the Armenian genocide and the US's problematic relationship with its long history of racial exploitation. Given citizens' strong attachment to a 'glorious' vision of their community's past, many doubt the capacity of state apologies to effectively propose an alternative, more accurate account of history. Moreover, the fact that it is mostly liberal democracies that are inclined to say 'sorry' – at both home and abroad – has led conservative commentators to sneer at the 'tyranny of guilt': liberals should give up the obsession with self-flagellation and proudly celebrate their societies' historical achievements.[13]

Third, confronted with the current 'apology mania',[14] many observers have become suspicious of the bombastic rhetoric of many apologies. Thus, a cynical posture often prevails: apologies that exacerbate '"gestural politics" awash in self-interest and crocodile tears [...] enable governments and leaders to defuse angry minority groups without committing any actual resources to the problems of injustice and exclusion'.[15] Sceptics see such official acts as nothing but a 'smoke screen'[16] that serves as a 'seductive, feel-good strategy contrived and promoted by governments'[17] to compensate for the lack of redistributive measures.

Notes

1. In this introduction, we draw heavily on two recently published articles. For a full account of how we conceive of political apologies see: Mihaela Mihai, 'When the State Says "Sorry": State Apologies as Exemplary Political Judgments', *Journal of Political Philosophy* 21, no. 2 (2013): 200–220 and Mathias Thaler, 'Just Pretending: Political Apologies for Historical Injustice and Vice's Tribute to Virtue', *Critical Review of International Social and Political Philosophy* 15, no. 3 (2012): 259–278.
2. Nicolaus Mills, 'The New Culture of Apology', *Dissent* 48, no. 4 (2001): 113–116; Mark Gibney *et al.* eds., *The Age of Apology: Facing up to the Past*, Pennsylvania Studies in Human Rights (Philadelphia: University of Pennsylvania Press, 2008).
3. Stanley L. Engerman, 'Apologies, Regrets, and Reparations', *European Review* 17, no. 3–4 (2009): 593–610.
4. Trudy Govier, 'Forgiveness and the Unforgivable', *American Philosophical Quarterly* 36, no. 1 (1999): 59–75; Trudy Govier, *Taking Wrongs Seriously: Acknowledgement, Reconciliation, and the Politics of Sustainable Peace* (Amherst, N.Y: Humanity Books, 2006); Gibney *et al.*, *The Age of Apology*; Ari Kohen, 'The Personal and the Political: Forgiveness and Reconciliation in Restorative Justice', *Critical Review of International Social and Political Philosophy* 12, no. 3 (2009): 399–423.
5. Nicholas Tavuchis, *Mea Culpa: A Sociology of Apology and Reconciliation* (Stanford, CA: Stanford University Press, 1991); Charles L. Griswold, *Forgiveness: A Philosophical Exploration* (New York: Cambridge University Press, 2007).

notes

6. 'Harper's Apology "Means the World": Arar', *CBC News*, 26 January 2007, accessed 1 May 2013, http://www.cbc.ca/canada/story/2007/01/26/harper-apology.html.
7. Barbara L. Solow, 'Introduction', in *Slavery and the Rise of the Atlantic System*, ed. Barbara L. Solow (Cambridge: Cambridge University Press, 1991), 1–20; Marika Sherwood, *After Abolition: Britain and the Slave Trade Since 1807* (London/New York: I.B. Tauris, 2007), 8.
8. Sherwood, *After Abolition*, 10. Sherwood shows that 1807 did not actually mark the end of slave trading at British hands. It took a series of subsequent laws and a lot of international negotiations with the other European traders before the abominations stopped.
9. For the immediate reaction to the content of this piece, see: Greg Hurst and Elsa McLaren, 'Blair "Regret" Over Slavery Not Enough, Say Campaigners', *The Times*, 27 November 2006, accessed 1 May 2013, http://www.thetimes.co.uk/tto/news/uk/article1906772.ece; David Smith, 'Blair: Britain's "Sorrow" for Shame of Slave Trade', *The Guardian*, 26 November 2006, sec. Politics, accessed 1 May 2013, http://www.guardian.co.uk/politics/2006/nov/26/race.immigrationpolicy.
10. 'Slave Trade Shameful, Blair Says', *BBC*, 25 March 2007, sec. UK, accessed 1 May 2013, http://news.bbc.co.uk/1/hi/uk/6493507.stm.
11. For a report on the discontent surrounding the events in 2007, see: Amanda Kirton, 'Discontent Voiced Over Slavery Events', *BBC*, 3 April 2007, sec. UK, accessed 1 May 2013, http://news.bbc.co.uk/1/hi/uk/6523327.stm.
12. Nick Smith, *I Was Wrong: The Meanings of Apologies* (Cambridge: Cambridge University Press, 2008), 155.
13. Pascal Bruckner, *The Tyranny of Guilt: An Essay on Western Masochism* (Princeton: Princeton University Press, 2010).
14. Gorman Beauchamp, 'Apologies All Around', *The American Scholar* 76, no. 4 (2007): 87; Lee Taft, 'Apology Subverted: The Commodification of Apology', *The Yale Law Journal* 109, no. 5 (2000): 1135.
15. Alice MacLachlan, 'The State of "Sorry": Official Apologies and Their Absence', *Journal of Human Rights* 9, no. 3 (2010): 347.
16. Gary Foley, 'Duplicity and Deceit: Rudd's Apology to the Stolen Generations', *Melbourne Historical Journal* 36 (2008), accessed 1 May 2013, http://www.kooriweb.org/foley/essays/essay_28.html.
17. Gillian Cowlishaw, 'A Multiplicity of Meanings: An Ethnographic Reflection on Kevin Rudd's Apology on Behalf of the Nation, to Australia's Indigenous Peoples in January 2008', *Critique of Anthropology* 29, no. 3 (2009): 358.

16

POLITICAL APOLOGIES AND CATEGORICAL APOLOGIES

Nick Smith

I Was Wrong: The Meanings of Apologies attempted to differentiate the central meanings provided by 'categorical apologies', a term I offered to stipulate a regulative ideal for acts of contrition.[1] That book also considered how these meanings map onto collective apologies, which added many layers of complexity to the discussion. Research for my forthcoming book on the role of apologies in legal contexts introduced additional complications. In both individual and collective harms, a pattern – subject to many disclaimers regarding cultural specificity – becomes evident. A victim suffers harm. She wants something like an apology. She may not have an exact sense of what a sufficient apology would entail, but something like a categorical apology motivates her: she wants to know what happened, she wants someone to admit wrongdoing, she doesn't want to stand by while someone 'gets away with' violating a moral principle she cares about, she wants to be respected and recognised as wronged, she wants the wrongdoer to feel badly, she wants to know this isn't going to happen again to her or anyone else and she wants the wrongdoer to take practical responsibility for redressing her injury. This chapter will identify a few of the questions I find most helpful to ask when evaluating the meanings provided by – and avoided by – political apologies.

Note that I limit discussions of political apologies here to contrition for acts performed in an official capacity rather than the more personal failures that politicians often confront. Thus I am more concerned here with occasions like Clinton's apology for the Rwandan genocide than with his response regarding his sexual scandals. This chapter also does not address issues about how one's tendency to apologise corresponds to one's political affiliations. In the US, for example, the right can seem allergic to apologies: G. H. W. Bush once declared 'I will never apologise for the United States of America, I don't care what the facts are,' while Mitt Romney titled his autobiography *No Apologies*.

1. Has the political apology corroborated the factual record?

We can first ask whether the offender explains what she did with an appropriate degree of specificity so as to establish a record of the events salient to the injury. In many cases 'what happened' will be obvious to both the victim and the offender, but the victim desires a public admission confirming her account. In other cases, much of the story may be opaque to the victim. Vague assertions that 'mistakes were made' will typically not provide the explanations we seek. Those who volunteer information regarding adverse events early in the process gain credibility; those who concede damaging facts only after they can no longer deny them lose credibility.

Harms caused by collectives such as nations can present particularly challenging factual investigations as webs of causation weave throughout the organisation and over time, such that even leaders of the group may be unclear regarding exactly how they came to be causing such harms. Establishing a record may take time. In some situations of large-scale harm that occurs over a prolonged period – consider civil claims against the US for its programme of 'Mexican Repatriation' – documenting a sufficient record can occupy teams of historians. Leaders may genuinely not know of the wrongdoing within their organisation's past or present and only learn the extent of the problem after reading reports from internal or external investigators. Victims should be especially wary of representatives of collectives assuring that they will 'get to the bottom of what happened' but who never actually report sufficient findings or provide a schedule for when they will report such findings.

In some situations, cataloguing a full record may no longer be possible; for instance, the names and stories of many victims of the US African slave trade are lost to history. Some opportunities for meaning die with the victims or offenders. If someone goes to her grave with a secret regarding what actually happened, no apology from the living can resurrect that particular form of meaning.

We should also pay attention to the possibilities of offenders confessing to certain events, only to later deny them. The Japanese government's retraction of its apology for its use of Korean sex slaves during World War II provides a particularly shocking example of this dynamic, with the Prime Minister undermining a previous administration's expressions of remorse by claiming that there was 'no evidence to prove that there was coercion' of the wartime sex slaves.[2] History, in this sense, can be temporary. Such telling and un-telling of wrongs can cause renewed pain for victims and they should maintain awareness of the tenuousness of such historical accounts.

Also note that establishing a factual record will often include explanations of the offenders' mental states at the time of the offence, including accounts of the intentions motivating the harmful actions.

2. Has the political apology accepted blame for the offence?

The acceptance of blame constitutes a core meaning of apologies. It also presents some of the most complex challenges, especially when applied to groups that commit mass injuries and where tenuous chains of command obscure moral networks. I devoted a considerable amount of time in *I Was Wrong* to debates regarding collective responsibility, and I will not revisit those contentious issues in any detail here.

Good reasons point towards holding collectives as such responsible for civil harms. Leftists in particular like to attribute responsibility to non-individuals, partly due to their sympathy towards arguments for structural causation and because within such a worldview corporations stand as the fountainhead of so many social ills. Even those on the right who recite the absolute inviolability of 'individual responsibility' help themselves to notions of collective blame when they speak of 'The Government' or 'The Liberal Media' as the proximate cause of various negative phenomena. Collectives like corporations and governments also have deeper pockets than individuals. If we find such groups responsible for harm we can tap their resources for redress. When we speak of collective blame in the political context, however, we should not lose sight of a few key points.

Most basically, a categorically apologetic offender will accept that the injury is her fault. She does not offer mere sympathy for the harm, nor does she view herself as an innocent or even heroic person 'taking responsibility' for solving problems not of her making. Rather, and in accordance with commonsense notions of proximate causation, she admits to unjustifiably causing the harm. Wrongdoers sometimes attempt to avoid accepting fault by claiming that no one deserves blame because the harm was somehow accidental or unintentional. Too many historical examples demonstrate how wrongdoers attempt to bury their intentions deep within faceless institutional forces to deflect blame away from themselves and into faceless institutions. The soldier claims she did not intend genocide; the executive that she did not will the deaths.

Another common strategy for minimising blame takes the form of denying culpable intentions by casting the harms as accidental. Intentions become especially opaque when speaking of collectives. When we refer to collective intentions, do we refer to an aggregation of the mental states of individuals or something located within the institution as such and irreducible to members? Within organisations individuals may hold conflicting intentions, with some deviously scheming to profit by causing suffering, while others in the group are ignorant of the potential consequences or work tirelessly to prevent these consequences. Some individual members may experience a variety of intentions, some days being unaware of potential consequences, some days working to avoid potential consequences and at other times feeling they should do whatever it takes to make money. Some may settle into apathy, not intending to cause harm but thinking that there is not much they can do to stop it, so they might as well make some money.

This wide spectrum of culpable intentions within organisations points towards the importance of apologies that capture the specific roles played by individuals. Although groups of people can act together in various respects, victims should be wary of those who attempt to shift blame from the individual to the collective. In many cases we can rather easily identify who within a collective deserves blame. Often many individuals will deserve blame for their specific causal contributions. Some will intentionally order underlings to value profit over life. Others will execute those orders. Some will look the other way. Some should have paid more attention. Some will lie to cover it up. Several individual people committing multiple interlocking wrongs cause most of the cases discussed in this chapter, but often in collective apologies the individuals disappear into the collective, as if the institution had a will entirely of its own: as if the institution took the wheel and no one could do anything about it. This, of course, is often a lie shrouded in a metaphor. The hypocrisy of allowing the collective to shoulder one's culpability becomes especially odious when we see it from those who are first in line to demand recognition – especially in the form of pay rises and elections – when things go well. Like most of us, leaders are quick to accept credit for their work in the form of demanding high salaries or re-election; when the pendulum of accountability swings, we should be equally willing to accept blame.

I therefore advise victims to take extra care when those who injured them avoid providing individual apologies that accept personal blame and instead offer some form of collective apology, where no one in particular admits culpability. Many victims know full well who caused their suffering, especially if the institution has provided the salient details. Watching the guilty outsource their moral work to the corporate mantle can add insult to injury.

Specificity in moral causation can also help to shatter claims that victims should view large-scale events caused by human agents as somehow accidental. Rather than viewing the harms as accidents for which we can prepare but which we cannot prevent, precise attributions of blame identify the need for reform at various levels. Differentiating culpability in these senses offers a much greater awareness of how individual actions aggregate to cause large-scale harm and thereby increase our chances of preventing further harm.

I do not want to overstate these points, as institutional apologies and admissions of collective guilt can have considerable value. Collective apologies can, for instance, declare or renew a group's core values. They can also provide examples for individuals within the group to follow to confess their own role in the wrongdoing, in part by ensuring that blame is shared and no individual will be scapegoated or blamed disproportionately to her actions. Collectives can also synthesise apologies from many individuals into a coherent narrative that pieces together how many minor failings added up to major harms.

A binocular view that simultaneously appreciates how individual blame and structural causation combine to result in harm provides the best vantage for understanding what happened, who deserves blame and how to best fix the problem. Too often, however, collective apologies provide neither an individual taking personal responsibility for the harm and changing her ways accordingly, nor an institution undertaking the sorts of structural reform that would prevent similar harms. Collective apologies often actively avoid attributing blame in order to insulate wrongdoers – and often the most powerful players who held the authority then initiate the behaviour – from the consequences of their actions.

3. Does the political apology possess appropriate standing to apologise and accept blame?

A categorically apologetic wrongdoer accepts blame and provides the apology, rather than outsourcing the work of contrition to a proxy, such as an attorney or spokesperson. Third parties can express important meanings, for instance corroborating the victim's account of the event, apportioning blame, vindicating moral principles, legitimating suffering and providing redress. In most cases, however, apologies from third parties fail to convey certain kinds of important meanings. Just as my public relations manager cannot exercise for me, she cannot undergo moral transformation and the entailed negative emotions on my behalf. I cannot offload my blame onto her.

Questions of standing in collective apologies become more nuanced when, rather than hiring an outsider to perform the deed, the apologiser occupies a position that allows her to make a more credible claim to have contributed to causing the harm. Modern institutions interrelate in baroque organisational charts, with some entities overseeing hundreds of large subsidiaries. Each of these subsidiaries probably has its own clusters of departments, branches and other subgroups over which it exercises varying degrees of control and oversight.

Generally speaking, individuals with obvious membership in the organisation, as well as a high rank in that organisation – what I call 'membership with rank' – make the strongest claims to possess standing to apologise for the organisation. Yet even such standing suffers from oversimplification. President Obama surely has membership with rank to speak for the US, but to say he 'speaks for me' regarding any number of positions overstates his authority. Issues of consensus surface here: for many controversial issues, only about half of US voters agree with Obama on any number of issues. If I disagree and it becomes important for another to know that I disagree with Obama – for instance if I am travelling in the Middle East and wish to make clear to my hosts that I do not support his policy on drones – then my statements clarifying my views override what my hosts might expect to be my 'American' view, as articulated by Obama. Many forms of collective membership do not require a member to endorse the views of its leaders. Thus when a member with rank asserts standing to apologise on behalf of the group, we understand the leaders' contrition most clearly when we appreciate how their assertions track the actual views of their constituencies, as well as the degree of disagreement tolerated within the organisation. Disagreeing with a leader's apology could be considered a grave offence in some authoritarian regimes. Publicly challenging your boss' expression of contrition might get you fired.

After establishing the relevant group to which the apologiser should belong in order to hold a credible claim to standing, additional questions arise regarding the temporal nature of the collective. We often act as if leaders occupy unbroken chains of causation, for example as if the president of the US is effectively one moral agent from Washington to Obama. Although apologies from current leaders for the mistakes of past leaders convey important meanings regarding the contemporary values and intentions of the institution, this differs considerably from an executive possessing the sort of standing that allows her to accept blame on behalf of her predecessors. If we stretch notions of group membership and moral causation too thin, I might assert standing to accept blame for the destruction of Carthage because I share it by membership in humanity – and perhaps also my wife's Italian-American heritage – with the Romans of 146 BCE. If, upon learning of my apology, modern Tunisians filed a claim against me to recover their ancient losses, I would be quick to explain that I did not intend to imply that I deserved blame for the ancient genocide.

Situations will arise where victims will not place much importance on whether the apologiser possesses standing to accept blame or speak on behalf of the wrongdoers. The current member with rank may lack culpability but, more importantly, have the ability to make the future look different from the past. If victims seek primarily redress, they may not care who writes the checks so long as they clear.

4. Does the political apology identify each harm and the principles underlying each harm, and share a commitment to the principles underlying each harm?

Does she take care to identify all of the harms involved rather than collapsing multiple wrongs into an undifferentiated assertion that she somehow acted badly, such that we cannot discern precisely what she admits? Does she only name the most undeniable offence in light of the accumulated evidence? Does she apologise for only the lesser offence, perhaps because doing so maximises the strategic advantage of appearing contrite, while minimising the political risks?

Note here how insufficiently specific apologies allow leaders to obscure their own culpable actions under an umbrella of overly-generalised harm. One might object that such a standard expects too much precision in documenting harms and presents an impractical task for many injuries. I appreciate such difficulties, but I cannot find a compelling standard according to which we can distinguish between harms that deserve recognition and those that do not. In practice, those who demand recognition are typically most likely to find their harms recognised, and we should worry that this only further compounds inequality: harms against those without the resources or wherewithal to bring action go unrecognised.

Here we can also seek to understand the extent to which the offender understands why the offence is offensive and therefore makes explicit the values at issue. This can occur at two levels: comprehending the prevailing state of the law or registering the offence according to a deeper moral code. When the offender understands the principle, this helps her identify other behaviours that fall within its provenance. Collective harms may trigger many principles given the range of their activities, the many morally laden posts within their institutions and the extent of the harms they cause.

The process of identifying the principles at issue can bring substantial benefit for a community, even if the offender ultimately refuses to endorse the value as subsequently discussed.[3] Whether through internal discussions within organisations or in the public discourse surrounding the harms, the process of understanding why actions invoke the demand for an apology can occasion self-reflection and institutional review regarding first principles. Sometimes this process provides an opportunity for an institution to reflect on norms endorsed by its predecessors, norms that have since become less generally accepted.

Identifying the principles differs from endorsing those principles. If the offender rejects the principle, she will not think that she has done anything wrong. Charges against her may fortify her resolve to act in accordance with the offending beliefs, leading her to double down in defence thereof. By contrast, awareness of and commitment to the underlying principle provides reason to speak the signature phrase of the categorical apology: 'I was wrong.' My actions deserve blame because they violated values that I share with the victims. An offender who explains why she commits to the principle at stake provides a glimpse into her character and motivations.

In collective contexts, apologies can serve as declarations of institutional policy. A group might update their charter to conform to evolving social norms or to reflect changes in leadership. A declaration can also restate and emphasise a commitment to long-held values from which members have deviated. Again, the process of discussing, revising and renewing commitments to core values supports important objectives even if the collective or individual does not accept blame for the harm at issue.

5. Does the political apology recognise victims as moral interlocutors?

When offenders treat their victims as moral interlocutors, they treat them with respect. They treat them as humans deserving dignity rather than as mere means to some end. They understand and interact with the injured not as abstractions – numbers on a balance sheet or statistical misfortunes – but as concrete and particular individuals who think and feel. The wrongdoers understand the need to reach out and apologise specifically to the victims, rather than to express general contrition to the media or some third party that they believe holds the most power over them. When I harmed you, I saw you as somehow unworthy of sufficient consideration, but now I turn to you in humility to discuss the very values and principles that give meaning to my life.

Collective harms present various challenges and opportunities in this regard. Often in cases of large-scale injuries the offence stems not from an aberrant misdeed somehow out of character for the offender, but rather from a kind of systematic disregard of the interests of a group of people. Recognising victims and members of the community with equal worth can provide especially important meaning in the aftermath of such degradation.

In some cases, interlocution with the victim will not be possible. The victim may be long dead. She may refuse to participate in dialogue. Offenders may be left to recognise an interlocutor who rejects them. Victims may desire that recognition come not from those responsible for the harm, but rather from their replacements or superiors. If I suffered discrimination at your hands, I may want you fired, as well as an apology, not from you, but from the highest ranking person in the organisation who will declare that I am a person of equal worth and who has the power to ensure that this never happens again. Some may reasonably desire the recognition from the highest ranking official in the collective because this confers the greatest elevation of their status. When Bill Clinton offered his apology for the Tuskegee experiments, he lacked certain kinds of standing to accept blame for the atrocities. As a standing president publicly recognising the moral status of poor black Southerners, however, he does more to elevate their standing and bring attention to the injustices against them than would actions from lower ranking officials, better positioned to accept blame for their own role in authorising or conducting the experiments.

For those who view these issues along a more Continental axis, Levinas and Adorno were my first philosophical loves and they lurk beneath the surface of my treatment of apologies. For Levinas and Adorno, the ethical relation is always between singulars: the face or the non-identical other and the 'subject'.[4] As soon as we introduce the abstractions of politics (the nation, an ethnicity, any collection of faces) we lose sight of the concrete singularity and vulnerability that both Adorno and Levinas believe must be the concrete living sources of ethical life. Levinas has a distinctive treatment of apologies as a kind of perpetual undoing of conceptual violence (the apology of unsaying the said, in his terminology). Part of my caution with respect to collective apologies lies in their abstraction from concrete particular individuals who have been harmed. Apologies to demographic clusters risk losing sight of the individual victim in all of her complexity and vulnerability.

6. Does the political apology express and demonstrate categorical regret?

Categorical regret requires the offender to understand that she has committed a moral error that she wishes she could reverse. Categorical regret thus differs from empathy for the consequences of what the actor continues to endorse as a justified decision. Categorical regret for institutional harms can raise complex issues when such organisations look back on their multivariable cost-benefit analyses that sought to balance many variables.

Institutions often attempt to invoke exculpatory background facts to mitigate the wrongness of their decisions. We should take care to distinguish between those who offer this information as an excuse and those who demonstrate increased self-awareness by reconstructing the decision-making process in a manner that helps them understand the wrongness of the choice so that they can avoid similar mistakes going forward: I clearly understand why I did it, I see why it was wrong, and this knowledge allows me to explain how I will avoid those pitfalls.

In some cases, the harm at issue may effectively be the proximate cause of the apologisers' power and identity. In the case of categorical regret for African slavery or genocide against Native Americans, so much of the US' current wealth can be traced to those events that wishing that such injustices did not happen might imply wishing the non-existence of the nation in its current form.[5] We should also appreciate that the accused sometimes stand by their decisions and make it clear that they do not regret their actions because they would make the same choice again if faced with the same variables.

7. Has the political apology been performed properly?

The instance of uttering an apology is in many ways the beginning of a process rather than the end and we should not look too narrowly at apologies as speech acts, but here we can reconsider the features clustered around the speech act and how they lay foundations for the meanings they promise. A full discussion of the who, what, where and when of political apologies is beyond the scope of this chapter but two points merit brief mention.

Public apologies can suffer in various ways from failing to address the victims directly. Some political offenders seem to apologise to the media, regulatory bodies or other third parties rather than to victims. Failing to acknowledge victims in this way can cause new harms by denying victims status as moral interlocutors. In cases with thousands of victims, reaching individual victims presents obvious logistical challenges, especially if they are dead.

Public apologies for political harms can accomplish many objectives, including explaining to the community what happened, removing suspicions that the victim deserves blame, honouring and reaffirming the breached values, elevating the status of historically subordinated classes of victims and triggering a process of reform across similarly situated institutions. Note however that victims may have good reasons for wanting to keep apologies provided to them private, perhaps because public knowledge of the apology would bring undesired attention to them and their injuries, thereby causing further pain. In some cases, victims may find an offender's desire to broadcast an apology to amount to moral grandstanding that serves offenders interest's at the expense of the victims' desire for discretion: 'Look at me. I am apologetic. I am good. Recognise my goodness and confer benefits.'

8. To what extent does the political apology demonstrate reform?

Apologies are treatments not cures, beginnings not conclusions. Apologies make promises. The individual categorically apologetic offender forbears from reoffending over her lifetime; the collective forbears from reoffending for the remainder of its existence. The categorically apologetic offender demonstrates reform with a record of resisting temptations to reoffend. The more temptations she overcomes over a longer duration, the more evidence we have of her reform and the more confidence we can have in our ability to predict her behaviour. The process of publicly or privately performing an apology therefore sets a stage. The lifetime of behaviour enacts the moral transformation. Such covenants set forth the conditions of future relations and can lay the foundations for large groups to live in peace rather than in retribution and fear.

Who makes and keeps the promise to reform in political apologies? Current leadership may embrace reform but, over time, politicians with less resolve to honour promises to reform replace them. A systematically corrupt institution may concentrate all of its blame onto a single individual, scapegoating her and acting as if firing her solves the problem. Here an institution might argue that all reform falls upon that lone bad apple and, once it removes her, the organisation has completed its corrective actions. Alternatively, collectives may deflect blame so deeply into the collective as such that no particular members believe they have personally done anything wrong or that they must personally reform.

If the apologising institution will soon cease to exist, it shares with deathbed apologies limited ability to provide a meaningful commitment to reform because it won't be around long to fulfil its promise to reform and suffer the consequences of the transformation.

Promises to reform can be both too collective – such that no one takes responsibility, or too individual – such that the need to reform falls entirely on one scapegoat who can be ritually excised. A sufficiently precise accounting of moral causation and blame – identifying individual actors as well as those who promulgate blameworthy policies – affords the best perspective on who should undertake which reforms. The binocular approach of individual reform plus structural renovation offers the most effective means for achieving and sustaining institutional reform.

This makes attempts to dissociate apologies from blame especially problematic. If we construe an apology as something other than an admission of guilt, the apologising party need not admit to having done anything wrong. If they have not transgressed, they need not reform their behaviour. Thus a party can simultaneously offer a 'safe apology' and continue to commit the same offence against the plaintiff or others.

In addition to expecting the apology to promise reform, victims should be sure that apologisers honour these promises. Just as we should exercise a healthy scepticism towards criminal offenders who promise change, victims should not overvalue bald assurances from political entities that they will 'do everything within their power to make sure it never happens again'. Rather than accepting such ambiguous and non-committal assertions at face value, reviewers should evaluate as many data points as possible to judge the commitment. Have they begun the reform? How do they plan to undertake the changes? What measures ensure that they will complete the changes? How will they audit individual behaviour and institutional design, culture and decision-making processes? Should we trust internal audits or would public transparent external reviews be more reliable? How will they evaluate progress towards reform on the individual and collective level? How does it incentivise the desired behaviours? What happens if they fail, for instance because of changes in leadership or dissolution? How will the institution punish those who fail to honour the principles? Will the institution report its failures to external regulators? What sanctions will apply, and do these penalties provide sufficient deterrent? Does anyone take personal responsibility for overseeing the reform? What if she leaves? Like many aspects of apologies, answers to these questions benefit from the passage of time as offenders demonstrate or undermine their commitment to reform.

9. Has the political apology provided appropriate redress?

The categorically apologetic offender provides appropriate redress for the harms she caused. In most cases, the sooner she provides this redress the better, because victims will typically continue to suffer the unmitigated effects of the harm until some form of redress assuages the injury. The sooner she returns property, for example, the shorter the duration of the deprivation. Determining what constitutes appropriate redress often proves contentious. We can address qualitative and quantitative issues here: what kinds of redress are appropriate? how much redress suffices?

The most seemingly obvious kind of redress ceases the harm at issue. If you apologise for taking something, you return it. Reform and redress intertwine in this regard. Consider the US Supreme Court's 2008 ruling in Hawaii v. Office of Hawaiian Affairs where it considered the US Congress' 1993 apology for the overthrow of the Hawaiian government 100 years earlier.[6] The apology resolved 'to acknowledge the historic significance of the illegal overthrow of the Kingdom of Hawaii, to express its deep regret to the Native Hawaiian people, and to support the reconciliation efforts of the State of Hawaii [...] with Native Hawaiians'.[7] The apology went on to recognise 'the suppression of the inherent sovereignty of the Native Hawaiian people', to 'apologise [...] to Native Hawaiians on behalf of the people of the United States for the overthrow [...] with the participation of agents and citizens of the United States, and the deprivation of the rights of Native Hawaiians to self-determination', and to express a 'commitment to acknowledge the ramifications of the overthrow of the Kingdom of Hawaii, in order to provide a proper foundation for reconciliation between the United States and the Native Hawaiian people'.[8]

The Supreme Court of Hawaii interpreted the apology as recognising that Native Hawaiians held claims to a specific 1.2 million acres of land, stating that 'based on a plain reading of the Apology Resolution [...] Congress has clearly recognised that the native Hawaiian people have unrelinquished claims over the ceded lands, which were taken without consent or compensation'.[9] Writing for a unanimous US Supreme Court, Justice Alito reversed the Hawaiian Supreme Court's decision by explaining that the apology provided no more than 'conciliatory or precatory' language. 'Such terms are not the kind that Congress uses to create substantive rights,' and therefore the apology did not impact the status of the contested land. As one of the Justices previewed the ruling at oral argument, 'Why isn't it sufficient just to say that this resolution has no substantive effect, period ...?'[10] Thus in the Supreme Court's view, even though Congress' apology declared the illegality of the overthrow and the taking of the land this did not mean that they meant to return it or otherwise admit that they lacked legitimate ownership of it: 'We're sorry we took it from you and we know that was wrong and illegal. But we're keeping it.'[11]

Although 'returning' the Hawaiian land presented many complexities, it offered a fairly simple solution compared to other collective harms. Imagine returning to Native Americans or African Americans what the US wrongfully took from them and their ancestors. Something like full reparations for African slavery might require such a massive amount of resources that it could shift the balance of global power from the northern to the southern hemisphere.

Some victims may seek punitive redress sufficient to provide stronger deterrents, or more substantial retributive punch. Due to deontological fears that it entails causing suffering to innocent members of a group and to consequentialist concerns that it hinders deterrent effects of penalties, collective punishment lacks popularity. It also runs counter to favoured notions of individual moral responsibility that locates blame singularly in the choices of free agents. Punitive redress from collectives, however, can take many forms beyond fines. For victims primarily concerned with their claim triggering reform, the institution might transform their charter or operating procedures, submit to periodic external reviews or expend considerable resources publicising their wrongdoing in order to raise awareness and hopefully change the behaviours of peer institutions.

Redress also conveys different meanings depending on who provides it. Unlike someone who pays a delegate to do her dirty work, the offender who works on the front lines of remediation offers several kinds of meaning. Taking practical responsibility requires the offender to directly confront the harm she caused and to invest her own life in caring for her victim. She subjects herself to the emotional pain of grappling with the consequences of her actions. Victims may consider this pain important on retributive grounds because she deserves to take a hard look and be haunted by the suffering. Offenders should not, in other words, enjoy the psychological comforts of their offices, while others live in the emotional maelstrom of post-offence trauma. If we understand redress as a process that offenders should undergo as a means to the end of their moral transformation – or as some essential element of their moral transformation – then delegating redress frustrates that objective. The offender's direct participation in providing redress also reinforces her treatment of the victim as moral interlocutor, enacting the understanding that her time is too valuable or that somehow she is too important to care for the person she harmed.

Where the money comes from should still matter, even for those who maintain a strictly financial view of redress. Those who profited from causing suffering should be those who take the loss. If former executives or politicians who grew rich from blameworthy activity leave their successors holding the bag, this starts to look like the child serving time for the parent's crime. In some cases, the offending organisation will offload the burden of redress onto taxpayers. The Japanese government, for instance, diverted public funds to Chisso, so that it could continue compensating victims of Minamata disease.[12] In this regard, consider the practice of apologetic corporate offenders who cite their redress payments as evidence of the sincerity of their reform, while they receive tax windfalls by deducting those costs. British Petroleum enjoyed a $10 billion tax benefit by writing off $37.2 billion in Blackwater Horizon cleanup expenses.[13]

The temptation to seek redress from the collective rather than the individual often makes strategic sense because institutions tend to hold greater resources than individuals. Indeed, this practical matter tends to influence the metaphysics of collective responsibility: we often act as if collectives bear moral responsibility because we know this belief affords the best chance of compensation. Victims should keep in mind, however, that such 'deeper pockets arguments' may leave them taking from the innocent. While the architects of the 2008 financial crisis enjoy new corporate, academic and governmental leadership positions, the US citizens feel the pain of 'austerity' and 'sequestration' cuts designed in part to clean up the mess created by bank executives.

In addition to determining the kinds of redress, the amount of redress and who should undertake that redress, civil claims raise questions regarding who receives the benefits of redress. Here issues of standing arise regarding to whom redress should be paid. Do only survivors receive redress, or can relatives or descendants collect on behalf of deceased victims? In cases involving harms against classes such as African or Native Americans, do we determine compensation according to race, ethnicity, citizenship, social and economic status, biology, self-identification or some other criteria? Do all victims deserve the same amount or do we index redress to amount of harm or cost of living?

10. What intentions motivate the civil offender's apology?

The categorically apologetic offender undertakes the work of apologising for the sake of the offender and the community, and in recognition of the breached value. We can distinguish this from an apology provided primarily, if not exclusively, for self-serving objectives. Even if all of the other aspects of the apology remain the same, intentions matter.

Political apologies suffer from a crisis of credibility as candidates and parties consult focus groups and pollsters to decide the extent to which various kinds of apologies confer strategic advantages. Although typically determining an individual or group's intentions requires highly fallible inferences as we look for clues to the offenders' mental states, sometimes organisations leak a smoking gun by explaining – in internal documents – precisely why they apologise. The issue of an apology for the Chinese head tax – a fee levied against Chinese immigrants to Canada beginning in 1888 – has been a political battleground for decades, with Conservatives and Liberals spinning the issue and leaving victimised groups perennially unsatisfied with previous apologies and redress. In 2013, a leaked memo shattered the appearance that politicians would address the issue in good faith. The memo from the office of British Columbia's (BC) Liberal Party outlined a campaign strategy of using public funds to apologise to Chinese and Indian voters to secure 'quick wins' with those ethnic groups.[14] Outrage ensued. The now transparent attempt to intentionally use expressions of contrition for historical injustice in order to gain political support led the president of the Union of British Columbia Chiefs to explain that the intention expressed in the memo 'represents a deep sense of betrayal and we find it highly offensive that now the moves on the part of the BC provincial Liberals are tainted by this revelation, and it brings into question their efforts at reconciliation with respect to historical wrong doings'. The president of the Head Tax Families Society of Canada summarised his position: 'Don't pander to me by saying that "Hey we have a strategy. We are going to apologise." Well you know what? Take your apology and shove it where the sun don't shine.'[15]

Others seemed less concerned about the political manoeuvring motivating the apologies for the head tax and were more focused on securing meaningful redress for the thousands of families impacted. The executive director of the Chinese Canadian National Council equated a 'genuine apology' with one that provided substantial financial compensation to victims. 'If we wanted just an apology,' he explained, 'we would have got it back in 2011 or 2012 or early 2013.'[16] For some, sufficient payments might be a more reliable measure of genuineness – at least of genuine desire to pay redress – than noble intentions. Again, some victims may not care very much about the motivations for apologising, so long as they get what they seek. As I hope to have shown, however, some meanings central to categorical apologies rely on specific intentions. Parties interested in those sorts of meanings must pay especially close attention in order to gain insight into the political apologiser's mental states.

The notion that collectives as such can intend anything – as opposed to aggregation of the mental states of members – adds another layer of complexity that I will not consider here other than to note questions regarding consensus. One member of an organisation might apologise from the purest and most self-sacrificing of intentions. Others in the same organisation might support the apology for cynical and purely self-interested instrumental reasons. Or perhaps everyone in the organisation shares the same motivations for apologising. The standing issues discussed earlier resurface here, and those evaluating the intentions should parse meaning accordingly. A consensus of membership apologising for the sake of the victims provides the ideal motivation, but this will be a difficult standard to meet for large organisations with diverse memberships.

11. Does the political apology demonstrate appropriate emotions?

The emotional content of political apologies in civil law presents important but nebulous issues. The offender should experience an appropriate degree of the appropriate kinds of emotion, typically including sorrow, guilt, empathy and sympathy. An offender who fails to experience the proper apologetic emotions does not provide certain important kinds of meaning. She does not show she has understood and is disgusted with the pain she has caused. Negative emotions can also indicate deserved suffering. Beyond this baseline recognition that emotions play essential roles in apologetic meaning, questions abound. Which emotions should the offender experience, in what quantity and for how long? How should the emotions evolve over time as the offender better understands the extent of the harm she caused? How do cultural differences regarding emotional expression nuance any answers we provide?

Even though we may speak of corporations as persons in the eyes of the law, the idea that institutions as such experience emotions strains credibility. Members of the collective may feel grief, regret, remorse or shame, and in the aggregate all of these emotions may add up to meaningful expressions. But the notion that the collective experiences negative emotions in some sense irreducible to the mental states of its members humanises organisational structures too much. It would be as if we expected an animated corporate mascot to somehow embody the mind of the organisation: a remorseful Ronald McDonald means that McDonald's Corporation suffers negative emotions and therefore should be viewed as appropriately contrite, even if the blameworthy executives are unmoved. It is just such dissociation between the individual feelings and collective harms that leads some to view modern corporations as sociopathic.[17]

The idea that human spokespersons can embody the emotions of a collective faces similar problems. The spokesperson might actually feel any number of apologetic pangs. Even if she does not deserve blame or feel guilt, she can certainly sympathise with plaintiffs. But problems of standing arise: is she the person who should be experiencing the negative emotions on account of her blameworthiness? Does she even distinguish between her own emotional states and those allegedly attributable to the organisation? If we expect the political offender to suffer retributive punishment via experiencing negative emotions, surely expressions of shame from her paid ambassador causes pain to the wrong person. Acting as if we can emotionally punish a collective allows individual offenders to deposit their moral debts to soulless institutions, from which we will never collect. Likewise, if the spokesperson can absorb the organisation's shame or humiliation this would seem to significantly diminish any deterrent threat or rehabilitative impact of such negative emotions.

Even if a leading executive, who deserves blame, expresses the requisite emotions, does she speak for her own emotions or for the group's? Do all of the other blameworthy individuals also experience these emotions? What if only a few members of the group really feel bad, some feel bad for a while, some give it no thought and others think the victims deserve to suffer? Again, issues of consensus complicate matters, especially in apologies from the state when so many issues divide across party lines. As we noted previously, emotions provide one way to read the intentions of the apologiser. Deciphering the mental states of individuals via outward appearance is an inexact science; reading the face and emotions of a spokesperson to determine the feelings of an institution approaches folly.

The difficulty of mapping negative emotions onto collectives can have the benefit of forcing victims and offenders to evaluate apologies according to other, more substantive aspects of apologies. Rather than fixating on the emotional fits and starts that too often guide our evaluations of the quality of apologies, or drumming up pain for events long in the past and to which we have little emotional connection, once we recognise that emotions have a limited role in collective civil wrongdoing we can concentrate on whether the institution provides salient facts, accepts blame, provides redress and hits various other notes that do not require controversial attributions of collective mental states.

Conclusion

Although each deserves far more attention that I can provide in the scope of this chapter, the questions above will hopefully help actors understand political apologies so that they are better equipped to (a) identify deceptive uses of apologies and (b) insist on and negotiate for the meanings they desire. In particular, awareness of these tactics may go some way towards empowering disadvantaged victims in their conflicts with sophisticated political actors who use ambiguities surrounding the meanings of apologies to further compound their advantages.

Endnotes

1 This chapter expands upon arguments from *I Was Wrong: The Meanings of Apologies* (New York: Cambridge University Press, 2008). For a more thorough defence of the arguments suggested here, please see Part II of *I Was Wrong* on 'Collective Apologies'. See also my summary in 'An Overview of Challenges Facing Collective Apologies', in *Public Apology between Ritual and Regret*, ed. Daniel Cuypers, Daniel Janssen, Jacques Haersis, Barbara Segaert (Amsterdam: Rodopi, 2013), 29–34. This article also revisits material from: 'Against Court-Ordered Apologies', *New Criminal Law Review: An International and Interdisciplinary Journal* 16, no. 1 (2013): 1–49; 'Apologies in Law: An Overview of the Philosophical Issues', *Pepperdine Dispute Resolution Law Journal* (Forthcoming 2013); 'Apologies, Character, and Fitness: A Practical Framework for Evaluating Remorse in the Bar Admission Process', *ABA Journal of the Professional Lawyer* 21, no. 2, (2012): 37–78 (co-authored with Mitch Simon and Nicole Negowetti); and 'The Penitent and the Penitentiary: Questions Regarding Apologies in Criminal Law', *Criminal Justice Ethics*, Summer/Fall (2008): 2, 82–85.

2 Roy Brooks, 'Japan's Official Responses to Reparations', in *When Sorry Isn't Enough: The Controversy over Apologies and Reparations for Human Injustice*, ed. Roy Brooks (New York: New York University Press, 1999), 127–128. On Abe's subsequent denials, see 'Sex Slave Denial Angers S. Korea', *BBC News*, 3 March 2007, accessed 1 July 2013, http://news.bbc.co.uk/1/hi/world/asia-pacific/6414445.stm.

3 See Mihaela Mihai, 'When the State Says "Sorry": State Apologies as Exemplary Political Judgments', *Journal of Political Philosophy* 21, no. 2 (2013): 200–220.

4 For more on what I have in mind here, see my 'Questions for a Reluctant Jurisprudence of Alterity', in *Essays on Levinas and Law: A Mosaic*, ed. Desmond Manderson (New York: Palgrave Macmillan, 2008), 55–75, and 'Adorno vs. Levinas: Evaluating Points of Contention', *Continental Philosophy Review* 40, no. 3 (2007): 275–306.

5 Janna Thompson, 'The Apology Paradox', *Philosophical Quarterly* 55, no. 201 (2000): 470–475.

6 Hawaii v. Office of Hawaiian Affairs, 129 S. Ct. 1436 (2009).

7 Joint Resolution of Nov. 23, 1993, Pub. L. No. 103–150, 107 Stat. 1510–1513.

8 Ibid.

9 Office of Haw. Affairs v. Hous. & Cmty. Dev. Corp. of Haw., 177 P.3d 884, 922 (Haw. 2008).

10 *Hawaii v. Office of Hawaiian Affairs*, 129 S. Ct. 1436 (2009) (finding that Hawaii's apology did not take away its ability to sell or transfer ceded lands). For the bit from oral argument: Transcript of Oral Argument at 6, *Hawaii*, 129 S. Ct. 1436 (2009) (No. 07–1372), 2009 WL 462660.

11 As the editors of *Harvard Law Review* put it: 'We Apologise for Stealing Your Land, but it's Still Our Land'. 'The Supreme Court, 2008 Term: Leading Cases', *Harvard Law Review* 123 (2009): 310.

12 Andrew Jenks, *Perils of Progress: Environmental Disasters in the 20th Century* (Upper Saddle River: Pearson, 2010), 32.

13 Gretchen Morgenson, 'Paying the Price, but Often Deducting It', *The New York Times*, 12 January 2013, accessed 1 July 2013, http://www.nytimes.com/2013/01/13/business/paying-the-price-in-settlements-but-often-deducting-it.html.

14 'First Nations and Cultural Groups Reject Political Apologies: Leaders Reject B.C. Liberal's Plan for "Easy Wins" with Ethnic Groups', *CBC News*, 7 March 2013, accessed 1 July 2013, http://www.cbc.ca/news/canada/british-columbia/story/2013/03/07/bc-political-apology.html.

15 'First Nations', *CBC News*.

16 Tamsyn Burgmann, 'Head Tax Apology Advocates Tell B. C. Premier Not to Delay', *The Canadian Press*, 10 March 2013, accessed 1 July 2013, http://www.canada.com/news/Advocates+Chinese+head+apology+premier+should+delay/8076616/story.html.

17 See Joel Bakan, *The Corporation: The Pathological Pursuit of Profit and Power* (New York: Free Press, 2004).

17

Reconciliation as Ideology and Politics

Andrew Schaap

Since Marx's critique of Hegel, reconciliation has been suspected of being inherently conservative because it casts social conflict as always in the service of the unity of the state. As such, it dissimulates the fundamental contradictions at stake in class conflict, the consciousness of which would radically call into question the terms of political association.[1] Starting from an acknowledgement of this skepticism toward the concept of reconciliation within radical theory, I will outline six objections to the framing of politics in terms of reconciliation that emerged in popular and academic debates about reconciliation in Australia and elsewhere in the 1990s. The concept of reconciliation stands accused of being: too *vague* to form a coherent political project; *illiberal* because it looks forward to an ideal of community that is not compatible with the pluralism of modern societies; *question-begging* since it aims to restore a prior state of harmony that never actually existed; *assimilative* in that it represents the political claims of the ruled only in terms commensurate with the interests of the rulers; *quietist* insofar as it demands resignation to the injustices of the past and forgoing resentment of their continuing legacy; and *exculpatory* in that it provides an opportunity to redeem the good conscience of the nation primarily through symbolic gestures.

Each of these objections underwrites the legitimate concern that reconciliation might be ideological insofar as it invokes the common good to legitimate a particular order in which the interests of some are privileged over those of others. Consequently, there may be good strategic reasons for a party to a conflict to refuse to couch its political claims in terms of reconciliation.[2] Yet it might also be a strategic error to concede the ideological capture of the concept of reconciliation entirely to its conservative appropriators. In this article, I therefore seek to rehabilitate the concept of reconciliation for a radical politics by refuting several principled objections that are often raised by critics of reconciliation processes. By outlining and responding to these six negative claims against reconciliation as *ideology*, I aim to construct a positive account of reconciliation as *politics*. In doing so, I want to resist the conclusion that reconciliation, which might currently be considered a 'ruling idea' within the international community, is *necessarily* 'an idea of the ruling class' while allowing that it might *contingently* be so.[3]

As such, I follow what Costas Douzinas describes as a Gramscian form of critique, according to which:

> . . .political ideas and concepts are neither true nor false but the tools through which we make sense of our world. In law and politics, therefore, the task is not so much to discard wrong ideological concepts but to re-define them against whatever conservative connotations they may have acquired, adjust them to the project of popular politics and build around them a 'hegemonic' bloc.[4]

This is not to say that each of the objections outlined below are articulated in terms of the orthodox Marxist critique of ideology. However, taken together, these objections draw attention to a common division among observers and practitioners of reconciliation processes: on the one side we are often presented with an anodyne view of reconciliation as promising to redeem the fallen realm of politics; on the other side, there is a tendency toward totalising critique that views reconciliation as invariably masking the realities of power politics.

Against falling prey to either reduction, I agree with Stewart Motha that it is necessary to grapple with the "double move" of reconciliation as both an "emancipatory demand [politics] and device by which an enforced commonality can be reinscribed [ideology]."[5] Analyzing reconciliation as ideology and politics thus leads to the heart of the problem of the political (the thematization of commonality) and the staging of politics (the representation of conflict). While the politics of transitional justice bring the problem of the political to the fore, this problem also takes us beyond the particular dilemmas confronting 'transitional societies.' Indeed, the problem of the political, around which the politics of reconciliation turn, is the fundamental concern of political theory understood as inquiry into the origin of law and the end of political community.

1. *The Ambiguity Objection*

Reconciliation, it is often complained, means too many different things to too many different people to be a coherent ideal towards which members of a divided society might strive. For instance, Andrew Gunstone notes that during the formal reconciliation process in Australia there was "a multitude of differing definitions of reconciliation advocated by various individuals and organizations, that emphasized issues as diverse as indigenous rights, religion, assimilation, acknowledging history and the need for indigenous and non indigenous people to accept their current situation." Gunstone identifies the consequent "confusion within the wider Australian community over the meaning of reconciliation" as one of the factors that contributed to its failure as a public policy.[6]

To counter this objection, we need to distinguish the *concept* of reconciliation from its various *conceptions*. The *concept* of reconciliation might be defined in a non-controversial way, as for instance, a public reckoning with a history of political violence and oppression and their legacy in order to enable people divided by that past to coexist within one political community and to recognize the legitimacy of its law.[7] As with other political ideals, it is hard for political actors to oppose reconciliation when understood in these terms. Consequently, the politics of reconciliation become apparent in the competing *conceptions* of reconciliation that emerge in public debates about how it might be achieved, what 'real' or 'true' reconciliation would require. In other words, reconciliation is, like every other political concept, 'effectively contestable.'[8]

At least three conceptions of reconciliation emerged, for instance, in public debates in Australia in the 1990s. The self-proclaimed 'practical' conception of reconciliation favored by the Howard government was ostensibly premised on a universal ideal of distributive justice and focused on achieving equity between indigenous and non-indigenous citizens in terms of socio-economic indicators of well-being such as health, education, housing and employment.[9] The restorative conception favored by the Opposition (and derisively labeled 'symbolic' by the Government) was based on reparative justice and emphasized the collective responsibility of non-indigenous Australians for past injustices. Among other things, it required an official apology and reparations to the stolen generations and their families.[10] In mainstream debates about the merits of practical versus restorative reconciliation, the constitutional conception of reconciliation favored by most indigenous leaders often went unacknowledged. It appealed to the democratic ideal of self-determination and emphasized the importance of a treaty, indigenous rights, Aboriginal sovereignty and constitutional recognition.[11]

In such circumstances, it is not clear that greater definitional precision over the meaning of reconciliation would make its achievement more likely. Rather, it might polarize a population further by raising the stakes of the conflict in terms of whether to reconcile or not. In contrast, as Michael Freeden puts it, "ambiguity. . .is a recipe for political coexistence" since it enables support to be mobilized for a shared enterprise among plural constituencies.[12] Moreover, since it allows reconciliation to be a contestable project from the outset, the ambiguity of the concept can be understood as an enabling condition for politics among people in a divided society. If we had to agree on a definition of reconciliation before we could begin to reconcile, reconciliation would never be initiated. Yet a willingness to reconcile, enabled by the ambiguity contained within such a collective intention, might provide the basis for an overlapping dissensus in relation to which people can debate and contest the terms of their political association.

An overlapping *consensus* refers to a (public) agreement on the fundamental principles of legitimacy in a well-ordered society, which may be supported from a plurality of potentially competing (private) conceptions of the good. In contrast, an overlapping *dissensus* would refer to the bringing into view of the fundamental wrong that would unite the parties to reconciliation as members of the same political unity. Political unity would not be presupposed in terms of a shared commitment to those principles of justice according to which reasonable members of a well-ordered society would arbitrate their political disagreements. Rather it would be understood as a contingent possibility of politics that comes about through contesting the nature of the injustice that brought the parties to the conflict together in the first place. In this context, the contestability of the concept of reconciliation enables an agonistic politics that is potentially constitutive of political community: in contesting the significance of the social world according to the conflicting perspectives brought to bear on it, that world might become more common to those engaged in struggle. When brought to bear on political relations between indigenous and settler societies in Australia, for instance, the distributive, reparative and constitutional conceptions of reconciliation might intersect to reveal what is at stake in coming to terms with the legacy of colonization.

In contrast, reconciliation becomes ideological when its meaning is over-determined. For it then tends to function as a meta-political ideal that disciplines conflict. It interpellates subjects in a way that renders their disagreement resolvable in terms commensurate with the newly democratic or 'postcolonial' regime.[13] Drawing on the work of Althusser, for instance, Claire Moon describes how, in the work of the Truth and Reconciliation Commission, reconciliation functions as "an organising category that. . .imposes concordance in place of contestation, conditioning the way in which South Africa's history is related in symbolic and material ways": as a history of human rights violations rather than one of "oppression, exploitation, cruelty, just war, or revolution."[14] Similarly, in Australia, reconciliation was ideological to the extent that indigenous peoples' claim to self-determination could not be articulated in terms of the prevailing dispute over 'practical' verus 'symbolic' reconciliation within the settler society, which took for granted the co-citizenship of indigenous and non-indigenous people.[15] If reconciliation depends on a population within a state coming to think of itself as a people, then a particular conception of reconciliation cannot be determined in advance but must be worked out politically by those who would get together to reconcile in the first place.

2. *The Illiberal Objection*

Reconciliation, it is sometimes said, presupposes an ideal of community that is too demanding for any modern society, let alone one deeply divided by a history of political violence. While reconciliation might be an appropriate term within the theological discourse in which it originated it makes no sense to talk of reconciliation in political life, in which the most we can aspire to is the containment of conflicts rather than their resolution.[16] Hence Timothy Garton-Ash suggests that "taken to the extreme the reconciliation of all with all is a deeply illiberal idea" because "liberalism means living with unresolvable conflicts of values and goals."[17] Reconciliation is ideological, on this account, when it presupposes a comprehensive conception of community with which some members of society might reasonably take issue. Instead of seeking an unattainable social harmony, the argument goes, we should pursue more limited goals such as peaceful coexistence and mutual toleration.[18]

Underlying this objection is what Judith Shklar calls the 'liberalism of fear,' which is not predicated on any substantive idea of the common good. Rather it claims to begin from a recognition of "a *summum malum*, which all of us know and would avoid if only we could. That evil is cruelty and the fear it inspires, and the very fear of fear itself."[19] Liberalism, on this view, is premised on the negative promise 'Never Again' that is central to reconciliation processes. A thin liberal conception of reconciliation would be limited to a strong defense of equal rights and their legal protection and the affirmation of the rule of law, including the establishment of a culture of respect for human rights. The importance of reconciliation would be in commemorating the past as a history of violations of human rights in order to prevent their reoccurrence.[20]

I have already described the ideological aspect of reconciliation with which liberalism takes issue in terms of over-determination, to which I proposed effective contestability as a remedy. In this section, I will deal instead with the ideological aspect of the 'thin' liberal conception of reconciliation. While purporting to be grounded in politics, this conception disavows the problem of the political. Shklar gives us a clue to this ideological aspect of reconciliation when she describes the marriage of liberalism to democracy as one of convenience: democracy is only of instrumental worth to this variant of liberalism because it is the regime least likely to violate human rights. Reconciliation becomes ideological, when conceived in these terms, to the extent that it affirms human rights while only genuflecting to the ideal of popular sovereignty.

While rejecting the idea that the inalienability of human rights is self-evident, the liberalism of fear insists that the recognition of political violence as Evil is self-evident and it is with this that we must take issue. For, as Alain Badiou observes, if the promise 'Never Again' is construed in terms of an "ethical consensus founded on the recognition of Evil, it follows that every effort to unite the people around a positive idea of the Good. . .becomes in fact the real source of Evil itself."[21] As such, reconciliation would disavow its own politics (and violence) in the name of an 'ethics,' which posits human rights as the higher moral principles according to which politics should be ordered.

Consequently it fails to grapple with the problem of the political. Namely, why those who happen to live in proximity to each other should look to the same law and political institutions to secure their basic rights.[22] While it might be true that every person has an interest in securing certain basic rights for herself, each person also needs a reason why she should cooperate with others in a particular historical community to secure her rights in common. Conceived in terms of the liberalism of fear, reconciliation takes for granted the fact of an association of rights-bearing individuals because its interest in community is primarily instrumental: as a predictable environment in which legal persons can pursue their private freedoms.

Following a history of oppression in which the rights of some are denied in the name of political community, reconciliation minimally requires the legal recognition of all citizens of a new regime as entitled to equal rights. However, a politics of reconciliation must further address and articulate the substance of these rights and how they might come to be held in common by members of a divided society. It cannot take their interest in securing them collectively to be self-evident. As Rancière puts it, "the simple relationship between humanity and its denial never creates a community of political dispute."[23] Rather than simply appeal to the shared humanity of those divided by the past as the basis of political community, what is required is a *demonstration* of the wrong that would unite them in a particular historical community.

Writing in the context of Chile, Fernando Atria describes the articulation of reconciliation as politics and ideology by distinguishing between the legal conception of human rights ("grounding actionable claims against others") and their political aspect ("constitutive of the political community").[24] The problem with the legal conception of human rights is that it refers to the way in which human rights are instituted during normal times, whereas 'human rights violations' are always perpetrated during times of exception in which the law is suspended.[25] Human rights violations are not committed between co-members of the political unity on which a legal order rests but are typically justified in terms of the threat that internal or external enemies pose to the unity of the legal order. Consequently, Atria argues, the promise 'Never Again' cannot be redeemed by normal legal means because it is unable to take account of the political context in which violence was perpetrated, the "social drama' of inhuman treatment of fellow human beings in exceptional situations, when the legal is suspended."[26] A legal conception of rights deals with the past by depoliticizing the conflict as one among individual agents. In doing so, law cannot take account of what makes human rights violations so atrocious, namely, that they were collectively organized by the state and justified in the name of a people.

To the extent that a thin conception of reconciliation takes for granted individuals' private interests in securing human rights as already publicly shared it fails to address "terror as something that affects the self-understanding of the political community that suffers it, so that [for example] coming to terms with it is restoring the basis for the 'we' of 'we the Chileans.'[27] In other words, it fails to address the constitutive, foundational dimension of human rights that is implicit in the promise 'Never Again' insofar as it expresses a *collective intention*, an act of self-determination. A politics of reconciliation would be predicated on this political aspect of human rights, the declaration of which is itself a kind of exceptional politics that is constitutive of political community.

3. *The Question-Begging Objection*

Reconciliation, it is sometimes pointed out, refers to the 'restoration' of friendly relations after an estrangement. But in contexts of transitional justice there is often, in fact, no prior state of harmony that could be restored. In her analysis of the narrative framing of reconciliation by the TRC in South Africa, for instance, Claire Moon observes that:

> Tutu's words call upon the prelapsarian human condition – the moment of creation – and hail a return to a condition of harmony and unity that preceded 'The Fall'...Reconciliation...[suggests] that a condition of national harmony and accord in

> South Africa actually *did* exist prior to its alleged 'rupture'. All this...in the context of South Africa's 'stark circumstances' in which there is 'nothing to go back to, no previous state or relationship one would wish to restore'.[28]

In moral philosophy, the prior state of harmony refers to the moral community from which a wrongdoer becomes alienated in violating a communal norm and to which she or he is restored through a process of remorse, reparation and reaffirmation of the norm, followed by punishment and/or forgiveness.[29] The problem with applying this account of reconciliation to divided societies is, of course, that we cannot presuppose shared norms between the persecutors (including their beneficiaries) and the persecuted. In a context such as Australia, in which violence and oppression against the colonized was legitimated in terms of the shared moral norms of the colonizers, indigenous people might quite rightly be suspicious of the 're' in reconciliation.

As with the liberal notion of 'restoring' the rule of law in a divided society, the presupposition of an original commonality to be restored begs the question since it presupposes as given what is actually a contingent achievement of politics. Yet there is a crucial difference between the 'thin' community presupposed by liberalism and the apparently 'thicker' original harmony conceptually linked to the 're' in reconciliation. Whereas liberalism takes for granted the fact of a political society to secure the rights of individuals, reconciliation presupposes a counter-factual community of equals that is prior to the institution of any social order. As such, the restorative aspect of reconciliation brings into relief the paradox of representing 'the people' in any democracy. For the "we" that is invoked to legitimate or challenge existing institutions never actually exists prior to those institutions but is always the achievement of political action. The people whose will the laws of a democratic society are supposed to express cannot actually speak as a people but can only ever be represented by specific actors and institutions.[30] This is what Claude Lefort means when he claims that in a democracy the place of power is empty: the people is a quasi-transcendent subject of democratic discourse that, contra Schmitt, is irreducible to any particular determination.[31]

For society to represent itself as a unity it must refer to a point outside of its 'self' from which it can perceive itself as a whole. Or, as Hans Lindahl puts it, "polities can only particularise themselves in the process of positing boundaries, by projecting a boundless whole in which they locate themselves."[32] The 're' in reconciliation enables precisely this insofar as it refers to a counter-factual community of equals in terms of which members of a determinate political community might represent their society as a whole and imagine how it might otherwise be. Such reference to a counter-factual community is commonplace in political theory. For instance, it figures both in the state of nature in social contract theory and the pragmatic presuppositions of communication in Habermas' discourse ethics. But it originally derives from the religious imagination: the ideal of an original harmony provides a point of critique in terms of which we might understand how our actually existing society is and might otherwise be.

Reconciliation becomes ideological to the extent that this harmony that is to be 'restored' is reified and inscribed as an enforced commonality. Stewart Motha makes this point in his analysis of the (unratified) Declaration Towards Reconciliation in Australia, which begins: "We, the peoples of Australia, of many origins as we are, make a commitment to go on together in a spirit of reconciliation." Motha argues that the Declaration is "premised on a presumed and insistent commonality."[33] Despite the recognition of plurality in its reference to "peoples of many origins," he points out that this is held together by a singular 'We' that is premised on a concept of sovereignty in its "original imperial terms": "We recognise that this land and its water were settled as colonies without treaty or consent."[34] This explicit acknowledgement of the question-begging objection entails an admission of the facticity of the political community with its origin in violence and the fiction of any reference to an original harmony that might be restored. Yet, Motha argues, despite this confession there is also a "preservation of the sovereign assertion that is at once finite (an event that took place 'back then') and infinite ('it can never be parted from or addressed')."

As critique of the reconciliation process in Australia, Motha's analysis is astute. Yet, it tends toward totalizing critique in its insistence that the sovereign assertion can *never* be addressed. I agree that this sovereign assertion cannot be *legally* redressed.[35] Politically, however, the 're' in reconciliation is only potentially and not necessarily ideological and it can also serve to politicize and resist ideology by insisting on an unredeemed promise of equality that would enable us to imagine how the relation between indigenous and settler societies might be different, how the identities of colonizer and colonized might be resisted. [36] Importantly, the singular 'We' that opens the Declaration is an indexical term: it can only point to a collectivity that remains indeterminate. Because the 'we' cannot speak as a 'we', someone must claim to represent it. This representative claim inevitably entails a certain violence in positing community. Yet, in its invocation of the people, it may fail or succeed and, should it succeed, it may always be contested (if only in retrospect). Politically, the significance of the Schmittian conception of the political on which Motha's analysis partly relies, is that it recognizes the contingency of the substantive form of political unity that underlies every legal order. As such, it could always be otherwise.

A politics of reconciliation therefore requires distinguishing between the proto-political community of equals to which the 're' in reconciliation refers and the determinate political association that it potentially calls into question. As such, reconciliation would not be understood as the end of politics. As Valerie Kerruish argues, the unity to which the 're' in reconciliation refers should not be sought in terms of an ideal community that a determinate community might be made to approximate. Rather, it should be understood in negative terms as 'not in this world' and in this sense related to it. As such, the unity to which the 're' in reconciliation refers does not provide a blue print for a new society as utopias are sometimes interpreted to do. Rather, "its conceptual link is to freedom, in [the Australian] context, decolonisation."[37]

4. *The Assimilative Objection*

Perhaps the most common objection to the concept of reconciliation is that it privileges national unity and political stability over the requirements of justice. Reconciliation perpetuates assimilation to the extent that it takes for granted one nation that needs to be healed rather than recognizing two (or more) distinct political communities. Stewart Motha describes reconciliation as a "neo-imperial gesture, that amounts, in the Australian context, to a process of re-inscribing a 'post-colonial' political community under one law that "subordinates indigenous laws and customs, once again, in the name of 'civilisation', and its new effigies, democracy and human rights."[38] Reconciliation as nation-building may be viewed as assimilative since it seeks to overcome the state's crisis of legitimacy by *incorporating* the colonized into the political community as free and equal citizens rather than recognizing their right *not* to reconcile.

The fact that reconciliation was supposed to be achieved to coincide with the centenary of the Australian Federation in 2001, points to the close connection between the concept of reconciliation and nation-building in Australia in the 1990s.[39] As Andrew Gunstone discusses, the emphasis placed on improving relations between indigenous and non-indigenous people, on their being united as Australians, living together and sharing histories and cultures, served to marginalize or silence certain indigenous justice claims, such as the right to self-determination, which could not be articulated within the terms of settler nationalism.

This ideological use of the concept was particularly apparent in the fact that while indigenous people had called for a treaty with the Australian state since the 1960s, reconciliation is all they were offered in the 1990s. The reason why reconciliation was more palatable than a treaty to the settler society was clearly elucidated by the former Prime Minister John Howard while Opposition leader in 1988: "it is an absurd proposition that a nation should make a treaty with some of its own citizens."[40] A treaty suggests retrospective recognition that Aboriginal sovereignty existed at the time of settlement, which would call into question the validity (if not the fact) of the sovereignty of the Australian state now. In contrast, the concept of reconciliation seems to take for granted the sovereignty of the Australian state and co-membership of indigenous and non-indigenous Australians in one nation. While Prime Minisiter, John Howard responded to renewed calls for a treaty at the end of the official reconciliation process by saying that we should focus on "what unites us as Australians rather than what divides us."[41] Of course, even to focus mainly on what "divides us" as Australians would be assimilative to the extent that it presupposes that it is *as Australians* that "we" are divided.

Yet, while the concept of reconciliation often is employed in this ideological way by nation-states, it also has the potential to politicize the terms of association in a divided society. In particular, the new beginning that reconciliation seeks to enact draws attention to the political risk of (re)founding a political community. For the new beginning that we seek to enact can only be recognized as such in retrospect since it depends on the establishment of a lasting institution. As already discussed, the 'we' that is invoked to found a political community does not exist in the moment in which a new constitution is made, but only comes about to the extent that future generations continue to identify themselves as part of this historical community. If the 'backward-looking' dimension of reconciliation is presented in terms of 'restoring' the proto-community of equals, its 'forward-looking' dimension is presented in this attempt to found a community-to-come.[42] As Emilios Christodoulidis has observed, this risk that the beginning we seek to enact might fail should be celebrated since, in contrast to the reification of the nation, it "imports an awareness that keeps community both attuned to the aspiration of being-in-common and aware of its vulnerability."[43]

It is no coincidence that the revolutions in France and America and more recently in Eastern Europe and South Africa all tend to focus on the establishment of a constitution and the promise 'never again.' Constitution-making is historically associated with the attempt to memorialize a new beginning. Indeed, in South Africa, it was only *after* the establishment of a treaty and a provisional constitution that it was possible to talk of reconciliation. Only with the formal cessation of hostilities is it possible for former enemies to countenance civic friendship and to begin a process of reconciliation.

As such a treaty and reconciliation in Australia are not alternatives. Rather, it is only with the establishment of a treaty (or many treaties) between the settler society and indigenous peoples in Australia that a space for a reconciliatory politics is constituted. A treaty might thus establish the possibility of an *inclusion* that is not at the same time an *incorporation* of indigenous people within an Australian nation/state. In the absence of such a treaty, the new beginning that "we" seek to enact in the present is unlikely to be recognized as such by future generations. Indeed, as Rob Sparrow has argued, "we" (members of the settler society at the beginning of the twenty-first century) are more likely to be perceived by our successors (indigenous and non-indigenous) as one with those 'past generations' from whose actions and attitudes we so readily (and anxiously) distance ourselves in the present.[44] Similarly, in the absence of reconciliation, any treaty that we might make now is unlikely to stand the test of time.

5. *The Quietist Objection*

Reconciliation is often also objected to on the grounds that it places the burden of dealing with a history of political violence on the victims by demanding that they forgive and forget their oppressors when they are entitled to resent and resist them. This objection was strongly put by indigenous writer and activist, Kevin Gilbert when he asked:

> What are we to reconcile ourselves to? To a holocaust, to massacre, to the removal of us from our land, from the taking of land? The reconciliation process can achieve nothing because it does not. . .promise justice.[45]

Invoking the sense of reconciliation as resignation, this objection points to the ideological aspect of reconciliation insofar as it demands letting go of past grievances and, hence, being "reconciled to domination."[46]

The relation between reconciliation and justice is a difficult one. This becomes especially clear when we consider the relation between justice and forgiveness. Following Aurel Kolnai, the paradox of forgiveness can be stated as follows: on the one hand, forgiveness should be conditional on our wrongdoer repenting, repairing the wrong, reaffirming the norm violated, etc. For if we forgive before this we end up condoning the wrong. On the other hand, if forgiveness is conditional in this way on our wrongdoer deserving to be forgiven, it seems to become redundant.[47] For we seem only to be doing what justice requires. Indeed, to withhold our forgiveness from a person who deserves it would appear unjust or, at least, unvirtuous.[48]

Yet there is also another idea of forgiveness as unconditional, as something that we freely offer to the other, regardless of whether he or she deserves our forgiveness or not, for the sake of establishing or restoring a relationship with her or him. This idea of forgiveness was sometimes referred to in South Africa as a kind of higher morality that transcends the demands of retributive justice for the sake of restoring community. But to the extent that such unconditional forgiveness transcends justice it risks becoming unjust.[49] Indeed, critics of the Truth and Reconciliation Commission in South Africa argued that Desmond Tutu's insistence on the importance of forgiveness amounted to counselling the oppressed to resign themselves to the injustice of apartheid rather than demanding the distributive and reparative justice they were entitled to.

I agree with Bert van Roermund that political reconciliation requires a movement back and forth between these two sequences of forgiveness, which he describes in terms of 'rubbing on' and 'rubbing off.'[50] If it is not to amount to a form of quietism, then reconciliation should not be understood in opposition to justice. Rather, a willingness to reconcile should be understood as providing a political context in terms of which justice can be staged. This requires on the one hand seeking justice through, for instance, redistribution, reparations, criminal trials, apologies, indigenous rights, constitutional recognition, etc. and at the same time making possible a public reckoning with the past by the victims' willingness to "defer those justified claims of retribution that could obstruct peace in the future."[51] The relation between reconciliation and justice in this way points to the relation between politics and justice in any political society. Justice depends on political institutions for its (imperfect) realization and as such, is always worked out within a determinate political community. On the other hand, the possibility of political community depends, in the first place, upon a willingness to forgive on the part of those formerly oppressed.

In its ideological aspect reconciliation demands forgiveness from the victims of injustice as a condition of their recognition as free and equal co-members of the political community. As politics, in contrast, reconciliation would be predicated on gratitude that it is only due to a *willingness* of those formerly oppressed to forgive (in the political sense of being willing to countenance sharing the same political institutions with their former oppressors) that talk of reconciliation is possible at all. Such an awareness introduces a reflexivity into the politics of reconciliation in recognizing the right of those previously oppressed not to reconcile and hence the need to furnish reasons to reconcile. If reconciliation as ideology offers recognition of membership in the political community in exchange for acquiescence in the injustices in which that political community originated, a politics of reconciliation requires finding reasons to reconcile to in order to redeem the offer to forgive that made possible the foundation of a new political association. For, importantly, as Van Roermund points out, it is up to those formerly oppressed to determine "what could be obstructive for what they conceive as a worthy peace in their future society," what reasons are sufficient to defer their justified claims to retribution. In the absence of being able to determine what counts as an adequate reason to reconcile, those who forgive "would not be liberated from oppression to begin with".[52] Consequently, as Emilios Christodoulidis and Scott Veith put it, "the question [why reconcile?] that reconciliation presses us to ask. . .is whether certain conflicts and consequences are, or can be recognized and addressed within a reconciliatory politics. This question must be insisted on so that surrender of the experience for continuing harms and conflicts does not become the condition of any possible 'common' future."[53]

6. *The Exculpatory Objection*

Finally, reconciliation, it is sometimes said, enables those ordinary citizens collectively implicated in past injustices as beneficiaries of a regime to evade assuming any real responsibility by lapsing into a sentimental politics of guilt or shame. For instance, symbolic politics such as the signing of sorry books in Australia, emotional outpourings in Parliament, the displays of the 'Sea of Hands' and marches across the Sydney Harbour Bridge only serve to relieve colonial guilt without addressing the very real inequalities that continue to exist, the specific wrongs perpetrated or the particular people unjustly harmed. As Anthony Moran observes in relation to Australia:

> A new form of settler nationalism, itself responding to a perception of national illegitimacy, is one of the forces that stimulated the movement for reconciliation. Ideas and feelings about the nation, national belonging, and reconciliation vary, but what 'Aboriginal Reconciliation' means for many of its non-indigenous supporters is the opportunity to free the nation of the guilt or shame associated with its foundations.[54]

In its ideological aspect, reconciliation enables a sentimental avowal of responsibility in order to achieve a sense of belonging to a 'good' nation that is, in fact, an evasion of real liability that would incur material costs in the form of reparations.[55]

While sentimentality can be a way of evading political responsibility, however, we should be careful not to make the opposite mistake of insisting that politics requires reasonableness without passion. Politics begins from outrage at injustice. The sense of shame that many members of the settler society feel for the treatment of indigenous people in Australia, for instance, is an important impulse that can mobilize people to act to change a shameful situation. Yet, this sense of shame becomes sentimental when it centers attention on feeling good about ourselves and our nation rather than on what can be done to redress the situation.[56] Reconciliation is ideological when it becomes exculpatory in this sense.

For a politics of reconciliation, the feeling of shared responsibility needs to be thought of in terms of a responsibility that is *responsive to* the political claims of those who suffered previous injustice. Thomas Brudholm, attributes something like this notion to Jean Améry, who "held the Germans to the demand of *ressentiment* to turn back time and undo what happened." Given the impossibility of meeting this "absurd demand," Améry's notion of a justifiable reconciliation would depend not so much on Germans, "coming to terms with the past" as "coming to share the victims' unreconcilable attitude to the inexpiable evils of the past."[57] In the Australian context, such responsiveness would not take for granted the membership of indigenous people in the nation nor assume that the interests of the settler society and indigenous people could be reconciled. In recognizing the right of indigenous people not to reconcile, such political responsibility would be animated, as Johan van der Walt puts it, by a desire not *to be reconciled* but *to live in reconciliation*.[58]

In assuming responsibility in this way, the settler society would not be hoping for forgiveness from indigenous people that would relieve them of their guilt by bringing about a final settlement that would be paid to any future claims for reparative justice. Rather, as Colin Perrin and Scott Veitch suggest, the truth-telling and acknowledgement of systematic racial discrimination and genocide reported in *Bringing Them Home* in Australia, would continue to have an unsettling effect on the political association between settler and indigenous societies.[59] A politics of reconciliation would seek to realize political community while acknowledging the impossibility of any final settling of accounts.[60]

Conclusion

As Paul Ricoeur describes it, the autonomy of the political leads to a paradox in that the rationality of the political (the working out of human coexistence in relation to the good of community) gives rise to the evils of political power (violence against a part of the community legitimized by an appeal to the interest of the whole). Against the temptation to oppose two styles of political reflection – on the one side an insistence on 'the rationality of polity' and on the other an insistence on the 'violence and untruth of power', the task of political theory for Ricoeur is to recognize "that the greatest evil adheres to the greatest rationality, that there is political alienation because [the political] is relatively autonomous."[61] It is in this spirit that I have undertaken the analysis of the six objections to reconciliation above. Rather than responding to the realist critique of reconciliation as ideology with an opposing moral idealism, I have argued for reconciliation as politics that is reducible neither to violence nor consensus, although it is conditioned by the possibility of both.

Insofar as it tends to inscribe an enforced commonality, as Stewart Motha puts it, reconciliation probably has been ideological in every society in which it has been deployed as state policy. There may be a fundamental change in the membership of the ruling class between the regime that has been overturned and that which a politics of reconciliation has installed. There may be a cessation of overt political violence. As ideology, however, reconciliation would nevertheless still be complicit in the exercise of various forms of structural violence in its appeal to an idea of commonality to legitimate a social hierarchy.

As such, reconciliation is a form of what Rancière calls 'the police': "an order of the visible and the sayable [predicated on a division between rulers and ruled] that sees that a particular activity is visible and another is not, that this speech is understood as discourse and another as noise."[62] Within the order of the sayable of the ideology of reconciliation, what registers as speech is that which would confirm the unity of the political association. In contrast, any political claim that would question the substantive unity that underlies the political order in the first place could only be perceived as noise. As Rancière observes, the police "can procure all sorts of good, and one kind of police may be infinitely preferable to another."[63] The reconciliatory police order of Chile after the fall of Pinochet is obviously preferable to that of the long years of its authoritarian-capitalist regime.

Yet, as Rancière goes on to say, "Whether the police order is sweet and kind does not make it any less the opposite of politics."[64] Throughout this article I have therefore sought to recuperate the concept of reconciliation for a politics along something like the lines that Rancière proposes, as a mode of activity that is 'antagonistic to policing.' Politics always calls into question a social order by demonstrating the fundamental equality that it implicitly presupposes. Namely, that both parties to a conflict possess the same faculty of understanding: that to understand a speech as an order, to be able to obey, one must also already possess the capacity for understanding that the social order one claims is lacking. In this context, politics is the staking out of a speaking position that is not made available by a police order: it makes heard as speech what could only register as noise within that order. Politics is predicated on this assumption of equality that "demonstrates the sheer contingency of the order, the equality of any speaking being with any other speaking being."[65] Political activity always involves a process of subjectification to the extent that it brings into view this hidden presupposition of the police order, the ontological equality that underlies every social hierarchy. As such, politics is the "practice whereby the logic of the characteristic of equality takes the form of *processing of a wrong*."[66]

I have sought to develop an account of reconciliation as a processing of a wrong, a demonstration of the fundamental wrong on which the polity is founded which is brought into view by the friction between reconciliation as ideology and politics. Between: overdetermination and contestability; privatization and collectivization; reifying and invoking unity; certainty and risk; expectation and gratitude; accounting and responsiveness. The significance of the six aspects of reconciliation as politics that I have argued for come down to the possibility of the processing of a wrong or its demonstration, which depends on an awareness of the extent to which the foundation of political community both presupposes a fundamental equality of its members and represses this presupposition in its casting of social conflict as always in the service of a unity. There is both violence in the foundation of every social order (enforced commonality) and the inscription of an ideal equality (on which every emancipatory demand is predicated).

Rancière is an important theorist for us since he thinks through Ricouer's political paradox or what Stewart Motha refers to as the double move of reconciliation. As Rancière acknowledges, politics does not exist in a vacuum: its logic is heterogenous to that of the police but it is always also bound up with it. There is no issue or sphere that is inherently political and politics' guiding principle of equality is not essentially political. What the principle of equality does is "lend politics reality" in the staging of a conflict that brings into view the fundamental equality underlying every police order. What makes an action political is its form: "the form in which confirmation of equality is inscribed in the setting up of a dispute, of a community existing solely through being divided."[67] Reconciliation as politics would always concern this setting up of a dispute, the processing of the wrong on which political community is founded.

NOTES

I am grateful to Keith Breen, Emilios Christodoulidis, Hans Lindahl, Stewart Motha, Claire Moon, Kathy Smits, Ernesto Verdeja, Ian Zuckerman and two anonymous reviewers for their helpful comments on earlier drafts of this paper.

1. See, for instance, Mark Neocleous, "Let the Dead Bury Their Dead: Marxism and the Politics of Redemption," *Radical Philosophy* 128 (2004): 29.

2. Indeed, I believe this currently to be the case for indigenous people in Australia who remain under siege by the settler society.

3. Karl Marx and Frederick Engels, "The German Ideology," in David McLellan, ed., *Karl Marx: Selected Writings* (Oxford: Oxford University Press, 1977), 176.

4. Costas Douzinas, *The End of Human Rights: Critical Legal Thought at the Turn of the Century* (Hart Publishing: Oxford, 2000), 169.

5. Stewart Motha, "Reconciliation as Domination," in Scott Veitch, ed., *Law and the Politics of Reconciliation* (Aldershot: Ashgate, 2007), 88. John Borneman similarly arrives at a 'Janus-faced' vision of reconciliation, see John Borneman, "Reconciliation after Ethnic Cleansing: Listening, Retribution, Affiliation," *Public Culture* 14, no. 2 (2002), 301–302.

6. Andrew Gunstone, "Unfinished Business: the Australian Reconciliation Process from 1991–2000," *Journal of Australian Indigenous Issues* 8, no. 4 (2005); Brandon Hamber and Hugo van der Merwe, similarly identify a profusion of meanings of reconciliation in the South African context as a stumbling block toward the possibility of a lasting reconciliation, see Brandon Hamber and Hugo van der Merve, "What is This Thing Called Reconciliation?" *Reconciliation in Review* 1, no. 1 (1998), Centre for the Study of Violence and Reconciliation online paper, http://www.csvr.org.za/articles/artrcbh.htm, Accessed March 1, 2007.

7. Alternative definitions of the concept include "an agreement among antagonistic subjects to depart from violence in a shared present" (Borneman) and "building or rebuilding relationships today that are not haunted by the conflicts and hatreds of yesterday" (Hayner). Borneman, "Reconciliation after Ethnic Cleansing," 300; Priscilla Hayner, *Unspeakable Truths: Facing the Challenge of Truth Commissions* (Routledge: NY & London, 2002), 161.

8. Michael Freeden explains that, in contrast to being "essentially contestable" a concept is "effectively contestable because its contestability is not an essential property of the concept but a property of political discourse." See Michael Freeden, "Essential Contestability and Effective Contestability," *Journal of Political Ideologies* 9, no. 1 (2004), 5. I have previously argued that reconciliation is an essentially contestable concept but this stronger claim is not necessary for the argument made here in favour of reconciliation as politics. See Andrew Schaap, *Political Reconciliation* (London: Routledge, 2005), 12–13. Erik Doxtader argues that reconciliation is properly understood not as an essentially contestable concept but rather as a rhetorical one, i.e. a "concept that depends on speech to contest certain sorts of essentialism." While Doxtader's discussion of reconciliation is theoretically rich, his claiming of reconciliation for an anti-essentialist politics is itself effectively contestable in Freeden's terms. Erik Doxtader,"Reconciliation: A Rhetorical Conception", *Quarterly Journal of Speech* 89, no.4 (2003): 269, 287.

9. See John Howard, "Practical Reconciliation," in Michelle Grattan, ed., *Reconciliation: Essays on Australian Reconciliation* (Melbourne: Bookman Press, 2000), 88–96. It should be noted that this appeal to distributive justice was made in bad faith given the worsening disparity in the distribution of the benefits and burdens of social cooperation between indigenous and non-indigenous people in Australia under the Howard government.

10. See Paul Keating, "The Redfern Park Speech," in Grattan, ed., *Reconciliation: Essays on Australian Reconciliation*, 60–64.

11. See Geoff Clarke, "Not Much Progress," in Grattan, ed., *Reconciliation: Essays on Australian Reconciliation*, 228–234.

12. Freeden, "Essential Contestability and Effective Contestability," 10.

13. On this point see Emilios Christodoulidis, " 'Truth and Reconciliation' as Risks," *Social and Legal Studies* 9, no. 2 (2000): 179-204; and Damien Short, *Reconciliation and Colonial Power* (Aldershot: Ashgate, 2008).

14. Claire Moon, "Narrating Political Reconciliation: Truth and Reconciliation in South Africa," *Social and Legal Studies* 15, no. 2 (2006), 260, 272; and *Narrating Political Reconciliation* (Lanham: Lexington Books, 2008).

15. For analyses of the debate over an official apology in Australia see Marguerite La Caze, "The Asymmetry between Apology and Forgiveness," *Contemporary Political Theory* 5, no. 4 (2006): 447–468; Katherine Smits, "Deliberating Past Injustices: Apology, Historical Identity and Reconciliation in the Australian Case," *Constellations* 15, no. 2 (2008).

16. For discussions of the political significance of the theological meanings of reconciliation, critical of this too easy insistence on secularism, see Michael Phillips, "Aboriginal Reconciliation as Religious Politics," *Australian Journal of Political Science* 40, no. 1 (2005): 111–124; Andrew Schaap, "The Proto-Politics of Reconciliation," *Australian Journal of Political Science* 41, no. 4 (2006): 615–630; Fernando Atria, "Reconciliation and Reconstitution," in Scott Veitch, ed., *Law and the Politics of Reconciliation* (Aldershot: Ashgate, 2007).

17. Timothy Garton-Ash, "True Confessions," *The New York Review of Books*, July 17, 1997, 37.

18. On reconciliation conceived in terms of democratic reciprocity, conceived in terms of dialogical liberalism as opposed to the liberalism of fear that I discuss here, see Amy Gutmann and Dennis Thompson, "The moral foundations of truth commission," in Robert I. Rotberg and Dennis Thompson, eds., *Truth v Justice: The Morality of Truth Commissions* (Princeton: Princeton University Press, 2000). For a critique see my "Agonism in Divided Societies," *Philosophy and Social Criticism* 32, no. 2 (2006): 255–277.

19. Judith Shklar, "The Liberalism of Fear," in Stanley Hoffman, ed., *Political Thought and Political Thinkers* (Chicago: University of Chicago Press, 1998), 11. For recent restatements of this position see Michael Igantieff, *Human Rights as Politics and Idolatory* (Princeton: University of Princeton Press, 2001), 55–56; Jonathan Allen, "The Place of Negative Morality in Political Theory," *Political Theory* 29, no. 3 (2001): 337–363.

20. For a distinction between thin and thick conceptions of reconciliation see David Crocker "Truth Commissions, Transitional Justice and Civil Society" in Rotberg and Thompson, eds., *Truth v Justice: The Morality of Truth Commissions*. For a problematization of these distinctions in the colonial context see Damien Short, "Reconciliation and the Problem of Internal Colonialism," *Journal of Intercultural Studies* 26, no. 3 (2005): 267–282.

21. Alain Badiou, *Ethics: An Essay on the Understanding of Evil*, trans. Peter Hallward (London: Verso, 2001), 13.

22. Bert van Roermund, "Rubbing Off and Rubbing On: the Grammar of Reconciliation," in Emilios Christodoulidis & Scott Veitch, eds., *Lethe's Law: Justice, Law and Ethics in Reconciliation* (Oxford: Hart Publishing, 2001), 188. I discuss this issue in *Political Reconciliation*, ch. 2; see also Mahmood Mamdani, "Amnesty or Impunity?" in Seyla Benhabib, Ian Shapiro, and Danilo Petranovich eds. *Identities, Affiliations, and Allegiances* (Cambridge: Cambridge University Press, 2007).

23. Jacques Rancière, *Disagreement: Politics and Philosophy* trans. Julie Rose (Minneapolis: University of Minnesota Press, 1999), 138.

24. Fernando Atria, "The Time of Law: Human Rights between Law and Politics," *Law and Critique* 16 (2005): 137–159.

25. Ibid., 138.

26. Ibid., 153–154, citing Simone Weil.

27. Ibid.,140.

28. Claire Moon, "Prelapsarian State: Forgiveness and Reconciliation in Transitional Justice," *International Journal for the Semiotics of Law* 17 (2004) citing Antjie Krog. See also Neocleous, "Let the dead bury their dead. . ." 29; Rosalyn Diprose, *Corporeal Generosity: On Giving with Nietzsche, Merleau-Ponty and Levinas* (Albany: State University of New York Press, 2002), 148.

29. See, for instance, Christopher Bennett, "The Varieties of Retributive Experience', *The Philosophical Quarterly* 52, no. 207 (2002): 145–163.

30. See Bert van Roermund, "The Concept of Representation in Parliamentary Democracy," *Current Legal Theory*, 14, no. 1 (1996): 31–52 and "First-Person Plural Legislature: Political Reflexivity and Representation," *Philosophical Explorations* 6, no. 3 (2003): 235–250. The classic expression of the paradox is in Rousseau's *Social Contract* (2.7.9).

31. Claude Lefort, *Democracy and Political Theory* (Cambridge: Polity Press, 1988), 17. As Bernard Flynn explains, in a democracy, "there is no one who is *a priori* certified to speak in the name of the people. Each one does speak in the name of the people, but each is legitimately contradicted by others who, with as much right, also evoke the name of the people." Bernard Flynn, "Lefort," in Simon Critchley and William Schroeder, eds., *A Companion to Continental Philosophy* (Oxford: Blackwell, 1998), 489.

32. Hans Lindahl, "Agonistic Cosmopolitanism: Immigration, Justice and a Phenomenology of the Political World", unpublished manuscript.

33. Motha, "Reconciliation as Domination," 77.

34. Ibid.,78 citing the Declaration.

35. For reasons powerfully argued by Atria in "The Time of Law."

36. I develop this argument more fully in relation to the work of Lefort in "The Proto-politics of Reconciliation."

37. Valerie Kerruish, "Reconciliation, Property and Rights," in Christodoulidis and Veitch, eds., *Lethe's Law: Justice, Law and Ethics in Reconciliation*, 200.

38. Motha, "Reconciliation as Domination," 77, 69. See also Damien Short, "Australian 'Aboriginal' Reconciliation: The Latest Phase in the Colonial Project," *Citizenship Studies* 7, no. 3 (2003): 291–312.

39. For the connection between reconciliation and nation building in South Africa see, among others, Richard A. Wilson, *The Politics of Truth and Reconciliation in South Africa: Legitimizing the Post-Apartheid State* (Cambridge: Cambridge University Press, 2001) and Michael Humphrey, *The Politics of Atrocity and Reconciliation: From Terror to Trauma* (London: Routledge, 2002).

40. Cited in Paul Patton, "Reconciliation, Aboriginal Rights and Constitutional Paradox in Australia," *The Australian Feminist Law Journal* 15, no. 1 (2001), 37. For a discussion see Andrew Schaap, "The Absurd Proposition of Aboriginal Sovereignty" in Andrew Schaap, ed., *Law and Agonistic Politics*, (Aldershot: Ashgate, forthcoming); and "Aboriginal Sovereignty and the Democratic Paradox," in Adrian Little and Moya Lloyd eds., *The Politics of Radical Democracy* (Edinburgh: Edinburgh University Press, forthcoming).

41. Howard, 'Practical Reconciliation', 96.

42. I develop this argument more fully in "The Time of Reconciliation and the Space of Politics" in *Law and the Politics of Reconciliation*, Scott Veitch, ed. (Aldershot: Ashgate, 2007).

43. Christodoulidis, "Truth and Reconciliation as Risks," 198.

44. Robert Sparrow, "History and Collective Responsibility," *Australasian Journal of Philosophy* 78, no. 3 (2003): 346–359.

45. Cited by Kerruish, "Reconciliation, Property and Rights," 191.

46. Motha, "Reconciliation as Domination," 70.

47. Aurel Kolnai, "Forgiveness," in *Ethics, Value and Reality* (London: The Althone Press, 1977).

48. Jacques Derrida is probably better known than Kolnai for his thematisation of the aporia between a conditional forgiveness (which he associates with reconciliation) and an act of pure forgiveness arising from a Levinasian unconditional ethical injunction. See his "On Forgiveness," in *On Cosmopolitanism and Forgiveness* (London: Routledge, 2001). For a critical discussion see Ernesto Verdeja, "Derrida and the Impossibility of Forgiveness," *Contemporary Political Theory* 3, no. 1 (2004): 23–47; Richard J. Berstein, "Derrida: the Aporia of Forgiveness?" *Constellations* 13, no. 3 (2006): 394-406; Samir Haddad, "Arendt, Derrida and the Inheritance of Forgiveness," *Philosophy Today*, forthcoming.

49. See Peter Digeser, "Forgiveness and Politics: Dirty Hands and Imperfect Procedures," *Political Theory* 26, no. 5 (1998): 700–724.

50. Bert Van Roermund, "Rubbing Off and Rubbing On: the Grammar of Reconciliation," in *Lethe's Law: Justice, Law and Ethics in Reconciliation*, Christodoulidis and Veitch, eds.,.

51. Ibid., 180.

52. Ibid., 181.

53. Christodoulidis and Veitch, "Reconciliation as Surrender" in *Justice and Reconciliation in Post-Apartheid South Africa*, Du Bois and Pedain, eds.

54. Anthony Moran, "Aboriginal Reconciliation: Transformations in Settler Nationalism," *Melbourne Journal of Politics* 25 (1998).

55. See also Anne Orford, "Commissioning the Truth," *Columbia Journal of Gender and Law* 15, no. 3 (2006): 877–880.

56. For an Arendtian critique of collective guilt as sentimentality see my "Guilty Subjects and Political Responsibility," *Political Studies* 49, no. 4 (2001): 749–766.

57. Thomas Brudholm, "Revisiting Resentments: Jean Améry and the Dark Side of Forgiveness and Reconciliation," *Journal of Human Rights* 5 (2006), 21.

58. Johan Van der Walt, "Psyche and Sacrifice: An Essay on the Time and Timing of Reconciliation," *Journal of South African Law* 4 (2003): 635–651.

59. Human Rights and Equal Opportunity Commission, *Bringing Them Home: National Inquiry into the Separation of Aboriginal and Torres Straight Island Children from their Families* (Canberra: AGPS, 1997). For an insightful reading of the report see Anne Orford, "Commissioning the Truth".

60. Colin Perrin and Scott Veitch, "The Promise of Reconciliation," *Law, Text, Culture* 4, no. 1 (1998): 225–233.

61. Paul Ricoeur, "The Political Paradox," in *History and Truth* (Evanston: Northwestern University Press, 1965), 249.

62. Rancière, *Disagreement*, 29.

63. Ibid., 31.

64. Ibid., 31.

65. Ibid., 30.

66. Ibid., 35.

67. Ibid., 32.

Andrew Schaap is Lecturer in the Department of Politics at The University of Exeter. He is author of *Political Reconciliation* (2005).

Part III

THE PERMEABLE BOUNDARIES OF TRANSITIONAL JUSTICE

(i) In what transitions?

(ii) For what wrongs?

(iii) To what political ends?

18

Transitional justice and ongoing conflict

Par Engstrom

Introduction

The field of transitional justice (TJ) emerged out of attempts to give theoretical meaning to *ad hoc* accountability policies adopted as part of broader processes of political democratization in Latin America and Eastern Europe. From these beginnings TJ has dramatically expanded in scope and ambition. The hugely increased normative ambitions of TJ are nowhere more apparent than in practices of judicial intervention in situations of ongoing conflict. Such interventions have brought the field of TJ into much closer contact with the related, but distinct, fields of conflict resolution and peacemaking (or peacebuilding). Peacebuilders have also dramatically expanded their policy objectives beyond the cessation of armed conflict to include the establishment of a sustainable peace, the neutralization of the incentives for a return to conflict, and the realization of a variety of accountability and rule of law strategies. This chapter accounts for the expanding normative ambitions of the field of TJ and evaluates the implications for TJ of its involvement in ongoing conflicts. It also suggests some tentative ways for TJ to recast its engagement with ongoing conflicts.

The chapter is divided into three parts. The first examines the ways in which TJ is increasingly embedded in conflict resolution and peacebuilding efforts and evaluates the relatively recent trend towards judicial intervention in ongoing conflicts. It examines two main underlying trends that drive these developments: the intractability of contemporary armed conflict, and the dramatic development of the "global accountability regime" and the associated expansion of the rights of victims. It also briefly assesses the normative and operational overlaps inherent in the ambitious agenda of "liberal peacebuilding."

The second part analyzes three particularly significant aspects of judicial interventions in ongoing conflict. First, the move towards judicial interventions in ongoing conflict is anchored in a consequentialist logic that has generated increasingly strident demands for empirical evidence of TJ claims. Yet, in part because of the complex and indeterminate causal pathways of such claims, robust empirical evidence is still lacking. Second, the internationalization of transitional justice has created significant tensions between international and local agency. Yet, the problematic effects of international judicial pressures are also exacerbated by local institutional fragility and by attempts to implement TJ in highly inhospitable conditions, including in the absence of any discernible political transition. Third, the dominance of legal and judicial approaches to TJ has tended to privilege retributive forms of justice in ways that often are not conducive to conflict resolution or political and societal reconciliation. But the judicialization of TJ also runs the risk of obfuscating politics in ways that almost invariably benefit elite interests.

The final part of the chapter attempts to move beyond the current theoretical and policy impasse by outlining a proposal for a (possible) way forward that emphasizes the complexity inherent in the field of TJ. It also provides brief reflections on the contours of a prudent, incremental, and politically attuned strategy of TJ engagement with ongoing conflict.

I. The expansion of transitional justice

The trend towards judicial intervention in ongoing conflicts is relatively recent.[1] In the modern period, TJ developed as a field of theory and practice concerned with questions of truth, justice, and reconciliation in the context of political regime change: from military regimes to electoral democracy in South America; following the fall of communist regimes in Eastern Europe; and at the end of civil war in Central America. From these beginnings TJ has dramatically expanded both in terms of geographical coverage and in terms of normative ambitions. The hugely increased normative ambitions of TJ are nowhere more apparent than in practices of judicial intervention in situations of ongoing conflict. The intervention of the International Criminal Court (ICC) in Libya is but the most recent reflection of the emergence of the ICC as a key actor on the contested terrain of conflict resolution. As a result, there has been a discernible shift from the pursuit of accountability strategies after the cessation of armed hostilities on the one hand, and in the aftermath of political transitions on the other, to attempts to achieve accountability for atrocities even before a political settlement of armed conflict has been reached.

The practice of international judicial interventions in ongoing conflicts can be traced back to the beginning of the 1990s and the establishment of the International Criminal Tribunal for the former Yugoslavia (ICTY). The United Nations Security Council (UNSC) resolution that established the ICTY was adopted in the midst of ongoing conflict in Bosnia and before the start of peace negotiations at Dayton. Yet, the ICTY issued only few indictments during the armed conflict itself and cases only came to trial after the end of the war. Instead, the first significant attempt to pursue justice during ongoing conflict came with the indictment of Slobodan Milosevic during the NATO bombing of Kosovo. But, the pursuit of justice during ongoing conflict has become increasingly contentious since the adoption of the Rome Statute and the creation of the ICC. The ICC's temporal jurisdiction that limits potential prosecution to crimes committed after 1 July 2002 has pushed the Court and the ICC Prosecutor towards engaging with ongoing conflicts.[2] The increasing number of ICC indictments and investigations in recent years has led to the close involvement of international criminal justice in ongoing conflicts in Uganda, the Democratic Republic of the Congo, Sudan, Kenya, Colombia, and, most recently, Libya.

1. Contemporary conflict and transitional justice

The creation of the ICC represents a dramatic shift in the global accountability regime. While under the "Nuremberg model" the militarily victorious parties used their power to pursue justice after the cessation of conflict, under the "Rome model" interventions are undertaken by third-party judicial actors. As a consequence of this shift, judicial interventions are initiated not following military victories, but rather during ongoing conflict. Two main underlying trends underpin and drive these developments: the intractability of contemporary armed conflict; and the dramatic expansion of the international legal architecture.

Character of contemporary armed conflict

There has been a discernible shift from the industrialized total warfare of the first half of the twentieth century, to contemporary forms of low-intensity conflict in conditions of state breakdown. Interstate warfare, as part of foreign policy and with distinct lines between state, army, and society, has lost much of its institutional character. Wars have in this sense become more irregular, a trend further accentuated by the privatization of much contemporary warfare.[3] This can especially be seen in the division between civilians and soldiers. In contemporary warfare, uniforms are not always used, in part because of the increased use of irregular and paramilitary forces. Whilst most war fatalities in the early twentieth century were military personnel, at the turn of the century most war fatalities were civilian.[4]

For some, the underlying problem is the legitimacy of the state, and problematic or "weak" statehood as a legacy of the post-colonial era.[5] As long as major interstate war remains unlikely,[6] and legitimation problems of weak states continue, such conflicts are likely to persist. This is further exacerbated by the ethnic dimensions of contemporary conflicts, which have inscribed these conflicts with, as Shaw has noted, a genocidal impulse.[7] This is not to deny that identity in terms of distinguishing between "us" and "them" has always been important, especially since the advent of nationalism in the nineteenth century. Concerns surrounding identity are always present in any political community, and not only in the context of the breakdown of political legitimacy.

Nonetheless, these general patterns of contemporary conflict all have implications for attempts to resolve conflict, but also, crucially, questions of how to ensure accountability for atrocity crimes.[8] The centrality of ethnic identity and the specific organization of armed groups in conflict matter fundamentally both for the efforts to end hostilities and for accountability. In particular, the blurred lines between "war" and "peace" in much contemporary conflict have led to attempts to implement TJ policies in institutionally and politically very fragile and unstable situations, before any discernible transition (from "war" to "peace") has taken place.[9]

Development of the international legal architecture

There are two key dimensions to the development of the international legal architecture governing accountability efforts in the context of ongoing conflict. The first is related to the greatly increased normative ambitions inherent in the development of international human rights institutions in recent decades. The UN has assumed a prominent peacebuilding role, incorporating human rights protection into its operations as guiding principles. The more overtly coercive dimensions of human rights enforcement have emerged front and center in contemporary debates on the appropriate response of the international community to massive human rights violations. Movement towards politically legitimating humanitarian intervention based on collective action—including the use of force—is embodied in the principle of "Responsibility to Protect" or RtoP, and associated efforts to redefine threats to international peace and security that have pushed human rights compliance onto the agenda of the UNSC. This development reflects both the broadening of interpretations of threats to international peace and security, including mass atrocities, and the increased acceptability of the use of force for a broad range of policy objectives and associated beliefs in the utility of military power.

One remarkable feature of the normative development of international human rights in recent decades is the emergence of individual accountability as a guiding principle for TJ. This should be seen against the broader global trend, uneven as it may be, toward the criminal prosecution of those responsible for grave human rights violations. As a result, international criminal justice—with the ICC as its central institution—has emerged as a form of global governance, with specific underlying principles, values and norms, in the process reshaping human rights politics and institutions.[10] Liberal assumptions concerning the ability to individualize guilt, and the ability to deter violence absent the use of force, have become deeply embedded in the international criminal justice regime.[11]

In particular, the current development of international criminal law has tended to advance a rather narrow understanding of "accountability" that focuses on individual criminal accountability at the expense of broader alternative conceptions of accountability as conventionally enshrined in international human rights law (i.e. state, or public, accountability). Retributive approaches to justice have also gained a privileged position within the international criminal justice regime at the expense of restorative approaches, with "justice" primarily conceived of as "punishment" of transgressors. Moreover, the traditional distinctions between the different bodies of international law have become increasingly blurred, with the laws of war—regulating conduct in armed conflict—coming into a closer relationship with international human rights law on the one hand and international criminal law on the other.

Hence, overall, the expansion of the international legal architecture has created a much higher presumption against impunity and in favor of accountability than what existed one decade ago.[12] The UN Secretary-General has taken the view that UN-endorsed peace agreements can never grant amnesties for genocide, war crimes, crimes against humanity, or gross violations of human rights.[13] This presumption is also deeply embedded in the overarching objective of the Rome Statute, namely "to put an end to impunity for the perpetrators of [the most serious crimes of concern to the international community] and thus to contribute to the prevention of such crimes."[14]

The second dimension is related to the rise in "victim-centered" notions of justice. There has been a steady increase in provisions for victims' rights in recent years. This can be seen in the growth of reparations programs, in the creation of a victims' trust fund at the ICC, and in the adoption of UN guidance and principles pertaining to restorative justice.[15] The increased emphasis on victims' rights has brought criminal justice into a closer relationship with human rights in the field of TJ. The strengthening of victims' rights has also led to the incorporation of human rights into international criminal justice processes. The potential link between restorative and retributive forms of justice can most clearly be seen in the increasing trend in international criminal justice towards the recognition of the role of victims in these processes, especially in the design of reparation policies.

Clearly, expectations of victims for justice have increased, at least partly as a result of changes in international criminal law and the dramatic expansion of the TJ field. Nevertheless, giving privileged attention to victims' interests and demands also raises several complex issues. The participation of victims in TJ processes is often complicated, particularly since victims are not a homogeneous group, and the nature of abuses they have suffered may vary. In many cases, victims groups include relatives of those killed and/or disappeared, in some cases entire groups and communities of people have been victimized, and, in others, the primary group of victims are smaller groups of political activists. In some instances, individuals and groups who have suffered human rights violations may reject the term "victim" and prefer the term "survivor." There are also circumstances in which some "victims" were also "perpetrators" (e.g. child soldiers).

Yet, TJ processes are often driven by victims' groups. While victims' groups clearly have a legitimate role in shaping transitional institutions and processes that affect them directly, it is less clear to what extent their demands should be privileged when these collide with broader conceptions of the public interest, a category within which "peace," however understood, falls. Victims and affected communities may also demand types of justice and forms of punishment that may be unacceptable to those not directly affected and, in some circumstances, by external actors (such as the death penalty). The participation of victims raises therefore a host of intrinsically complex questions regarding definitions of what constitutes the "public interest," whose definition counts, and classical dilemmas in democratic theory between majoritarian interests on the one hand and individual rights and protections on the other.

2. Liberal peacebuilding and transitional justice: overlapping agendas and operational tensions

The practice of international judicial interventions in ongoing conflicts has brought the field of TJ into much closer contact with the related, but distinct, fields of conflict resolution and peacebuilding. The primary objective of peacemakers has traditionally been to secure a peace agreement that would ensure an end to the armed conflict. In recent decades, however, peacebuilders have dramatically expanded their policy objectives beyond the cessation of armed conflict to include the establishment of a sustainable peace, the neutralization of the incentives for a return to conflict, and the realization of a variety of accountability and rule of law strategies.[16] In the process, peacebuilding and human rights have also become an integral part of the agenda of the UNSC and the management of international peace and security more broadly. While traditionally based on principles of consent, neutrality and the limited use of force, the UNSC-mandated peacebuilding missions over the course of the last two decades have included election observation, provisional administration, and coercive rules of military engagement.

Hence, the expansion of both TJ and peacebuilding has created significant normative and operational overlaps between these traditionally distinct fields of theory and practice. There are indeed many shared features within the broader global context of enthusiasm for "liberal peacebuilding" that gained a certain momentum through the 1990s and into the 2000s. For some, TJ policies are closely associated with the rise of state-building.[17] For others justice plays a central role "in establishing the foundations for genuine and long-lasting peace."[18] Similarly, for former UN Secretary-General Kofi Annan, TJ and peacebuilding are based on mutually reinforcing imperatives: "Justice and peace are not contradictory forces. Rather, properly pursued, they promote and sustain one another. The question, then, can never be whether to pursue justice and accountability, but rather when and how."[19]

Yet, despite the partially overlapping development of TJ and peacebuilding, attempts to bring these fields together have generated significant tensions. Partly, this is due to the fact that not all components of liberal political practice can easily be reconciled and partly to institutional boundaries, professional trajectories, normative commitments, and policy preferences of these fields of theory and practice.[20] Demands for accountability have traditionally tended to be construed as obstacles to peace. Indeed, for the recently created UN Peacebuilding Commission (PBC), accountability is not a top priority. For the PBC, it seems, given the absence of TJ in its institutional mandate, accountability should, at best, be deferred until later in peacebuilding processes.

II. Judicial intervention in ongoing conflict

There has been a dramatic shift in the practice of TJ towards the pursuit of accountability, particularly through prosecutions, during ongoing conflict. This trend of (external) judicial interventions in the midst of conflict and the pursuit of TJ in the absence of an apparent transition can be explained by the combined effects of the developments examined in the previous section. However, from intervention in ongoing conflicts, a number of specific challenges have become particularly acute. First, international judicial interventions are underpinned and reinforced by the belief held by some proponents that the tool of indictments and the threat of prosecution can alter the prospects for achieving peace. Second, judicial interventions during conflict have exacerbated the internationalization of TJ in ways that risk undermining local accountability processes. Third, international judicial interventions have further strengthened the trend towards the increasing judicialization of TJ.

1. Rise of consequentialism and the empirical turn in transitional justice research

The shift in TJ debates over the course of the last two decades has been significant. For advocates such as Diane Orentlicher in the beginning of the 1990s the focus was on the legal status of a *duty* to prosecute.[21] Although TJ practitioners were indeed concerned with the potential impact of strategies adopted, particularly with regards to the potentially destabilizing effects of wide-ranging prosecutions on fragile transitional societies, both the policy and scholarly debate was overwhelmingly normative in character. This can be explained in large part by the fact that the TJ agenda was overwhelmingly driven by activists often with personal histories of suffering as opposed to the more professionalized cadre of actors who have subsequently been driving the policy agenda.

In recent years, however, with the practice of judicial interventions in ongoing conflicts, particularly through the ICC, combined with the rise of donors' "impact agenda," TJ advocates have increasingly justified their activities on the basis of utilitarian logics in general and the logic of deterrence in particular. Indeed, as Vinjamuri highlights, "recent arguments have emphasized the instrumental purposes of justice, essentially recasting justice as a tool of peacebuilding and encouraging proponents and critics alike to evaluate justice on the basis of its effects."[22] Hence, the decision to pursue justice during ongoing conflict has been justified primarily in terms of its capacity to alter the outcome of the conflict by enhancing the prospects for peace through judicial deterrence. For proponents, the deterrence effect of criminal punishment affects the cost-benefit calculations of potential perpetrators. Credible threats of punishment deter rights-violating behavior and encourage engagement with peace processes. Indicting abusive political leaders may also marginalize, delegitimize, and remove perpetrators and potential spoilers of peace processes.

Skeptics argue, however, that punishment for perpetrators of serious violations undermines efforts to bring violent conflict to an end and precludes the possibility of forgiveness, reconciliation, and other societal goals.[23] On this view, attempts to hold individuals to account may prevent possibilities of ending conflicts through negotiation and may provoke a backlash or intensification of political and societal divisions. The prospects of being held to account for violations leave potential spoilers with little choice than to undermine peace processes. Containing spoilers, not holding them to account, should, on this view, be the top priority of peace negotiators.

The turn towards empiricism

The shift from an emphasis on a putative duty to prosecute to a logic of consequences has shaped debates surrounding "deterrence effects" of international prosecutions in ongoing conflicts and prevention of future conflicts. Since the creation of the ICC the debate as to whether seeking justice for grave international crimes interferes with efforts to resolve armed conflict has undoubtedly intensified as the likelihood and credibility of prospects for prosecution have increased. In particular, the move towards judicial interventions in ongoing conflict, underpinned by a consequentialist logic, has led to demands for empirical support of TJ claims. However, the jury is still very much out when it comes to the empirical evidence to support claims regarding the impact of TJ (or lack thereof).[24] For example, several recent studies of the impact of TJ mechanisms on peace have failed to confirm the claim that the pursuit of international criminal justice leads to peace, or that justice initiatives are necessary for sustained peace.[25]

Undoubtedly, the causal pathways involved in these relationships are highly complex and indeterminate. Still, the lack of robust empirical evidence is clearly problematic for any claim based on the logic of consequences. By the same token, however, there is little evidence to suggest that the anticipated negative consequences of pushing for accountability actually materialize.[26] There is, in other words, not sufficient empirical evidence to conclude either that accountability strategies increase the risk of conflict or that they increase the likelihood of continuing conflict.

For some proponents of accountability, the absence of robust empirical evidence that shows that pushing for accountability undermines peace and leads to a deterioration of the human rights situation provides solid grounds for continued advocacy.[27] Yet, the absence of robust empirical evidence has forced accountability advocates towards the adoption of "faith-based" policy prescriptions.[28] After all, most TJ advocates often have neither the resources nor the training to conduct impact assessment exercises or to collect the necessary empirical evidence. There are also inherent difficulties in identifying and evaluating the many complex variables shaping TJ outcomes and a relative absence of long-term data sets that would allow for comparisons over time. But it is also the case, as argued by Clark and Palmer, that "[t]he field of TJ balances uneasily between analysis and advocacy ... [and the] fervent certainty of much human rights advocacy has often hampered the tasks of impartial research and informed policymaking."[29]

2. *Internationalization of transitional justice*

The early TJ efforts of the 1980s, particularly in Latin America, were distinctly local in origins and primarily driven by local actors. But starting in the 1990s the

Nuremberg precedent was revived in the form of *ad hoc*, international tribunals. Yet, these tribunals were soon criticized for being far removed from the populations affected by the violations and for the lack of support from domestic judicial systems. Partly in response to these criticisms, on the one hand, hybrid courts combining national and international law were established and, on the other, a permanent international tribunal, the ICC, was eventually created. Yet, the internationalization of TJ activities, in combination with the coercive and highly politicized character of international judicial processes, has created significant tensions between international and local agency.

Global solutions to local problems

The considerable influence of international actors in the TJ field jeopardizes local ownership of and participation in TJ processes. As argued by Nagy in this volume, TJ as a field of practice and "normative inquiry" has become increasingly institutionalized within the broader structures of global governance over the course of the last decade in particular. True, as a partial corrective to this globalizing force, many practitioners have embraced localized, or "traditional," forms of TJ. Still, considerable tensions and legitimacy deficits exist in the gaps between international and local agency.

First, the influence of international generalist "expertise," funds, and emphasis on global models tends to shape TJ agendas in ways that often are to the detriment of domestic actors. International donors and consultants, although well-meaning, wield considerable influence in ways that risk the "crowding-out" of local actors. Second, as pointed out by Vinjamuri, "[s]ecuring international justice, securing peace, and devolving justice to national actors are likely to be incompatible goals, especially in states where institutions are weak and a high degree of instability persists."[30] Hence, decisions to judicially intervene in ongoing conflict are likely to be taken by outsiders and may therefore undermine local ownership of justice initiatives. Third, international interventions are often overly ambitious and their ultimate objectives are rarely explicit. This is partly because there is little agreement on what constitutes success, but also the expectations on what TJ processes can achieve are often inflated.

The coercive character of international justice

There is also the problem of the coercive and highly politicized character of international judicial processes. As the vast literature on "humanitarian intervention" repeatedly points out, politicization and selectivity are inherent in the practice of intervention by powerful states. This can be seen, for example, in the uneven character of international responses to some of the most recent high-profile humanitarian/human rights crisis and conflict situations: Syria (weak condemnation and piecemeal UN sanctions regime); Libya (forceful and immediate ICC/NATO intervention); and Sri Lanka (delayed investigations). Moreover, as recently highlighted in the initial response by the UNSC to the outbreak of civil war in Libya to refer the situation to the ICC, judicial interventions can also be aimed at replacing diplomacy and attempts at political solutions, hence reinforcing the trend towards judicialization.

Similarly, international judicial interventions are intimately linked to the development of conceptions of "human security" that underwrote practices of interventions in humanitarian crises by Western states following the end of the Cold War. Scholars of "securitization" highlight that the move towards linking human rights with the high politics of international security has a number of problematic implications, including privileging coercive force over political responses to crisis situations. Another problem is related to the potential of international (judicial) interventions to alter power balances and thereby the relative power of the warring parties. Such interventions are of course highly political and, as Vinjamuri points out, "the assumption that justice can be pursued neutrally during conflict is inconsistent with the claim that justice can independently affect the prospects for peace by marginalizing some actors and empowering others."[31] As seen in international judicial interventions in, for example, Libya, Sudan/Darfur, and Uganda, such interventions are not perceived as neutral or driven by legal considerations of selecting situations and cases to investigate in accordance with the Rome Statute. Critics of the ICC also argue that it selectively applies international criminal justice against less powerful states. This criticism is bolstered by the predominantly African focus of investigations initiated thus far by the ICC's Office of the Prosecutor (OTP).

Transitional justice in inhospitable conditions

The problematic effects of international judicial pressures are exacerbated by domestic institutional fragility. In conflict situations, local capacity to implement accountability strategies is particularly limited. The sheer number of perpetrators in societies afflicted by mass atrocity would overwhelm even a well-functioning judicial system.[32] Similarly, the delivery of TJ, particularly when administered in conjunction with peacebuilding programs such as demobilization, is institutionally very complex and burdensome.[33] Trial justice, for example, requires robust domestic justice institutions, which in most (post-)conflict societies are absent. In addition, the pursuit of TJ in weakly institutionalized environments is particularly subject to political manipulations.[34]

As a result, TJ, on its own and without broader institutional and political reforms, is unlikely to assist where it is needed the most. Attempts to implement TJ in inhospitable conditions, including the pursuit of justice initiatives in the absence of any discernible political transition, may mean reaching for the most difficult. TJ as a distinct field of theory and practice emerged in the context of political transition from, primarily, military rule to democratic governments in Latin America. Processes of TJ in Latin America are, however, likely to be quite different from those in countries that are moving from internal armed conflict, or are still engulfed in conflict, in Africa and in other parts of the world. The applicability of TJ findings in the region of Latin America (and in post-Soviet states) may be limited for a number of reasons including differences in patterns of state formation, colonization and decolonization, civil society activism, legal and judicial traditions, democratization, and socio-economic development. Indeed, for some, "there are grounds to suspect that TJ is best suited to states with relatively strong institutions and a certain minimum level of democracy."[35] This seems to echo the early modernization literature on democratization that viewed only countries that had attained a certain level of socio-economic development as "fit" for democracy. Nonetheless, such tensions are bound to intensify as the attention of international actors is currently undergoing a regional refocus towards the Middle East and the Arab world more broadly.

Challenges of legitimacy

International actors and institutions have carved out a central role for themselves when dealing with mass atrocities. As an increasing number of TJ institutions are established around the world, the agency of the specific actors involved is central to the pursuit of TJ. Yet, the question remains on what grounds external interventions, and particularly judicial interventions, are legitimate. Indeed, "who should be deciding on these processes, implementing them and ultimately benefiting from them are deeply contested issues."[36] Human rights activists and legal professionals often assert the authority of international legal norms and institutions on positivist grounds. This may not be altogether surprising given the extensive mobilization of resources around the values underpinning the international human rights and criminal justice regimes. Conventional understandings of the legitimacy of international legal norms either focus on the procedural fairness (due process guarantees) of criminal justice, or adopt legal positivist positions, accepting the authority of international law. For some, the legitimacy of international criminal justice ultimately rests on both its procedural fairness and its sources of authority (in terms of the relevant community that can/should be able to hold perpetrators to account).[37]

Regarding the latter, the crucial question is: accountable to whom? The common justification for international sanction for international crimes is that such abuses constitute an affront to humanity as a whole. For scholars such as Henham, however, "whatever measures are taken in the name of humanity to 'penalise' or 'punish' or 'deter' perpetrators of international crimes, these must draw moral support from both global and local constituencies."[38] This highlights the importance of context and agency in TJ processes. As argued by Clark and Palmer, "[w]ho implements transitional justice processes, what needs they respond to, and how particular interventions are ultimately understood by affected populations, are critical in determining the legitimacy and efficacy of transitional responses."[39] There are, however, also pragmatic reasons for why the particular histories, social norms, and cultural practices of affected communities must shape the development and implementation of TJ policies. For, without giving such considerations due attention, the legitimacy deficits of internationalized practices of TJ inevitably determine their impact.

3. Judicialization of transitional justice

Legal and judicial strategies have become dominant in the field of TJ. For proponents, the increase in international prosecutions, even in the context of ongoing conflict in recent years, demonstrates that law can prevail over politics, and that the criminal prosecution of abuses can assist in breaking the "wall of impunity."[40] For some, as outlined above, there is a strong consequentialist rationale for criminal prosecution as a way to reassert the legitimacy of the state, to strengthen the rule of law, and to promote political democratization.[41]

Yet, there are significant limits to what legal and judicial mechanisms can achieve in relation to TJ outcomes. In the first instance, there are the limits inherent in the recourse to judicial procedures and logics in addressing complex social and political problems: the challenges inherent in processes of judicialization per se. It remains crucial therefore to recognize the limits of what judicial approaches to accountability can achieve, especially through international courts and tribunals. In response to the complex objectives of contributing to conflict resolution, increasing political stability, combating impunity, and promoting reconciliation, any positive contributions of trial-based approaches to accountability are likely to remain modest.

Moreover, the specific character of the development of international criminal justice has privileged retributive forms of justice in ways that often are not conducive to conflict resolution or political and societal reconciliation. The international criminal justice system, as encapsulated by the ICC, aims primarily at the prosecution and punishment of individuals, and retribution and deterrence have been promoted as the primary objectives of punishment. The development of international criminal justice has taken place, however, at the expense of restorative approaches of justice and of broader notions of human rights accountability. Yet, despite the prevalence of claims of effectiveness of the international criminal justice regime in terms of deterrence, there is a dearth of empirical evidence documenting such claims. Also, especially in the context of large-scale organized political violence, there are inherent limitations in retributive approaches to criminal justice. As mentioned before, simply given the vast number of cases in such contexts, attempts to establish individual criminal responsibility tend ultimately to be unsatisfactory. To focus on a handful of cases may invite accusations of selectivity and further contribute to the politicization of the judicial system. Although the prosecution of individual cases may be symbolically very significant, criminal prosecutions are not likely to bring about political reconciliation.

The judicialization of TJ also risks obfuscating politics in ways that almost invariably benefit elite interests. Clearly, judicial interventions do not cancel out politics; they are both fundamentally driven by politics and, in turn, shape politics. In other words, Moreno Ocampo's aspiration that the ICC statute would result in a move "from a world based on power to one based on law,"[42] veers towards an attempt at depoliticization. As seen in Uganda, for example, the intervention of international tribunals can be manipulated by local elites for their own political ends. Hence, the potential for dislocation of politics that processes of judicialization entail may lead to elite capture and local power structures to condition the impact of TJ processes.

III. Recasting transitional justice and conflict resolution in an imperfect world

The final part of the chapter outlines some possible ways for TJ to recast its engagement with ongoing conflicts. In the first instance there is the need to recalibrate TJ strategies in the context of ongoing conflict in terms of: management of expectations; acknowledgement of the limits of the "transitional" paradigm when applied to ongoing conflicts; recognition that consensus is unlikely and probably undesirable; embracing of complexity and the blurred boundaries inherent in the field of TJ; and recognition that any gains made are prone to reversals.

1. Prudence, incrementalism and the constant potential for reversal

The theory and practice of TJ has its roots in the understanding that transitional contexts constitute disruptions of "politics as usual" that offer opportunities to recast justice and its foundations.[43] Yet, TJ issues are invariably complex. At the core of TJ debates is a set of moral and political dilemmas, which are not readily reduced to general theories. As with any morally fraught subject there are very rarely any straightforward solutions available. Consensus surrounding most issues relating to TJ remains elusive and, as with any morally thorny issue, probably undesirable.

There is still a need, nonetheless, to go beyond the binary debates that tend to dominate the field (peace vs justice, law vs politics, local vs international, etc.) and recognize the complexity and blurred boundaries inherent in the field of TJ. On the one hand the tensions between, say, peace and justice are likely to be less pronounced than what is often maintained. On the other, there are fertile grounds to explore useful ways forward beyond sterile dichotomies.[44] It is also important to better manage the expectations of what TJ mechanisms can realistically achieve. For many critics, the pursuit of TJ in the early stages of a political transition, or even in the absence of a transition, may be considered premature.[45] Indeed, it is crucial to recognize the limits of the "transitional" paradigm (as developed in the context of democratic transitions) when applied to ongoing conflicts. In particular, the paradigm may be misleading, as it implies that countries moving away from a difficult past will necessarily make the transition toward democracy and stability. Overburdening TJ mechanisms with excessive roles tends to give rise to inflated expectations of what TJ can deliver. In the context of ongoing conflict, rather than there being a rupture with the past, the legacies and challenges of the past are likely to fundamentally shape any future developments.

There is also the need to recognize that any normative progress with regards to TJ is prone to reversals. Consider the framework of Responsibility to Protect (RtoP) that increasingly underpins, both discursively and institutionally, attempts to intervene in ongoing conflicts. RtoP highlights the reality of constant renegotiations of state sovereignty in matters of human rights and the legitimate form and scope of international interventions in the domestic affairs of sovereign countries. It has shifted understandings of what sovereignty entails towards a less absolutist understanding of sovereignty over the course of the last decades. These trends also invoke understandings of sovereignty not as entitlement but as status, understandings of what it means to be a legitimate member of an international society, and the capacity to engage in increasingly complex transactions with other members of the system.[46]

However, if one accepts that normative understandings of the legitimate scope for intervention in conflict are prone to change, there will also be the potential for pushback, reversal, and stagnation. As Welsh observes, "[c]fforts to implement norms open up new areas of contestation for those sceptical of the norm's provisions, and can lead to either backsliding or differential interpretations of the norm's meaning."[47] What does this mean for the pursuit of accountability strategies by external actors during ongoing conflict? There may indeed be broad recognition of certain fundamental principles enshrined in the international criminal justice system and the associated concept of RtoP concerning state responsibility and intervention. But criticism from rising powers, such as Brazil, India, and China, suggests that these states are not yet willing to fully accept the compatibility between the principle of non-interference and international criminal justice. More generally, resistance to the more coercive efforts to enforce international criminal justice—in Libya and Sudan/Darfur for example—needs to be seen in the context of an uncertain future for the global human rights regime more broadly in light of the wider implications of the rise of non-Western states and shifting global power balances. As power shifts globally, therefore, competing understandings of sovereignty that emphasize sovereign equality may reassert themselves, challenging the demands and expectations of accountability advocates.

2. *Strategizing transitional justice*

Against this background of challenges, in the spirit of "strategizing" TJ, five points are highlighted in summary form:

First, any morally defensible strategy of TJ would include not only legal considerations, but also the inherently political context in which the strategy is developed and implemented. According to some, international judicial actors, and particularly the ICC Prosecutor, should openly admit the political nature of their activities, which would enable them to make more informed political decisions. Yet, most advocates of international criminal justice tend to maintain that their role is to operate autonomously from political influences. Clearly, justice actors and institutions are both affected by and effect politics. Judiciaries, whether domestic or international, do not operate in a political vacuum. They are often attuned to and generally accommodate political shifts. The law, however, and the interests and normative preferences of its practitioners, cannot be simply reduced to politics. Developments in international law fundamentally shape the normative environment in which political actors operate. More specifically, the force of legal norms does not merely manifest itself in the form of constraints. Legal norms also have important creative, generative and constitutive influences on political practice. For Finnemore and Toope, for example, international law is more than merely a matter of cases and courts, or formal treaty negotiation. It has a constructive dimension in which actors participating in law's construction "contribute to legitimacy and obligation, and to the continuum of legality from informal to more formal norms."[48] Law in this view draws attention to those rules, norms, and decision-making procedures of institutions that shape expectations, interests, and behavior.

Second, and building on this last point, by considering "the interests of justice" the complexities of sequencing and timing must be better understood. In the first instance, further research on the causal effects of TJ mechanisms, including indictments and amnesties, on the dynamics of ongoing conflict is required. Recent research findings suggest that the timing of TJ mechanisms matter, but it remains unclear exactly how and why this is the case.[49] Indeed, Article 53 of the Rome Statute provides that the ICC Prosecutor may desist from opening an investigation if it appears to him that this would be in the "interests of justice."[50] However, the Rome Statute gives little guidance on what criteria the OTP should apply to determine what these constitute. Beyond the obligation to consider the gravity of the crime and the interests of victims, the Rome Statute makes no reference to the interests of peace and security, for example. Still, the notion of the interests of justice suggests that there is a strong rationale to defer prosecutions, i.e. delay justice, in times of political instability.

A better understanding of the dynamics of time also includes a recognition that incentives and norms tend to change over time, and hence also what is both normatively desirable and politically/practically possible. Accountability measures are not likely to serve short-term interests of bringing violent conflict to an end. Accountability norms may very well complicate peace negotiations. TJ, therefore, is quite clearly a moving target. Political circumstances change as power balances shift, consequently altering the incentives facing relevant political actors. But more subtle changes also occur over time in the normative environment in which actors operate. In other words, what is both possible and desirable is prone to change over time. Hence, although accountability claims have a tendency to persist over time, timing is important, rendering what may seem as a morally desirable sequencing of TJ mechanisms difficult to implement.

Third, TJ strategies must be clearer on objectives. What objectives do and should TJ mechanisms accomplish and for whom? In terms of TJ policies, there are some hard questions that need to be addressed: what is it for, what social and political functions should the particular approach adopted fulfill, and what actors are—and should be—the beneficiaries? Does the specific mechanism actually deliver what it is set out to deliver; for example, does it bring the citizenry together (reconciliation) or in fact divide or further polarize the population between the beneficiaries and supporters of the *ancien régime* and its victims? Do trials not only combat impunity and establish accountability but also satisfy that powerful human instinct—revenge? Moreover, what are the institutional implications of court prosecutions for a judiciary that may already be under considerable institutional strain and political pressure? That is, do the policies on TJ strengthen or debilitate state institutions mandated to develop and implement these policies? A wide variety of mechanisms are now included in the TJ "toolkit"—investigations to establish the truth and identify perpetrators, reparations programs for the victims of human rights violations (financial and symbolical, in terms of memory sites), institutional measures to establish mechanisms to prevent recurrence of violations, and of course prosecutions and trials. However, the last few decades of accumulated TJ experience show that it is often not a simple matter of choosing between different TJ mechanisms.

Fourth, when engaging with ongoing conflicts, TJ advocates might consider a stronger focus on rights-abusing behavior in conflict rather than on the broader political dynamics of the conflict itself. Violent conflict is of course part of human history and is likely to remain so for the foreseeable future. Instead, advocates are better served by focusing on certain types of behavior in armed conflict—i.e. atrocity crimes—and to aim to hold perpetrators accountable for having committed grave crimes. That is, more focus should be given to the actual conduct of armed conflict rather than to the broader conflict per se. Too often this distinction is lost in both scholarly and policy debates. This is ultimately a principled (and modest) position that is not easily reduced to impact assessments. True, international criminal law targets the type of behavior (war crimes, crimes against humanity, genocide) that is the result of planning and systematic execution. Hence, it might not be easy to separate individual crimes from the broader conflict dynamics. Yet, making the case for accountability for perpetrators of grave human rights crimes does not have to lead advocates to exaggerated claims that TJ can end or prevent armed conflicts. It is therefore important to focus on abusive behavior in conflict, rather than merely participation in the conflict itself.

Finally, there is a strong normative case that some form of accountability ought to be part of efforts to end ongoing conflict and to build peace. Many TJ advocates argue that peace is not sustainable without some form of accountability. Although there is a lack of compelling evidence to support this claim, the key point to note here, however, is that accountability measures can take different forms. Article 53 of the Rome Statute, for example, highlights the question of whether prosecution is the only appropriate response to international crimes, or whether other mechanisms (such as amnesties and truth commissions) are acceptable alternatives. Non-retributive TJ mechanisms such as truth commissions and other alternative mechanisms also have potential accountability effects. Accountability measures may indeed complicate efforts to reach an end of armed conflict. But without any type of accountability measures as part of a peace settlement, serious doubts are likely to be cast on the character of the "peace" obtained. In particular, there is a need to expand the focus beyond individual criminal accountability. For example, the relative advantages of human rights mechanisms over criminal justice mechanisms in the context of post-conflict societies include: locating victims at the center; a demonstrated capacity to deal with a larger caseload; and a focus on state accountability, rather than individual accountability. From this perspective, redress goes beyond the individual case and highlights the needs of broader institutional and structural reforms.[51]

Amnesties, for instance, when appropriately designed, can constitute a legitimate form of accountability. It is generally recognized that international law obligates countries to prosecute genocide, crimes against humanity, and war crimes. Developments in international criminal law, in particular, have limited the ability of negotiators to trade off justice for a peace deal (e.g. in the form of blanket amnesties and explicit impunity deals). But, international law and norms also potentially provide common discursive grounds for the formulation of conflict resolution policies and appropriate TJ mechanisms. International law provides norms to enable the formulation of amnesty policies that could assist in efforts to end conflict while staying within its strictures: for example, with regards to certain types of conditional amnesties. The accumulated result of several decades of TJ practice is a broad set of duties of states, rights of victims and families, and obligations to provide reparations that limit the discretion of governments and mediators. Accountability constitutes therefore a key component of any efforts to achieve peace and eventual reconciliation and raises the possibility to promote accountability by other means than criminal prosecutions, such as truth commissions, lustration, reparations, etc. For Snyder and Vinjamuri, for example, properly designed and enforced amnesties have a better track record than trials and truth commissions of ending civil wars and encouraging human rights, democracy, and the rule of law (at least as measured by Freedom House and Polity IV). According to their study, trials only contribute to the ending of abuses when spoilers are weak and where domestic justice institutions are robust.[52]

Yet, certain measures are neither legitimate nor appropriate. This raises the question of what criteria should be used to evaluate legitimacy. At the minimum, accountability measures should be sensitive to local contexts and must be driven by and respond to local demands and needs. Therefore, to inform our understanding of what is possible, and even desirable, in societies engulfed in conflict it remains imperative to adequately and modestly recognize local political and historical particularities before using any general "lessons" to advance specific policy recommendations. An emphasis on local needs does not, however, exclude international efforts per se. On the contrary, this may demand such efforts in order to support local attempts to push accountability against entrenched interests. As argued by Seils and Wierda:

> [t]he existence of an external body with both the will and the means to achieve accountability means that negotiators are no longer hostage only to domestic realities. It may be that in some situations this will allow for greater

> clarity in persuading parties to conflicts that some degree of meaningful accountability in respect of serious crimes will have to form part of the solution.[53]

However, to really bring conflict to an end, root causes need to be addressed. This is beyond the will and capacity of outsiders and a very long-term process for which there are no quick policy fixes.

Conclusion

The normative expansion of the field of TJ is particularly evident in practices of judicial intervention in situations of ongoing conflict. The combined effect of an increasingly intrusive international legal architecture, the rise of victims' movements and their NGO support networks worldwide, and the intractability of contemporary armed conflict, has moved international judicial proceedings forward, with interventions taking place not after, but during, ongoing conflict. International judicial interventions are also spearheaded by practical constraints posed by the ICC's temporal limitation in investigating cases prior to July 2002. As a result, TJ has become an integral part of the political and legal context in which conflict resolution and peacebuilding strategies are formulated and implemented.

This chapter has highlighted a number of particularly pressing challenges that have become increasingly apparent in the cases of international judicial interventions in ongoing conflict to date, including: the dearth of robust empirical evidence to support the belief held by many advocates of judicial interventions that the tool of indictments and the threat of prosecution can alter the prospects for achieving peace; the risks of undermining local accountability processes inherent in international interventions, particularly in situations characterized by ongoing conflict and institutional fragility; and the privileged status of retributive forms of justice and the judicialization of TJ strategies at the expense of other potentially complementary strategies.

These challenges notwithstanding, the TJ field is undoubtedly continually evolving and the practice of judicial intervention in ongoing conflict is fairly recent. It may therefore be an opportune juncture to reflect on what prudent, incremental, and politically attuned strategies of TJ engagement with ongoing conflict may look like. This chapter has sought to outline some of the key dimensions that such an engagement might need to consider. Yet, whatever the merits of this approach to the complex issues that shape the pursuit of accountability strategies during ongoing conflict may be, the complexity inherent in the field of TJ means that consensus regarding foundational issues is unlikely and probably undesirable.

Notes

The author is grateful to Olga Martin-Ortega for helpful comments on earlier drafts and for coaxing the chapter from me. Chandra Lekha Sriram, Caroline Holmqvist-Jonsäter, and Thomas Pegram offered very constructive comments on a previous draft.

The participants at the authors' workshop at the School of Oriental and African Studies, University of London, provided the ideal intellectual environment for the discussion of many of the themes covered in this chapter. The author has also greatly benefitted from the discussions over the years with members of Oxford Transitional Justice Research (OTJR), particularly Phil Clark and Nicola Palmer, and the co-chairs of the London Transitional Justice Network, Chandra Lekha Sriram, Iavor Rangelov, and Leslie Vinjamuri. The usual caveats apply.

1 For analysis of justice trends, see Leslie Vinjamuri and Aaron P. Boesenecker, "Accountability and Peace Agreements: Mapping Trends from 1980 to 2006, *Centre for Humanitarian Dialogue Report*, September 2007.

2 When it comes to the scope of the ICC's prosecutions, Moreno Ocampo argues: "The ICC's mandate to select the most serious crimes committed after July 1, 2002, requires that we engage in judicial proceedings in relation to conflicts even before they have ended. Working in these circumstances can mean conducting investigations in situations where physical access is sometimes impossible or where there is a total collapse of functioning institutions. My Office has to pursue its justice mandate when there are negotiations for peace with the worst perpetrators or when the allegations are against the members of the government." Luis Moreno Ocampo, "Transitional Justice in Ongoing Conflicts," *International Journal of Transitional Justice*, vol. 1 (2007), p. 8.

3 On the role of private economic interest in such wars, see further: Kal Holsti, *The State, War, and the State of War* (Cambridge: Cambridge University Press, 1996), and Mary Kaldor, *New and Old Wars: Organized Violence in a Global Era* (Cambridge: Polity Press, 2002).

4 With regard to civilian casualties in contemporary armed conflict, figures in the range of 80–90 percent of civilian war victims are frequently cited. For a nuanced discussion of these figures and the inherent difficulties assessing civilian war casualties, see Adam Roberts, "Lives and Statistics: Are 90% of War Victims Civilians?" *Survival: Global Politics and Strategy*, vol. 52 (2010), pp. 115–36.

5 For Freedman: "the prototypical conflict now is a function of the weak state. States are weak because of the fragile nature of the civil society upon which they have been built, their undeveloped institutional structures, which are often unable to contain and channel political tensions, and their problems of poverty and economic adjustment. These weaknesses can lead to breakdowns of law and order, to secessionist movements, to outright civil war." Lawrence Freedman, *War* (Oxford: Oxford University Press, 1994), p. 359.

6 For an opposing perspective and for the likelihood of inter-state war, see John J. Mearsheimer, "The Gathering Storm: China's Challenge to US Power in Asia," *The Chinese Journal of International Politics*, vol. 3 (2010), pp. 381–96.

7 Martin Shaw, *War and Genocide* (Cambridge: Polity Press, 2003).

8 For an excellent analysis of post-Cold War narratives of conflict from the perspectives of primarily Anglo-American theorists, see Caroline Holmqvist-Jonsäter, *Policing Wars: A Twenty-First Century Discourse on War* (PhD dissertation, King's College London, 2010), Chapter 1.

9 Some studies show, for example, that about half of all countries that emerge from war lapse back into violence within five years. Paul Collier *et al.*, *Breaking the Conflict Trap: Civil War and Development Policy* (Washington: World Bank, 2003).

10 Paige Arthur, "How 'Transitions' Reshaped Human Rights: A Conceptual History of Transitional Justice," *Human Rights Quarterly*, vol. 31 (2009), pp. 321–67. On TJ as a form of global governance see, further, Rosemary Nagy's chapter in this volume.

11 Bruce Broomhall, *International Justice and the International Criminal Court: Between Sovereignty and the Rule of Law* (Oxford: Oxford University Press, 2004).

12 Paul Seils and Marieke Wierda, "The International Criminal Court and Conflict Mediation," *International Center for Transitional Justice Occasional Paper Series*, June 2005.

13 United Nations Secretary-General, *The Rule of Law and Transitional Justice in Conflict and Post-conflict Societies*, UN Doc. S/2004/616 (3 August 2004).

14 Rome Statute, preamble, available at <*http://untreaty.un.org/cod/icc/statute/99_corr/preamble.htm*>, accessed 12 October 2011.

15 See, further, Chandra Lekha Sriram's contribution to this volume.

16 For an excellent overview, see Richard J. Ponzio, *Democratic Peacebuilding: Aiding Afghanistan and Other Fragile States* (Oxford: Oxford University Press, 2011).

17 Gerhard Thallinger, "The UN Peacebuilding Commission and Transitional Justice," *German Law Journal*, Part I/II, 8 (2007), pp. 681–710, available at <*www.germanlawjournal.com/index.php?pageID=11&artID=843*>, accessed 12 October 2011. The literature on state-building is extensive; see, for example, Richard Caplan, *International Governance of War-Torn Territories: Rule and Reconstruction* (Oxford: Oxford University Press, 2005); Simon Chesterman, *You, The People: The United Nations, Transitional Administration, and State-Building* (Oxford: Oxford University Press, 2004); and Dominik Zaum, *The Sovereignty Paradox: The Norms and Politics of International Statebuilding* (Oxford: Oxford University Press, 2007).

18 M. Cherif Bassiouni, "Searching for Peace and Achieving Justice: The Need for Accountability," *Law and Contemporary Problems*, vol. 59 (1996), pp. 9–28.

19 United Nations Secretary-General, *The Rule of Law and Transitional Justice*, op. cit., para. 21.

20 On the limits of transitional justice vis-à-vis peacebuilding, see Wendy Lambourne, "Transitional Justice and Peacebuilding after Mass Violence," *International Journal of Transitional Justice*, vol. 3 (2009), pp. 28–48.

21 Diane Orentlicher, "Settling Accounts: The Duty to Prosecute Human Rights Violations of a Prior Regime," *Yale Law Journal*, vol. 100 (1991), pp. 2537–615. Orentlicher has subsequently partly revised her position by emphasizing the *scope* of the duty to prosecute. Diane Orentlicher, "'Settling Accounts' Revisited: Reconciling Global Norms with Local Agency," *International Journal of Transitional Justice*, vol. 1 (2007), pp. 10–22. See also Carlos Nino's reply to Orentlicher: Carlos Nino, "The Duty to Punish Past Abuses of Human Rights Put into Context: The Case of Argentina," *Yale Law Journal*, vol. 100 (1991), pp. 2619–40.

22 Leslie Vinjamuri, "Deterrence, Democracy, and the Pursuit of International Justice," *Ethics and International Affairs*, vol. 24 (2010), pp. 191–211.

23 Jack Snyder and Leslie Vinjamuri, "Trials and Errors: Principle and Pragmatism in Strategies of International Justice," *International Security*, vol. 28 (2003/04), pp. 5–44.

24 For an overview, see Oskar N. T. Thoms *et al.*, "State-level Effects of Transitional Justice: What Do We Know?" *International Journal of Transitional Justice*, vol. (2010), pp. 1–26.

25 See: Tove Grete Lie, Helga Malmin Binningsbo, and Scott Gates, "Post-Conflict Justice and Sustainable Peace," *Post-Conflict Transition Working Paper*, World Bank Policy Research Working Paper (April 2007); Eric Brahm, "Uncovering the Truth: Examining Truth Commission Success and Impact," *International Studies Perspectives*, vol. 8 (2007), pp. 16–35; Oskar N. T. Thoms, James Ron, and Roland Paris, "The Effects of Transitional Justice Mechanisms: A Summary of Empirical Research Findings and Implications for Analysts and Practitioners," *Centre for International Policy Studies Working Paper*, April 2008.

26 See, however, James Meernik, "Justice or Peace: How the International Criminal Tribunal Affects Societal Peace in Bosnia," *Journal of Peace Research*, vol. 42 (2005), pp. 271–90.

27 Payam Akhavan, "Are International Criminal Tribunals a Disincentive to Peace? Reconciling Judicial Romanticism with Political Realism," *Human Rights Quarterly*, vol. 31 (2009), pp. 624–54.

28 Thoms *et al.*, "State-level Effects," op. cit., p. 5.

29 Nicola Palmer, Phil Clark and Danielle Granville (eds.), *Critical Perspectives in Transitional Justice* (Antwerp: Intersentia, 2011).

30 Vinjamuri, "Deterrence," op. cit., p. 202.

31 Vinjamuri, "Deterrence," op. cit., p. 203.
32 In Liberia, as pointed out by Raddatz in her contribution to this volume, the capacity of the domestic legal system to try alleged perpetrators remains constrained.
33 As highlighted by García-Godos in this volume.
34 See, for example, Brown's chapter in this volume.
35 Thoms *et al.*, "State-level Effects," op. cit., p. 25.
36 Clark and Palmer, "Challenging," op. cit.
37 See, further, Roberto Gargarella, "Human Rights, International Courts and Deliberative Democracy," in Palmer, Clark and Granville (eds.), *Critical Perspectives*, op. cit.
38 Ralph Henham, "International Sentencing as a Force for Achieving Peace through Justice," in Oxford Transitional Justice Research (OTJR) (eds), *Critical Perspectives in Transitional Justice* (Antwerp: Intersentia, 2011).
39 Clark and Palmer, "Challenging," op. cit.
40 See, for example, Jo-Marie Burt, "Accountability after Atrocity in Peru: The Trial of Former President Alberto Fujimori in Comparative Perspective," in Palmer, Clark and Granville (eds.), *Critical Perspectives*, op. cit. See, more generally, Kathryn Sikkink, *The Justice Cascade: How Human Rights Prosecutions are Changing World Politics* (New York: W.W. Norton & Company, 2011).
41 See, generally, Juan Méndez, "Accountability for Past Abuses," *Human Rights Quarterly*, vol. 19 (1997), pp. 255–82.
42 Moreno Ocampo, "Transitional Justice in Ongoing Conflicts," op. cit. p. 8.
43 Ruti G. Teitel, *Transitional Justice* (Oxford: Oxford University Press, 2000).
44 Take the example of retributive and restorative forms of justice. Carolyn Hoyle argues that "[w]hile there is by no means consensus on the compatibility of restorative and retributive justice, it is clear that restorative justice (on the whole) does not necessarily reject all punitive measures associated with retributive justice and *vice versa*, and that there is more common ground between the two forms of justice than is often recognised." Carolyn Hoyle, "Can International Justice Be Restorative Justice? The role of Reparations," in Palmer, Clark and Granville (eds.), *Critical Perspectives*, op. cit.
45 See, for example, Snyder and Vinjamuri, "Trials and Errors," op. cit.
46 As Annan argued, "sovereignty implies responsibility, not just power." Kofi Annan, "Intervention," Ditchley Foundation Lecture XXXV, 1998, p. 2.
47 Jennifer Welsh, "Implementing 'The Responsibility to Protect': Where Expectations Meet Reality," *Ethics and International Affairs*, vol. 24 (2010).
48 Martha J. Finnemore and Stephen Toope, "Alternatives to 'Legalization': Richer Views of Law and Politics," *International Organization*, vol. 55 (2001), pp. 744–47.
49 Tricia D. Olsen, Leigh A. Payne, and Andrew G. Reiter, *Transitional Justice in Balance: Comparing Processes, Weighing Efficacy* (Washington: United States Institute of Peace, 2010).
50 Article 53(1)(c) of the Rome Statute expressly recognizes that a prosecutor must consider whether "taking into account the gravity of the crime and the interests of victims, there are nonetheless substantial reasons to believe that an investigation would not serve the interests of justice."
51 On this point, see further, Antoine Buyse, "Hybrid Human Rights Mechanisms in Post-conflict Transitions: The Experience of the Bosnian Human Rights Chamber" in Palmer, Clark and Granville (eds.) *Critical Perspectives*, op. cit.
52 Snyder and Vinjamuri, "Trials and Errors," op. cit.
53 Seils and Wierda, "The International Criminal Court and Conflict Mediation," op. cit.

19

Transitions in the Middle East and North Africa: new trajectories and challenges for transitional justice?

Hugo van der Merwe

Transitional justice has emerged as a body of study and practice in response to the practical challenges faced in promoting various goals during a political transition. It is, this concluding chapter argues, a contested field to which activists, social movements and political actors seek to lay claim in order to promote particular agendas. We thus have another set of competing scholars and practitioners – domestic and international – from human rights, international law, conflict resolution, peace building, public health, etc seeking to establish particular goals as priorities to be pursued in a context of rapid political flux. On the one hand, this is a disagreement about norms – what goals and values should prevail in a particular context. On the other hand, it is a debate about what is feasible – what can realistically be achieved during this window of opportunity.

In order to assess the contribution of the Middle East and North African uprisings to the trajectory of the transitional justice field, this chapter first sketches out the key developments of the field up until 2011, and attempts to explain how the field has grown out of particular transitional challenges. The continuities and shifts presented by the Middle East and North African contexts are then assessed in order to gain some understanding of how they are impacting on the meaning of transition and transitional justice.

Evolution of the field of transitional justice

The term 'transitional justice' was first coined in response to debates among scholars and human rights advocates in relation to the set of challenges faced by transitions from dictatorship to democracy in the Southern Cone of America.[1] The starkest challenge presented in these contexts was how to promote human rights in a democratising context that was still so fragile – where military authority had been replaced by democratic rulers, but where these autocratic forces still posed a threat to new democracies. The position of conventional human rights advocacy was to pursue criminal accountability; but doing so in this political context was seen as a threat to consolidating democracy. The policy debate therefore focused upon how to balance the promotion of human rights with the need to consolidate a new democracy (Arthur 2009).

The initial focus of transitional justice was thus the theory and practice of balancing prosecutions and democracy. How much prosecution is feasible – or at what stage should it be pursued? What kind of amnesties would offer the least threat to consolidating democracy? What other forms of accountability can assist in promoting human rights? A key policy alternative that emerged in the Latin American context was that of truth commissions.[2] The argument presented was that truth could serve some of the same goals as prosecutions, particularly in terms of establishing certain facts, holding perpetrators accountable in the public eye and establishing new norms. Activists, scholars and policy makers were confronted both by moral dilemmas (how much should justice and democracy be compromised?) and by practical challenges (how far can justice be pushed before there is a backlash?).

After the focus on Latin America, the transitions in Eastern Europe in the early 1990s were also drawn into the ambit of transitional justice, and the scope of mechanisms used took on additional intervention alternatives and permutations. In the context of many of these transitions the key challenge was the need to deal with deeply politicised and authoritarian institutions which dominated many aspects of public life. Transitional justice here took on a range of new permutations. Vetting, for example, emerged as a critical tool in the transitional justice toolbox to pursue accountability of a broader set of perpetrators and promote institutional transformation.

The South African Truth and Reconciliation Commission took the transitional justice debate into a new realm. While drawing on the Latin American and Eastern European experience, South African policy makers set themselves a new agenda – promoting reconciliation while balancing human rights and consolidating democracy. Recognising that the South African context of racial oppression demanded different solutions, the model used in South Africa reformulated the transitional justice challenges as something that could be packaged into a theologically inspired amnesty–truth–forgiveness–reconciliation model, which supposedly trumped the need for justice (or at least justice understood as focusing on prosecutions).

As enthusiasm for transitional justice has grown, we find it being increasingly applied in various countries emerging from violent civil war, where transitional justice has to broaden its scope even more to incorporate a larger peace-building agenda that seeks to transform society, not just reform an autocratic state. The scale of the problems is much greater, including challenges related to dealing with hundreds of thousands of victims, devastated economies, failed states and displaced populations. Transitional justice interventions now also have to take into account a new set of challenges: historical division between ethnic groups, refugee resettlement, demobilisation and reintegration of conventional armies and rebel groups, and building democratic institutions where there is little pre-existing institutional capacity or democratic tradition.

The agenda for what was to be achieved in the transition phase had thus grown to include not just human rights and democracy, but also healing, reconciliation, social reconstruction and nation building. In turn, the toolset that had emerged in a range of contexts to address an array of transitional challenges had gradually taken on the more hegemonic form of a defining framework for transitional justice practice. Instead of being a field that sought to address a set of transitional challenges, transitional justice was increasingly understood as the application of a set of predefined instruments to a context vaguely defined as transitional. Rather than asking what the goals or needs of transition are in a particular context, the question being asked had become: how does one apply prosecutions, truth commissions, vetting reparations and memorialisation mechanisms? This is still true today – thus instead of asking what Egyptians want from their transition and how that can be best secured, scholars are asking 'Does Egypt need a truth commission', or even 'What form of truth commission does Egypt need?' The debate, as a result, becomes constrained by the already-existing set of tools established in other (possibly unrelated) transitional contexts.

Another element of transitional justice that has become increasingly dominant over the last 20 years is the role of international law and, alongside this, the increasing role of the international community in promoting and facilitating particular transitional justice mechanisms. The focus on the legal framework and mechanisms guiding transitional justice is particularly illustrated by the establishment of the International Criminal Court (ICC). A more worrying aspect of this shift is the increasing use and abuse of international norms and multilateral institutions by global actors to promote regime change under the guise of protecting human rights.

Since the turn of this century, the United Nations has increasingly endorsed and promoted transitional justice and adopted many of its mechanisms. The United Nations defines transitional justice as 'the full range of processes and mechanisms associated with a society's attempts to come to terms with a legacy of large-scale past abuses, in order to ensure accountability, serve justice and achieve reconciliation' (UNSC 2004). The United Nations Development Programme (UNDP) has also developed guidelines on a range of transitional justice mechanisms, or what it calls its 'Rule of Law Toolkit' (see UNHCHR 2006).

Transitional justice was also taken up by regional bodies, such as the African Union (AU), which took on an increasing role in supporting national efforts to deal with issues of accountability and peace-building. While wary of the international justice agenda, the AU played a supporting role in transitional justice initiatives in various countries.[3]

Inevitably it became obvious that all the hype about the 'magic' of transitional justice sounded too good to be true. Could all of these goals really be achieved through the right combination and sequencing of transitional intervention tools? Scholars and practitioners have cautioned against the search for quick-fix solutions to complex challenges such as mass trauma (Weinstein 2011; Mendeloff 2009) and reconciliation (Chapman 2009). Much of the assumed knowledge of the transitional justice field (the link between truth and reconciliation, the therapeutic value of testimony, the restorative potential of public hearings, etc) has been challenged as simplistic and not transferable to other political or cultural contexts. Even assumed 'best practice' models have been increasingly questioned, such as the effectiveness of truth commissions and other transitional justice interventions in preventing the recurrence of torture (McGregor 2013).

The enthusiasm of its promoters, however, has often meant that caution is thrown to the wind. Transitional justice has in many respects become a bandwagon (Editorial Note 2013) and is being promoted by a host of international technical experts and a transitional justice industry that stands accused of prioritising its own growth rather than the delivery of benefits for affected societies (Madlingozi 2010). In Chapter 3, Habib Nassar also cautions about the danger of international actors being rapidly deployed to devise transitional justice intervention at the expense of thorough local consultations with key stakeholders. The point here is that while international resources and expertise can be very valuable, the danger of marginalising local knowledge and broad local participation as well as local priorities in the rush to secure immediate policy gains is deeply problematic.

A second, deeper set of questions that has emerged asks: What are the ultimate goals of these transitions and what should be seen as appropriate priorities in a context of political flux? Viewing transitions as contested spaces where the trajectories of change are subject to violent conflict involving a range of stakeholders means that transitional justice needs to be understood in relation to its role in furthering or mediating between particular agendas. While transitional justice potentially presents a space for fair and peaceful engagement with a contested past, it may also open up new contestations over the values that will guide a future social order.

By 2009, the field of transitional justice was clearly showing signs of dissension and fundamental strains about its legitimacy. Is it still a coherent field of study and practice (Bell 2009)? And who defines its goals and boundaries? Critical questions emerged about its links to neo-liberal agendas (Nagy 2008), whether it was in fact responsive to local victim needs (Robins 2012; Madlingozi 2010) and whether it does in fact contribute to longer-term social justice concerns (including gender justice and social inequality[4]).

Established scripts for transition – the dominant one being a liberal peace with its focus on early elections, rule of law and market reforms – are often presented as uncontested or incontestable. Transitional justice had seemingly been co-opted by a liberal agenda that prioritised market regulation, international integration and political stability. It was thus a set of tools that was often seen as more closely associated with the transfer of power between elite groups rather than transforming structures of exclusion, inequality and oppression (Gready et al. 2010).

By reflecting on the historical roots of transitional justice, some scholars pointed out its emergence in the 1980s as linked to a global context of the retreat of the Left (Arthur 2009), the Washington consensus around neo-liberal economic models and a narrow global engagement with civil-political rights rather than socio-economic concerns. As Klaus Bachmann, Robert Stewart and Kirsten Fisher point out in their contribution to this volume, the transitions in Central and Eastern European countries occurred in a particular global environment that provided an implicit framework for understanding transition goals. While the starting point for the transition trajectory is different in various contexts, there is still a very clear assumed common end-point for transitions wherever they occur.

Alongside the growth (and conflict around) the economic model consensus that underlies much of the transition debates, we have also seen the emergence of international criminal law as the dominant framework for viewing how human rights abuses should be handled. This model for framing rights and wrongs and establishing responsibility for prevention and punishment introduced complex challenges regarding how powerful countries can and should interfere in local conflicts. It also raises deeper questions about how conflict and the re-establishment of peace and justice are to be achieved. Using the law (both international and national) as a defining framework for norms and values is a potentially powerful force for correcting historical imbalances and addressing recent injustices. It is also, however, a very blunt tool that often undermines more restorative processes, overwrites traditional understandings of community cohesion and shifts power in sometimes unexpected ways. Much recent debate has thus focused on the need for transitional justice to be guided by local knowledge and priorities rather than allowing international templates to dictate practice.

Transitional justice in the Middle East and North Africa

This brings us to the Arab Spring in the Middle East and North Africa (MENA). While the situations in these countries as analysed in this volume show some similarity with other transitional contexts, they also show interesting and instructive contrasts in how transitions and transitional justice is being conceptualised.

The MENA transitional contexts reflect many of the same challenges experienced by other recent transitions, and their transitional justice debates have spawned similar policy alternatives that have also become contentious. The specific character of these transitions does, however, crystallise certain debates that will help shape and define the future boundaries and fault lines of transitional justice.

Before the Arab Spring, transitional justice in the MENA was marked by two extremes – Morocco and Sudan.[5] These cases provide interesting contrasts in the taxonomy of transitional justice. Morocco presented the first example of a truth commission in an Arab country (generally praised as a positive contribution but within a very circumscribed transitional process), and Sudan is hailed as an example of a new frontier (or a dismal failure) of international justice. Neither is a useful template for engaging with policy options to address the transitions in Libya, Tunisia and Egypt, and perhaps Syria at some point in the future.

Other transitional justice contexts may offer more parallels, but that does not mean that their transitional justice models provide obvious examples to inform policy. As argued above, transitional justice interventions should not be guided just by the nature of past abuses, but more fundamentally depend upon the transformation goals being sought. Debates about the future of MENA societies appear to be subject to more fundamental questions about the nature of a future social order. As Salloukh suggests in Chapter 1, the rules of the game of being a free people are at stake. It is indeed a 'struggle over alternative visions of the politics, moral and social orders' which calls into question the form of government and law. This is particularly relevant given the push-pull of competing visions presently playing out between advocates of political Islam and those who support liberal democracy, a point that is emphasised very strongly by Khatib in Chapter 7.

The level of contestation over the future of the new society in these countries was for many years masked by an oppressive government which presented a facade of consensus that stifled public debate. Transitional justice debates thus occur against a backdrop of deeply divided visions of where the transitions are supposed to lead. In contrast to many transitional societies where transitional justice seeks a return to democracy or is guided by a consensus or imposition of a clear political and economic framework, the MENA transitions remain subject to passionate debate and violent confrontations over the fundamental shared basis of the society.

Transitional justice processes do not enter the picture as neutral tools to achieve clearly framed objectives. As Manea aptly points out in Chapter 8, one way to make sense of transitional justice is to look at it as 'justice with an instrumental purpose' (quoting Bell and O'Rourke 2007: 24). In Chapter 9, Hanna also cautions that notions of transitional justice have informed discourses of transition (rather than vice versa). Given that transitional justice is conceived as a tool of liberal peace-building (approvingly by some authors and with scepticism by others in this volume), it is understandable that it becomes a terrain of struggle which pits different ideological approaches against each other.

Salloukh and others in this volume have also warned about the continuities that limit the scope of transition being pursued. Rather than a process of fundamental transformation of the social order, there are elements of the old order that have managed to survive and redefine themselves. In Chapter 6, Bachmann, Stewart and Fisher note that the survival of certain elites is not an uncommon phenomenon. Transitions create new opportunities and some, due to their previously privileged positions, are well placed to avoid sanction and reinvent themselves in this new environment. Just as certain groups and individuals may shed their *ancien regime* skins effectively, institutions can also survive largely unscathed. As Salloukh indicates, new political groups can take over institutions and simply replicate the previous regime's hegemonic practices (an accusation that was made against Egypt's President Morsi during his one year of rule). Institutional cultures of abuse and exclusion all too easily survive in an environment where they are subject to new, narrow political agendas. Without a clear vision for a new society, it is also not surprising that some states have retreated to the old regime's abusive practices, including the neo-liberal economic policies that many blame for the social inequalities that gave rise to mass protests in the first place.

International concepts and policy recommendations are clearly not being taken at face value by local actors. The goals, appropriate intermediaries or relevant expertise and best practices that have guided much international transitional justice is treated with more than the usual amount of scepticism by local stakeholders in these countries. It is also a context where the role of the international community is more controversial and not necessarily viewed as benign (as a result of colonial legacies in particular). The historical role and responsibility of international actors for human rights abuses and their interests in promoting particular transitional outcomes are important considerations for national transitional justice debates.

How to conceptualise and address the role of international actors in human rights abuses committed in a country dealing with transition is a critical transitional justice question that has not been effectively unpacked in other contexts. Rather than treat countries as insulated and autonomous, transitional justice needs to engage with the reality of international involvement in internal conflicts and foreign interests in how transitions are managed.

This point emerges in the Lebanese case explored by Szekely in Chapter 5, who points out the danger of being caught up in regional agendas. It is not just the historical roles of outside actors that raise concerns about foreign intervention in transitional justice policy developments, but also the future regional and international interests in the transitional outcomes. As so clearly illustrated by Szekely's analysis of Lebanon's struggle with its violent legacy, regional engagement comes with powerful strings attached and presents a double-edged sword. Alignments between local stakeholders and foreign sponsors only make this relationship much more complex and dangerous. Moreover, the intervention of the UN through the Lebanon Criminal Tribunal seems to present a continuation of this trend rather than a break with the past. In Chapter 10, Kersten's examination of the Libyan context highlights the thirst for transitional justice to bolster a sense of sovereignty that is particularly resonant against the backdrop of centuries of colonialism. Where human rights abuses committed by colonial powers were never subjected to accountability mechanisms, the transitional justice policy recommendations now presented by these ex-colonialists is understandably treated with scepticism.

The challenge of building legitimacy for international actors, particularly the UN organs, is one that is likely to face particular challenges in the MENA context. As Fisher, in Chapter 11, spells out, the legitimacy of international bodies such as the ICC and frameworks of international criminal law more generally require a better track record of intervention to prove that these constitute a fair and responsive system that can be drawn on and constructively engaged with in these contexts. Given the AU's challenge to the legitimacy of the ICC in other African contexts and the appointment of an African head prosecutor in the ICC, North Africa will provide an important testing ground for the credibility of these interventions.

Truth commissions, prosecutions and reparations programmes have increasingly sought to engage actors beyond the narrow national boundaries that conventionally shaped their jurisdiction. Given the internationalised nature of human rights abuses and exploitative economies, the artificiality of national transitional justice boundaries has been increasingly questioned (Sriram and Ross 2007). The ability of human rights abusers to secure international financial support and to hide their illegal gains outside their borders directly challenges the conventional conceptions of accountability for abuses and responsibility for reparations.

The accountability of other countries for their role in human rights abuses committed by the MENA authoritarian regimes, or in the conflict to rid the countries of these regimes, has been raised by several authors in this volume. Nassar, for instance, questions whether and how international financial institutions can be held responsible for their role in financing the exploitative policies that abused social and economic rights of citizens. The transitional justice field is yet to confront the question of foreign profits generated by investment in or through exploitative and oppressive regimes. Nassar suggests the possibility of treating loans to such regimes as 'odious debt' for which new democracies do not have a legal responsibility to repay. This presents a new boundary that governments in other contexts have been fearful of crossing when pursuing transitional justice.[6]

Foreign direct involvement in conflict (such as collaboration with state security through intelligence and extraditions, and the killing of civilians in NATO bombings in Libya, as mentioned by Fisher) are also more central to or more overtly highlighted in transitional justice debates in MENA than in previous transitional contexts. Difficult questions are being asked about how international actors can be held accountable for their actions and what type of actions should be included in such accountability. This speaks very directly to questions of accountability of more powerful international actors. Whether transitional justice is to remain a process that mainly targets the defeated side will again be tested. While transitional justice policies have sought to present themselves as impartial and inclusive, global powers have up to now generally managed to avoid scrutiny (as Reiter, in Chapter 4, shows was the case with the US role in Latin America).

Western cultural assumptions underlying certain interventions and policy recommendations are also a matter of huge concern. A fear of this cultural imperialism is legitimate in a field where international transitional justice norms have framed the problems and solutions to present a very Western and sometimes Christian ethos of individual morality, social order and understanding of the meaning of citizenship and nationhood. However, to reject transitional justice ideas as un-African or un-Islamic because of this tainted association is not intellectually feasible or productive. These challenges need to be confronted sooner or later, preferably through more locally grounded conceptualisations of the problems and solutions. As pointed out by Reiter, Bachmann, Stewart and Fisher, as well as Szekely in other regional contexts, these challenges cannot be avoided by a withdrawal into amnesia about abuses or a denial of the damage that has been done.

Many of the conventional historical transitional justice mechanisms do seem to have some relevance in the MENA context. Processes to address accountability and punishment of perpetrators of mass human rights abuses, healing and reparations for victims, reconciliation initiatives among historically divided sections of society, and institutional transformation (particularly judicial and security sector reform) are clearly applicable in these contexts. The obvious similarities make simple transfers of lessons from other contexts tempting, but the nuanced and sometimes important differences in terms of how each context shapes these processes require serious reconsideration (and even reconceptualisation) of 'best practice' models. The meaning of healing, reconciliation and even the role of public institutions can be conceptualised in very different ways depending on historical, political and cultural contexts.

These are the issues that have been prioritised in many recent transitions and which have become the conventional defining features of transitional justice or even of transition. Prioritising these concerns over others or seeing them as indicators of successful transitions, however, is highly problematic. Ultimate goals and immediate priorities need to be locally determined, particularly in contexts where other immediate safety and survival needs may be paramount (Robins 2011; Vinck and Pham 2008). The prioritisation of certain abuses over others is directly reflected in the time frame used by transitional justice mechanisms. Focusing on more recent events (as pointed out by Massagee in Chapter 2) prioritises correcting only a small sample of abuses and avoids a more systematic review of the past.

While there may be important similarities between the case studies in this volume and previous transitional justice contexts, in other respects they present important contrasts. The temptation to look at transferring lessons learned elsewhere thus needs to be treated with serious caution. Transitional justice mechanisms developed in other contexts have not provided clear answers for key concerns raised by the MENA region, such as how to deal with socio-economic rights or broader issues of social justice and systematic economic inequalities. While this has been increasingly recognised as a challenge, those who have advocated an expansion of transitional justice to include such concerns have not provided clear answers for how they can be incorporated, and transitional justice mechanisms have been slow in expanding their mandates. While he calls for an expanded mandate for transitional justice in the MENA context, Nassar questions the availability of appropriate practical models for providing such accountability and relief. The civil-political rights focus of conventional transitional justice mechanisms do not seem to lend itself to an easy expansion to incorporate this broader mandate. Processes for engaging with corruption, land redistribution and social equality have thus generally been treated as parallel concerns rather than incorporated as part of more formal transitional justice mechanisms (Powell 2010).

While some transitional justice processes have expanded their human rights agendas to include issues of corruption and land allocation,[7] the conventional approach of most transitioning states has been to view such broader justice agendas as a second stage of transition after civil-political rights are secured, treating political rights as a foundation for promoting socio-economic rights. Given the closely intertwined nature of abuses, such as corruption, with civil and political rights abuses, some have strongly argued that they need to be addressed in a more integrated manner (Carranza 2008). However, there is a growing recognition of the need to treat social inequalities and economic exploitation as systematic abuses that qualify as central transitional justice priorities in international law. Former UN High Commissioner for Human Rights, Louise Arbour (2006: 2), has argued that transitional justice:

> must reach to, but also beyond the crimes and abuses committed during the conflict which led to the transition, into the human rights violations that pre-existed the conflict and caused, or contributed to it. When making that search, it is likely that one would expose a great number of violations of economic, social and cultural rights and discriminatory practices.

The protests that ushered in the transitions in the MENA highlighted the illegitimacy of economic systems that have entrenched a wealthy elite and have left large sections of the population destitute. The centrality of these concerns challenges transitional justice to speak to this broader agenda in a more immediate manner. Ongoing popular protests that highlight the lack of progress on these issues will be difficult for transitional justice policy makers to set aside as beyond their mandate (Abou-El-Fadl 2012).

Another challenge to conventional conceptions of transitional justice is that of gender justice. Gender-based and sexual violations that occurred in the context of conflict are now firmly established as a critical component of transitional justice. How to develop mechanisms that are appropriately structured, staffed and skilled to address these violations, however, is a constant challenge that has to be faced anew in each context, and it is difficult to transfer lessons from other contexts and apply them in a situation where the patterns of abuses and the local processes of recovery and empowerment are very different. In a context where women do not have a strong voice, where systematic and structural vulnerability to future abuses are not addressed and where services for victims are driven by a patriarchal structure, these challenges are likely to require serious prioritisation and advocacy efforts.

Yet the more fundamental gender justice concerns are not clearly spelled out in conventional transitional justice approaches. If transitional justice is narrowly conceived as a process to deal only with the overt political violence of the past, it will not address the issue of structural inequalities and social norms which oppress women. In order to include a broader gender justice agenda, transitional justice would need to be conceptualised as a process that seeks to address the root causes of violence in transitioning societies.

As Manea points out, conflicts and transitions present a rupture in traditional roles for women. It presents new opportunities for political engagement that disrupt old patterns and provide a glimpse of a different future. The challenge for transitional justice is to provide spaces to consolidate change, not just a mechanism to return society to some false ideal of the past.

A related set of questions with which transitional justice has increasingly grappled relates to the challenge of deepening democracy. Rather than just expanding democracy to include the participation of women, democratic institutions and processes are themselves being questioned as insufficiently open and engaging.

While democracy is a unanimous goal, the failure of representational governance through regular elections means that such a system is increasingly challenged as an adequate space for citizens' agency in the political life of their communities. The spontaneous nature of the uprisings in many countries, and the continued upsurge of this public involvement in voicing concerns, raises questions about whether democratic elections are a sufficient arena for the public to hold representatives accountable. Particularly in a context where political parties and public institutions have been discredited, simply creating space for new parties and ensuring the fairness of elections does not appear to address the gap between the state and its citizens. Transitional justice is itself presented as a foundation of this transformation by Manea, who proposes societal trust and inclusive participation as essential elements of these processes.

The challenge is thus not only to develop transitional justice policies in a more consultative manner, but to develop policies that affirm and create arenas for citizen engagement, dialogue and empowerment beyond the traditional political spaces that have compartmentalised and sterilised political life.

Conclusion

The Arab Spring in the MENA region is clearly pushing the boundaries of transitional justice and sharpening debate about its motives, its control and its feasibility. In many ways these tensions in the transitional justice debate echo developments in other regions, but it also seems to take the debate back to its roots. Are we still looking at promoting the twin goals of democracy and human rights? While these are still held up by the various stakeholders and over-arching goals in the Arab context, the meaning given to these concepts has become more contested. Which rights are seen as absolute or priorities, and what does democracy mean in practice?

Have we come full circle? Are we returning to a point where the basic legitimacy of transitions are themselves being questioned, and where a new consensus on the meaning of economic justice and political democracy needs to be forged for transitional justice to be viewed as an appropriate intervention by all sides? Transitional justice initially emerged at a time of international political shifts, when the Cold War was cooling down and the focus had shifted to strengthening individual human rights. Has the discourse of rights and globalisation of systems of abuse shifted to the extent that this narrow focus on civil and political rights and electoral democracy has lost its ability to frame transitional aspirations? Or are we entering a new stage where transitional justice, in each of its new manifestations, takes on more ambitious transformative goals that push existing boundaries? What seems clear is that the debates in the MENA present opportunities for developing transformative justice processes which prioritise local agency, resources and participatory policy processes and challenges unequal power relations and structures of exclusion. Whether these opportunities will be acted upon remains to be seen.

Notes

1 Some scholars trace the development of transitional justice to the Nuremburg trials or even ancient times. These analyses, however, look at post-conflict justice in broader terms (usually more focused on crimes of aggression, treason and war crimes), rather than through a specific human rights lens. See, eg Huyse 2012.

2 The emergence of truth commissions set (some of) the Latin American examples apart from the European countries that also struggled with democratic transitions in the 1970s (Spain, Portugal and Greece), where similar challenges of balancing democratisation and justice produced similar debates but different solutions.

3 While initially inconsistent in its stance, the AU has also gradually developed its own principles and framework for engaging with transitional justice intervention, which promises a more coherent and engaged approach. See 'African Leadership and Ownership in Transitional Justice' 2012.

4 The lack of transformation evidenced by the continued inequality and persistence of high levels of violence in South Africa has raised serious questions about the supposed success of the truth commission in that country. See, eg Editorial Note 2013.

5 In Ch 3, Habib Nassar focuses on Morocco as well as Iraq and Algeria as important regional precedents.

6 Even after the transition to democracy in South Africa, the new government chose to honour the debts incurred by the Apartheid government.

7 For example, the Kenyan Truth, Justice and Reconciliation Commission (Truth Justice and Reconciliation Commission Act No 6 of 2008).

Bibliography

Abou-El-Fadl, Reem (2012) 'Beyond Conventional Transitional Justice: Egypt's 2011 Revolution and the Absence of Political Will', 6(2) *International Journal of Transitional Justice* 318.

'African Leadership and Ownership in Transitional Justice' (2012) 3(1 and 2) *African Governance Newsletter* 4.

Arbour, Louise (2006) 'Economic and Social Justice for Societies in Transition', 40(1) *International Law and Politics* 1.

Arthur, P. (2009) 'How Transitions Reshaped Human Rights: A Conceptual History of Transitional Justice', 31(2) *Human Rights Quarterly* 321.

Bell, C. (2009) 'Transitional Justice, Interdisciplinarity and the State of the "Field" or "Non-Field"', 3(1) *International Journal of Transitional Justice* 5.

Carranza, R. (2008) 'Plunder and Pain: Should Transitional Justice Engage with Corruption and Economic Crimes?' 2(3) *International Journal of Transitional Justice* 310.

Chapman, Audrey (2009) 'Approaches to Studying Reconciliation', in Hugo van der Merwe, Victoria Baxter and Audrey Chapman (eds), *Assessing the Impact of Transitional Justice: Challenges for Empirical Research* (USIP Press).

Editorial Note (2013) 7(1) *International Journal of Transitional Justice* 1.

Gready, P., Boesten, J., Crawford, G and Wilding, P. (2010) 'Transformative Justice

– A Concept Note', October, at http://www.wun.ac.uk/sites/default/files/transformative_justice_-_concept_note_web_version.pdf.

Huyse, L. (2012) *Transitional justice after war and dictatorship: Learning from European experiences (1945–2000)*, Centre for Historical Research and Documentation on War and Contemporary Society, CEGES-SOMA, Brussels.

McGregor, Lorna (2013) 'Transitional Justice and Torture', 7(1) *International Journal of Transitional Justice* 29.

Madlingozi, Tshepo (2010) 'On Transitional Justice Entrepreneurs and the Production of Victims', 2(2) *Journal of Human Rights Practice* 208.

Mendeloff, D. (2009) 'Trauma and Vengeance: Assessing the Psychological and Emotional Effects of Post-Conflict Justice', 31(3) *Human Rights Quarterly* 592.

Nagy, Rosemary (2008) 'Transitional Justice as Global Project: critical reflections', 29(2) *Third World Quarterly* 275.

Powell, P. (2010) 'The Role of Constitution Making and Institution Building in Furthering Peace, Justice and Development: South Africa's Democratic Transition', 4(2) *International Journal of Transitional Justice* 230.

Robins, Simon (2011) 'Towards Victim-Centred Transitional Justice: Understanding the Needs of Families of the Disappeared in Postconflict Nepal', 5(1) *International Journal of Transitional Justice* 75.

Robins, Simon (2012) 'Challenging the Therapeutic Ethic: A Victim-Centred Evaluation of Transitional Justice Process in Timor-Leste', 5(1) *International Journal of Transitional Justice* 75.

Sriram, C.L. and Ross, Amy (2007) 'Geographies of crime and justice: contemporary transitional justice and the creation of "zones of impunity"', 1(1) *International Journal of Transitional Justice* 45.

UN Security Council (2004) *The rule of law and transitional justice in conflict and post-conflict societies: Report of the Secretary-General*, 23 August,

UNSCR (2006) 'Rule-of-Law Tools for Post-Conflict States: Truth Commissions', at http://www.ohchr.org/Documents/Publications/RuleoflawTruthCommissionsen.pdf.

Vinck, P. and Pham, P. (2008) 'Ownership and Participation in Transitional Justice Mechanisms: A Sustainable Human Development Perspective from Eastern DRC', 2(3) *International Journal of Transitional Justice*, 398.

Weinstein, Harvey M. (2011) 'Editorial Note: The Myth of Closure, the Illusion of Reconciliation: Final Thoughts on Five Years as Co-Editor-in-Chief' 5(1) *International Journal of Transitional Justice* 1.

20

"Inescapable Networks of Mutuality": The Development of Transitional Justice in the United States

Abstract Having demonstrated in Chaps. 3–5 how the Greensboro Truth and Reconciliation Commission used the rhetorical mechanisms of transitional justice in an attempt to establish its authority, this chapter looks more broadly at the development of the field of transitional justice in the United States. It surveys several US-based initiatives to explore how the rhetorical tradition of transitional justice is being reaccentuated elsewhere in the country. Through this examination, it considers the place of transitional justice in liberal democracies, and it discusses the ramifications of the book's central arguments for scholars and practitioners working in the field of transitional justice.

"I love it that in my home state of North Carolina we are taking leadership from the ANC [African National Congress], from people in South Africa, and of course making it our own as we will. I believe that the death of hope is an act of violence. I hope that we re-establish a level of hope. And I think it can begin in Greensboro, I think it can spread to other places."

Si Kahn, executive director of Grassroots Leadership in Greensboro ("Testimony," 2005, p. H1)

Introduction

Advocates of the Greensboro Truth and Reconciliation Commission often championed it as "the first of its kind" in the United States (GTCRP, 2004). However, while the Commission may have been the first of its kind *in* the United States, it was not solely *of* the United States. This book has explored how the GTRC drew upon the rhetorical tradition of transitional justice—a tradition with roots outside of the United States—to garner the authority to bring about change in Greensboro. In making this claim, I do not mean to suggest that the Commission did not rely on other rhetorical traditions in its bids for authority; it certainly did.[1] However, the GTRC's authorization was bound up, in significant ways, with the discursive practices of the SATRC and the ICTJ—organizations whose members included Desmond Tutu, Bongani Finca, Lisa Magarrell, Peter Storey, Louis Bickford, and Pricilla Hayner.

Chapter 1 of this book provided an overview of these arguments and contextualized them historically, socio-politically, and theoretically. Chapter 2 made the case that the field has, in fact, given rise to a rhetorical tradition, and it surveyed the work of other scholars to highlight some of the prominent features of that tradition at the level of word, argument, and genre: the ideograph of reconciliation (and its relationship to other important terms, such as *ubuntu*), the *ethos* of representivity and unrepresentivity, and the genre of the final report. Chapters 3–5 then demonstrated how the GTRC and its advocates reaccentuated those features in Greensboro. More specifically, Chap. 3 explored Bongani Finca's performance of *ubuntu* in his speech

[1] This book has focused primarily on the ways in which the GTCRP and GTRC reaccentuated the rhetorical resources of past truth commissions—and, in particular, of the SATRC. There were, however, other rhetorical traditions circulating in Greensboro during the operation of the GTRC, not all of which were consistent with those of the rhetorical tradition of transitional justice. As Murphy (1997) noted of rhetorical traditions more generally, "[T]here are layered and dissonant voices within and between traditions. Traditions 'speak' to each other and to pressing problems of the day. No one tradition can finalize the world or itself" (p. 73). Thus, one possible avenue for future research would be to consider the interplay between various traditions and how the GTCRP and GTRC orchestrated them (p. 74). Such work would benefit from a sustained exploration of the ways in which the GTCRP and GTRC drew upon the rhetorical traditions surrounding the civil rights movement, the practices of civil religion in the United States, and the research practices of the academy. It might also consider whether or not the reaccentuation of these traditions amplified or attenuated the effects of the rhetorical tradition of transitional justice.

at the GTRC's Swearing In and Seating Ceremony, which functioned to endorse the commissioners and position them as authorities in the community. Chapter 4 showed that the GTRC, like the SATRC before it, constructed its organizational *ethos* in two, seemingly incongruous ways throughout its operation: as both representative and unrepresentative of the Greensboro community. This *ethos* allowed commissioners to seek widespread public support even as it suggested that the Commission was a model for community members to follow. As Chap. 5 demonstrated, not all members of the community were receptive to the Commission. In the introduction of their *Final Report*, commissioners used Pricilla Hayner's widely accepted definition of "truth commissions" to position themselves alongside past truth commissions and lend credibility to their narrative about systemic racism in Greensboro.

In the present chapter, I begin by considering what my findings suggest about the development of transitional justice in the United States and in other liberal democracies. To illustrate how the field is developing in these contexts, I survey several US-based initiatives. Following this survey, I discuss the ramifications of the book's central arguments for scholars and practitioners working in the field of transitional justice, and I suggest how these stakeholders might use rhetorical knowledge to promote transitional justice more effectively elsewhere.

The Shape of the Rhetorical Tradition in the United States

To date, most of the world's TRCs have operated in emerging democracies and have enjoyed state-sponsored support. Because the TRC model has relied on a centralized authority structure, the rhetorical tradition of transitional justice has been propagated, in large part, by state spokespersons and tied, unsurprisingly, to the state interests of the emerging democracies.[2] However, in the United States and other countries where democracies are already in place, TRCs have not gained nearly as much traction at the national level. One plausible reason for this is that the goals of political reconciliation offered by TRCs are, as Daniel Philpott (2006) has pointed out, often seen as incompatible with the values of liberalism (pp. 11–44).

Philpott (2006) listed several reasons why the two are often seen as incompatible. For one thing, many view political reconciliation as inconsistent with the notion that criminals should be punished for their crimes. Mechanisms of political reconciliation, such as TRCs, typically do not provide accountability in the form of punishment, or they suggest that criminals should be punished in ways that vary from the punishment practices of the liberal tradition (p. 26). Another reason political reconciliation and liberalism are often seen as incompatible is because the former—and all it entails, including forgiveness, repentance, etc.—is viewed as an "improper concern of the state" (p. 27). The tradition of liberalism demarcates "spheres of activity in

[2] As Salazar (2002) illustrated with respect to the SATRC, the work of TRCs is often implicated in projects of nation building and democratization.

which the state is not to interfere"; and reconciliation, with its ties to personal belief, is one of those spheres (p. 27). A third, more practical reason that Philpott mentioned is that calls for political reconciliation do not guarantee social unity: if the public views attempts at political reconciliation as unsuccessful or as "depriving victims of their due," then "it will regard political reconciliation as a drain on the legitimacy of the new regime" (p. 34).

Despite these reasons, some scholars have claimed that political reconciliation and liberalism could be made more compatible, although, as Jonathan VanAntwerpen (2010) highlighted, there are different perspectives about how best to do so (pp. 41–45). One perspective surveyed by VanAntwerpen—which was put forward by Amy Gutmann and Dennis Thompson (2000)—is that the answer lies in rejecting conceptions of reconciliation that understand it to mean "comprehensive social harmony" and that expect "an entire society to subscribe to a single comprehensive moral perspective"—which Gutmann and Thompson described as "an illiberal aim" and "deeply undemocratic" (as cited in VanAntwerpen, 2010, p. 41). The other perspective VanAntwerpen surveyed—which was advanced by Daniel Philpott (2006)—is that what is required for greater compatibility is not a thinner account of reconciliation but "a reconfiguration of widely held liberal understandings of democratic deliberation and public reason, a rethinking of liberal theory prompted by both the promise and the challenge associated with political theologies of reconciliation" (as cited in VanAntwerpen, 2010, p. 45).

Given the challenges facing both of these approaches, a national truth and reconciliation in the United States seems to me somewhat unlikely. However, as the work of the Greensboro Truth and Reconciliation Commission illustrated, the apparent incompatibility between liberalism and political reconciliation has not closed off all possibilities for the development of the field of transitional justice in the country. I would argue, moreover, that the case of the GTRC provides an indication of how the field might continue to develop, both in the United States and in other liberal democracies. Some of the GTRC's defining features included the following: it operated independently of government authority; it developed through grassroots means and community-based partnerships; it received support from NGOs (such as the ICTJ) and philanthropic organizations (such as the Andrus Family Fund); and it drew upon the rich rhetorical resources of past truth commissions. These features of the Greensboro initiative suggest that, in the United States and other liberal democracies, the field of transitional justice will be much more decentralized. Rather than looking solely to the government for support, future truth-seeking initiatives will likely find their support in a developing transnational network of local stakeholders, non-governmental organizations, and those affiliated with past transitional justice initiatives. This network will likely take the place of the nation-state as the primary means of TRC authorization, and—to the extent that new TRC initiatives gain traction—it will foster the proliferation and development of the rhetorical tradition of transitional justice in these contexts and beyond.

Recent truth-seeking initiatives in the United States help to substantiate these claims about the development of the field. In what follows, I provide brief sketches of several of these initiatives, some of which are ongoing: the Mississippi

Truth Project (MTP), the Maine Tribal-State Child Welfare Truth and Reconciliation Commission (METRC), the Metropolitan Detroit Truth and Reconciliation Commission on Racial Inequality (DTRC), the Liberian Truth and Reconciliation Commission Diaspora Project (LTRC), and two short-term truth commissions that addressed poverty-related issues. While these examples are not, of course, sufficient to provide a comprehensive picture of the field of transitional justice in the United States, they do offer an indication of the ways that the field is developing, particularly in relation to the authorization of the TRC mechanism.[3]

The Mississippi Truth Project

The Mississippi Truth Project has stated that its origins are a 2005 open letter from Rita Bender—the widow of murdered civil rights worker Michael Schwerner—to Mississippi Governor Haley Barbour, challenging him on his belief that the recent conviction of her husband's killer "closed the books on the crimes of the civil rights years, and that we all should now have 'closure'" ("Timeline of the MTP," n.d., para. 2). In response to Bender's letter, a diverse group of individuals formed the Mississippi Coalition for Racial Justice, aimed at promoting statewide conversations about race. Two years later, the Coalition began to consider the prospects of a statewide truth and reconciliation commission, and eventually created the MTP—the goal of which would be to establish the Mississippi Truth and Reconciliation Commission (para. 9). Since that time, the MTP has written, revised, and circulated a Declaration of Intent for the Commission (para. 12–15); applied for and received funding; hired and trained part-time staff members (para. 13); and begun collecting oral histories from individuals around the state (para. 27, 29, 31–32). It is hoped that the yet-to-be-formed Commission, along with the ongoing work of the project, will "create a culture of truth telling that will bring to light racially motivated crimes and injustices committed in Mississippi between 1945 and 1975" ("What is the MTP," n.d., para. 1).

Like the Greensboro initiative, the MTP began as a grassroots operation. It is telling that, instead of receiving a charge and support from the State of Mississippi, the initiative was born in response to the governor's claims. As a grassroots operation, the MTP has been garnering authority through local engagement: its statewide oral

[3] Given the scope and focus of this book, I have chosen to limit my survey to initiatives that include the words "truth project," "truth commission," or "truth and reconciliation commission" in their titles. There have, of course, been other types of transitional justice initiatives as well. For example, in "A Sampling of Truth-seeking Projects in the United States," Magarrell (n.d.) compiled a list that included—but was not limited to—national inquiries (e.g., the Commission on Wartime Relocation and Internment of Civilians and the Tuskegee Syphilis Study Ad Hoc Advisory Panel to the Assistant Secretary for Health and Scientific Affairs), state inquiries (e.g., the Oklahoma Commission to Study the Tulsa Race Riot of 1921 and the 1898 Wilmington Race Riot Commission), and academic inquiries (e.g., the Brown University Steering Committee on Slavery and Justice). Such initiatives are a fertile ground for future study.

history project and Welcome Table initiative—which aims to promote dialogue about race among members of diverse communities ("Welcome Table," n.d.)—serve as a means of raising awareness and support for its work, in addition to fostering its long-term goals. The MTP has also garnered authority by identifying itself with the civil rights movement. In July 2007, for example, the initiative received endorsements from "[c]ivil rights veterans and scholars of the civil rights movement" to establish a truth and reconciliation commission ("Timeline of the MTP," n.d., para. 8).

More importantly for my purposes, the initiative has been connected with the network of support that helped authorize—and now includes—the GTRC. The MTP's website, for example, includes a video endorsement from Archbishop Emeritus Desmond Tutu ("MTP Partners," n.d.), as well as many resources from the International Center for Transitional Justice ("Basic Information," n.d.). The website also includes links to a documentary about the GTRC by filmmaker Adam Zucker, along with a guide—produced in partnership with both the ICTJ and the Andrus Family Fund—for facilitating discussion about the film ("MTP Partners," n.d.). In April of 2008, representatives from the GTRC attended a meeting of the MTP ("Timeline of the MTP," n.d., para. 11), and, in late 2009, the Reverend Peter Storey—who served as Nelson Mandela's prison chaplain and was involved in the Greensboro initiative—met with MTP stakeholders to discuss the project (para. 23). Through these individuals, documents, and media, the rhetorical tradition of transitional justice has again been reaccentuated. To give just one example, it is clear that the MTP has worked to establish an *ethos* of representivity. The project's members have noted that they are "composed of leadership from diverse faith and social communities and organizations" (para. 3). At one point during their operation, they even sought to reinforce their claim to representivity by becoming more inclusive in terms of youth participation. In one of the entries on their timeline, they wrote, "Aware of an absence of youth participation, the Coalition reaches out to the Jim Hill Civil Rights/Civil Liberties Club (CRCL)—consisting of students from Jim Hill High School, Murrah High School, and St. Andrew's Episcopal School" (para. 5).

Maine Tribal-State Child Welfare Truth and Reconciliation Commission

In addition to the MTP, there is currently an initiative underway in the State of Maine to establish a TRC to address injustices committed against people indigenous to the region: members of the Wabanaki tribes. Leaders and supporters of the Maine initiative have traced the origin of the injustices against the tribes to the arrival of Europeans in the fifteenth century ("History & Background," n.d., para. 1). Since that time, 16 of 20 Wabanaki tribes have been destroyed (para. 1), resulting in "a 90-percent population depletion since first contact with Europeans" (Attean & Williams, 2011, para. 8). More recently, in the 1950s and 1960s, the Indian Adoption

Project relocated children from their families by placing them in the foster care system (para. 10). Esther Attean and Jill Williams (2011)—who are both involved in the initiative—have noted, "In Maine, Wabanaki children were removed from their homes and communities at a per-capita rate 19 times higher than that of non-Native children. Agencies in charge of child protection often removed children first and asked questions later, if they asked questions at all. Many tribal members lived in fear of losing their children" (para. 10). While the initiative's leaders have admitted that there has been some progress to address these issues—such as the 1978 Indian Child Welfare Act—they have also observed that "Maine's child welfare history continues to impact Wabanaki children and families today" ("History & Background," n.d., para. 3).

Like the MTP, the Maine initiative is a grassroots operation—a point which Attean and Williams (2011) emphasized by contrasting it with other TRCs; they wrote, "[U]nlike other official truth commission projects in the Americas that were conceived of and instituted by high-level politicians, this one is being initiated and planned by a group of Indigenous women working in and around the child welfare system, some of whom were taken from our families by the state as children" (para. 3). Support for the project has been garnered, in part, from the existing Wabanaki tribes and from the Maine Indian Tribal-State Commission. Once again, however, support has also come from the transnational network of those working in the field of transitional justice. Like the GTRC and MTP, the Maine initiative received funding from the Andrus Family Fund, and Jill Williams—who works with the fund and is assisting those in Maine—was the executive director of the GTRC. The initiative's website also mentioned the "guidance and support" that it has received from the ICTJ ("TRC Partners & Supporters," n.d., para. 9–10).

The Maine initiative's distance from the state—and its reliance on the field of transitional justice for support—may be more directly tied to its ultimate goals than was the case for the GTRC or the MTP. For those currently working on the project, some of the key goals include "developing a new type of relationship between the state and the tribes, as well as deepening a sense of autonomy and self-determination within the Native communities" (Attean & Williams, 2011, para. 21). To begin to achieve these goals, stakeholders have been reaccentuating the rhetorical tradition of transitional justice—particularly through the use of the ideograph reconciliation. For instance, Williams and Attean wrote, "While the reconciliation-related goals of other truth commissions have largely been about finding ways for Indigenous and non-Indigenous people to live together on the same land without violence, the reconciliation goals in Maine run deeper" (para. 21). In this passage, Williams and Attean invoked the term "reconciliation"; however, they chose not to define the term as "peaceful co-existence." Instead, they reaccentuated the term to advance the goal of decolonization: "[W]hile we use the term 'reconciliation' to describe the effort, we see the commission as a piece of a larger effort towards decolonization, undoing the centuries of harms inflicted upon the Wabanaki people" (para. 7). In other words, the ideograph reconciliation, for the Maine initiative, has been used in an attempt to bring about the restoration of national autonomy.

Metropolitan Detroit Truth and Reconciliation Commission on Racial Inequality

The Metropolitan Detroit Truth and Reconciliation Commission on Racial Inequality was impaneled in November of 2011 to investigate "racial oppression of people of color by individuals, structures and institutions" in Detroit and Southeast Michigan (Michigan Roundtable for Diversity & Inclusion [MRDI], 2011a, p. 1). As the DTRC's charter has highlighted, this oppression has caused economic and wage disparities, fewer employment opportunities, higher poverty rates, more restricted access to education and health care, higher incidences of illness, and lower life expectancies (p. 2). To seek the truth about racial oppression and begin to address the many associated problems, the nine-member DTRC will engage both individuals and institutions, inviting them to bear witness to the injustices and to address "their own individual histories of conscious or unconscious perpetuation of patterns of racial privilege and oppression" (p. 3). Like other TRCs, the DTRC will conclude its work by issuing findings and making recommendations about ways to address the past and to create a better future (p. 3).

There are several ways in which the DTRC initiative has already reaccentuated the rhetorical tradition of transitional justice. The initiative's website, for example, notes, "This model of a Truth and Reconciliation Commission is based upon similar efforts around the world, most notably in South Africa, and Greensboro, North Carolina" (MRDI, 2011b, para. 5). Additionally, the organization's charter begins with the motto "Without Truth, no Healing; without Forgiveness, no Future" (MRDI, 2011a, p. 1)—drawing upon the common sayings of past truth commissions and, more specifically, upon the title of Desmond Tutu's (1999) book *No Future without Forgiveness*. Furthermore, Desmond Tutu's daughter Naomi Tutu gave the keynote address at the Commission's impaneling ceremony.

The Detroit initiative also reaccentuated the rhetorical tradition of transitional justice in and through its mandate—which drew upon much of the language of GTRC's mandate. The GTRC's mandate began as follows:

> There comes a time in the life of every community when it must look humbly and seriously into its past in order to provide the best possible foundation for moving into a future based on healing and hope. Many residents of Greensboro believe that for this city, the time is now. (GTCRP, 2003, p. 1)

The Detroit initiative's mandate echoed much of this language:

> There comes a time in the life of every community when it must look honestly and seriously into its past in order to provide the best possible foundation for moving into a future based on healing and hope; a future that is consistent with the United States of America's founding promise of equality and opportunity for all. (MRDI, 2011a, p. 1)

The GTRC's mandate, which began and ended with references to the Commission's timeliness, helped establish an opening, an opportunity, for the initiative and suggested its necessity. Beginning with the phrase "There comes a time" and ending with "opportunity for all," the Detroit initiative's mandate utilized language from the Greensboro mandate to establish a similar opening; however, it marshaled this opportunity for a slightly different goal—namely, to promote equality. The mandate endings shared much as well. The GTRC mandate read:

> The passage of time alone cannot bring closure, nor resolve feelings of guilt and lingering trauma, for those impacted by the events of November 3, 1979. Nor can there be any genuine healing for the city of Greensboro unless the truth surrounding these events is honestly confronted, the suffering fully acknowledged, accountability established, and forgiveness and reconciliation facilitated. (GTCRP, 2003, p. 2)

The DTRC's mandate made similar claims:

> Truth and Reconciliation will begin when individuals and institutions come together in a spirit of honest reflection to promote racial justice and equality. The passage of time alone cannot cure these ills. There can only be genuine healing for the residents of Detroit and Southeast Michigan when the truth surrounding the structural causes and consequences of racial privilege and oppression are honestly confronted and understood, the suffering caused by such inequality fully acknowledged and forgiveness and reconciliation facilitated. (MRDI, 2011a, p. 6)

In these passages, there was an emphasis on the ways that healing does and does not come about. Both mandates suggested that what is necessary to bring about change is a *kairotic* moment—a moment of opportunity or crisis. To temper the force of what was a potentially threatening notion for some audience members, both mandates employed the passive voice to make these claims.

There were, moreover, less explicit examples of reaccentuation, of which I will only mention one. During the Commission's impaneling ceremony, members of the Detroit initiative constructed the *ethos* of the DTRC in ways that reaccentuated the *ethos* established for the GTRC. In their oath, the commissioners were asked to pledge to do their work without bias or prejudice—thereby establishing their objectivity (Michiganroundtable, 2011). But they were also positioned in terms of representivity. Peter Hammer, the director for the Damon J. Keith Center for Civil Rights, introduced the commissioners as follows:

> I think you are already getting the sense of how powerful they are, and the hope throughout this entire process is that each one of you can see parts of yourselves in each one of them, and that—conversely—each one of them represents a different part of our communities, and—collectively—I think you can see the power and the wisdom that this commission is going to bring in terms of their life experience. (Michiganroundtable, 2011)

In these remarks, Hammer began by calling attention to the issue of authority, claiming that the commissioners were "powerful." According to Hammer, this power was grounded in a two-fold representivity: the commissioners represented individual residents of Detroit and Southeast Michigan, and they represented different parts of the region. Like the *ethos* constructed for the GTRC, the *ethos* constructed for the DTRC both distanced commissioners from the community and aligned them with the community, setting them up to accomplish different facets of a complex mandate.

Liberian Truth and Reconciliation Commission Diaspora Project

One of the most striking examples of a truth commission that has operated in the United States is the Liberian Truth and Reconciliation Commission. Liberia formed a Truth and Reconciliation Commission in 2005; and, while Liberia's political history is too complex to adequately recount here, a few remarks about this history are necessary to understand what the LTRC has to do with the development of transitional justice in the United States. Liberia was originally established in the 1820s by the American Colonization Society as a colony for freed African-American slaves. These Americo-Liberians settlers, as they came to be called, established their country's independence in 1847. However, like most colonial narratives, this one involved conflict and marginalization of peoples: the West-African region that would become Liberia was not unoccupied when it was settled by the Americo-Liberians, and the history of Liberia from the middle of the nineteenth century to the end of the twentieth century involved a series of conflicts between the indigenous Liberians (who made up the vast majority of the Liberian population) and the Americo-Liberians. The latter controlled Liberia for much of the twentieth century, and they often imposed their cultural beliefs on the former. However, in 1980, a military coup, led by indigenous Liberians, gave way to a shift in political power. The new leadership took a more authoritarian approach to governing than the previous regime, and two civil wars followed, lasting from 1989 to 1996 and from 1999 to 2003 (Dunn-Marcos, Kollehlon, Ngovo, & Russ, 2005, p. 4). It has been estimated that, during these wars, over two hundred thousand people were killed and hundreds of thousands were displaced from their homes (p. 2). In response to these forced displacements, the United States developed a resettlement program for Liberian refugees. More than 24,000 Liberians have traveled to the United States since 1989 (p. 1).

The authoritarian government was ousted in 2003, and a transitional government was formed in the country, leading to peaceful, democratic elections in 2005. Following the elections, President Ellen Johnson-Sirleaf called for the establishment of a truth and reconciliation commission to address the mass atrocities committed in the country; and, on May 12, 2005, the Liberian National Transitional Legislative Assembly (NTLA) established the LTRC. Its aim was to investigate "gross human rights violations and violations of international humanitarian law as well as abuses that occurred, including massacres, sexual violations, murder, extrajudicial killings and economic crimes, such as the exploitation of natural or public resources to perpetuate armed conflicts, during the period January 1979 to October 14, 2003" (NTLA, 2005, sect. 4a).

What is important for my purposes is the fact that the truth-seeking process was not limited to those living within Liberia but was extended to include displaced Liberians. The non-governmental organization Minnesota Advocates for Human Rights (MAHR) partnered with the LTRC to collect statements from Liberians living in the United States and elsewhere (MAHR, n.d.).[4] Statement-taking began in

[4]The Minnesota Advocates for Human Rights also collected statements in the United Kingdom and in Ghana.

Minnesota in 2006, and statements were subsequently collected from Liberians living in other US cities, including Atlanta, Chicago, New York, Newark, Philadelphia, Providence, and Washington (Barry, 2007; MAHR, n.d.).

The case of the LTRC highlighted another way that the field of transitional justice may develop in the United States. In this case, the US-based non-governmental organization gathering testimony had even stronger international ties than the GTRC did; its authority was warranted, in large measure, by the Liberian government. Despite this difference with the GTRC, the case of the LTRC confirmed the importance of transnational affiliations in the authorization of transitional justice endeavors in the United States. If political reconciliation proves to be incompatible with liberalism in the country, the US may see a growing number of TRCs that operate inside its borders but are authorized from without.

Poverty Truth Commissions

Two additional, short-term truth commissions were formed to address questions of poverty in the United States, and these truth commissions, too, speak to the importance of transnational affiliations as a means of authorization. From July 15 to 17, 2006, the Poor People's Economic Human Rights Campaign (PPEHRC) held a 3-day truth commission in Cleveland, Ohio, attended by over 500 people. The Commission's website noted that it was "modeled after similar commissions in Africa and Latin America" and that it "brought people from all across the USA and the world to bring to light the actual suffering and economic human rights violations that many Americans endure on a daily basis" (PPEHRC, 2006). The Commission was comprised of both domestic and international commissioners—one of which was South African Winnie Mandela. In addition to the PPEHRC's truth commission, a smaller poverty truth commission was organized by Union Theological Seminary in New York City on April 13, 2007. The day-long truth commission was, according to its website, "inspired by the Truth and Reconciliation work done in places such as South Africa and Peru" and "based on the United Nations' Universal Declaration of Human Rights" (Poverty Initiative, 2007). As the truth commissions' websites highlighted, both of the initiatives drew upon the resources of the field of transitional justice. In fact, one of the commissioners at Union Theological Seminary's Poverty Truth Commission was Nelson Johnson, who helped organized the November 3, 1979 rally in Greensboro and was later instrumental in forming the GTRC.

Implications for Scholars and Practitioners of Transitional Justice

The findings in this book—and, more specifically, the claims about the development of the field of transitional justice in the United States—have implications for scholars and practitioners of transitional justice. This penultimate section of the book highlights some of these implications, with the hope that those working in the field of transitional justice might be able to draw upon my work in their future endeavors. The implications sketched in the next section attest to the value of attending, with care, to the rhetorical activity surrounding truth commissions and other mechanisms of transitional justice.

Implications for Scholars Studying Transitional Justice

There has been a tendency, in the study of truth commissions, to conceptualize these institutions as national projects that operate, largely, in and through the civil society of a given country. For example, Hayner (2001) surveyed twenty-one truth commissions in *Unspeakable Truths*, and she arranged her descriptions of these truth commissions by the country in which they were instituted. Given that most truth commissions are instituted by national governments, such divisions are not surprising. However, what these divisions elide, and what my study has brought into relief is the importance of transnational forces in the development and authorization of truth commissions. While I do not mean to suggest that all past truth commissions relied on international affiliations to the extent that the GTRC did (although many certainly may have), I think there is a need among scholars studying truth commissions—including those studying national commissions—to pay greater attention to the transnational forces that have given rise to and sustained these institutions. Such a research agenda may be generative in furthering our understanding about how truth commissions work (or don't work) as political and social tools to bring about change.

The need for a more thorough account of the ways that transnational forces have given rise to and sustained truth commissions is predicated, in part, on the emergence of a global civil society. Civil society has typically been defined as the sector of society comprised of voluntary groups and organizations—which include, but are not limited to, religious institutions, trade unions, mass media, and political parties—that are not controlled by the government. It has been understood to provide some protections against the interests of the state even as it frequently serves state interests. In recent years, however, expanded and enhanced networks of communication have developed, which have given rise to "an interweaving and strengthening of ties between multiple civil societies" (DeChaine, 2005, p. 5). The result has been the development of what some are calling global civil society—the societal sphere comprised of multiple civil societies that are interconnected by common values and interests, often across geographical spaces and nationally defined territories. As D. Robert DeChaine's (2005) work on humanitarian NGOs has highlighted, global civil society offers a viable source of political authority for non-governmental actors (like those who founded the GTRC as well as the commissioners themselves), and the political authority garnered through global civil society may serve to further attenuate the authority of the nation-state. DeChaine has written, "'Through its circumnavigation of political boundaries, the transnational social forces that make up global civil society 'undermine states' monopoly of legitimate authority over a territorially defined populace, which is one of the central ideas of sovereignty'" (p. 6).[5] This undermining of the "legitimate authority"—the sovereignty—of the nation-state means that, for some members of the state, "global identifications begin to displace, and sometimes override, national ones" (p. 30).[6] Authority is thereby redistributed so that "national governments are increasingly sharing traditionally sovereign powers with nonstate actors, signifying a weakening of state powers in relation to national autonomy" (p. 50). (Take, as just one example from my study, Bongani Finca's attempts at the Swearing In and Seating Ceremony to establish global identifications between the people of Greensboro and the people of South Africa. While it is unlikely that Finca's remarks alone overrode the audience's national identifications, they, together with the many other global identifications established through the truth commission process, may have attenuated some individuals' alignments with the city and strengthened alignments with the Commission.) To avoid looking at international forces in the study of the development of truth commissions is to risk missing important ways in which these institutions act in their communities and nations.

We should, then, focus on truth commissions not simply as national projects operating in civil society but also as transnational phenomena that operate in and through global civil society. DeChaine's (2005) conceptualization of NGOs has provided an excellent model for how we might begin to think about truth commissions, at least as they are emerging in the United States context. For DeChaine, the emphasis on NGOs as "monolithic organizational 'structures'" has been problematic, insofar as it has presupposed that such organizations are isolated from one another and has obscured the "ever-shifting currents, nonlinear interconnections and interimbrications, and often less than tangible imaginative energies" between them (p. 155). To address this problem, DeChaine, referencing Arjun Appadurai's notion of "new neighborliness," recommended reconceptualizing NGOs as "shifting flows of people, ideas, resources, and most of all, power"—an act of definition that DeChaine claimed would allow scholars to better attend to the ways in which resources, both material and non-material, travel in and among organizations (p. 155). Studying truth commissions not as monolithic organizational structures but as shifting flows of resources may help us better understand how they function as social tools—and, perhaps more importantly, how they might function as *more effective* social tools—to redress inequalities. Moreover, to the extent that the interconnections that DeChaine mentioned are discursively constructed (as many of them are), there is an ongoing need to attend to the rhetorical activity surrounding transitional justice initiatives.

The bulk of *Remaking Transitional Justice in the United States* has focused on *ethos*, the subject position constructed by and for the GTRC through discourse. Future research might unpack other aspects of the rhetorical tradition surrounding truth commissions, including its characteristic commonplaces, appeals to *pathos*

[5]DeChaine quoted Deibert (1998, p. 35) here.

[6]DeChaine quoted Hall (1992, p. 302) here.

and *logos*, genres, and figures of speech and thought. In describing the rhetorical tradition surrounding truth commissions in more detail, such research promises to offer communities a much more robust model for action, both at and below the institutional level. Communities and countries looking to institute truth commissions would, I think, find it exceedingly valuable to have detailed descriptions not simply of typical committee structures and their functions but of the genre conventions of public hearings and final reports; the characteristic commonplaces employed by truth commissions (e.g., "bygones will not be bygones" or "the truth makes free"); the reoccurring ideographs (e.g., truth, reconciliation, *ubuntu*); the common appeals to *ethos*, *pathos*, and *logos*; and other distinctive rhetorical moves. Ultimately this research might enable communities to take up the rhetorical tradition of transitional justice in new ways.

Implications for Practitioners of Transitional Justice

To other communities and individuals looking to address past violence or injustices, this book highlights the importance of establishing affiliations outside of the community in order to garner the authority to act—i.e., the importance of working in and through global civil society to bring about change. A second, and no less significant, thing at stake here for practitioners of transitional justice is the way in which they conceptualize how truth commissions—and, by extension, other forms of transitional justice—function as models for other countries and communities.

There has been a tendency among those who advocate for (and those who study) truth commissions to describe them as models at the structural or institutional level. For example, Elizabeth Kiss (2000) noted that it is the "institutional repertoire of truth commissions [that] may be helpful in developing innovative approaches to a variety of moral and political challenges" (p. 92). Furthermore, to the extent that truth commissions have been conceptualized as models for action, there has been a tendency to focus on the large-scale, pragmatic policies implemented by truth commissions, such as amnesty, reparations, etc. While these tendencies have not been unproductive, they may have given short shrift to some of the other ways that truth commissions have functioned as models.

What has often been elided in the current model talk surrounding truth commissions are the patterned ways of using language, the figurative and argumentative devices, and the genres—all of which may be used as *rhetorical* models for subsequent rhetorical performances. In bringing into relief the ways in which the rhetorical tradition surrounding truth commissions has been reaccentuated in a new context, *Remaking Transitional Justice in the United States* has served to complement the emphasis on truth commissions as institutional models or models of large-scale policy: it has suggested that truth commissions also provide countries, communities, and individuals with models of rhetorical action at the level of discourse, clause, and even grammar. In making explicit the different ways that the GTRC and GTCRP constructed the tension between representivity and unrepresentivity, this study may better allow subsequent truth commissions to use these subject positions strategically as they work to establish broad community support. While I am not advocating that subsequent truth commissions make rhetorical moves identical to those of the GTRC, my findings suggest that members of future truth commissions may benefit from paying careful attention to the figurative and argumentative devices of past commissions.

Furthermore, in some cases it may actually be more effective to perform facets of the rhetorical tradition of transitional justice without establishing a truth commission at the institutional level. As Magarrell and Wesley (2008) have noted, implementing a truth commission is not easily accomplished, and it is not "always appropriate" given the context (p. 242). Truth commissions require considerable financial resources, as well as volunteers who are willing to give of their time and energies, often without compensation. Moreover, establishing these institutions to "dig up" the past is likely to engender resistance—and even open hostility—from various sectors of the community. Given these constraints, communities might choose to perform *one* of the many genres of truth commissions (e.g., they might hold a one-day discussion to address a particular concern). Or they might reaccentuate aspects of the rhetorical tradition in novel institutional configurations (e.g., they might facilitate a working group, comprised of representatives from different sectors of the community, to investigate racial or economic inequities and offer recommendations to the city government).

These suggestions are not inconsistent with recent calls for truth and reconciliation in the United States.[7] For instance, in her call for the use of truth and reconciliation processes to address the history of lynching in the United States, Sherrilyn Ifill (2007) spoke to the variety of institutional forms that truth and reconciliation processes may take:

> Without question, conversations within communities about racial violence will have to take many forms. Some discussions may take the form used by the Truth and Reconciliation Commission in South Africa, in which witnesses come forward to give written or oral statements to a group of commissioners. In other instances, a form of town hall meeting may be appropriate. But productive conversations on race must provide opportunities for community members—black and white—to…talk to one another. (p. 152)

In addition to the town hall, another form for performing the rhetorical tradition of transitional justice that Ifill proposed was community conferencing, which she described as "facilitated discussion that enables those who have been 'affected by behavior that has caused serious harm' to work together to find solutions and to repair harm" (p. 151). Similarly, Southern Truth and Reconciliation—an organization to which Ifill belonged and served on the advisory board—advocated for truth and reconciliation forums—one of "a 'menu of options' from which constituent communities might discover and develop their own ideas for community-building events, programs and activities to promote restorative justice, healing, and dialogue"

[7]Moreover, as Gready (2011) noted, instead of trying to negotiate multiple genres and methodologies, privileging "one genre tributary or form of truth" may help ensure that a truth commission's products are not "fragmentary and mutually undermining" (p. 56).

(Southern Truth & Reconciliation, 2007). Kiss (2000) proposed yet another alternative form: the short-term public hearing. Such a hearing would incorporate "some of the institutional aspects of a truth commission" and could offer members of broken communities the opportunity "to air grievances, educate the public, offer reparations, and create opportunities to move forward in a spirit of reconciliation" (p. 93). Each of these options—town halls, community conferencing, truth and reconciliation forums, and short-term public hearings—may be viable alternatives to formal truth commissions. While developing these alternatives may be difficult, making the resources of the rhetorical tradition of transitional justice transparent is, I think, a productive first step.

There are, of course, potential risks to such work. Even as the rhetorical tradition of transitional justice provided resources for the GTRC, it also created constraints that may have limited the GTRC's effectiveness. For example, adopting the language of reconciliation and forgiveness may have created unrealistic expectations about what counted as success for the Commission. When Virgil Griffin refused to express any remorse about his actions on November 3, 1979 during his testimony to the Commission, some in the community wondered whether the GTRC was simply providing a platform to perpetuate the November 3rd confrontation and tarnish Greensboro's image. Moreover, in framing the endeavor in Greensboro as a "Truth and Reconciliation Commission," the initiative tied itself to an institutional model that, by definition, was to have an end date. Past truth commissions had operated for finite periods of time and concluded by releasing reports, so the Greensboro initiative did so as well. While the commissioners did invite groups to read and discuss their *Final Report* before disbanding, it may have been that the initiative, framed in different terms, could have better enabled *ongoing* dialogue.

Erik Doxtader (2004) has raised additional concerns about transposing reconciliation initiatives from South Africa to other contexts, such as Greensboro:

> Reconciliation appears to have come into its time. Talk of its potential is widespread, and calls for its practice are now heard as a serious alternative to realist doctrines that offer little solace to those caught in the grip of total violence…In all of this, there is little doubt that reconciliation's current cachet has much to do with its prominent role in the South African transition from apartheid to constitutional democracy. Over the last decade, South Africa's 'unique experiment' has been read by many as a precedent, the basis for a model that can be installed and employed productively in other situations. Among a number of larger efforts, the mandate for the recently created Truth and Reconciliation Commission (TRC) in Greensboro, North Carolina, shows a strong family resemblance to the charge that was handed to the South African TRC in 1995. Imitation may not be risk-free. While it is still [in its] early days, reconciliation's (over)claimed potential may harbor some significant costs. Backed by multimillion-dollar budgets, several international organizations currently devote themselves to advocating reconciliation and providing resources for its formal development, work that has led some to question whether reconciliation represents a new mode of colonial logic. (pp. 379–380)

The fact that calls for reconciliation—and, by extension, all aspects of the rhetorical tradition surrounding truth commissions—may represent a "new mode of colonial logic" is a legitimate risk. Truth commissions may impose particular ways of thinking, acting, and being on others, and they may serve as a means of exploiting—or maintaining power over—individuals, groups of people, or entire countries.[8] Note, however, that the fact that this risk exists does not in and of itself mean that countries and communities should simply eschew the truth commission approach: in a world increasingly characterized by deterritorialization and globalization, many strategies for addressing past human rights violations run the risk Doxtader articulates. What is necessary is to be actively engaged, throughout any truth-seeking process, in identifying and working to mitigate the ways that the process may be harmful, while attempting to meet the contingent demands of the new context and bring about positive change.

On Last Words

Did the Commission work? Was it successful? These are the questions that I am asked more than any others when talking to people about the GTRC, and they are some of the most difficult questions to answer. One of the reasons evaluating the success of the Commission proves difficult has to do with the nature of the Commission's mandated objectives, which tended to be abstract and subjective. How does one gauge the extent to which the Commission reconciled the community, clarified people's confusion, acknowledged people's feelings, or facilitated changes in social consciousness? Does it matter that people defined reconciliation and healing in different ways? And what is the extent of the Commission's impact that would count as success? If 500 people claim to have benefited from the process is that sufficient to count the Commission as a success? If two people claim to have been reconciled is that sufficient? And should we even evaluate the Commission based on its own objectives?

As these questions imply, the question of the Commission's success depends on the criteria one chooses to evaluate success. If one chooses to evaluate the success of the Commission based on the response of city government, the Commission would likely be deemed a failure: the Greensboro City Council voted "to oppose" the Commission's work, and many of the Commission's recommendations for the city have not been implemented. But if one chooses to evaluate the Commission based on its ability to prompt public engagement and community dialogue, the case could be made that the Commission was, at least somewhat, successful. The public events of the GTRC generated a modest, but not insignificant, audience turnout.

---

[8] Similarly, Gready (2011) highlighted that the diffusion of the practices of transitional justice may not always have positive effects. In *The Era of Transitional Justice*, for example, he noted that testimonies from truth commission hearings that circulate beyond their immediate contexts may get appropriated by human rights discourse in ways that "erase" and "decontextualize" the stories (p. 79). "The reification of victimhood," he continued, is "almost a condition of hearability," leading to further marginalization of those who have testified (p. 79). Given that the reception of testimony "can easily create new contexts of vulnerability and violation," Gready argued for "greater control for the testifier in the realms of representation, interpretation and dissemination" of his or her testimony (p. 82).

Attendance at both the Swearing In and Seating Ceremony and the Report Release Ceremony was over five hundred people, and there were several hundred individuals who attended the Commission's three public hearings. Moreover, as Magarrell and Wesley (2008) have noted, despite the fact that the council voted not to endorse the Commission, they were forced to publicly consider—and discuss—the events of November 3, 1979 (p. 174).[9] With regard to the *Final Report*, many organizations pledged to read and discuss it, and several have done so. Furthermore, a few of the Commission's recommendations have been or are being taken up by Greensboro citizens. For example, the Commission's recommendations prompted a minimum wage campaign in Greensboro, led the Department of Social Services in Guilford County to institute Undoing Racism workshops, and resulted in a number of college course offerings devoted to the events of November 3, 1979 and the work of the Commission.

Another measure by which one might deem the Commission successful was in its creation of a public forum for survivors of November 3, 1979 to tell their stories and be heard. Given that former CWP members' stories were not validated by the city or the judicial system, the creation of such a forum was not insignificant. In her book *Shattered Voices: Language, Violence, and the Work of Truth Commissions*, Phelps (2004) persuasively argued that the public testimonies prompted by truth commissions affect a kind of justice, balancing the destruction of language that results from physical violence. She wrote, "The processes by which truth commissions gather stories have great potential for creating a kind of justice that not only publicly exposes truth and vindicates people, but also a kind of justice that is dynamic and ongoing, not perfect of course, but a visible manifestation of an ethical and political commitment that honors truth, individual worth, dignity, and equality" (p. 72). In creating a space for survivors to speak and be heard, the GTRC may have helped to constitute the kind of justice Phelps mentioned here—a justice that involved the restoration of language to those who had been previously silenced.

One might also claim that the Commission was a success to the extent that its advocates, with the help of the AFF and the ICTJ, were able to build a transnational network of individuals and organizations. This network, which helped the GTRC establish its authority, may have positive implications for people beyond those living in Greensboro. I have already mentioned several initiatives that are drawing upon the work of the Greensboro initiative to garner authority for themselves. Moreover, as a result of the relationship forged with Bongani Finca, members of the GTCRP sent a 23 person delegation to South Africa for 10 days in November 2007, during which time "participants both shared the Greensboro Truth and Reconciliation process with their South African counterparts and learned from the rich struggle that has emerged out of apartheid" (GTCRP, 2007, para. 1).

[9]Magarrell & Wesley (2008) wrote, "[T]he fact that the 'official' city engaged at all, even in this negative way, was an important part of the process of revealing the truth about November 1979 and its aftermath in the community. The process was so present in the community that it *did* matter, it could *not* be ignored. And despite the discomfort of the city…they entered the dialogue about what the report and recommendations meant" (p. 174).

One might also evaluate the success of the GTRC with regard to its long-term impact; however, I believe there are reasons to resist doing so. For one thing, as Magarrell and Wesley (2008) have noted, it may be too early to say what the long-term impact of the Commission will be (p. 207). A second, perhaps more important, reason to resist doing so is that it could be perceived as a "last word" about the Commission. Setting aside the presumptuousness of a general pronouncement about the Commission's efficacy, I worry that such "last words" risk closing off future possibilities and serving to undermine, however slightly, the ways in which the work of the GTRC may yet shape the community. There is, in other words, a finality to "last words" that risks contributing to inaction: to the extent that the Commission is understood to be a failure, community members may choose not to engage its findings seriously; to the extent that it is deemed a success, community members may be tempted to view the Commission's work as sufficient.

What is the alternative to issuing a presumptuous "last word"? I believe that the appropriate critical stance in response to questions about the overall success of the Commission is the stance taken by the commissioners themselves—namely, hope. In her wonderful book *Tactics of Hope: The Public Turn in English Composition*, Paula Mathieu (2005) distinguished wishing from hoping, and, drawing upon the work of Ernst Bloch, she defined the latter as follows: "To hope," she wrote, "is to look critically at one's present condition, assess what is missing, and then long for and work for a not-yet reality, a future anticipated" (p. 19). For me, this definition exemplifies the stance taken and promoted by GTRC commissioners, who, throughout the entirety of their operation, attempted to critically assess their situation, to work actively for a better future through their speeches and writings, and to prompt others to do the same. Even at their last public event, the Report Release Ceremony, commissioners resisted dwelling on their successes and emphasized the work yet to be done by members of the community. Here I am reminded, in particular, of the words of Commissioner Muktha Jost, who, in describing the challenges faced by the Commission, made the following observation:

> Our work shows that there is much from the past about November three that needs to be redeemed. When we consider how this past can be redeemed, we realize the immensity of the work ahead for you. As we present our findings and conclusions, we want to remind you that this is the result of a modest but spirited and sincere approach for the truth around November three. We believe that it's important to recognize that we are not free from human rights abuses and injustice here in the United States, and we hope that the truth about the past will help us understand the present better and build a safer, more just, and inclusive future. It is in that spirit that we present to you our findings, conclusions, and recommendations. (Seel, 2006)

It is this stance of hope, as defined by Mathieu and performed by Jost and the other commissioners, which I believe we would do well to emulate.

Such a stance does not mean withholding any and all judgments: we can and should critique the ways in which the Commission was problematic and validate the ways in which it was exemplary. Nor does such a stance mean that we cannot or should not speak of the particular successes and failures of the Commission. But it does mean that, in making these judgments, we should avoid issuing the last words on the matter. The question of the Commission's long-term success is best treated as an open question. It is, I think, in this spirit that commissioners concluded their *Final Report*:

> We believe the truth and reconciliation process in Greensboro opened up the debate around Nov. 3, 1979, in a positive way and has successfully engaged a broad spectrum of the community in an effort that offers hope for reconciliation. As a Commission that looks a bit like Greensboro in microcosm, we found that this process—and our own struggle to hear and understand each other—had a profound impact on our perceptions of the issues we explored. Our individual and collective commitment to the truth helped us persevere. And the human stories and emotions we encountered along the way moved us to do our best to leave behind a legacy we hope will serve Greensboro for years to come. We cannot say what the future will hold for this community or what the long-term impact of this process will look like, but we hope that this process also serves as a learning tool for others in this county who, like Greensboro, are burdened by a legacy of hurt and inspired by the possibility of honestly coming to terms with their own history. (GTRC, 2006)

In this excerpt—which serves as the commissioners' own last words—one can find evidence for many of the arguments made in the preceding pages of this book; that said, when reading this passage, I am moved most of all by the commissioners' hopefulness, which cuts through the text fiercely and confidently.

References

Attean, E., & Williams, J. (2011). Homemade justice. *Cultural Survival Quarterly. 35*(1). Retrieved March 1, 2012, from http://www.culturalsurvival.org/publications/cultural-survival-quarterly/united-states/homemade-justice

Barry, E. (2007, September 18). From Staten Island haven, Liberians reveal war's scars. *The New York Times*. Retrieved October 17, 2007, from http://www.nytimes.com/2007/09/18/nyregion/18liberians.html?_r=2&oref=slogin&oref=slogin

Basic information on truth commissions. (n.d.). Retrieved March 5, 2012, from http://www.mississippitruth.org/pages/truth-comms.htm

DeChaine, D. R. (2005). *Global humanitarianism: NGOs and the crafting of community*. Lanham, MD: Lexington.

Deibert, R. J. (1998). Altered worlds: Social forces in the hypermedia environment. In C. J. Alexander & L. A. Pal (Eds.), *Digital democracy: Policy and politics in the wired world* (pp. 23–43). Oxford: Oxford University Press.

Doxtader, E. (2004). The potential of reconciliation's beginning: A reply. *Rhetoric & Public Affairs, 7*(3), 378–390. doi:10.1353/rap. 2005.0005.

Dunn-Marcos, R., Kollehlon, K. T., Ngovo, B., & Russ, E. (2005). *Liberians: An introduction to their history and culture*. Washington, DC: Center for Applied Linguistics.

Gready, P. (2011). *The era of transitional justice: The aftermath of the truth and reconciliation commission in South Africa and beyond*. New York, NY: Routledge.

Greensboro Truth and Community Reconciliation Project. (2003). Mandate for the Greensboro Truth and Reconciliation Commission. Retrieved October 5, 2007, from http://www.greensborotrc.org/mandate.php

Greensboro Truth and Community Reconciliation Project. (2004, June 12). The swearing in and seating ceremony of the Greensboro Truth and Reconciliation Commission [Ceremony program]. Copy in possession of author.

Greensboro Truth and Community Reconciliation Project. (2007). Delegation to South Africa. Retrieved June 2, 2008, from http://www.gtcrp.org

Greensboro Truth and Reconciliation Commission. (2006). *The Greensboro Truth and Reconciliation Commission final report: An examination of the context, causes, sequence and consequence of the events of November 3, 1979.* Retrieved March 1, 2012, from http://www.greensborotrc.org/

Gutmann, A., & Thompson, D. (2000). The moral foundations of truth commissions. In R. I. Rotberg & D. Thompson (Eds.), *Truth v. justice: The morality of truth commissions* (pp. 22–44). Princeton, NJ: Princeton University Press.

Hall, S. (1992). The question of cultural identity. In S. Hall, D. Held, & T. McGrew (Eds.), *Modernity and its futures* (pp. 273–316). Cambridge: Polity.

Hayner, P. B. (2001). *Unspeakable truths: Confronting state terror and atrocity.* New York, NY: Routledge.

History & Background. (n.d.). Retrieved March 5, 2012, from http://www.mainetribaltrc.org/history.html

Ifill, S. A. (2007). *On the courthouse lawn: Confronting the legacy of lynching in the twenty-first century.* Boston, MA: Beacon.

Kiss, E. (2000). Moral ambition within and beyond political constraints: Reflections on restorative justice. In R. I. Rotberg & D. Thompson (Eds.), *Truth v. justice: The morality of truth commissions* (pp. 68–98). Princeton, NY: Princeton University Press.

Magarrell, L. (n.d.). A sampling of truth-seeking projects in the United States. Retrieved March 1, 2012, from http://www.mississippitruth.org/documents/sampling.pdf

Magarrell, L., & Wesley, J. (2008). *Learning from Greensboro: Truth and reconciliation in the United States.* Philadelphia, PA: University of Pennsylvania Press.

Mathieu, P. (2005). *Tactics of hope: The public turn in English composition.* Portsmouth, NH: Boynton/Cook.

Michigan Roundtable for Diversity & Inclusion. (2011a). Charter for the Metropolitan Detroit Truth and Reconciliation Commission on Racial Inequality. Retrieved March 1, 2012, from http://www.miroundtable.org/Roundtabledownloads/FinalMandate2011.pdf

Michigan Roundtable for Diversity & Inclusion. (2011b). Race, residence and regionalism. Retrieved March 1, 2012, from http://www.miroundtable.org/raceresidenceregionalism.htm

Michiganroundtable. (2011). Race2Equity conference. Retrieved March 1, 2012, from http://www.youtube.com/watch?v=l4BBcpegrRA&feature=player_embedded

Minnesota Advocates for Human Rights. (n.d.). Liberian Truth and Reconciliation Commission Diaspora Project. Retrieved October 17, 2007, from http://liberiatrc.mnadvocates.org/Home.html.

MTP Partners. (n.d.). Retrieved March 5, 2012, from http://www.mississippitruth.org/pages/partners.htm

Murphy, J. M. (1997). Inventing authority: Bill Clinton, Martin Luther King, Jr. and the orchestration of rhetorical traditions. *Quarterly Journal of Speech, 83*(1), 71–89. doi:10.1080/00335639709384172.

National Transitional Legislative Assembly. (2005). Truth and Reconciliation Commission of Liberia Mandate. Retrieved June 2, 2008, from https://www.trcofliberia.org/about/trc-mandate.

Phelps, T. G. (2004). *Shattered voices: Language, violence, and the work of truth commissions.* Philadelphia, PA: University of Pennsylvania Press.

Philpott, D. (2006). Beyond politics as usual: Is reconciliation compatible with liberalism? In D. Philpott (Ed.), *The politics of past evil: Religion, reconciliation, and the dilemmas of transitional justice* (pp. 11–44). Notre Dame, IN: University of Notre Dame Press.

Poor People's Economic Human Rights Campaign. (2006). National truth campaign: Shining a light on poverty in the U.S.A. Retrieved October 17, 2007, from http://www.economichumanrights.org/ntc_report1.shtml

Poverty Initiative. (2007). Poverty truth commission. Retrieved October 17, 2007, from http://www.povertyinitiative.org/events/event_pages/4-13-07_truth_commission/4-13-07_truth_commission_main.html

Salazar, P. J. (2002). *An African Athens: Rhetoric and the shaping of democracy in South Africa.* Mahwah, NJ: L. Erlbaum.

Seel, Laura (Producer). (2006). *Greensboro Truth and Reconciliation Commission report release ceremony* [DVD]. Greensboro, NC. (Obtained from Laura Seel.)

Southern Truth and Reconciliation. (2007). About us. Retrieved October 17, 2007, from http://www.southerntruth.org/index.htm

Testimony in search of truth. (2005, October 30). *News & Record*. p. H1.

Timeline of the Mississippi Truth Project. (n.d.). Retrieved on March 5, 2012, from http://www.mississippitruth.org/pages/timeline.htm

TRC Partners & Supporters (n.d.). Retrieved on March 5, 2012, from http://www.mainetribaltrc.org/links.html

Tutu, D. (1999). *No future without forgiveness*. New York, NY: Doubleday.

VanAntwerpen, J. (2010). Reconciliation reconceived: Religion, secularism, and the language of transition. In W. Kymlicka & B. Bashir (Eds.), *The politics of reconciliation in multicultural societies* (pp. 25–47). New York, NY: Oxford University Press.

Welcome Table. (n.d.). Retrieved on March 5, 2012, from http://www.welcometable.net/index.htm

What is the Mississippi Truth Project? (n.d.). Retrieved on March 5, 2012, from http://www.mississippitruth.org/

21

Justice for what?

Recognising a web of gender-based harms against women in transitional justice

INTRODUCTION

So far, this book has used the term 'human rights outcomes for women' in the context of transitional justice rather uncritically. Chapter 1 signposted the evolution of human rights and international law in the recognition of women's experiences of political violence, from women as secondary victims to women as primary victims of the same – and different – physical harms as men. The definition of women's human rights in transitional justice is, therefore, a moving target. Moreover, efforts to expand the definition of women's human rights have been critical terrain in feminist engagement with transitional justice.[1] Feminist engagement with human rights and transitional justice has always worked on two fronts, seeking both the protection of the human rights framework for violations against women, while also seeking to challenge and redefine the narrow understandings of violations that fall within the human rights frame.

In this same spirit of simultaneous engagement and critique, this chapter sets out the understanding of women's human rights that underpins the remainder of the book. The chapter seeks to work creatively within the strictures of the human rights canon, to reveal a web of public *and* private harms against women in contexts of political violence.

'Starting from women's lives'[2]: public and private harms as different, though complexly related

The approach advocated here is a nuanced understanding of how gender hierarchies interact with other political cleavages and dynamics to determine women's experiences of harm in contexts of political violence. In the account of women's experiences of public and private harms that follows, this chapter sets out the manner in which public harms of violent conflict and political repression

1 See further Ní Aoláin and O'Rourke (2010).

2 Bunch (1990: 496).

exacerbate and alter the nominally 'private' harms of violence against women in the home, on the body, the repressive regulation of women's reproductive lives, and the manipulation of women's collective organising. In capturing this account of different though complexly related public and private harms, a web of harms against women is proposed. The image of the web is apt: the web describes the connections between different types of harms against women, identifying the relationship of public to private harms. However, the collapse of those harms into a single indistinguishable set is eschewed.

Four aspects of how the context of political violence exacerbates women's private experiences of harm are emphasised and documented in the case studies:

1 First, political violence has a negative impact on the state's capacity to prohibit, prevent and punish private harms against women.
2 Second, political violence gives rise to the militarisation of everyday life, which erodes any notion of a private sphere for women free from the state's negative infringement of her bodily integrity. This manifests in sexualised harms to women political activists.
3 Third, heightened gender ideologies in periods of political violence lead to the acute public regulation of women's private reproductive lives.
4 Fourth, women often enter the public sphere during periods of political violence on the basis of the private maternal role and the need to provide for one's family and community. However, recognition of the subversive potential of women's collective action results in the public political manipulation of women's organising.

While this account of harms in the case studies is necessarily brief, the discussion identifies and articulates the relationship between private and public harms against women in contexts of political violence on which analysis in the remainder of the book relies.

Private violence against women and the state's deficient public response

In each of the cases under study, the context of political violence exacerbated the private incidences of domestic violence against women. In particular, the state's prioritisation of political violence over and above private violence meant that victims of domestic violence could not rely on the state's protective role against their victimisers. Through state inaction, this violence was invisible and implicitly condoned. The manifold deficiencies of public institutions exacerbated private incidences of violence. As this section will detail, whereas deficiencies in the police response were particularly evident in Northern Ireland, in Chile the complicity of the judiciary in perpetuating domestic violence was particularly significant. Moreover, in particular in Colombia, the militarisation of society created a climate of impunity for violence generally, that had a specifically gendered impact on the manifestation of domestic violence in the country.

Chile

In Chile, the socialist presidency of Salvador Allende was deposed by military coup in 1973 (Borzutzky and Oppenheim 2006). Political opposition was brutally suppressed under the military regime. Following the coup, approximately 6,000 individuals were arrested in a mass round-up by the new regime in Santiago. In this period repressive methods were unpredictable: courts-martial, summary executions, trial or indefinite detention (Frühling 1983). On 17 June 1974 the Bureau of National Intelligence (DINA) was created and empowered to arrest and detain people in secret locations. This marked the centralisation of the state's repressive apparatus. Within six months of the coup, the military had arrested 80,000 persons, and 160,000 suffered politically motivated job dismissals. An estimated 200,000 persons, including political refugees and their families, went into exile. The regime expelled 30,000 students, and replaced thousands of university professors with military personnel (Baldez 2002: 125). In the regime's first 18 months, one in every ten Chilean families was affected by arrest, detention or exile, and thousands of Chileans were executed (Americas Watch 1983a: 3). Detentions, disappearances and deaths continued at a high level until 1977.

In Chile, the impact of military rule on domestic violence was most pronounced in the response of the judiciary. The military junta formally respected the independence of the judiciary.[3] In practice, however, the courts were almost idle in respect of supervision of the legality of the regime's activities. Indeed, of over 5,400 habeas corpus petitions filed with the Chilean courts between 1973 and 1983, all but 10 were rejected, as the courts willingly accepted the official explanation that detained individuals had gone missing only after they had been released by the military or police (Hilbink 2007: 1). Judicial complicity in the perpetration of violence was not confined to habeas corpus petitions. Feminist organisations such as *La Morada* and DOMOS were active on the issue of domestic violence during the dictatorship. The first legal survey on domestic violence in Chile, carried out between October 1987 and December 1988, demonstrated the extent of judicial complicity in the impunity surrounding domestic violence in the country (Gonzales 1989). The study analysed the files of court cases from three regions for the crimes of injury, parricide and homicide of a wife or companion filed in 1986, and reviewed the rulings of the Court of Appeals and the Supreme Court from 1980 to 1986 for these same crimes. The study found that in the cases of the lower courts examined, no case resulted in a punishment set for the assailant. Analysis of judicial reasoning in the Court of Appeals and Supreme Court found that domestic violence tended to be justified or excused, rather than punished. Clear patterns

3 Decree Law No. 1, Diario Oficial, 11 September 1973.

were evident in the judicial response to domestic violence and more widespread failure of the Chilean judiciary to protect the human rights of individuals during this period.[4]

Northern Ireland

In Northern Ireland, the political conflict has lengthy historical roots, but hinges on the competing national aspirations of the minority Irish (largely Catholic) nationalist community, who seek a united Ireland, and the majority British (largely Protestant) unionist community, who seek to remain part of the United Kingdom. In parallel with the emergence of peaceful civil rights agitation in the 1960s (Northern Ireland Civil Rights Association 1978), the prospect of physical force resistance to the state gathered momentum. The response both directly by the state and by pro-state mobs was hostile, often violent. As civil unrest and violence spiralled, the British government authorised the mobilisation of units from the garrison force of the British Army in August 1969. In 1970 the recently remobilised paramilitary organisation, the Irish Republican Army, split into the Official IRA and the Provisional IRA (IRA or 'the Provisionals'), the latter of which was to pursue Irish independence through a campaign of violence. In response to continued unrest, the Northern Ireland executive introduced internment without trial on 9 August 1971 under the Civil Authorities (Special Powers) Act 1922 with British government approval. Within the first six months of its operation, sweeps by the police and army led to the arrest of almost two-and-a-half thousand individuals, all but a handful from the Catholic/Nationalist community (Foster 1988). It was the shooting dead of 13 unarmed civilians by the British Army at a banned anti-internment march in the city of Derry in 1972 that finally prompted the prorogucment of the Northern Irish parliament. Northern Ireland was to be governed through direct rule by the British government in London.

Over the course of the conflict, political violence in Northern Ireland was to pose the most grave of challenges to a liberal democracy: 'how can a country cope with organised lawlessness pursued for ostensibly political purposes?' (Ewing and Gearty 1990: 211). A policy of 'criminalisation' was to be used toward proponents of political violence. A slew of anti-terrorist legislation followed. Although internment would continue until 1976, as many cases as possible were to be processed through the courts as criminal charges. The British government's longer-term legislative response to the political violence in Northern Ireland was to set in train the steady erosion of due process requirements within the criminal justice system, most notoriously through the suspension of jury trials for paramilitary offences,[5]

4 The Chilean Truth and Reconciliation Commission found that 'During the period in question the judicial branch did not respond vigorously enough to human rights violations' (Chilean National Commission on Truth and Reconciliation 1993: Chapter 4A).

5 See further Jackson and Doran (1995).

but also through making confessions given involuntarily more easily admissible in criminal trials, allowing convictions based solely on the testimony of informers,[6] allowing inferences from the accused's silence,[7] and the extensive empowerment of the police and army.

In Northern Ireland, the impact of the conflict on individual experiences of domestic violence was most pronounced in relation to the policing of domestic violence. The greater number of legally and illegally held guns in Northern Ireland meant that guns were more commonly used in physical attacks on women than in either Britain or the Republic of Ireland (McWilliams and McKiernan 1993). The policy of 'criminalisation' pursued by the state in response to political violence, and the continued operation of the criminal justice system adjusted by emergency legislation, meant that the police operated at the frontline of the state's response to conflict violence in the jurisdiction.[8] The police were considered a 'legitimate target' of Republican violence. This highly militarised police role (the Royal Ulster Constabulary was the only routinely armed police force in the UK; the police were accompanied by the military on patrol; and police vehicles were heavily armed) (Walker, 2000: 175) gave rise to broad alienation of the police from the community. This alienation was experienced most acutely by the Catholic community. The overwhelmingly Protestant composition of the police force (Independent Commission on Policing for Northern Ireland 1999: 2), compounded by recurrent allegations of security force collusion in Loyalist violence,[9] led to perceptions – and compelling evidence – of one community (Protestant) policing the other major ethnic group (Catholic). The position of the police force at the frontline of the conflict led, unsurprisingly, to a 'suspicion of outsiders',[10] a suspicion that limited opportunities for constructive collaborative relationships with women's organisations such as Women's Aid that addressed domestic violence in the jurisdiction.

The absence of confidence in the police meant that domestic violence reporting remained very low throughout the period of the conflict.[11] The security concerns of the police around entering Catholic communities exacerbated the situation. For example, when a report of domestic violence was made, it was common practice to wait an hour and phone the number from which the call was made, in order to ensure that the phone call was not intended to lure police officers to

6 See further Greer (1995).

7 Criminal Evidence (Northern Ireland) Order 1988.

8 The dynamics are comprehensively described in Ní Aoláin (2000b: 26–71).

9 Aspects of these allegations concerning the deaths of Patrick Finucane, Robert Hamill, Rosemary Nelson and Billy Wright are documented in Cory (2004).

10 Eileen Calder, Director of Belfast Rape Crisis Centre, Belfast, personal communication, 29 June 2007.

11 Avila Kilmurray recounts that during the 1970s, there was simply no reporting to the police. Further, in Women's Aid's dealings with the Housing Association, there was no expectation from them that any reporting was taking place. Kilmurray, personal communication, 2 July 2007.

harm. There are recorded incidents of police responding to domestic violence reports in rural Republican areas with the support of snipers and army helicopters (McWilliams and McKiernan 1993). In the context where even to call the police resulted in great stigma, these sort of police responses further eroded women's confidence in reporting incidences of violence. The question 'don't you know there's a war going on?' was often posed in similar terms to women reporting domestic violence (Montgomery and Bell 1985: 53; McWilliams and McKiernan 1993). It captured the prioritisation by the police of the security situation over women's experiences of intimate violence.

Colombia

Colombia has endured the longest-running armed conflict in the Western Hemisphere. Successive waves of confrontation among guerrilla groups (most notably, the Fuerzas Armadas Revolucionarias de Colombia (Revolutionary Armed Forces of Colombia), or FARC, but also the urban-based M-19[12] and the Cuban-inspired Ejército de Liberación Nacional (ELN)), the armed forces (which have traditionally maintained a high degree of autonomy from government, allowing them to block attempts by the government to reach a negotiated settlement with the guerrilla groups, while being heavily complicit in the violence and criminality of paramilitary groups)[13] and paramilitary groups that emerged in the 1960s as part of a counter-insurgency tactic of the state to stem the spread of the perceived communist threat, have caused enormous loss of life and forced displacement and weakened the rule of law. The conflict has been marked by patterns of victimisation, drug trafficking and political crime. The new Colombian Constitution of 1991 was a landmark attempt to bring all political factions within the country into a reformed and reconstituted political infrastructure. The peace agreement character of the new Constitution was evident in its drafting, in the broad participation in its negotiation, and most literally in the 'right to peace' enshrined in the resulting constitutional text.[14] The Colombian Constitutional Court was called upon to facilitate Colombia's movement away from violence and injustice. However, the political pact that underpinned the 1991 Constitution, and initially held the political and military elites to principles of non-violence, quickly disintegrated. Increasing violence by paramilitary actors occurred in parallel with the diminution of state capacity in the country. By the end of the 1990s Colombia teetered on the verge of failed statehood. The collapse of a peace process with the FARC guerrillas coincided with heavy US investment in the

12 The group's full title was Movimiento 19 de Abril (19 April Movement). It took this title from the date of the presidential elections of 1970, in which the populist candidate Gustavo Rojas Pinillo was denied an electoral victory in an outcome that the group regarded as fraudulent.

13 For an early account of this relationship, see Amnesty International (1988a).

14 Constitution of Colombia, 1991, Article 22.

Colombian military, and renewed state determination to achieve a military defeat of the guerrilla forces. While levels of violence have waxed and waned, and its chief protagonists have varied, political violence has been a constant in Colombia since the 1940s (Welna and Gallon 2007).

The widespread impunity that surrounds violence perpetrated by the state and armed groups has contributed to a broader climate of impunity for all types of violent acts. The state's almost exclusive concern with political violence and narcotrafficking permitted the increase of other forms of violence. Research in 1987 found that the percentage of murders in Colombia resulting from subversion did not exceed 7.51 per cent in the years under analysis, and therefore over 90 per cent of violent killings were not considered to be of a political nature (Comisión de Estudios sobre la Violencia 1987: 18). Feminist and civil society organisations have long resisted the state's prioritisation of guerrilla-perpetrated violence. In the 1980s Latin American women's organisations began to raise the issue of domestic violence. The Colombian Casa de la Mujer in Bogotá, established in 1982, was one of the very first such organisations.[15] CAMI Mujeres was established in Cali in the same year, with the three political priorities of increasing women's political participation, advancing women's reproductive rights and ending violence against women.[16] Further, one of the first studies on the prevalence of domestic violence in Latin America was conducted in Bogotá in 1985.[17] These women's organisations have consistently sought to articulate the connections between the economic, social and political context of conflict violence, and levels of violence in the private ambit:

> [I]ntrafamily violence has not been the focus of attention for profound investigation in the way that political violence has, nor has it been sufficiently criminalized, which has permitted its reproduction under a climate of impunity and, why not say it, tacit social acceptance.
>
> (Casa de la Mujer 1988: 12)[18]

15 Larrain Heiremans (1994) (listing Casa de la Mujer in Colombia and La Morada in Chile as the first two Latin American women's organisations to advocate on domestic violence). Examples of Casa de la Mujer publications addressing domestic violence in this period include: Casa de la Mujer, *La Violencia: lo Impensable lo Impensado* (Bogotá, Colombia: 1990), Casa de la Mujer, *Nuevos Espacios y Otros Retos: Propuesta a Las Mujeres* (Bogotá, Colombia: 1986), Casa de la Mujer, *Violencia en la Intimidad* (Bogotá, Colombia: 1988).

16 See http://www.camimujeres.org/ (last accessed 1 March 2013).

17 The study was conducted by A. Berenguer on the basis of 233 interviews with women who had personal injuries attended to by the Instituto de Medicina Legal Bogotá in 1982. He recorded the civil status, age and socio-economic level of the women. The study also uncovered child abuse. Domestic violence was associated with alcoholism, irritability and accusations of infidelity against the woman. A. Berenguer, *Violencia Conyugal*, edn Colectivo Cuéntame tu Vida, No. 9, Cali, Colombia 1986, cited in Larrain Heiremans (1994).

18 Comments of the advisor to the President for the Plan Nacional de Rehabilitacion (the Plan proposed by the reformer President Barco in 1988 for social investment in conflict zones).

The consequences for Colombian women of this impunity and disregard was heightened vulnerability to staggering levels of violence, including domestic violence, illustrated by the address of the Colombian delegation to the 1987 Feminist *Encuentro* (meeting) in Taxco, Mexico, which opened with the words:

> We, Colombian women, have brought in our suitcases, in our backpacks, in our bodies, pieces, fragments from the moment our country is living . . . We couldn't nor wanted to leave behind, at the border, the trace of violence in Colombia.
>
> (Quoted in Morgan 1992: 367)

Privatised violence against women by public actors

In the discussion of human rights law in Chapter 1, it was observed that the classic political actor was understood to be male. This has had grave consequences for the construction of human rights protections around the needs of the male political actor. The assumption of political activity as male has meant that, in addition to being punished for political subversion, female political dissidents have been targeted for gender-specific forms of violence to punish their deviance from received gender norms (Corcoran 2006). Moreover, the sex-based nature of the harms has allowed perpetrators to portray this harm as 'private' and a manifestation of individual personal motivation ('lust'), and to resist its inherently political character as violence perpetrated by state actors against female political dissidents. These same gender dynamics can be traced in Chile and Northern Ireland, in terms of the deliberate targeting of female political dissidents for sexualised brutality, and in Colombia in the brutal regulation of the reproductive lives of female combatants through compulsory contraception and forced abortions. While these sexualised harms against combatant women and women in detention fit most neatly within the range of gender-specific harms against women currently recognised in transitional justice, the political character of these harms was in fact contested and resisted in each of the case studies.

Chile

In Chile, the repression by the military dictatorship was experienced directly and violently by women, most notably by women in detention. Female dissidents were systematically targeted for sexual violence and torture (Bunster 1985, 1991). Their departure from the traditional maternal role provoked a brutal and highly sexualised response from the state (Acuña Moenne 2005). The work of Ximena Bunster was particularly important in bringing this violence to light in the 1980s, exposing the torture of women that was consciously and systematically directed at her female sexual identity and female anatomy (Bunster 1985: 307; 1991). Physical and psychological sexual violence was inflicted on women by the military, either for direct involvement in dissident activities, or for her relationship to a politically active male. Further, 'family torture' was perpetrated by the military regime, whereby state agents tortured children in front of their mothers in order to coerce information from these women about the subversive activities of their husbands (Bunster 1985). The regime's brutal practice of torture thereby reinforced the regime's gendered ideology of maternity and family: deviance from the maternal role was violently suppressed, and the valorised protected family bond was used against individual dissident women who were forced to witness the torture of a family member.

Ideologies and ideals of womanhood were not exclusive to the military regime. They were replicated in the attitudes of the women's fellow political prisoners, as is graphically illustrated by the account of former political prisoner Hernán Valdés of the sexual relations between female detainees and soldiers he witnessed while in detention:

> We couldn't figure the women's behaviour out. Were they participating [by consorting with the soldiers] out of fear, sheer despair, cynicism or pleasure? . . . We [the men] were all outraged. Someone recalled how in the National Stadium the women prisoners had preferred to be shot rather than let the soldiers lay a finger on them. We couldn't explain this kind of collusion.
>
> (Hernán Valdés, quoted in Baldez 2001: 29)

The modes of survival adopted by these women were condemned for their deviation from the pure and self-sacrificing feminine 'ideal'. Further, the women's behaviour was presumed to emanate from their private personal preference, and not the public political circumstances of their detention.

Northern Ireland

In Northern Ireland, against a backdrop of emergency powers and high levels of imprisonment, prisons have always been key sites of the political conflict.[19] In 1976 the British government withdrew political status from prisoners arrested for paramilitary activity in Northern Ireland, prompting prison protests as Republican prisoners refused to wear the newly assigned prison uniform (they instead wore only blankets, in a protest that became known as the blanket protest). The blanket protest escalated into a 'no wash' protest, then the 'no slop-out' protest, and finally the 'dirty protest', which involved prisoners spreading excrement along the walls of their prison cells. Republican prisoners in Armagh women's prison joined the protest for political status first by refusing to work, and later in the adoption of a 'no wash' protest in 1980. While these prison events were landmarks in the escalation of the conflict in Northern Ireland, it was the strip-searching of women

19 For the authoritative account of the relationship of prisons to the political conflict, see McEvoy (2001).

prisoners that has been the lightning-rod issue of the political detention of women in Northern Ireland.

In 1982 the normal procedural practice of strip-searching a prisoner on reception at Armagh women's prison was extended on a random and frequent basis to prisons in Northern Ireland. Strip-searching was carried out with much greater frequency on female inmates in Northern Ireland than in prisons in England and Wales (National Council for Civil Liberties 1986). According to the women subjected to the practice, the searches were being used to discipline and punish female prisoners.[20] Amnesty International routinely condemned the practice of strip-searching female prisoners in Northern Ireland, voicing concerns that the practice was being carried out 'with the deliberate intention of degrading and humiliating the women' (Amnesty International 1986: 4; 1991b: 22). The women prisoners themselves publicly condemned the practice:

> What we are saying is that, in Armagh, intensive strip searching is currently being used in a way that constitutes sexual harassment, specifically to break the spirit of women who are regarded by the authorities as a political threat to the British state.
>
> (Letter from Armagh women prisoners, cited in Hackett 1995: 111)

The prevalent conservative ideologies of womanhood dominated the campaign against strip-searching at Armagh (Father Dennis Faul 1983). One campaign pamphlet states:

> This new procedure has been a traumatic experience for young Catholic girls and older women, all of whom were reared and educated in Catholics houses and schools where the strictest standards of modesty were impressed upon them as a matter of conscience . . . they were taught to be pure and chaste like the Blessed Virgin and St Brigid and St Maria Goretti.
>
> (Father Dennis Faul 1983)

This language reified cultural values deeply antithetical to women's autonomy and stands in stark contrast to the language with which women experiencing strip-searching condemned the practice. This characterisation of the treatment as antithetical to the passive and chaste images of Catholic femininity evacuated the women and their treatment of its clearly political character.

Colombia

In Colombia, the First Report on the Human Rights Situation in Colombia conducted by the Inter-American Commission on Human Rights in 1981

20 *The Irish Times* (1980) as quoted in Loughran (1988: 64).

catalogued civil and political rights violations in the country during the previous four years. The report was particularly concerned with the executive's capacity to declare states of emergency,[21] extra-judicial killings,[22] habeas corpus,[23] ordinary and military justice[24] and military operations in rural zones.[25] 'Other rights' included freedom of religion and conscience, freedom of thought and expression, the right to assemble, freedom of association and political rights.[26] With strong resonance to Chile and Northern Ireland, specific mention of women's human rights was confined to female prisoners. Allegations of the abuse and torture in detention of a small number of female members of M-19 and FARC were investigated. The Commission noted the 'vile insults' that were made against 'the honour and dignity' of these women, while naked and enduring 'every type of abuse'.[27]

Much later reports noted similar sexualised victimisation of female combatants. In her 2001 Report, the UN Special Rapporteur on Violence Against Women noted the sexualised violence experienced by women within armed groups, in particular in terms of sexually transmitted infections, forced contraception and abortions.[28] The public political activity of these female combatants was giving rise to the brutal regulation of their private reproduction, as women's reproductive roles were deemed incompatible with their public combatant roles.

In terms of the gendered binary of public and private harms in transitional justice, these sexualised harms against combatant women and women in detention fit most neatly within the range of gender-specific harms against women currently recognised in transitional justice. Nevertheless, as the foregoing account illustrated, the political character of these harms was in fact contested and resisted in each of the case studies.

The public regulation of women's private reproductive lives

The control of women's reproductive functions by men and/or the state has long been critiqued by feminists as the cornerstone of women's oppression (see especially Petchesky 1986). The denial of women's reproductive autonomy can result in compulsory maternity for women, confining them to the private domestic sphere and restricting their access to the public sphere, as the gendered construction of the public sphere excludes women with caring roles. This analysis neatly

21 Inter-American Commission on Human Rights, 1981: Chapter 1, Political and Normative System.
22 Ibid, Chapter 2, Right to Life.
23 Ibid, Chapter 3, Right to Personal Liberty.
24 Ibid, Chapter 5, Right to Due Process.
25 Ibid, Chapter 7, Military Operations in Rural Zones.
26 Ibid, Chapter 6, Other Rights, A.
27 Ibid, Chapter 4, Right to Security and Personal Integrity, D.6.
28 United Nations Special Rapporteur on Violence Against Women: Radhika Coomaraswamy, 2001: para 56. See also Human Rights Watch (2003: 56–8).

reveals the highly public nature and consequences of the ostensible private matter of reproduction and mothering. Further, the heightened gender ideologies that tend to prevail in contexts of political violence mean that public political ideologies often involve the politicisation of a private maternal role (Yuval-Davis 1997). These observations on the centrality of reproduction to the political status of women bear particular resonance in times of heightened political change or threat. As 'the bearers of the collective' (Yuval-Davis 1997: 26), when the collective is threatened through insurgency or other forms of widespread political violence, regulation of women's fertility and reproduction can become central to maintenance of the collective. These dynamics manifested in distinct though related ways across each of the three case studies.

Chile

In developed and developing nations, the regulation of women's reproductive functions has been effective shorthand for revealing the ideology of the governing regime. This was nowhere more obvious than in the institution of a cult of maternity, and the practice of compulsory maternity, by the military junta in Chile. The militarisation of everyday life in Chile under the military junta led directly to further restrictions on women's reproductive freedom. Official state pro-natalism was motivated and justified by appeals to 'national security'. The size of families was a priority concern of the military regime, as evidenced in a 1979 Office of Planning (ODEPLAN) publication that stated:

> It should be kept in mind that every threat to the integrity of the family seriously affects the quality and quantity of the population, arthrologically reducing the number of inhabitants and their integral formation. It has been proven that the birth rate decreases substantially with the disintegration of the family and increases with family stability. An affectionate, stable family life is the best environment for the development of children.
>
> (Parson 2005: 83)

In 1980 the military's Director of Health, General Eduardo Diaz, expressly linked the regime's concern with family size to the doctrine of national security: 'We need conscription, but who is going to put on a uniform if we only have men of 60 or boys of 15?' (*Revista Hoy*, 23 July 1980, quoted in Acuña Moenne 2005: 156).

Against this backdrop, advancements made under the Allende government in public health family planning programmes, and reducing the number of backstreet abortions, were immediately and dramatically reversed with the installation of the military regime.[29] Therapeutic abortion was finally criminalised by the

29 For discussion see Casas (2004).

military regime in 1989; however, accounts of the evolving approach to abortion within the Chilean health system note that the 1989 legal development marked the logical conclusion of the medical practice ushered in by the military usurping power in 1973 (Red Chilena contra la Violencia Doméstica y Sexual 2008). It did not constitute a dramatic change in medical practice from the previous 17 years. Rather, the coup had been the critical moment in the change of behaviour of medical practitioners towards abortion. The considerably more sympathetic approach of medical practitioners that prevailed under the Allende administration, respectful of women's wishes and their socio-economic circumstances, ended with the installation of the military regime.[30] The coup marked the onset of the punitive public regulation of women's private reproductive lives.

Northern Ireland

Spiralling political violence in Northern Ireland in 1972 prompted the British government to prorogue the Northern Irish parliament, and to institute direct rule of the jurisdiction from ministers in central government in London. The circumstances of inter-communal political violence resulted in a high degree of deference by central government to what were perceived to be shared local sensibilities on social issues in the jurisdiction. Cross-religious consensus against women's reproductive autonomy, in particular in terms of access to abortion, has been consistently used by the state to shore up otherwise fragile political consensus in the jurisdiction. Central government demonstrated a reluctance to legislate progressively on issues in Northern Ireland contrary to the preferences expressed by the main religious communities. This was most clearly demonstrated in respect of liberalising legislation on abortion.

This unwillingness to institute progressive legal change has had particular gendered consequences for women, as, in respect of abortion, this issue was not even cited for possible legislative action by the British government. Liberalising legislation was introduced in England and Wales in 1967, and this was not extended to Northern Ireland by the local parliament. According to the administrative headquarters for the exercise of executive power in the jurisdiction, the Northern Ireland Office (NIO):

> Since the introduction of direct rule in 1972 the view has been taken not to introduce a measure to change the abortion laws in Northern Ireland unless it is likely to command broad support among the people of the Province. Such support does not exist at present.
>
> (Letter of Northern Ireland Office Minister Nicholas Scott to Ken Weetch MP, 21 March 1985, cited in Furedi 1995: 97)

30 Gloria Maria Vargas, Santiago, September 2008 at launch of Red Chilena contra la Violencia Doméstica y Sexual (2008).

The NIO relied on a motion passed the previous year by the Northern Irish Assembly and affirmed by 14 of the 26 local district councils stating their opposition to the extension of the Abortion Act 1967 to Northern Ireland. Thus, in deference to these overwhelmingly male-dominated political fora, restrictive legal regulation of women's reproductive lives continued in the jurisdiction, to devastating effect on women living there. Between 1967 and 1994, it is estimated that 40,000 women travelled from Northern Ireland to England and Wales to obtain an abortion, with the added financial, health and emotional burden entailed by that travel (Rossiter 2001: 6). In the context of inter-communal political violence, central government preferred to defer to perceived shared local sensibilities on private matters, irrespective of the impact on women.

Colombia

In Colombia, also, the struggle for public order and the state's survival during violent conflict has operated to limit the reproductive autonomy of individual women. During the 1990s violence spiralled and Colombia verged on failed statehood. Against this backdrop, the Constitutional Court's interpretation of the right to peace as a collective right served to permit the state to reassert its authority and to monopolise violence within the national territory. In consistent jurisprudence during the 1990s, the Court interpreted the right to peace as collective rather than individual, and consequently imposed a duty on all citizens to accept, for example, the violent consequences of having a police station in close proximity to their homes.[31]

The Court's determination to support the state in establishing public order in this period extended into the reproductive lives of individual women. In 1994 the Court first considered the constitutionality of the blanket prohibition of abortion in the country.[32] The Court was asked to consider whether a blanket ban on abortion was in violation of the state's duty to protect the right of citizens to freedom of conscience and religion, given that there was a diversity of beliefs in the country on when life begins. In affirming the constitutionality of the blanket ban, the Court noted that rights to freedom of conscience and religion can be constitutionally limited on the grounds that they pose a threat to public order. Further, the Court noted, 'public morality forms part of the concept of public order.'[33] Thus,

31 This rationale was clear in two cases decided by the Court in 1993, in which *tutela* applications by citizens seeking the removal of recently installed police stations, because they were targets for guerrilla violence, were rejected by the Constitutional Court. Corte Constitucional de Colombia, *Sentencia No. T-139/93*, magistrado ponente Jorge Arango Mejía, Corte Constitucional de Colombia, *Sentencia No. T-255/93*, magistrado ponente Fabio Morón Diaz.

32 Corte Constitucional de Colombia, *Sentencia No. C-133/94*, magistrado ponente Martha Sachica de Moncaleano.

33 Corte Constitucional de Colombia, *Sentencia No. C-133/94*, magistrado ponente Martha Sachica de Moncaleano, 10.

the individual's right to freedom of conscience and religion was subject to restriction where it clashed with perceived societal consensus on particular issues of 'public morality'. Giving express legal protection to the position of anti-choice opinion in the country was deemed constitutive of maintaining public order. In effect, the state worked to maintain its authority by submitting individual reproductive autonomy of women to the collective public morality.

Women's public political organising on the basis of private reproductive roles

There is a theoretical and practical tendency to counterpose women and private domesticity with the major political concerns of international politics.[34] However, the patterns in which women in repressive or conflicted times enter the public realm through the politicisation of their private interests have attracted substantial feminist analysis.[35] The maternal identity ('militant motherhood') (Alvarez 1990: 57) and the need to provide for one's family and community ('consumption-based mobilisation') (Craske 2003: 65) were the leitmotifs of this mobilisation. Feminist scholars are divided as to the potential of this sort of privately motivated mobilisation to secure a feminist reorganisation of political life, concerned that it reifies understandings of women's caring roles as natural and inevitable.[36] Whatever one's position on the question of feminine versus feminist political mobilisation by women, there is a much clearer distinction between women's self-organisation in the pursuit of collectively agreed goals and the manipulation of women's collective action to pursue externally decided goals by state or non-state armed actors (Molyneux 1985). In each of the cases under analysis, political elites were alert to the significance and subversive potential of women's political organising, and consequently sought to manipulate its political character. Women entered the public sphere often on the basis of their private maternal roles, but were met by public attempts to diminish the political character and to reassert the private character of women's collective action.

Chile

The circumstances surrounding the military coup in Chile fostered the heavy politicisation of women's maternal role from the outset of the regime. Women were perceived to have been key instigators in the military's usurpation of power.[37]

34 For discussion and critique of the distinction between 'big-P' and 'little-P' politics, see Cockburn (1998: 3).

35 See, for example, the paradigmatic work of Molyneux (1985, 1998).

36 For an overview of this debate, see Molyneux (1998).

37 See the discussion of the March of the Empty Pots in Baldez (2002: 76–97).

The Allende government's dramatic programme of wealth redistribution prompted unrest in commercial and agricultural spheres, leading to massive shortages of food and other consumer goods. The food shortages, and the perceived attack on the Catholic Church, mobilised a large female constituency in opposition to the Allende government, culminating in a massive protest of women from the upper, middle and popular sector on 1 December 1971. They marched to the Presidential Palace, banging their empty pots and pans. In this heavily gendered symbolism, the Allende administration was being condemned for forcing women – through its failure to guarantee adequate provision of food – to neglect their familial duties and to enter the public world of protest and politics. In 1972 the leaders of the march formed 'Feminine Power' (El Poder Femenino) to co-ordinate women's groups in opposition to Allende. This mobilisation sealed popular perceptions of the coup as motivated by the demands of women on the Chilean military. Indeed, in the early aftermath of the coup, junta leader General Pinochet specifically invoked the mobilisation of women in order to legitimate the military's actions:

> They knew even then, the Chilean women, that the country was in danger and that, with the inefficiency of political action thus demonstrated, only in the Forces of Arms and of Order existed the salvation of Chile. Now that the path of our history has been rectified by the military *movimiento* of the 11th of September, it would not be right to forget the agreement we made with the women of our country. Their voice was for us the voice of the country, that called upon us to save it.
>
> (Augusto Pinochet, *El Mercurcio*, 24 April 1974, quoted in Baldez 2002: 118)

Within the context of highly restricted political expression, General Pinochet sought to marshal women's political activity, in their private maternal role, behind the military regime. Just as the military had drawn on heavily gendered ideology of the Chilean mother to justify overthrowing the democratically elected government, protection and valorisation of the Chilean family was to prove a potent ideological force in maintaining the dictatorship. The dictatorship actively sought to recruit Chilean women to this ideology of family. Thus, the theme of abnegation[38] and sacrifice by women (principally mothers) was to prove popular and enduring. The extensive network of Mothers' Centres (Centros de Madres, CEMAs), established in the 1950s by church and charity groups to train women in crafts, and thereby to allow them to earn an extra family income, proved ready recruiting ground for the military regime. By 1973 30,000 such centres existed through the country. Immediately after the coup, in October 1973, Pinochet created the National Secretariat of Women (Secretaría Nacional de la Mujer,

38 To refuse, relinquish or deny oneself certain rights.

SNM). Also during October 1973, he reorganised the Mothers' Centres. Pinochet's wife, Lucia Hiriart de Pinochet, became the director of both organisations. These efforts were designed to build on support provided by 'Feminine Power', and to marshal the support of Chilean women behind the military regime:

> The Chilean woman has understood how to achieve her duties, reestablishing in the soul of the people her role as a mother, the feeling of nationality, and faith in the destiny of our Fatherland.
>
> (Lucia Hiriart de Pinochet, at the inauguration of the International Year of Women, 4 April 1975, quoted in Parson 2005: 82)

The private maternal role of women was manipulated to further the public political objectives of the military regime.

Northern Ireland

Since the re-escalation of conflict in the 1960s, women's organising has been a mainstay of the jurisdiction (Roulston 1997: 65). However, the emergence and evolution of women's civil society organisations in Northern Ireland has not been immune to the political divisions that structured violent conflict in the jurisdiction (Roulston 1997: 56). Rather, women's civil society organising in Northern Ireland has been very largely determined by these prevailing political divisions. As Rick Wilford has observed: '[E]fforts to forge [a united] women's movement in Northern Ireland ha[ve] foundered over the mutually reinforcing cleavages of nationality and religion' (Wilford 1996: 41). The detention conditions of women in Armagh prison prompted intense pressure on the Northern Ireland Women's Rights Movement (NIWRM), as the Republican women engaged in 'dirty protests' in order to receive official recognition of their imprisonment as political. Nell McCafferty captured the dilemma confronting feminists with graphic detail as she wrote in the *Irish Times* that year: 'the smell of menstrual blood on the walls of Armagh prison smells to high heaven. Shall we turn our noses up?' (McCafferty 1980). Nevertheless, the NIWRM refused to take a position on political status, as it was 'not a feminist aim' (Loughran 1988: 59). There were concerns that supporting the women's protest would be perceived as supporting the IRA's armed campaign. The inadequacy of feminism as a unifying political agenda was painfully apparent, as 'Armagh became a metaphor for everything that has kept Irish women divided from each other' (Ward, 1991: 156). The fraught political backdrop of ethnic divisions, inter-communal violence, and routine presence of highly militarised security forces, meant that women's mobilisation in Northern Ireland during the conflict came to be defined by the practical co-operation of women on issues of material survival for the family and community (Rooney 1995: 45). Hence, rather than a 'women's movement' per se, Northern Ireland has been home to a 'women's sector' since the 1970s. This 'women's sector' consists of a large network of organisations of, and for, women, defined not by their avowed feminist commitments, but by their common concern for material survival issues of women and families.

In Northern Ireland, the proroguement of the local parliament and the institution of direct rule from London over the jurisdiction in 1972 resulted in an absence of obvious sites and targets of political participation. Consequently, alternative sites of political participation had to be forged in order to influence state decision-making. Civil society organisations flourished during the period of direct rule. Tenant associations, trade unions, civil rights movements, Left politics and community development emerged initially in a spirit of self-help. Over time, these organisations gained capacity and the 'professional' bodies responsible for decision-making in health and social services, employment and training, education, the environment and agriculture sought broader input in their decision-making. Consequently, in the interests of 'getting the business of government done', several civil society organisations came to have significant policy influence in Northern Ireland.[39] Further, this development of a vibrant civil society was not without gender implications. Women proliferated in these organisations, as volunteers, staff members and service-users (Meehan 2003). The response of state institutions was to selectively include and validate certain forms of women's organising, while attempting to exclude and delegitimate other forms, principally in order to depoliticise women's organising. The state wielded its influence in this regard through government funding and regulating access to public decision-making.

In 1985 the British government introduced the *Hurd Principles* for determining the eligibility of community organisations for state funding, in which organisations deemed to be directly or indirectly advancing the aims of paramilitary groups were precluded. In the implementation of these principles, various community organisations, largely from the Catholic community, were either denied funding or had their funding withdrawn. The specifically gendered impact of this political vetting became apparent in 1990 when Belfast City Council refused to continue to grant aid to the Falls Women's Centre in Republican West Belfast. This prompted the coming together of the Downtown Women's Centre and the Shankill Women's Centre in Loyalist West Belfast in solidarity with the Falls Women's Centre to protest at the City Council's decision, and ultimately the decision was reversed.[40]

The general trend in non-governmental organisations, as they have increased in size and influence, was to move from advocacy work to service-provision.[41] With this institutionalisation of their role as service-providers, they have increasingly become government 'partners' in state provision of social services, with attendant influence in state decision-making (Morison and Livingstone 1995). However, the privileging of women's activism in social service provision over

39 See further Hadfield (1989: Chapter 5).

40 See further Cockburn (1998: 76).

41 Avila Kilmurray, Director of the Community Foundation for Northern Ireland and Founder Member of Northern Ireland Women's Coalition, personal communication, 2 July 2007.

more overtly political activity works to reinforce notions of women's caring role as both natural and inevitable.

Colombia

The threat to women's political organising in Colombia has been of a more overtly violent nature. Writing in 2001, the UN Special Rapporteur on Violence Against Women noted the heavy toll that the conflict violence was taking on women's organisations, as the groups were losing their organisational processes and also losing their autonomy to armed actors (UN Special Rapporteur on Violence Against Women 2001: 23). This concern over the impact of the conflict on the autonomy of women's organisations has been reiterated in feminist analysis of the reinsertion element of the current demobilisation process of paramilitaries taking place under the auspices of the 2005 Justice and Peace Law. A Report examining the reintegration process of paramilitaries in Tierralta concluded that the process was imposing further limitations on the rights of free associations and expression of women as a consequence of the hegemony of paramilitarism in the zone (Corporación Humanas 2007).

There is overwhelming evidence of the more direct targeting of women civil society leaders for violence and threats of violence. This violence is generalised across women's movements making demands through the justice and peace process. It reached a head in 2007 with the four high-profile assassinations of women leaders within a period of two months.[42] In response to these assassinations, women's peace organisation Iniciativa de la Mujeres por la Paz (IMP) brought a *tutela* application for the protection of 13 named women, drawn from IMP leaders and high-profile victims being supported by IMP. The application ultimately reached the Constitutional Court. The Court held that the existing programme for protection of victims and witnesses[43] was inadequate to protect the applicants' constitutional rights to life and security, and that the Minister for Justice and National Office of the Prosecutor were under a legal obligation to establish a programme of protection within six months that specifically addressed the added vulnerability of women victims seeking to avail themselves of the justice and peace process.[44]

These examples demonstrate not just the direct targeting of women political activists by paramilitaries, but the failure of state institutions to effectively protect and defend the rights of those women to politically organise.

42 Yolanda Izquierdo Berrio, Carmen Cecilia Santana Romaña, Osiris Jacqueline Amaya Beltrán, Judith Vergara Correa.

43 Established further to Presidential Decree 3570 of 2007.

44 This account is taken from Iniciativa de Mujeres Colombianas por la Paz (2009).

Table 2.1 The Web of Harms: the relationship of public to private harms against women in contexts of political violence

	Chile	*Northern Ireland*	*Colombia*
Private violence and deficient state response to that violence	Deferential judiciary, failing to protect rights and security of individuals	Police neglecting domestic violence, prioritising political violence	State's prioritisation of conflict violence, general climate of impunity for violence against women
Privatised violence against women by public actors	Sexualised torture of female political dissidents	Strip-searching of women political prisoners	Brutal regulation of the reproductive functions of combatant women
The public regulation of women's private reproductive lives	Linking 'national security' and state pro-natalism	Conservative political consensus on women used to balance otherwise violently opposed parties	Privileging 'public morality' over women's individual autonomy
Women's political organising on the basis of a private role	Manipulating mothers' centres	Privileging women's apolitical organising	Direct targeting of women civil society leaders for violence and threats of violence

THE WEB OF HARMS: NORM, DOCTRINE, POLITICS

This final section of the chapter elaborates the normative, doctrinal and political merits of placing the notion of a web of gender-based harms against women at the centre of feminist engagement with transitional justice.

The web of harms: a normative construct

Chapter 1 outlined the grounds for sustained feminist critique of the public/private divide, namely the tendency for this divide to neatly separate the harms in women's lives from the concerns (and obligations) of the state, and to consign women to an apolitical space. Notwithstanding this critique, feminists have seldom completely rejected the public/private distinction. Instead, feminist focus has attached to the mutability of the public/private divide (Landes 1998), and how individuals and groups with resources have great discretion in determining where the divide is drawn.[45] Those without resources, however, must endure the most exploitative probing of the 'private', in particular to access the public resources of the state (Fineman 1995). The control of women's reproductive functions reflects this exploitative drawing of the public/private divide. For example, the requirement that, in order to access abortion services restricted to cases of rape and incest or fatal foetal abnormality, individual women must endure investigation of the most intimate areas of their lives. Consequently, rather than a rejection of the public/private divide altogether, many feminists have called for the distinction to be drawn in a way that is less exploitative of women (see especially Lacey and Frazer 1993).

The value of a private sphere, respected by the state, resonates all the more in cases of transition. Often the prior regime was characterised by the perpetration of violence in the 'private' sphere, for example through house searches of civilians or strip-searching prisoners. In this context, establishing a private sphere, free of interference from a state of still dubious legitimacy, is an understandable priority. Further, for women's movements seeking to make gains through the transitional state, the overall project of rehabilitating the public sphere is helpful. The state can thereby become a legitimate site of feminist activity and feminist gains.

The public/private divide is a potent theoretical tool in gender analysis of political violence and transitions out of such violence. To surrender such a tool can only weaken gender analysis of transitions. Rather, the web of harms retains the public/private divide, and focuses on revealing the relationship of the public to the private and the ways in which this relationship changes during transition.

The web of harms: a doctrinal framework

The doctrinal motivation for the web of harms against women, which is also – admittedly – a pragmatic motivation, is rooted in the understanding of harm within established legal categories in transitional justice. As noted, transitional justice is typically concerned with widespread human rights violations of a 'most serious' nature. Even mechanisms ostensibly more flexible than courts, such as truth commissions, borrow from established legal categories in their definition of harm (Ní Aoláin and Turner 2007). Similarly, administrative reparations programmes in transitional justice respond to a 'traditional catalogue of civil and political rights violations' (de Greiff 2006: 7). Thus the common legal devices of transitional justice turn upon the very designation of public civil and political rights violations, as explicitly distinct from private harms that occur in contexts of political violence. Against this backdrop, the strategic wisdom of articulating the commonality in women's experiences of harms before, during and after political

45 See especially Nancy Fraser's (1998) enlightening analysis of the Anita Hill–Clarence Thomas hearings, in which Thomas could successfully assert the 'private' nature of his behaviour, while Hill's behaviour was exposed to repeated and intense scrutiny.

violence is questionable. As Margaret Urban Walker observes: 'In a perspective that looks to violence with an eye to *reparations* for victims, the individual victim's experience of catastrophic *discontinuity* needs to hold central place' (Urban Walker 2009: 29, emphasis in original).

Efforts to establish a continuum of state responsibility for public and private harms against women have secured remarkable gains in recent years, in terms both of state obligations to prohibit, prevent and punish violence perpetrated against women by private actors, and in the responsibility of states to guarantee the physical integrity of women carrying pregnancies. States are now bound by overlapping positive obligations in respect of private harms against women. While, formally, political violence does not exempt states from their due diligence obligations, in practice the political exigencies that pertain in contexts of political violence result in the loosening of legal obligations on those states in respect of their positive obligations. As experience tells us, in the context of transitional justice instituted in the aftermath of widespread political violence, these legal devices rely on a traditional, smaller and less exacting catalogue of negative obligations on states to refrain from the direct perpetration of harms against its citizens.

By articulating the qualitative impact of political violence on private harms against women, as undertaken in this book, it may be possible to articulate a different, though related, set of obligations on the transitioning state in respect of violence against women and women's reproductive rights. The web of harms provides a framework for nuanced engagement with legal categories in transitional justice that emphasises the importance of ensuring accountability for past public harms against women, but by also revealing the impact of past political violence on women's private experiences of harm, demonstrates the need for transitional justice to provide some form of redress also to those exacerbated private harms.

The web of harms: a political tool

The final, and most significant, reason for adopting a web of harms thesis concerns the political context for feminist engagement with transitional states. Advancing the notion of state responsibility for private harms against women is a difficult political agenda. The length of time required to secure today's modest gains is a vivid illustration of the challenges involved in making private harm a public responsibility. Nevertheless, securing state accountability for the public harms of the past is also a thorny political agenda in transitional states. Demands to 'look to the future' and to 'move on' and 'close the book' on harms of the past are potent in contexts in which the past is deemed difficult, divisive and potentially destabilising to a transition (Fletcher *et al* 2009). It is important, therefore, for feminists to avoid an undifferentiated approach to seeking accountability for past 'public' harms and ongoing 'private' harms. This sort of undifferentiated approach would be insufficiently sensitive to the deeply *political* context in which demands for state accountability are made in transitional contexts. States, eager to break from the past, may view any question of state liability in past harms as antithetical to the transitional project and damaging to the recuperation of state legitimacy. Conversely, demands to address ongoing private harms, such as domestic violence, may offer the new state an opportunity to demonstrate its commitment to human rights and non-violence without costly reminders of the state's relationship to past harms. Women's movements would be well advised against being naive about the extent to which feminist demands can legitimate powerful political narratives of states in transition. To draw on Elizabeth Spelman's groundbreaking feminist analysis of overlapping systems of disadvantage:

> Ironically, the categories and methods we may find most natural and straightforward to use as we explore the connections [between harms may] confuse those connections rather than clarify them.
>
> (Spelman 1990: 115)

The web of harms, by contrast, encourages political sensitivity to the differential position of the state to past and future harms, and to public and private harms, and for feminists to strategise accordingly, in order to ensure the recognition and redress of the widest possible range of harms against women, both public and private.

CONCLUSION

Defining harms in transitional justice has been one of the key sites of feminist intervention and contestation in this field. This chapter has sought to draw empirical analysis of women's experiences of violence, infringements of reproductive autonomy and political manipulation, together with feminist theoretical elaboration of those harms, in order to speak to dominant categories of harms in transitional justice. Findings and analysis in this chapter underpin the remainder of the book, as it examines human rights outcomes for women in terms of this web of harms against women. Normatively, do transitional justice processes recognise the exacerbating impact of public on private harms against women? Doctrinally, do transitional justice processes provide accountability for this web of harms? Politically, do transitional justice processes affirm women's agency as they mobilise around a web of harms against women?

22

Anticipating the Past: Transitional Justice and Socio-Economic Wrongs

Lars Waldorf

Abstract

Even as transitional justice struggles to deliver on its original promises of truth, justice and reconciliation, more demands are being placed on it. Over the past several years, the transitional justice 'industry' has embraced holistic approaches that have it doing ever more. This article critically examines transitional justice's recent attention towards historically constructed socio-economic inequalities. It begins by looking at the shift in transitional justice discourse and practice with respect to economic and social rights. Next, it discusses the arguments made for transitional justice's engagement with those rights and looks at efforts by truth commissions and administrative reparations programmes to address them. Finally, it argues that transitional justice should avoid directly addressing past socio-economic wrongs and explores some alternate paths.

> We will not anticipate the past! ... our retrospection will be all to the future.
>
> (Sheridan, 2008: n.p.)

Introduction

Writing in 2002, one scholar bemoaned the fact that transitional justice was 'not concerned with measuring and overcoming the persistent effects of unjust advantage from the past on social and economic relations under the successor regime' (Meister, 2002: 97). That is no longer the case. In an influential public lecture in 2006, Louise Arbour, then United Nations High Commissioner for Human Rights, called on transitional justice to 'make the gigantic leap' that would enable justice to be fully realized in post-authoritarian and post-conflict societies:

> Transitional justice must have the ambition of assisting the transformation of oppressed societies into free ones by addressing the injustices of the past through measures that will procure an equitable future. It must reach to, but also beyond the crises and abuses committed during the conflict which led to the transition, into the human rights violations that pre-existed the conflict and caused, or contributed to it. When making that search, it is likely that one would expose a great number of violations of economic, social and cultural (ESC) rights and discriminatory practices. (2006: 3–4)

Several scholars and practitioners have heeded that call.[1] The *International Journal of Transitional Justice* devoted a special issue to transitional justice and development in 2008, and the International Center for Transitional Justice (ICTJ) published an edited collection on the same topic in 2009 (in the aptly named series 'Advancing Transitional Justice'). In the past several years, Morocco (with funding from the European Union) has provided community reparations to 11 regions that were economically marginalized (i.e. excluded from development programmes) during the period from 1956 to 1999 (ICTJ, 2009: 24–28, 42).

Even as transitional justice struggles to deliver on its original promises of truth, justice and reconciliation (see Olsen et al., 2010; Thoms et al., 2010), more and more demands are being placed on it. Rama Mani, for example, insists that transitional justice 'will lose credibility in the predominantly impoverished and devastated societies where it operates' if it does not tackle social injustice, corruption, resource exploitation and criminal violence (2008: 253–254). Mani is in good company (see Carranza, 2008; Cavallaro and Albuja, 2008; Duthie, 2008; Gready, 2010; Laplante, 2007; Miller, 2008; Muvingi, 2009). Over the past several years, the transitional justice 'industry' has embraced holistic approaches that have it doing ever more (Gready, 2010: 7; see Fletcher and Weinstein, 2002; UN, 2004: para. 26). This is exemplified by the ICTJ's recent efforts to link transitional justice to the development and peace-building enterprises (which also happen to be better funded).[2]

I am wary of efforts to have transitional justice tackle historically constructed socio-economic inequalities. For, as Mani herself acknowledges, 'existing TJ mechanisms are already overcharged, their responsibilities too heavy, public expectations too unrealistic and finances already too lean' (2008: 255). In this article, I examine transitional justice's turn towards economic and social wrongs. I start by looking at the recent shift in transitional justice discourse and practice with respect to economic and social (ESC)[3] rights. Here, I explain why transitional justice initially ignored ESC rights and why it is now considering them. Next, I critically discuss transitional justice's engagement with ESC rights, with an emphasis on the two mechanisms that have gone the furthest in addressing violations of ESC rights: truth commissions and administrative reparations programmes. Finally, I raise several concerns about well-meaning efforts to have transitional justice address past socio-economic wrongs and then consider alternate approaches.

Neglecting Economic and Social Rights

There are several reasons why transitional justice has historically tended to neglect economic and social wrongs. First, transitional justice has been heavily influenced by human rights and, as such, has replicated that discipline's longstanding legalistic bias towards civil and political rights, which are seen as more amenable to both 'naming and shaming' (in the court of public opinion) and more justiciable (in a court of law) (Arbour, 2006: 6–7, 10–13).[4] In Ken Roth's (2004) classic (and heavily contested) formulation, it is easier to identify violations, violators, and remedies when it comes to civil and political rights. Furthermore, a violations approach does not easily lend itself to remedying structural inequalities and exclusions (see Hayner, 2010: 166).

Second, the rise of transitional justice has been profoundly shaped by criminal justice (Arbour, 2006: 3), particularly the concomitant development of international criminal law, which mostly treats those civil and political rights linked to bodily integrity (see Rome Statute of the International Criminal Court, 1998: articles 6–8). International criminal law emphasizes individual criminal responsibility rather than structural causes (Miller, 2008: 275). Not surprisingly then, there have been very few prosecutions under international criminal law for massive violations of ESC rights (but see Arbour, 2006: 16–17; UN OHCHR, 2008: 1–2, n. 5). Overall, international criminal law conceptualizes justice in narrow terms as accountability and procedural fairness (due process). In her speech, Arbour criticized United Nation Secretary General Kofi Annan for adopting this narrow formulation of justice in his important 2004 report on transitional justice (2006: 4–5; see also UN, 2004: para. 7).

Third, transitional justice has often played the role of handmaiden to 'liberal peacebuilding', which applies the liberal peace thesis – that market democracies are less likely to go to war – from inter-state to intra-state conflicts. The notion is that political and economic liberalization promotes sustainable and 'positive' peace. Consequently, liberal peacebuilding efforts are directed at building the rule of law, instituting electoral democracy, and carrying out neoliberal economic reforms (see Newman et al., 2009; Paris, 2004). Gready (2010a: 233) faults transitional justice for having been partly co-opted by the globalized neoliberal agenda, which largely ignores ESC rights.

Finally, the initial absence of ESC rights is explicable in terms of transitional justice's intellectual history. Transitional justice emerges out of the late 20th-century political transitions from authoritarian to democratizing regimes in Eastern Europe and the Southern Cone. At the time, those transitions were conceptualized as relatively short-term affairs. As such, economic change was something for successor regimes to tackle *after* the transition period had produced new (and presumably more democratic) constitutions, laws, and institutions. In addition, scholar-activists working on transitions focused on 'legal-institutional reform, rather than transformation at the socio-economic level' (Arthur, 2009: 347). Furthermore, communism's collapse and the Left's decline had discredited redistributive politics. As John Torpey points out, 'reparations politics' (which includes transitional justice)

> is a product of particular historical circumstances – in particular, it is a response to a post-utopian context that differs sharply from the period that preceded it – and seeks to achieve

> some of the aims of the progressive agenda through a focus on righting the past rather than on the basis of the kind of idealized vision of the human future that drove much that went before it. (2006: 7; see also Galanter, 2002: 121)

This historical and intellectual context helps explain why 'prosecutions, truth-telling, restitution, and reform of abusive state institutions – not some other measures of justice, such as those associated with claims for distributive justice – were recognized as the legitimate justice initiatives' in political transitions (Arthur, 2009: 326, emphasis in the original).

Engaging Economic and Social Rights

Over the past few years, there has been increasing criticism of transitional justice for its neglect of socio-economic wrongs and a related push to have it deal with those wrongs. As noted above, Arbour's call for transitional justice to engage with such wrongs has resonated with influential transnational advocacy networks (including the International Center for Transitional Justice and the *International Journal of Transitional Justice*). So, how do we explain this shift? First, the international human rights movement has increasingly championed socio-economic rights and their justiciability, which has enhanced its appeal and relevance in the Global South.[5] Second, recent years have seen the 'end of the transition paradigm' as many post-authoritarian and post-conflict regimes have stalled in a political 'grey zone' that is neither authoritarian nor democratic (Carothers, 2002). As a result, the emphasis on legal-institutional reforms (typified by rule of law programmes) is being supplemented by more socio-economic interventions (such as legal empowerment) (see Carothers, 2006; Golub, 2010). Third, the global economic crisis has taken the shine off neoliberal economics, which forms a pillar of liberal peacebuilding. Fourth, post-conflict programming (including transitional justice) increasingly emphasizes the need for holistic, complementary approaches (see Boraine, 2006). The United Nations has championed 'integrated' strategies that bring together peace, justice, development, and security considerations (see UN, 2011). For transitional justice scholars and practitioners, holism appears to offer a way out of hard dilemmas (truth versus justice, peace versus justice). It also promises to replace competition over donor funding (transitional justice *versus* development) with complementary linkages (transitional justice *and* development).

Arbour makes both a normative and an instrumental case for including gross violations of ESC rights in transitional justice. First, she argues for the indivisibility of human rights. While states have repeatedly affirmed that principle (most fatuously at the Vienna World Conference on Human Rights in 1993), it has yet to become anything approaching customary international law. Even if we assume rights are indivisible, that offers no guidance on which rights to prioritize in the context of fragile transitions and limited resources.[6] A recent empirical study found that a successor regime's choice of transitional justice mechanism is positively correlated with its economic health: poorer countries were more likely to select cheaper transitional justice mechanisms (amnesties and truth commissions) over more expensive ones (trials) (Olsen et al., 2010: 77).

Second, Arbour argues from an instrumental perspective that transitional justice will not have a sustainable impact if it ignores ESC rights:

> Given transitional justice's additional objective of bringing about social transformation that will prevent a resurgence of conflict, it is not only important to build dispute resolution institutions, but perhaps even more effective to attack the sources of the legitimate grievances that, if unaddressed, are likely to fuel the next conflagration. (2006: 8)

This argument is problematic on two grounds. For one thing, the extent to which poverty, inequality, and ESC wrongs drive armed conflict is highly debated among social scientists (see Berdal and Malone, 2000; Stewart, 2008; Thoms and Ron, 2007). For another thing, Arbour assumes what she needs to demonstrate: that transitional justice actually has the aim and ability to '[bring] about social transformation'.

What is conspicuously absent from Arbour's speech is any mention of what the victims supposedly served by transitional justice actually want (see Shaw and Waldorf, 2010; Nee and Uvin, 2010; Weinstein et al., 2010). When asked, victims often prioritize present economic needs. For example, an attitudinal survey of Nepalese victims found that they listed their 'immediate needs' as compensation (24%), education (17%), housing and clothing (12%), employment (8%), locating the disappeared (7%), and punishing perpetrators (3%) (ICTJ, 2008; see Robins, 2009). In other words, victims wanted reparative and distributive justice more than retributive justice. Surveys in Kenya (Robins 2011b), northern Uganda (Pham et al., 2007) and the Democratic Republic of Congo (Vinck and Pham, 2008) have produced similar results. As the authors of the Congo study wrote: 'As long as basic survival needs are not met and safety is not guaranteed, social reconstruction programs, including transitional justice mechanisms, will not be perceived as a priority and will lack the level of support needed for their success' (Vinck and Pham, 2008: 404; see also de Greiff, 2009: 31). These findings suggest that everyday injustices rooted in historical inequalities may be as important, if not more important, for many survivors than the extraordinary injustices of gross human rights abuses. Or as one young Rwandan genocide survivor put it, 'We've got used to the genocide; it's daily life that's the problem' (Pells, 2009).

Using Transitional Justice Mechanisms to Address Socio-Economic Wrongs

The strongest rationale then for transitional justice addressing socio-economic wrongs is where that reflects the needs and priorities of victims and survivors (in specific contexts). However, the question remains whether transitional justice mechanisms are practically suited for correcting such wrongs. To date, the two mechanisms that have gone furthest in handling economic and social wrongs are truth commissions and reparations.

Truth commissions

In general, truth commissions have been hesitant to remedy economic and social wrongs. The South African Truth and Reconciliation Commission (TRC) focused narrowly on 'bodily integrity rights' rather than on apartheid (a crime against humanity) and its violations of ESC rights. In so doing, the TRC acknowledged its own limitations:

> The consequences of human rights violations [due to apartheid] ... cannot be measured only in the human lives lost through deaths, detentions, dirty tricks and disappearances, but in the human lives withered away through enforced poverty and other kinds of deprivation. (Truth and Reconciliation Commission of South Africa, 2003: vol. 1, ch. 4, p. 65)

Mahmood Mamdani famously criticized the TRC for not treating the 3.5 million individuals who underwent forced removals as victims:

> The Latin [American] analogy obscured what was distinctive about apartheid. For the violence of apartheid was aimed less at individuals than at entire communities, and entire population groups ... The point of torture, terror, death, was even more far-reaching: its aim was to dispossess people of means of livelihood. (2000: 179)

The TRC's narrow focus on perpetrators of extra-judicial killings, disappearances, and torture let apartheid's many beneficiaries off the hook all too easily. As Mamdani further commented: 'Whereas the focus on perpetrators fuels the demand for justice as criminal justice, that on beneficiaries shifts the focus to a notion of justice as social justice' (quoted in Torpey, 2006: 55).

At times, truth commissions have addressed the economic and structural underpinnings of gross human rights abuses in three inter-related ways: through their hearings, reports and recommendations. The South African Truth and Reconciliation Commission did hold specialized hearings on the business sector's role in human rights violations, even if the resulting testimony was not sufficiently incorporated into the final report or its recommendations (Gready, 2010: 213). More ambitiously, the Timor-Leste truth commission held hearings on famine and forced displacement, and then linked 'the right of people to food' with the denial of other rights, such as freedom of movement (Commission for Reception, Truth and Reconciliation in East Timor, 2005: chap. 7(3), p. 3).

Other truth commission reports (e.g. Guatemala, Peru and Sierra Leone) addressed the socio-economic factors behind the conflicts, including dispossession, inequality, exclusion, and even the colonial legacy. Yet, socio-economic factors were mostly relegated to the sections on historical background, where they could be more easily ignored. As Lisa Laplante observes, 'presenting socioeconomic root causes of conflict as historical context leaves policy change to the discretion of political leaders, while presenting them as rights violations makes redress and reform a political imperative' (2008: 341).

Finally, truth commission recommendations are often a long laundry list that extends from human rights protections to good governance to micro-credit financing. Mani contends that 'truth commissions should go further than analysis of causes and should propose workable solutions for these [social] injustices' (2008: 256). Gready is rightly sceptical, stating that while truth commissions could do more to name and analyse ESC violations, it is unrealistic to expect them to offer 'informed strategic recommendations on everything from torture to education' – they simply lack the expertise for such policy formulation (2010: 215). More fundamentally, though, truth commission recommendations are often ignored, not because they are unworkable, but because those commissions are inherently weak institutions with short life-spans (see UN OHCHR, 2008: 11–12).

Some argue that truth commissions can, and should, do more to remedy socio-economic wrongs. In particular, several scholars propose that truth commissions should investigate corruption and economic crimes as a way of delegitimizing past regimes and consolidating successor regimes (Carranza, 2008: 315–316, 320–321; Cavallaro and Albuja, 2008: 140). However, the UN Office of the High Commissioner for Human Rights counsels a fairly cautious approach:

> Those drafting the mandate should be conscious of the dangers and difficulties of including economic crimes within a truth commission's scope. The methodology and timing required for investigating corruption and economic crimes are quite different from those required for investigating individual or systematic practices of torture or killings, for example. Furthermore, a broad focus on 'violations of economic and social rights' might suggest the need to look into poverty, homelessness, education policy failures and other social ills. Although these are critically important subjects, this could risk expanding the mandate of the commission so broadly that it may be impossible to reasonably complete its task. (2006: 9)

In addition, the inclusion of economic crimes could provoke wider opposition to transitional justice – not just from the political and economic elites who benefitted from those crimes (de Greiff, 2009: 41), but also from complicit beneficiary groups (see Mamdani, 2000: 179). Like the UN OHCHR, the International Center for Transitional Justice has recommended that successor regimes deal with economic crimes outside truth commissions (Hayner and Bosire, 2003).

Reparations

Reparations are the most victim-centred transitional justice mechanism (see UN, 2005). As such, they have the potential to respond more directly to victims' needs and priorities. Indeed, when victims' attitudes are surveyed, a majority often ranked compensation as more important than trials (see Robins, 2009: 324). Yet, the very fact that 'reparations are explicitly and primarily carried out *on behalf of victims*' (UN OHCHR, 2008: 2–3) goes some way to explaining why there is so little political will among successor regimes and donors to provide reparations (see Segovia, 2006) – for victims usually have little political clout. Successor regimes frequently ignore, evade and delay implementing the reparations programmes recommended by truth commissions or other bodies. Tellingly, only 14 of the 84 transitions between 1970 and 2004 implemented reparations programmes (Olsen et al., 2010: 53).

Instead of spending scarce resources on reparations to individuals, successor regimes (even those nominally controlled by victims and survivors) prefer to promote future-oriented development that will benefit larger social groups (see Colvin, 2008: 418–419). According to the UN OHCHR: 'Governments in developing countries facing demands for reparations are strongly inclined to argue that development *is* reparation ... Beneficiaries perceive them, correctly, as programmes that distribute goods to which they have rights as citizens, and not necessarily as victims' (2008: 26; see also de Greiff, 2006: 470; Roht-Arriaza, 2004: 130). Development-as-reparations also undermines the ability of reparations to function as state acknowledgement of wrongdoing (Roht-Arriaza and Orlovsky, 2009: 172–173).

Debate over reparations can also preclude or obscure the larger political debates to be had over redistribution. As Miller observes, reparations 'allow the state to redistribute wealth only in a strikingly narrow manner, frequently compensating only those named by the transitional justice mechanism' (2008: 284–285; see also Gready, 2010: 216; Muvingi, 2009: 180). Reparations programmes are inherently divisive, pitting individuals and groups against one another over who gets compensated and by how much. Such conflict can inhibit collective political action against the successor regime over economic policies (Miller, 2008: 284–285).

Peru offers an illuminating example of the difficulties in using reparations to address socio-economic wrongs. Peru's Truth and Reconciliation Commission found that most victims 'requested redress for their current needs, which arose from inequitable social and economic conditions and not necessarily the war' (Laplante, 2008: 351–352). That many victims prioritized needs over damages suggested they were not satisfied with a reparations model that returned them to the status quo ante – an inequitable status quo that had contributed to the conflict (see Laplante, 2009: 90).

In a fascinating account, Lisa Magarrell (2003) described the Commission's internal debates over whether reparations should address civil and political rights or ESC rights; past violations or present consequences; direct or indirect harms; and individual or collective reparations. Some Commission staff initially proposed remedying consequences (rather than the initial violations) through 'collective reparations measures in the form of social services, infrastructure and economic development for the affected population' (Magarrell, 2003: 93). This ambitious proposal quickly proved impracticable. As Magarrell recounts:

> First, the universe of harm it intended to redress was enormous and the victim population particularly difficult to define ... At the same time, the categories of harm became very generalized ... Causation issues became mixed with other underlying social problems that exacerbated or coincided with harms caused directly by the abuses experienced ... Thus, in one fell swoop, one can lose the specific recognition of human rights victims as such, and frustrate those who suffer the same problems but are not included in the [reparations] program. (2003: 93)

These concerns, among others, pushed the Commission to eventually adopt a programme that limited itself to remedying victims for past violations of civil and political rights through a mix of individual and collective benefits. The Commission's final report stated that its reparations programme 'does not seek to resolve problems of poverty, exclusion and inequality', noting that these were better left to the state's social development policies (quoted in Magarrell, 2003: 95). When it came time to implement a reparations programme, however, the state started off with community reparations – 'taking the approach the TRC had first considered and decided against' (Hayner, 2010: 174) – until pressured to provide individualized reparations. From 2007 to 2009, the community reparations programme identified nearly 1000 communities affected by violence that were to receive investment projects worth up to $33,000 per community (ICTJ, 2009: 31).

Practical Difficulties

As the discussion above demonstrates, there are enormous practical difficulties with having transitional justice mechanisms tackle historically constructed socio-economic inequalities. First, those mechanisms are already over-stretched and under-funded. Reparations programmes, for example, do not have the funds to cover victims of massive economic and social wrongs and are unlikely to acquire such funds (de Greiff, 2009: 40). Second, there is a danger of raising already inflated expectations of what transitional justice mechanisms can accomplish. Truth commissions have already suffered self-inflicted wounds by over-promising reconciliation. Third, transitional justice mechanisms have a relatively short life-span during periods of political transition. By contrast, the remedying of socio-economic injustices is a long-term political project. As Williams notes:

> Short-term, provisional reparations programs conceived in response to specific waves of human rights violations are probably not the best tool for addressing long-term patterns of inequality. The latter involve human rights issues, but are essentially political questions ... they merit deliberation, sensitivity to local political factors, and democratic accountability. (2007: 49)

In other words, the reduction of longstanding inequality is necessarily 'post-transitional' – something to be accomplished as part of creating a new and hopefully more democratic order.[7] Finally, transitional justice scholars and practitioners have no expertise in designing and implementing programmes to reduce socio-economic inequalities.

Conclusion

In my view, transitional justice is inherently short-term, legalistic and corrective. As such, it should focus on accountability for gross violations of civil and political rights. This is not to deny the importance of addressing past and present socio-economic inequalities as a matter of both justice and potential conflict prevention. But that should be done through democratic politics and distributive justice – not through elite bargains and transitional justice (see Howard-Hassmann, 2008: 184). Well-meaning efforts to have transitional justice tackle socio-economic wrongs will simply freight it with yet more unrealizable expectations.

If, as I have argued, transitional justice in its current form is ill-suited to addressing socio-economic wrongs, then where does that leave us? One option is to re-conceptualize transitional justice. For example, Wendy Lambourne has called for 'a transformative justice model of transitional justice' that brings together economic justice along with legal, psychosocial, and political justice in an effort to transform both structures and relations (2009: 46). In a footnote, Lambourne acknowledges that her 'model risks trying to include too much ... thus becoming analytically overstretched and impractical'

(2009: 46, n. 61). That is indeed the case. Lambourne's model ends up conflating (rather than linking) transitional justice with Rami Mani's (2002: 3–22) conception of peacebuilding (which combines legal, rectificatory and distributive justice). By contrast, Paul Gready et al. propose a narrower concept of transformative justice that is analytically distinct from transitional justice. In their formulation, transformative justice supplements transitional justice by 'seek[ing] to change pre-conflict structures in ways that are more inclusive, less unequal and more fair' (2010). Still, what this would look like in practice and how it differs from rights-based, conflict-sensitive development remains unclear.

A second option would involve linking transitional justice and development while respecting their differences and distinct domains (de Greiff, 2009: 29, 63; Lenzen, 2009: 84). After all, there is a fundamental difference between transitional justice and development: the former mostly emphasizes corrective justice, while the latter mostly focuses on distributive justice (de Greiff, 2009: 63). Rather than having transitional justice directly tackle socio-economic inequality, it might benefit development indirectly by promoting inclusive and participatory citizenship (or social integration), especially for victims and survivors (de Greiff, 2009: 62). What this actually means in terms of developing 'programmatic links' between transitional justice and development has yet to be seen (de Greiff, 2009: 61; see also DFID/ICTJ, 2007). There is a risk, however, that such links may make transitional justice even more state-centric than it is already (especially given the current trend in development towards providing budget or sector support).

A third option is to reorient transitional justice so it becomes more responsive to the immediate priorities of victims themselves (see Robins, 2011a). A recent survey of 376 victims of Kenya's 2007–2008 post-election violence found 'The basic economic needs that drive the reparative demands of victims can be summarized in terms of homes and livelihoods; without these, particularly the latter, victims perceive the impact of the violation as continuing' (Robins, 2011b: 28). Once these needs are met, then victims can be consulted about other transitional justice mechanisms (such as trials and truth commissions). This would be a capabilities approach to transitional justice.

One innovative proposal for addressing the economic needs of victims is to provide them with reparations in the form of shares in microfinance institutions (MFIs). Hans Dieter Seibel and Andrea Armstrong favour a scenario in which

> governments could issue smaller collective grants to villages or subdistricts as the start-up capital for local MFIs, but also individual cash payments, with which beneficiaries may choose to buy shares or open accounts in the newly created microfinance institution ... This option does recognize individual suffering, but also provides a neutral space where, finances permitting, other members of the community may also participate. Low-level perpetrators would indeed be allowed to participate, but their cash contribution to an organization that at least initially would be owned by victims could contribute to restoring the inequalities of power within the community. Particularly for victims that have suffered abuse which led to their subsequent ostracism ... these types of institutions can promote social inclusion and participation by facilitating interpersonal contact. (2006: 687)

There are several other advantages to such a reparations scheme. First, it increases the likelihood that reparations payments will contribute to sustainable income-generating activities. Second, it provides 'safe savings for the poor, enhancement of agency, expansion of services, and civic repair through the building of financial institutions' (Bernstein, 2009: 310). Third, it is more likely to be financed by international donors than other reparations programmes (Bernstein, 2009: 310; Seibel and Armstrong, 2006: 694; see Segovia, 2006). Finally, such microfinance institutions often give women greater access to credit. In this way, transitional justice can make a limited contribution to the process of chipping away at historically entrenched gender inequalities (Bernstein, 2009: 315).

Notes

The author thanks Paul Gready for incisive comments on an earlier draft and Scott Straus for the opportunity to present some of the ideas here to faculty and graduate students at the University of Wisconsin-Madison (as part of the Mellon Sawyer Seminar series, 'Vulnerability and Resilience: Rethinking Human Rights for the 21st Century'). He is grateful to Gerry Johnstone and Joel Quirk for the invitation to join both the workshop on 'Repairing Historical Wrongs' and this special issue, as well as for their helpful comments on earlier drafts. Finally, he appreciates the comments of two anonymous reviewers.

1. Some go further, arguing that transitional justice should remedy colonial injustices, such as the colonial state's land grabbing (see Muvingi, 2009). Typically, most transitional justice mechanisms (such as Kenya's Truth, Justice, and Reconciliation Commission) limit their temporal reach (jurisdiction) to the period after European decolonization in the mid-20th century (the obvious exception is the settler colonialism in South Africa). Other scholars and practitioners have criticized the use of transitional justice instruments to provide accountability for the long histories of violent dispossession and marginalization of indigenous communities in established democracies (see Corntassel and Holder, 2008; Jung, 2009).
2. The author worked with ICTJ, helping to extend transitional justice into adjacent domains (see Patel et al., 2010).
3. I use the common abbreviation for economic, social and cultural rights (ESC) even though this article does not address cultural rights.
4. There have been several trenchant critiques of the legalistic bias in human rights (see Gearty, 2006: 60–98; Meckled-García and Çali, 2006) and transitional justice (see McEvoy, 2007), as well as the related phenomenon of the judicialization (or juridification) of politics (see Simpson, 2007: 137–140). Arguably, though, a legalistic approach is better suited to a transitional period in which democratic institutions and accountability are (presumably) being established.
5. For accounts of Amnesty International's turn to socio-economic rights, see Goering (2006), Hopgood (2006) and Khan and Petrasek (2009).
6. Arbour's (2006) argument is rather ambivalent on this score. At one point, she contends that 'transitional justice … has shown itself vulnerable to the proposition that human rights can be "sequenced" and that some should systematically be accorded greater priority over others' (Arbour, 2006: 10). Yet, later on, she acknowledges the need to develop 'specific criteria … to determine which [ESC] violations should be addressed, either as a matter of priority, or not at all' (Arbour, 2006: 14). She further recognizes that those criteria 'focus first and foremost on discriminatory violations' in 'the context of transitional justice' (Arbour, 2006: 14).
7. Cath Collins has proposed 'post-transitional justice' as a new analytical category that is distinct from transitional justice in the following ways (among others):

> First, where transitional justice is centrally concerned with attaining and preserving the minimum institutional requirements of formal democracy, post-transitional justice focuses on subsequent questions of the quality, reach, and perfectibility of that democracy. Second, post-transitional justice accordingly questions the comprehensiveness and sufficiency of initial transitional justice compromises ... Third ... post-transitional justice has been largely non-state, driven by private actors operating both 'above' and 'below' the state. (2010: 22)

References

Arbour L (2006) Economic and social justice for societies in transition. Second Annual Transitional Justice Lecture hosted by the Center for Human Rights and Global Justice at New York University School of Law and the International Centre for Transitional Justice. New York University Law School, New York, 25 October.

Arthur P (2009) How 'transitions' reshaped human rights: A conceptual history of transitional justice. *Human Rights Quarterly* 31: 321–367.

Berdal M and Malone D (eds) (2000) *Greed and Grievance: Economic Agendas in Civil Wars*. Boulder, CO: Lynne Reiner.

Bernstein A (2009) Tort theory, microfinance, and gender equality convergent in pecuniary reparations. In: Rubio-Marín R (ed.) *The Gender of Reparations: Unsettling Sexual Hierarchies while Redressing Human Rights Violations*. Cambridge: Cambridge University Press.

Boraine A (2006) Transitional justice: A holistic interpretation. *Journal of International Affairs* 60: 17–27.

Carothers T (2002) The end of the transition paradigm. *Journal of Democracy* 13: 1–21.

Carranza R (2008) Plunder and pain: Should transitional justice engage with corruption and economic crimes? *International Journal of Transitional Justice* 2: 310–330.

Cavallaro J and Albuja S (2008) The lost agenda: Economic crimes and Truth Commissions in Latin America and beyond. In: McEvoy K and McGregor L (eds), *Transitional Justice from Below: Grassroots Activism and the Struggle for Change*. Oxford: Hart, pp. 121–141.

Collins C (2010) *Post-Transitional Justice: Human Rights Trials in Chile and El Salvador*. University Park, PA: The Pennsylvania State University Press.

Colvin CJ (2008) Purity and planning: Shared logics of transitional justice and development. *International Journal of Transitional Justice* 2: 412–425.

Commission for Reception, Truth and Reconciliation in East Timor (2005) *Chega! The Report of the Commission for Reception, Truth and Reconciliation in East Timor*. Dili.

Corntassel J and Holder C (2008) Who's sorry now? Government apologies, truth commissions and indigenous self-determination in Australia, Canada, Guatemala, and Peru. *Human Rights Review* 9: 465–489.

Carothers T (ed.) (2006) *Promoting the Rule of Law Abroad: In Search of Knowledge*. Washington, DC: Carnegie Endowment for International Peace.

de Greiff P (2006) Justice and reparations. In: de Greiff P (ed.) *The Handbook of Reparations*. Oxford: Oxford University Press, pp. 451–477.

de Greiff P (2009) Articulating the links between transitional justice and development: Justice and social integration. In de Greiff P and Duthie R (eds), *Transitional Justice and Development: Making Connections*. New York: Social Science Research Council and the International Center for Transitional Justice, pp. 28–75.

DFID/ICTJ (Department for International Development/International Center for Transitional Justice) (2007) *Donor Strategies for Transitional Justice: Taking Stock and Moving Forward*. London and New York: DFID/ICTJ.

Duthie R (2008) Toward a development-sensitive approach to transitional justice. *International Journal of Transitional Justice* 2: 292–309.

Fletcher L and Weinstein H (2002) Violence and social repair: Rethinking the contribution of justice to reconciliation. *Human Rights Quarterly* 24: 573–639.

Galanter M (2002) Righting old wrongs. In: Minow M (ed.) *Breaking the Cycles of Hatred: Memory, Law and Repair*. Princeton, NJ: Princeton University Press, pp. 107–131.

Gearty C (2006) *Can Human Rights Survive? The Hamlyn Lectures 2005*. Cambridge: Cambridge University Press.

Goering C (2006) Amnesty International and economic, social and cultural rights. In: Bell D and Coicaud J-M (eds) *Ethics in Action: The Ethical Challenges of International Nongovernmental Human Rights Organizations*. Cambridge: Cambridge University Press, pp. 204–217.

Golub S (ed.) (2010) *Legal Empowerment: Practitioners' Perspectives*. Rome: IDLO.

Gready P (2010) *The Era of Transitional Justice: The Aftermath of the Truth and Reconciliation Commission in South Africa and Beyond*. London: Routledge.

Gready P, Crawford G, Boesten J and Wilding P (2010) Transformative justice: A concept note. Unpublished draft, September.

Hayner PB (2010) *Unspeakable Truths: Transitional Justice and the Challenge of Truth Commissions*, 2nd edn. London: Routledge.

Hayner P and Bosire L (2003) *Should Truth Commissions Address Economic Crimes? Considering the Case of Kenya*. New York: ICTJ.

Hopgood S (2006) *Keepers of the Flame: Understanding Amnesty International*. Ithaca, NY: Cornell University Press.

Howard-Hassmann RE (2008) *Reparations to Africa*. Philadelphia, PA: University of Pennsylvania Press.

ICTJ (International Center for Transitional Justice) (2008) *Nepali Voices: Perceptions of Truth, Justice, Reconciliation, Reparations and the Transition in Nepal*. New York: ICTJ.

ICTJ (International Center for Transitional Justice) (2009) *The Rabat Report: The Concept and Challenges of Collective Reparations*. New York: ICTJ.

Jung C (2009) *Transitional Justice for Indigenous People in a Non-transitional Society*. New York: ICTJ.

Khan I and Petrasek D (2009) *The Unheard Truth: Poverty and Human Rights*. London: Amnesty International.

Lambourne W (2009) Transitional justice and peacebuilding after mass violence. *International Journal of Transitional Justice* 3: 28–48.

Laplante LJ (2007) On the indivisibility of rights: Truth commissions, reparations, and the right to development. *Yale Human Rights and Development Law Journal* 10: 141–177.

Laplante LJ (2008) Transitional justice and peace building: Diagnosing and addressing the socioeconomic roots of violence through a human rights framework. *International Journal of Transitional Justice* 2: 331–355.

Laplante LJ (2009) From theory to practice: Implementing reparation in Post-truth Commission Peru. In: Johnston BR and Slyomovics S (eds) *Waging War, Making Peace: Reparations and Human Rights*. Walnut Creek, CA: Left Coast Press, pp. 75–94.

Lenzen M (2009) Roads less traveled? Conceptual pathways (and stumbling blocks) for development and transitional justice. In: de Greiff P and Duthie R (eds) *Transitional Justice and Development: Making Connections*. New York: Social Science Research Council and the International Center for Transitional Justice, pp. 76–109.

McEvoy K (2007) Beyond legalism: Towards a thicker understanding of transitional justice. *Journal of Law and Society*, 34: 411–440.

Magarrell L (2003) Reparations for massive or widespread human rights violations: Sorting out claims for reparations and social justice. *Windsor Yearbook of Access to Justice* 22: 85–98.

Mamdani M (2000) The truth according to the Truth and Reconciliation Commission. In: Amadiume I and An-Naim A (eds) *The Politics of Memory: Truth, Healing, and Social Justice*. New York: Zed Books, pp. 176–183.

Mani R (2002) *Beyond Retribution: Seeking Justice in the Shadows of War*. Cambridge: Polity.

Mani R (2008) Editorial: Dilemmas of expanding transitional justice, or forging the nexus between transitional justice and development. *International Journal of Transitional Justice* 2: 253–265.

Meckled-García S and Çali B (eds) (2006) *The Legalization of Human Rights: Multidisciplinary Perspectives on Human Rights and Human Rights Law*. London: Routledge.

Meister R (2002) Human rights and the politics of victimhood. *Ethics and International Affairs* 16: 91–108.

Miller Z (2008) Effects of invisibility: In search of the 'economic' in transitional justice. *International Journal of Transitional Justice* 2: 266–291.

Muvingi I (2009) Sitting on powder kegs: Socioeconomic rights in transitional societies. *International Journal of Transitional Justice* 3: 163–182.

Nee A and Uvin P (2010) Silence and dialogue: Burundians' alternatives to transitional justice. In: Shaw R and Waldorf L (eds) *Localizing Transitional Justice: Interventions and Priorities after Mass Violence*. Stanford, CA: Stanford University Press, pp. 157–182.

Newman E, Paris R and Richmond OP (eds) (2009) *New Perspectives on Liberal Peacebuilding*. Tokyo: United Nations University.

Olsen TD, Payne LA and Reiter AG (2010) *Transitional Justice in Balance: Comparing Processes, Weighing Efficacy*. Washington, DC: United States Institute of Peace Press.

Paris R (2004) *At War's End: Building Peace after Civil Conflict*. Cambridge: Cambridge University Press.

Patel A, de Greiff P and Waldorf L (eds) (2010) *Disarming the Past: Transitional Justice and Ex-Combatants*. New York: Social Science Research Council and the International Center for Transitional Justice.

Pells K (2009) We've got used to the genocide; it's daily life that's the problem. *Peace Review* 21: 339–346.

Pham P, Vinck P, Stover E, Moss A, Wierda M and Bailey R (2007) *When the War Ends: A Population-based Survey on Attitudes about Peace, Justice and Social Reconstruction in Northern Uganda*. New York: International Center for Transitional Justice.

Robins S (2009) Whose voices? Understanding victims' needs in transition. *Journal of Human Rights Practice* 1: 320–331.

Robins S (2011a) Towards victim-centred transitional justice: Understanding the needs of families of the disappeared in postconflict Nepal. *International Journal of Transitional Justice* 5: 75–98.

Robins S (2011b) *'To Live as Other Kenyans Do': A Study of the Reparative Demands of Kenyan Victims of Human Rights Violations*. New York: International Center for Transitional Justice.

Roht-Arriaza N (2004) Reparations in the aftermath of repression and mass violence. In: Stover E and Weinstein H (eds), *My Neighbor, My Enemy: Justice and Community in the Aftermath of Mass Atrocity*. Cambridge: Cambridge University Press, pp. 121–139.

Roht-Arriaza N and Orlovsky K (2009) A complementary relationship: Reparations and development. In: de Greiff P and Duthie R (eds) *Transitional Justice and Development: Making Connections*. New York: Social Science Research Council and the International Center for Transitional Justice, pp. 170–213.

Rome Statute of the International Criminal Court (1998) 2187 U.N.T.S. 3.

Roth K (2004) Defending economic, social and cultural rights: Practical issues faced by an international human rights organization. *Human Rights Quarterly* 26: 63–73.

Segovia A (2006) Financing reparations programs: Reflections from international experience. In: de Greiff P (ed.) *The Handbook of Reparations*. Oxford: Oxford University Press.

Seibel HD with Armstrong A (2006) Reparations and microfinance schemes. In: de Greiff P (ed.) *The Handbook of Reparations*. Oxford: Oxford University Press.

Shaw R and Waldorf L (2010) Introduction: Localizing transitional justice. In: Shaw R and Waldorf L (eds) *Localizing Transitional Justice: Interventions and Priorities after Mass Violence*. Stanford, CA: Stanford University Press, pp. 3–26.

Sheridan RB (2008) *The Rivals: A Comedy*. Project Gutenberg Ebook. Available at: http://www.gutenberg.org/cache/epub/24761/pg24761.html.

Simpson G (2007) *Law, War & Crime*. Cambridge: Polity.

Stewart F (ed.) (2008) *Horizontal Inequalities and Conflict: Understanding Group Violence in Multiethnic Societies*. Basingstoke: Palgrave.

Thoms ONT and Ron J (2007) Do human rights violations cause internal conflict? *Human Rights Quarterly* 29: 674–705.

Thoms ONT, Ron J and Paris R (2010) State-level effects of transitional justice: What do we know? *International Journal of Transitional Justice* 4: 329–354.

Torpey John (2006) *Making Whole What Has Been Smashed: On Reparation Politics*. Cambridge, MA: Harvard University Press.

Truth and Reconciliation Commission of South Africa (2003) *Truth and Reconciliation Commission of South Africa Report*. Cape Town: Juta.

UN (United Nations) (2004) *Report of the Secretary-General on the Rule of Law and Transitional Justice in Conflict and Post-conflict Societies*. UN Doc. S/2004/616. New York: UN.

UN (United Nations) (2005) *Basic Principles and Guidelines on the Right to a Remedy and Reparations for Victims of Gross Violations of International Human Rights Law and Serious Violations of International Humanitarian Law*. A/Res/60/147. New York: UN.

UN (United Nations) (2011) *Integrated Disarmament Demobilization and Reintegration Standards*. New York: UN.

UN OHCHR (United Nations Office of the High Commissioner for Human Rights) (2006) *Rule-of-Law Tools for Post-Conflict States: Truth Commissions*. Geneva: UN.

UN OHCHR (United Nations Office of the High Commissioner for Human Rights) (2008) *Rule-of-Law Tools for Post-Conflict States: Reparations Programmes*. Geneva: UN.

Vinck P and Pham P (2008) Ownership and participation in transitional justice mechanisms: A sustainable human development perspective from eastern DRC. *International Journal of Transitional Justice* 2: 398–411.

Weinstein HM, Fletcher LE, Vinck P and Pham PN (2010) Stay the hand of justice: Whose priorities take priority? In: Shaw R and Waldorf L (eds) *Localizing Transitional Justice: Interventions and Priorities after Mass Violence*. Stanford, CA: Stanford University Press, pp. 27–48.

Williams RC (2007) *The Contemporary Right to Property Restitution in the Context of Transitional Justice*. New York: ICTJ.

23

Plunder and Pain: Should Transitional Justice Engage with Corruption and Economic Crimes?

Ruben Carranza

Abstract

This article examines the various points at which accountability for economic crimes, including large-scale corruption, intersects with accountability for human rights violations. To date, transitional justice has largely compartmentalized legacies of abuse into those based on a narrow set of human rights violations and those based on economic crimes, which the author argues is an inadequate way to address both sets of abuses. Because corruption and human rights violations are mutually reinforcing forms of abuse, the field of transitional justice should approach economic crimes in the same way it approaches civil and political rights violations. The author suggests that traditional transitional justice mechanisms would be strengthened by an engagement with corruption and economic crimes, which would allow for both sources of impunity to be confronted.

Introduction

To some of its practitioners, transitional justice and its mechanisms of truth seeking, prosecution, reparations and institutional reform were meant solely to apply to holding the perpetrators of massive violations of human rights accountable while providing their victims with some measure of truth and justice. The prevailing assumption seems to be that truth commissions, human rights trials and reparations programs are meant to engage mainly, if not exclusively, with civil and political rights violations that involve either physical integrity or personal freedom, and not with violations of economic and social rights, including such crimes as large-scale corruption and despoliation. To a growing number of transitional justice advocates, particularly those who work in or come from impoverished postconflict or postdictatorship countries, this traditional view is inadequate. It ignores the experience of developing countries abused by dictators or warlords who have been *both* brutal and corrupt. It perpetuates an impunity gap by focusing on a narrow range of human rights violations while leaving accountability for economic crimes to ineffective domestic institutions or to a still evolving international legal system that deals with corruption.[1]

[1] For the purposes of this article, economic crimes are defined as offenses committed by both state and nonstate actors that may constitute violations of the human rights enumerated in the International Covenant on Economic, Social and Cultural Rights.

The first part of this article looks at how accountability for human rights violations and accountability for economic crimes have intersected, and the impact of this on impunity. The second part examines the reasons behind the compartmentalization of human rights and economic crimes and its consequences for anticorruption and transitional justice initiatives. The third part explores the limits of existing anticorruption mechanisms, as well as the potential of transitional justice mechanisms as an alternative. The fourth part shows that engaging with economic crimes can have a significant effect on truth seeking and reparations and can contribute to more effective means of combating impunity. The last part of the article addresses the strategic policy questions that transitional justice advocates ought to answer when confronted with legacies of economic crimes and large-scale corruption.

The Intersection of Human Rights Violations and Economic Crimes

The legacies of large-scale corruption and other economic crimes committed by politically exposed persons[2] or by leaders and members of nonstate armed groups have been, with a few exceptions, ignored in transitional justice initiatives. The few exceptions – such as the initiatives carried out in Chad, the Philippines, Sierra Leone, East Timor, Peru and, most recently, Liberia – and some concepts underlying the International Criminal Court's Trust Fund for Victims (ICC-TFV) demonstrate that transitional justice can be strengthened and can confront impunity more effectively if it engages with accountability for corruption and economic crimes.

The relationship between a state's human rights record and the extent of corruption in its government can be as simple as one of mutual reinforcement. As Transparency International asserts:

> A corrupt government which rejects both transparency and accountability is not likely to be a respecter of human rights. Therefore, the campaign to contain corruption and the movement for the promotion and protection of human rights are not disparate processes. They are inextricably linked and interdependent.[3]

In many cases, the relationship is more complex. Not all transitions are from corrupt dictatorships to relatively democratic societies, and whether emerging from authoritarian rule or armed conflict, many developing countries that have undergone human rights-focused transitional justice processes still face the consequences of unresolved legacies of economic crimes, legacies that have for the

[2] A frequently used definition of a politically exposed person is that of the Financial Action Task Force (FATF): 'Individuals who are or have been in the past entrusted with prominent public functions in a particular country. This category includes, for example, heads of State or government; senior politicians and government, judicial or military officials; senior executives of State owned corporations and important political party officials.' FATF, 'Report on Money Laundering Typologies 2003–2004,' http://www.fatf-gafi.org/dataoecd/19/11/33624379.pdf (accessed 13 August 2008).

[3] Lawrence Cockcroft, 'Corruption and Human Rights: A Crucial Link,' Transparency International working paper (1998).

most part been ignored by past transitional justice processes and were not seen as having significant implications for defeating impunity.

As the examples below demonstrate, while the main motivation behind large-scale corruption might be greed, the availability of resources to maintain impunity is clearly just as important a motive. These examples show that economic crime pays at least insofar as it helps perpetrators defeat or delay attempts at prosecution and even ultimately escape accountability for human rights violations.

Pinochet's Legacy of Corruption

A significant part of Chilean society long regarded the late Augusto Pinochet as 'honest in money matters,'[4] as if to mitigate his regime's human rights record. The discovery of substantial Pinochet-owned offshore bank accounts has decisively broken the myth of his incorruptibility. The funds in these accounts, discovered in the course of a US congressional investigation, were moved while Pinochet was the subject of extradition efforts in Europe.[5] Pinochet died without being convicted of any crime. The corruption charges against him were brought too late,[6] certainly long after he had already used his ill-gotten assets to avoid accountability. Nonetheless, Pinochet's death does not prevent the recovery of those assets – a possibility that, as discussed below, has an impact for other transitional justice mechanisms such as reparations and truth seeking.

Post-Abacha Nigeria and Post-Mobuto DRC

In Africa, massive human rights violations and large-scale corruption not only intersect but also overlap across various political transitions. The death of Nigeria's Sani Abacha made it impossible to hold him accountable for human rights violations, so the recovery of some $4 billion in assets he and his family amassed became the focus of the post-Abacha government.[7] Although some of these assets were turned over by Swiss and American banks, a Swiss-brokered, global compromise fell through in 2001. To this day, the Abacha family continues to use these assets to maintain influence in Nigerian politics and to preserve the impunity of those who could still be held accountable.[8]

In the Democratic Republic of Congo (DRC), the legacy of Mobuto Sese Seko remains unaddressed, including the estimated $12 billion in funds he embezzled.[9] Despite their magnitude, Mobuto's economic crimes have been ignored in

[4] 'Pinochet's Secret Millions Tarnish His Image,' *New Zealand Herald*, 19 October 2004.

[5] See, United States Senate Permanent Subcommittee on Investigations, 'Money Laundering and Foreign Corruption: Enforcement and Effectiveness of the Patriot Act, Case Study Involving Riggs Bank' (July 2004).

[6] See, 'Pinochet Family Cleared of Embezzlement Charges,' *Reuters*, 27 October 2007.

[7] Elizabeth Olson, 'Nigeria to Recover $1 Billion from Late Dictator,' *New York Times*, 18 April 2002.

[8] In 2002, the author conferred with the Nigerian government's Swiss lawyer in Geneva, who admitted to difficulties in obtaining evidence of Abacha's stolen wealth given the family's considerable political power in Nigeria.

[9] Tim Daniel, 'Repatriation of Looted State Assets: Selected Case Studies and the UN Convention Against Corruption,' in *Global Corruption Report 2004* (Berlin: Transparency International, 2004).

transitional justice initiatives. Instead, the focus has been on the cycles of violence that have taken place since Mobuto's fall. By leaving unexamined the relationship between Mobuto's economic crimes and the enduring violence in the DRC, transitional justice has been boxed into a small corner, dwelling on the violent consequences of an unresolved past while mostly ignoring its structural causes.

Post-Suharto Indonesia and Post-Marcos Philippines

Transitional justice remains elusive in Asia, and the examples of Indonesia and the Philippines show how economic crimes and human rights violations have mutually reinforced impunity in the region. Indonesia's Suharto died without being convicted of any crime involving human rights, or for the corruption that allowed his family to amass an estimated \$9 billion.[10] While Ferdinand Marcos was held civilly liable in the US to pay damages to approximately 10,000 victims of human rights violations in the Philippines,[11] no one among his associates, including his widow, Imelda Marcos, has been imprisoned for those violations or for the corruption they perpetrated.

In both cases, the postdictatorship governments not only failed to hold the former dictators criminally accountable for corruption but also employed flawed measures to hold them and their military subordinates liable for human rights violations.[12] Marcos and Suharto enjoyed impunity until they died. Their military conspirators remain unaccountable and their families continue to enjoy the fruits of their economic crimes.

South Africa and the Post-TRC Impunity Gap

This pattern of mutually reinforcing impunity has emerged across different countries. It should prompt honest reflection on the adequacy of an approach in which accountability for civil and political rights violations is privileged over an approach that engages with both this narrow set of human rights and economic crimes.

Post-apartheid South Africa illustrates this inadequacy well. The country's Truth and Reconciliation Commission (TRC) did not address corruption simply because it claimed that corruption fell outside its mandate. Whether or not the exclusion of economic crimes may have had more substantive reasons, its consequences, as articulated in a South African civil society report from 2006, should be a lesson for other countries, especially those seeking to emulate the TRC process. The report demonstrates the link between human rights violations and corruption, pointing out that 'when the apartheid state was at its most repressive, it was also at its

[10] Agung Putri, 'Evading the Truth: Will a Truth and Reconciliation Commission Ever be Formed?' *Inside Indonesia* 23 (2003); John Colmey and David Liebhold, 'The Family Firm,' *Time*, 24 May 1999.

[11] See, Maria Glenda Ramirez, 'The Philippines: Assessing the Need for a Truth Commission Fifteen Years After' (paper presented at 'Human Rights and Law in Asia,' Asia Society, New York, 27 March 2001).

[12] See, for example, David Cohen, *Intended to Fail: The Trials Before the Ad Hoc Human Rights Court in Jakarta* (New York: International Center for Transitional Justice, 2008).

most corrupt.'[13] The author contends that by not addressing corruption under apartheid, the TRC lost a historic opportunity, as

> [E]vidence of these [economic] crimes will be further erased over time and money stolen will continue to enrich the beneficiaries of corruption. In taking this path, we choose to close the book on the past. Such a decision will not threaten the South African elite and will no doubt be welcomed by many. It will, however, probably always haunt us as a society.[14]

Mutually Reinforcing Impunity

The ongoing trials of Peru's Alberto Fujimori and Liberia's Charles Taylor also show that prosecution in itself may not decisively break the mutually reinforcing walls of impunity built in the pretransition period. Most of these dictators' ill-gotten assets were hidden while they were in power, so that Fujimori can even claim that since his exile 'no foreign bank accounts have been found.'[15] If the kind of zeal shown in prosecuting human rights cases is not applied to denying ex-dictators access to their ill-gotten assets, these assets will be used to derail trials and asset recovery efforts. Taylor's hand is apparent in the effort to intimidate prosecution witnesses appearing in the Special Court for Sierra Leone (SCSL),[16] as it is in the defeat of proposed Liberian legislation that would have frozen some of his assets.[17]

Using their ill-gotten assets, the likes of Pinochet, Marcos and Suharto have financed destabilization and intimidation, stifled investigations, delayed trials, fought extradition and sponsored political proxies to counter attempts at holding them accountable for human rights violations. With more than enough in such assets, they can do this until the political tide changes in their favor or until their deaths, whichever comes first. These examples show how impunity for economic crimes reinforces impunity for human rights violations.

The Compartmentalization of Transitional Justice

In theory, there seems to be no fundamental obstacle to applying the key elements of transitional justice to large-scale corruption and economic crimes. In practice, however, the predominant approach in the transitional justice field tends to view human rights as narrower than the range of human rights violations that actually occur. The field compartmentalizes the unresolved legacies faced by transitioning societies, particularly in developing countries. It constructs one compartment for human rights violations and another for economic crimes and corruption. Economic crimes thus are treated as if they do not constitute rights violations in themselves. Not only does this compartmentalization oversimplify the relationship

[13] Hennie van Vuuren, *Apartheid Grand Corruption: Assessing the Scale of Crimes of Profit in South Africa from 1976 to 1994* (Cape Town: Institute for Security Studies, 2006), 3.

[14] Ibid., 87.

[15] 'Peru's Former President Plots His Return to Power,' *New York Times*, 22 December 2002.

[16] Sheriff Z. Adams, 'Moses Blah Returns from the Hague,' *News*, 29 May 2008.

[17] 'Liberian Lawmakers Reject Bill to Freeze Taylor's Assets,' *Associated Press*, 23 September 2007.

between those unredressed legacies but it also does not reflect the reality of the societies that seek to address them.

Some transitional justice practitioners from Africa have pointed out that 'the traditional definition of transitional justice [is] too narrow.' In their view, a more meaningful definition must recognize contexts where 'mass poverty and socio-economic concerns inform the needs of victims and the object of justice.' Specifically, these practitioners see corruption as a *principal* subject of the field:

> [Transitional justice advocates in] countries such as Nigeria, Kenya and Liberia . . . have included issues of corruption as a key crime to be addressed, making the argument that this 'structural violence' has had far wider implications than direct violence, and that it has been and continues to be a fault-line for violent conflict.[18]

This dissonant view of transitional justice evokes a previous challenge to the universalist assumptions of the human rights movement,[19] which was based on the argument that certain Asian values affect the way some Asian states apply human rights standards. In the present case, the challenge comes by way of African activists asserting ownership over local transitional justice initiatives.

Transitional justice advocates often speak of nurturing a sense of ownership among the people of societies in which transitional justice mechanisms are pursued. Yet, the predominance of civil and political rights-focused transitional justice initiatives in many developing countries struggling with what the African practitioners describe as 'mass poverty and socio-economic concerns' creates doubt that a complete sense of ownership can be inculcated as long as economic crimes and large-scale corruption are excluded from mainstream transitional justice advocacy.

This focus on civil and political rights violations and corresponding hesitation to address violations of socioeconomic rights may be an extension of the larger dichotomy in human rights discourse. Civil and political rights violations are seen not only as justiciable but also as susceptible to being redressed through transitional justice. Socioeconomic rights violations, meanwhile, usually are considered non-justiciable and therefore better addressed by a catch-all reference to development programs.

Thus, most truth commissions, which are often seen as the most iconic mechanisms of transitional justice, have ignored corruption and economic crimes. By one count, 34 truth commissions were established worldwide between 1974 and 2004.[20] Of these commissions, only three appear to have expressly engaged with economic crimes,[21] socioeconomic rights violations or a set of crimes that necessarily incorporates past acts of corruption. The rest have *tacitly* assumed corruption and

[18] See, African Transitional Justice Research Network, 'Mapping Exercises, Key Findings and Challenges: Definition of Transitional Justice in Africa,' http://www.transitionaljustice.org.za/index.php?option=com_content&task=view&id=314&Itemid=36 (accessed 24 August 2008).

[19] See, Randall Perenboom, 'Human Rights and Rule of Law: What's the Relationship?' *Georgetown Journal of International Law* 36(1) (2005): 809–945.

[20] Kathryn Sikkink and Carrie Booth Walling, 'Errors about Trials: The Emergence and Impact of the Justice Cascade' (paper presented at the Princeton International Relations Faculty Colloquium, 27 March 2006).

[21] These are Chad, Liberia and Sierra Leone.

economic crimes to be outside the ambit of truth seeking, as truth commissions are described as 'bodies set up to investigate a past history of violations of human rights in a particular country.'[22]

International, hybrid and regional human rights tribunals, including the ICC, have been set up to try heads of state and other political or military leaders, with many prosecutions founded on the concept of system crimes.[23] The range of crimes that form part of this prosecutorial strategy assumes the exclusion of economic crimes, despite the otherwise strategic role of these crimes in maintaining systems of abuse. The assumption seems to be that someone else will address those 'other' systemic violations and that something else can provide redress.

The transitional justice tools prescribed by the UN for its field missions partly reflect this narrow view. The UN Office of the High Commissioner for Human Rights (OHCHR) acknowledges that truth commissions 'traditionally' have focused 'on serious human rights abuses . . . as well as violations of international humanitarian law and war crimes.'[24] It acknowledges, however, that 'in some countries, economic crimes have been as prominent – and in the public's mind as egregious – as the civil and political rights violations by a prior regime.' OHCHR declares that, in such cases, one 'option' is to engage in 'discussion of including corruption and other economic crimes within a truth commission's mandate.'[25] The fact that OHCHR notes that economic crimes can be as prominent and, 'in the public's mind,' as egregious as violations of civil and political rights may be indicative of a perspective that takes the public's mind standard of egregiousness less seriously than the standard officially adopted by an international human rights institution. This perspective implies a hierarchy of egregiousness that places economic crimes below civil and political rights violations. The gravity of these two forms of abuse seems to be equal only in the public's mind, and not in the minds of international institutions or nongovernmental organizations (NGOs), which, by their practice, significantly define the conventions of human rights and prescribe to the rest of the world how human rights violations are to be redressed.

The former UN High Commissioner of Human Rights Louise Arbour began to move away from this view. She made an explicit statement that transitional justice should engage with socioeconomic rights violations, noting that:

> Transitional justice should take up the challenge that mainstream justice is also reluctant to rise to: acknowledging that there is no hierarchy of rights and providing protection for all human rights, including economic, social and cultural rights . . . A comprehensive transitional justice strategy would therefore want to address the gross violations of all

[22] Priscilla Hayner, 'Fifteen Truth Commissions – 1974 to 1994: A Comparative Study,' *Human Rights Quarterly* 16(4) (1994): 598.

[23] System crimes have been described as 'crimes such as genocide, crimes against humanity and war crimes [that] differ from ordinary crimes in that they are generally of such a scale that they require a degree of organization or system to perpetrate.' International Center for Transitional Justice, *Pursuing Justice In Ongoing Conflict: A Discussion of Current Practice* (May 2007), 21.

[24] See, UN Office of the High Commissioner for Human Rights (OHCHR), *Rule of Law Tools for Post-Conflict States: Truth Commissions* (2006), 9.

[25] Ibid.

> human rights during the conflict and, I suggest, the gross violations that gave rise or contributed to the conflict in the first place.[26]

How (or even whether) UN agencies and NGOs engaged in transitional justice work will incorporate this view remains to be seen.

The Limits of Anticorruption Initiatives and the Potential of TJ Mechanisms

Because it must respond to different types of transitions, victims and perpetrators, transitional justice has become increasingly nuanced and has evolved into the multidisciplinary field it is now. It embraces not only law and human rights but also the reform of police and military bureaucracies,[27] healthcare and psychology, education, children's rights, gender, media and communications, and even art and filmmaking. As a result, a wide range of international actors with a varied set of skills now work within the field. Yet, despite the expansion in the disciplines it employs, transitional justice has remained narrow in the range of injustices with which it deals, avoiding engagement with legacies of corruption and economic crimes and leaving them for fragile posttransition governments to address.

The paths along which human rights advocacy and anticorruption initiatives evolved might partly account for this situation. While transitional justice was still a nascent field in the 1990s, nongovernmental anticorruption initiatives, such as Transparency International, emerged at the international level.[28] This was after the 'justice cascade' had already been set in motion by human rights activists,[29] with the cascade's direction fixed on civil and political rights violations. The human rights movement gave rise to the subfield of transitional justice. The international anticorruption movement, meanwhile, did not develop its own analog to that subfield. The anticorruption movement was more forward looking, seeking to prevent corruption rather than push for accountability for past actions. It promoted the nebulous notion of 'good governance' instead of confronting legacies of large-scale corruption and economic crimes.

International financial institutions (IFIs) eventually caught up with the anticorruption movement and have since been influential in shaping its direction. The IFIs' anticorruption agenda is driven in part by criticism of the role they played in lending to corrupt, repressive regimes. Their current anticorruption rhetoric notwithstanding, it is unlikely that IFIs will look at the past to examine their roles in sustaining authoritarian regimes, given the empirically proven correlation

[26] Louise Arbour, 'Economic and Social Justice for Societies in Transition' (lecture given as the Second Annual Transitional Justice Lecture, New York University School of Law Center for Human Rights and Global Justice and the International Center for Transitional Justice, New York, 25 October 2006), 14.

[27] See, for example, Eirin Mobekk, *Transitional Justice and Security Sector Reform: Enabling Sustainable Peace* (Geneva: Geneva Center for the Democratic Control of Armed Forces, 2006).

[28] Transparency International was formally established in 1993.

[29] See, Sikkink and Walling, supra n 20.

between foreign debt and abusive dictatorships.[30] As one critic asked about the World Bank's stance, 'How far can the Bank really go with this agenda, in particular where the Bank itself has been the cause of corruption, and odious and illegitimate debts, in the past?'[31]

Since the social and economic impact of large-scale corruption is of such magnitude that posttransition governments can hardly ignore them, a common initiative among victim countries has been to seek the recovery of assets amassed by corrupt former leaders. Victim countries often find themselves in the predicament of lacking both the kind of proof and the political leverage necessary to deal with the states in whose banking and financial institutions their embezzled funds are kept. Although countries like Switzerland and the UK have been trying seriously to rid themselves of the reputation of being laundering centers for ill-gotten wealth, the challenges to recovering assets have not decreased significantly for victim countries.[32]

Most victim countries simply cannot afford the costs of foreign litigation; in many cases, they cannot even match the resources available to perpetrators. This increases the importance of finding an alternative means of ferreting out the truth regarding corruption (including the whereabouts of proceeds), obtaining the cooperation of 'low-level' perpetrators (for instance, through selective conditional amnesties, as discussed below) and procuring a trail that can stand as evidence in prosecutions of higher level perpetrators. Victim countries would benefit from having a transitional justice mechanism as an alternative means for dealing with legacies of corruption and economic crimes. As stand-alone asset recovery efforts are not often part of a comprehensive agenda to extract accountability from former rulers, situating these initiatives in a transitional justice context could only be beneficial.

Two recent developments could take transitional justice in this direction. First, the UN Convention Against Corruption (UNCAC)[33] took effect in 2005 and explicitly made asset recovery a 'fundamental principle.'[34] Second, the US has begun enforcing anti-money laundering regulations, including criminal law enforcement against non-American perpetrators of large-scale corruption. The US president

[30] See, David Gray, 'Devilry, Complicity, and Greed: Transitional Justice and Odious Debt,' *Law and Contemporary Problems* 70 (2007): 137–164.

[31] Gail Hurley, 'Wolfowitz Needs to Look at Corruption of Yesterday, Not Just Today and Follow the Positive Example of Norway,' European Network on Debt and Development (1 June 2006), http://www.eurodad.org/whatsnew/articles.aspx?id=338 (accessed 27 August 2008).

[32] It has been said that 'asset recovery is a costly and time consuming enterprise. It requires lawyers, forensic accountants, expert opinions, translators, travel expenses, etc. Private law firms often prove helpful in tracing and recovering assets abroad, as in the efforts of the Philippines against Ferdinand Marcos and Nigeria against the estate of Sani Abacha. Such firms are expensive, generally charging from $200 to $600 per hour. Corruption offenders can be relied upon to spare no expense to keep their ill gotten gains.' Excerpted from Jack Smith, Mark Pieth and Guillermo Jorge, *The Recovery of Stolen Assets: A Fundamental Principle of the UN Convention Against Corruption*, (International Center for Asset Recovery brief for the U4 Anti-Corruption Resource Center, February 2007), 2.

[33] United Nations Convention Against Corruption, UN General Assembly Resolution A/RES/58/4, *entered into force* 14 December 2005.

[34] Ch. V, art. 51, of the UNCAC states: 'The return of assets pursuant to this chapter is a fundamental principle of this Convention, and States Parties shall afford one another the widest measure of cooperation and assistance in this regard.'

has, for example, issued a proclamation prohibiting entry into America for foreigners linked to corruption abroad.[35] One US official describes this as a policy of 'prosecuting kleptocrats' and of 'denying safe haven to corrupt officials and their illicitly-acquired assets.'[36]

In addition, the World Bank's Stolen Asset Recovery Initiative (StAR)[37] and the UN Office of Drugs and Crime (UNODC) explicitly connect asset recovery efforts with accountability for large-scale corruption and the level of a victim country's development. They do not, however, connect them to extracting accountability for massive human rights violations. StAR proposes to support 'coordinated, international requests to freeze assets in relation to a specific Politically Exposed Person.' It cites as exemplary the asset recovery experiences of Nigeria, Peru and the Philippines. Neither the World Bank nor UNODC has (yet) linked its anticorruption initiatives with its own or outside transitional justice mechanisms. Nonetheless, the fact that StAR has singled out the experiences of Nigeria, Peru and the Philippines specifically because of these countries' histories of repressive *and* corrupt rule shows the potential for combining these mechanisms.

Value Added by Addressing Economic Crimes

A Fuller Account of the Legacy of Abuse

The human rights focus of transitional justice determines the way in which a repressive regime or a brutal conflict is remembered. Most transitional justice mechanisms focus on civil and political rights violations, which means that accounts of abuse and injustice invariably focus on violations committed by police, military and paramilitary personnel. In the process, nonphysically violent abuses committed by civilians (or military officials) connected to the regime, including spouses, children, other relatives or even finance and budget ministers and advisers, are glossed over. An engagement with corruption would allow transitional justice mechanisms, particularly truth commissions, to frame their work within a larger factual context. By exposing the extent of corruption or the scale of economic crimes, these mechanisms would reveal that the depth of the damage caused by perpetrators goes beyond violence directed against their opponents or against citizens targeted by repressive measures.

In proposing that truth commissions look into economic crimes, this author's assumption is not that past truth commissions that dealt with civil and political rights violations were completely effective in resolving those injustices. That point

35 United States of America Presidential Proclamation No. 7750, 'Proclamation by the President: To Suspend Entry as Immigrants or Non-Immigrants of Persons Engaged in or Benefiting From Corruption' (12 January 2004).

36 David Luna, 'Prosecuting Kleptocrats: Denying Safe Haven to Corrupt Officials and Their Illicitly-Acquired Assets' (remarks at the 'International Recovery of the Proceeds of Corruption' seminar, American Bar Association Section of International Law Anticorruption Initiatives and Compliance Issues Committee, Washington, DC, 9 December 2005).

37 World Bank, *Stolen Asset Recovery (StAR) Initiative: Challenges, Opportunities, and Action Plan* (June 2007).

is still open to debate, and the debate will always be framed by different contexts, such as whether prosecutions, reparations and other measures accompanied or followed a truth commission's findings and whether amnesties or steps to overcome the impunity of perpetrators identified by truth commissions were taken. There are those who argue that truth commissions should not be a substitute for prosecutions,[38] but this stance assumes that once truth is revealed, individual criminal accountability follows. In that respect, it would make little difference to the process if truth commissions were *also* to address economic crimes, establishing, for example, individual criminal accountability for large-scale corruption. But there are those who fear that the political bargaining that surrounds a truth commission can end up blocking prosecution. In cases of civil and political rights violations, the South African experience shows this to be a valid apprehension. In cases of economic crimes and corruption, the prospect of recovering assets following a TRC process could offset the risk of prosecution being bargained away, a choice that seems acceptable in the case of Kenya[39] and Bangladesh.[40]

Two additional features would distinguish a truth commission with a mandate to look into both human rights violations and economic crimes from past commissions. The first would be its capacity to establish a more complete truth. The second, which is discussed below, would be its potential to harness resources for reparations and to counter the ability of perpetrators to maintain their impunity.

Even though it did not have an explicit mandate to look into economic rights violations, the Commission for Reception, Truth and Reconciliation (CAVR) in East Timor addressed famine and forced displacement. By holding hearings on these economic rights violations,[41] CAVR was able to establish that, of the estimated 102,800 victims who died during the Indonesian occupation, approximately 84,200 died of hunger and illness rather than being killed outright or forcibly disappeared.[42] More important, it established a far more truthful account of the Indonesian occupation than it would have had it limited itself to physical integrity violations tied to civil and political rights.

The incorporation of economic crimes into accounts of past abuses allows the myth of clean dictatorships to be shattered,[43] giving society an opportunity to reflect on the relationship between the economic crimes and the human rights violations committed by former rulers and other perpetrators. By reflecting on the relationship between plunder and pain, the various manifestations of transitional justice – prosecutions, conditional amnesties, reparations programs as well as

[38] Michael P. Scharf, 'The Case for a Permanent International Truth Commission,' *Duke Journal of Comparative and International Law* 7(2) (1997): 375–410.

[39] Gakuu Mathenge, 'Githongo's Cure for Impunity,' *The Standard*, 24 August 2008.

[40] 'Bangladesh Sets Up Corruption Truth Commission,' *Agence France Presse*, 30 July 2008.

[41] See, 'CAVR Public Hearing on Famine and Forced Displacement 28–29 July 2003 Dili, Timor-Leste,' CAVR press release (23 July 2003).

[42] See, Human Rights Data Analysis Group, 'Timor-Leste FAQs,' http://www.hrdag.org/resources/timor-leste_faqs.shtml#1 (accessed 20 August 2008).

[43] 'Chile Sets Precedent for Holding Dictators Accountable for Corruption: Pinochet Facing Charges on Corruption,' Transparency International press release (25 November 2005).

vetting and other institutional reforms – are informed by a more comprehensive account of the crimes that were committed by perpetrators, including data on the wealth they amassed, the resources available for reparations and the kind of punishments or measures of forgiveness that society should impose or can afford.

Experience Indicates that a Compartmentalized View of TJ Is Untenable

OHCHR suggests that a difference in methodology and the possibility of 'not completing its task' are obstacles to integrating economic crimes and corruption into a truth commission's mandate.[44] As only a handful of more than 30 past truth commissions incorporated economic crimes into their truth-seeking work,[45] OHCHR does not seem to have sufficient empirical basis to conclude that if other commissions had done the same, they would have been unable to overcome the anticipated obstacles.

In any event, those commissions mandated to look into economic crimes, as well as those that construed their role as requiring an examination of socioeconomic rights violations alongside other types of abuses, did in fact establish findings regarding corruption or other socioeconomic rights violations. Doing so did not appear to have hindered them from simultaneously looking at their countries' legacy of massive human rights violations.

The Chad Commission's mandate included identifying 'the financial operations and bank accounts,' as well as other assets, of former President Hissène Habré and his associates.[46] The Commission's report includes a list of plunderers and their assets and recommends the vetting of these persons and the sequestration of their assets. Its recommendations regarding both human rights and economic crimes were not implemented, although some of those named in the report as Habré accomplices were removed from office, albeit more than a decade later.[47] The Sierra Leone TRC report, meanwhile, declares 'years of bad governance, endemic corruption and the denial of basic human rights' as among the causes of armed conflict. It even identifies specific diamond mining companies that had links to armed groups in the country.[48] As mentioned earlier, CAVR conducted thematic hearings on forced displacement and famine. Its report links the violation of

> the [economic] right of people to food with … the denial of freedom of movement, the violation of the right of individuals to live where they want, the denial of access to relief, the destruction of food sources, and ultimately the violation of the right to life.[49]

44 OHCHR, supra n 24 at 16.

45 Sikkink and Booth Walling, supra n 20.

46 Chad Council of State Decree No. 014/P.CE/CJ/90 (29 December 1990).

47 Human Rights Watch, 'Habré Henchmen Ousted from Government,' press release (12 August 2005).

48 *The Final Report of the Truth and Reconciliation Commission of Sierra Leone* (Freetown: Truth and Reconciliation Commission of Sierra Leone, 2004) [hereinafter 'Sierra Leone TRC report'].

49 *Chega! Final Report of the Commission for Reception, Truth and Reconciliation in East Timor* (Dili: Commission for Reception, Truth and Reconciliation in East Timor, 2005), ch. 7(3), p. 3.

These examples show that truth commissions *can* examine and report on legacies of corruption, economic crimes and other socioeconomic rights violations. They also show, however, that, as with truth commission recommendations on civil and political rights violations, the implementation of recommendations regarding accountability for economic crimes depends on the political will of the succeeding government.

The broader mandates of the abovementioned truth commissions did not lead to unreasonable delays in the completion of their work or the submission of their reports. It could be argued that the few commissions that addressed economic crimes and corruption acted more expeditiously than their strictly human rights-oriented counterparts, considering the 'dual' coverage of their mandates. Given the different contexts in which transitional justice measures are applied, it may not even be reasonable to compare the effectiveness of truth commissions on the basis of their mandates; it may be more useful to strongly encourage local ownership of the truth-seeking process and to let local actors resolve issues involving the inclusion of economic crimes within a commission's mandate. By that standard, whatever may be said about the ongoing truth-seeking process in Liberia, the inclusion of economic crimes in the law that created the truth commission[50] was characterized by the relatively active engagement of Liberian civil society, as well as of the international community.

The ongoing process of establishing the Truth, Justice and Reconciliation Commission (TJRC) in Kenya should be informed by the debates that took place in 2003 surrounding the recommendations of the Task Force on the Establishment of a TJRC.[51] One side of the debate recommended that the proposed truth commission exclude corruption and economic crimes from its mandate because their inclusion would enlarge the breadth of investigation and distract from human rights violations.[52] In response, the Task Force took the position that 'the investigation of past economic crimes should be included [because, otherwise, it would] represent such a yawning gap in the record of truth of Kenya.'[53] The Task Force then proposed a method of truth seeking that was significantly similar to the Philippines' means of addressing its conjoined legacies of corruption and human rights abuse.[54] The task force proposed that the truth commission be 'organized into two chambers, one to look into past gross violations of human rights abuses and another to deal with past grave economic crimes.'[55] OHCHR's position in the Kenya debate represents a compromise of sorts. In particular, the High Commissioner has noted that:

50 Liberia Truth and Reconciliation Commission Act (May 2005), art. 4, sec. 4.

51 The Task Force was referred to as the 'Mutua Commission,' after its chairperson, Prof. Makau Mutua.

52 These debates are chronicled in detail in, Priscilla Hayner and Lydiah Bosire, *Should Truth Commissions Address Economic Crimes? Considering the Case of Kenya* (New York: International Center for Transitional Justice, 2003).

53 Ibid., 207.

54 In 1986, two commissions were established in the Philippines: one to investigate and prosecute human rights violations and another, the Presidential Commission on Good Government (PCGG), to do the same for economic crimes under the Marcos dictatorship. The first commission was dissolved in 1989 and the other still exists.

55 Hayner and Bosire, supra n 52 at 207.

> Economic matters certainly should not be excluded per se. If there is a clear link between economic issues and violence – such as land conflicts that erupt in violence or the State confiscates property when persons are arrested or disappear – then a truth commission should clearly recognize, inquire into and report on these matters.[56]

While engaging with corruption would require an entirely different pool of investigators with a different set of skills and experiences, this does not differ significantly from what investigations in other transitional justice contexts would require. For example, OHCHR's 'tools' on prosecutions and transitional justice suggest:

> Effective investigation requires appropriate analysis of the ways in which such organizations are legally required to work, as well as how they actually operated during the time in question. Lawyers may lack all the skills necessary to carry out such analyses, and *significant input from other experiences and disciplines can be very beneficial*.[57]

Transitional justice institutions invariably need experts in areas other than law or human rights. In fact, transitional justice should already have moved beyond its legalistic origins given that the varied contexts in which the field operates requires it to transcend a reliance on law as an instrument of justice. A transitional justice-based truth-seeking process that addresses economic crimes might be a sounder approach than the predominantly litigation-based process utilized, to their frustration, by the Philippines, Nigeria and Pakistan.

A study on lustration programs implemented in post-Soviet Eastern Europe compared the effectiveness of two distinct approaches to truth revelation.[58] It concluded that an 'incentive-based truth revelation' (ITR) process, which provides those who collaborated or worked in the former regimes with 'incentives for revealing themselves,' works better than an 'evidence-based truth revelation' (ETR) procedure, which 'operates in a fashion similar to an ordinary court system' and does not provide incentives. Processes that include ITR, the study points out,

> create incentives for perpetrators to step forward and testify against themselves. The reward offered to the perpetrator or ex-collaborator is usually immunity from criminal charges or serious sentence reduction. Using such procedures allows for the extraction of statements from those wrongdoers for whom evidence does not even exist. Such effectiveness is impossible in the case of ETRs, which resemble traditional prosecution methods by relying on extricating evidence of collaboration from archival resources or from victims' testimonies.[59]

As discussed below, an ITR approach would be useful if a judicious amnesty policy for economic crimes were combined with efforts to recover assets from perpetrators.

[56] OHCHR, supra n 24 at 16.

[57] Emphasis added. OHCHR, *Rule of Law Tools for Post-Conflict States: Prosecution Initiatives* (2006), 21.

[58] Marek Kaminski and Monika A. Nalepa, *Judging Transitional Justice: An Evaluation of Truth Revelation Procedures* (Irvine: Center for the Study of Democracy, 2004).

[59] Ibid.,15.

Asset Recovery as a Resource for Reparations

Most postconflict or postdictatorship developing countries cannot, on their own, finance transitional justice measures. This predicament has plagued the SCSL,[60] the Extraordinary Chambers of the Courts of Cambodia (ECCC)[61] and Liberia's Truth and Reconciliation Commission.[62]

While this is not a comprehensive solution to the problem of financing transitional justice initiatives, it seems both just and practical for the recovery of assets amassed by perpetrators of economic crimes to be used in part to fund those initiatives, particularly reparations programs. In the Philippines, reparations for victims of the Marcos dictatorship are anchored in proposed domestic legislation, as well as a competing initiative that relies on the enforcement of the US Alien Tort Claims Act judgment against the Marcos family.[63] Both approaches depend on about $680 million in assets recovered by the Philippine government in 2003 from Marcos bank accounts in Switzerland.[64] The Philippine experience also shows that paths that were closed to transitional justice can be opened when reparations and asset recovery intersect. As though opening a backdoor to truth seeking, the proposed reparations law calls for the establishment of a commission that would 'ensure that the truth behind all human rights violations is thoroughly documented.'[65]

In Peru, a special fund, *El Fondo Especial de Administración del Dinero Obtenido Ilicitamente en Perjuicio del Estado* (FEDADOI), was created to govern the use of assets confiscated from Fujimori and his close associates.[66] Under the FEDADOI law, recovered assets have been used for both anticorruption and transitional justice measures, including truth seeking and reparations.[67] The truth commission hearings in Peru, coming off revelations of widespread corruption by the Fujimori regime, created the political conditions that prompted Switzerland[68] and the US[69] to return to Peru $77 million and $20.2 million in ill-gotten assets, respectively.

[60] Integrated Regional Information Network (IRIN), 'Donors Pledge Less than Half Funds Needed for War Crimes Court,' 3 October 2005.

[61] Pepe Escobar, 'Rouge Justice,' *Asia Times Online*, 14 April 2005.

[62] Rob DeVries, 'Liberia Truth Commission on Hold Due to Lack of Funds,' *Jurist*, 28 November 2006.

[63] Decision of the US Ninth Circuit Court of Appeals in *Hilao v. Estate of Ferdinand Marcos et al.*, No. 03-16934, DC No. MDL-00840-MLR (28 December 2004) contains a summary of the relevant US court decisions.

[64] See, *Republic of the Philippines v. Estate of Ferdinand Marcos*, G.R. No. 152154, Supreme Court of the Philippines (15 July 2003).

[65] Thirteenth Philippine Congress, House of Representatives House Bill No. 3315, sec. 8(B)(4).

[66] Funds confiscated from Fujimori and Vladimiro Montesinos may be used already under the FEDADOI law, 'even before it is judicially determined [that the assets] have been illicitly acquired.' Nelly Calderón Navarro, 'Fighting Corruption: The Peruvian Experience,' *Journal of International Criminal Justice* 4(3) (2006): 507–508.

[67] Decree of Urgency No. 122-2001, art. 10 (iii) and (iv).

[68] Swiss Federal Office of Justice, 'Montesinos Case: Switzerland Transfers 77 million US dollars to Peru,' press release (20 August 2002).

[69] US Department of State, 'Transfer to Peru of Assets Derived From Corruption,' press release (12 January 2004).

The possibility of using recovered assets to finance reparations programs is not limited to situations involving fallen dictators. The Sierra Leone Truth and Reconciliation Commission, for example, distinguishes between 'the revenue generated from mineral resources' and 'seized assets from convicted persons.'[70] The former contemplates a mining tax to finance reparations, while the latter refers to the possibility that assets of perpetrators who 'profited from the conflict' will be used to fund reparations programs.

With the indictment of Taylor for the war crime of pillage,[71] this might be possible, but it is not necessarily assured. A conviction for pillage can lay the basis for the forfeiture of Taylor's ill-gotten profits,[72] but because the SCSL is aimed only at accountability for war crimes and gross human rights violations, it does not bridge the gap between Taylor's economic crimes and the legal obligation to provide reparations for victims. The statute states that forfeited assets will be turned over to 'their rightful owner' or to the government of Sierra Leone, but not necessarily used for reparations. The prosecutor argues that while they may be 'morally connected,' Taylor's ill-gotten assets and the victims' right to reparations are not 'expressly legally connected.'[73]

The Judicious Use of Conditional Amnesties Can Contribute to Asset Recovery

While amnesty-for-truth mechanisms have often immediately (and justifiably) triggered concerns that they encourage impunity with respect to human rights violations, a similar approach with respect to large-scale corruption and economic crimes may not be as controversial, especially if it results in the recovery of assets amassed through those crimes.

An ITR-based approach clearly motivated some of the approaches to corruption investigation and asset recovery that are now in the UNCAC.[74] The treaty contemplates the possibility of granting amnesty for providing truth in connection with corruption investigations.[75] This was not a hard choice to make, as granting amnesties and other incentives in exchange for information arguably is not as difficult a dilemma in corruption cases as in cases involving gross human rights violations. In many states, anticorruption legislation in general already offers

70 Sierra Leone TRC report, supra n 48 at vol. II, ch. 4, p. 269.

71 SCSL statute, art. 3(f).

72 SCSL Rules of Procedure, Rule 104(c).

73 From remarks made by SCSL prosecutor Stephen Rapp at a briefing for NGOs on 14 July 2008.

74 See, for example, art. 37(1) of the Convention: 'Each State Party shall take appropriate measures to encourage persons who participate or who have participated in the commission of an offence established in accordance with this Convention to supply information useful to competent authorities for investigative and evidentiary purposes and to provide factual, specific help to competent authorities that may contribute to depriving offenders of the proceeds of crime and to recovering such proceeds.'

75 See, art. 37(3): 'Each State Party shall consider providing for the possibility, in accordance with fundamental principles of its domestic law, of granting immunity from prosecution to a person who provides substantial cooperation in the investigation or prosecution of an offence established in accordance with this Convention.'

whistleblower protection. Some states even allow *qui tam* actions in corruption cases.[76]

Even if the truth-seeking process can be used to establish a perpetrator's complicity in large-scale corruption, truth commissions clearly are not in themselves a means for recovering assets. When combined with amnesties and anticorruption instruments, such as the UNCAC and mutual legal assistance treaties, however, an incentive-based truth commission policy can create conditions conducive to asset recovery. For instance, immunity offered in the Philippines by a commission of inquiry-type agency led to disclosures of hidden Marcos assets and hastened asset recovery litigation in Switzerland.[77]

Expanding the Role of Human Rights Courts

The Taylor case shows that factual and legal issues that involve evidence of an economic crime can be addressed in a trial for war crimes and human rights violations. As discussed earlier, human rights courts reflect a compartmentalized view of human rights and transitional justice and do not see themselves as mandated to address corruption and other economic crimes.

That being said, most existing tribunals can take measures that address economic crimes even if this is not seen as their principal mandate. By doing so, they can go beyond their specific but limited role of holding individual perpetrators liable for a narrowly defined set of human rights violations and fulfill two other possible roles: enhancing victims' right to reparations and expanding the range of tools against impunity.

Under the ICC statute, victims of crimes tried before the ICC can obtain reparations from the ICC's Trust Fund for Victims.[78] Among the penalties in the ICC statute is the 'forfeiture of proceeds, property and assets derived directly or indirectly from that crime.'[79] Thus, perpetrators who amassed assets through the crimes and human rights violations for which they are convicted can be held accountable not just for those crimes expressly within the Court's jurisdiction but also for economic crimes.

The regulations applicable to the TFV provide for a number of ways in which the assets of a convicted perpetrator can be used for reparations.[80] The ICC prosecutor, or even victims, may request a freeze on assets that might be susceptible to being

[76] A good example is the US False Claims Act, 31 U.S.C., sec. 3729, which allows citizens to file cases against persons involved in fraudulent government contracts and to obtain a portion of the damages recovered.

[77] The Presidential Commission on Good Government has both investigatory and immunity-granting powers.

[78] See, Article 79: 'A Trust Fund shall be established by decision of the Assembly of States Parties for the benefit of victims of crimes within the jurisdiction of the Court, and of the families of such victims.'

[79] ICC statute, art. 77(2)(b).

[80] See, Marieke Wierda and Pablo de Greiff, *Reparations and the International Criminal Court: A Prospective Role for the Trust Fund for Victims* (New York: International Center for Transitional Justice, 2005).

used for reparations.[81] In the issuance of an arrest warrant for Thomas Lubanga, for example, the ICC's Pre-Trial Chamber requested that states trace, freeze or seize Lubanga's assets. In issuing its request, the Chamber noted that 'the reparation scheme provided for in the Statute is not only one of the Statute's unique features . . . it is also a key feature,' and that 'the success of the Court is, to some extent, linked to the success of its reparation system.'[82]

The ECCC, meanwhile, has two unique features. First, it can award 'collective and moral reparations'[83] to victims of the Khmer Rouge, unlike the *ad hoc* tribunals for the former Yugoslavia and Rwanda, which had no reparations mandates. Second, it can receive civil party claims, marking the first time that victims have been granted a clear *locus standi* before a hybrid human rights court.[84] While any judgment to provide reparations is to be 'borne by convicted persons,'[85] this should not limit the court's discretion in defining what kind of 'collective' and 'moral' reparations would be meaningful for victims. Of the handful of accused, only one has relatively significant assets that can be applied toward reparations for almost two million Khmer Rouge victims.[86] This circumstance should prompt the ECCC to look at how the Khmer Rouge's profitable history of massive illegal logging and mining[87] can be tied to the court's reparations mandate.

A less obvious but more strategic way in which human rights courts can develop their role in the field of transitional justice is by exploring approaches through which they can assume jurisdiction over economic crimes and large-scale corruption. As argued earlier, the concept of system crimes should be an opportunity for human rights courts to prosecute and try human rights violations and economic crimes together.[88] Certain crimes, such as the appropriation of property,[89] pillage[90] and starvation,[91] are already both violations of socioeconomic rights and war crimes that fall within the mandate of human rights courts. The concept of system crimes arguably could go further, lending itself to the inclusion of large-scale corruption and despoliation when carried out in conjunction with gross human rights violations. The ICC prosecutor has indicated the possibility of undertaking

81 ICC statute, art. 57(3)(e).

82 Situation in the Democratic Republic of the Congo: In the Case of *Prosecutor v. Thomas Lubanga Dyilo*, Decision of the Pre-Trial Chamber 1, No. ICC0-01/04-01/06 (31 March 2006).

83 Rule 23, para. 11, of the ECCC's Internal Rules states: 'The Chambers may award only collective and moral reparations to Civil Parties. These shall be awarded against, and be borne by convicted persons.'

84 Internal Rules of the ECCC, Rule 23, para. 1(a) and (b).

85 Ibid.

86 As of writing, five accused are before the ECCC. Only Ieng Sary appears to have some assets that may be described as substantial.

87 Philip Shenon, 'Now It's the Jungle that the Khmer Rouge Decimates,' *New York Times*, 7 February 1993. See also, Global Witness, 'Forests: The Khmer Rouge and the Funding of the Civil War,' http://www.globalwitness.org/pages/en/khmer_rouge_and_civil_war.html.

88 See, OHCHR, supra n 57.

89 ICC statute, art. 8(iv).

90 Ibid., art. 8(xvi).

91 Ibid., art. 8(xxv).

an investigation of 'money-laundering and other crimes' connected to resource extraction associated with armed conflict.[92]

A bolder step is to characterize large-scale corruption as a crime against humanity in itself, which some anticorruption advocates have proposed.[93] Some argue that, even now, 'in certain cases, corruption may take the form of a crime against humanity,' so that this 'possibility extends significantly the jurisdictional ambit of national courts and empowers the International Criminal Court to consider a case.'[94] This approach would not be unprecedented, as transitional justice has contributed to the recognition of certain sexual offenses as war crimes.[95] There is room to argue that certain economic crimes committed by a repressive regime or in the context of an armed conflict should fall within the ICC's jurisdiction.

The abovementioned possibilities would not only contribute to the progressive development of international human rights law but also advance international anticorruption mechanisms. No international tribunal has explicit jurisdiction over large-scale corruption. The UNCAC does not create any organ that might perform this function.[96] Some domestic courts might possess jurisdiction over specific corrupt acts committed outside their territorial jurisdiction, but this is defined by domestic law,[97] or, in some cases, by a regional treaty.[98] Moreover, longstanding principles of immunity and extradition that no longer pose as insurmountable an obstacle to foreign prosecution in cases of gross human rights violations are still obstacles in cases of corruption committed abroad.[99]

Unlike the international legal regime for protecting human rights, the international legal regime that governs corruption is relatively new. In the drafting of the UNCAC, no consensus emerged on the definition of corruption.[100] The growing

92 See, ICC Prosecutor press release, No. pids.009.2003-EN (16 July 2003).

93 At the 11th International Anti-Corruption Conference in South Korea, organized in May 2003 by various states' anticorruption agencies, the former Kenyan minister of justice, Kiraitu Murungi, proposed that large-scale corruption be declared a crime against humanity. See, 'Seoul Findings,' a summary of conference findings, http://www.11iacc.org/download/finish/11IACC_Seoul_Findings.doc

94 See, Ilias Bantekas, 'Corruption as an International Crime and Crime against Humanity: An Outline of Supplementary Criminal Justice Policies,' *Journal of International Criminal Justice* 4(3) (2006): 1.

95 *Prosecutor v. Dragoljub Kunarac, Radomir Kovač, Zoran Vuković (Foča)*, Appeals Chamber Judgment, No. IT-96-23 (12 June 2002).

96 In a chapter entitled 'Mechanisms for Implementation,' the UNCAC creates a 'Conference of State Parties.' However, this body has no adjudicative power or any capacity to create a tribunal to act on actual corruption cases.

97 An example would be the US Foreign Corrupt Practices Act, 15 U.S.C., sec. 78dd-1, *et seq.*

98 Such as the Organisation for Economic Co-operation and Development's (OECD) Convention on Combating Bribery of Foreign Public Officials in International Business Transactions, 37 I.L.M. 1 (18 December 1997).

99 Veronica Pujas, 'Immunity and Extradition: Obstacles to Justice,' in *Global Corruption Report 2004* (Berlin: Transparency International, 2004).

100 The author participated in the discussions of the UN Ad Hoc Committee on how corruption should be defined. Once the impossibility of getting members to agree on a definition was established, none was used in the Convention.

number of regional conventions against corruption[101] and the taking into effect of the UNCAC obviously will contribute to combating impunity for corruption. Still, this pales in comparison to the relative robustness of the international mechanisms that can already extract accountability for human rights violations.

Conclusion: The Scope of 'Justice' in Transitional Justice

The theories at the center of transitional justice are broadly drawn and susceptible to varying interpretations, including that mechanisms that address corruption and economic crimes should be incorporated into its mainstream. The practice of transitional justice to date, however, has been associated with a very narrow paradigm of what constitutes human rights violations. Any engagement with socioeconomic rights issues would require transitional justice advocates to disabuse themselves of the overemphasis on civil and political rights that Balakrishnan Rajagopal attributes to 'the dominance of Western scholars and NGOs,' arguing that it has in turn allowed a 'bias . . . [to be] built into the normative corpus of human rights.'[102]

Both civil and political rights and socioeconomic rights abuses are committed against overlapping sets of victims by an invariably overlapping set of perpetrators. An impunity gap is created when transitional justice mechanisms deal with only one kind of abuse while ignoring accountability for large-scale corruption and economic crimes. It is true that resolving the nearly intractable social and economic inequities that bring about or exacerbate human rights violations and conflict are not explicit aims of transitional justice. Nonetheless, addressing poverty and social inequality must be regarded as among the strategic goals of any transitional justice undertaking.[103] At the very least, it should be an overarching aim of any attempt at truth seeking, criminal prosecution, reparations and institutional reform. It may be stating the obvious to say that whatever gains may be made from transitional justice initiatives could be unmade if the conditions that led to or aggravated repression and conflict are left to fester, allowing repression to reemerge and conflict to recur.

Whether the engagement with corruption is founded on the premise that corruption is a human rights violation,[104] or on the theory that economic crimes are part of an indivisible system of crimes committed by the same set of

[101] Examples are the Inter-American Convention Against Corruption, the OECD Convention on Combating Bribery of Foreign Public Officials in International Business Transactions and, most recently, the African Union Convention on Combating Bribery and Corruption.

[102] Balakrishnan Rajagopal, 'Human Rights and Development: Legal and Policy Issues with Special Reference to Dams,' in *Regulation, Compliance and Implementation*, ed. Angela Cropper, Daniel Bradlow and Mark Halle (Cape Town: World Commission on Dams, 2000), pp. 4–5.

[103] Which is not to say that transitional justice has been effective thus far in arriving at this goal. A study for the UK's Department for International Development (DFID) concludes that 'the impact of [transitional justice mechanisms (TJMs)] on poverty reduction will be particularly limited as long as reparative measures that address the economic and social consequences of human rights violations continue to be neglected, and while violations of economic and social rights remain largely excluded from the focus of TJMs.' Jane Alexander, 'A Scoping Study of Transitional Justice and Poverty Reduction,' final report for DFID (January 2003), 3.

[104] See, for example, Nihal Jayawickrama, 'Corruption: A Violation of Human Rights?' Transparency International working paper (June 1998).

perpetrators or regime,[105] the mechanisms used in transitional justice can in fact be applied. The question, then, is under what conditions they should be applied. So far, transitional justice has largely avoided this question. It wants to look at abuses committed under dictatorships and during armed conflict, but it looks away when it sees the economic crimes and social injustices that breed or worsen poverty, conflict and repression.[106] Posttransition developing countries that are chronically poor *and* conflict-ridden are likely to remain so notwithstanding the introduction of transitional justice measures. By allowing these structural inequities to persist through evasion, the field of transitional justice can rightly be accused of creating and then frustrating expectations of meaningful change.

To be fair, the exclusion of corruption and economic crimes from transitional justice mechanisms does not necessarily mean that the role of these violations in abuse and conflict is being diminished. A popular view is that transitional justice is meant to address one part of the problem with the hope that it can contribute to the solution of the whole. This view accounts for the policy argument that bringing in a nonhuman rights component could become a distraction in the work, for instance, of a truth commission. It also explains the apprehension that looking into large-scale corruption and economic crimes could divert the public's attention from the gravity of human rights violations and spread the limited resources for pursuing transitional justice mechanisms too thin. Furthermore, some validity can be found in the concern that the field of transitional justice, as it is, lacks the capacity to investigate and extract accountability for corruption. This precisely begs the question: Is capacity lacking because transitional justice is inherently incapable of engaging with economic crimes and corruption, or is it lacking because the field has not paid attention to such abuses?

These policy arguments, founded as they are on what transitional justice is perceived to be and has achieved so far, do not answer the questions of what transitional justice should aim to become and what it can still do. While transitional justice promotes accountability by what it chooses to confront, it may reinforce impunity by what it chooses to ignore.

[105] For a useful and practice-oriented view of the indivisibility of rights and Peru's experience with truth seeking in the context of both socioeconomic rights as well as civil and political rights violations, see, Lisa J. Laplante, 'On the Indivisibility of Rights: Truth Commissions, Reparations, and the Right to Development,' *Yale Human Rights and Development Law Journal* 10 (2007): 88–140.

[106] According to Jane Alexander, 'An approach to transitional justice that incorporates the goal of poverty reduction calls for particular attention to be paid to the perspectives of victims. It requires an examination of the linkages between poverty and human rights violations, and of structural inequalities as a root cause of conflict.' Alexander, supra n 103 at 48.

24

Justice after the war: The International Criminal Court and post-Gaddafi Libya

Mark Kersten

In contrast to other Arab Spring uprisings, the International Criminal Court (ICC) intervened in Libya and has subsequently played an important, if controversial, role in the country's political transition. This chapter provides a critical overview of key events pertaining to the ICC's role and impact in post-Gaddafi Libya. It offers some tentative conclusions on how Libya's experience with international criminal justice may affect the broader field of transitional justice.[2]

Libya has clearly indicated that its actions regarding post-Gaddafi accountability are aimed at maintaining its sovereignty and establishing itself as an equal member of the international community, able and willing to prosecute senior members of the Gaddafi regime. The ICC has striven to show that it is an effective institution that can have positive effects on conflict and post-conflict justice and accountability. However, as this analysis makes clear, the pursuit and politics of justice in post-Gaddafi Libya has been characterized by ongoing mistrust and rancour among key figures and actors. This animosity has been consistently stoked by a lack of interest among the concerned parties to seek, identify and pursue judicial avenues where their interests could converge and complement each other. Ultimately, this may hamper the objectives and interests of both the ICC and Libyans.

The chapter proceeds in three sections. Section one examines the capture of Abdullah al-Senussi in Mauritania and Saif al-Islam Gaddafi[3] as well as the controversies over where they should be tried. Section two details efforts to represent Saif, focusing in particular on the controversial arrest and detention of ICC defence counsel following their visit to Zintan in June 2012. Section three offers some reflections on the implications of the pursuit of post-Gaddafi justice on the field of transitional justice.

Saif and Senussi: will they stay or will they go?

The decision of where to hold post-conflict trials has always been politically contentious; the dilemmas it poses are part of the hardwiring of international criminal justice. Divorcing justice from the communities in which atrocities have occurred is replete with trade-offs and controversy (Simpson 2007: 30–53). Extracting evidence, protecting witnesses and contextualizing crimes becomes an immensely difficult process when adjudication takes place far away from where atrocities were perpetrated. But in many cases, post-conflict states do not have the resources or the judicial and political stability to adjudicate serious breaches of international criminal justice. This dilemma is captured by the ICC's principle of complementarity wherein the Court can only investigate and prosecute crimes when national authorities are unable or unwilling to do so.

Following the death of Muammar Gaddafi, Abdullah al-Senussi and Saif al-Islam Gaddafi were the only remaining individuals wanted by the ICC for their roles in the Gaddafi regime's brutal crackdown against civilians. The fate of Saif and Senussi became the locus of a potent and polarizing debate on where post-conflict justice in Libya should be served. This section provides background on both Saif and Senussi before delving into the polarizing fight over where to try them, a battle which has created an acrimonious rift between those actors who see The Hague as the only legitimate venue for trial and those who believe that Libya has the sovereign prerogative to try Saif and Senussi.

'The Senussi Sweepstakes'[4]

Abdullah al-Senussi was a key member of Gaddafi's most trusted circle of advisors, having served as both Libya's external and internal intelligence chief. As one observer suggests, 'Senussi's association with the worst excesses of the Libyan regime stretch back to the early days of Col. Gaddafi's dictatorial rule' (Sherlock 2011). With the exception of Muammar Gaddafi, Senussi may have been 'the most feared man in Libya' (Hilsum 2012a). Notably, Senussi is widely believed to bear responsibility for the infamous 1996 Abu Salim Massacre (where at least 1,200 Libyan prisoners were killed) and the Lockerbie bombing in 1988. Because of his position as the gate-keeper of the regime's secret, Geoffrey Robertson (2011a) called Senussi the 'crown jewel' of justice in Libya. For his role in the crackdown on Libyan demonstrators, the ICC issued an arrest warrant against Senussi for being an 'indirect perpetrator' on two counts of crimes against humanity – murder and persecution (ICC 2012k).

In March 2012 it was reported that Senussi had been arrested in a joint operation between French and Mauritanian officials in Nouakchott, Mauritania. Immediately following his arrest, Senussi's fate emerged as the centrepiece of what was described as a 'three-way custody battle' (Mark 2012) and an 'extradition race' (Hirsch 2012) between Libya, France and the ICC. In seeking Senussi's surrender, Libyan authorities took an aggressive and ultimately successful approach, applying concerted diplomatic pressure and offering Mauritania substantial incentives in order to gain custody of Gaddafi's right-hand man. Finally, on 5 September 2012, Senussi was extradited to Libya, 'on the basis of guarantees given by the Libyan authorities' (see Harding and Black 2012). It was reported that Senussi's transfer cost Libya $200 million (see Sydow 2012).

Saif in Zintan

Prior to the Libyan uprising – and even in its early stages – many observers and diplomats saw Saif al-Islam Gaddafi as a moderating force in Libya. The London School of Economics-educated Saif had been instrumental in Libya's rapprochement with the West, played a key role in negotiating the surrender of the country's weapons of mass destruction and nuclear programme, helped to secure compensation for victims of the Lockerbie bombing, and spearheaded efforts to de-radicalize and make peace with the Libyan Islamic Fighting Group (LIFG). As Lindsey Hilsum (2012b: 156) writes, in the 2000s 'it became clear that he was his father's heir apparent, and anyone who wanted to do business in Libya had to do business with him'. Consequently, many saw Saif as a reform-minded successor to his father, someone who could continue Libya's transformation from a pariah state to a legitimate and respected member of the international community.

It quickly became clear, however, that Saif was willing to play a significant role alongside his father. As with Senussi, the ICC issued an arrest warrant for Saif, accusing him of being an indirect co-perpetrator on two counts of crimes against humanity – murder and persecution. After fleeing Tripoli, on the night of 19 November 2011, Saif was arrested by a militia brigade from Zintan where he remains at the time of writing. The drama over where he and Senussi would be tried, however, had long since commenced.

Where to try Saif and Senussi?

Discussions on where to try Saif and Senussi began as early as August 2011, when the prospect of bringing senior Libyan officials to justice became a distinct possibility (see Bosco 2011; Jillions 2011; Kersten 2011a; Kaye 2011). The debate has been characterized by a polarizing battle between proponents of trying them in Libya, on the one hand, and those who believe that only the ICC should try them impartially and legitimately, on the other. Within these camps, however, is a curious constellation of actors and positions. Predictably, Libyan authorities have made clear their intentions to try Saif on Libyan soil with Libyan judges, while international human rights NGOs have insisted that Gaddafi's son be tried in The Hague (see Amnesty International 2011; Parliamentarians for Global Action 2011). However, somewhat paradoxically, the Office of the Prosecutor (OTP) has been supportive of Libya's claims to try Saif, while the Office of Public Counsel for the Defence (OPCD) has vociferously worked to demonstrate that a fair trial in Libya is all but impossible.

From the outset, the National Transitional Council (NTC) maintained that Saif would be investigated and tried in Libya. Doing so, it has been consistently claimed, is essential to establishing the country as a sovereign member of the international community (see, for example CNN 2012; Al Jazeera 2012). For example, in October 2011, a month prior to the arrest of Saif, Colonel Ahmed Bani, the military spokesman for Libya's interim rulers, explained why the ICC could not gain custody of Saif:

> We will not accept that our sovereignty be violated like that. We will put him on trial here. This is where he must face the consequences of what he has done. We will prove to the world that we are a civilised people with a fair justice system. Libya has its rights and its sovereignty and we will exercise them. (See Chulov 2011)

Libya's desire to try Saif should also be understood within the context of prevalent fears that surrendering Saif or Senussi to the ICC could undermine Libya's revolution and potentially destabilize the country. There is a concern that Saif could be found innocent or released after serving a short sentence if tried at the ICC. This concern is likely a result of a combination of the relatively minor charges against him at the ICC, his young age (41 years old as at the time of writing) and the possibility of a lenient sentence. Notably, the Libya Working Group, an assembly of experts on Libya, has opined that it would be politically impossible for the NTC to allow Saif to receive an innocent verdict because it would be seen to 'betray the revolution' (see Chatham House 2012a: 3). And, according to Geoffrey Robertson (2011b), an innocent verdict at the ICC is a real possibility: 'Saif has the makings of an arguable defense ... His judges would be independent and his conviction on the basis of proof beyond reasonable doubt would by no means be a foregone conclusion'. In contrast, Libya could charge Saif with additional offences, such as corruption, and impose the death penalty.

Remarkably, the OTP has, by and large, sided with the NTC's plans to try Saif, demonstrating a leniency that appears unprecedented in the history of the Court. During a November 2011 visit to Tripoli, Moreno-Ocampo capitulated to the inevitability of the NTC's demands to try Saif:

> The standard of the ICC is that it has to be a judicial process that is not organised to shield the suspect ... and I respect that it's important for the cases to be tried in Libya ... and I am not competing for the case. (See BBC 2012a)

Rather than standing by the orthodox standard of complementarity, whereby a state has to convince ICC judges that it is actively able and willing to prosecute the same individuals for the same crimes, the OTP has seemingly calculated that it is best positioned to argue that it contributed positively to Libya's pursuit of justice.[5] There are a number of plausible explanations for this position.

As suggested above, it is not a given that Saif would be convicted at the ICC. The Libya Working Group noted in February 2012 that '[t]here is speculation that the ICC does not want Saif to be put on trial in The Hague as they do not have a strong case against him' (see Chatham House 2012c). Timothy William Waters (2011) has argued, alternatively, that Moreno-Ocampo's acquiescence was a pragmatic response aimed at ensuring the cooperation of Libyan authorities so as 'to have any hope of influencing the process'. In this context, it is important to note that the ICC has received scant support from the international community which has been largely unconcerned with the pursuit of post-Gaddafi accountability, periodically reaffirming that the ICC and Libya should cooperate but that it is up to Libya to decide the fate of Saif and Senussi. Indeed, the general consensus among the states that intervened has been that Libya should prosecute Saif and Senussi, irrespective of the ICC's indictments (see Lynch 2011; McGreal 2012; Kersten 2013).

Rather than demanding the surrender of Saif and Senussi, the OTP has shifted its focus away from seeking custody of Saif or Senussi towards claiming that they can achieve 'positive complementarity' in Libya. In this context, Moreno-Ocampo argued that 'the ICC is still providing an important service, because we will ensure justice in Libya, whoever will do it' (see Papenfuss 2012). The OTP, moreover, appeared on numerous occasions at the side of NTC leaders, reaffirming the perception that his role is to support – and not challenge – Libya's efforts to try Saif. As Waters (2011) suggests, this may be a pragmatic calculation on the part of Moreno-Ocampo. Claiming some responsibility for bringing both Saif and Senussi to justice in Libya by couching arguments in the rhetoric of positive complementarity may soften the blow – and deflect criticism – of the ICC appearing largely impotent in contributing to accountability in post-Gaddafi Libya. Still, the attitude of the OTP has not been shared by all organs of the Court.

By working to defend the ICC's right to prosecute Saif and Senussi, it has been the Office of Public Counsel for the Defence (OPCD) which has most adamantly sought to ensure that Saif and Senussi be tried in The Hague. As a result, on a number of occasions the OPCD has taken aim at the OTP's acquiescence with Libya's demands to prosecute Saif and Senussi. Just days after Saif's arrest on 28 November 2011, the OPCD asserted that the OTP was employing double-standards with regards to its conception of complementarity:

> … it is in the general interests of the Defence that the standard and criteria for determining the existence of investigations and prosecutions be interpreted and applied uniformly throughout the different ICC cases: it would be unfair to apply a more stringent standard to cases in which admissibility is challenged by the Defence, whilst applying a more relaxed standard in the present case due to the apparent coalescence of Prosecution and State interests (ICC 2011c; see also Stahn 2012: 12).

The OPCD also took issue with Moreno-Ocampo's public comments and appearances with members of the NTC which, they argued, appeared to reaffirm the validity of the NTC's desire to prosecute Saif in Libya. In May 2012, the OPCD filed a motion with the ICC's Appeals Chamber to disqualify Moreno-Ocampo from the Libyan case due to 'an objective appearance that the Prosecutor is affiliated with both the political cause and legal positions of the NTC government' (ICC 2012c para 28). While the motion was ultimately unsuccessful, just four days before the end of Moreno-Ocampo's tenure as Chief Prosecutor the Appeals Chamber issued a scathing ruling which claimed that the Prosecutor's behaviour was clearly inappropriate in light of the presumption of innocence. 'Such behaviour not only reflects poorly on the Prosecutor but also, given that the Prosecutor is an elected official of the Court and that his statements are often imputed to the Court as a whole, may lead observers to question the integrity of the Court as a whole' (ICC 2012h).

Libya's admissibility challenge

In May 2012, Libya filed an admissibility challenge at the ICC in which the government argued that because it was actively investigating and willing to prosecute Saif and Senussi, ICC judges had an obligation to rule in favour of Libya's admissibility challenge (ICC 2012b). At the same time, Libya unveiled a refurbished courtroom in Tripoli (see Al Shalchi 2012) and a prison custom-made for Saif (Stephen 2012b). The application, and the commitment to demonstrating that it was actively investigating and willing to prosecute Saif and Senussi, is an indication of the Libyan government's interest in having the ICC and the international community more broadly endorse Libya's efforts at achieving transitional justice.

Prior to Senussi's extradition from Mauritania to Libya, it was widely believed that Libya's admissibility challenge would be fundamentally undermined by the fact that it did not have custody of Senussi and that Saif remained in the custody of a Zintani militia. With Senussi's extradition to Libya, a significant obstacle to Libya's admissibility challenge was removed. However, the Court rejected Libya's admissibility challenge in Saif's case, relying heavily on the fact that Gaddafi's son remains in the custody of a Zintani brigade and not the central government.[6] Yet while the admissibility challenge has precipitated a fascinating political and legal debate which will undoubtedly have implications on the future functioning and practices of the ICC, it should not deter from a recognition that other options were available with regards to prosecuting Saif and Senussi.

A missed opportunity

The polarizing battle between proponents of a trial in Libya versus those advocating justice in The Hague deflected attention away from existing alternative legal and political options, which could have served the interests of all parties. Two distinct options could have satisfied the interests of both the ICC and Libya: an *in situ* trial and a sequencing of trials. Unfortunately, neither was sufficiently explored.

The Rome Statute envisages the possibility of *in situ* trials under Article 3(3), which states that proceedings may take place 'elsewhere, whenever [the

ICC] considers it desirable'. Indeed, the potential of holding trials away from The Hague has been explored by the ICC in other contexts.[7] Such trials have numerous advantages: their proximity to the victims, witnesses and evidence; acting as a demonstration that justice is being done; contributing to the building of the rule of law by training lawyers and providing a material legacy; and maintaining the standards of international criminal justice (see Kaye 2011; Kersten 2011a).

The OTP initially saw the option of an *in situ* trial favourably and presented it to the NTC during a visit in November 2011 to discuss the fate of Saif. On the eve of the visit, ICC spokesperson, Fadi El Abdallah, suggested that a trial by ICC judges in Libya was indeed a viable option (see Murphy 2011). The OTP subsequently reported that it had offered such an option to the NTC (ICC 2012b). Importantly, holding an *in situ* trial in Tripoli (or perhaps even Zintan) could have satisfied the need of both parties. The NTC would be able to reaffirm itself as a sovereign entity able to hold fair trials as well as demonstrate its commitment to international law. The ICC would hear a key case and demonstrate that it was sensitive to the desire of Libyans to see justice served where crimes occurred rather than divorcing proceedings from victims and survivors. Nevertheless, the NTC rejected the possibility of an *in situ* trial and stated that it would only accept a trial in Libya, by Libyan judges (see Murphy 2011; Stephen 2012a). Rather than defending this option and presenting its benefits to the Libyan public or the international community, the possibility of an ICC trial in Libya appears to have been subsequently ignored by the ICC, international human rights NGOs and the Libyan government itself.

During the November meeting, the OTP also suggested that the ICC and the NTC could sequence prosecutions. Sequencing, envisioned under Article 94 of the Rome Statute, would entail the ICC trying Saif and Senussi for the alleged crimes outlined in their indictment and subsequently transferring them to Libya to be tried for other alleged crimes (see Stahn 2012: 325–49). As Carsten Stahn writes, the sequencing of trials could have been 'settled on a negotiated basis, i.e. through consultation and agreement' (2012: 340). The trial at the ICC would have provided time for Libya to stabilize the country and build an independent judiciary capable of subsequently trying Saif and Senussi domestically for crimes beyond the ICC's temporal jurisdiction (see Robertson 2011b). Moreover, sequencing could have ensured that alleged crimes committed before and after 15 February 2011[8] were investigated and prosecuted. However, as with an *in situ* trial sequencing remained insufficiently explored.

Of course, neither an *in situ* trial nor a sequencing of trials is a perfect or risk-free option; each has its own drawbacks. But these were real options which could have avoided the animosity of the current debate regarding the fate of Saif and Senussi by potentially satisfying the interests of all actors involved – not to mention the interests of justice. While Libya may not have looked upon any option other than a local trial favourably, it is important to note that the ICC did very little to communicate or demonstrate its work locally or to establish any kind of local presence during the conflict (Chatham House 2011: 10). This point was noted by the director of Lawyers for Justice in Libya, Elham Saudi (Chatham House 2011: 10):

> The press and NGOs were in Libya and were gathering evidence but there was no visible presence of the ICC. People were not clear as to what should happen after the indictments and did not understand why, for example, the BBC was in Libya but the ICC was not.

The ICC thus had little leverage when it came to influencing where Saif and Senussi would be tried. The Court appeared alien to Libyans and, as a consequence, many find absurd the notion of handing over prized detainees from the Gaddafi regime to a Court that had a minimal presence during their struggle against Gaddafi.

But there should be no confusion: the polarizing nature of the debate regarding where to try Saif and Senussi was not inevitable. It was an extension of the fact that the OTP, international human rights groups and the international community did not effectively communicate the existence of other options. As Saudi adds:

> It is not an either or of having a trial in The Hague or a trial in Libya. There's a multitude of options in between as well and that's where the education is lacking and the ICC is failing because they have an active responsibility and a positive duty to inform Libyans of all their options and to assist them in achieving those options. (See BBC 2012b)

The OPCD detention debacle

From the moment the former heir to the Libyan regime was captured, efforts to represent Saif have been fraught with controversy and characterized by an accumulation of mistrust, bitterness and animosity between the OPCD and the OTP and between the ICC and Libya. Nothing demonstrated this reality as vividly as the detention of four ICC staff members from June to July 2012.

On 7 June 2012 four staff members of the OPCD – Melinda Taylor (Australia), Helene Assaf (Lebanon), Alexander Khodakov (Russia) and Esteban Peralta Losilla (Spain) – were arrested following a meeting with Saif al-Islam Gaddafi in Zintan. The four staff members had been granted access to Saif by the office of Libya's General Prosecutor but were detained by members of the Zintani militia which had held custody of Gaddafi since his arrest. Describing their arrest, Ajmi al-Atiri, a commander from the Zintani brigade, explained: 'We tricked the ICC team by presenting them with one of our men who we told them was deaf and old and illiterate but he is actually a wise man who can speak four languages including English' (see Shuaib and Al Shalchi 2012). In describing the actions of the ICC staff as 'a homeland security issue', al-Atiri further claimed that numerous blank documents, a coded letter to a close confidante of Saif, Mohammed Ismail, as well as spying and recording devices, had been retrieved from the lawyers. The four were arrested, it was maintained, because their actions threatened Libyan national security. It subsequently came to light that at least some members of the NTC were seeking to leverage the staff's freedom. On 12 June, NTC spokesperson Mohammed al-Hareizi declared that Taylor was free to leave in exchange for information regarding the location of Ismail:

> We want this guy. It is very important to catch this guy because this guy is very, very, very danger[ous] for us ... We don't have anything against this woman. Just we need some information from her, after that she will be free. (See Al Arabiya 2012a)

In response to these developments, ICC President Judge Sang-Hyun Song declared that ICC staff enjoyed immunity from arrest and prosecution in their capacity as the defence counsel for Saif and demanded that Libyan authorities 'take all necessary measures to ensure their safety and security and to liberate them' (ICC 2012g). Following this initial reaction, the Court became engaged in a series of negotiations with Libyan authorities aimed at guaranteeing the return of Taylor and her staff. Additionally, the Australian government and, in particular, Foreign Minister Bob Carr and Australia's ambassador to Libya, David Ritchie, played an intimate role in efforts to have the ICC staff released. For its part, the international community was largely silent. A week after the arrest of the ICC staff, NATO Secretary-General Anders Fogh Rasmussen, on an official visit to Australia, declared: 'I strongly regret that certain groups in Libya have arrested or withheld representatives of the International Criminal Court. I would urge them to release these individuals as soon as possible' (see Al Arabiya 2012b). More than a week after the arrest of the ICC staff and in response to pressure from Russian Foreign Minister Sergei Lavrov, who believed that the staff's detention was in violation of UN Security Council Resolution 1970 (see RIA Novosti 2012), the Security Council finally issued its own statement where it 'express[ed] serious concern over the detention' of the staff and 'urge[d] Libyan authorities at all levels and all concerned to work towards immediate release of all the ICC staff members' (Security Council 2012b). Notably, the Council's statement did not demand that Libya release the staff members, nor did it criticize the arrest and detention of an international delegation that enjoyed diplomatic immunity.

In working for Taylor's release, Carr began to publicly voice criticism of the ICC for not having adequate protocols and procedures in place for lawyers working in fragile, highly volatile contexts (see ABC 2012; *Telegraph* 2012). He consequently suggested that the ICC apologize for any 'misunderstandings' it had caused. The notion of an apology was criticized by a number of observers. Amnesty International's Widney Brown stated that Carr's public suggestion that the Court owed Libya an apology for illegally detaining ICC staff was short-sighted and would 'undermine the independence of the International Criminal Court and create a precedent where governments think well, if we just lock somebody up then we'll get them to back off' (see Flitton and Lester 2012; see also Heller 2012a). Richard Goldstone (2012) wrote that any '[t]alk of securing a "deal" for the release of the four risks compromising the global authority of the court, which is backed by the full authority of the UN and the international community'.

Carr's declaration that the Court should apologize to Libya put the ICC in an immensely difficult position: either the Court apologized and risked undermining its authority and legitimacy or it refused to apologize and risked being blamed for prolonging Taylor's detention. Consequently, on 22 June 2012, the Court released a statement which declared that:

> The ICC deeply regrets any events that may have given rise to concerns on the part of the Libyan authorities. In carrying out its functions, the Court has no intention of doing anything that would undermine the national security of Libya (ICC 2012i).

The statement furthermore promised that any wrongdoing on the part of the ICC staff would be investigated,[9] and noted that the Court was 'extremely grateful to the Libyan authorities for their commitment to take all necessary action for the release of the Court's staff members' (ICC 2012i).

On 3 July, ICC President Song arrived in Zintan, where he, again, publicly expressed regret on behalf of the Court, declaring that he wished 'to apologise for the difficulties which arose due to this series of events' (see Simons 2012). All of the four staff were then flown in a plane organized by the Italian government to Rome and subsequently transferred to The Hague.

A game with no winners

The arrest of the ICC staff should be understood within the context of a fragile state protective of its sovereign prerogatives. As Barak Barfi and Jason Pack (2012) argue, '[i]n arresting Taylor and her colleagues, the NTC has sought to hamstring the ICC's investigation while sending the court a message Libya will not tolerate an infringement of its sovereignty'. Libya's Deputy Foreign Minister, Abdel Aziz, responded to the international outcry by defending the country's ability to govern itself: 'I would say the international community should be fair to Libya. You cannot continue to always push Libya to do this, to do that. There is the other side of the coin that has to be addressed too' (see Gumuchian and Shuaib 2012). Still, the arrest and detention of the ICC staff is likely to hinder the aims and interests of both the ICC and the new Libyan state.

The Court's apology is likely to undermine its authority. The Court effectively apologized to Libya for arresting staff members who enjoy immunity from arrest and prosecution and thanked them for their cooperation in the process.

Moreover, the ICC's response to Libya may undermine the capacity for defence lawyers to work in fragile political contexts. It may also now prove impossible for any staff from the ICC to effectively represent Saif in proceedings before the Court. Not long after the release of the ICC staff, the Libyan government cast doubt on 'the OPCD's ability to properly and genuinely represent Mr Gaddafi's views' and stated that 'communications between the Libyan Government and the OPCD appear to have irretrievably broken down' (ICC 2012j: paras 8 and 10).

A thorough report filed by the OPCD in August 2012 is indicative of the extent to which the relationship between Saif's defence counsel and the Libyan government has been tarnished. The OPCD noted that their point-man in Libya 'informed both the Counsel for Mr. Gaddafi and the ICC interpreter on independent occasions that the actions of the Libyan authorities were "retaliation" for the allegations, which had been set out in the OPCD report of 7 March 2012' (ICC 2012l: para 265). Earlier, Nick Kaufman similarly suggested that the animosity within the ICC filings put Taylor and her delegation at risk, stating that she had 'fallen victim of this hostility which is because of the intensity of the litigation', and that '[t]here is no doubt that these filings contributed to cementing the, shall we say, anger of the local authorities holding Saif, against Melinda and her superior [Keïta]' (see Callinan 2012). The bad blood appears to have spread into the OTP as well. In learning about the arrest of Taylor and her colleagues, Moreno-Ocampo refused to defend the OPCD staff members, blaming them instead for their predicament: 'It's not what we would expect of the court, of the defence' (see Gumuchian 2012). His statement was in stark contrast to other respected international lawyers.

The debacle over the arrest of the ICC staff likely tarnished Libya's international reputation and its case to prosecute Saif and Senussi in Libya. In the wake of the arrest of the ICC staff, high profile legal figures publicly voiced concern over Libya's commitment to international justice and human rights standards. Numerous international legal scholars demonstrated that *regardless* of what occurred during the meeting between the OPCD delegation and Saif, the staff members were entitled to diplomatic immunity (see Akande 2012; Heller 2012d; Cronin-Furman and Taub 2012). By refusing to release the delegation, Libya flouted its international legal obligations and may have made it less likely that the Court would be inclined to accept the government's admissibility challenge, once described as 'a brilliant piece of work [which] stands a good chance of success' (Heller 2012b). While ICC judges did not touch on the detention of the ICC staff in their judgment on Libya's admissibility challenge regarding Saif, siding with Libya would have risked reaffirming numerous contraventions of international law and the illegal treatment of ICC staff. In this context, Richard Goldstone (2012) wrote that '[w]hat is effectively an act of kidnapping also regrettably demonstrates that there is as yet no rule of law in Libya domestically. Ultimately, what has happened has justified the insistence by the ICC that Saif should be tried in The Hague'.

The ICC and post-Gaddafi Libya: implications and questions for transitional justice

A number of tentative conclusions regarding the implications of post-Gaddafi justice on the wider field and pursuit of international criminal and transitional justice can be drawn. This section considers three implications of the ICC's intervention on post-conflict justice in Libya and the field of tranitional justice more broadly: the ever-present risk of post-conflict victor's justice; the politics of complementarity; and the capacity of the ICC to function in fragile contexts.

Victor's justice

The pursuit of post-Gaddafi justice in Libya has played directly into perceptions that post-conflict accountability inevitably devolves into victor's justice. Not only have prosecutions almost exclusively targeted Gaddafi regime officials, but a blanket amnesty has been granted for any 'military, security or civil actions dictated by the February 17 Revolution that were performed by revolutionaries with the goal of promoting or protecting the revolution' (HRW 2012). With regards to the ICC, only Saif and Senussi remain indicted by the Court and, while other senior Gaddafi-era officials have been put on trial in Libya, there is little-to-no indication that serious violations by pro-revolution militias will be held to account.[10] Importantly, the OTP has contributed to the perception of one-sided justice and accountability. The public appearance of Moreno-Ocampo with leaders of the NTC and with rebels in Misrata, for example, has reaffirmed the OTP's positions of siding with the NTC and the rebels as well as its apparent lack of interest in investigating allegations of crimes by the rebels.

For the field of transitional justice, there is a need to conduct more research into the relationship between how conflicts end and subsequent approaches to achieving justice and accountability. Libya's approach to transitional justice is a direct result of the manner in which the conflict ended; the victor's peace of the rebels over the Gaddafi regime has largely translated into post-conflict victor's justice.

The politics of complementarity in post-conflict settings

Libya demonstrates that questions pertaining to where prosecutions should and can take place will remain a subject ridden with controversy. The country's experience with post-conflict accountability poses difficult questions for the field of transitional justice. Two, in particular, are worth highlighting. First, how are we to comprehend shifting interpretations of complementarity? The Libyan situation exposes the reality that the principle and practice of 'complementarity' is not understood in the same way across cases. Second, and relatedly, are the expectations of a state's capacity to prosecute perpetrators of international crimes following a significant period of atrocity and autocracy fair and feasible? Put another way, how long should a state transitioning out of a period of conflict have in order to prove that it is able and willing to prosecute members of a former regime? The experience of Libya would seem to indicate that *no* state that emerges from decades of autocratic rule, where an independent judiciary is non-existent, can be judged able and willing to prosecute key figures itself. In such contexts, the state will be expected simply to 'flip' individuals indicted by the ICC to The Hague at the earliest possible opportunity. If it does not, it risks being judged in contravention of its obligations under international law and castigated by the international human rights community. This may be deeply problematic and will surely be unacceptable to states emerging from periods of heightened political violence seeking to reassert their sovereign capacity and status. Indeed, such states face a difficult quandary: on the one hand, they view prosecuting their own citizens as a matter of upholding or rescuing their status as legitimate and sovereign members of the international community; on the other, their international reputation may be undermined by their insistence that they can prosecute ICC indictees themselves. These issues make exploring alternative, justice-sharing solutions between states and the ICC all the more relevant and pressing. Many of the tensions that emerge in the fight over where to try ICC indictees can be avoided by exploring and pursuing middle-ground options (for example an *in situ* trial or the sequencing of trials) where the interests of all parties can be met. However, as the case of Libya has demonstrated, such middle-ground options are too often neglected.

The ICC in fragile settings

It is entirely possible that the ICC's intervention in Libya will ultimately have greater effects on the Court itself than on Libya. This finding is of significance as it contradicts a generally held assumption that whenever the ICC intervenes in ongoing and or recently concluded conflicts, it will have a significant impact on the decision-making of state actors. In Libya, however, this does not appear to be the case.

The ICC's decision-making in Libya may have palpable ramifications on its future capacity to function effectively in fragile conflict and post-conflict contexts. First, the Court's apology to Libya may affect the capacity of ICC staff to operate in such situations in the future (see Cronin-Furman and Taub 2012). The apology appeared to send the message that the illegal arrest and detention of ICC staff was, at least in part, the fault of the Court. The danger is that this will set a precedent and encourage states to abuse the rights of ICC staff in the future. As Geoff Taylor has stated: if the ICC 'can't protect their own people when they go into these dangerous places, how will it work? Unless they can protect their staff, these courts can't function' (see Kyriacou 2012). Second, the OTP's leniency towards Libya and its currying favour with the NTC is something that must be more critically addressed as it has diminished the Court's ability to appear impartial and independent. Third, the bitter divisions that have emerged within the Court need to be addressed. In order, ultimately, to be a successful, independent and impartial Court, the ICC must have a well-functioning OTP *and* OPCD. Together, these developments and issues will have long-term implications on the capacity of the ICC to contribute to the pursuit of transitional justice in post-conflict settings.

Conclusion

Post-Gaddafi Libya has been a battleground for legitimacy and effect. The ICC has striven to demonstrate that it is a viable international institution which can positively affect the pursuit of post-conflict justice. Libya has sought to demonstrate that it is a functioning sovereign state able and willing to execute justice. In the end, however, both the Court and the Libyan state may be left disappointed.

This chapter has sought to provide a critical overview of events pertaining to the ICC's role and impact in post-Gaddafi Libya. In doing so, a precarious narrative emerges, one where Libya is viewed as a lawless country, uninterested in justice, versus a Court trying to maintain relevance and desperately seeking to have a positive effect on post-accountability justice in Libya. Critically, this narrative is an extension not simply of ongoing events, but deep-seated mistrust, prevalent animosity and poor lines of communication between Libya and the ICC. None of this was inevitable and, in numerous instances, aggravations of this tenuous relationship could have been avoided. Despite this, much can be, and remains to be, learned from the ICC's experience in Libya. The Court's intervention and its impact on the pursuit of post-conflict justice and accountability pose many important questions for the Court's role in fragile post-conflict contexts and for the field of transitional justice more broadly. How these questions are answered is likely to have profound effects on the future functioning of the ICC.

Notes

2 Shorter versions of this article can be found at Kersten 2012a and 2012b
3 Henceforth referred to as Saif, although he is not to be mistaken with his brother, Saif al-Arab Gaddafi.
4 This phrase was authored by David Bosco in his 2012 article 'The Senussi Sweepstakes: Who gets Libya's former intelligence chief?'.
5 It should be noted that, in response to Libya's admissibility challenge, the OTP has expressed some concern about the fact that Saif is not in the custody of Libya. See ICC 2012e.
6 Libya has since appealed the Pre-Trial Chamber's decision.
7 The possibility of holding *in situ* ICC trials was explored for both the Democratic Republic of Congo and Kenyan cases.

8 In referring the situation in Libya to the ICC in Resolution 1970, the UN Security Council restricted the Court's temporal jurisdiction to 15 February 2011.
9 At the time of writing there is no indication that an investigation has been conducted.
10 See Ch 11.

Bibliography

ABC (2012) 'Libya set to free Melinda Taylor if ICC apologises: Carr', available online at www.abc.net.au/am/content/2012/s3528077.htm.

Akande, D. (2012) 'The Immunity of the ICC Lawyers and Staff Detained in Libya, EJIL: Talk!', available online at www.ejiltalk.org/the-immunity-of-the-icc-lawyers-and-staff-detained-in-libya/.

Al Arabiya (2012a) 'Aussie lawyer free if she reveals Libyan outlaw: report', available online at http://english.alarabiya.net/articles/2012/06/12/220148.html.

Al Arabiya (2012b) 'NATO chief urges ICC team release in Libya', available online at http://english.alarabiya.net/articles/2012/06/14/220592.html.

Al Jazeera (2011) 'Gaddafi's son in civil war warning', available online at www.aljazeera.com/news/africa/2011/02/201122023272596625l.html.

Al Jazeera (2012) 'Libya rules out ICC trial for Saif al-Islam', available online at www.aljazeera.com/news/africa/2012/04/2012499216767703.html.

Al Shalchi, H. (2012) 'Libya snubs ICC, unveils courtroom ahead of Gaddafi son trial', Reuters, available online at http://af.reuters.com/article/topNews/idAFJOE83908N20120410.

Amnesty International (2011) 'Saif Gaddafi must be transferred safely to ICC', available online at www.amnesty.org/en/news/saif-gaddafi-must-be-transferred-safely-icc-2011-10-28.

Amnesty International (2012) 'Amnesty International Condemns Libyan Law Restricting Freedom of Speech as "Eerie Reminder" of Gaddafi Era', available online at www.amnestyusa.org/news/news-item/amnesty-international-condemns-libyan-law-restricting-freedom-of-speech-as-eerie-reminder-of-gaddafi.

Barber, B. (2011) 'The fate of Saif Gaddafi', *Guardian*, available online at www.guardian.co.uk/commentisfree/2011/dec/04/saif-gaddafi-no-fraud.

Barfi, B. and Pack, J. (2012) 'Libya wants ICC hamstrung via Aussie's capture', *The Australian*, available online at www.theaustralian.com.au/news/world/libya-wants-icc-hamstrung-via-aussies-capture/story-e6frg6ux-1226398005984.

BBC (2011) 'Libya: Gaddafi son Saif al-Islam in contact with ICC', available online at www.bbc.co.uk/news/world-africa-15496608.

BBC (2012a) '"No Libyan response" on Gaddafi son as deadline nears', available online at www.bbc.co.uk/news/world-africa-16479494.

BBC (2012b) 'Unreliable Evidence – Transitional Justice', Radio 4, available online at www.bbc.co.uk/programmes/b01gh8n2.

Bosco, D. (2011) 'Can Libya try the Qaddafis?', *Foreign Policy*, available online at http://bosco.foreignpolicy.com/posts/2011/08/22/can_libya_try_the_gaddafis.

Bosco, D. (2012) 'The Senussi Sweepstakes: Who gets Libya's former intelligence chief?', *Foreign Policy*, 17 March, available online at http://bosco.foreignpolicy.com/posts/2012/03/17/libyan_intelligence_chief_nabbed_in_mauritania.

Callinan, R. (2012) 'Lawyers warned of risks in Libya', *The Sydney Morning Herald*, available online at www.smh.com.au/world/lawyers-warned-of-risks-in-libya-20120614-20d63.html.

Chatham House (2011) 'Milestones for International Criminal Justice', Chatham House, 22 September.

Chatham House (2012a) 'Libya: Establishing the Rule of Law', Chatham House – MENA Programme: Libya Working Group Meeting Summary.

Chatham House (2012b) 'Libya: Re-establishing the State', Chatham House (transcript), available online at www.chathamhouse.org/sites/default/files/public/Meetings/Meeting%20Transcripts/250512elkeibQ&A.pdf.

Chatham House (2012c) 'Libya's Recovery: Prospects and Perils', Chatham House – MENA Programme: Libya Working Group Meeting Summary.

Chulov, M. (2011) 'Libya insists Saif al-Islam Gaddafi should be tried at home', *Guardian*, available online at www.guardian.co.uk/world/2011/oct/29/libya-saif-gaddafi-justice.

CNN (2012) 'Libya appeals ICC order to hand over Saif Gadhafi', available online at http://articles.cnn.com/2012-04-10/africa/world_africa_libya-saif-gadhafi-appeal_1_libyan-people-moammar-gadhafi-libyan-government?_s=PM:AFRICA.

Cronin-Furman, K. and Taub, A. (2012) 'Is the International Criminal Court Facing Its "Black Hawk Down" Moment?', *The Atlantic*, available online at www.theatlantic.com/international/archive/2012/06/is-the-international-criminal-court-facing-its-black-hawk-down-moment/258528/.

Flitton, D. and Lester, T. (2012) 'Amnesty cautions against "apology" to Libya', *National Times*, available online at www.theage.com.au/opinion/political-news/amnesty-cautions-against-apology-to-libya-20120619-20m5v.html.

Goldstone, R. (2012) 'ICC's Libyan crisis shows Saif Gaddafi should be tried in The Hague', *Guardian*, available online at www.guardian.co.uk/law/2012/jun/22/icc-libya-crisis-saif-gaddafi-hague.

Grant, G. (2012) 'Government struck financial deal with Mauritania over Senussi handover', *Libya Herald*, available online at www.libyaherald.com/2012/09/05/govt-struck-financial-deal-with-mauritania-over-senussi-handover/.

Gumuchian, M.-L. (2011) 'EXCLUSIVE – The capture of Gaddafi's son', *Reuters*, available online at http://af.reuters.com/article/energyOilNews/idAFL5E7MK01720111120?sp=true.

Gumuchian, M.-L. (2012) 'UPDATE 2 – ICC team visit detained colleagues in Libya', *Reuters*, available online at http://af.reuters.com/article/libyaNews/idAFL5E8HCI1C20120612?sp=true.

Gumuchian, M.-L. and Shuaib, A. (2012) 'Libya says it wants ICC's cooperation over detained staff', *Reuters*, at www.reuters.com/article/2012/06/16/us-libya-icc-idUSBRE85F0IW20120616.

Harding, L. and Black, I. (2012) 'Mauritania extradites Gaddafi spy chief Senussi to Libya', *Guardian*, available online at www.guardian.co.uk/world/2012/sep/05/mauritania-gaddafi-senussi-libya.

Heller, K.J. (2012a) 'Foreign Minister Bob Carr Goes Shopping in the Department of Bad Ideas', *Opinio Juris*, 20 June, available online at http://opiniojuris.org/2012/06/20/foreign-minister-bob-barr-goes-shopping-in-the-department-of-bad-ideas/.

Heller, K.J. (2012b) 'Libya Challenges the Admissibility of the Cases Against Gaddafi and

Al-Senussi', *Opinio Juris*, 2 May, available online at http://opiniojuris.org/2012/05/02/libya-challenges-the-admissibility-of-the-cases-against-gaddafi-and-al-senussi/.

Heller, K.J. (2012c) 'Libya's Dorda Prosecution – and My Modified Due Process Thesis', *Opinio Juris*, 18 September, available online at http://opiniojuris.org/2012/09/17/libyas-prosecution-of-buzeid-dorda-and-my-modified-due-process-thesis/.

Heller, K.J. (2012d) 'Why I Think the Detained ICC Personnel Are Entitled to Diplomatic Immunity', *Opinio Juris*, 15 June, available online at http://opiniojuris.org/2012/06/15/why-are-the-detained-icc-personnel-entitled-to-diplomatic-immunity/.

Hilsum, L. (2012a) 'Abdullah al-Senussi, Gaddafi's "black box"', *FT Magazine*, available online at www.ft.com/cms/s/2/a55d465e-aab1-11e1-9331-00144feabdc0.html#axzz20nZOCQNj.

Hilsum, L. (2012b) *Sandstorm – Libya in the Time of Revolution* (Faber and Faber).

Hirsch, A. (2012) 'Mauritania likely to extradite Libyan spy chief to France', *Guardian*, available online at www.guardian.co.uk/world/2012/mar/20/mauritania-likely-extradite-libyan-france.

HRC *Report of the International Commission of Inquiry on Libya*, A/HRC/19/68, 2 March 2012.

HRW (2012) 'Libya: Amend New Special Procedures Law', available online at www.hrw.org/news/2012/05/11/libya-amend-new-special-procedures-law.

ICC (2011a) *Warrant of Arrest for Saif Al-Islam Gaddafi*, ICC-01/11-14 (27 June).

ICC (2011b) *Prosecutor's Submissions on the Prosecutor's recent trip to Libya*, ICC-01/11-01/11 (25 November).

ICC (2011c) *OPCD Request for Authorisation to Present Observations in Proceedings concerning Mr Saif Gaddafi*, ICC-01/11-01/11 (28 November).

ICC (2012a) *Public Redacted Version Urgent Report Concerning the Visit to Libya*, ICC-01/11-01/11-69 (2 March).

ICC (2012b) *Application on behalf of the Government of Libya pursuant to Article 19 of the ICC Statute*, ICC-01/11-01/11 (1 May).

ICC (2012c) *Request to Disqualify the Prosecutor from Participating in the Case Against Mr. Saif Al Islam Gaddafi*, ICC-01/11-01/11 (3 May).

ICC (2012d) *Press Conference by Prosecutor of International Criminal Court on Libyan Situation* (16 May), at www.un.org/News/briefings/docs/2012/120516_ICC.doc.htm.

ICC (2012e) *Prosecution response to Application on behalf of the Government of Libya pursuant to Article 19 of the ICC Statute*, ICC-01/11-01/11 (5 June).

ICC (2012f) *Lawyers for Justice in Libya and Redress Trust's Observations Pursuant to Rule 103 of the Rules of Procedure and Evidence*, ICC-01/11-01/11 (8 June).

ICC (2012g) *Four ICC staff members detained in Libya; Immediate release requested*, ICC-CPI-20120609-PR805 (9 June), available online at www.icc-cpi.int/NR/exeres/82F7D00E-500E-46FE-BE04-906B269DCDB2.htm.

ICC (2012h) *Decision on the Request for Disqualification of the Prosecutor*, ICC-01/11-01/11 OA 3 (12 June).

ICC (2012i) *Statement on the detention of four ICC staff members*, ICC-CPI-20120622-PR815 (22 June).

ICC (2012j) *Libyan Government Requests for Status Conference and Extension of Time to file a Reply to the Response to its Article 19 Admissibility Challenge*, ICC-01/11-01/11 (30 July).

ICC (2012k) *Situations and Cases: Libya*, available online at www.icc-cpi.int/menus/icc/situations%20and%20cases/situations/icc0111/situation%20index?lan=en-GB.

ICC (2012l) *Public Redacted Version of the Corrigendum to the 'Defence Response to the "Application on behalf of the Government of Libya pursuant to Article 19 of the ICC Statute"'*, ICC-01/11-01/11 (31 July).

Jillions, A. (2011) 'Trying the Tripoli Three: Justice at Home or Away?', *Justice in Conflict*, available online at http://justiceinconflict.org/2011/08/24/trying-the-tripoli-three-justice-at-home-or-away/.

Kaye, D. (2011) 'What to Do With Qaddafi', *New York Times*, 31 August, available online at www.nytimes.com/2011/09/01/opinion/what-to-do-with-qaddafi.html?_r=2.

Kersten, M. (2011a) 'Having Cake and Eating it Too: An ICC Trial in Libya?', *Justice in Conflict*, available online at http://justiceinconflict.org/2011/08/26/having-cake-and-eating-it-too-an-icc-trial-in-libya/.

Kersten, M. (2012a) 'Libya vs. The ICC: Stalemate over Saif and Senussi', *Think Africa Press*, available online at http://thinkafricapress.com/libya/icc-game-no-winners-rome-statute-saif-gaddafi-senussi-ntc-zintan.

Kersten, M. (2012b) 'No winners in ICC-Libya standoff', *Foreign Policy – Middle East Channel*, available online at http://mideast.foreignpolicy.com/posts/2012/10/08/no_winners_in_icc_libya_standoff.

Kersten, M. (forthcoming) 'Between Justice and Politics: The International Criminal Court's Intervention in Libya', in C. Stahn, C. De Vos and S. Kendall (eds), *International criminal justice and 'local ownership': Assessing the impact of justice interventions* (Cambridge University Press).

Kyriacou, K. (2012) 'Husband of Brisbane lawyer Melinda Taylor says arrest in Libya puts all ICC workers at risk', *Herald Sun*, available online at www.heraldsun.com.au/news/victoria/husband-says-all-icc-workers-at-risk/story-e6frf7lf-1226396128427.

Lawyers for Justice Libya (2012a) 'LFJL Applauds the Supreme Court of Libya's Decision on Law 37', available online at www.libyanjustice.org/news/news/post/28-lfjl-applauds-the-supreme-court-of-libya%E2%80%99s-decision-on-law-37.

Lawyers for Justice Libya (2012b) 'LFJL strongly condemns new laws breaching human rights and undermining the rule of law', available online at www.libyanjustice.org/news/news/post/23-lfjl-strongly-condemns-new-laws-breaching-human-rights-and-undermining-the-rule-of-law.

Lynch, C. (2011) 'Rice says Libyan people can decide whether to try Qaddafi; ICC says not so fast', *Foreign Policy*, available online at http://turtlebay.foreignpolicy.com/posts/2011/08/23/rice_says_libyan_people_can_decide_whether_to_try_qaddafi_icc_says_not_so_fast.

Mark, M. (2012) 'Abdullah al-Senussi central figure in three-way custody battle', *Guardian*, available online at www.guardian.co.uk/world/2012/may/25/abdullah-al-senussi-custody-battle.

McGreal, C. (2012) 'US backs Libya in dispute over trial location for Saif al-Islam Gaddafi', *Guardian*, available online at www.guardian.co.uk/world/2012/jun/06/us-libya-saif-al-islam-gaddafi-trial.

Murphy, F. (2011) 'Libya vows it, not ICC, will try Saif, Senussi', *Reuters*, available online at www.reuters.com/article/2011/11/21/us-libya-icc-idUSTRE7AK08K2011112.

Olsen, T.D., Payne, L.A. and Reiter, A.G. (2010) *Transitional Justice in Balance – Comparing Processes, Weighing Efficacy* (United States Institute of Peace).

Papenfuss, T. (2012) 'Interview with Luis Moreno-Ocampo, Chief Prosecutor of the International Criminal Court, Global Observatory', available online at www.theglobal

observatory.org/interviews/197-interview-with-luis-moreno-ocampo-chief-prosecutor-of-the-international-criminal-court.html.

Pargeter, A. (2012) *Libya – The Rise and Fall of Qaddafi* (Yale University Press).

Parliamentarians for Global Action (2011) 'Parliamentarians for Global Action (PGA) calls for the prompt surrender of Saif Al Islam Gaddafi and Abdallah Al Senussi to the International Criminal Court (ICC)', available online at www.pgaction.org/uploaded-files/PGA%20PR%20ICC%20Libya%20arrest%20nov%202011%20ENG.pdf.

Prieur, L. and Al Shachi, H. (2012) 'Mauritania agrees to Senussi extradition, Libya says', *Reuters*, available online at www.reuters.com/article/2012/03/20/us-libya-senussi-idUSBRE82J0X120120320.

RIA Novosti (2012) 'Lavrov Pushes for UN Feedback on ICC staff detentions in Libya', available online at http://en.ria.ru/world/20120613/174009325.html.

Robertson, G. (2011a) 'Ending Impunity: the struggle for global justice', remarks given at The School of Oriental and African Studies, London, 21 November.

Robertson, G. (2011b) 'Why Libya Must Send Saif Gaddafi to The Hague', *The Daily Beast*, available online at www.thedailybeast.com/articles/2011/11/21/why-libya-must-send-saif-gaddafi-to-the-hague.html.

Security Council (2012a) 'International Criminal Court Chief Tells Security Council Libya Wants Domestic Courts to Handle Proceedings against Son of Former Libyan Leader Gaddafi', SC/10651, 16 May, available online at www.un.org/News/Press/docs/2012/sc10651.doc.htm.

Security Council (2012b) 'Security Council Press Statement on International Criminal Court Staff Detained in Libya', SC/10674 (15 June).

Sherlock, R. (2011) 'Libya: "the executioners" Abdullah al-Senussi captured', *Telegraph*, available online at www.telegraph.co.uk/news/worldnews/africaandindianocean/libya/8902861/Libya-the-executioner-Abdullah-al-Senussi-captured.html.

Shuaib, A. and Al Shalchi, H. (2012) 'ICC lawyer meeting Gaddafi son detained in Libya', *Reuters*, available online at www.reuters.com/article/2012/06/09/us-libya-icc-idUSBRE8580FH20120609.

Simons, Marlise (2012) 'Libya Frees Four From International Court's Team', *The New York Times*, available online at www.nytimes.com/2012/07/03/world/africa/libya-frees-four-from-international-criminal-court.html?_r=0.

Simpson, G. (2007) *Law, War and Crime – War Crimes Trials and the Reinvention of International Law* (Polity Press).

Smith, D. (2011) 'Gaddafi's son claims Nato wants deal with Libya', *Guardian*, available online at www.guardian.co.uk/world/2011/jul/01/gaddafi-son-nato-libya-deal.

Stahn, C. (2012) 'Libya, the International Criminal Court and Complementarity – A Test for "Shared Responsibility"', 10(2) *Journal of International Criminal Justice* 325.

Stephen, C. (2012a) 'Saif Gaddafi sets Libya's new rulers a test of commitment to human rights', *Guardian*, available online at www.guardian.co.uk/world/2012/jan/07/saif-gaddafi-libya-human-rights.

Stephen, C. (2012b) 'The secrets of Saif Gaddafi's jail: chef, satellite TV and a basketball court for just one', *Guardian*, available online at www.guardian.co.uk/world/2012/mar/18/said-gaddafi-libya-international-criminal-court.

Sydow, C. (2012) 'Libyens Ex-Geheimdienstchef Sanussi – Der Mann, der zu viel weiß', 7 September, available online at www.spiegel.de/politik/ausland/abdullah-al-sanussi-koennte-ueber-libyens-kooperation-mit-cia-berichten-a-854366.html.

Telegraph (2012) 'Australian lawyer held in Libya "could be freed with apology"', available online at www.telegraph.co.uk/news/worldnews/africaandindianocean/libya/9340696/Australian-lawyer-held-in-Libya-could-be-freed-with-apology.html.

Waters, T.W. (2011) 'Let Tripoli Try Saif al-Islam – Why the Qaddafi Trial is the Wrong Case for the ICC', *Foreign Affairs*, available online at www.foreignaffairs.com/articles/136726/timothy-william-waters/let-tripoli-try-saif-al-islam.

25

Transitional Justice as Global Project: critical reflections

ROSEMARY NAGY

ABSTRACT *This article critically reflects on the ways in which the global project of transitional justice is channelled or streamlined in its scope of application. Using the categories of* when, *to* whom *and for* what *transitional justice applies, it argues that transitional justice is typically constructed to focus on specific sets of actors for specific sets of crimes. This results in a fairly narrow interpretation of violence within a somewhat artificial time frame and to the exclusion of external actors. The article engages themes of gender, power and structural violence to caution against the narrowing and depoliticisation of transitional justice.*

Transitional justice as a field and practice has grown tremendously over the past 15 years or so to include: the institution of international criminal tribunals, hybrid courts and the International Criminal Court (ICC); the development of a 'right to truth' and 'right to reparation' under international law; the transnational proliferation of truth and reconciliation commissions (TRCs); the expansion of transitional justice scholarship such that it now has a dedicated journal, research centres and academic programmes; and the birth of international and regional transitional justice NGOs. In other words, transitional justice has become a well established fixture on the global terrain of human rights. It entails an insistence against unwilling governments that it is necessary to respond to egregious violence and atrocity. The international community provides fragile new governments with important financial, institutional and normative support for reckoning with the past, attending to the needs of victims, and setting the foundations for democracy, human rights and the rule of law.

Yet there also appear worrisome tendencies of the international community to impose 'one-size-fits-all', technocratic and decontextualised solutions. To what extent does transitional justice appear from on high as 'saviour' to the 'savagery'[1] of ethnic, especially African 'tribal', conflict? Steeped in Western liberalism, and often located outside the area where conflict occurred, transitional justice may be alien and distant to those who actually have to live together after atrocity. It is accused of producing subjects and truths that are blind to gender and social injustice. And, in a post-9/11 world, transitional justice may increasingly be shaped by 'the appropriation of the language of "transition" and "democratization" in furtherance of an apparently global project [that has] few effective international legal constraints'.[2]

All this suggests a timely need to reflect critically upon transitional justice as a global project. By 'global project', I refer to the fact that transitional justice has emerged as a body of customary international law and normative standards. I call it a 'global' project rather than an 'international' one in order to capture the three-dimensional landscape of transitional justice (local, national, global) and its location within broader processes of globalisation. It is a 'project' by virtue of the fairly settled consensus—a consensus that has largely moved past the initial debates of 'peace versus justice' and 'truth versus justice'—that there can be no lasting peace without some kind of accounting and that truth and justice are complementary approaches to dealing with the past. The question today is not *whether* something should be done after atrocity but *how* it should be done. And a professional body of international donors, practitioners and researchers assists or directs in figuring this out and implementing it.

In the first section of this article I critically introduce the way the scope of transitional justice is typically defined and implemented. In the remaining sections I employ the categories of *when*, to *whom* and for *what* transitional justice applies in order to challenge troubling features of its standardisation. I do not wish to deny that national governments and local actors are active agents in their own transitional processes. Rather, my concern is to call attention to the ways in which their horizon of options may be channelled or streamlined. Engaging themes of gender, power and structural violence, the article offers a cautionary investigation of the worrying ways in which the scope of transitional justice can be depoliticised and narrowed. The reflections undertaken here are intended to be suggestive in nature and to raise questions for further research. For the sake of convenience, I presume a fairly singular (Westernised) international community, acknowledging here its rather nebulous and frequently divided nature.

Defining the scope of transitional justice

It is not often remarked that figuring out how to implement transitional justice is necessarily a task of first determining the problem. Transitional justice seeks to redress wrongdoing but, inevitably, in the face of resource, time and political constraints, this is a selective process. Transitional justice thus involves a delimiting narration of violence and remedy. This raises, as Bell and O'Rourke put it, 'fundamental questions about what exactly transitional justice is transiting "from" and "to"'.[3] Although there is no single definition of transitional justice, I suggest that predominant views construct human rights violations fairly narrowly to the exclusion of structural and gender-based violence. There is a privileging of legal responses which are at times detrimentally abstracted from lived realities. Little attention, if any, is paid to the role that established, Western democracies have in violence. Together, these tendencies profoundly affect perceptions of the nature of violence, victimhood and perpetration, and they skew the direction of truth, justice and reconciliation. I develop these claims below by first comparing several representative definitions of transitional justice.

In one of the narrower definitions, Teitel explains transitional justice as 'the view of justice associated with periods of political change, as reflected in the phenomenology of primarily legal responses that deal with the wrong-doing of repressive predecessor regimes'.[4] Although Teitel rightly provides a normative challenge to Schumpeterian notions of a successful transition (marked by fair elections), she focuses almost exclusively on (re)establishing the rule of law through legal mechanisms—prosecutions, historical inquiry, administrative justice, reparation, and constitutional justice.[5] Her argument for law's 'independent potential' to shape political change may be an impressive work of legal theory, but gender, customary law, culture, and social justice are virtually absent as categories of analysis. Teitel's cases are largely confined to post-authoritarian or post-communist regimes, rather than to war-torn societies. Her explicit concern with bringing 'illiberal' regimes into the fold of liberal democracy, as well as her argument that transitional justice applies in 'extraordinary' periods between regimes, treats established liberal democracies as benevolent models.

Roht-Arriaza, in her introduction to *Transitional Justice in the Twenty-First Century*, widens the context of transitional justice by defining it as 'that set of practices, mechanisms and concerns that arise following a period of conflict, civil strife or repression, and that are aimed directly at confronting and dealing with past violations of human rights and humanitarian law'.[6] Although she dismisses Teitel's 'problematic' definition for 'overvaluing' law and underestimating periods of flux, Roht-Arriaza nonetheless takes a 'narrower' view. The edited collection focuses on truth commissions, criminal prosecution, vetting and reparation; it largely leaves aside things such as memorialisation, police and court reform, or tackling distributional inequities. Roht-Arriaza acknowledges that 'a narrow view can be criticized for ignoring root causes and privileging civil and political rights over economic, social and cultural rights, and by doing so marginalizing the needs of women and the poor'. But she nonetheless argues that 'broadening the scope of what we mean by transitional justice to encompass the building of a just as well as peaceful society may make the effort so broad as to become meaningless'.[7]

Mani provides one of the broadest understandings and critiques of what she terms 'restoring justice within the parameters of peacebuilding'.[8] Her prime concern is low-income, war-torn societies, and she argues, contrary to Roht-Arriaza's position above, that building peace and building a just society are inseparable processes. Drawing on Galtung's twin objectives of negative peace (cessation of conflict) and positive peace (removing structural and cultural violence), Mani is clear that a holistic approach is necessary. She argues for a three-fold view of 'reparative' justice: restoring the rule of law through reforms to prisons, police and judiciary; rectifying human rights violations through trials, truth commissions, reparation and traditional mechanisms; and redressing the inequalities and distributive injustices that underlie war. Mani is particularly attuned to the importance of drawing on local knowledge and culture for sustainable peace. She also analyses the way that international financial institutions have exacerbated the socio-economic inequalities that underlie conflict. Yet Mani could go further in examining the involvement of Western states in conflict,[9] and gender is surprisingly and inexplicably absent from an otherwise astute and ambitious analysis.

As should become clear, my sympathies lie with an approach that understands violence and its transitional response fairly broadly. However, it is important to note that the prevailing view of transitional justice's scope is largely confined within a fairly specific set of mechanisms. Even Mani explicitly positions her approach as a 'broader conceptual and contextual framework' that does not 'attempt to replace or "overthrow" transitional justice' but would 'include all existing methods of transitional justice'.[10]

According to the UN Secretary General's 2004 *Report on the Rule of Law and Transitional Justice in Conflict and Post-conflict Societies*, the full range of methods 'may include both judicial and non-judicial mechanisms, with differing levels of international involvement (or none at all) and individual prosecutions, reparations, truth-seeking, institutional reform, vetting and dismissals, or a combination thereof'.[11] The International Centre for Transitional Justice (ICTJ), an NGO which is involved in transitional justice initiatives in over 30 countries, defines the major approaches as: prosecution, truth-telling, reparation, institutional reform, promoting reconciliation and social reconstruction, memorialisation and taking into account gendered patterns of abuse.[12]

For reasons of space my analysis will focus on the predominant institutions—trials and truth commissions. International criminal justice operates far more 'from above' than do truth commissions, although the move towards hybrid courts and the provision that the ICC be of 'last resort' have sought to reverse this trend. While truth commissions are more localised in nature, they nonetheless tend to operate with extensive donor and international NGO support or, as in El Salvador, Guatemala, East Timor and Sierra Leone, with UN involvement.

My main concern is how the implementation of trials and truth commissions tends to structure conceptions of violence and justice. Their implementation ought to be assessed within the context of an overarching assumption 'that a focus on legal processes is adequate to resolve individual and social harm', as Fletcher and Weinstein put it.[13] Furthermore, the privileging of legalistic approaches occurs within an international climate where, as Mani notes, 'the prevalent liberal–democratic ideal . . . tends to favour freedom and liberty over equality'.[14] This means there has been a tendency to underrate the gendered and socioeconomic ramifications of violent conflict, which may include HIV/AIDS, widowhood and poverty. Instead, transitional justice has been heavily influenced by the 'international legalist paradigm', which focuses on generating elite and mass compliance with international humanitarian norms.[15] Notably the international legalist paradigm has extended beyond the push for prosecution. This can be seen in the emergence of the rights to truth and reparation under customary international law, in the transnational proliferation of truth commissions, which are quasi-judicial bodies mandated to investigate gross violations of human rights, and in the emphasis within the international donor community on 'doing justice' over other forms of development.[16]

Oomen convincingly argues that one of the reasons for the prominence of the legalist paradigm is that law is perceived as a safe, neutral, universal way to engage with other countries.[17] But these are false and problematic assumptions about the law that transitional justice must guard against. The problem is not with law and human rights *per se* but with the depoliticised way in which 'justice' can operate. A technocratic focus on 'the law' abstracts from lived realities. For instance, gendered advances in international criminal law still mean that 'any woman' could serve as a witness in landmark cases because individuals are subsumed under 'larger principles which their testimony helps establish'.[18] Compiling databases for 'trend analysis' of gross human rights violations, as many truth commissions do, or convicting top perpetrators will not necessarily contribute to community-based truth or reconciliation.[19] Furthermore, challenges to Westernised international criminal justice have emerged with Rwanda's neo-traditional *gacaca* courts and a call in Northern Uganda to use *mato oput* and other traditional cleansing ceremonies rather than the ICC. And, as a final example, a narrow fixation on judicial mechanisms in Iraq shields analysts from asking normative questions about the illegitimacy or justifiability of the occupation or about whether 'justice' is even possible in such a context.[20]

In the following analysis I point to general trends and draw on several prominent country examples to illustrate the ways in which the scope of transitional justice is channelled. These cases include the 'standard-setting'[21] South African Truth and Reconciliation Commission (1996–2003), which looms large on the transitional justice landscape as a model or lesson. Sierra Leone and East Timor each represent significant developments in global practice because they pair trials with truth commissions. Moreover, the Special Court for Sierra Leone (established in 2002 and still in operation) and the Special Panel for Serious Crimes in East Timor (1999–2005) are hybrid courts. Sierra Leone's Truth and Reconciliation Commission (2000–05) and East Timor's Commission for Reception, Truth and Reconciliation (2001–05) both demonstrate tentative advances in the ability of truth commissions to provide extensive accounts of gender-based violence, social injustice and external influence. Finally, Iraq and Afghanistan present troubling situations of seeking truth, justice and reconciliation in the midst of occupation and conflict.

I turn now to the categories of *when*, to *whom* and for *what* transitional justice applies. I argue that these categories function to hone transitional justice into a particular kind of solution to address particular kinds of problems. The focus on specific sets of actors for specific sets of crimes channels transitional justice towards a fairly narrow interpretation of violence within a somewhat artificial time frame and to the exclusion of external actors.

When transitional justice applies

The *when* of transitional justice is tied to the very conception of transition. Whether transiting from authoritarianism to democracy or from war to peace (to democracy), transitional justice has typically appeared salient only after massive direct violence has been brought to a halt. In part, this appearance has to do with the emphasis within the literature on prosecution, truth-telling, reparation, reconciliation and reform, and less so on peace accords, transitional administration, or disarmament, demobilisation and reintegration. Transitional justice also implies a fixed interregnum period with a distinct end; it bridges a violent or repressive past and a peaceful, democratic future. Notions of 'breaking with the past' and 'never again', which align with the dominant transitional mechanisms, mould a definitive sense of 'now' and 'then'.

This can problematically obscure continuities of violence and exclusion. For example, the efforts of the South African TRC to promote the 'new' South Africa met with considerable challenge and resistance in the face of ongoing police violations of human rights, political violence, racialised socioeconomic inequalities, *de facto* geographic apartheid, and general racism and xenophobia.[22] More generally, to construct transition as a break with past violence also neglects the domestic violence that many women face in a militarised society and after male combatants return home. There is some evidence to suggest that violence against women actually increases in the 'post-conflict' period.[23] This can occur as a result of post-traumatic stress, of the need of men to reassert control in their homes, which had been headed by women during the war, or because of the sense of dislocation, powerlessness and unemployment that combatants may face upon return.[24]

In Iraq and Afghanistan the transition is constructed as being 'from' a repressive police state under Saddam Hussein or 'from' cycles of war and repression culminating in the Taliban regime.[25] This neatly avoids the current matter of foreign military intervention and implies that the transitional problem has to do with 'then' and not the 'now' of occupation, insurgency, and the war on terror. (And, as I discuss below, it implies that the problem has to with 'them', not 'us'). Although prosecution, vetting, reparation and truth-telling are taking or will take place in the midst of violence and insecurity, the concern of these transitional mechanisms is the history before 2001 in Afghanistan and before 2003 in Iraq. The 'to' of transitional justice is thus insulated from the current reasons for instability.

Of course, with the ICC's indictments in Uganda, the DRC and Darfur, we do see prosecution being purposefully used to address current violence. Yet it appears that the ICC is facing situations where actual prosecution cannot not take place because of difficulties of arrest and, even if trials begin, they may be to little or even detrimental political effect. For instance, some Acholi leaders in northern Uganda have opposed the ICC's actions because they fear it will jeopardise peace talks[26] (and, as noted earlier, because it contravenes traditional values). This raises questions about what exactly makes a mechanism or process 'transitional' in the first place. However, even if the 'to' of the ICC's contribution to transitional justice is uncertain, the 'from' is not: it is a transition from the context of 'conflict and war'.

The concern with this consistent emphasis on applying transitional justice only *when* there is massive repression, conflict or war is, as Orford argues, that 'the literature gives the sense that large-scale human rights violations are exceptional' and that 'the focus is not on genocide or human rights violations in liberal democratic states'.[27] She 'unsettles' this assumption by examining the 'the everydayness and bureaucratization of genocide and of massive human rights violations' through a reading of Australia's (1997) *Bringing Them Home* report on the separation of Aboriginal and Torres Strait Islander children from their families.[28] Similar examples can be found in Canada and the USA: the Royal Commission on Aboriginal Peoples (1996); the planned Residential Schools Truth and Reconciliation Commission; and the Greensboro (North Carolina) Truth Commission. However, while it is important to acknowledge and address systemic human rights abuse, it is also rather awkward to affix the label 'transitional' to justice long denied in liberal democracies. To say that the transition to democracy is as yet incomplete or that we are transitioning to a reconciled, more just society, may overly broaden notions of democratisation or transition.

To *whom* transitional justice applies

The more pressing concern, to follow on from the above, has less to do with *when* justice is transitional than with *to whom* transitional justice applies. Because transitional justice almost always applies to non-Western, developing countries, it is vulnerable to the general challenge that critics raise against the supposed universalism of human rights. The general thrust of this challenge is that the West arrogates the universal to itself and then brings all others into its fold of humanity.[29] The case of Iraq is most obviously liable to this charge. As noted above, the artificial time frame of transitional justice applies only to Saddam's Iraq. This glosses over the illegality of the US-led invasion, the damage caused by the corrupt UN oil-for-food programme, ongoing insurgency, and human rights abuses committed by US soldiers at Abu Ghraib and elsewhere. Furthermore, as Chandler writes, when Paul Bremer created the Iraqi Special Tribunal:

> Commentators everywhere insisted on the importance of a fair trial, on 'justice being seen to be done,' not so much for Saddam's benefit as for the political and educational benefit of the Iraqi people. Implicit in this discussion was the idea that the Iraqi people could not move on without a thorough accounting of the past; that without this process they were not ready for the freedom their Western liberators offered them. Here responsibility for chronic violence and instability of the Iraqi people was shifted away from the actions of the intervening powers and placed with the psychological immaturity of the Iraqi people.[30]

Prosecution and other transitional mechanisms are put in place to teach Iraqis, and not the USA and its allies, about the rule of law and human rights.

Neither paternalism nor asymmetry is confined to the Iraqi case. Charges of paternalism have been voiced, for example, regarding the transitional administrations run by the international Peace Implementation Council in Bosnia–Herzegovina and by the UN in East Timor. The different High Representatives to Bosnia have used their sweeping authority to impose legislation that was rejected by democratically elected parliamentarians, to ban political parties, and to dismiss elected officials.[31] In East Timor, Orford documents how postcolonial reconstruction treats the country as a 'blank slate in terms of existing knowledge and experience, marked by cronyism, incompetence and corruption. The people of East Timor are portrayed as lacking a state, ethics, skills and respect for human rights.'[32] Katzenstein notes that, in the building of the Special Panels for Serious Crimes, 'many East Timorese in the judiciary felt sidelined by the UN staff' because of a lack of consultation on institutional design. Mentoring programmes quickly disintegrated when UN personnel entirely took over the tasks at hand, and East Timorese became 'sick of internationals coming in and conducting "workshops"'.[33]

As for the asymmetrical features of globalised transitional justice, these go right back to the Nuremburg precedent of victor's justice. In more recent history, victor's justice has prevailed in the International Criminal Tribunal for Former Yugoslavia's (ICTY) refusal to investigate alleged violations of international humanitarian law committed by NATO during its bombing campaign in Kosovo and in the International Criminal Tribunal for Rwanda's (ICTR) halted investigation of the governing Rwandan Patriotic Front (RPF) for war crimes. Furthermore, geographic 'zones of impunity'[34] are being created thanks to the state-centric nature of international law. For instance, the ICC does not apply to non-state parties except in the instance of Security Council referral, which will inevitably be limited by veto politics. There is also the USA's active campaign against the ICC. Over 100 countries, some of which have poor human rights records and have shown little ability or interest in domestic criminal procedures, have been induced by the USA to sign bilateral agreements refusing extradition to the ICC.

Third country prosecution can overcome the jurisdictional limits of other institutions or domestic amnesties. But, as Wilke points out, the universality of 'justice without borders' is fairly particularistic: 'either some of the victims have the citizenship of the prosecuting state, or the perpetrators (and some of the victims) are physically present in the country'.[35] The result is highly uneven globally speaking: the likelihood of pursuing justice is largely confined to liberal democracies that have the resources and political interest to mount a case. Even when a case is mounted, the challenges of extradition and lining up different legal systems can result in a watering down of charges, as seen when the British House of Lords reduced Spain's draft charges against Pinochet from 30 to three.[36] (And, of course, Home Secretary Jack Straw let Pinochet go home.)

International criminal justice also appears frequently unable to respond to violent conflict that spills across borders. Currently, as Sriram and Ross explain, the ICC is mandated to investigate human rights violations in northern Uganda but not Lord's Resistance Army (LRA) activities in southern Sudan or support by the Sudanese government to the LRA during Sudan's North–South civil war. The ICC has no jurisdiction in Sudan except in Darfur and only there for Sudanese nationals.[37] As another example, former Liberian leader Charles Taylor is not facing trial for crimes he committed in Liberia, his own country, or neighbouring Côte d'Ivoire, because the Special Court for Sierra Leone does not have extraterritorial jurisdiction.[38]

The pursuit of transitional justice in East Timor is especially illustrative of zones of impunity. From 1974 to 1999 the people of East Timor suffered death and destruction under the illegal Indonesian occupation, with violence culminating during the 1999 plebiscite on autonomy. Under the subsequent United Nations Transitional Administration (UNTAET), the Serious Crimes Investigative Unit was created to investigate and prosecute crimes at the Special Panel for Serious Crimes (comprised of two international and one East Timorese judge). Although Indonesia and UNTAET signed a memorandum of understanding regarding the exchange of evidence, the Serious Crimes Unit was unable to gain access to Indonesian suspects, and thus those with the 'greatest responsibility' remained out of reach of the Dili-based court.[39] The UN did not set up a process to address those responsible in Indonesia, indicating that Indonesia is obligated to do so. Under severe pressure the Indonesian government has established an *ad hoc* court to deal with violations in East Timor, but so far it has acquitted all Indonesians, and some military officers implicated in atrocities have actually been promoted.[40]

The Indonesian president's treatment of East Timor's independence as national humiliation,[41] combined with the limited mandate of East Timor's hybrid court, have resulted in a 'near universal perception within Indonesia that the 1999 violence was the result of conflict between two opposing East Timorese factions, rather than a military-orchestrated terror campaign'.[42] But the problem is not simply Indonesia's intransigence. The problem also lies with the international community. Hybrid courts are touted as a means of doing 'justice on the cheap', and there was a widespread perception among the East Timorese that the international community did not care about their plight.[43] Indeed, the Special Panel was shut down in 2005 because of a lack of international political and donor support. (The UN Secretary-General has since recommended the resumption of the tribunal's investigative but not judicial functions.[44]) The UN Commission of Experts recommended in its 2005 report that an international tribunal be established under Chapter VII of the UN Charter if Indonesia's 'manifestly inadequate' *ad hoc* courts do not improve.[45] Yet, even if an international tribunal were created, which appears unlikely, it would not address the broader injustices of occupation and exploitation. It would say little about Australian, American, British and Japanese support of Indonesia's occupation or how Indonesian control and impoverishment of the East Timor coffee sector (a major reason for occupation) fitted into cold war politics and volatile price shifts after 1989.[46]

The East Timor situation thus points to a further concern that transitional justice operates in such a way that 'the international community is absent from the scene of violence and suffering until it intervenes as the heroic saviour'.[47] Foreign involvement in violence—through indifference, funding, training, cross-border raids, or conflict economies in arms, diamonds or oil—is largely absent from or negligible in official transitional justice records. This occurs most starkly with prosecution because trials create fairly individualised accounts of human rights crimes. Truth commissions are better equipped to paint the larger picture of violence. But, as Hayner reports, for the most part truth commissions do not investigate the role of outside actors in internal human rights violations.[48] In recent exceptions, the Sierra Leone truth commission addresses quite extensively the role of foreign actors in the conflict, including Liberia's Charles Taylor, Libya, the diamond industry, and the international community for abandoning Sierra Leone in its hour of need. And, to return to the East Timor case discussed above, the Commission for Reception, Truth and Reconciliation (CAVR) holds the international community accountable for providing military backing to the Indonesian government and holds Indonesia and other states liable for reparation.

To *what* transitional justice applies

Even if truth commissions do investigate the role of outside actors—and the majority do not—their primary focus are the direct perpetrators and direct victims of crimes against humanity and violations of international humanitarian law. The issue therefore is not only to *whom* transitional justice applies, but also to *what* it applies. By and large transitional justice pertains to genocide, torture, disappearance, massacre, sexual violence and other war crimes. In the privileging of legalistic approaches, transitional justice tends to focus on gross violations of civil and political rights (arbitrary or indefinite detention, severe assault, ill-treatment, etc) or on criminal acts (property destruction, abuse of children, etc). Consequently, structural violence and social injustice are peripheral in the 'from' and 'to' of transitional justice.

The social and political costs of this narrow framing are vividly apparent in the South African experience. Although the TRC clearly recognised apartheid as a crime against humanity, its mandate narrowly defined victims and perpetrators as those who had suffered egregious bodily harm. Apartheid thus featured as the context to crime rather than the crime itself.[49] The everyday violence of poverty and racism—and consequently the ordinary victims and beneficiaries of apartheid—were placed in the background of truth and reconciliation. Because the TRC report largely appeared as a depoliticised chronicle of wrongful acts, it did not sufficiently depict the ways that illegal acts of torture, killing and terror were intrinsic to legally sanctioned apartheid.[50] Admittedly, there were understandable logistical reasons for limiting the scope of inquiry, and the TRC did hold a series of hearings on the role of civil society. But, as I have argued elsewhere, the overall effect was to relieve beneficiaries of obligations pursuant to national reconciliation and to pass over the suffering of millions in the 'new' South Africa. This has had lasting effects on perceptions of justice and racial reconciliation in South Africa, including the ongoing debate and lawsuit over corporate reparations.[51]

In thinking of the costs elsewhere of a similarly narrow framing of *what* transitional justice addresses, I point to an important speech given by the UN High Commissioner for Human Rights, Louise Arbour. She argues that the failure thus far of transitional justice to pay sufficient attention to economic, social and cultural (ESC) rights or discriminatory practices 'was eminently predictable' given the heavy influence of criminal law in transitional justice and the 'hidden assumption that ESC rights are not entitlements but aspirations'.[52] Arbour makes a powerful call for a significant shift in praxis:

> Without losing its raison d'être, I believe that transitional justice is poised to make the gigantic leap that would allow justice, in its full sense, to make the contribution that it should to societies in transition. Transitional justice must have the ambition of assisting the transformation of oppressed societies into free ones by addressing the injustices of the past through measures that will procure an equitable future. It must reach to, but also beyond the crimes and abuses committed during the conflict which led to the transition, into the human rights violations that pre-existed the conflict and caused, or contributed to it. When making that search, it is likely that one would expose a great number of violations of economic, social and cultural (ESC) rights and discriminatory practices.[53]

East Timor's CAVR shows how a truth commission might widen the scope of *what* transitional justice addresses. CAVR's statistical accounting of fatal human rights violations looks beyond the direct result of military operations to include death from hunger and illness.[54] There is a separate chapter on forced displacement and famine, which affected nearly every person living in that period. (In contrast, the South African TRC could only sneak in findings of specific violations of ESC rights by treating arson as 'severe ill-treatment'. There was considerable criticism of its refusal to treat forced displacement similarly.) CAVR, in its chapter on violations of social, cultural and economic rights, addresses the use of the education system as a propaganda tool, the manipulation of the coffee market, de-development and environmental degradation.[55] It also provides recommendations regarding the rights to freedom from hunger, to an adequate standard of living, education, culture, basic health and to a sustainable environment. Unfortunately, as too often seems the case with truth commissions, the East Timorese government and the international community have largely ignored its report.[56]

Engendering transitional justice will be an important corollary to taking up Arbour's call. Until very recently women and gender have been glaringly absent from transitional justice programmes. Masculinist determinations of the transitional problem have centred on political violence with, as noted above, an emphasis on 'extraordinary' violations of civil and political rights.

This construction disregards and treats as 'ordinary' the private or intimate violence that women experience in a militarised, unequal society. It also fails to reflect the myriad of social and economic harms that are disproportionately placed upon women, widows in particular, during and after repression or armed conflict.[57]

When 'truth' is structured around extraordinary violence, women predominantly bear witness on behalf of deceased partners, children and grandchildren, that is, as indirect or secondary victims. Consequently women's stories of violence and suffering do not fully emerge. Jolly remarks in the South African case that 'the TRC lacked the social and structural context to be able to conceive of these women as victim-survivors, authors and subjects of their own narratives'.[58] When women do appear as victim-survivors in their own right,[59] it is overwhelmingly as victims of sexual violence, something that is incredibly difficult to give public testimony about. Women-only workshops and hearings can alleviate this difficulty, but, as Levine argues in the East Timorese context, women-centred hearings should not neglect other forms of gender-based suffering, such as losing a limb to a landmine when searching for food or facing discriminatory inheritance laws.[60]

Certainly, it is an important advance for women's rights to recognise that sexual violence constitutes a crime against humanity, war crime, or genocide, rather than simply being a spoil of war or violation of honour. But international criminal jurisprudence, as Franke points out, has problematically created 'mis-recognition' or 'over-recognition' of women. It pins female victims of sexual violence to an essentialised identity that makes it difficult to 'script new social possibilities', particularly where rape is highly stigmatised. Furthermore, 'it fails to capture the array of manners in which women suffer gross injustice'.[61] As Park puts it, 'international law is not a silver bullet to alleviate the structural barriers, constraints and challenges that entrench girls' vulnerability in peacetime and wartime'.[62]

Truth commissions are better positioned to address the marginalisation of women and girls because they look at patterns of violations. For example, the Sierra Leone TRC's extensive and far-reaching recommendations include the repeal of discriminatory inheritance, marriageable age, and other customary laws, amendments to laws pertaining to domestic and sexual violence, promotion of skills training, education and economic empowerment of women, and setting up of a Gender Commission.[63] These recommendations follow extensive gendered analysis in other sections of the report and reach well beyond a sexualised accounting of gender-based violence to challenge structural inequality. Unfortunately the Sierra Leone government has done 'next to nothing' to implement these recommendations, despite being legally bound to do so, and despite the recent provision of external debt relief.[64]

Conclusion

In the determination of *who* is accountable for *what* and *when*, transitional justice is a discourse and practice imbued with power. Yet, it can be strikingly depoliticized in its application. Artificial time frames and zones of impunity produce restricted accounts of violence and remedy. A narrow, legalistic focus on gross violations of civil and political rights overlooks the ways in which structural violence and gender inequality inform subjective experiences of political conflict, injustice and their consequences. Where structural violence enters the picture, it is largely in the background. Where gender enters the picture, it is fixated on sexual violence against women, neglecting sexual violence against men and non-sexual violence against women.

Efforts within the global project of transitional justice to retract from one-size-fits-all solutions must guard against the kinds of channeling highlighted in this paper. To do so requires a broader approach that encompasses structural violence, gender inequality and foreign involvement. This challenge speaks to the very legitimacy of a globalized transitional justice as well as to the efficacy and legitimacy of mechanisms designed to help those who must live together after atrocity. International law and transnational norms must have a heightened role in transitional circumstances precisely because national legal and political systems are weak or corrupt. At the same time, remote institutions and narrowly conceived mechanisms and analyses will not change ordinary people's lives for the better.

Notes

1 M Mutua, 'Savages, victims and saviors: the metaphor of human rights', *Harvard International Law Journal*, 42, 2001, pp 201–242.

2 C Bell, C Campbell & F Ní Aoláin, 'Justice discourses in transition', *Social & Legal Studies*, 13 (3), 2004, p 307.

3 C Bell & C O'Rourke, 'Does feminism need a theory of transitional justice? An introductory essay', *International Journal of Transitional Justice*, 1 (1), 2007, p 35.

4 RG Teitel, 'Theoretical and international framework: transitional justice in new era', *Fordham International Law Journal*, 26 (4), 2003, p 893, see also fn 1. Teitel's succinct definition of transitional justice draws from her seminal book, *Transitional Justice*, New York: Oxford University Press, 2000.

5 See Teitel, *Transitional Justice*.

6 N Roht-Arriaza, 'The new landscape of transitional justice', in N Roht-Arriaza & J Mariezcurrena (eds), *Transitional Justice in the Twenty-First Century*, New York: Cambridge University Press, 2006, p 2.

7 *Ibid*.

8 R Mani, *Beyond Retribution: Seeking Justice in the Shadows of War*, Malden, MA: Polity, 2002, p 17.

9 R Lui, 'Beyond retribution: seeking justice in the shadows of war [book review]', *Australian Journal of Political Science*, 38 (3), 2003, pp 589–590.

10 R Mani, 'Rebuilding an inclusive political community after war', *Security Dialogue*, 36 (4), 2005, p 524.

11 United Nations Secretary-General, *Report on the Rule of Law and Transitional Justice in Conflict and Post-Conflict Societies* (2004), para 8.

12 See The International Centre for Transitional Justice's website, 'Where We Work', at http://www.ictj.org/en/where/overview/; and 'Transitional Justice Approaches', at http://www.ictj.org/en/tj/, both accessed 20 July 2007.

13 LE Fletcher & HM Weinstein, 'Violence and social repair: rethinking the contribution of justice to reconciliation', *Human Rights Quarterly*, 24 (3), 2002, p 584.

14 Mani, *Beyond Retribution*, p 151.

15 See L Vinjamuri & J Snyder, 'Advocacy and scholarship in the study of international war crimes tribunals and transitional justice', *Annual Review of Political Science*, 7, 2004, p 347.

16 B Oomen, 'Donor-driven justice and its discontents: the case of Rwanda', *Development and Change*, 36 (5), 2005, p 890.

17 *Ibid*, p 893.

18 KM Franke, 'Gendered subjects of transitional justice', *Columbia Journal of Gender and Law*, 15, 2006, pp 813, 820.

19 See RA Wilson, *The Politics of Truth and Reconciliation in South Africa: Legitimizing the Post-Apartheid State*, Cambridge: Cambridge University Press, 2001.
20 For example, E Stover, H Megally & H Mufti, 'Bremer's "Gordian Knot": transitional justice and the US occupation of Iraq', in Roht-Arriaza & Mariezcurrena, *Transitional Justice in the Twenty-First Century*, pp 229–254, are completely agnostic on these points.
21 RI Rotberg, 'Truth commissions and the provision of truth, justice, and reconciliation', in RI Rotberg & D Thompson (eds), *Truth V Justice*, Princeton, NJ: Princeton University Press, 2000, p 4.
22 R Nagy, 'The ambiguities of reconciliation and responsibility in South Africa', *Political Studies*, 52, 2004, pp 709–727; K Lalloo, 'Citizenship and place: spatial definitions of oppression and agency in South Africa', *Africa Today*, 45 (3–4), 1998, pp 439–460; and Nahla Valji, *Creating the Nation: The Rise of Violent Xenophobia in the New South Africa*, 2003, at http://www.csvr.org.za/papers/papnv1.htm, accessed April 2004.
23 C Duggan & AM Abusharaf, 'Reparation of sexual violence in democratic transitions: the search for gender justice', in P de Greiff (ed), *The Handbook of Reparations*, Oxford: Oxford University Press, 2006, p 627. F Ní Aoláin, 'Political violence and gender during times of transition', *Columbia Journal of Gender and Law*, 15, 2006, pp 829, 848, notes that there may be an increase in reporting rather than in incidents.
24 C Chinkin & H Charlesworth, 'Building women into peace: the international legal framework', *Third World Quarterly*, 27 (5), 2006, p 946. See also Ní Aoláin, 'Political violence and gender during times of transition'.
25 For example, see Democratic Principles Working Group, 'Iraqi opposition report on the transition to democracy', *Journal of Democracy*, 14 (3), 2003, pp 14–29; USIPeace Briefing, *Establishing Justice and the Rule of Law in Iraq: A Blueprint for Action*, 2003, at http://www.usip.org/pubs/usipeace_briefings/2003/0801_ESIraq_law.html; and Afghanistan Independent Human Rights Commission, *A Call for Justice*, 2005, at http://www.aihrc.org.af/Rep_29_Eng/rep29_1_05call4justice.pdf.
26 See T Allen, *Trial Justice*, London: Zed Books, 2006. A similar fear was voiced in 1995 when the ICTY indicted Milosevic prior to the conclusion of a diplomatic solution.
27 A Orford, 'Commissioning the truth', *Columbia Journal of Gender and Law*, 15, 2006, p 863.
28 *Ibid*, p 854.
29 See P Fitzpatrick & E Darian-Smith, 'Laws of the postcolonial: an insistent introduction', in E Darian-Smith & P Fitzpatrick (eds), *Laws of the Postcolonial*, Ann Arbour, MI: University of Michigan Press, 2002, pp 1–15; and Mutua, 'Savages, victims and saviors'.
30 D Chandler, *Empire in Denial: The Politics of State-building*, London: Pluto, 2006, p 172.
31 A Orford, *Reading Humanitarian Intervention*, Cambridge: Cambridge University Press, 2003; and Chandler, *Empire in Denial*.
32 Orford, *Reading Humanitarian Intervention*, p 139.
33 S Katzenstein, 'Hybrid tribunals: searching for justice in East Timor', *Harvard Human Rights Journal*, 16, 2003, p 256.
34 CL Sriram & A Ross, 'Geographies of crimes and justice: contemporary transitional justice and the creation of "zones of impunity"', *International Journal of Transitional Justice*, 1 (1), 2007, pp 45–65.
35 C Wilke, 'A particular universality: universal jurisdiction for crimes against humanity in domestic courts', *Constellations*, 12 (1), 2005, p 84.
36 F Webber, 'The Pinochet case: the struggle for the realization of human rights', *Journal of Law and Society*, 26 (4), 1999, pp 523–537.
37 Sriram & Ross, 'Geographies of crimes and justice', p 57.
38 *Ibid*, p 59.
39 See CL Sriram, *Globalizing Justice for Mass Atrocities: A Revolution in Accountability*, London: Routledge, 2005; and Human Rights Watch, 'East Timor: UN Security Council must ensure justice', *Human Rights News*, 29 June 2005, at http://hrw.org/english/docs/2005/06/28/eastti11231.htm, accessed 30 July 2007.
40 Human Rights Watch, *Justice Denied for East Timor*, 2004, at http://www.hrw.org/backgrounder/asia/timor/etimor1202bg.htm.
41 See *ibid*.
42 J Nevins, 'Restitution over coffee: truth, reconciliation and environmental justice in East Timor', *Political Geography*, 22, 2003, p 684.
43 Sriram, *Globalizing Justice for Mass Atrocities*, p 88.
44 Human Rights Watch, *2007 World Report: East Timor*, at http://hrw.org/englishwr2k7/docs/2007/01/11/eastti14856.htm, accessed 25 July 2007.
45 UN Commission of Experts, *Summary of the Report to the Secretary-General of the Commission of Experts to Review the Prosecution of Serious Violations of Human Rights in Timor-Leste (Then East Timor) in 1999*, S/2005/458, paras 17, 29.
46 See Nevins, 'Restitution over coffee', pp 682, 690–693.

47 Orford, 'Commissioning the truth', p 862.

48 P Hayner, *Unspeakable Truths: Confronting State Terror and Atrocity*, New York: Routledge, 2000, pp 75–76. Some earlier exceptions include the truth commissions in Chad, Chile, El Salvador and Guatemala.

49 See M Mamdani, 'Reconciliation without justice', *South African Review of Books*, 1996, 46, pp 3–5.

50 Wilson, *The Politics of Truth and Reconciliation in South Africa*; and R Nagy, 'Violence, amnesty and transitional law: "private" acts and "public" truth in South Africa', *African Journal of Legal Studies*, 1 (1), 2004, pp 1–22.

51 See R Nagy, 'Postapartheid justice: can cosmopolitanism and nation-building be reconciled?', *Law and Society Review*, 40 (3), 2006, pp 623–652; and Nagy, 'The ambiguities of reconciliation and responsibility in South Africa'.

52 L Arbour, 'Economic and social justice for societies in transition', speech at New York University of Law School, 2006, p 2, at http://www.chrgj.org/docs/Arbour_25_October_2006.pdf, accessed 12 October 2007.

53 *Ibid*, p 3.

54 East Timor CAVR, *Chega! Final Report of the Commission for Reception, Truth and Reconciliation in East Timor*, 2005, ch 6.12, p 5, at http://www.ictj.org/en/news/features/846.html. CAVR is the first truth commission to use a retrospective mortality survey.

55 *Ibid*, ch 7.9, p 3ff.

56 Human Rights Watch, *2007 World Report: East Timor*.

57 See E Rehn & E Johnson Sirleaf, *Women, War and Peace: The Independent Experts' Assessment on the Impact of Armed Conflict on Women and Women's Role in Peace-building*, New York: UNDP, 2002.

58 RJ Jolly, 'Desiring good(s) in the face of marginalized subjects: South Africa's truth and reconciliation commission in a global context', *South Atlantic Quarterly*, 100 (3), 2002, p 623.

59 Discussion of women as combatants, perpetrators or collaborators is beyond my scope.

60 C Levine, 'Gender and transitional justice: a case study of East Timor', Canadian Consortium for Human Security, 2004, pp 29–30, at http://www.humansecurity.info/sites/cchs/files/pdfs/Fellow%20Papers/levine_corey_paper.pdf.

61 Franke, 'Gendered subjects of transitional justice', p 822.

62 ASJ Park, '"Other inhumane acts": forced marriage, girl soldiers and the special court for Sierra Leone', *Social & Legal Studies*, 15 (3), 2006, p 316.

63 Sierra Leone TRC, *Witness to Truth: Report of the Sierra Leone Truth and Reconciliation Commission*, vol 2, ch 3, Accra: Graphic Packaging, 2004, paras 107–111, 316–376, at http://www.trcsierraleone.org/drwebsite/publish/index.shtml.

64 L Graybill, 'Debt relief: a panacea for Sierra Leone?', *CSIS Africa Policy Forum*, 9 February 2007.

26

The Violence of Peace: Ethnojustice in Northern Uganda

Adam Branch

ABSTRACT

Traditional justice, or what this article refers to as 'ethnojustice', claims to promote social reconstruction, peace and justice after episodes of war by rebuilding traditional order. Ethnojustice has become an increasingly prominent mode of transitional justice in northern Uganda. As such interventions multiply throughout Africa, it is essential to probe their political and practical consequences. This article situates ethnojustice theoretically within the broader discourse, practice and institutions of transitional justice, and historically within the reaction against orthodox liberal transitional justice from within the industry. Through an engagement with ethnojustice texts and interventions in the Acholi region of northern Uganda, the article argues that ethnojustice can end up extending forms of unaccountable, patriarchal power within Acholi society, funded and supported by the Ugandan state and international donors. In addition to underpinning this project of social discipline, ethnojustice also benefits the Ugandan state in its effort to avoid accountability for its violence during the war.

INTRODUCTION

The guns have fallen silent, and peace has returned to northern Uganda after two decades of vicious war between the Ugandan government and the Lord's Resistance Army (LRA). With the rebels' reign of brutality a thing of the past, the Acholi have left the squalid camps where they lived for years and returned to their land, and the long process of reconstruction and reconciliation has begun. Instead of war and humanitarianism, peace and justice — often combined within 'transitional justice' — are the signs under which interventions can now occur. Or so the official narrative proclaims — just as it had proclaimed the war to be a black-and-white struggle in which the Ugandan government, together with their Western partners, sought to rescue the civilian population from the terrorist Lord's Resistance Army.

The author would like to thank the faculty and students at MISR and SDSU where previous versions of this paper have been discussed, as well as the editors of this special issue for their encouragement and the anonymous referees for their suggestions.

However, given the gulf between the official narrative about the war and the actual course of the war, it may not be surprising that today's declared peace is rife with violence. Fighter jets roar overhead almost every day. The political protests in the wake of the 2011 presidential elections — for which the military had deployed extensively — were met with extreme force, as they were in other areas of Uganda. Strange diseases erupt among the rural population, for whom the state has disavowed almost all responsibility, as it did during the war. Land, the only thing left to most people, is being lost through often violent dispossession. Paramilitaries occupy rural schools, game wardens have killed farmers, and the military is staking out land for its own use. The main town in the region Gulu is seeing rapid urbanization into slums, increasing poverty, inequality and crime. The Uganda People's Defence Force (UPDF) is spread throughout the region in the name of hunting the remnants of the LRA as American military contractors fly reconnaissance missions overhead and US Special Forces carry out operations on the ground. Rumours circulate of new rebel groups and there is widespread talk of another war.

How do we make sense of the fact that today's peace is shot through with violence and that a regime of transitional justice is accompanied by the emergence of new — and not so new — forms of injustice? I argue that this peace-time violence should not be seen as a vestige of the war or as a product of social breakdown caused by the war, which could be solved through the consolidation of peace and more extensive transitional justice and reconstruction. Instead, I argue that violence is a central element in the re-constitution of structures of power and inequality in post-war northern Uganda. Violence and peace are not antithetical: the violence of peace is not residual, destructive and non-political, but rather is productive political violence, pushing towards specific possible futures, while cutting off others.

The irony is that some forms of today's political violence and the injustices they support are legitimated and put into practice through transitional justice itself. This is the central paradox explored by this article: how practices of justice that claim to enable the transition from war to peace can instead violently entrench the very forms of domination and inequality that gave rise to war in the first place. The article focuses on one particular modality of transitional justice that has risen to prominence in northern Uganda: traditional justice promotion or what I call, drawing on Paulin Hountondji's critique of ethnophilosophy, 'ethnojustice' (Hountondji, 1996). Today, numerous state- and donor-driven ethnojustice projects can be found, ranging from discovering lost chiefs, to building a palace for the so-called Acholi paramount chief, providing development funds for redistribution by the Acholi council of chiefs, and providing money for reconciliation rituals. Before discussing ethnojustice itself, I will first critically examine the discourse of transitional justice more broadly in order to show how ethnojustice, although conceived of as a reaction against the limitations of orthodox liberal transitional justice, embodies the same political logic as the latter and can lead to similarly counterproductive results.

TRANSITIONAL JUSTICE IN QUESTION: VIOLENCE AND POLITICAL ORDER

Hannah Arendt provides a seminal account of the paradoxical relation between founding violence and political order, as the editors to this volume point out (Anders and Zenker, 2014). In her words, 'violence was the beginning and, by the same token, no beginning could be made without using violence, without violating' (Arendt, 1990: 20). Founding violence, of course, is a long-standing problematic in political theory, one reflected upon by thinkers ranging from Machiavelli to Walter Benjamin. A common point of entry is the dilemma posed by the fact that every normal political–legal order must rely on extra-legal, exceptional violence for its own foundation. Founding violence thus cannot be assimilated within the order that it, *de facto*, founds, because it is antithetical to the very norms and laws that, *de jure*, underpin that order. It is the violence of fratricide, parricide, extermination, primitive accumulation or mass expulsion. It can be revolutionary violence in which the forms of domination and inequality that upheld one order are destroyed and new forms of power and modes of distribution are established. The problem of founding violence can be dealt with by placing that violence in the unspeakable past; however, that past can always return to haunt the present and its pretension to non-coercive, ordinary legality.

Transitional justice denotes a different relationship between founding violence and post-violence political order.[1] Instead of founding violence being relegated to the unspeakable past, it is incessantly invoked in the present, whether for the purpose of redress or forgiveness. Instead of attempting to forget the past, it is used to provide the present order with legitimacy, derived from this order's claim to deal justly with the past through legal, political and social mechanisms. The ideals and norms informing transitional justice for past wrongs are thus advanced as the legitimate framework of today's political community. In short, today's political order establishes its legitimacy by claiming to justly assimilate the violence of the past to the present.

In its claim to remedy the injustice of the past through justice today, transitional justice has a certain resonance with notions of revolutionary justice. Revolutionary justice is given a classic formulation in Lenin's *State*

1. My use of the phrase 'transitional justice' refers to a specific discourse, set of practices and institutions that have emerged as a coherent framework in the last twenty years. Even if there are practices that today's scholars of transitional justice might place under that rubric (Teitel, 2003), I am interested in those practices and institutions that understand themselves specifically as 'transitional justice'. As I argue, these have a specific normative underpinning, with specific political consequences. See Huyse (1995) for a reminder of how recent the phrase 'transitional justice' is.

and Revolution: subsequent to a violent revolution, the state, which was the '"special coercive force" for the suppression of the proletariat by the bourgeoisie, of millions of working people by handfuls of rich, must be replaced by a "special coercive force" for the suppression of the bourgeoisie by the proletariat (the dictatorship of the proletariat)' (Lenin, 1964: 397). The new order, brought to power through revolutionary violence, will continue to carry that revolution to completion using the coercive instruments of the state in the name of revolutionary justice. In the legal terrain, this can be seen as 'victor's justice' without the bad conscience that often afflicts liberal legalists when faced with post-transition trials.[2]

Similar to revolutionary justice, transitional justice claims to rectify past injustices through political institutions today. It, too, may use coercion to effect this justice, whether by preventing attempts at extra-legal remedy or by punishing those who cannot be forgiven. The difference is the commitment of orthodox transitional justice to a specific normative order: a liberal-legalist, human rights-based order to be founded in a 'responsible' sovereign state — what some have termed the model of 'liberal peace' (Chandler, 2006; Duffield, 2001; Paris, 2004). This order's supposed universal validity means that transitional justice will represent itself not as a radical transformation, but as establishing or re-establishing a proper, legitimate, liberal order which is presumed to enjoy consent from all proper, modern, liberal subjects. Thus, while transitional justice can proceed from many starting points — 'rogue states', 'failed states', crimes against humanity, civil wars, insurgencies, or other situations that are presented as violating liberal norms — it all leads to the same end point, that of liberal peace.

The consequence is that the necessary link between transitional justice and actual political transition is severed. Transitional justice can be called upon to rectify any declared threat to liberal norms, past or present, as its instruments are even used to actively *promote* the transition to a liberal order (Teitel, 2003), for example, when the International Criminal Court (ICC) is deployed as a complement to Western military intervention. Transitional justice becomes a set of technical instruments that can be employed by states, donors or international organizations in the name of ending or rectifying declared transgressions of liberal norms. There is no requirement that transitional justice grows from or responds to a social demand in order to be valid, as transitional justice is divorced from any necessary connection to social or democratic forces. Thus, when transitional justice invokes forgiveness in the name of reconciliation and peace, it is forgiveness for those who are deemed to be aligned with the liberal framework or redeemable within it.

2. For an illumination of this bad conscience, it is useful to compare, for example, Merleau-Ponty's (1980) description of the show trials in *Humanism and Terror*, or the Soviet jurists' position at Nuremberg, with the discomfort that trials from Nuremberg to Tadic have created in liberal jurists. For seminal, critical contributions to the debate, see Kirchheimer (1961), Koskenniemi (2002), Shklar (1964) and Simpson (2007).

When it invokes punishment in the name of accountability, ending impunity, and peace, that is for those who are accused of having irredeemably violated the liberal order.

The politics of transitional justice are thus determined from two directions. First, the range of harms from the past that can be designated as injustices, and thus deserving of rectification, is limited by the liberal transitional justice framework. Certain forms of power or inequality that are deemed unjust, even by the majority, may be placed off-limits from remedy or transformation by those states, donors or experts who claim to put transitional justice into practice. Robert Meister argues that the South African Truth and Reconciliation Commission (TRC) did precisely this by providing a guarantee for whites to retain the economic benefits they gained under apartheid (Meister, 2011). The tools or modes of action that can be used legitimately to realize justice are also limited by the transitional justice framework. Long, expensive and risky court proceedings displace more immediate and clear forms of retribution; or a revolutionary upsurge that drove the political transition is demobilized and forced to abandon its more radical demands in the name of a just, inclusive political order. Additionally, the statist orientation of transitional justice, in which the end goal is to build 'responsible' states, can give it an anti-popular dimension. In short, the internal logic of transitional justice can define and restrict what can be done in the name of justice and how it can be done, rendering it a disciplining process.

A second set of political effects stem not from the disciplinary internal logic of transitional justice, but from its potential for instrumentalization. Given the inherent ambiguity of the liberal human rights framework and its capacity for polyvalent invocation and strategic manipulation, decisions about who is aligned with liberal order and who is a threat to it will be politically determined (Douzinas, 2007). Similarly, decisions determining which parties to forgive and which to punish can easily be steered by the interests of the politically powerful, nationally or internationally. Thus, for example, the ICC decides to prosecute the LRA, aligned with Khartoum, but to grant effective immunity to the Ugandan government, aligned with the US and Western donors. Or, the siege on Benghazi is responded to through an R2P military intervention and criminal prosecution, while the siege on Sirte is ignored (Grovogui, 2011).

Through these two routes — discipline and instrumentalization — transitional justice can end up reinforcing the injustices of the past instead of remedying them. Moreover, this reinforcement may itself be violent when it needs to overcome resistance by those whose demands for justice are silenced or not met. Forgiveness can mean protecting certain privileged groups or individuals from demands for substantive justice and may also be effected through coercion. Punishment can mean using violence to enforce sanctions against those deemed irredeemably criminal — usually the losers of the conflict, which may further perpetuate grievances. Transitional justice can be counter-revolutionary when it silences demands for justice that transgress the liberal framework (Meister, 2011). It can be conservative when it re-enforces structures of domination and inequality in the name of reconciliation and forgiveness. It can also be vengeful when it is the victors continuing war by legal means in the name of ending impunity and ensuring accountability — the accusation levelled by liberal legalist Hans Kelsen at the Nuremberg trials (Zolo, 2009).

Thus, transitional justice can end up reinforcing the very injustices and modes of domination and inequality that gave rise to episodes of violence in the first place. This tendency goes beyond what the editors of this volume refer to as 'tensions and contradictions between the often lofty and abstract ideals of (transitional) justice and their actual enactments and realizations in practice' (Anders and Zenker, 2014). The problem faced by transitional justice is more fundamental than a disjuncture between rhetoric and reality. The tendency of transitional justice to employ violence to help establish unjust political order is not due to the messiness of reality — it is inherent to transitional justice and has a specific political valence.

While the orthodox liberal transitional justice discourse and practice has occupied a significant place in Uganda, perhaps the most prominent demand within the scope of transitional justice has been for a different, non-liberal form of justice — so-called traditional justice, what I refer to as ethnojustice. However, as I explain, the same political tendencies that are found in liberal transitional justice — the way in which its disciplinary internal logic and its instrumentalization create the possibility to violently reinforce the very forms of domination and inequality that gave rise to upheaval in the first place — are also found in ethnojustice.

THE TURN TO TRADITION

Interventions claiming to promote traditional reconciliation and justice are found throughout Africa, and the increasing interest in African tradition as part of the transitional justice agenda can be seen as part of a broader cultural turn in development, justice, state building and counterinsurgency (Gregory, 2008). In the words of one proponent of this new embrace of tradition, there has been a beneficial 'renaissance in the concept of "the indigenous" and the concepts of "traditional" and "indigenous" . . . offer possible advantages of sustainability and participation, the "elixir" that orthodox approaches to peace-making seek to attain' (MacGinty, 2008: 140).

The logic informing traditional reconciliation and justice interventions is a familiar one that derives from the broader field of peace building. Violence is seen as emerging from the breakdown of war-affected societies, the etiology of which is located in the collapse of traditional values and social harmony, the disappearance of ritual practices that ensured such harmony, and the loss of authority among elders and other traditional leaders. Thus, the breakdown of war-affected society, where that society is defined as traditional, is cause and consequence of violence. Traditional reconciliation and justice interventions are to help rebuild this lost authority structure so that it can preside over reconstructed traditional societies, as Africans are to be 'empowered' as tribes, under customary chiefs. This is the ethnojustice agenda, in which the fulfilment of justice is equated with the establishment of what is considered a traditional social order.

This turn to traditional culture represents a radicalized attempt to institute more genuine 'participation' in peace building with a view to improving the legitimacy and efficacy of Western intervention. It follows the logic of the liberal understanding of transitional justice, namely that there is an absolute and legitimate social-political order that needs to be re-established in the wake of violence. However, this absolute order that is to be re-established, instead of being based in a universal human rights framework, is based in a particular cultural framework. This switch is grounded in the idea that in certain parts of the world, the most important, authentic identities are cultural identities, particularly traditional, customary or tribal identities. Participation should thus take place within this cultural framework or risk being rejected as an alien imposition (Chopra and Hohe, 2004; Richmond, 2008; Zartman, 2000). The West has long conceived of Africa in tribal terms, thus it comes as small surprise that Africa finds itself at the cutting edge of this multifaceted turn toward cultural intervention.

The invocation of culture and tradition in the service of peace and justice also reflects a deeper mistrust among interveners regarding the extent to which Africans are prepared for modernity. It represents an effort to transcend the problems they see as arising from the attempt to impose liberal Western models on supposedly 'illiberal' places like Africa. From this perspective, violence in Africa is most fundamentally derived from the disruption caused by the clash between a timeless, still-present and ineradicable African tradition and an imposed Western modernity. It follows that the promotion of liberal peace would exacerbate the underlying causes of conflict by intensifying modernity's disruptive force and by marginalizing those whose participation is needed to successfully promote peace and justice. Ethnojustice thus appeals to Western audiences by basing its legitimacy on claims to represent and work with authentic African identity and difference, treat Africans with dignity as Africans and avoid imposing Western ideas and models.

However, because ethnojustice conceives of Africans as possessing an unspoken unanimous worldview, it cannot but impose a Western imagination of African institutions. During the colonial period the instrumental identification and use of African tradition was based upon the notion that a too-fast transition to modernity would introduce destructive upheaval into African cultures. Today, the idea of an eternal African tradition is again imagined and deployed instrumentally. The history of Western instrumentalization of imagined notions of African tradition as the basis of indirect-rule colonialism should itself give pause to those promoting this new phase of transitional justice intervention. In this sense, ethnojustice represents the revival, not of African tradition, but of the British tradition of indirect rule in Africa under which African tribes were to be civilized. As Tim Allen puts it, 'efforts were made to do the same thing rather more systematically in the past, when "tribal" customs were incorporated into the indirect administration of the British protectorate through government-appointed chiefs and other local agents' (Allen, 2010: 253).

Not all calls for traditional justice come from Westerners seeking better purchase for intervention in Africa, however. African critics of Western involvement in Africa have also made clear the need to go beyond orthodox transitional justice in seeking futures of peace, development and justice (Lekha Sriram and Pillay, 2009). As the Zimbabwean human rights activist Brian Kagoro argues, transitional justice needs to be divorced 'from its neo-liberal and neo-imperial hue to guarantee its success in Africa' (Kagoro, 2012: 15). In its place, he continues, African activists should advance 'a self-sustaining Afro-centric transitional justice that takes on board the historiography of African conflicts as well as the broader geo-political and geo-economic contexts of such conflicts' (ibid.: 9). Despite the often wide-ranging and radical statements calling for an African transitional justice that recognizes the continent's particular historical experience, this literature tends to reduce what is specifically 'African' to the cultural. It fails to problematize the tradition–modernity dichotomy that underlies both orthodox transitional justice (which values the modern) and ethnojustice (which values the traditional). The literature tends to assume that a particularly 'African' transitional justice would lead to 'a healthy balance between tradition and modernity when it comes to the strategies deployed to promote justice and reconciliation' (Murithi, 2012: 214). Creating such a balance would require a complementary merger of formal legal mechanisms and traditional mechanisms, whereby each corrects the shortcomings of the other. This approach begs the question of why the concept of 'transitional justice' should be retained at all, and why other, less ideologically burdened political concepts aren't employed instead.

My argument will be that, despite its self-proclaimed distance from the liberal peace model, the political consequences of so-called Africanized interventions can end up hewing closely to the outcomes of so-called liberal transitional justice interventions. First, both forms can be effectively instrumentalized by states. The instrumentalization of liberal transitional justice enables states to deploy violence in the name of human rights at the national and international level. Likewise, the instrumentalization of ethnojustice enables states to insulate themselves from demands for accountability or justice after periods of conflict. Second, the internal logic of both can lead to reinforcing forms of inequality or domination through discipline. Liberal transitional justice puts private property and the capitalist market economy off-limits and consolidates a liberal political and economic order. Similarly, the internal logic of ethnojustice insulates gender and age-based structures of domination from challenge and can thus consolidate a patriarchal, gerontocratic social order. The remainder of this article provides a critique of the theory and practice of ethnojustice as it has been instantiated in the response to the war in northern Uganda.

TRANSITIONAL JUSTICE IN UGANDA

Civil war began in the Acholi region of northern Uganda soon after Yoweri Museveni, the commander of the southern-based National Resistance Army (NRA), seized power from a principally northern government in 1986. Museveni's NRA proceeded to occupy the Acholi region of northern Uganda and launched a violent campaign there against the civilian population, partly in a misguided attempt to prevent the eruption of insurgency, partly in revenge for the atrocities for which the south held northerners responsible during the civil war of 1981–86. Instead of preventing a rebellion, this state violence provoked that very rebellion, as a series of primarily Acholi rebel movements emerged in 1986–88, including the Uganda People's Democratic Army and the Holy Spirit Movement (HSM), which led to a further escalation of government violence against Acholi civilians. After the failure of those early movements, by the end of the decade a new rebel group, which combined orthodox guerrilla tactics with a blend of political and spiritual orientations, the LRA, had arisen as the most potent rebel force.

By that time, the support that previous rebel groups had enjoyed among the Acholi peasantry had diminished due to the rebels' military failures and the government's brutal counterinsurgency. In that atmosphere, the LRA interpreted reduced popular support as Acholi civilian support for the government and directed their violence at suspected government collaborators. The LRA soon became infamous for its massacres, maiming, and the forced recruitment of tens of thousands of Acholi, many of them children. The Ugandan government's counterinsurgency was also brutal, focused on destroying suspected popular rebel support. Hundreds, if not thousands, of Acholi were killed by direct state violence. The most devastating aspect of the government's counterinsurgency was its policy of mass forced displacement and internment. Starting in 1996, the government forcibly displaced the entire rural Acholi population, over a million people, driving them out of their homes and into internment camps through a campaign of threats, murder and bombing and burning down entire villages. Once in the camps, the government failed to provide adequate relief aid or protection, which led to a massive humanitarian crisis with excess mortality levels reaching approximately 1,000 people per week. The violence did not end until 2006, when the LRA departed from Uganda, apparently for good, and the dominant discourse concerning the north shifted to one of reconstruction and justice.

The broader structural conditions that gave rise to and prolonged the war were twofold. First and foremost were national political issues which centred around grievances the Acholi community held against the post-1986 Museveni-led government. The Acholi were largely excluded from the new government, and their political leaders were subject to state violence and repression. Economically, the Acholi demanded compensation for the massive looting of cattle, one of their main sources of livelihood, which was carried out by the NRA troops soon after their arrival in the north. And then there was the massive violence of the counterinsurgency itself, especially forced displacement, which the Acholi demanded be brought to an end and for which they demanded compensation.

Second were social upheavals within the Acholi community. These comprised everyday, and not-so-everyday, forms of resistance, primarily by women and youth, against the assertion of patriarchal, gerontocratic power within clan and household structures. Resistance to the power of older men helped to give rise to phenomena such as spirit possession, manifesting largely among young women, which provided a space of authority beyond the control of older men. This resistance can also be seen in the social composition of the rebel groups, especially the HSM and LRA. The former was led by a young woman spirit medium and the latter by a young male spirit medium, both drawing their support largely from young men and women. The war was the result of a confluence of national and internal political crises which were further exacerbated during the course of the war (Branch, 2011). Thus, any form of justice in the post-war period would have to address both the domination and inequality imposed by the state against the Acholi as a community, and the domination and inequality imposed by older men against youth and women within the Acholi community. I will argue that ethnojustice tends to worsen these two forms of injustice instead of remedying them.

Debates over justice were triggered by the intervention of the ICC, which commenced its investigation in July 2004 in response to a referral from the Ugandan government in late 2003. With the ICC's intervention, the international transitional justice industry quickly got involved as well. In the debate that followed, a number of divergent demands were heard: that the ICC prosecute all parties involved, that the ICC leave Uganda, that a blanket amnesty be guaranteed, that a combination of national and international trials be used, or that a truth commission be established. But the position that received the most attention was voiced by Acholi activists and political leaders who, with increasing support from international donors, demanded that legal procedures be replaced by Acholi traditional justice. Controversy has raged since then, with supporters of the ICC accusing proponents of traditional justice of condoning impunity, and supporters of traditional justice accusing the ICC of prolonging the war and destructively imposing Western ideas of justice upon the Acholi. Both sides comprise alliances between local, national and international political actors; both can locate consent within Acholiland; and each accuses the other of being promoted by foreign donors (Allen, 2006; Branch, 2007). Since the end of the war in 2006, traditional justice has received further institutional support at the Juba Peace Talks, in particular in Agenda Item 3, and in the Peace, Recovery and Development Plan (Komakech, 2012: 67). It is to the early articulations of traditional justice that I turn next.

ETHNOJUSTICE IN THEORY[3]

Ethnojustice is a discourse that combines elements from ethnography and from the study of law and ethics to describe what it claims are traditional systems of justice of non-Western cultures. In describing a traditional system of justice, ethnojustice purports to present a single, coherent, positive system that is consensually and spontaneously adhered to by all members of that culture; what Hountondji calls the myth of unanimism (Hountondji, 1996: xviii). Moreover, from an ethnojustice perspective such a culture, even if in abeyance today, remains valid and should be revived. Against this ethnojustice discourse, I will try to meet Hountondji's demand that, instead of 'African traditional thought', we consider 'African *traditions* of thought' — or, in this case, traditions of justice — where those traditions are themselves plural, contrasting and contested (ibid.: xxiv, emphasis added). In so doing, I argue that peace and justice will not be found through the imposition of an inert, authoritarian order upon societies. It will emerge through the ongoing and contentious process of including more groups, interests and voices in the deliberations over the shape of those societies.

The outline of the ethnojustice approach can be found in the first major ethnojustice text on northern Uganda, Dennis Pain's *The Bending of the Spears* (1997), which purports to give an account of the 'traditional authority structure' of the Acholi. At the heart of Pain's account is his assertion that, among the Acholi, conflicts were traditionally regulated and resolved by the *rwodi-moo*, or traditional elders. He writes, 'The principle of conflict resolution in Acholi is to create reconciliation which brings the two sides together' and involves both paying compensation for harm done and ritually drinking a 'bitter root extract drink', known as *mato oput* (Pain, 1997: 56). In the current conflict, as in any conflict among the Acholi, according to Pain, the *rwodi-moo* should meet and decide on a route for its resolution. He then confidently proclaims, 'as with any idea in Acholi, if the proposal is good, all will accept and Acholi can then speak with one voice' (ibid.: 54). Reconciliation can proceed through the 'traditional approach to "cooling" the situation and healing the land and restoring relationships, far beyond the limited approaches of conservative western legal systems' (ibid.).

Today's crisis, according to Pain, is the result of 'social break-down', in particular a 'collapse of traditional networking and values' in which 'the elders have failed to take on the responsibility which they should have

3. The following sections draw on Branch (2011).

taken' (ibid.). The war is thus represented as an intra-Acholi conflict that has escaped the limits traditionally imposed by elders. Even though 'all clans (and subclans) are both victims and perpetrators' (ibid.: 51), the most important task is the reconciliation of LRA fighters: 'although the rebels are seen to have rejected society, if society now establishes the means of reconciliation, the rebels will accept that authority' (ibid.).

Pain thus internalizes the war as an intra-Acholi problem, while also counterproductively misrepresenting the politics of the internal crisis. He reduces the national politics of the war to a social crisis brought about by the breakdown of traditional authority, embodied in a patriarchal regime of elders and chiefs, and reduces the resolution of the war to the re-incorporation of the young, alienated LRA into that unreformed regime. Although it is true that there has been a significant loss of authority by male elders as a result of the war and displacement, to reduce the local and national political crises faced by the Acholi to that loss of authority is unwarranted. When a misconception like this informs transitional justice interventions, it can have counterproductive political consequences, entrenching the very forms of domination and inequality that gave rise to the crises. First, ethnojustice can be counterproductive as a result of its own internal logic, which empowers older men at the expense of youth and women. Second, ethnojustice is counterproductive as a result of its instrumentalization by the state, which uses ethnojustice to evade accountability for violence or repression and to entrench its power within Acholi society by manipulating a regime of unaccountable 'chiefs'. Ethnojustice also prevents the international dimensions of war from being rectified or even comprehended.

ACHOLI ETHNOJUSTICE

The ICC intervention sparked a flurry of research within the ethnojustice paradigm. One of the earliest and most important studies is *Roco Wat i Acholi: Restoring Relationships in Acholi-land: Traditional Approaches to Justice and Reconciliation* (Liu Institute for Global Issues and Gulu District NGO Forum, 2005), funded by the John D. and Catherine T. Macarthur Foundation and by the Royal Embassy of the Netherlands.[4] The purpose of *Roco Wat* was 'to provide an initial assessment of how traditional rituals and ceremonies could be further adapted to address the crimes committed during the 19-year old conflict in Uganda' (ibid.: 1). To this end, it seeks principally to 'identify and describe: a) Justice from the perspective of Acholi traditional culture; [and] b) the processes and mechanisms of traditional justice' (ibid.: 7). *Roco Wat* attributes the importance of ethnojustice to the fact that: 'After nearly two decades of conflict, social relationships and trust

4. Other, more nuanced accounts have been produced since this initial period; for example, see Komakech (2012) and Oola (2012).

within a traditionally communal culture have been severely degraded. Consequently, so has Acholi culture, and the prominent role cultural leaders (Chiefs, Elders and Mego) once held in society. Due to mass displacement, youth have little opportunity to learn about their history or culture' (ibid.: 2).

The report presents the recently created body of Acholi chiefs and elders, Ker Kwaro Acholi (KKA), as key to this process of reviving traditional justice mechanisms in order to help restore relationships in Acholiland. *Roco Wat* intended to begin the project of the positivization and formalization of so-called Acholi traditional justice by collecting and writing down practices, rituals and ceremonies, which was to proceed in tandem with the empowerment of KKA as the privileged body that was to apply this formalized traditional justice system.

The ethnojustice of *Roco Wat* does not allow Acholi themselves to fully articulate their own traditional justice system. Instead, it is up to experts and outsiders, with the assistance of Acholi academics and elders, to compile and formalize the traditional justice system as a coherent whole, subsequent to which it will be up to outsiders to help revive those traditions among the Acholi. Although *Roco Wat* recognizes that some elders have considerable knowledge of the traditional justice system, it also implies that they still need additional instruction, and it notes that outside organizations, funded by foreign donors, are conducting 'leadership training on traditional practices' (ibid.: 31). The situation of the youth is even more deplorable from the ethnojustice perspective; indeed, 'one Elder remarked that the younger generations do not know how to be Acholi' (ibid.: 22). The strangeness of foreign organizations teaching old men how to be proper elders is compounded by the fact that elders are then expected to teach recalcitrant youth and women how to be proper Acholi. This, as we will see, is a recipe for a potential disciplinary project, one based on the silence of actually existing Acholi people in favour of the 'true' traditional Acholi identity articulated and promoted by foreign actors with local partners.

The Unanimism of Acholi Tradition

So what are the characteristics of this Acholi traditional justice system, from an ethnojustice perspective? First, ethnojustice relies on the idea of a radical break with traditional culture as a result of British colonialism. Moreover, it assumes that before colonialism, a timeless, unchanging and clearly defined Acholi identity and set of cultural practices existed. In this spirit, *Roco Wat* repeatedly refers to 'how traditional justice was once practiced in Acholi prior to colonialism' (ibid.: 9). It thus displays the ethnojustice tendency to equate a pure, essential cultural identity and set of practices with the pre-colonial, and to contrast it with an impure colonial and post-colonial society that has been contaminated by Western ideas and practices. On the one side is the traditional, pre-colonial, non-state, communal, consensual and restorative. On the other is the Western, colonial/post-colonial, individualist and punitive which supposedly disrupted this earlier harmonious traditional justice system (ibid.: 16). However, the idea that a self-regulating, harmonious Acholi culture existed throughout the pre-colonial period in which a traditional Acholi justice system held sway, fails to take into account what many have described as the British invention of the Acholi as tribe. Furthermore, even if a pre-colonial Acholi identity did exist, it also fails to acknowledge the century of extensive violent conflict and upheaval that preceded the advent of British colonialism. This was a period not of primitive harmony and cultural purity, but of destructive foreign incursion, slave raiding and internecine warfare.

The report goes on to describe Acholi traditional justice as being rooted in the spiritual (ibid.: 3), whilst simultaneously being socially functional: 'in traditional Acholi culture, justice is done for *ber bedo*, to restore harmonious life' (ibid.: 14). In traditional Acholi culture, according to *Roco Wat*, belief in and consent to this justice system and the social order it supports is unanimous. All Acholi value the unity of the Acholi, or the clan, before they value themselves as individuals. The typical Acholi, then, believes absolutely in the spiritual world and in the punishment that the spiritual world sends down when rules are violated. Ethnojustice relegates the spiritual to the functional, in the service of reproducing a static social order. This is achieved by rendering the spiritual domain positive, that is, capable of being formalized in writing and codified in a series of specific normative rules and prescriptions.

Such positivization, however, is contrary to the very nature of the spiritual. As Allen (2010: 253) explains, through this process, rituals 'will lose their flexibility, and will no longer have all the many resonances and associations of lived ritual actions. They will have status that is at least partly based on their externally supported authority. They will become privileged rites and, most likely, the preserve of certain figures of male authority recognized by the government'. The spiritual is inherently a realm of surplus, a domain from which the potential for social or political rupture can always emerge. The idea that it can be contained in positive form without remainder, making it perfectly functional to an existing social order, is a fiction that those in power often want to maintain. Numerous examples can be found within Acholi society of the disruptive potential of the spiritual, a potential that ethnojustice denies.

Ethnojustice and Power

As Allen suggests, the ethnojustice discourse and its reification of the spiritual serve to legitimate the power of a specific social group: male elders, who are presented as the privileged repositories and guardians of tradition and the exclusive mediators with the spiritual world. They are in charge of 'a series of rituals within village settings and household compounds in order to appease the ancestors and ensure the moral order was upheld' (Liu Institute, 2005: 11). Thus, elders and *rwodi* are assigned the exclusive role of regulating Acholi society through their access to the spiritual domain.

Just as in the Pain report, ethnojustice here conceives of the empowerment of male elders as a project of reconstruction or rebuilding an authentic order that is in crisis, as ethnojustice is explicitly phrased in terms of 'reviving' traditional authority. There is truth to the crisis of older male authority. However, the attempt to resolve that crisis by forcefully re-imposing an imagined order of the past is bound to exacerbate the broader social crisis in which the breakdown of male authority is situated. The reason for this is because, at present, the lineage- and clan-based structure of patriarchal, generally gerontocratic, male leadership, which had held significant internal authority in Acholi society at various times over the last century, has been thrown into crisis by the war and displacement. Male Acholi elders and chiefs have largely lost their power of social regulation and political leadership, and while men have seen their authority and status within Acholi society wane, women, and to a lesser extent youth, have seen their economic, social and political authority and status rise. These latter groups have benefited from new business and educational opportunities, human rights interventions and associations made possible in the environment of displacement. Young people also found a form of sometimes ambiguous empowerment in the rebel groups and paramilitaries. Ethnojustice thus represents an opportunity for older men to assert their power under the guise of tradition and to dismiss challenges to that power as non-traditional and non-authentic.

The recently invented KKA is the main beneficiary of this. As *Roco Wat* favourably reports: 'Participants at the Consultative Workshop agreed that Acholi culture was in decline, and in need of revival, especially for youth. Ker Kwaro Acholi and its supporters should embark upon a cultural revival through the recommendations below, which should be supported by donors and the Government of Uganda' (Liu Institute, 2005: 74). The motivation is clear: to channel donor and state funding to the promotion of 'traditional authorities' who can lead a cultural revival and, through mechanisms of traditional justice, restore social order among the Acholi. It is a supposedly empowering, participatory project — where Acholi are empowered to participate as proper, 'responsible' Acholi under the authority of chiefs. The World Bank was among the donors who responded to the call. Their Northern Uganda Social Action Fund (NUSAF) envisioned two thousand 'interventions targeted at traditional institutions' to promote social order by reviving traditional authorities, in particular chiefs and elders. In the process, it was to stimulate inter-clan meetings and dialogue in order to help the process of reconciliation between the LRA and the Acholi. The Bank hired NGOs and individuals to identify the traditional leadership.[5]

A key assumption of the ethnojustice perspective is that these older men, as the proper guardians of tradition and the spiritual, will enjoy universal consent to their authority. A glance at social reality in Acholi, however, reveals this to be far from the case. Instead, following Hountondji's critique of ethnophilosophy, this putatively unanimous adherence to Acholi traditional justice and the social order it upholds is a mystification. It mystifies one particular version of traditional justice, which is in fact part of a dominant ideology and upholds the power of a specific group who claim exclusive access to the spiritual domain in order to ensure the reproduction of their preferred social order. The consequence is that ethnojustice can legitimize a disciplinary social project, one which imposes the same forms of domination and inequality that gave rise to conflict in the first place. As Erin Baines puts it, 'although local mechanisms emphasize reconciliation in a way that punitive approaches do not, it could potentially increase violence rather than restore relationships' (Baines, 2009: 184).

The Violence of Ethnojustice

Although some revival of traditional authority seems to be widely supported among Acholi, there is controversy over just what that authority should comprise and what its domain should be. In interviews conducted among the Acholi soon after the end of the war, it was found that for women and youth, especially those in towns, a return to the idealizations of pre-war order advocated by many male elders would be neither practical nor just. For their part, however, elders and many men tended to demand a comparatively vast increase in their authority once back in the village in a bid to correct the corruption introduced into Acholi society during displacement. In the most extreme versions, elders saw themselves occupying a dominant and all-encompassing role in regulating society in the post-conflict period and dealing with everyone from ex-rebels to thieves, government informants, prostitutes, foreigners and all troublemakers. This revival of their traditional authority, men and elders explained, would take place by imposing discipline at the family and clan levels through warnings, fines, corporal punishment and, if all else fails, expulsion from the clan and curses.

Therefore, there is a possibility that post-war Acholi society may see a coercive project carried out by men, especially men with family or clan authority, designed to eliminate what they see as the corruption that had infected Acholi society during the war and displacement. This produces the potential for violence and upheaval within Acholi society around this kind of systematic exclusion of certain categories of people from clan membership

5. Interview with project coordinator, Office of the Prime Minister, Kampala, 5 March 2003.

and land possession. Indeed, many older men framed the re-establishment of traditional authority explicitly in terms of undoing the power gained by women and youth and imposing the power of men and elders over these formerly subjugated groups. This project could involve physical violence, as caning and other punishments can take place within the family or else at the clan level, administered by the husband or by clan enforcers. As a result, women's and youths' public space and the social and economic opportunities they enjoy with it may be erased as they are confined to the private world of the home, whereas the public space of older men re-opens through social interaction within the lineage and clan.

Ex-LRA returnees, often representing the most marginalized youth or those most unwilling to conform to the demands of older male authorities, could face particular difficulties under the imposition of an ethnojustice agenda. Indeed, tensions between male lineage-based authorities and armed young men have been one of the roots of the wars that have plagued northern Uganda for over two decades, so there is no historical precedent that would imply that ex-members of the LRA would necessarily submit to this older male authority now. Moreover, there is no guarantee that traditional authorities will not use their new authority *against* ex-members of the LRA whom they see as undesirable or who are without firm family or clan connections. In short, a number of factors — fear of revenge, refusal to submit to male authority and the possibility that male authorities may exclude them from clan membership and access to land — meant that ex-LRA members, especially those who had been in the bush the longest and were without strong family relations, could end up facing discipline and exclusion.

Indeed, as soon as movement out of the camps began in 2007, so former LRA began to report being dispossessed of their land by other members of the community, sometimes with the collusion of clan authorities. According to a study of the International Organization for Migration, 90 per cent of the male former LRA they surveyed in post-war Gulu towns 'reported experiencing acute isolation and/or fear of revenge upon return', and over 90 per cent of 'former Lord's Resistance Army combatants surveyed in Gulu municipality reported being unable to access land upon return' (McKibben and Bean, 2010: 8; see also Branch, 2013). Many took refuge in town, further adding to the poverty and social pressures there.

Therefore, the externally funded ethnojustice project could enable a wider project of imposing disciplinary male authority on an Acholi society where that male authority lost much of its legitimacy decades ago. This could amount to a transitional justice project carried out by men to redeem what they saw as a deeply corrupted Acholi society, an agenda that would ride on the coat-tails of the more public transitional justice agenda promoted by foreigners and the Ugandan government. However, because it would represent peace built on the backs of women and youth, there is the potential for further crisis within Acholi society around the exclusion of certain categories of people from clan membership and land possession, reinforcing the very forms of inequality and domination that helped drive on the conflict.

Just as ethnojustice effects a positivization of the spiritual, therefore, it also effects a reification of justice and social order, excising from each its inherent plurality and possibility for rupture. In fact, neither the spiritual, the moral, nor the social are the positive, singular and unanimous domains that ethnojustice insists they are, and they cannot exist in the closed, mutually supporting circuit that ethnojustice claims to identify. Each is a terrain where there is contradiction, conflict and struggle between dominant and non-dominant opinions, ideas and projects.

Importantly, it is not only male elders who benefit from the promotion of ethnojustice: its advantages can also redound to the Ugandan government. As discussed, the two-decade war stemmed from and exacerbated grievances both internal to the Acholi community, of youth and women against older men's power, and between the Acholi community and the Ugandan state. From this angle, the Ugandan government is instrumentalizing ethnojustice in ways that re-enforce the very forms of injustice that gave rise to the war and that will need to be rectified if the legacy of the war is to be overcome. For one thing, it seems likely that the Ugandan government is interested in promoting Acholi traditional justice precisely because traditional justice may guarantee state impunity. Indeed, rituals presided over by male lineage-based Acholi authorities are inadequate to deal with crimes committed by a modern state (Baines, 2007). Ethnojustice also fails to take into account the international dimensions of the war, including the role of the donors in funding Uganda's militarization, and the role of the aid agencies in collaborating with forced displacement. The assertion of a uniquely Acholi traditional justice further tribalizes the conflict, making it an 'Acholi problem', and can make national political justice even more difficult (Allen, 2010: 257–60).

Second, the government has often made successful efforts to co-opt the newly established, and foreign-supported, set of chiefs whose unaccountable authority makes them good candidates for state manipulation. It remains to be seen whether this cadre of chiefs supported by foreign donors and the government will be able to establish legitimacy within Acholi society or if their dependence on external funds will make them tools of outsiders seeking political control or economic benefits. For these reasons, we might expect ethnojustice to appeal to other states that are involved in political violence and seeking to avoid demands for accountability. In these contexts, the promotion of ethnojustice can entrench the forms of state-driven inequality and injustice that give rise to political grievances and violent conflict.

The Plurality of the Spiritual and the Social

The lack of consensus among Acholi on the particular version of the spiritual and the social promoted by ethnojustice is very apparent even in recent

Acholi history. Indeed, the spiritual domain has offered a wide scope for alternative and oppositional ideologies among the Acholi, most notably in the form of spirit possession and the work of the *ajwaka* (a medium or 'tamer' of spirits). The HSM and LRA can be seen as embodying counterhegemonic spiritual claims in part against the power of male elders. The spiritual is a terrain on which women and youth have asserted claims to power and authority beyond that of the male elders, and it is by no means the exclusive preserve of those elders, as ethnojustice would have it. Ethnojustice ignores the disruptive power of *ajwaka* and the fact that many *ajwaka* today come from outside Acholiland, and thus may draw on the spiritual to articulate national or even cosmopolitan identities and projects. Ethnojustice instead imposes the tribe, under the customary power of the chief, as the essential political and social unit, ignoring how the spiritual may rupture not only the power of the male chief but also the boundaries of the tribe as collective identity. Ethnojustice may retribalize political identity in the name of justice and social order, when it is a movement towards the national that may be needed to overcome the legacy of violence.

The domain of justice is a terrain of social struggle in northern Uganda at present and cannot be reduced to being functional to a certain patriarchal model of social order. This is seen with the contestation over what justice should mean in the wake of the war. Indeed, in one 2010 survey, only half of the respondents said that 'traditional justice ceremonies' were 'useful for transitional justice', and only 39 per cent said that they were useful for community reconciliation (Oola, 2012: 55–56). *Roco Wat*'s insistence on the 'consensual' nature of all 'traditional' Acholi justice should draw our attention to how that consent is enforced and at whose expense. The monopolization of justice and reconciliation by an externally supported male authority structure, as dictated by ethnojustice, fails to address the fact that different groups within Acholi society, in particular women and youth, might have their own particular demands for justice. Furthermore, these demands may be centred around alternative spiritual mechanisms or have nothing to do with the spiritual at all, oriented instead toward formal, state-based legal processes, non-spiritual community-based processes or other alternatives. As a result, ethnojustice has the potential to silence those who do not identify with this revived male authority and the version of the spiritual that it claims to uphold. It also has the potential to silence community demands for justice made against the state. Chiefs, empowered through state largesse, may be willing to serve as proponents of forgiveness, repressing claims for justice against the state.

Women, in particular, could be prevented from deciding for themselves what justice means in response to their own specific experiences during the war. It is unreasonable to assume that women would agree to male elders deciding what justice means for them, or to assume that women would be satisfied with men deciding that the perpetrators of violence against women should simply be forgiven, as male elders may very well do under the mantle of tradition. Men may be satisfied with a negotiated, ritualized solution among themselves that does not involve punishment or compensation, whereas women may not be willing to accept that as a just solution at all. The imposition of such justice could create a peace among men built on a reinforced regime of gendered violence.

The external promotion of this form of traditional authority does not enjoy unanimous support even among men. Some men see the project not as the redemption of a corrupt Acholi society, but as part of that corruption itself. Foreign and state sponsorship of traditional authority has provided supposed chiefs with the opportunity to grab land and enrich themselves under the mantle of KKA. Whites and their money are seen as promoting dependency among the Acholi, turning Acholi against Acholi within the NGO job market and creating a new breed of *Acholi matar*, or 'white Acholi'. Foreign agencies are accused of paying people sitting allowances to participate in workshops and sensitizations, a practice that has corrupted the traditional Acholi practice of sitting and meeting to resolve problems without concern for monetary compensation. So there are certainly those men who see ethnojustice not as a revival of traditional Acholi society with external assistance, but as corrupting Acholi society even further.

In short, community-based justice cannot be reduced to a male-dominated version of traditional justice because the community itself, especially now after two decades of war, is not reducible to those who would claim traditional authority (not that it was before the war either). Acholi society, like any society, is not a homogeneous, coherent whole. Acholi traditional justice as identified and celebrated by ethnojustice is only one ideology supporting a claim to power by one group, legitimated through an appeal to a singular tradition and Acholi identity. It is promoted at the expense of alternative traditions of justice and of the spiritual, social and political order *within* Acholi society.

CHALLENGING ETHNOJUSTICE

'The process of reviving traditional justice is not an easy task', *Roco Wat* admits (Liu Institute, 2005: 3), and at one point the report does indeed recognize that the imposition of a gerontocratic, patriarchal order on contemporary Acholi society might not be an unmitigated good. *Roco Wat* appears uncomfortable with the fact that physical punishment of women and youth through beating is a widely prevalent aspect of the traditional culture being promoted by older men — a traditional justice that supposedly rejects justice through punishment as Western. Indeed, this brings to light the double standards of the ethnojustice discourse and it belies the claim that traditional justice is restorative and non-punitive. Women and youth can be 'traditionally' subjected to punishment, physical violence, expulsion, even fatal curses by male elders, whereas men's transgressions — or really a certain category of men's transgressions of interest to male elders — are dealt with through the lofty language of reconciliation, forgiveness, and restorative justice.

Finding a way forward would require a refutation of the ethnojustice discourse and its assumptions. It must recognize that the changes produced by upheaval represent not a deviation from a genuine Acholi traditional order, but rather opportunities for new forms of local and national democratization and political inclusion — forms that go beyond the reduction of the local to the customary and Ugandan citizens to tribespersons. It requires the admission that internal plurality, conflict and contestation have always characterized Acholi society, and the recognition of the many traditions found *within* Acholi society pertaining to the spiritual world and to justice. Indeed, there are many African and many Acholi traditions of justice. Some may find their origins in the pre-colonial period, others find their origins in the colonial, and others in various times during the post-colonial period. Some are tied to the symbolic and embedded in the cultural, others are tied to local and national state-based institutions and others derive from international norms. These different traditions emerged at different times in response to different circumstances and reflect different configurations of power and authority. *All* these traditions can be drawn on now in order to deal with the legacy of the war. For this reason, it is better to speak not of traditional justice but of *traditions of justice* among the Acholi, where the Acholi are historicized, not essentialized, within pre-colonial, colonial and post-colonial political and social processes.

Just as traditional justice, as described by the ethnojustice discourse, is not really traditional, so is it not really justice. Justice by its nature must always be open, never closed, must always be plural and unfinished, and cannot be the preserve of a single group. Justice is 'yet to come', in Hountondji's phrase, in the sense that it is open to new voices, new opinions, new formulations and ideas into the indefinite future. There is no single true justice, for justice is a domain of ultimate uncertainty, a fact that ethnojustice rejects. Justice, spirituality, tradition and society are all realms of internal contradiction and struggle, and only if that is recognized can democracy have a chance to emerge. Then, justice will not be functional to the project of imposing an authoritarian social order, but rather will be the subject for deliberation, organization and action in an inclusive, open, contentious social order.

Times of violent upheaval represent opportunities for the emergence of new political and social orders. If the initiative in such situations falls into the hands of international donors, NGOs and the state, then transitional justice may end up equivalent to discipline and coercion and may set the stage for future conflict. If the community that has survived the conflict takes up the initiative, new forms of inclusive popular organization may emerge that reject the oppression of the past, demand that international intervention come into line with democracy, and lay the foundation for peace in the future.

REFERENCES

Allen, T. (2006) *Trial Justice: The International Criminal Court and the Lord's Resistance Army*. London: Zed Books.

Allen, T. (2010) 'Bitter Roots: The "Invention" of Acholi Traditional Justice', in T. Allen and K. Vlassenroot (eds) *The Lord's Resistance Army: Myth and Reality*, pp. 242–61. London: Zed Books.

Anders, G. and O. Zenker (2014) 'Transition and Justice: An Introduction', *Development and Change* 45(3): 395–414.

Arendt, H. (1990/1963) *On Revolution*. London: Penguin.

Baines, E. (2007) 'The Haunting of Alice: Local Approaches to Transitional Justice in Northern Uganda', *International Journal of Transitional Justice* 1(1): 91–114.

Baines, E. (2009) 'Complex Political Perpetrators: Reflections on Dominic Ongwen', *Journal of Modern African Studies* 47(2): 163–91.

Branch, A. (2007) 'Uganda's Civil War and the Politics of ICC Intervention', *Ethics and International Affairs* 21(2): 179–98.

Branch, A. (2011) *Displacing Human Rights: War and Intervention in Northern Uganda*. New York: Oxford University Press.

Branch, A. (2013) 'Gulu in War ... and Peace? The Town as Camp in Northern Uganda', *Urban Studies* 50(15): 3152–67.

Chandler, D. (2006) *Empire in Denial: The Politics of Statebuilding*. London: Pluto Press.

Chopra, J. and T. Hohe (2004) 'Participatory Intervention', *Global Governance* 10(3): 289–305.

Douzinas, C. (2007) *Human Rights and Empire: The Political Philosophy of Cosmopolitanism*. New York: Routledge-Cavendish.

Duffield, M. (2001) *Global Governance and the New Wars: The Merging of Development and Security*. London: Zed Books.

Gregory, D. (2008) '"The Rush to the Intimate": Counterinsurgency and the Cultural Turn', *Radical Philosophy* (150): 8–23.

Grovogui, S. (2011) 'Looking Beyond Spring: An African Perspective on the Arab Revolt in World Order'. CIHA Blog. http://sites.uci.edu/cihablog

Hountondji, P. (1996) *African Philosophy: Myth and Reality* (2nd edn). Bloomington, IN: Indiana University Press.

Huyse, L. (1995) 'Justice after Transition: On the Choices Successor Elites Make in Dealing with the Past', *Law & Social Inquiry* 20(1): 51–78.

Kagoro, B. (2012) 'The Paradox of Alien Knowledge, Narrative and Praxis: Transitional Justice and the Politics of Agenda Setting in Africa', in M. Okello et al. (eds) *Where Law Meets Reality: Forging African Transitional Justice*, pp. 4–52. Cape Town: Pambazuka Press.

Kirchheimer, O. (1961) *Political Justice: The Use of Legal Procedure for Political Ends*. Princeton, NJ: Princeton University Press.

Komakech, L. (2012) 'Traditional Justice as a Form of Adjudication in Uganda', in M. Okello et al. (eds) *Where Law Meets Reality: Forging African Transitional Justice*, pp. 64–79. Cape Town: Pambazuka Press.

Koskenniemi, M. (2002) 'Between Impunity and Show Trials', *Max Planck Yearbook of United Nations Law* 6: 1–35.

Lekha Sriram, C. and S. Pillay (eds) (2009) *Peace versus Justice? The Dilemma of Transitional Justice in Africa*. Scottsville: University of KwaZulu-Natal Press.

Lenin, V. (1964) *Collected Works: Volume 25*. Moscow: Progress Publishers.

Liu Institute for Global Issues and Gulu District NGO Forum (2005) *Roco Wat I Acholi: Restoring Relationships in Acholi-land: Traditional Approaches to Justice and Reintegration*. Vancouver: University of British Columbia Press.

MacGinty, R. (2008) 'Indigenous Peace-Making versus the Liberal Peace', *Cooperation and Conflict* 43(2): 139–63.

McKibben, G. and J. Bean (2010) *Land or Else: Land-based Conflict, Vulnerability, and Disintegration in Northern Uganda*. Kampala: International Organization for Migration.
Meister, R. (2011) *After Evil: A Politics of Human Rights*. New York: Columbia University Press.
Merleau-Ponty, M. (1980) *Humanism and Terror: An Essay on the Communist Problem*. Boston, MA: Beacon Press.
Murithi, T. (2012) 'Towards African Models of Transitional Justice', in M. Okello et al. (eds) *Where Law Meets Reality: Forging African Transitional Justice*, pp. 200–17. Cape Town: Pambazuka Press.
Oola, S. (2012) 'A Conflict-Sensitive Justice: Adjudicating Traditional Justice in Transitional Contexts', in M. Okello et al. (eds) *Where Law Meets Reality: Forging African Transitional Justice*, pp. 53–63. Cape Town: Pambazuka Press.
Pain, D. (1997) *'The Bending of the Spears'. Producing Consensus for Peace and Development in Northern Uganda*. London: International Alert/Kacoke Madit.
Paris, R. (2004) *At War's End: Building Peace after Civil Conflict*. Cambridge: Cambridge University Press.
Richmond, O. (2008) *Peace in International Relations*. London: Routledge.
Shklar, J. (1964) *Legalism*. Cambridge, MA: Harvard University Press.
Simpson, G. (2007) *Law, War and Crime: War Crimes, Trials and the Reinvention of International Law*. London: Polity Press.
Teitel, R. (2003) 'Transitional Justice Genealogy', *Harvard Human Rights Journal* 16: 69–94.
Zartman, I.W. (ed.) (2000) *Traditional Cures for Modern Conflicts: African Conflict 'Medicine'*. Boulder, CO: Lynne Rienner.
Zolo, D. (2009) *Victors' Justice: from Nuremberg to Baghdad*. London: Verso.

Adam Branch (e-mail: abranch2@mail.sdsu.edu) is Senior Research Fellow at the Makerere Institute of Social Research in Kampala, Uganda, and Associate Professor of political science at Department of Political Science, San Diego State University, 5500 Campanile Drive, San Diego, CA 92182, USA. His work has focused on political violence and international intervention, leading to the book, *Displacing Human Rights: War and Intervention in Northern Uganda* (Oxford University Press, 2011), as well as numerous articles and chapters on the ICC, humanitarianism and regional security.

27

On Transitional Justice Entrepreneurs and the Production of Victims

TSHEPO MADLINGOZI

Abstract

What kinds of politics are (re)produced when a transitional justice expert seeks out the victim, elects to rescue him from his marginality, categorizes him and represents him on the world stage? More specifically, given the fact that transitional justice experts legitimize their existence on the basis of speaking about and for victims, is it ever possible for the expert to exercise 'responsibility' to the victim's story in ways that contribute to the genuine empowerment of the victim? The main aim of this contribution is to make some tentative remarks on how, and what kind of, victims are 'produced' by the transitional justice industry. In the first section I make some generalized observations regarding the political subjectivity of victims produced when transitional justice experts speak about and for victims. In the second section I then look at how Khulumani Support Group, a South African-based social movement of over 55,000 members, has negotiated the contradictions brought about by the transitional justice industry and its representations – in a sense of speaking both about and for victims. I conclude that since 'the story' is the main point of encounter between the authoritative expert and the marginalized victim, 'responsibility to the story' should mean more than being nice to victims or adhering to rigorous scientific and ethical standards; it should also, if not principally, be about redistribution of resources and power. In exercising responsibility to the story experts need to dismantle trusteeship and reproduction of colonial relations.

> The production of authentic victims, or victim authenticity, is an inherently voyeuristic or pornographic practice that, no matter how carefully or sensitively it is done, transforms the position of the 'victim' in his or her society and produces a language of victimization for him or her to speak on the international stage... The remove between the human rights professionals and the people they purport to represent can reinforce a global divide of wealth, mobility, information and access to audience. Human rights professionals consequently struggle, ultimately in vain, against a tide of bad faith, orientalism and self-serving sentimentalism. (Kennedy, 2002: 121)

> *I am not educated. Nomarussia Bonase is uneducated. I don't have a degree. But I can tell you I have a degree. I went to a university; the university of East Rand. My lecturers are the citizens of South Africa, especially the people of East Rand. That is where I got educated. Nobody can come and tell me anything. I can beat the experts, the professionals who have those degrees.* (Nomarussia Bonase, Khulumani Support Group East Rand Coordinator, Thokoza, Interview, 10 October 2009)

Background

The main aim of this contribution is to make some tentative remarks on how, and what kind of, victims are 'produced' by the transitional justice industry. More specifically this contribution has two central concerns: first, I would like to recast Spivak's question and ask: Can the victim speak?[1] Second, I would like to look at the kind of political subjectivities produced by transitional justice experts. This contribution originates from the premise that, as far as victims are concerned, the ultimate goal of transitional justice processes and interventions is not just to 'heal', compensate, and honour victims' memories, but it is ultimately to contribute to the transformation of the political subjectivity of victims in ways that enable them to engage as active citizens, whose capacity to think, to speak, to act, and to revolt is acknowledged and respected.

In the first section I make some generalized observations regarding the political subjectivity of victims produced when transitional justice experts speak about and for victims. In the second section I then look at how Khulumani Support Group (www.khulumani.net), a South African-based social movement of over 55,000 members, has negotiated the contradictions brought about by the transitional justice industry and its representations.

Discursive and Political Violence in Transitional Justice

To illustrate how dominant discourses and institutions, in both the First World and the Third World, marginalize and disempower the 'subaltern', Spivak focuses on the practice of widow-sacrifice (sati) – an act in which a widow immolates herself at the husband's funeral pyre as an act of ultimate loyalty and devotion. During colonial India the British abolished the practice on the basis of a 'civilizing mission' to India. Famously, Spivak saw this as an example of 'White men saving brown women from brown men' (1988: 92). On the other hand, Hindu men excused this practice by arguing that the widows wanted to die. Spivak shows how each of these representations legitimized the other: one purports to be a civilizing mission, saving Hindu

1 See Gayatri Chakravorty Spivak, 'Can the Subaltern Speak?' (1988) (looking at how dominant discourses and institutions marginalize and disempower the Third World 'subaltern').

women from Hindu men, the other a reward, permitting the women to commit a 'pure' and 'courageous' act. All the while, the widow's *own* voice is ignored (Kapoor, 2004: 627). As Kapoor (2004: 628) surmises, the crux of Spivak's argument is that the above representations conflate two related but discontinuous meanings of 'representation': '1) "speaking for" in the sense of political representation; and 2) "speaking about" or "re-presenting" in the sense of making a portrait'. I want to submit that because the transitional justice industry chiefly operates on the basis of these kinds of representations, any discussion of 'responsibility to the story' should seriously engage with the political implications of these representations.

Whether it is through 'fact finding' reports, conference papers, academic journal articles, 'field notes', or more egregiously, funding proposals, the core task of a transitional justice entrepreneur is to speak about or for victims. In this article I would like to reflect on the question of whether the transitional justice expert can *ever* exercise 'responsibility' to the victim's story. In doing so, therefore, we should not only ask whether the victim can ever speak, but whether it is ever legitimate for others to speak about or for the victim. In discussing 'the problem of speaking for others', Alcoff (1991: 7) poses the following question:

> Is the discursive practice of speaking for others ever a legitimate practice, and if so, what is the criterion for its validity? In particular, is it ever valid to speak for others who are unlike me, or who are less privileged than me?

Kapoor (2004: 628), writing in the context of the field of development, adds the following questions:

> What are the ethico-political implications of our representations for the Third World, and especially for the subaltern groups that preoccupy a good part of our work? To what extent do our depictions and actions marginalise or silence these groups and mask our own complicities? What social and institutional power relationships do these representations, even those aimed at 'empowerment', set up or neglect?

It is true that in some post-conflict situations or in situations of prolonged authoritarianism victims often lack the space or skills to speak for themselves vis-à-vis elites – both state and others such as aid workers, NGO officials, and 'academic migrant workers'. But the practice of speaking for and about victims further perpetuates their disempowerment and marginality. To be sure, as transitional justice experts, both from the First World and Third World, we appropriate the right to speak for victims by dint of our geopolitical and institutional privilege. In fact we must go further and assert that the transitional justice entrepreneur gets to be the speaker or representative on behalf of victims, not because the latter invited and gave her a mandate but because the entrepreneur sought the victim out, categorized her, defined her, theorized her, packaged her, and disseminated her on the world stage. Having 'mined' the story in order to use it in the First World – a practice others aptly refer to as cultural imperialism – the entrepreneur reinforces her status as the authoritative knower who is ordained to teach, civilize and rescue the benighted, hapless victim. Despite writing critically and passionately about the situation of *the* victim, the victim is not only left in the same position but this encounter could be an act of further violence and dispossession. Razack (2007) aptly refers to this as 'stealing the pain of others', dehumanizing victims further and reinstalling First Worlders as morally and racially superior in relation to them.

While it might be true that most experts appropriate the story with the intention of helping the victim and that most genuinely attempt to exercise 'responsibility to the story', parenthetically, we might ask: is it even possible for the expert to get to know the reality of the victim-other? When a researcher comes to Africa to conduct research, she faces many constraints which make the task of 'knowing' her subject very difficult. First, she does not speak the local language and, not unlike the missionary or colonial anthropologist, she has to rely on an English-speaking local informant and translator. Other sets of constraints include submission deadlines, academic writing and referencing styles, as well as the inherited ideological and theoretical baggage she is coming with. Ratele (2008) therefore asserts that researchers need to quit pretending that existing or traditional research methodological and analytical frameworks tell us anything about African people worth knowing.[2]

The 'theft of victims' pain' occurs more clearly in the work of international non-governmental organizations (INGOs) concerned with lobbying and advocacy in the area of transitional justice. To be effective in their work, these INGOs speak about and for victims with the aim of inviting others to do something to end victims' suffering. In this sense then, transitional justice NGOs are part of the international human rights movement aimed at saving victims everywhere. Mutua (2002) and others have shown how this mission is a continuation of the missionary impulse to civilize and save the Third World. Mutua (2002: 19) thus concludes:

> Once again, the allegedly superior Europeans and North Americans descend on supposedly backward natives in the Third World with the human rights mission to free them from the claws of despotic governments and benighted cultures.

2 An example of the difficulty in 'knowing' the researched subject and understanding their narrative is discussed in a brilliant book by Krog et al. (2009). Antjie Krog (2009: 91) confirms that it was only after the testimony of their research subject was closely retranslated by her co-investigators and read from an African indigenous cultural and psychological standpoint that she could 'come to the awareness that her testimony was a narrative of exceptional power'.

Mutua (2002: 10–38) presents this through a metaphor he terms the 'savages-victims-saviours (SVS) construction': the victim sandwiched between 'the ogre' (the state) and the 'redeemer, the good angel' (INGO officials).

For Kennedy (2002: 111) this practice is bad for both 'victims' and human rights 'advocates'. The tendency of human rights to articulate good and evil in abstract terms is extremely limiting for victims, Kennedy points out, because

> differences among 'victims', the experience of their particularity and the hope for their creative and surprising self-expression, are erased under the power of an internationally sanctified vocabulary for their self-understanding, self-presentation and representation as 'victims' of human rights abuses. (Kennedy, 2002: 112)

At the same time, for advocates of human rights the knowledge that they are 'heroic agents for an authentic suffering elsewhere' kills any chance of genuine solidarity with those cast as victims (Kennedy, 2002: 112). As reproduced at the head of this article, for Kennedy, this representational dimension of human rights advocacy is the most despicable thing – he calls it voyeuristic and pornographic – about using human rights as the language of emancipation and empowerment.

To further understand how transitional justice actors often rob victims of their agency in ways that are inimical to victims' empowerment, let alone active citizenship, we need to view 'transitional justice' as a global project aimed at reconstructing Third World states in Western liberal democratic terms (Lundy and McGovern, 2008). Another key point is the fact that the whole enterprise of transitional justice has become 'overdominated by a narrow legalistic lens' (see McEvoy, 2007, for a review of this literature). McEvoy (2007: 421) shows that one way in which legalism is discernible 'is a tendency towards an understanding of transitional justice that is both state-centric and 'top down'.' Further, and more significant, McEvoy (2007: 424) argues that this tendency has come to see justice and its delivery as the business of state and state-like institutions. Local communities are therefore robbed of agency and are merely seen as either victims to be rescued or perpetrators to be prosecuted: 'entire post-war populations [are viewed] either as traumatized victims lacking the ability to make decisions about the future, or as people driven by destructive psychosis that renders them incapable or morally unworthy of positive contributions to peace-building' (Lundy and McGovern, 2008: 265).

The transitional justice industry, especially that which is part of the 'international human rights movement/community', could therefore be accused of producing a racially inferior and politically disempowered subject. In this regard, Neocosmos (2006) has argued that the human rights discourse is part of a project to substitute emancipatory politics based on active citizenship with 'statism', that is, politics of demobilization and passivity reliant on 'state-delivery' or delivery by other institutions like NGOs whose mode of operation is, despite rhetoric to the contrary, overwhelmingly top-down. The politics and practice of human rights discourse, he argues, are actually disempowering as they produce 'passive citizenship dependent on power (states, empire, NGOs, etc.) for its existence' (Neocosmos, 2006: 357). Understood in this way the human rights discourse is actually often detrimental to the empowerment of victims as it produces a lack of agency (the notion that 'victims' or oppressed people cannot wage the struggle by and for themselves) and trusteeship (the idea that others must 'represent' or 'take up the cause on behalf' of 'victims') (Neocosmos, 2006; Meister, 2002; Mutua, 2002). Despite all the talk about victim empowerment then, the victim produced by transitional justice NGOs and others in the international human rights movement is a hapless, passive victim dependent on NGOs and others to speak for her and argue her case.

To sum up, it can be argued that the encounter between the victim and expert reproduces relations of inferiority and superiority. In this encounter, the one is the victim and the other is the saviour. Politics of disempowerment and trusteeship – with a heavy missionary slant – are reproduced. If we agree that 'the story' is the entry point to appropriation, 'theft of pain' and cultural imperialism, what is the transitional justice expert's responsibility? Responsibility should certainly extend beyond issues of ethics in research and advocacy. Confronting our own responsibility should also encompass the kinds of political subjectivity we produce. In the next section I look at the attempt by a social movement of victims to overturn these unequal power relations, reject their representation by others, and 'speak out' for themselves.

Khulumani Support Group

> *They just want us to be victims and tell our stories so they can help us. I am sick of telling my story. It makes them feel good to show that they are helping us. They don't really want to change things and what good does telling our stories over and over do? They are just white professionals who want to keep their jobs.* (Western Cape Khulumani member, cited in Colvin, 2000)

> We do not want to be the recipients of services provided by government, when we are capable of providing these services ourselves once the necessary resources have been allocated to us. We have proven our capacity to take our future in our hands. We demand to play our part in rebuilding our own lives. (Khulumani, 2006b)

Khulumani Support Group (Khulumani), a national organization of victims and survivors of gross human rights violations committed during apartheid, was established in 1995, just before the setting up of the Truth and Reconciliation Commission (TRC), with two main aims: firstly to ensure that victims took part in the TRC and that the Commission functioned in a 'victim-centred' manner; and secondly to contribute to the empowerment of victims. Victims and survivors settled on the name Khulumani – 'Speak Out' – because they had decided that silence was not an option and that they needed to speak out about what had been done to them and what they had witnessed being done to others (Khulumani, 2009).

Historical Origins of Khulumani Support Group

Khulumani's origins can be traced back to the separate creation of two organized groupings of victims, which later coalesced into Khulumani Support Group. The Gauteng grouping of victims was assisted by the Centre for the Study of Violence and Reconciliation (CSVR) in order to establish itself as an organization of victims. In order to teach victims about the impending TRC process, CSVR ran educational workshops across Gauteng and neighbouring provinces. In March 1996 Khulumani set up a 'central Khulumani advice office' based in Johannesburg (Hamber et al., 2000). As far as the Western Cape grouping is concerned, the Cape Town Trauma Centre for Survivors of Violence and Torture was instrumental in bringing together groupings of victims which eventually affiliated with Khulumani. Starting from 1998, the Trauma Centre's Torture Project started reaching out to ex-political prisoners and torture survivors. Colvin (2000) reports that in order to assist ex-political prisoners and torture survivors, the Trauma Centre began holding monthly meetings. The meetings were organized into a two-part structure. The first part of the meeting was devoted to advocacy issues and the second part was reserved for storytelling. Colvin (2000) reports that as the organizations became two independent but collaborating entities, there was also a split between the advocacy activities and the storytelling component. The latter component was seen as the work of the Trauma Centre, while the former was seen to fall within the domain of Khulumani. As time went on, some Khulumani members started to get tired of just telling their stories without that having an impact on their socio-economic needs. Khulumani Western Cape developed into an independent and assertive organisation.

As already stated, Khulumani was created in order to enable victims and survivors to access the TRC and to make sure that their rights in terms of the TRC Act were protected. Throughout the TRC process Khulumani helped victims obtain and fill out applications and appeals, coordinated meetings with TRC officials, and provided individual and group counselling for victims as they delivered their testimonies. The organization hoped that the official process of truth telling would help them reclaim their dignity. However, for a variety of reasons, the TRC process has left a bitter taste in the mouths of Khulumani members. Khulumani members repeatedly point out that the TRC was a 'perpetrator-friendly' process; it betrayed victims in that the promises regarding reparations and truth recovery were never met; and they felt that they were forced to forgive perpetrators while perpetrators and beneficiaries of the apartheid system did not show any remorse.[3]

Organizational Dynamics of Khulumani Support Group

Membership of Khulumani is by way of filling out a Needs Assessment Form (NAF), outlining the details of violation(s) of human rights that the individual has suffered and what their needs are. The fact that membership is by way of self-identification as a victim or survivor, as opposed to being 'certified' by some state agency or NGO, reaffirms members' sense of agency. The NAFs are collated onto the Khulumani Apartheid Reparation Database that is used to inform and challenge government policy on reparations and its other policies relating to the needs of victims. The database was initiated in 2001 with the aim of getting a very comprehensive picture of victims in South Africa – that is, where they are located and what their most urgent needs are.

As can be expected, Khulumani members were involved in the struggle against apartheid in a variety of ways. Consider the following from Khulumani Free State (Provincial Workshop 29 and 30 September 2006):

- we were political activists and we belonged to different parties;
- we were part of the community uprisings;
- we became involved through our siblings, our relatives, and our friends;
- we were involved in trade union activities as organized workers;
- we participated in political activities at school and we joined the student political movements;
- we fought the apartheid regime through the underground movement;
- we suffered the vandalizing of our property and physical and emotional abuse;
- we advocated for the rates and rent boycotts;
- as Christians, we were victimized by white people, especially by Afrikaners.

Constitutionally, the highest decision-making structure in Khulumani is the National Steering Committee. This Committee, which also elects the Board of Trustees, is made up of representatives from different Provincial Steering Committee structures. All Khulumani regional structures, incorporating various districts, make provincial structures. It is expected that most of the work of the organization should be carried out by these local structures.

3 Despite the fact the TRC was the most resourced truth commission ever, that it held more than 100 public hearings and collected more than 22,000 testimonies from survivors, a study edited by Chapman and van der Merwe (2008) entitled 'Did the TRC Deliver?' found that the TRC failed to achieve all its objectives.

A National Contact Centre (NCC), with only a handful of full-time staff, provides support to provincial and local structures that are in charge of implementing programmes and campaigns. The organization is also quick to point out that it is not an NGO. In its 2005 strategic plan articulating the 'distinct competitiveness of Khulumani', staff made the following point: 'Most NGOs are driven by people with high standards who make decisions on behalf of others. But Khulumani has a bottom-up approach. In Khulumani survivors speak on behalf of victims'. Coming back to the issue of representation and (dis-)empowerment, as we shall see below, Khulumani has had to tread carefully to ensure that while it mobilizes on the basis of victimhood, the ultimate goal for such mobilization should be the building of a strong, vibrant collective of empowered activists.

There is general agreement amongst Khulumani staff (Khulumani, 2009) that the organization has undergone the following three phases in its development:

Phase 1: 1995–1998: support to victims to engage with the TRC and to attend its hearings, and the provision of assistance in outreach activities and in statement-taking;

Phase 2: 1998–2006: mobilization and advocacy around reparations issues, with strategic research into community reparations and policy recommendations as a means of reconstructing damaged communities and rebuilding the lives of victims and survivors;

Phase 3: 2006, ongoing:

- in-depth documentation and archival work on the lives of ordinary citizens who gave their lives in the struggle and the building of a history from 'the ground' of the struggle beyond the existing narratives of exile and incarceration;
- development of livelihoods activities using an economic rights framework;
- increased engagement in the intersections of violence and gender and the healing of sexual wounds sustained in the struggle;
- implementation of legal strategies to address key issues of impunity;
- deepened connections with efforts within the African continent to support emerging victims' groupings across the continent;
- ongoing efforts to expand the use of the public sphere by victims, as opposed to researchers/experts.

As is clear from this history, Khulumani has grown from just being a support group concerned with helping members to meaningfully engage with the TRC to being a movement concerned with issues of social justice and transitional justice, broadly defined. Since 2006 the organization has broadened its scope to deal with the felt needs of members and to deal with various issues emerging from transitional justice processes. More recently the organization has declared that its 'real goals' beyond the TRC are to make the following real: 'to end impunity, to ensure reconciliation, and to create agency and not dependency' (Khulumani, 2006a).

Today some of the organization's programmes focus on the following:

- Khulumani survivors of gender-based violence at the hands of both state agents and fellow comrades;
- victim and survivor-led community memorials;
- implementation of community reparations programmes through the securing of community investment grants for local sustainable livelihoods activities;
- addressing the direct needs of victims for prostheses, healing from torture, and adult basic literacy training;
- offering after-school care in poor township schools;
- youth participation in social reconciliation;
- getting the names of people who died in the 'mass struggle' onto the *Sikhumbuzu* wall (wall of remembrance) at Freedom Park (a state-initiated national monument and memorial).

Apart from the Khulumani Apartheid Reparation Database, a key mobilizing tool that the organization uses is its Charter for Redress. The idea behind the Charter for Redress was first mooted in 2005. The organization sought to draw inspiration from the 1955 Congress of the People's Freedom Charter – a powerful rallying document during South Africa's liberation struggle. Between July and December 2006 staff from the NCC travelled to all provincial structures as well as the majority of its regional structures to hold participatory workshops with members. The main aim of the workshop was for victims and survivors to identify the issues that in their opinions still had to be resolved by the government. At the end of the process, these were collated into a Charter (see Khulumani, 2007a). In a press statement (Khulumani, 2007b) announcing the launching of the Charter the organization stated:

> The Charter identifies the fact that reconciliation has a price – the price is the cost of redressing the terrible wrongs done to individuals and communities across South Africa. The Charter provides a checklist for all South Africans to explore what it is that victims and survivors require if they are to experience a sense of justice and to become restored to active participation in the ongoing construction of a society that benefits and includes all its citizens, not only the 45% who presently live above Minimal Living Standards.

How Successful has Khulumani Been?

Briefly the following could be said, that at the macro and policy levels, issues of reparations, sustainable livelihoods, social reconciliation, and impunity regarding apartheid era crimes remain unresolved and constitute the bases of ongoing struggle. However, success at a policy level is not the only way to assess the effectiveness of a social movement. In his study of why people participate in social movements, Klandermans (2004: 361) distinguishes between three 'dynamics of movement participation', namely instrumentality, identity, and ideology:

> *Instrumentality* refers to movement participation as an attempt to influence the social and political environment; *identity* refers to movement participation as a manifestation of identification with a group; and *ideology* refers to movement participation as a search for meaning and expression of one's views.

Assessing the success of a social movement should thus go beyond just looking at whether the movement has been able to make an impact at the policy-making level. This especially applies to identity-based movements campaigning for the rights of marginalized groups like sexual minorities, immigrants, 'the poor', and of course victims of past human rights abuses. For these movements, evaluating 'success' must go beyond an evaluation that begins and stops at the 'instrumental' level, and must seek to see how far the organization has been able to afford members the dignity and sense of worth in belonging to a group and being able to express their moral outrage.

Turning to Khulumani, its mission is to contribute to the transformation of its members from victims to active citizens. When one looks at the three phases of the movement's development one notices that in phases one and two the main objective of the organization was getting the state to recognize victims and survivors and afford relief to its members. As it became clear that this process will be a long and ongoing process of engagement and struggle, the organization shifted its attention to programmes and activities that could help in the empowerment of its members. So, although the reparations campaign is still the central public campaign of the organization, at the branch level members are involved in a number of activities that are aimed at self-empowerment so that they could become 'change-agents' within their communities. In the past two years, culminating in the recently articulated mission of the organization, the theme of 'empowerment' has featured a lot in the organization's language and slogans. For example, Khulumani's latest psychosocial workshop manual, co-developed with Marie Kilroe (2009), stresses that the aim of these workshops is individual and group empowerment. 'Empowerment processes' are defined in the manual in the following terms:

> Empowering processes are those where people create or are given opportunities to control their own destiny and influence the decisions that affect their lives. Empowering processes are a series of experiences in which individuals learn to see a closer correspondence between their goals and a sense of how to achieve them and to gain greater access to and control over resources. Efforts to gain control, access to resources,

and a critical understanding of one's sociopolitical context are fundamental aspects of empowering processes.

Organizational activities such as storytelling, group counselling for family members of those who disappeared, 'history from below', and sustainable livelihoods projects are frequently seen and assessed through an empowerment lens.

Most Khulumani members speak of the sense of pride and dignity in belonging to Khulumani when previously they felt neglected, marginalized, and disempowered. In a most vivid demonstration of the merging of 'instrumental', 'identity', and 'ideology' dynamics, one member of Khulumani has gone so far as officially naming her son – now four years old – 'Khulumani':

> *My baby Khulumani … [Laughing]. I got pregnant while being an activist in this organization. What made me name my baby Khulumani is because of this government that does not want to listen. I would like that even when he is old they must look at him as a Khulumani member, whose mother was so active trying to get into the heart of government in order to help the citizens of South Africa.* (Nomarussia Bonase, Thokoza, Interview, 10 October 2009)

Another member explains what being a member of Khulumani has meant for him:

> *Being with Khulumani has taught me a lot, especially to discover the uniqueness in victims and survivors of human rights violations…. [Interacting] with other members on a daily basis is really really significant to me because it really reminds me that sharing, through experience, [is good] hence the saying 'company in distress makes sorrow less'. So in a nutshell I would say it has been an uplifting experience throughout these past years.* (Zweli Mkhize, Braamfontein, Interview, 8 November 2007)

Jobson and Mthetwa (2009) explain this sense of agency further by asserting that in Khulumani those who 'cross over' to the side of the 'victors'

> are the ones who take the lead in organizing meetings, counselling, participating in activities that promote human rights, organizing memorials and participating in democracy enforcing activities such as information sharing, voting, protesting against the violation of rights, striving for financial independence, etc. They empower those behind them who then rise to empower others.

From my observations, I see that a lot of members now demonstrate a certain sense of empowerment and active citizenship as a result of their involvement with Khulumani. A detailed exposition of how Khulumani members demonstrate this on a day-to-day basis in their communities is impossible here. The following summary, which appears in Khulumani's organizational profile booklet (Khulumani, 2009), adequately captures some of the instances that demonstrate the acquisition of 'civic competence' through involvement with the organization:

- the monitoring of the performance of local governments through application of the Promotion of Access to Information Act (PAIA) by 15 groups across Gauteng, and now extended to the Western Cape;
- the provision of safety and security support services as active members of Community Police Forums and as trauma counsellors based at local police stations;
- the monitoring of the 2009 General Election as Election Observers, accredited and trained by the Independent Electoral Commission to provide oversight at local polling stations in all nine provinces;
- assistance to former combatants to apply for Special Pensions in recognition of the years of service given for the struggle for democracy as registered members of liberation movements;
- the monitoring of prison conditions and the treatment of prisoners as Independent Correctional Centre visitors;
- advocacy in support of victims of violations of the past as well as victims of current violations such as sexual violence;
- Khulumani members have made written and oral submissions to Parliament and to the TRC Unit (a unit set up by the state to monitor how government departments are implementing the recommendations of the TRC) in relation to issues that affect them;
- door-to-door visiting to care for vulnerable children and their caretakers when they are ill;
- organization and hosting of community commemoration and heritage-related events.

Too often experts claim that a movement that organizes on the basis of 'victimhood' perpetuates feelings of disempowerment and dependency. The history and ongoing struggle of Khulumani Support Group shows that it does not have to be so. The movement does frame its collective identity on the basis of yet-to-be-redressed violations experienced by members, not to perpetuate dependence and feelings of disempowerment, but to build a self-reliant collective movement able to challenge government and others. In this regard, I have previously referred to Khulumani members as 'bad victims' who are not willing to be wheeled out during national days, to cry, sing and tell their stories, and in Fanonian terms then 'go back to the cave' (Madlingozi, 2007).[4] Khulumani members refuse to accept their situation as

4 At an official function in February 2010 to rebury four liberation combatants who were buried in unmarked graves, a government spokesperson referred to Khulumani as 'like a toothache that refuses to go away'.

natural, and actively struggle for their legal and moral entitlements and assert their right to be heard – thus taking responsibility for their own stories and how they should be used, as we shall see below.

From 'Dependency to Agency': Refusing Representation

A typical NGO can be described as having the following characteristics: a not-for-profit organization made up of professional office bearers who draw up programmes and raise funds on behalf of certain beneficiaries or 'clients'. The structure of a typical NGO is hierarchical, with policies and other decisions being drawn up by the salaried staff members or board of directors of the organization and/or donors. NGOs do not normally have a membership base – the leadership of the organization itself identifies 'stakeholders' or 'beneficiary communities' that it would like to 'provide' or 'deliver' certain services to and to 'empower'. Critical commentators (Shivji, 2007; Neocosmos, 2004; Mutua, 2002; Wood, 1990) have argued that this kind of relationship produces dependency and inevitable passivity.

Looking at the characteristics above, it would be incorrect to say that Khulumani is an NGO. Khulumani Support Group is a national membership-based organization. This is how two members explained the concept:

> *I remember last year there was a workshop attended by the women members of Khulumani where they amended Khulumani policy. It made me very happy because it was not just members from Gauteng, there were members from all provincial structures. Which means Khulumani's constitution or policy is not just something that emanates from the [national] office, it is something that comes from provincial structures and those provincial structures are made up of people from branches. Which means everything that happens in Khulumani comes from the ground, from the communities until it reaches the national level.* (Nesta Ndebele, Braamfontein, Interview, 5 August 2007)

> *When we say Khulumani is membership-based, we mean it is an organization that is sustained by the people; its decisions are made by the people not by a clique or whoever. Even though we have a board that is directing us, its purpose is just to oversee that Khulumani is disciplined and that it follows its code of conduct. But when it comes to decision-making it is directed by its constitution and the people. The leadership is elected by the people. It begins democracy from the local level.* (Mohloaua Monnye, Bloemfontein, Interview, 24 February 2007)

Coming back to the issue of 'representation' and production of dependent victims, Khulumani members are not content with just being 'represented' by the staff at the NCC. Khulumani members constantly and consistently seek to hold the organization to account for activities done on behalf of the members. A resolution that is always adopted at provincial and national meetings relates to 'improving communication between the Contact Centre and the provincial and regional structures'. Towards this end, mobile phone text messages are sent, although infrequently, to members in order to give updates and deliver 'breaking news'. A quarterly newsletter is also sent to local structures. All staff members, not just provincial and regional coordinators, complain that members call them all the time demanding information and claiming their right to inform programmes and strategies – notwithstanding the fact that staff members receive their mandate from resolutions adopted at the AGM or National Steering Committee meetings. One staff member recently put it thus: 'working for Khulumani means you forgo your privacy. Members from all over South Africa call 24/7 demanding information and wanting to give advice.' (Zweli Mkhize, author's notes, 15 January 2010)

Most branches hold meetings every fortnight where members receive updates, mandate branch coordinators, give general strategic advice and raise grievances. At one such meeting held on 9 September 2009 in Sharpeville, members were angry that they had not received any updates in a long time from the NCC and felt that they were not consulted when important decisions were taken. Some of the comments made included the following:

> *When it comes to things where our input is needed ... we are called in but when it comes to 'luxurious' things like workshops and trips to other regions we are not needed.*
>
> *The rot is up there at the office not down here. Locally branches are working hard.*
>
> *The Board is ineffective. It must be 'fixed'.*
>
> *Even though people are volunteering, they must carry out their work in a 'straight manner'.*
>
> *You Tshepo might be a qualified lawyer or whatever but you don't know the pain of losing your loved one, having your family torn asunder. You do not know the pain!*

The move from 'dependency to agency' is both internal (between members and mandated staff) and external (between Khulumani and other civil society organizations and state agencies) and is therefore also shaping Khulumani's interaction with NGOs. Although, as we have seen above, some NGOs played a key role in shaping the initial strategic direction of the organization, over the years Khulumani has grown in confidence and now seeks to direct its engagement with others. The organization now seeks to conclude a memorandum of understanding when it enters into partnerships with civil society organizations and government agencies – setting out rights and responsibilities of each partner. The organization also has a research protocol document in which it asks potential researchers not only to submit their thesis proposals and ethics clearance from the university but also to explain how the envisioned research will make a contribution towards victim empowerment. While some transitional justice experts, eager to have an encounter with victims, have charged that these measures mean that the NCC staff are 'obstructive gatekeepers' or are holding members 'hostage', given a history of exploitation and unaccountability on the side of some researchers and NGO officials, members feel that these measures are necessary.[5]

As far as responsibility to victims' stories is concerned, increasingly members seek to alter the unequal power relations that are produced during encounters with experts. An example of this new assertiveness is this resolution from Khulumani Grahamstown:

> University students should know that copyright of any data that they will be researching belongs to Khulumani Support Group and not to the university and that any document to be documented (sic) by the university on Khulumani Support Group should benefit the latter. (Khulumani, Grahamstown, Workshop, 5 May 2007)

This repudiation of researcher–victim power relations is also evident in this call by Khulumani Mpumalanga provincial workshop participants:

> The selling of victims' stories or inviting of film companies to make documentaries about victims' stories in return for the payment of R50 or R100 should end because it destroys the dignity of victims and survivors throughout the continent.

Moving beyond the representation of its members by others, as part of its community memorialization and 'history from below' projects, the organization has started a process where branches, working with a staff member from the NCC, engage in a participatory process of telling their stories. With funding from the Rosa Luxemburg Foundation the organization is publishing booklets wherein members tell their stories. This process builds upon an earlier, mutually affirming and beneficial partnership with the South African History Archive which documented the history and stories of Khulumani members in the East Rand.

I would like to argue that the objections raised above do not only concern issues of ethics and responsibility towards victims' stories, but attempt to restructure the power relations between transitional justice entrepreneurs and victims. It must be stated, however, that the move from 'dependency' to 'agency' and the various 'gatekeeping' measures that the organization has undertaken has not meant that the organization does not collaborate with

5 To circumvent organizational protocol, some experts approach members directly, outside of organizational protection, individualizing them as victims and negating their identity as active members of a social movement.

transitional justice scholars and practitioners. Quite to the contrary, the organization is now more than ever before granting interviews and engaging in collaborative projects with others. However, in doing so the organization has endeavoured to ensure that its members' stories are 'used' in ways that do not lead to the disempowerment of members and the demobilization of the organization. This perspective can be summed up in the following email response written by Khulumani's director to a PhD candidate:

> Victims and survivors are quite able to express for themselves what needs to be done. An organization like Khulumani, values immensely the intellectual perspectives that researchers can bring, but we wish to see these researchers working from within the organization, not applying an external lens, to advance their own careers, to some extent at the expense of victims and survivors. (Marjorie Jobson, Email correspondence, 2007)

The aim of this section was not to make out that Khulumani is a movement without any internal hierarchies and tensions. As evident above, members sometimes feel that those they have given a mandate to represent them do not act in a democratic and accountable manner. On those occasions, Khulumani members are never shy to voice their dissatisfaction and prescribe corrective measures. As with any social movement, the process of building a cohesive, democratic, and participatory collective is forever an ongoing process. Nonetheless, the case study of Khulumani shows that key to the transformation and empowerment of victims is the building of their own movement that does not rely on transitional justice experts and other elites that government and others consider 'legitimate interlocutors' to speak about and for them. This is therefore key to the shift from dependency to agency, that is, victims having greater control over their encounters with expert-others and not allowing themselves and/or their stories to be used as fodder to sustain the industry and its entrepreneurs.

Conclusion

> *We have everything. When people come here, we want to know who are these people, what is their objective? What are they doing here? What do they want? Because we don't want people to come and get rich on our stories. We are not playing here. The stories are our hearts.* (Nomarussia Bonase, Thokoza, Interview, 10 October 2009)

> Politics begins when one decides not to represent victims ... but to be faithful to those events during which victims politically assert themselves. (Badiou, 1985, as cited by Neocosmos, 2007: 18)

In this article I have been concerned to argue that 'responsibility to the story' is not simply about faithfully representing what victims say or their reality –

as if that were ever possible. I have argued that 'the story' is usually the entry point towards reconstituting victims as hapless, disempowered and lacking in any rational thought and action. 'The story' is also the central device in sustaining the transitional justice industry. This industry is made up of constantly mushrooming transitional justice academic centres and think tanks, ('peer-reviewed' and subscription-based) journals and books, mail listserves, blogs, newsletters, fellowships, workshops and conferences. Most of these are based in the First World but also include big, influential Third World transnational NGOs and local informants/'point men'. A well-travelled international cadre of actors – what I have called transitional justice entrepreneurs – theorize the field; set the agenda; legitimize what constitute appropriate transitional justice norms and mechanisms; influence the flow of financial resources; assist governments in transition; invite, collaborate with and capacitate 'relevant' local NGOs and 'grassroots organizations'; and ultimately not only represent and speak for victims but 'produce' *the* victim.

Although done with the best intention in the world, the 'global apartheid' – on one side white knowledgeable experts and on the other side black victims who need saving – re-enacts and perpetuates the civilizing mission of the past centuries. Whether it is through field reports, policy papers, or academic papers and manuscripts, transitional justice experts' professional advancement is based on being able to 'speak about' and 'speak for' victims. Despite the constant references to the need to have 'victims' voice be heard', to have 'victim-centered or bottom-up transitional justice processes', and to 'victim empowerment', transitional justice scholars and practitioners have not genuinely interrogated how their programmes and interventions have led to the disempowerment or empowerment of victims.

Since 'the story' is the main point of encounter between the authoritative expert and the marginalized victim, 'responsibility to the story' should mean more than being nice to victims or adhering to rigorous scientific and ethical standards (standards set by the benign entrepreneur and her peers in academia and the NGO world). It should also be about the kinds of politics and political subjectivities reproduced by those encounters. Critical self-reflexivity, and an awareness of the power relations at play during these encounters, could be the starting point.[6] Helping to come up with an epistemology that promotes victim consciousness and is faithful to the world view of victims is also an urgent task. All of this might go a long way in

6 While the practice of 'reflexivity' might be useful in opening up avenues for the expert to come to terms with his ideological and epistemological baggage, the power relations involved in the encounter, and his complicity in perpetuating the marginality of the victim, Ratele (2008: 553, original emphasis) sounds a warning regarding the assumption of power ironically reinforced: 'At the most basic, but not unimportant, level the assumption is in how the researcher looks at the object of study, and how he is never looked at. When he remembers to look at himself, it is called **reflexivity**. Even here though, it is the researcher who is looking at himself, it is not those he is studying looking at him'.

starting a process, as Badiou (1985) counsels, by which the 'expert' becomes faithful to those events in which victims politically assert themselves, thus enabling the emergence of truly emancipatory politics constituted of equals. In order to achieve the latter goal, transitional justice experts should move away from the view that says that 'theory is white and metropolitan, while experience is black' (Gordon, 2006, cited in Pithouse, 2009: 162). This does not mean that victims possess all knowledge or truth, or that they do not deploy their victim identity opportunistically and situationally. It simply means that 'responsibility to the story' should also, if not principally, be about redistribution of resources and power. In exercising our 'responsibility to the story' we need to dismantle the trusteeship and reproduction of colonial relations; failure to do so would be 'to turn solidarity into imperialism' (Mgnxitama, 2004).

At the risk of romanticizing the organization, the work of Khulumani Support Group shows that it is possible to have victims empower themselves and reject unequal power relations that come with encounters between victims and transitional justice experts. Khulumani members endeavour to reject the culture of trusteeship and demand that their stories be used in a responsible manner, a politically responsible manner that leads to their empowerment so that they can participate in activities that concern them as equals. Khulumani members have not allowed others to simply represent them – they have chosen to 'speak out' for themselves, thereby transforming their political subjectivities into those of thinking, acting and protesting human beings. Indeed, the victim *can* speak and do much more.

Acknowledgements

An earlier version of this paper was delivered at the Taking Stock of Transitional Justice Conference, Oxford University, United Kingdom, 26–28 June 2009. Participation at the conference was made possible with kind support of the Oxford Transitional Justice Research network. Although inspired by my work at Khulumani, I have not discussed this article with anyone from the organization and as such I have written it in my personal capacity. I am grateful to the editors of this special edition for inviting me to share my thoughts and for the comments they made on an earlier draft. All errors and misrepresentations are solely mine.

References

Alcoff, L.M. 1991. 'The Problem of Speaking for Others'. *Cultural Critique*, 20 (Winter 1991–1992): 5–32.

Arthur, P. 2009. 'How "Transitions" Shaped Human Rights: A Conceptual History of Transitional Justice'. *Human Rights Quarterly*, 31 (2): 321–367.

Chapman, A.R. and van der Merwe, H. 2008. *Truth and Reconciliation in South Africa: Did the TRC Deliver?* Philadelphia: University of Pennsylvania Press.

Colvin, C. 2000. 'We Are Still Struggling: Storytelling, Reparations and Reconciliation after the TRC'. http://www.csvr.org.za/wits/papers/papcolv.htm (referenced 13 October 2008).

Hamber, B., Mosikare, N., Friedman, M., and Maepa, T. 2000. 'Speaking Out: The Role of Khulumani Victim Support Group in Dealing with the Past in South Africa'. http://www.brandonhamber.com/publications/pap_khulumani.doc (referenced 13 October 2008).

Jobson, M. 2007. Presentation to Kirchentag Centre on Africa, 9 June 2007, on Conflict Resolutions in Africa, by Dr Marjorie Jobson, Director, Khulumani Support Group.

Jobson, M. and Mthetwa, Z. 2009. The Memorialisation of Historical Crimes – Constraints, Possibilities and New Directions – the Case of the Sharpeville Massacres between 1960 and 1992. Khulumani Support Group.

Kapoor, I. 2004. 'Hyper-self-reflexive Development? Spivak on Representing the Third World "Other"'. *Third World Quarterly*, 25 (4): 627–647.

Kennedy, D. 2002. 'The International Human Rights Movement: Part of the Problem?' *Harvard Human Rights Journal*, 15: 101–125.

Khulumani Support Group. 2001. Constitution. www.khulumani.net.

———. 2006a. *Khulumani! Speak Out!* Booklet.

———. 2006b. *Reparations: The Perspective of Khulumani Support Group*. Powerpoint Presentation.

———. 2007a. *Charter for Redress*.

———. 2007b. 'Khulumani Support Group Launches its Charter for Redress'. 13 August 2007 Press Statement.

———. 2009. *Organizational Profile*.

Kilroe, M. 2009. Psychosocial Workshop Manual: Facilitators' Manual for Khulumani Support Group.

Klandermans, B. 2004. 'The Demand and Supply of Participation: Social-Psychological Correlates of Participation in Social Movements'. In: D.A. Snow, S.A. Soule, and H. Kriesi (eds). *The Blackwell Companion to Social Movements*. Malden, MA: Blackwell Publishing: 360–379.

Krog, A., Mpolweni, N., and Ratele, K. 2009. *There was this Goat: Investigating the Truth Commission Testimony of Notrose Nobomvu Konile*. Pietermaritzburg: University of KwaZulu–Natal Press.

Lundy, P. and McGovern, M. 2008. 'Whose Justice? Rethinking Transitional Justice from the Bottom Up'. *Journal of Law and Society*, 35 (2): 265–292.

Madlingozi, T. 2007. 'Good Victims, Bad Victims: Apartheid Beneficiaries, Victims and the Struggle for Social Justice'. In: W. Le Roux and K. Van Marle (eds). *Law, Memory and Apartheid: Ten Years after AZAPO v President of South Africa*. Pretoria: Pretoria University Law Press: 107–126.

McEvoy, K. 2007. 'Beyond Legalism: Towards a Thicker Understanding of Transitional Justice'. *Journal of Law and Society*, 34 (4): 411–440.

Meister, R. 2002. 'Human Rights and the Politics of Victimhood'. *Ethics and International Affairs*, 16 (2): 91–106.

Mngxitama, A. 2004. 'Let Black Voices Speak for the Voiceless'. *Mail and Guardian Online*, 22 June 2004.

Mutua, M. 2002. *Human Rights: A Political and Cultural Critique*. Philadelphia: University of Pennsylvania Press.

Neocosmos, M. 2004. 'The State of the Post-Apartheid State: The Poverty of Critique on the South African Left'. *Politeia*, 23 (3): 137–157.

———. 2006. 'Can a Human Rights Culture Enable Emancipation? Clearing the Theoretical Ground for the Renewal of a Critical Sociology'. *South African Review of Sociology*, 37 (2): 356–378.

———. 2007. 'Civil Society, Citizenship and the Politics of the (Im)possible: Rethinking Militancy in Africa Today'. http://www.abahlali.org/files/Neocosmos%202007%20citizenship%20and%20politics.pdf (referenced 15 June 2009).

Pithouse, R. 2009. 'Shifting the Ground of Reason'. In: H. Jacklin, and P. Vale (eds). *Re-imagining the Social in South Africa: Critique, Theory and Post-apartheid Society*. Pietermaritzburg: University of KwaZulu–Natal Press: 141–175.

Ratele, K. 2008. 'Postcolonial African Methods and Interpretation'. In: M.T. Blanche, K. Durrheim, and D. Painter (eds). *Research in Practice: Applied Methods for the Social Sciences*. Rondebosch: University of Cape Town Press: 538–555.

Razack, S.H. 2007. 'Stealing the Pain of Others: Reflections on Canadian Humanitarian Responses'. *Review of Education, Pedagogy, and Cultural Studies*, 29 (4): 375–394.

Shivji, I.G. 2007. *Silences in NGO Discourse: The Role and Future of NGOs in Africa*. Oxford: Fahamu.

Spivak, G.C. 1988. 'Can the Subaltern Speak?' http://www.mcgill.ca/files/crclaw-discourse/Can_the_subaltern_speak.pdf (referenced 15 March 2010).

Wood, E.M. 1990. 'The Uses and Abuses of "Civil Society"'. *Socialist Register*, 26 (1990): 60–84.

Interviews

Nomarussia Bonase, Thokoza 10 October 2009
Zweli Mkhize, Braamfontein 8 November 2007
Mohloaua Monnye, Bloemfontein 24 February 2007
Nesta Ndebele, Braamfontein 5 August 2007

28

Impact Assessment, Not Evaluation: Defining a Limited Role for Positivism in the Study of Transitional Justice

Geoff Dancy

Abstract

Discussions of impact assessment and evaluation are the newest installment in the brief history of the field of transitional justice. Noticeably, a positivist logic of inference is being favored in these discussions. This article argues that a distinction should be made between impact assessment and evaluation, and that the role of positivist approaches is best conceived of as contributing to the former. Evaluation, on the other hand, should be undertaken by those analysts willing to embrace and promote normative ideals, to which they compare practices on the ground. This type of 'comparison to the ideal' is the province of interpretive-critical logics of inference. After carving out a modest role for positivism, the article presents a quantitative analysis of transitional justice impact to show how such a logic is good for grounding observers' expectations for different types of transitional cases. The analysis demonstrates that transitional justice mechanisms do not have a uniquely destabilizing effect across such cases. The article concludes with a syncretist view – that interpretive, ideal-based evaluations should proceed alongside positivist impact assessments.

Introduction

Practices deployed and administered in the name of justice do not readily lend themselves to simple empirical evaluation. Justice is not easily observed or measured, its attached meanings and symbols cannot escape cultural particularity and it will always be the controversial subject of ideological and political contestation, rather than causal certitudes. This does not mean that justice is not among the worthiest of considerations, or that it should be thrown into the rubbish bin with other 'hopelessly naïve' utopic aims. What it does mean is that, as Socrates intimates in an answer to a query posed by Glaucon, justice should not be considered solely in consequentialist terms.[1] Justice is good in itself as well as because of its salutary consequences. Using the language of contemporary social theory, one might further extrapolate that justice, like other goods such as equality or emancipation, will never be a singular outcome but is an ongoing relational process involving an

[1] Socrates states, 'I, for my part, suppose . . . that [justice] belongs in the finest kind [of good], which the man who is going to be blessed should like both for itself and what comes out of it.' Allan Bloom, trans., *The Republic of Plato*, 2nd ed. (New York: Basic Books, 1991), 36.

exchange between people's 'ideals' and the structural 'realities' that limit action.[2] Social scientific inquiry tends repeatedly to elide and rediscover these lessons, and the study of transitional justice is no exception.

Since its inception, the field of transitional justice has moved seamlessly from a cataloging of those structural realities within political transitions that harness the possibilities for victims' justice,[3] to functionalist renderings that assert the social purpose of transitional justice mechanisms[4] and back to a reflective pessimism concerning the ability of those limited mechanisms to realize ideals.[5] Now, two decades after transitional justice was discursively born, the talk is of evaluation.[6] How do we know if transitional justice efforts have 'worked'? How might practitioners show donors a return on their investments? I put forth in this article that there are roles for both positivist and interpretive modes of thinking in addressing these and related questions. However, positivist approaches are of late being advertised as the premier way to evaluate transitional justice, with too much emphasis being placed on causal generalization at the expense of critical political judgments. This has the paradoxical effect of placing too big a burden on useful but constrained analytical techniques. After outlining the limits of a positivist approach to transitional justice, I gesture toward a quantitative, consequentialist assessment of transitional justice impact that embraces its own inadequacies. I do so for the expressed purpose of not only filling holes left by the literature on transitional justice impact but also laying the foundation for a circumscribed positivist agenda within the field.

I divide this article into five remaining sections. The second section will draw a crucial distinction between evaluation and impact assessment of complex transitional justice interventions. Where questions of evaluation imply a progressive, means–end instrumentalism, questions of impact can be more agnostic as to the achievement of ideals. The third section will argue that this first distinction can

[2] E.H. Carr, *The Twenty Years' Crisis, 1919–1939*, ed. Michael Cox (Basingstoke: Palgrave Macmillan, 2001).

[3] Guillermo A. O'Donnell, Philippe C. Schmitter and Laurence Whitehead, *Transitions from Authoritarian Rule: Comparative Perspectives* (Baltimore, MD: Johns Hopkins University Press, 1986); Samuel P. Huntington, *The Third Wave: Democratization in the Late Twentieth Century* (Norman, OK: University of Oklahoma Press, 1991); Jose Zalaquett, 'Balancing Ethical Imperatives against Political Constraints: The Dilemma of New Democracies Confronting Past Human Rights Violations,' in *Transitional Justice: How Emerging Democracies Reckon with Former Regimes*, ed. Neil J. Kritz (Washington, DC: US Institute of Peace Press, 1995).

[4] Margaret L. Popkin and Naomi Roht-Arriaza, 'Truth as Justice: Investigatory Commissions in Latin America,' *Law and Social Inquiry* 20(1) (1995): 79–116; Robert I. Rotberg and Dennis Thompson, eds., *Truth v. Justice: The Morality of Truth Commissions* (Princeton, NJ: Princeton University Press, 2000); Priscilla B. Hayner, *Unspeakable Truths: Confronting State Terror and Atrocities* (New York: Routledge, 2001).

[5] David Mendeloff, 'Truth-Seeking, Truth-Telling, and Postconflict Peacebuilding: Curb the Enthusiasm?' *International Studies Review* 6(3) (2004): 355–380; Gary J. Bass, *Stay the Hand of Vengeance: The Politics of War Crimes Tribunals* (Princeton, NJ: Princeton University Press, 2000); Jelena Subotić, *Hijacked Justice: Dealing with the Past in the Balkans* (Ithaca, NY: Cornell University Press, 2009).

[6] For a comprehensive history of the transitional justice 'subfield,' see, Paige Arthur, 'How "Transitions" Reshaped Human Rights: A Conceptual History of Transitional Justice,' *Human Rights Quarterly* 31(2) (2009): 321–367.

be grafted onto a split between positivism and interpretive-critical epistemologies, one that finds expression in the corpus of transitional justice research. Using a 2008 report funded by the Canadian government, the section will also present evidence of positivism's newfound popularity and limitations. In the fourth section, I will attempt to define the role of positivist approaches in the study of transitional justice. Part of this defense will hinge on my own syncretist understanding of diverse ways of knowing. In the fifth section, I will present new summary statistics on transitional cases and accompanying transitional justice interventions. These statistics show that those cases in which we observe transitional justice, on average, are not more likely to witness negative impacts, though results vary by type of transition. In the sixth and concluding section, I will offer guiding principles for future research.

Evaluation versus Impact Assessment

Before 1990, only 10 countries in the world had prosecuted human rights violators and only five had formed truth commissions to investigate their troubled pasts. By 2007, these figures had spiked: trials had been initiated for 59 state jurisdictions and at least one official truth-seeking body had been established in 33 states.[7] With these upward trends, transitional justice shifted from a narrow and specialized area of advocacy to the strategic forefront of transnational democratic state building, rule-of-law promotion and postconflict peacebuilding. Codifying this transformation, organs of the UN have in the last half-decade started to commission reports on 'best practices' in transitional justice.[8] A definitive statement came with the publication of a report on transitional justice and rule of law by the secretary-general in 2004, which was followed by the unofficial delegation of UN operations concerning transitional justice to the Office of the High Commissioner for Human Rights (OHCHR) in 2006.[9] Transitional justice remains one of OHCHR's foremost priorities.[10]

By the end of the 1990s, claims concerning the potential worth of trials and truth commissions abounded. Many times such claims were scaffolded onto moral abstractions, analogies about social health and hidden assumptions about the systematic operation of the body politic. 'Just as wounds fester when they are not exposed to the open air,' one scholar wrote, 'so unacknowledged injustice can

[7] This article will make use of a dataset compiled by the author. See, Geoff Dancy, 'Choice and Consequence in Strategies of Transitional Justice,' in *The Handbook of the Political Economy of War*, ed. Christopher J. Coyne and Rachel L. Mathers (Chaltenham: Edward Elgar Publishing, forthcoming).

[8] See, the UN secretary-general's 'The Rule of Law and Transitional Justice in Conflict and Postconflict States,' UN doc. S/2004/616 (23 August 2004). See also, UN, *Guidance Note of the Secretary-General: United Nations Approach to Transitional Justice* (March 2010).

[9] See, Office of the High Commissioner for Human Rights, *Strategic Management Plan, 2008–2009* (2009).

[10] See, 'Address by Ms. Navanethem Pillay, United Nations High Commissioner for Human Rights' (address given at the annual conference, FDFA Political Affairs Division IV, Human Security, Geneva, Switzerland, 15 October 2009).

poison societies and produce cycles of distrust, hatred, and violence.'[11] Left unclear, however, were the reasons that such claims might be revealed to be coherent or correspondent to happenings in a variety of contexts.[12] As it should be, the use of transitional justice mechanisms has invited calls for greater scrutiny and general skepticism toward 'templatization.' What has become apparent is that practice has largely escaped reflection, and that observers must start to take stock of common sense undertakings. Have trials and truth commissions been influential? Have they really worked?

Such questions are normally brought to bear in policy discussions regarding transitional justice 'impact assessment' or 'evaluation.'[13] These terms are often used interchangeably or even combined into 'impact evaluation.'[14] However subtle the differences in wording, they are important.[15] Evaluation involves, most broadly, determining 'the worth of a thing.'[16] More specifically, the definition could be extended to include 'assessing the strengths and weaknesses of programs, policies, personnel, products, and organizations to improve their effectiveness.'[17] Importantly, such an appraisal must take place based on a list of chosen criteria, or imposed metrics. Impact assessment, meanwhile, is the 'tracking of change as it relates to an identifiable source or set of factors.'[18] Whereas an evaluation must first delineate how and on what basis certain intentionally produced features of transitional justice mechanisms are going to be assessed, an impact assessment must simply monitor the externalities associated with their operation.[19] To draw on an analogy, if a rock were dropped in a pond, impact assessment would mean noting the dimensions of the rock and documenting the amplitude and frequency of the ripples it produces. Evaluation would be much the same, but with a key addition: it would assess how *well* the rock produced the desired effect of creating waves.

[11] Elizabeth Kiss, 'Moral Ambition with and Beyond Political Constraints: Reflections on Restorative Justice,' in Rotberg and Thompson, supra n 4 at 72.

[12] An oft-cited example is David Mendeloff's 14-point problematization of the notion that truth seeking contributes to postconflict peacebuilding. Mendeloff, supra n 5.

[13] Hugo van der Merwe, Victoria Baxter and Audrey R. Chapman, eds., *Assessing the Impact of Transitional Justice: Challenges for Empirical Research* (Washington, DC: US Institute of Peace Press, 2009).

[14] Oskar N.T. Thoms, James Ron and Roland Paris, *The Effects of Transitional Justice Mechanisms: A Summary of Empirical Research Findings and Implications for Analysts and Practitioners* (Ottawa: Centre for International Policy Studies, University of Ottawa, 2008).

[15] I am not the first to note a distinction. See, Emery Brusset, 'Suggestions for the Evaluation of Transitional Justice,' International Development Research Centre PowerPoint presentation (August 2008), http://www.idrc.ca/en/ev-114543-201-1-DO_TOPIC.html (accessed 10 August 2010).

[16] Blaine R. Worthen, 'Program Evaluation,' in *The International Encyclopedia of Educational Evaluation*, ed. Herbert J. Walberg and Geneva D. Haertel (New York: Pergamon Press, 1990), 42.

[17] See, American Evaluation Association, 'About Us,' http://www.eval.org/aboutus/organization/aboutus.asp (accessed 10 August 2010).

[18] Brusset, supra n 15.

[19] Some literature on professional evaluation would reject this distinction. 'Goal-free evaluation,' for example, is an approach very close to what I call impact assessment. In goal-free evaluation, an evaluator remains purposefully ignorant of the program's goals; this way, (s)he can measure the actual outcomes of the program without bias. See, Blaine R. Worthen and James R. Sanders, *Educational Evaluation: Theory and Practice* (Worthington, OH: Charles A. Jones Publishing, 1973).

For 'simple' problems, like producing clean drinking water, evaluation is straightforward and can proceed on the basis of precise measurement.[20] For what might be referred to as 'complex' social problems – which reject simple recipes for action, must be sensitive to unique contexts and are always infused with a degree of uncertainty – evaluation becomes much more difficult.[21] Transitional justice is in the latter category.[22] In such cases, evaluation implies judgment of the goal-reaching capabilities of mechanisms and requires two basic activities: first, selection of a set of appropriate objectives toward which a body aims (that is, establishment of performance criteria) and, second, review and judgment of a body's performance based on those criteria. A great deal of nuance exists in literature on evaluation science, but in reference to transitional justice, I split evaluation into two stages, the process stage and the outcome stage.[23] Process-based evaluation involves the quality of actions and enactments undertaken by a transitional justice mechanism. An evaluator might assess whether methods of investigation are appropriately suited to obtaining accurate information on human rights violations committed in the past.[24] He or she might also judge, positively or negatively, whether trial and truth-seeking procedures are fair to both victim and perpetrator elements. Furthermore, process-oriented program directors and consultants can attempt 'participatory evaluation,' wherein focus turns to involving targeted populations, building capacity and producing local ownership.[25] Alternatively, outcome evaluations focus on a mechanism's overall production or nonproduction of aimed-for goals. A majority of writings on transitional justice, at least implicitly, present this second type based on aspirational notions of what ought to be. In this vein, authors have tended to ask questions such as, 'Is transitional justice just?' or, 'When does reconciliation turn into a denial of justice?'[26]

An impact assessment performs different tasks. Instead of necessarily judging based on a specific set of performance-based criteria, those who assess the impact of institutions engage in two different activities: first, they isolate those social or political factors that might plausibly be disrupted or altered by the operation of the institution and, second, they attempt to explain how and why institutions

[20] The World Health Organization has actually calculated \$3–\$34 returns for each dollar invested in clean water. See, UN Educational, Scientific and Cultural Organization, *Third UN World Water Development Report: Water in a Changing World* (2009).

[21] I thank Colleen Duggan for alerting me to the complex–simple distinction.

[22] On simple, complicated and complex problems, see, Sholom Glouberman and Brenda Zimmerman, 'Complicated and Complex Systems: What Would Successful Reform of Medicare Look Like?' Commission on the Future of Health Care in Canada Discussion Paper No. 8 (July 2002).

[23] Phuong Pham and Patrick Vinck, 'Empirical Research and the Development and Assessment of Transitional Justice Mechanisms,' *International Journal of Transitional Justice* 1(2) (2007): 231–248.

[24] Patrick R. Ball and Audrey Chapman. 'The Truth of Truth Commissions: Comparative Lessons from Haiti, South Africa, and Guatemala,' *Human Rights Quarterly* 23(1) (2001): 1–43.

[25] On participatory evaluation, see, Ann Zukoski and Mia Luluquisen, 'Participatory Evaluation: What Is It? Why Do It? What Are the Challenges?' *Community-Based Public Health Policy and Practice* 5 (April 2002), http://depts.washington.edu/ccph/pdf_files/Evaluation.pdf.

[26] Charles T. Call, 'Is Transitional Justice Really Just?' *Brown Journal of World Affairs* 11(1) (2004): 101–113; Mahmood Mamdani, 'When Does Reconciliation Turn into a Denial of Justice?' Sam Nolutshungu Memorial Lecture Series 15 (1988).

did or did not produce change in those factors. For example, an impact assessor might analyze how the pursuit of domestic trials further polarizes existing social cleavages, affects levels of party support or leads to increased public confidence in courts. Implied in this type of assessment is a counterfactual judgment about what might have happened in the absence of transitional justice efforts. In the world of development assistance, one tool of such impact assessment increasingly advocated is randomized control trials (RCTs). An RCT applies a program to one sector of the population and then compares it to a similar but untreated control sector in order to observe impacts. Because they involve direct social experimentation, RCTs have been criticized on ethical and methodological grounds.[27] Moreover, for complex interventions like transitional justice, which necessitate political negotiation prior to establishment and usually aspire to have the greatest impact possible across the population, the selective application required by RCTs seems both less plausible and less desirable. Instead of manufacturing social experiments, transitional justice impact assessors must study what the world gives them.

In transitional justice interventions, evaluation and impact assessment are highly related, but differences between the two are real. Impact assessment does not deal well with processes, primarily because it is oriented toward those social phenomena surrounding proceedings, bracketing the proceedings themselves. In comparison, evaluators might explicitly establish at the outset various process-based aims of a transitional justice mechanism, such as to engage in fair, equal, nonselective and nonretrospective indictments; to maintain appropriate evidence collection methodologies; or to maintain linkages to community-based, local efforts at reconciliation. Efforts at evaluation typically entail a greater degree of normativity, in addition to what Kathryn Sikkink refers to as 'comparison to the ideal.'[28] In contrast to examining positive or negative *externalities* of a process, the act of developing performance metrics is almost by its very nature awash in normative commitments. The evaluator might ask whether transitional justice mechanisms provide justice for victims and their families, generate social cohesion and reconciliation, establish the rule of law and democracy, promote a positive 'culture of human rights' or nudge transitional states in the direction of development.[29]

[27] See, Angus Deaton, *Instruments of Development: Randomization in the Tropics, and the Search for the Elusive Keys to Economic Development* (Princeton, NJ: Center for Health and Wellbeing, Princeton University, 2009); William Easterly, 'Development Experiments: Ethical? Feasible? Useful?' Aidwatch blog (16 July 2009), http://aidwatchers.com/2009/07/development-experiments-ethical-feasible-useful/ (accessed 10 August 2010).

[28] Kathryn Sikkink, 'The Role of Consequences, Comparison, and Counterfactuals in Constructivist Ethical Thought,' in *Moral Limit and Possibility in World Politics*, ed. Richard M. Price (New York: Cambridge University Press, 2008), 103.

[29] On social cohesion and reconciliation, see, Mark R. Amstutz, *The Healing of Nations: The Promise and Limits of Political Forgiveness* (Lanham, MD: Rowman and Littlefield Publishers, 2005). On rule of law and democracy, see, A. James McAdams, ed., *Transitional Justice and the Rule of Law in New Democracies* (Notre Dame, IN: University of Notre Dame Press, 1997). On the culture of human rights, see, Rotberg and Thompson, supra n 4. On development, see, Pablo de Greiff and Roger Duthie, eds., *Transitional Justice and Development: Making Connections* (New York: International Center for Transitional Justice, 2009); 'Special Issue: Transitional Justice and Development,' *International Journal of Transitional Justice* 2(3) (2008).

Each of these questions presents a goal construct that is by nature normative and progressively oriented toward a teleological social aim.[30]

Comparison to the Ideal

Outcome-based evaluations often carry with them ethical predispositions on notoriously difficult-to-define social concepts, all of which are objects of widespread political contestation. Take rule of law, for example. While it is one of the primary organizing principles of contemporary global public policy, and of transitional justice specifically, it has also been the subject of spectacular definitional disagreement, international legal proselytizing and UN turf wars.[31] To say, for example, that building rule of law should be a goal of transitional justice is a statement of an ideal, the content of which needs to be filled with a particular instrumentalism. This act of filling is the establishment of evaluative criteria. Ideal-based comparisons and judgments can be the stuff of engaged social and political activism, and of 'emancipatory' critical theorizing.[32] However, of particular concern to practitioners of transitional justice is the fact that a wide variety of ideals can be ushered into discussions of evaluation. One occluded feature of this variety is that observers typically orient their focus toward a level of societal structure that they prefer to be targeted by transitional justice efforts. In other words, no consensus exists over *for what* and *for whom* transitional justice is pursued.

Two general groups of perspectives have formed around these issues. One consists of those who highlight top-down or state-level goals. In this group, some argue that transitional justice mechanisms should serve apparatuses of state authority. This evaluative approach, characteristic among self-described 'realists,' promotes the stability of rule over the pursuit of victim-based justice,[33] holding that if justice mechanisms do not somehow buttress order, they should be scrapped or highly modified. Another perspective is that transitional justice should contribute to the consolidation of newly installed democratic regimes. If mechanisms can encourage societal actors to play by the rules of the democratic game, to engage *pro forma* in participatory and electoral politics, then they have served their purpose of promoting liberal democracy. A third perspective is that the mechanisms should

[30] See, Colm Campbell and Catherine Turner, 'Utopia and the Doubters: Truth, Transition, and the Law,' *Legal Studies* 28(3) (2008): 374–395. The authors make a similar point that many times claims about transitional justice are utopic in nature.

[31] See, Thomas Carothers, 'The Rule of Law Revival,' *Foreign Affairs* 77(2) (1998): 95–106. See also, Brian Z. Tamanaha, *On the Rule of Law: History, Politics, Theory* (Cambridge: Cambridge University Press, 2004). On the UN's approach to rule of law, some might see progress in the recent establishment of the Rule of Law Coordination and Resource Group under the auspices of the deputy secretary-general. Still, that such an effort is being made to coordinate across nine different operational entities hints that, until recently, various UN strategies concerning rule of law were largely program specific, disconnected and at times in disagreement.

[32] See, 'The Tasks of Emancipatory Social Science,' in Erik Olin Wright, *Envisioning Real Utopias* (New York: Verso, 2010).

[33] See, Huntington, supra n 3. See also, Jack Snyder and Leslie Vinjamuri, 'Trials and Errors: Principle and Pragmatism in Strategies of International Justice,' *International Security* 28(3) (2003–2004): 5–44; Roland Paris, *At War's End: Building Peace after Civil Conflict* (Cambridge: Cambridge University Press, 2004).

foster conflict resolution between rival groups in society and that justice efforts pay insofar as they produce reconciliation and discourage recourse to political violence.[34]

The second group of perspectives privileges a bottom-up approach.[35] Some see the purpose of justice properly conceived to be the alteration of unfair or unequal relations between groups in localized contexts. In places like Guatemala, where formerly victimized indigenous populations are still being marginalized, justice cannot rightly be said to exist.[36] Others focus on individuals' perceptions of justice and the ways in which people may or may not look favorably on the operation of transitional justice mechanisms.[37] Many observers and survey researchers highlight people's testimonies and recorded opinions, implicitly advancing evaluative criteria that are simultaneously individualistic and majoritarian. According to them, if samples of the targeted population agree in their positive evaluations, then transitional justice must have been served. If not, it must have been left wanting.[38]

Impact assessors are less drawn to ideal comparisons and more drawn to comparison across actual cases that can be grouped together. A sample question would be whether Northern Ireland's 'inquiries' into the past drummed up a good deal less political mobilization than South African processes of reconciliation. Another would be whether postconflict states that have instituted some variant of transitional justice are more vulnerable to the resumption of violence between armed groups. The list of questions in this vein is endless, but impact assessments hinge on two assumptions. The first is that empirical social phenomena can be divvied up into observable things (variables) that exhibit similar characteristics. The second is that the impact of some variables on other variables can be studied within similar contexts, out of which one might come to lessons applicable across all such contexts. These assumptions, generally, are epistemological, in that they reflect an approach to knowing. Specifically, they are positivist. Positivist thinking, I argue in the following section, is increasingly being given the nod in literature on transitional justice evaluation. However, as I will try to illuminate, the positivist logic

34 William J. Long and Peter Brecke, *War and Reconciliation: Reason and Emotion in Conflict Resolution* (Cambridge, MA: MIT Press, 2003). See also, Tom Hadden, 'Human Rights and Conflict Resolution,' in *Judges, Transition, and Human Rights*, ed. John Morison, Kieran McEvoy and Gordon Anthony (Oxford: Oxford University Press, 2008).

35 For a similar effort at splitting the literature by which level it highlights, see, van der Merwe, Baxter and Chapman, supra n 13.

36 Laura Arriaza and Naomi Roht-Arriaza, 'Social Reconstruction as a Local Process,' *International Journal of Transitional Justice* 2(2) (2008): 152–172.

37 See, generally, the work of James Gibson, including James L. Gibson, 'Does Truth Lead to Reconciliation? Testing the Causal Assumptions of the South African Truth and Reconciliation Process,' *American Journal of Political Science* 48(2) (2004): 201–217; James L. Gibson, Jeffrey Sonis and Sokhom Hean, 'Cambodians' Support for the Rule of Law on the Eve of the Khmer Rouge Trials,' *International Journal of Transitional Justice* 4(3) (2010): 377–396.

38 See, for example, David Backer, 'Evaluating Transitional Justice in South Africa from a Victims' Perspective,' http://sitemaker.umich.edu/backer/files/backer.saio.article.pdf (accessed 10 August 2010); David Backer, 'Watching a Bargain Unravel? A Panel Study of Victims' Attitudes about Transitional Justice in Cape Town, South Africa,' *International Journal of Transitional Justice* 4(3) (2010): 443–456.

of inference is more appropriately used when in the service of impact assessment, not of evaluation based on ideals.

Positivism and Interpretivism in the Field of Transitional Justice

Positivism is not the same as quantitative social science, though positivist thinking is usually conflated with numeracy.[39] The latter is almost always in service of the former, but it is common to have positivist work that avoids complex statistical models or sticks to comparisons across only a few cases.[40] In other words, various methods can employ a positivist logic of inference. These include formal modeling, survey research, cross-case statistical research, large-*n* case comparisons and small-*n* qualitative case analysis.[41] What these all share is a belief in unit homogeneity – that unit groups can be formed out of social facts like truth commissions, center-right parties, military regimes or spoilers – and in the ability to study such units across contexts – with spoilers in Argentina seen as categorically similar to those in Uganda. Moreover, in positivism's contemporary incarnation, proving between-variable causality is seen as the *sine qua non* of good research.[42] This logic of inference may be contrasted with logics that, at risk of oversimplifying, may be called interpretive-critical.

Interpretive and critical logics of inference resist the above assumptions, arguing that units are hardly ever alike (for example, no two truth commissions are the same) and, more important, that cultural contexts are so vastly different that even if units were alike, they would have effects that are bound by particular meanings. Moreover, such thinking has the added benefit of casting light on the way people understand themselves (subjectivity), the way they share understandings (intersubjectivity) and the way disparate understandings of the same symbols often collide. In this respect, interpretivists can actually study the ways in which positivist assumptions produce subjectivities or, more negatively, ingrain certain relations of domination.[43] Methodologically, interpretivism often involves hermeneutical 'textual' analysis that aims at promoting an understanding of difference. Where positivism aims at emphasizing patterns and continuity to the subordination of deviation, interpretivism aims at understanding the ways in which deviation can be construed as purposive or meaningful.

39 David Dessler, 'The Positivist-Interpretivist Controversy,' *Qualitative Methods* 1(2) (2003): 21–24.

40 See, Gary King, Robert Keohane and Sidney Verba, *Designing Social Inquiry: Scientific Inference in Qualitative Research* (Princeton, NJ: Princeton University Press, 1994).

41 See, Oskar N.T. Thoms, James Ron and Roland Paris, 'State-Level Effects of Transitional Justice: What Do We Know?' *International Journal of Transitional Justice* 4(3) (2010): 329–354.

42 For an excellent general history description of positivism, see, Fred Chernoff, *Theory and Metatheory in International Relations: Concepts and Contending* (New York: Palgrave Macmillan, 2007). See also, James Johnson, 'Consequences of Positivism: A Pragmatist Assessment,' *Comparative Political Studies* 39(2) (2006): 224–252.

43 See, for example, Steve Smith, 'The United States and the Discipline of International Relations: "Hegemonic Country, Hegemonic Discipline,"' *International Studies Review* 4(2) (2003): 67–85.

Hard boundaries cannot be drawn around these logics of inference, and methodological allegiances do not have to form around such binaries. Positivism and interpretivism exist on a continuum, and methods can be combined or mixed in service of either.[44] However, it would be naïve to deny that preferences for the relative intellectual merits of generalization over complication exist. In fact, practitioners in peacebuilding and transitional justice have taken note of this schism, one that Reina Neufeldt has referred to as pitting 'logical frameworkers' against 'complex circlers.'[45] Where the former group 'favors linear, cause and effect thinking, and attempts to use easily measurable indicators which are thought to apply to a variety of situations,' the latter thinks that 'due to the complexity of development, or in this case, transitional, settings, it is impossible to create a simple framework that can be used to evaluate all transitional justice work.'[46]

The split is all too present in current transitional justice research. A new vanguard of cross-national comparative research is performing the task of Neufeldt's logical frameworkers, weighing out the independent and interactive impacts of transitional justice measures on aggregated state features like democratic institutionalization, human rights compliance and absence of violent conflict. Some have generated positive impact assessments. In a study of 93 democratizing countries, Hunjoon Kim and Kathryn Sikkink find that trials drive down quantitatively measured repression levels, even controlling for the presence of violent conflict.[47] The authors further argue that, theoretically, the threat of future trials serves to deter leaders from considering repressive policies. On the other side are those that issue a negative impact assessment based on the unnecessary risks accountability poses to peace. Most notably, Jack Snyder and Leslie Vinjamuri have issued an incisive statement against trials, claiming that they impose avoidable risks during peace processes by antagonizing potential spoilers.[48] In their analysis of 32 postconflict cases, they also write that whatever successes have been assigned to truth commissions are more likely attributable to amnesties, which facilitate bargaining between fighting groups.[49] Other large-*n* analyses have produced mixed results, showing for example that truth commissions correlate with lower human

[44] Some wonder, however, whether quantitative methods can be used effectively in interpretive research. See, Laura Stoker, 'Is It Possible to Do Quantitative Survey Research in an Interpretive Way?' *Qualitative Methods* 1(2) (2003): 13–16.

[45] Reina C. Neufeldt, *"Frameworkers" and "Circlers" – Exploring Assumptions in Peace and Conflict Impact Assessment* (Berlin: Berghof Research Center for Constructive Conflict Management, 2007).

[46] See, International Center for Transitional Justice (ICTJ) and UK Department for International Development (DFID), 'Donor Strategies for Transitional Justice: Taking Stock and Moving Forward' (report of the seminar, 'Donor Strategies for Transitional Justice: Taking Stock and Moving Forward,' London, UK, 15–17 October 2007).

[47] Hunjoon Kim and Kathryn Sikkink, 'Explaining the Deterrence Effect of Human Rights Prosecutions for Transitional Countries,' *International Studies Quarterly* (forthcoming).

[48] See, Snyder and Vinjamuri, supra n 33.

[49] Louise Mallinder comes to a similar conclusion about the use of amnesties in particular. In a magisterial work, she carefully categorizes amnesty types while also arguing that they can be put to use in particular strategic contexts to facilitate demobilization and power-sharing arrangements. See, Louise Mallinder, *Amnesty, Human Rights and Political Transition: Bridging the Peace and Justice Divide* (Oxford: Hart Publishing, 2008).

rights scores when established in isolation, and that trials combined with amnesties are linked to more positive democracy and human rights practices.[50]

On the interpretive side are a large and growing mass of rich, context-specific studies that are pushing back against such attempts at generalization. Notable examples include Greg Grandin's critical reading of Latin American experiences with liberalism-inspired truth commissions, which worked to suppress the memory of political, leftist challenges that gave rise to internal conflicts in favor of simplistic, parable histories.[51] Another is Rosalind Shaw's ethnographic work on the localization of a global truth regime in Sierra Leone, which faced the complication that many survivors found forgetting to be paramount to truth in the search for reconciliation.[52] A third is Christine Bell, Colm Campbell and Fionnuala Ní Aoláin's reading of hegemony in the US' 'yoking' of transitional justice to the 'war on terror' in Iraq.[53] Related to this is Catherine Turner's concern that transitional justice practice, when linked to the recognitional legitimacy of states, unfolds in a way that supports a liberal, neoimperial order.[54] A fourth place to look for emblematic interpretive-critical works is in feminist studies of transitional justice, which have demonstrated how justice and reconciliation practices, among other things, entrench gendered, masculinist discourses.[55] Although their works are widely disparate, these authors share a desire to ignore or repulse grand theories about the ability of justice efforts to 'work.' To determine if they 'work,' one must first theorize who they serve and document the way mechanisms are understood in their given historical and discursive contexts.

Unfortunately, the positivist–interpretivist divide has three important drawbacks for the complex field of transitional justice. First, perhaps because positivism reinforces political-economic statist thinking with its emphasis on control and the elimination of disruptions to order, it is generally favored by government actors

[50] Eric Brahm, 'Uncovering the Truth: Examining Truth Commission Success and Impact,' *International Studies Perspectives* 8(1) (2007): 16–35. Tricia D. Olsen, Leigh A. Payne, and Andrew G. Reiter, *Transitional Justice in the Balance: Comparing Processes, Weighing Efficacy* (Washington, DC: US Institute of Peace Press, 2010). On the truth commission finding, see, Eric Wiebelhaus-Brahm, *Truth Commissions and Transitional Societies: The Impact on Human Rights and Democracy* (London: Routledge, 2010). See, also, Tricia D. Olsen, Leigh A. Payne, Andrew G. Reiter and Eric Wiebelhaus-Brahm, 'When Truth Commissions Improve Human Rights,' *International Journal of Transitional Justice*, 4(3): 457–476.

[51] Greg Grandin, 'The Instruction of Great Catastrophe: Truth Commissions, National History, and State Formation in Argentina, Chile and Guatemala,' *American Historical Review* 110(1) (2005): 46–67.

[52] Rosalind Shaw, 'Memory Frictions: Localizing the Truth and Reconciliation Commission in Sierra Leone,' *International Journal of Transitional Justice* 1(2) (2007): 183–207.

[53] Christine Bell, Colm Campbell and Fionnuala Ní Aoláin, 'The Battle for Transitional Justice: Hegemony, Iraq, and International Law,' in *Judges, Transitions, and Human Rights*, ed. John Morison, Kieran McEvoy and Gordon Anthony (Oxford: Oxford University Press, 2008).

[54] Catherine Turner, 'Delivering Lasting Peace, Democracy and Human Rights in Times of Transition: The Role of International Law,' *International Journal of Transitional Justice* 2(2) (2008): 126–151.

[55] See, Brandon Hamber, 'Masculinity and Transitional Justice: An Exploratory Essay,' *International Journal of Transitional Justice* 1(3) (2007): 375–390. See also, Catherine O'Rourke, 'The Shifting Signifier of "Community" in Transitional Justice: A Feminist Analysis,' *Wisconsin Journal of Law, Gender and Society* 23(2) (2009): 269–291.

and organizations they fund.[56] This means that positivism is being promoted as the primary or apposite logic to be applied in evaluation of transitional justice. Second, because studies vary sharply in epistemology, it is hard to coordinate or talk about important lessons that have been learned so far. Third, favoritism for positivist logic stacks the deck against evaluation. Because within this framework evaluation can only be based on central tendencies within observable, factual data, the richness of perception-based social phenomena across contexts is passed over. To illustrate these points, I turn to a comprehensive report that was commissioned by the Canadian Department of Foreign Relations and International Trade. This report shows favoritism toward a positivist epistemology in service of evaluation. In the following section, I describe the report and problematize some of its conclusions, my aim being to show why positivist approaches alone cannot fill the evaluation gap in the practice of transitional justice.

The CIPS Report

In 2008, Oskar Thoms, James Ron and Roland Paris conducted an extensive critical review of the transitional justice literature for the Centre for International Policy Studies (CIPS) at the University of Ottawa, a concise version of which is reproduced in this special issue.[57] The report would almost immediately reverberate through the community of transitional justice practitioners, inspiring defensive reactions from some. It would also be instrumental in framing my own thinking about these issues. One reading of my following analysis is that I disagree with the authors wholesale and aim to diminish their contribution. This is not my intent. In fact, I agree with the authors on many points, and I hope our pieces are considered to be in conversation.[58] However, I intend to highlight two viewpoints in their report that I do not share. The first is that disputes in transitional justice literature boil down simply to causal claims and counterclaims. I believe this contention is made intentionally to render positivist what is a multiform literature. Second, while the authors gesture toward the value of a mixed-method approach, wherein both qualitative and quantitative methods are used together, they do so within an exclusively positivist framework, arguing that small-*n* and large-*n* studies should both aim toward producing causal probabilities. In contrast, I think this is the province of impact assessments; transitional justice evaluations can and should produce knowledge that is not exclusively causal in nature. In other words, where the authors argue for mixed methods informed by positivism, I argue for the use of mixed methods *and* mixed epistemologies to inform our understanding of transitional justice.

[56] See generally, James C. Scott, *Seeing Like a State: How Certain Schemes to Improve the Human Condition Have Failed* (New Haven, CT: Yale University Press, 1998). For a discussion relevant to transitional justice, see, Kieran McEvoy, 'Beyond Legalism: Towards a Thicker Understanding of Transitional Justice,' *Journal of Law and Society* 34(4) (2007): 411–440.

[57] Thoms, Ron and Paris, supra n 14.

[58] I agree with, among other things, their emphasis on establishing scope conditions for studies, supporting transitional justice with 'moral and legal rationales' and considering embeddedness of 'TJ in the context of wider peacebuilding policies.' Thoms, Ron and Paris, supra n 41 at 343.

The original CIPS report presents a critical review of current research on transitional justice, both highlighting key debates in the field – justice versus peace, truth versus justice – and demonstrating the inconclusiveness of empirical findings on either side of these debates. The report emphasizes the importance of 'fact-based discussions' and 'evidence-based evaluations of TJ options.'[59] According to the authors, these fact-based discussions should center on the location of 'causal effects of TJ mechanisms,' with the ultimate purpose of generating strong conclusions or law-like causal statements concerning the impact of transitional justice tactics. Only on the back of such empirical conclusions, the report argues, can 'good international public policy' be formed.[60]

The report's critique of current work, oriented within a paradigm that promotes generally accepted standards of positivist science, is not internally inconsistent or fallacious on its own terms, although the authors do present the reasons that such an approach to evaluation is incomplete. The first is that, by themselves highlighting the importance of macrosocial goals like democratization, rule of law and the absence of political violence, the authors are setting hard-to-meet standards of proof for practitioners of transitional justice. To show across cases that use of trials and truth commissions, holding other things constant, *increases* democratic participation or the peaceful resolution of conflict would be a Sisyphean task. Methodologically, stable democratic practice and peace are subject to equifinality, that is, they are the product of many simultaneously operating processes. Demonstrating that the proceedings of a three-year truth commission or the passage of one amnesty law lead to democracy, stripped of every other factor changing during a transition, is near impossible. This means that the positivist end of confirming causal relationships is not really reachable.[61]

The second reason that the report does not offer good guidance for evaluators is that ideals at stake in debates over transitional justice cannot all be operationalized, or converted into singular, variable entities. The authors note that 'some TJ outcomes are inherently difficult to measure, such as reconciliation, justice, and healing . . . Better conceptual clarity is thus essential.'[62] That scholars cannot agree on what justice or reconciliation 'look like' is unsurprising. Notions like reconciliation mean different things to different people; in fact, as one scholar details, there are many varieties of reconciliation.[63] For instance, Lesley McEvoy, Kieran McEvoy and Kirsten McConnachie have demonstrated that for ex-combatants in Northern Ireland, reconciliation is a 'dirty word,' viewed by Republicans as a construct of the British state that only paints over a historical legacy of intentional subjugation and denial of rights, and by Loyalists as a paradigm which

59 Thoms, Ron and Paris, supra n 14 at 5–6.

60 Ibid., 12–14.

61 The authors recognize that it is extremely difficult to isolate what are ultimately 'endogenous TJ outcomes' because transitional justice mechanisms are established at the same time as countries are undergoing multiple conflict resolution or democratization processes. Thoms, Ron and Paris, supra n 41.

62 Thoms, Ron and Paris, supra n 14 at 28.

63 Jens Meierhenrich, 'Varieties of Reconciliation,' *Law and Social Inquiry* 33(1) (2008): 195–231.

demonizes their own legitimate political claims.[64] For the authors of the CIPS report, however, the lack of agreement on the referents to which words like reconciliation correspond is a failure on the part of objective observers, a problem of 'clarity' that could be corrected with a sounder conceptual architecture. I suggest that terms like justice and reconciliation by their very nature resist conceptual exercises like operationalization and call out for contextual or idealist understandings, rather than forced objective definitions. This means that the hope for unit homogeneity, and singularity of purpose, in transitional justice is thwarted.

An extension of this problem, and a third reason that such a positivist approach to outcome evaluation cannot be fully realized, is that without conceptions of what substance constitutes concepts like 'justice,' one cannot conduct data-driven research. Variable-based methods are based on a substantialist ontology, wherein the assumption is that concepts correspond to materials that can be counted, measured and effectuated by causes.[65] Some concepts correspond better to constitutive relationships. Justice, reconciliation and peace are notions that, rather than being conceived as discrete goals, would be more properly understood as 'epiphenomenal' conditions that 'supervene' on life once other social prerequisites are met.[66] Other phenomena are more quantifiable, however, and may be construed properly as having common substance. Examples include the number of people disappeared by a military regime, the amount of money provided to families of victims and the number of casualties of gruesome internal wars. I contend that these are riper for data-driven impact assessment, rather than outcome evaluation, *per se*.

A fourth and final reason that evaluation cannot be fully supported by data-driven positivist research is that even when correlations may be discovered between substantive social facts, they cannot fully capture the causal mechanisms at play. Why and how do truth commissions correlate with higher or lower levels of abuses to physical integrity rights? What is it about them that brings this relationship to life across cases? The CIPS report notes that 'TJ analysts conflate correlation with causation.'[67] This is true, but the tendency is not a problem of transitional justice research specifically – it is endemic to all statistical research. Multivariate regression and maximum likelihood estimation focus on covariation: when one measurable social fact is changing, another is changing within the same unit of time and space. However, the ways in which those changes are related to one another must be breathed in by the analyst's theories. Here, interpretation becomes

[64] Lesley McEvoy, Kieran McEvoy and Kirsten McConnachie, 'Reconciliation as a Dirty Word: Conflict Community Relations and Education in Northern Ireland,' *Journal of International Affairs* 60(1) (2006): 81–106.

[65] On substantialism, see, Mustafa Emirbayer, 'Manifesto for a Relational Sociology,' *American Journal of Sociology* 103(2) (1997): 281–317.

[66] In this respect, argues Pablo de Greiff, 'reconciliation' is a term very similar to 'happiness.' See, Pablo de Greiff, 'The Role of Apologies in National Reconciliation Processes: On Making Trustworthy Institutions Trusted,' in *The Age of Apology: Facing Up to the Past*, ed. Mark Gibney, Rhoda E. Howard-Hassmann, Jean-Marc Coicaud and Niklaus Steiner (Philadelphia, PA: University of Pennsylvania Press, 2008).

[67] Thoms, Ron and Paris, supra n 14 at 28.

imperative for even positivist social scientists. If a statistical researcher finds that the use of domestic human rights trials decreases violations of human rights, for example, she must forward a particular interpretation of events to argue, say, that what is occurring is a form of 'deterrence,' or that some unobservable thing called deterrence is the motor generating simultaneous change among units.

This last point, along with those before, speaks to the need for mixed approaches. Although the authors of the CIPS report pin the hopes of future evaluation on data-driven, positivist thinking, they go on to convey to us the very reasons that interpretive-critical theorizing must supplement such a logic. In the next section, I intend to show both the virtues and the limits of positivist applications in transitional justice research, with an eye toward framing puzzles that a positivist framework *can* address.

Defining a Limited Role for Positivism

Interpretation and comparison to the ideal are both needed for enriching evaluation. Now that I have presented a discussion of the limitations of positivist approaches, I turn a critical eye to interpretive evaluations. Well-executed evaluations are present in a good deal of comparative studies. Perhaps ironically, such comparisons are many times employed in service of an assertion of the restraining features of political 'realities.' For instance, in the introduction to her powerful and engaging book, *Hijacked Justice: Dealing with the Past in the Balkans*, Jelena Subotić writes that her aim 'is to show that what happens in real politics differs significantly from the ideals set out by international justice entrepreneurs.'[68] After presenting well-researched evidence from Serbia, Croatia and Bosnia, she writes in her conclusion that in these cases full justice was not reached. One passage is worth quoting at length:

> This domestic commitment to justice that is the basis of much of transitional justice literature is very fickle and narrow; it does not extend to a full commitment to universal criminal accountability that pays no attention to identity politics (issues of ethnicity, religion, or race) and the victim/aggressor matrix. In plain words, the domestic public is much more likely to support transitional justice if its political opponents (the other guys) are put on trial.[69]

Rather than comparing Serbia, Croatia and Bosnia to other cases of transitional justice, the author self-reflexively bases her judgment on a 'maximalist' position: justice must be universal, equal and color blind. Thus, her conclusion is that transitional justice does not deliver.[70] Subotić's work does many things superbly. For example, for each state context, she traces the arc of nationalist party politics, including the two-level game between shaping the message to constituents

[68] Subotić, supra n 5 at 23.

[69] Ibid., 170.

[70] However, in the book's coda, Subotić takes a surprising, optimistic turn: the world with transitional justice is better than a world without it. This is because leaders like former Serbian President Slobodan Milošević have been delegitimized and removed from politics.

and responding satisfactorily to pressure from the international community. She posits that contagious nationalism spreads to and infects well-intended institutional practices. Although she at times genuflects toward generalization, Subotić's interview-based, thick descriptions are interpretive work at its best.

Nonetheless, work like this still cannot accomplish some things. First, because all of the cases she analyzes are subject to the jurisdiction of the International Criminal Tribunal for the former Yugoslavia (ICTY), Subotić's analysis cannot extend to those places where no such trials have taken place. Thus, we are not sure what would, or does, happen in similar places where no international tribunals prosecute former war criminals. Second, the work cannot establish a baseline for what our expectations should be. Sure, justice as Subotić defines it was not achieved, but is it ever? If, with Judith Shklar and other legal realists, we accept the premise that all law is politics on some level, then is it fathomable to expect that her standards would ever be met anywhere? Intriguingly, this type of evaluation, which has assumed a larger role in recent analysis, is Janus-faced: it is a reaction to the 'overselling' of the legalist promise that legal proceedings can trump the political challenges of transitional societies, while also being partly an extension of this promise.[71] It suggests that law, if only better institutionalized and practiced better by state politicians, would produce macro-level desiderata.

These two issues are why positivist transitional justice impact assessments have a crucial partnering role to play with interpretive outcome evaluations. First, they can extend the scope of research a good deal, allowing for consideration of transitional cases where certain social facts are present alongside cases where they are not. Second, positivist impact assessment can ground our expectations by providing baselines through correlative evidence: in many cases where X was in place, impact Y happened. Third, positivist transitional justice research can abandon the search for law-like causality and embrace correlation as a kind of broad-brushstroke history. Without arguing that the past is necessarily prologue, one can still issue comprehensive statements about what has, for instance, transpired since Argentina's 1983 *Nunca Más* report, allowing for the presentation of both trends and the events that have accompanied those trends.

Unresolved Issues for Positivists

Even within this limited role for positivist research, much remains to be done. First, just about every positivist comparative assessment of transitional justice effects examines a different universe of cases. Where some look specifically at countries transitioning to democracy,[72] others analyze solely postconflict or postatrocity states.[73] Ambiguities over what 'a state is supposed to be transitioning *to*' have

[71] On this overselling, see, McEvoy, supra n 56.

[72] See, for example, Neil Kritz, ed., *Transitional Justice: How Emerging Democracies Reckon with Former Regimes* (Washington, DC: US Institute of Peace, 1995).

[73] See, for example, M. Cherif Bassiouni, ed., *Postconflict Justice* (Ardsley, NY: Transnational Publishers, 2002).

been built into the field since its emergence.[74] The expansive range of contexts in which transitional justice might apply has created inconsistency among positivist impact assessments. In the words of one scholar, confusion exists over the questions of 'when to compare' and 'how to compare,' which bear directly on the results of policy assessment.[75] Without explicit statements about the similarity of contexts, positivist inference cannot move forward.

Second, scholars diverge in impact assessments based on the same evidence. For example, Jack Snyder and Leslie Vinjamuri deem the Argentine case to be a failure because trials 'risked provoking disturbances or even a coup by unreconciled elements of the officers corps.'[76] In other words, Argentine efforts created, on balance, negative externalities. Kathryn Sikkink and Carrie Booth Walling disagree on this score. They frame Argentine attempts at justice as having on balance positive externalities because no actual interruption of democracy ever occurred and repression scores indicate that abuses of rights are lower in the aftermath of trials and that trials allowed citizens to 'discover law.'[77] An explanation for this divergence is that empirical researchers observe different dependent variables or impacts. Some focus on the sustainability of peace among rival groups, while others examine the maintenance of institutional democracy and the protection of rights by government actors.

Third, newer empirical assessments face a negativity bias. Impact assessors are saddled with the burden of proving a progressive impact of embedded mechanisms, rather than simply proving the negative – that they do no unique damage amid larger processes. Assessors must show that increases in transitional justice causally generate increases in democratic institutionalization, peace and so on. Many times the injunction to transitional justice practitioners is to 'do no harm,' and one of the major arguments against justice-seeking tactics is that they are in fact counterproductive or harmful. However, few to no studies have convincingly shown, using statistical controls or counterfactuals, that accountability mechanisms actually create substantively negative effects for the polity. Instead, those studies that issue negative assessments simply elaborate the political difficulties of pursuing accountability or the methodological uncertainty of affirmative findings that illustrate their rationale.

[74] Naomi Roht-Arriaza, cited in Bronwyn Anne Leebaw, 'The Irreconcilable Goals of Transitional Justice,' *Human Rights Quarterly* 30(1) (2008): 100 (emphasis in original).

[75] David Backer, 'Cross-National Comparative Analysis,' in van der Merwe, Baxter and Chapman, supra n 13.

[76] Snyder and Vinjamuri, supra n 33 at 26.

[77] Kathryn Sikkink and Carrie Booth Walling, 'The Impact of Human Rights Trials in Latin America,' *Journal of Peace Research* 44(4) (2007): 427–445. On the 'discovery of rule of law' concept, see, Catalina Smulovitz, 'The Discovery of Law: Political Consequences in the Argentine Case,' in *Global Prescriptions: The Production, Exportation, and Importation of a New Legal Orthodoxy*, ed. Yves Dezalay and Bryant G. Garth (Ann Arbor, MI: University of Michigan Press, 2002).

Reassessing Transitional Justice Impact

Positivist scholars of transitional justice, to date, have failed on the basics: they have not been clear about which cases they study and why, and they have not detailed and summarized which transitional justice cases they deem to have had negative impacts. In this section, I attempt to do both of these things, and I focus on the macro, state level of analysis. I do so for two reasons. First, because comparativists have the tendency to think in terms of country years, I establish cases in which 'transitional justice' might apply on the basis of type and timing of state-wide political transitions. Second, because the central axis of contention among proponents and detractors of transitional justice is over whether accountability mechanisms grease or derail larger democratic and peacebuilding processes of transition, a first order of business should be macrosocial impact assessment. Value should be placed on retrospectively determining whether accountability policies were part of a conglomerate strategy that has ultimately managed to sustain moves toward institutional liberal democracy or the lack of violence in the wake of transition. For this reason, I highlight 'failure' and the avoidance thereof. If accountability mechanisms are not uniquely correlated with the breakdown of larger transitional processes, then it can at least be argued that they, *en masse*, do not have generally destabilizing impacts.

Classifying Type of Transition

The most exhaustive effort to generate a universe of potential transitional justice cases is provided by David Backer, who lists 114 transitional cases based on their shared 'experience of initiating a transition that could in principle permit or induce increased scrutiny of past injustices.'[78] Vague in this account, however, is what satisfies the 'transition' or 'in principle' clauses. I reproduce a list of cases using more explicit inclusion criteria. Authors like Ní Aoláin and Campbell argue for 'the need to conceive of transitional situations not as involving one single transition, but in terms of at least two primary sets: a movement towards democracy . . . and that towards peace.'[79] I share this view. But cross-national comparativists normally select one or the other, either postconflict or democratizing countries exclusively. As far as I know, no one has yet systematically catalogued all transitional cases or analyzed how they overlap. Simply for the purposes of selecting cases that fit either of these descriptions, one might conceptualize both democracy and peace as ongoing processes that are minimally present when they are institutionalized and when adverse disruptions like widespread violence are avoided. One can theorize transitional cases as those that have only recently begun to satisfy such minimum requirements.

Widely available quantitative data can be used conservatively to locate which cases fit these descriptions. First, if a regime exhibited a three-point move toward institutional democracy on the often-used Polity IV scale, it might be considered

[78] Backer, supra n 75 at 27.

[79] Fionnuala Ní Aoláin and Colm Campbell, 'The Paradox of Transition in Conflicted Democracies,' *Human Rights Quarterly* 27(1) (2005): 183.

Table 1. Summary Statistics on Failures of Transitional Regimes[a]

	(I) Total	(II) Failure	(III) % Total	(IV) TJ regime	(V) % TJ failure[b]	(VI) TJ failure
Democratization	103	40	38.8	48	16	33.3
Major termination	45	15	33.6	20	4	20.0
Double transitions	19	7	36.8	12	2	16.7
Total transitions	**129**	**50**	**38.8**	**56**	**18**	**32.1**
Pretransitions	27	–	–	8	6	75.0

[a]The number of 'total transitions' is not a sum of the three above categories because that would count double transitions twice. This number is the total of democratic transitions and major violent conflict transitions summed.
[b]These include Algeria (2004), the Central African Republic (1991), Haiti (1991), Haiti (1993–1994), Indonesia (1999), Mali (1990–1992), Nepal (1990), Niger (1991–1992), Nigeria (1998–1999), Philippines (1986), Sierra Leone (1996), Spain (1975), Thailand (1992), Turkey (1983), the Democratic Republic of Congo (2001), Ethiopia (1991–1993), Serbia/former Yugoslavia (1995), Rwanda (1994), Burundi (1993), Chad (1990), India (1977), Iraq (2003), Sri Lanka (1994) and Uganda (1986).

to be liberalizing (see Table 1 for details).[80] Second, to observe peaceful transitions, data on internal wars collected by the Peace Research Institute of Oslo (PRIO) is suitable. Those states that experienced at least 25 individual deaths in fighting between government and the opposition in one year, followed by fewer than 25 deaths for a spell of two years, might be considered to be undergoing a peaceful transition. Finally, if one also includes those listed by Backer, but which do not meet either requirement, a list of quasi- or pretransitional cases emerges. Following these procedures using data from 1972–2007 produces a universe of 156 total regime transition cases, some of which simultaneously undergo decreases in political violence and liberalization, some of which occur repeatedly in the same state jurisdiction and some of which experience elements of either but neither in full. Figure 1 presents this universe of transitional regimes, organized along these two dimensions.

A Glance at Negative Impacts

Within the entire universe of cases selected, 64 of 156 total transitional regimes have made use of at least one measure to achieve human rights accountability. Within the regimes that have experienced either of the two forms of transition, the number is 56. These can be quantified by the mere presence of transitional justice mechanisms in countries year by year.[81] Although this approach passes over a good deal of variation within mechanisms, one could say that the onset of trials or truth

[80] To define 'democratic transitions,' I chose all of those cases that had a three-point increase over the threshold of zero. If the three-point change was incremental, I began coding in the year of the first signs of upward movement. For a summary of the Polity IV data, see, Monty G. Marshall, Keith Jaggers and Ted Robert Gurr, *Polity IV Project: Political Regime Characteristics and Transitions, 1800–2004* (College Park, MD: Center for International Development and Conflict Management, 2006).

[81] I refer to these as transitional justice regimes. I include international trials, hybrid trials, domestic trials, truth commissions and lustration in the category of accountability mechanism. I do not include reparations because of limited data availability. In my aggregate measure, I am interested in whether any form of accountability was sought. I do not consider amnesty to be a strategy of accountability, so it is coded separately.

Figure 1. **Universe of Transition Regimes, 1972–2007**[82]

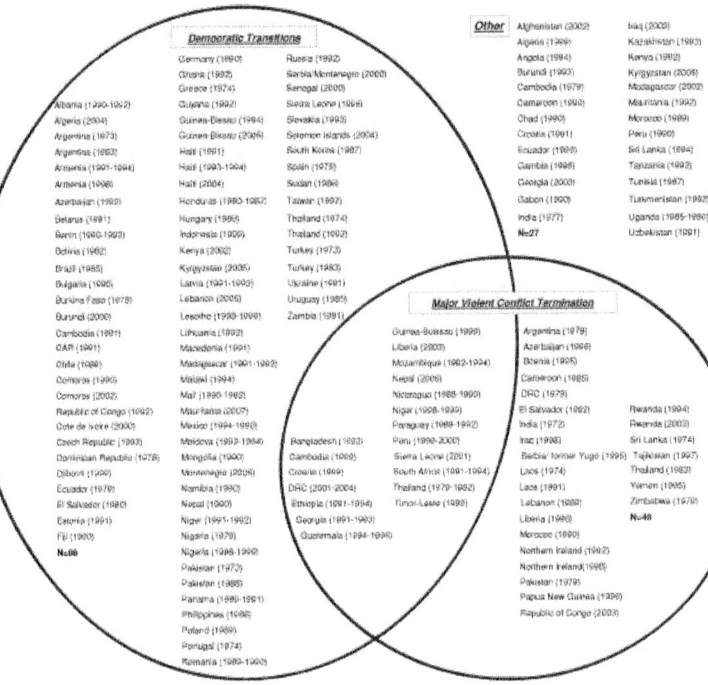

commission proceedings is still an observable social fact that can be minimally characterized as being present or absent in a given country at a given time. Judging the impact of these mechanisms is harder, but one can proceed pragmatically. I use a hard test in reference to the 103 democratic regime transitions. If they

[82] Reproduced from Geoff Dancy, 'Choice and Consequence in Strategies of Transitional Justice,' in *The Handbook of the Political Economy of War*, ed. Christopher J. Coyne and Rachel L. Mathers (Chaltenham: Edward Elgar Publishing, forthcoming).

To define 'democratic transitions,' I chose all of those cases which had a three-point increase over the threshold of zero. If the three-point change was incremental, I began coding in the year of the first signs of upward movement. For a summary of the Polity IV data, see M.G. Marshall, Keith Jaggers and Ted Robert Gurr, *Polity IV Project: Political Regime Characteristics and Transitions, 1800–2004* (College Park, MD: Center for International Development and Conflict Management, 2006).

I define 'major violent conflict termination' using the UCDP/PRIO Armed Conflict Dataset, version 4–2009. See, Nils Petter Gleditsch, Peter Wallensteen, Mikael Eriksson, Margareta Sollenberg and Håvard Strand, 'Armed Conflict 1946–2001: A New Dataset,' *Journal of Peace Research* 39 (2002): 615–637. These cases were generated using the following steps: (1) I selected out all years before 1970; (2) I chose those conflicts that were coded by the UCDP/PRIO Armed Conflict Dataset Codebook, version 4–2009, as 'internal' or 'internationalized internal' wars using the 'Type' variable; (3) I selected as major all of those conflicts that reached a historical threshold of 1,000 deaths using the cumulative intensity ('CumInt') variable; (4) I coded as 'one' every country year that reached a threshold of 25 battle deaths within that major conflict (derived from 'Startdate2'); and (5) I applied a two-year rule to determine the conflict's end, meaning that if the conflict did not resume in time (t) through time (t+2), it was considered to be terminated starting at time (t).

either reverted to nondemocratic forms of governance or saw the continuation or resumption of violent conflict, I list them, for the sake of simplicity, as 'failures.' For the 45 cases of conflict termination, I list them as failures simply if they later resumed violent patterns of conflict.

Table 1 presents summary numbers on regimes that have experienced failure so defined. Three tentative conclusions can be drawn from these basic statistics. First, for each type of transition, the baseline failure percentage is lower for those regimes that instituted some form of transitional justice. For democratization, this percentage is only slightly lower (by 5.5%). Among regimes emerging from major conflicts or experiencing double transitions, however, those that use transitional justice mechanisms have much lower failure percentages (13.6% and 21.1% lower, respectively). That it is possible to reach different conclusions about failure – and thus the impact of accountability efforts – depending on what sample of regimes is analyzed shows the importance of being careful and lucid when selecting which types of cases to compare. Also, from these findings one could argue that transitional justice is not necessarily as ill-placed in postconflict situations as some expect. In fact, in those cases where countries are simultaneously undergoing the termination of violent conflict and democratization, transitional justice strategies have a fairly consistent, nondisruptive track record.

Second, when totaled, the failure percentage for all transitional justice regimes is still lower by 6.7 percent. The data also shows that any transitional strategies, including accountability mechanisms, generally avoid failure around 68 percent of the time. Third, pretransitional regimes that pursue some form of accountability are much more likely to fail, which indicates that, arguably, accountability fits better in the context of existing transitions, rather than prior to their existence. Not shown in the table are similar figures on amnesty processes. Fifty-five transitional regimes used amnesties, of which 25 experienced failure (45.5%). However, it should be noted that of the 36 cases coded as nonfailing transitional justice regimes, a clear majority of 21 also used amnesty somewhere in their processes (58.3%).

I make no pretense that these cross-tabulated statistics are overwhelmingly robust, or that they are intended to be. At best, they are suggestive. Moreover, they will likely displease both those in the positivist and those in the interpretive-critical camp. The former would argue that I have done nothing to control statistically for the effects of other variables. Additionally, they cannot account for time, causality, the sequence of events or variation in accountability measures themselves. The latter camp would argue that I am engaged in a process of reifying problematic categories in my construction of what constitutes a transition and what amounts to regime failure. I would accept both of these criticisms. Still, I think that even this cursory exposition makes a valuable contribution. First, it shows how one might go about casing regime transitions and failures in a systematic and summary fashion. This means advancing an argument that basic commonalities do in fact exist across wholly different contexts. Second, it makes the case that accountability mechanisms, embedded within larger strategic efforts, do not seem to produce uniquely insuperable costs for peace or democracy, or at least costs that go beyond those transitional regimes already face.

Concluding Remarks

The analysis I perform in the previous section is not a complicated model. Because it defines common cases and then points to variation within observable units among those cases, however, it *is* positivist. The summary statistics defend against the claim that transitional justice mechanisms have uniquely destabilizing impacts within transitional contexts – a claim that has been made repeatedly within the justice-versus-peace debate. Unfortunately, such an impact assessment, and even those that are much more technically sophisticated, can do very little by way of *evaluation*, or determining the 'worth' of transitional justice interventions. Looking at these numbers, lost are crucial considerations, like whether formerly victimized citizens of Timor-Leste or Rwanda or Peru understand 'justice' to have been achieved or whether they can feel 'reconciled' with their neighbors. Political judgments about each of these cases would require that one talk with people in these places and get a feel for their understandings of what is at stake in their locales. Even further, broad generalizations give short shrift to concerns that leaders the world over are capturing practices of transitional justice in service of ignoble ends. One recent example is the Sri Lankan government's use of transitional justice rhetoric to target former Tamil militants without investigating the abuses committed during the 2008–2009 army offensive.[83] This, for obvious reasons, falls short of aimed-for human rights ideals.

What the numbers presented here can do is show what we might expect in which circumstances, based on extensive historical research that has informed a database. Settling the notion that transitional justice is uniquely dangerous at least opens a space for prudent political judgments about what it *does* contribute. Thus, this kind of positivist impact assessment must be taken in conjunction with interpretive work in evaluation that takes place on the ground. Observers should continue to use positivist logic to make arguments about consequences, building on correlations that otherwise might not have been noticeable, but they should do so with clearly stated assumptions about the way in which they choose their cases and why they understand these cases to be of a certain type. Interpretivists and critical theorists should continue to vivisect the body of assumptions on which these statements of correlation are based, while also attempting to discover the relations between observables and unobservables that constitute the social world. Without contributions from each way of thinking, responsible judgments about programs in the pursuit of social goods like justice cannot be made.

[83] 'Sri Lanka Seeks Foreign Judicial Network to Deal with Tamil Tiger Suspects,' *BBC Monitoring South Asia*, 23 September 2009.

29

"Show me your impact": Evaluating transitional justice in contested spaces

Colleen Duggan[1]

International Development Research Centre, Evaluation Unit, 150 Kent Street, PO Box 8500, Ottawa, Ontario, Canada K1G 3H9

ABSTRACT

This paper discusses some of the most significant challenges and opportunities for evaluating the effects of programs in support of transitional justice – the field that addresses how post-conflict or post authoritarian societies deal with legacies of wide spread human rights violations. The discussion is empirically grounded in a case study that assesses the efforts of the International Development Research Centre (IDRC) and one of its Guatemalan partners to evaluate the effects of a museum exposition that is attempting to recast historic memory and challenge racist attitudes in post-conflict Guatemala. The paper argues that despite the increasing trend to fund transitional justice programs, many international aid donors are stuck in traditional and arguably orthodox paradigms of program evaluation. This is having a negative effect not only upon the administration of aid but also upon how transitional justice research is perceived and valued by local populations. The case study experience indicates that there is no perfect evaluation model or approach for evaluating transitional justice programming – only choices to be made by commissioners of evaluation, evaluators, and those being evaluated. These are profoundly influenced by the extreme politics and moral values that define transitional justice settings as contested spaces in which calls to remember the tragic past must be balanced with aspirations to re-build a hopeful future.

1. Introduction

Transitional justice – the field that addresses how post-conflict or post authoritarian societies deal with legacies of wide spread human rights violations – has come to occupy a position of increasing importance in the administration of international aid[2]; so too has the menu of mechanisms or interventions called for by governments, international organizations, scholars and civil society advocates. Although there is no established model for transitional justice, it is generally understood to have moved beyond the realm of the juridical to the political, to embrace a suite of mechanisms that include criminal prosecutions of individual perpetrators (tribunals), truth seeking initiatives to address past abuse and clarify historical accounts of the past (truth commissions and investigative bodies), material and/or non-material reparations to victims, memorialisation initiatives that commemorate victims, reforms to key institutions (including the judiciary, army and police and vetting, dismissals and barring from public office) (Bickford, 2004, p. 1045) and most recently, reforms to history education.[3]

Transitional justice is arguably one of the most controversial, complex and unpredictable processes undertaken by governments and citizens in the politically charged and socially contested environments that accompany the transition from conflict or repressive rule. The use of mechanisms for transitional justice has proliferated throughout the world over the last decade, and especially over the last five years.[4] However, actors involved in the business of international aid are coming to realize that the record for evaluating the effects that these interventions are having on the lives of people has not matched enthusiasm for promoting, designing and financing them. As a field, it would seem that transitional justice is now coming of age. With this maturation, those who have a stake in the outcomes of transitional justice – governments, perpetrators, victims, ordinary citizens and the international aid community – are beginning to ask difficult

[1] The views and opinions expressed in this paper are those of the author and do not represent those of IDRC.

[2] A recent report by the International Centre for Transitional Justice notes that funding for programs on transitional justice has increased in recent years. By a very conservative U.S. private foundations alone have invested close to $93 million dollars in the transitional justice field from 2003 to 2007 (Bickford & Schultz, 2008, p. 24).

[3] Cole (2007) makes a convincing case for including history education as one of the institutions that should appear in frameworks for transitional justice. In the latter part of this paper, I will examine a case study that focuses on history education in Guatemala.

[4] A review of the website of the International Center for Transitional Justice indicates that transitional justice mechanisms are currently operating in no less than 37 countries in Africa, the Americas, Asia, Europe and the Middle East. See http://www.ictj.org/en/where/overview/index.html.

questions about the success or failure of the transitional justice project.

This paper is motivated by three recent trends that are influencing academic, policy and practitioner debates about the merits and pitfalls of transitional justice. The first relates to the social science literature on transitional justice, which is calling into question some of the core assumptions or change theories that tie together transitional justice mechanisms and their potential to identify causal relationships with wider processes for social change, including (but not restricted to) conflict prevention, reconciliation or 'social healing', democratization and consolidation of the rule of law (Brahm, 2007; Mendeloff, 2004; Vinjamuri & Snyder, 2004). The fact of the matter is that scholars, policymakers and advocates have all been weak in consolidating a compelling body of theoretical and empiric evidence that assesses both the positive and negative effects of these mechanisms upon larger processes of peacebuilding and development.[5]

In parallel to this debate, there is a re-kindling of methodological discussions around the effectiveness of aid and impact evaluation (and what constitutes acceptable or credible evidence). This manifests itself in one of two ways: a continuing tendency by donors to cling to linear, ill-adapted methods and approaches to the evaluation of international development aid, despite a tacit (or explicit) recognition of their limitations[6]; or seizing upon the use of experimental and quasi-experimental methods as a "gold standard" for impact evaluation, with little consideration for the need for multi-method approaches that account for the many complex factors that actually lead to changes in governance and human relationships in transitional societies.[7] As both a researcher and a donor, I have seen these dramas being played out in international and national organizations (both governmental and non-governmental) working in human rights and transitional justice in developed and developing world.

The third significant development that underpins this paper is the growing interest among social science researchers working on transitional justice to make use of the principles and methods emerging from program evaluation research and practice to sharpen applied empiric research on transitional justice.[8] Researchers and advocates alike are increasingly looking to program evaluation for new learning and clues that might help lead them out of the impact quagmire. At the level of practice, civil society and non-governmental organizations – particularly those working with victims in the developing world – are demanding legitimate approaches to better understand if and how transitional justice processes are helping or harming their societies. At the same time, they are anxious to respond to donor demands for evidence of "impact" in ways that are balanced and accountable – not only to donors, but also to the local populations in whose name transitional justice is being undertaken. Clearly, the single biggest dilemma facing all those working in the area of transitional justice is the urgent need to build an evidence base to underpin policy and practice.

In this paper, I will discuss some of the most significant challenges and opportunities for evaluating the effects of programs in support of transitional justice objectives. By means of a case study, I will empirically ground this discussion and share learning emerging from the efforts of the International Development Research Centre (IDRC) and one of its Guatemalan partners to track and evaluate the effects of a museum exposition that is attempting to recast historic memory and challenge racist attitudes and beliefs in post-conflict Guatemala. I will argue that despite the rapid growth of transitional justice and the increasing trend among bilateral and multilateral development assistance donors to fund transitional justice programs, many of these donors are stuck in traditional and arguably orthodox paradigms of program evaluation. This is having a profound effect not only upon the administration of international aid but also upon how transitional justice research is perceived and valued by local populations. The experience of IDRC indicates that there is no perfect evaluation model or approach for evaluating transitional justice programming – only choices to be made by evaluators and those being evaluated. These will continue to be profoundly influenced by the extreme politics and moral values that define transitional justice settings as contested spaces in which calls to remember the tragic past must be balanced with aspirations to re-build a hopeful future.

2. Historic Memory and Racism in Guatemala: Evaluating the Effects of the "*Why are we the way we are?*" Museum Exposition

2.1. How the story begins

Transitional justice processes most often take place in socially and politically fragile contexts that are characterized by high and increasing complexity. These settings are fluid, highly sensitive and often can be prone to relapses into violence. Guatemala is no exception to this characterization. The Guatemalan internal armed conflict ended in 1996, leaving about 2% of the national population dead or disappeared – 83% of who were indigenous (Commission for Historical Clarification, 1999). In 1999, Guatemala's Truth Commission concluded that the Guatemalan state had committed acts of ethnic genocide against the indigenous population. In the spirit of "nunca más" (never again), the Truth Commission report also highlighted the need for initiatives for historic memory and the reform of primary, secondary and university level education to include instruction on the causes, development and consequences of the war. The transformation of Guatemala's education system was also clearly recognized as a priority in the Peace Agreements[9] signed between the Government of Guatemala and the URNG guerrilla. Although most Guatemalans recognize that racism is a problem, spaces are limited for debating how Guatemalans might construct a nation in which ethnic diversity is celebrated and everyone is a citizen in the fullest sense of the word. The open discussion of racism in either the public or private domain remains a contentious and complex issue.

It was in this context that the Centro de Investigaciones Regionales de Meso América (CIRMA,) a research centre and library decided to dedicate major attention to developing research and educational strategies around the issue of racism, as a contribution to the social reconstruction of Guatemala in the post-conflict period (Adams, 2007a). The International Development Research Centre (IDRC), a publically funded Canadian institution that funds research in the developing world, was also interested in supporting innovative peacebuilding research in Guatemala. IDRC's relationship with CIRMA actually pre-dated the release of the Truth Commission report. Between 1998 and 2003, IDRC had supported CIRMA to produce an exhaustive multi-volume ethnographic study

[5] Scholars who are interested in problematizing transitional justice point out that what we have is largely anecdotal or inconclusive evidence. For a thorough review of some of the major studies to date on truth commissions, criminal trials and vetting see Thoms, Ron and Paris (2008).

[6] See for example Bakewell and Garbutt (2005) and United Nations General Assembly (2008). The by-line of this report is as follows: "results-based management at the United Nations has been an administrative chore of little value to accountability and decision-making".

[7] Renewed interest in such methods emerged in the advent of the Centre for Global Development's report. Since the release of the CGD report, debates for and against experimental methods, especially randomized controls trials have continued to rage. See for example, Ravallion (2009).

[8] See Pham and Vinck (2007).

[9] See Agreement on Identity and Rights of Indigenous Peoples (1995). Available from: http://www.usip.org/resources/peace-agreements-guatemala [cited 02.01.10].

of the history and current tendencies of interethnic relations in Guatemala. In 2003, CIRMA began discussing with IDRC and other donors the potential for using this research to reconstruct a new Guatemalan narrative around race relations and the history of the conflict. CIRMA's research formed the basis for an ambitious nation-wide effort to stimulate public reflection and dialogue, called the "National Campaign for Interethnic Dialogue: *Our Diversity is Our Strength!*" The campaign was developed on the basis of a national consultation, which detected strong interest in addressing the issue of racism in Guatemala, and just as strong a fear as to how to do this without exacerbating existing tensions (Adams, 2007a, p. 4).

This challenge – how to create a mechanism for dialogue which would foster, and not hinder, social reconciliation – was at the heart of the design of the Campaign that was launched in June of 2004 (Adams, 2007a, p. 3). Developed with help from international experts on social violence and reconciliation, and based on learning emerging from museums of conscience and race consciousness training experiences, the centre piece of the Campaign was a 5000 square-foot interactive museum exposition called *Por Qué Estamos Como Estamos?* (*Why are we the way we are?*)[10] Using photographic images, videos and interactive games that invited people to reflect on their own lives in Guatemalan society, the expo presented an animated, colourful portrayal of the history and current state of interethnic relations in Guatemala.

2.2. *Monitoring the effects of historic memory and education; original intentions*

As CIRMA contemplated the content and structure of the campaign, IDRC's Evaluation Unit offered to support CIRMA in conceptualizing and putting into place a comprehensive system for monitoring and evaluating results, including the effects of the campaign on those who would view it. Monitoring peoples' reactions to the campaign was seen as a critical first step in assessing how the campaign might contribute to changing peoples' attitudes and behaviors towards racism. Through a series of peer support meetings and training in a planning, monitoring and evaluation methodology known as Outcome Mapping,[11] IDRC worked with CIRMA staff in order to help them identify those individuals and groups in present day Guatemala who the campaign most hoped to influence: high school teachers in public and private schools, regional university authorities, university professors in the regions and social and political leaders in NGOs (Evaluation Unit, 2008, p. 8).

IDRC supported CIRMA to put together a global monitoring and evaluation strategy that included a series of monitoring and data collection instruments drawn from Outcome Mapping and other methodologies (questionnaires for dialogue participants, records of attendance at the expo, weekly reports by expo museum guides and exit interviews with expo attendees). All of this data was collected and tracked through a specially designed database. Monitoring efforts were largely focused upon the "*Why are we the way we are?*" museum expo which was considered by CIRMA to constitute the heart of the national campaign operation. IDRC and CIRMA each had interests – some of them shared – on issues of learning and accountability for results around the museum expo. Some within CIRMA wanted to use its research to catalyze a process of national reflection and deep social transformation. IDRC's Evaluation Unit wanted to know if its funding was achieving its desired outcomes and was also interested to see how Outcome Mapping might be successfully grafted onto a process for transitional justice and reconciliation. Both CIRMA and IDRC harbored the hope that data harvested from the monitoring and evaluation framework could be used to inform CIRMA's continued research on inter-ethnic relations and social reconciliation in Guatemala. As will be discussed further on, this lack of clarity around the use of monitoring data generated significant problems that affected attitudes around the value of monitoring and evaluation and the adoption and ownership of the M&E framework within CIRMA.

2.3. *What actually happened?*

Results from the first two years of the deployment of the museum expo in three regions of the country exceeded expectations, generating a wave of reactions both inside Guatemala and internationally. Between mid-2004 and mid-2006, the expo reached more than 117,000 visitors (nearly 1% of the national population). More people visited the exposition than visited Guatemala's other twenty-two museums combined over the same period of time. The campaign received support from seventeen national and international donors and from of a broad cross-section of Guatemalan society, an extremely rare achievement in this post-conflict society (Adams, 2007b, p. 6).

The data gathered by the campaign indicated that in general, the effort was received with high levels of acceptance and legitimacy. About 90% of the visitors to the exposition responded "positively" while 5% on either side viewed it as either too "light" or too "radical" (Adams, 2007a, p. 5). Reactions tended to be positive although a minority of the visitors were defensive and negative. The range of reactions to the expo underscores the deep complexity inherent in recasting historic memory and cultural identity in contested spaces, as illustrated in the following descriptions:

Reflections on personal identity and existing ambiguity[12]:

> "After visiting the expo, I thought more about it, and I am in fact, indigenous because my grandmother came from..."

Validation and feelings of comfort with the expo's message and content:

> "At last, somebody is telling it like it is."

> "I was a soldier in the 1980's and I had to leave Guatemala, and that made me think about our living situation."

Surprise, doubt and curiosity around the issue being presented in a new light:

> "I was foolish to teach absurd things to my students; the true history is quite different, and here I finally recognized that."

Discomfort and a desire for more profound and convincing arguments:

[10] The campaign also included two other components: a guided process for group dialogue of community leaders on the topic of interethnic relations and a series of university teaching activities oriented toward designing an effective teaching package on the history racism and social inequality. This paper will be restricted to a discussion of the museum exposition.

[11] Outcome Mapping is a planning, monitoring and evaluation methodology that assumes that people control change and that, as external agents, development programs only facilitate the process by providing access to new resources, ideas or opportunities for a certain period of time. The originality of the method is its shift away from attribution to contribution; and from assessing the products of a program (e.g. poverty alleviation and reduced conflict) to focus on changes in behaviours, relationships, and actions of the people and activities with whom a development program works directly. See Earl, Carden and Smutylo (2001).

[12] The following reflections are taken from Adams (2007a).

"We need to talk about structural discrimination in this country;"

"They don't say anything about reverse discrimination."

Fear in the face of the explicit presentation of the problem of racism:

"This expo is a double-edged sword, because by trying to create awareness it can also awaken a sleeping consciousness that could turn into a monster."

Annoyance and denial:

"What are you trying to do with this?"

"I don't think things are quite the way you show them."

The Campaign also received broad support from diverse segments of the population that seldom agree on any issue. Media support – written press, television, and radio – went well beyond simple reporting. The media became key allies, almost always providing the campaign with ample and positive coverage (Adams, 2007a, p. 7). The exposition also awakened the interest of diverse international organizations working in the field of human rights and research and education in post-conflict societies. A number of international foundations and donors requested presentations on the campaign or visited the expo with a view to documenting it as a model for reconciliation and educational innovation in a host of countries including Ethiopia, Eritrea, Serbia, Romania, Macedonia, Burma, Cambodia, Bolivia and Argentina (International Development Research Centre, 2008, p. 9).

3. What was learned about historic memory and education in Guatemala?

In developing and implementing the monitoring and evaluation strategy for the museum expo, CIRMA and IDRC faced a number of methodological and contextual challenges. These were navigated with varying degrees of success. In some instances, CIRMA was able to collect useful data that yielded significant learning around the effectiveness of the campaign and the nature of inter-ethnic relations, as well as how to approach the issue for greater reach. Four important pieces of learning stand out:

a. Mass exposure to the exposition: The Campaign reached 25% of the local population and 40% of the school population in two of the three Guatemalan departments where the expo was set-up, creating an important unanticipated effect. By saturating a specific population, the exposition apparently created a neutral external reference point enabling people to safely discuss what had been a virtually taboo subject. This is an effect that the expo is seeking to repeat by focusing on one social group in order to create a critical mass during the next five years (Adams, 2006, p. 6).
b. Young people are a critical group and are especially open: The original idea of targeting the expo to young people from 13 to 25 years of age was validated, as this group generally showed a special ability to interrogate their ideas and reflect upon reality. However, the expo organizers also observed that children from ten years of age were just as responsive. Despite their openness, however, these young Guatemalans would seem to require more formal facilitation (Adams, 2007b, p. 6).
c. Teachers are strategically place – and especially resistant: At the other extreme were the teachers, who as a group were among the most ambivalent and resistant visitors to the expo, with a tendency to stifle the reflection that their students were generating on their own. This is perhaps not surprising; the structural discrimination that underpins Guatemalan society is sustained no less by the education system than by the police or judiciary, the more common target institutions of transitional justice programming.
d. The exposition's efficiency and efficacy could be improved: Finally, an analysis of the costs involved in the first phase of the deployment of the expo enabled CIRMA to develop a plan to maximize financial and programmatic efficacy and efficiency for the final phase. An analysis of reactions to different parts of the exposition also allowed CIRMA to identify certain changes to make to the presentation of content and form of the installations (Adams, 2007b, p. 7). For example, it was noted that a number of urban youth who viewed the expo were unable to relate to the history of Guatemala's conflict, perceiving it as something that would be better to leave in the past. This suggested the need to adjust some of the content in a way that would be more accessible and immediately relevant to younger generations of Guatemalans (CIRMA, 2008, p. 6).

Despite the encouraging progress noted above, IDRC and CIRMA missed some major opportunities to track and understand the effects of the museum expo as a tool for social reconciliation. In mid-2006, CIRMA closed the expo in order to evaluate its results and plan for its re-design and re-launch.[13] As part of that process of reflection, IDRC commissioned an external summative evaluation of the monitoring and evaluation framework experience. While many important lessons emerged from that evaluation, three learnings in particular merit discussion here.

3.1. *The critical importance of defining use of findings*

During the planning phase, IDRC invested much time in working with CIRMA personnel in order to define how the data and analysis that would emerge from the monitoring and evaluation framework would be used and who exactly would use it. Based on the premise of Utilization Focused Evaluation (Patton, 2008) the M&E framework endeavored not to dictate any particular evaluation model, method, theory or use of findings. Rather, the expectation was that in guiding CIRMA through an interactive process, they would be better positioned to collect the data that the organization would need for accountability purposes vis-à-vis its donors and for learning purposes around the effectiveness of the expo.

The implementation of the framework over a period of two years gave rise to a series of unexpected outcomes. The first was a lack of agreement within CIRMA whether the framework and data collected should be used to inform decision-making for improving the operations of the expo, thus informing program effectiveness and fulfilling accountability requirements with donors; or whether the data should be used to feed and inform CIRMA's research activities (CIRMA, 2008, p. 23). Although the emerging data could arguably serve both purposes, the reality was that these were two fundamentally different groups of uses and users. A division also developed between those who wanted to use the expo as a sort of research laboratory or generator of interesting empirical data that could then inform a future research agenda within the organiza-

[13] In mid 2006, the National Campaign including the expo, was closed. A large multi-donor summative evaluation of the project was conducted at the end of 2006. One of the recommendations of the evaluation was that the expo be devolved from CIRMA.

tion and those who viewed and wanted to use the expo as a dynamic instrument for igniting a transformative process of social change among individuals and groups who viewed the expo. These differences contributed to ongoing organizational tensions which paved the way to the eventual devolvement of the expo and its operation to a separate organization.[14]

A second (and related) difficulty was the absence of sufficient spaces within CIRMA for reflection and analysis of emerging data. The daily operation of the National Campaign was an all consuming activity for CIRMA and its staff. The massive amount of rich qualitative data collected on the immediate effects that the expo was having on visitors' attitudes tended to be inconclusive, due to weak baseline data. Despite this problem, informal daily exchanges between staff allowed CIRMA to incorporate some process changes during execution and did significantly contribute to the re-design of content and process for the re-launch of the expo in 2009.

3.2. Balancing power relationships

The challenges around use were exacerbated by power differentials at two different levels: externally, between CIRMA and the seventeen national and international donors who were financing the Campaign; and internally between the CIRMA staff who were directly involved with the expo and those who continued to be occupied by CIRMA's traditional research and education activities.

Throughout the Campaign, CIRMA was forced to spend an inordinate amount of time ensuring that its donor relationships stayed on an even keel. Multiple donors with different reporting requirements called upon CIRMA to report on diverse outcomes (and anticipated impacts) with differing data. This resulted in an ongoing tug of war between those who valued quantitative vs. qualitative data; and those who insisted upon more linear approaches to planning and evaluation (logical framework analysis and results-based management) vs. those who espoused systems approaches. IDRC unwittingly played a part in this drama: the summative evaluation of the monitoring and evaluation project commissioned by IDRC in 2008 discovered that CIRMA staff involved in the M&E work felt obligated to maintain an exclusive focus on Outcome Mapping tools and their qualitative focus because IDRC (the principal creator of Outcome Mapping) was funding the M&E project (Ortiz, 2008). This happened at a time when the organization was under pressure for more quantitative data.

Part way through the project, the coordinator of the monitoring and evaluation work departed, taking with him his knowledge of Outcome Mapping. While the new coordinator made laudable efforts to get up to speed on the methodology, his research background was decidedly quantitative in nature. Although he managed to collect an impressive volume of quantitative (and largely demographic) data, opportunities to drill down to uncover qualitative considerations were lost. Nevertheless, much of the quantitative data collected did allow CIRMA to speak with authority to the outside world about the breadth and reach of the campaign, if not its effectiveness in influencing attitudes among the viewing public.

As mentioned, within CIRMA, both the National Campaign itself and the monitoring and evaluation project generated unexpected tensions. The high profile of the Campaign and related donor enchantment with the museum exposition resulted in the creation of two groups: those who were in the Campaign and those who were not. The Campaign was like a donor magnet, reproducing within CIRMA all of the worst deformations of international aid. The management of the daily of operations of the monitoring and evaluation project was highly centralized in the coordinators who oversaw this work. Despite their best efforts, the coordinators were unsuccessful in generating excitement and building ownership for monitoring activities. The museum guides who were working in the expo collecting and entering monitoring data saw this work as a burden and an imposition at the end of a long day. This was exacerbated by the fact that the data collection system was too large and ambitious. Data was being collected merely for the purpose of data collection, in the hopes that in the future, it would serve the purposes of research and program improvement.

3.3. Theories of change can be illusive when new ground is being broken

Transitional justice mechanisms are not unlike other international development interventions that aspire to facilitate or promote complex social change processes requiring multifaceted interventions and multiple national and international actors. In other words, change will always be the result of a multi-causal package and both the funders and the funded will be faced with the perpetual problem of attribution of results to a single project or program. The current state of the transitional justice field suffers from a very particular problem, however: as a relatively new and emergent field, we are in the early days of theory building and many of the theories of change that underpin transitional justice initiatives are either untested or inconclusive. Typical change processes or implicit (and often untested) assumptions about the goals of transitional justice include social healing (through truth-telling initiatives); reducing recidivism (through criminal trials for human rights abusers); or facilitating the formation of new identities (through educational reform, as in the case of the Guatemalan museum exposition).

The museum expo is not unlike other transitional justice initiatives: social change will be a long term process that will arguably take generations to become fully rooted. In other words, those working in support of transitional justice share the same impact dilemma that faces many international development actors working for governance and social change in transitional, socially and politically contested settings. In the Guatemalan case, we admittedly fell into the 'project trap'; both IDRC and CIRMA were perhaps caught up in the short timeline of the project and its interventions, looking for larger impact pay-offs. We also assumed a more linear process of knowledge transfer which would result in attitudinal change. Ironically, the Outcome Mapping framework which was built on the basis of systems theory was inadvertently extracted out of the wider system.

Although both CIRMA and IDRC had a general idea of the expo project's theory of change, not enough time was spent explicitly articulating assumptions and intentionality, or mapping out the potential complexities and variables – psychological, social/class, gender, political – that would influence the reactions of the individual visitors who would view the museum expo. Both organizations assumed a causal relationship between exposure to the content of museum and the subsequent formation or evolution of attitudes and values. In hindsight, it is now easy to see that the implied theory of change was far too simplistic. Using the expo to induce behavior change among individuals was viewed as an important proxy for assessing social change and was one of the motivating factors behind the selection of Outcome Mapping as a central methodology. Much of the power of Outcome Mapping is rooted in the participatory values that underpin the methodology. In this case, the assumed theory of change was never externally validated with other interested stakeholders. External validation

[14] Following up on the recommendations of the multi-donor evaluation, in June of 2007, the administration of the National Campaign was moved to the newly created Instituto Internacional de Aprendizaje para la Reconciliación Social-IIARS (International Institute for Learning on Social Reconciliation).

may well have uncovered the cracks in the theory of change and allowed us to view and understand the expo as a tool for cognitive reframing (confronting individuals with information discrepant or contradictory to their expressed attitudes or self-image to induce cognitive dissonance and create opportunities for re-framing these attitudes) (Shapiro, 2005). As it was, we missed the mark, and in this case, behavior change was never an appropriate indicator of social change – mainly because the viewing of the expo was in itself a passive activity which would have needed to be accompanied by longer term strategies for social action among targeted groups, if actual changes in behavior among the viewers were to be the final outcome.

Poor mapping of the theory of change is a common trap into which we ought not to have fallen. IDRC's accompaniment and mentoring of CIRMA could also have been tighter. However, given the cutting edge nature of the National Campaign and the fact that both CIRMA and IDRC were breaking new ground, it was only through the evaluation process that both organizations were able to fully grasp the complexity of the theory of change underlying the expo and its use. This error has now been rectified. With its re-design and re-launch in February of 2009, the expo is now being used as a teacher training tool for educating primary and secondary teachers and public servants on issues of race relations. The focus of the re-design has been on the development of a pedagogic strategy both to help teachers to digest the issue and to become constructive participants in post-exposition dialogues and investigation in the classroom. In using the expo in a more targeted manner, the expectation is that with the necessary incentives, teaching professionals in Guatemala might begin to move away from more traditional forms of emphasizing historic facts, not enquiry, and that students will begin understand and problematize why accounts of the same event – Guatemala's tragic conflict – might differ. IDRC has been working with the International Institute for Learning on Social Reconciliation (IIARS) in the design of a new monitoring and evaluation framework for the expo.

4. Lessons learned from Guatemala: key principles and approaches to evaluating transitional justice

It is hoped that learning from the "*Why are we the way we are?*" project can be used to improve planning, monitoring and evaluation of transitional programming in other countries emerging from violent pasts. Programming in these contested, complex contexts will almost always be accompanied by high levels of unpredictability. Co-existing and being comfortable with ambiguity is an important aspect of working in contested spaces – this does not come easily for most of the large donors and grantmakers who underwrite transitional justice programming and want visible, short term returns on their investments. Transitional justice, as we are often reminded, it far from "tried and true". Programming in this area is not for the risk adverse. Embracing risk in international aid administration is a tall order when there are multiple accountabilities at play. Since there still appear to be many questions around whether transitional justice 'works' (e.g. whether it promotes social reconciliation and contributes to peacebuilding), it seems that one of the most intelligent ways to manage the risks effectively would be increase learning. This implies going beyond the "yes" or "no" question of if transitional works to ask the question of how transitional justice works. Good program evaluation can help answer this question.

Those involved in transitional justice programming – civil society organizations, governments and donors of different persuasions – will need to abandon orthodox approaches to linear planning, monitoring and evaluation and embrace new approaches for dealing with complexity through adaptive management. In light of this reality, the following principles and approaches to the evaluation of transitional programming for social reconciliation should be considered.

4.1. Combine research and evaluation

Theory-based evaluation,[15] because of its focus on exploring both successes and failures, could be of particular importance for evaluating transitional justice. Theory-based evaluation as its name implies, has more often than once uncovered the difficulties or deficiencies underlying the original theory underpinning a program or project's logic. Because theory-building around the long term impacts of transitional justice is still in its infancy, it is also critical that transitional justice program evaluation be accompanied by deeper empirical research that sheds light on the social change processes and theories that underpin transitional justice as a concept.

4.2. Prioritize local stakeholder accountability not just donor accountability

As seen in the Guatemalan case, improving trust in strained inter-group relationships needs to be seen as a priority. Externally imposed approaches to program evaluation can often unwittingly play a role of undermining the long-term goals (or hoped for impacts) of transitional justice. Those being evaluated often view the parachuting of external evaluators into highly charged contexts as an imposition and a liability to be managed, since they assume that any negative findings will be taken up and exploited by adversaries to transitional justice. In such cases, the potential for doing more harm than good is very real. The success or failure of a program in support of transitional justice must pay heed to the equally important imperatives of vertical accountability to the donor and horizontal accountability to a wider base of civil society stakeholders.

4.3. Empower disadvantaged groups, including victims

Evaluation of programs designed to serve disadvantaged groups such as victims of human rights violations may actually be threatening to stakeholders in those groups. Program beneficiaries have often suffered bad experiences with the management of international aid, including evaluation. For many of these people, evaluation has been a highly disempowering experience. Whatever form of M&E that is chosen, it should be conflict-sensitive and not exacerbate tensions, making a socially and emotionally fraught situation worse. These contexts could greatly benefit from development evaluation approaches that build rather than erode the social capital of the organizations and beneficiaries involved in transitional justice programs.

While we often dwell upon the importance of evaluation for evidence, in contexts dealing with a violent past, it is important to remember the linkages that exist between findings as evidence, the process use benefits of evaluation[16] and the potential to recuperate lost social capital. Findings alone are of limited use and rarely (if ever), is an evaluation report sufficient to support social change. Because such a large part (although not all) of transitional justice programming is about re-building broken relationships, donors and evaluators need to double their efforts to straddle the intersect between the use of evaluation findings for articulating evidence based decision-making and good participatory process that

[15] See Weiss (1997).

[16] Process use refers to "individual changes in thinking, attitudes, and behaviour, and in program organizational changes in procedures and culture that occur among those involved in evaluation as a result of the learning that occurs during the evaluation process". Patton (2008, p. 115).

implants a deeper respect for the utility of evaluation in the user as a vehicle for organizational learning on the ground.

4.4. Use participatory approaches to offset power imbalances

Transitional justice contexts are often characterized by intense feelings of distrust at many levels. The ideological divisions of civil society are deep and are particularly difficult for an outsider to understand, let alone navigate. Recipients of transitional justice programs (governments, NGOs, and victims groups) may distrust bilateral or multilateral donors, who have in the past, played a direct or indirect role in the conflict. In such contexts, external evaluation is (not surprisingly) viewed as an extension of repressive tactics. Many of the long term goals of transitional justice suggest that participatory evaluation approaches such as self-assessment and peer review could play a constructive role in the achievement of the longer term, ambitious aspirations that underlie the transitional justice project. Participatory approaches that support evaluative thinking also build learning capacities into the organizations of transitional justice stakeholders.

5. Concluding remarks

At the end of the day, it is local actors who need to be convinced that transitional justice 'works'. Uptake and ownership of the well-intentioned goals of transitional justice will depend upon whether local actors perceive the achievement of results that are important to them and their constituencies – not the international donors who fund these processes and their evaluators. This reality has perhaps been most aptly summed up by the former President of the African Evaluation Association: "*It is not about your project; it is about my country*".[17]

Acknowledgements

The author would like to thank the Instituto Internacional de Aprendizaje para la Reconciliación Social (IIARS) and the Centro de Investigaciones Regionales de Meso América (CIRMA) for their openness and constructive attitude toward evaluating the monitoring and evaluation framework of the National Campaign. Within those organizations, special thanks go to Vivian Salazar and Tani Adams. Thanks also to Fred Carden, Stephen Brown, Joanna Quinn, Brynton Lykes and members of the editorial and international advisory boards of the International Journal of Transitional Justice for comments on earlier drafts of this paper.

References

Adams, T. (2007a). *Notes on the social impacts of the campaign to date, lessons learned and challenges for the future*. Guatemala: Instituto Internacional de Aprendizaje para la Reconciliación Social (IIARS). (Internal document).

Adams, T. (2007b). *Proposal to develop an educational strategy or teaching about racism and ethnic equality in Guatemala: Por Qué Estamos Como Estamos? 2007–2011* Guatemala: Instituto Internacional de Aprendizaje para la Reconciliación Social (IIARS). (Internal document).

Agreeent on Identity and Rights of Indigenous Peoples. (1995). Washington: United States Institute for Peace, Peace Agreements, Digital Collection.

Bakewell, O., & Garbutt, A. (2005). *The use and abuse of the logical framework approach*. Stockholm: SIDA.

Bickford, L. (2004). *Transitional justice in the encyclopaedia of genocide and crimes against humanity* (Vol. 3, pp.).). New York, USA: MacMillan.

Bickford, L., & Schultz, D. (2008). *Memory and justice confronting past atrocity of human rights abuse*. New York: International Centre for Transitional Justice.

Brahm, E. (2007). Uncovering the truth: Examining truth commission success and impact. *International Studies Perspectives*, *8*, 16–35.

Centre for Global Development. (2006). When will we ever learn? Improving lives through impact evaluation. Report of the Evaluation Gap Working Group, Washington.

Centro de Investigaciones Regionales de Meso América – CIRMA. (2008). *Final technical report for project 'global monitoring proposal for CIRMA's national campaign for dialogue and interethnic relations'*. Ottawa: International Development Research Centre.

Cole, E. A. (2007). Transitional justice and the reform of history education. *International Journal of Transitional Justice*, *1*(1), 115–137.

Commission for Historical Clarification. (1999). *Guatemala memory of silence: The report of the commission for historical clarification – Summary and conclusions*. Washington: AAAS Science and Human Rights Data Center. Available from: http://shr.aaas.org/guatemala/ceh/report/english/toc.html.

Earl, S., Carden, F., & Smutylo, T. (2001). *Outcome mapping building learning and reflection into development programs*. Ottawa: International Development Research Centre.

Evaluation Unit. (2008). *Annual corporate evaluation report*. Ottawa: International Development Research Centre.

Mendeloff, D. (2004). Truth-seeking, truth-telling, and postconflict peacebuilding: Curb the enthusiasm? *International Studies Review*, *6*(3), 355–380.

Ortiz S N.. (2008). *Participatory evaluation of the monitoring and evaluation system of the national campaign for dialogue and interethnic relations 'our diversity is our strength'*. Guatemala: Instituto Internacional para la Reconciliation Social.

Patton, M. Q. (2008). *Utilization focused evaluation, The new century text* (4th ed.). Sage.

Pham, P., & Vinck, P. (2007). Empirical research and the development and assessment of transitional justice mechanisms. *International Journal of Transitional Justice*, *1*(2), 231–248.

Ravallion, M. (2009). Should the Randomistas rule? Economists voice, February. Available from: http://www.bepress.com/ev/vol6/iss2/art6.

Shapiro, I. (2005). Theories of change, January. Available from: www.beyondintractability.org/essay/theories_of_change/.

Thoms, O. N. t, Ron, J., & Paris, R. (2008). *The effects of transitional justice mechanisms. A summary of empiric research findings and implications for analysts and practitioners centre for international policy studies*. Ottawa: University of Ottawa.

United Nations General Assembly. (2008). Review of results-based management at the United Nations. 22 September 2008. A/63/268.

Vinjamuri, L., & Snyder, J. (2004). Advocacy and scholarship in the study of international war crimes tribunals and transitional justice. *Annual Review of Political Science*, *7*(May), 345–362.

Weiss, C. H. (1997). Theory-based evaluation: Past, present, and future. In D. Rog & D. Fournier (Eds.), *Progress and future directions in evaluation: Perspectives on theory, practice, and methods* (pp. 76–). San Francisco, CA: Jossey-Bass.

Colleen Duggan is a Senior Program at the International Development Research Centre (IDRC). She brings her expertise in human rights and the rule of law in divided societies to IDRC's Evaluation Unit. She has published works on early warning and conflict prevention, gender and transitional justice, and the evaluation of peacebuilding initiatives. Together with International Conflict Research-INCORE (University of Ulster), she is leading an evaluation research project on evaluating research in violently divided societies. Between 2001 and 2005, She developed IDRC's programming in Latin America on peace and conflict and women's rights. Before joining IDRC, she worked for more than a decade with the UN High Commissioner for Human Rights and for the United Nations Development Programme in Colombia, Guatemala, El Salvador, and New York. Issues she focused on with the UN included humanitarian response, security sector reform, transitional justice, human rights, and peacebuilding. She holds a master's in law (international human rights and humanitarian law) from the University of Essex (UK) and a graduate degree in international development and economic cooperation from the University of Ottawa.

[17] Oumoul Ba Tall, President of the International Organizational for Cooperation in Evaluation. Speaking at the European Evaluation Society Conference, October 2008.

INDEX

Note: Page numbers in **bold** type refer to **figures**
Page numbers in *italic* type refer to *tables*
Page numbers followed by 'n' refer to notes